# Hungary

## THE ROUGH GUIDE

written and researched by

## Charles Hebbert
## and Dan Richardson

with additional accounts by
Annabel Barber and Emma Roper-Evans

THE ROUGH GUIDES

# THE ROUGH GUIDES

## TRAVEL GUIDES • PHRASEBOOKS • MUSIC AND REFERENCE GUIDES

 We set out to do something different when the first Rough Guide was published in 1982. Mark Ellingham, just out of university, was travelling in Greece. He brought along the popular guides of the day, but found they were all lacking in some way. They were either strong on ruins and museums but went on for pages without mentioning a beach or taverna. Or they were so conscious of the need to save money that they lost sight of Greece's cultural and historical significance. Also, none of the books told him anything about Greece's contemporary life – its politics, its culture, its people, and how they lived.

So with no job in prospect, Mark decided to write his own guidebook, one which aimed to provide practical information that was second to none, detailing the best beaches and the hottest clubs and restaurants, while also giving hard-hitting accounts of every sight, both famous and obscure, and providing up-to-the-minute information on contemporary culture. It was a guide that encouraged independent travellers to find the best of Greece, and was a great success, getting shortlisted for the Thomas Cook travel guide award,

and encouraging Mark, along with three friends, to expand the series.

The Rough Guide list grew rapidly and the letters flooded in, indicating a much broader readership than had been anticipated, but one which uniformly appreciated the Rough Guide mix of practical detail and humour, irreverence and enthusiasm. Things haven't changed. The same four friends who began the series are still the caretakers of the Rough Guide mission today: to provide the most reliable, up-to-date and entertaining information to independent-minded travellers of all ages, on all budgets.

We now publish more than 100 titles and have offices in London and New York. The travel guides are written and researched by a dedicated team of more than 100 authors, based in Britain, Europe, the USA and Australia. We have also created a unique series of phrasebooks to accompany the travel series, along with an acclaimed series of music guides, and a best-selling pocket guide to the Internet and World Wide Web. We also publish comprehensive travel information on our Web site:

http://www.roughguides.com

## HELP US UPDATE

A lot of effort has gone into ensuring that the fourth edition of *The Rough Guide to Hungary* is accurate and up to date. However, things can change fast: new restaurants and hotels appear, and prices and opening hours change. Any suggestions, comments, corrections or updates towards the next edition would be much appreciated. All contributions will be credited, and the best letters will be rewarded with a copy of the new book (or any other Rough Guide, if you prefer). Please mark all letters "Rough Guide Hungary Update" and send to:
Rough Guides, 62–70 Shorts Gardens, London WC2H 9AB, or
Rough Guides, 345 Hudson St, New York NY 10014.
Or send email to: mail@roughguides.co.uk
Online updates about this book can be found on Rough Guides' Web site at http://www.roughguides.com

# Hungary

## THE ROUGH GUIDE

There are more than one hundred Rough Guide titles
covering destinations from Amsterdam to Zimbabwe

**Forthcoming titles include**
Alaska • Copenhagen • Ibiza & Formentera • Iceland

**Rough Guide Reference Series**
Classical Music • Country Music • Drum 'n' Bass • English Football
European Football • House • The Internet • Jazz • Music USA • Opera
Reggae • Rock Music • Techno • Unexplained Phenomena • World Music

**Rough Guide Phrasebooks**
Czech • Dutch • Egyptian Arabic • European Languages • French • German
Greek • Hindi & Urdu • Hungarian • Indonesian • Italian • Japanese
Mandarin Chinese • Mexican Spanish • Polish • Portuguese • Russian
Spanish • Swahili • Thai • Turkish • Vietnamese

**Rough Guides on the Internet**
www.roughguides.com

## ROUGH GUIDE CREDITS

**Text editor:** Sophie Martin
**Series editor:** Mark Ellingham
**Editorial:** Martin Dunford, Jonathan Buckley, Jo Mead, Kate Berens, Amanda Tomlin, Ann-Marie Shaw, Paul Gray, Chris Schüler, Helena Smith, Judith Bamber, Kieran Falconer, Orla Duane, Olivia Eccleshall, Ruth Blackmore, Jennifer Dempsey, Geoff Howard, Claire Saunders, Anna Sutton, Gavin Thomas, Alexander Mark Rogers (UK); Andrew Rosenberg, Andrew Taber (US)
**Production:** Susanne Hillen, Andy Hilliard, Link Hall, Helen Ostick, James Morris, Julia Bovis, Michelle Draycott, Cathy McElhinney

**Cartography:** Melissa Flack, Maxine Burke, Nichola Goodliffe, Ed Wright
**Picture research:** Eleanor Hill, Louise Boulton
**Online editors:** Alan Spicer, Kate Hands (UK); Geronimo Madrid (US)
**Finance:** John Fisher, Neeta Mistry, Katy Miesiaczek
**Marketing & Publicity:** Richard Trillo, Simon Carloss, Niki Smith, David Wearn (UK); Jean-Marie Kelly, SoRelle Braun (US)
**Administration:** Tania Hummel, Charlotte Marriott

## ACKNOWLEDGEMENTS

Thanks to Richard Aczél, Biber Krisztina, Simon Broughton for his musical expertise, Eileen G.P. Brown, Jennifer Brown, Egyedi András, Ian Fairley, Pearl R. Gluck, Ruth E. Gruber, Hajdú Éva, Hangyál Judit, Tom Howells, Eve Kahn, Kollár Katalin, Csörsz Sándor, and their ace children Máté, Áron and Anna, Kuzmich Anikó, Tony Lang, Lőrincz Anna, Terry McGuigan, Molnár Miriam, Noé Csilla, Rácz Regina & Zsemle, George Schöpflin, Peter Sherwood, Sulyok Máté, Szoboszlai János and family, Szűcs Dóra, Tálos Attila, Tamás Amaryllis, Mark Thompson, Tolnai Lea, Torda Márta, Tóth Csilla, Stefan Wenckheim, the staff in Tourinform offices across the country, Tim Bender and BMK for use of machines, the Merdzsó, and all the many, many others who made this work possible and worth doing.

Thanks, too, to Derek Wilde for his proofreading and comments, Henry Barkman, David Mills, Maxine Burke and Stratigraphics (maps), Link Hall (typesetting) and Eleanor Hill (pictures).

## PUBLISHING INFORMATION

This fourth edition published May 1999 by Rough Guides Ltd, 62–70 Shorts Gardens, London, WC2H 9AB.
Reprinted September 2000
Distributed by the Penguin Group:
Penguin Books Ltd, 27 Wrights Lane, London W8 5TZ
Penguin Books USA Inc., 375 Hudson Street, New York 10014, USA
Penguin Books Australia Ltd, 487 Maroondah Highway, PO Box 257, Ringwood, Victoria 3134, Australia
Penguin Books Canada Ltd, 10 Alcorn Avenue, Toronto, Ontario, Canada M4V 1E4
Penguin Books (NZ) Ltd, 182–190 Wairau Road, Auckland 10, New Zealand
Typeset in Linotron Univers and Century Old Style to an original design by Andrew Oliver.
Printed in England by Clays Ltd, St Ives PLC
Illustrations in Part One and Part Three by Edward Briant.

Illustration on p.1 by Hilary McManus; and on p.373 by Tommy Yamaha
© Charles Hebbert and Dan Richardson 1999.
No part of this book may be reproduced in any form without permission from the publisher except for the quotation of brief passages in reviews.
432pp – Includes index
A catalogue record for this book is available from the British Library
ISBN 1-85828-315-9

## THE AUTHORS

**Dan Richardson** was born in England in 1958. Before joining the Rough Guides in 1984, he worked as a sailor on the Red Sea, and as a commodities dealer in Peru. Since then he has travelled extensively in Egypt and Eastern Europe. While in St Petersburg in 1992, he met his wife, Anna, and they now have a daughter, Sonia.

**Charles Hebbert** has been hanging around Hungary for seventeen years. He spent two years learning the language, supporting himself by starring in dreadful language-teaching videos and doing anything else that would bring in money, and then began a PhD on the position of women in Hungary. However, in 1990, with research going everywhere and nowhere, he decided to try his hand as a journalist in Budapest. He returned to London in 1998, where he works as a freelance writer.

## READERS' LETTERS

A big thank you to the readers who took the trouble to write in with their comments and suggestions (apologies for any misspellings or omissions): Ro Sonnet, Michael and Hazel Wallis, Peter Henshaw, Christina Neill-Higgins and Stephen Ward, David Cutter, G. H. Brown, Faith Ressmeyer, Helen Close, Mark Cheltenham, Sara Young and Maurice Barchdrecht, Gary Nuttall, Leila and Harvey Woolf, Andrew and Agnes Ayton, Glynis Shepherd, Rosemary Langton, John Brindham, Edgar H. Locke, Dr Paul Caffrey, Chris Jones, Julian Pykett, Alice Goddard, Michelle Smith, G.V. Wildfeir-Field, John Bushry, Hannah Musisi, John Leslie, Lynette Wright Pinter, Joan Shortman, Anton Jansen, Marco Ciotti, David Key, Nick Tyldesley, John and Lynda Harris, Grant Roberts, D.F. Wilson, Duncan Light, Lorraine Eason and Mary Taylor, Sarah Vickerstaff, Bill Martin, M.A. Siklos, Peter Clarke, Pedro Rosa, Derek Wilde and P. van der Kroft.

# CONTENTS

Introduction ix

# ● CHAPTER 4: TRANSDANUBIA 205–266

# ● CHAPTER 5: THE NORTHERN UPLANDS 267–311

# ● CHAPTER 6: THE GREAT PLAIN 312–371

# *PART THREE* CONTEXTS 373

# LIST OF MAPS

## MAP SYMBOLS

| | | | |
|---|---|---|---|
| Motorway | | Campground |
| Road | | Archeological site |
| Pedestrianized street | | Church (regional maps) |
| Steps | | Mosque |
| Path | | Synagogue |
| Railway | | Mountain |
| Ferry route | | Peak |
| National border | | Cave |
| Chapter division boundary | | Marshland |
| River | | Gate |
| Metro stop | | Wall |
| Bus stop | | Building |
| Airport | | Church (town maps) |
| Parking | | Cemetery |
| Hospital | | Jewish cemetery |
| Lighthouse | | Park |
| Information office | | Beach |
| Post office | | |

# INTRODUCTION

Visitors who refer to **Hungary** as a Balkan country risk getting a lecture on how this small, landlocked nation of eleven million people differs from "all those Slavs". Hungary was likened by the poet Ady to a "river ferry, continually travelling between East and West, with always the sensation of not going anywhere but of being on the way back from the other bank"; and its people identify strongly with the West while at the same time displaying a fierce pride in themselves as Magyars – a race that transplanted itself from Central Asia into the heart of Europe. Any contradiction between nationalism and cosmopolitanism is resolved by what the Scottish expatriate Charlie Coutts called the Hungarian "genius for not taking things to their logical conclusion". Having embarked on reforming state socialism long before Gorbachev, Hungary made the transition to multi-party democracy without a shot being fired, while the removal of the iron curtain along its border set in motion the events leading to the fall of the Berlin Wall. The end of Communism has hastened the spread of glossy western capitalism, and on arrival in Budapest your first impressions will be of a fast-developing and prosperous nation. However, there is another side to post-Communist Hungary, and beyond the capital and Lake Balaton living standards have fallen sharply amongst many people, for whom the transition to democracy has brought very mixed blessings indeed.

Hungary's capital, **Budapest**, inspires a feeling of *déjà vu*. It's not just the vast Gothic Parliament and other monuments of a bygone imperial era that seem familiar, but the latest fashions on the streets, or a poster advertising something that was all the rage back home a year before. In coffee houses, Turkish baths, and the fad for Habsburg bric-à-brac, there's a strong whiff of *Mitteleuropa* – that ambient culture that welcomed Beethoven in Budapest and Hungarian-born Liszt in Vienna. Meanwhile a wave of new clubs and restaurants and a burgeoning sex industry reflect the advent of nouveau riche entrepreneurs, and a massive influx of tourists and foreign investment.

After Budapest, **Lake Balaton** and the **Danube Bend** vie for popularity. The Balaton, with its string of brash resorts, styles itself as the "Nation's Playground," and enjoys a fortuitous proximity to the Badacsony wine-producing region. The Danube Bend has more to offer in terms of scenery and historic architecture, as do the **Northern Uplands** and **Transdanubia**. The beautiful old parts of Sopron, Győr and Pécs are, rightfully, the main attractions in Transdanubia, though for castle enthusiasts the Zempléni range and the lowlands of southern Transdanubia also have several treats in store; while in the Uplands the famous wine centres of Tokaj and Eger are the chief draw. On the **Great Plain** Szeged hosts a major festival, and its rival city, Debrecen, serves as the jumping-off point for the archaic Erdőhát region and the mirage-haunted Hortobágy *puszta*. See the **chapter introductions** for more details about each region.

## When to go

Most visitors come in the summer, when nine or ten hours of sunshine can be relied on most days, sometimes interspersed with short, violent storms. The humidity that causes these is really only uncomfortable in Budapest, where the crowds don't help; elsewhere the **climate** is agreeable. Budapest, with its spring and autumn festivals, sights and

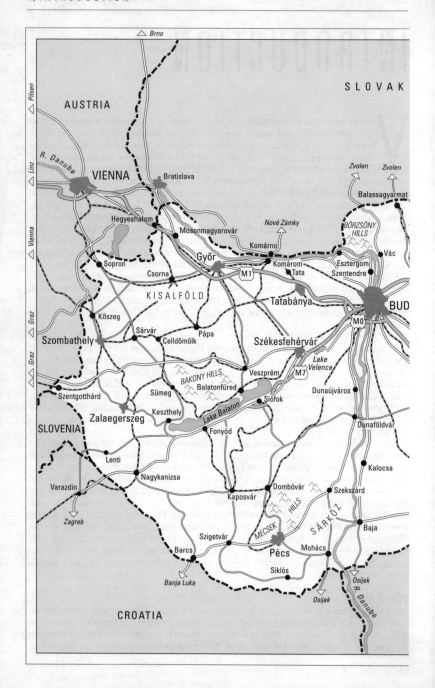

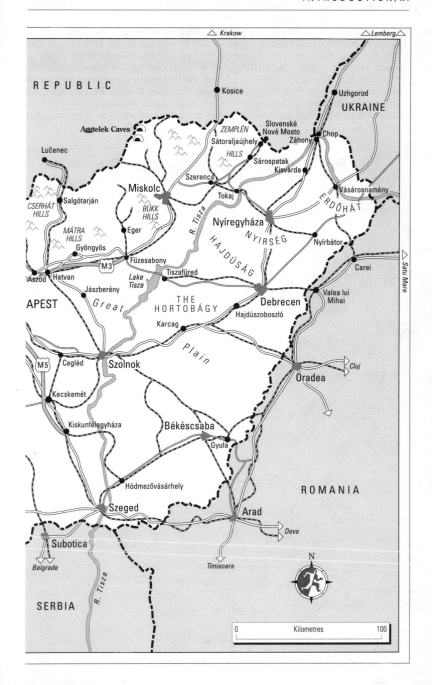

△ Krakow △Lemberg△

REPUBLIC

Kosice

Uzhgorod

UKRAINE

Aggtelek Caves

Lučenec

ZEMPLÉN

Slovenské Nové Mesto

Chop

Sátoraljaújhely

Záhony

HILLS

Sárospatak

Kisvárda

Szerencs

Vásárosnamény

Miskolc

Tokaj

ERDŐHÁT

CSERHÁT HILLS

Salgótarján

BÜKK HILLS

Nyíregyháza

MÁTRA HILLS

Eger

NYÍRSÉG

Gyöngyös

Nyírbátor

Füzesabony

HAJDÚSÁG

M3

Tiszafüred

Carei

Aszod

Hatvan

Lake Tisza

Jászberény

APEST

Great

THE HORTOBÁGY

Debrecen

Valea lui Mihai

Hajdúszoboszló

Karcag

Plain

M5

Cegléd

Szolnok

Oradea

Cluj

Kecskemét

Kiskunfélegyháza

Békéscsaba

Gyula

Hódmezővásárhely

ROMANIA

Szeged

Arad

Subotica

Deva

Belgrade

R. Tisza

Timisoara

N

SERBIA

Satu Mare

R. Tisza

0    Kilometres    100

culinary delights, is a standing invitation to come out of season. But other parts of Hungary have little to offer during the winter, and the weather doesn't become appealing until late spring. May, warm but showery, is the time to see the Danube Bend, Tihany or Sopron before everyone else arrives; June is hotter and drier, a pattern reinforced throughout July, August and September. There's little variation in **temperatures** across the country: the Great Plain is drier, and the highlands are wetter, during summer, but that's about as far as climatic changes go. The number of **tourists** varies more – the popular areas can be mobbed in summer, but rural areas receive few visitors, even during the high season.

| AVERAGE DAYTIME TEMPERATURES | | | | | | | | | | | |
|---|---|---|---|---|---|---|---|---|---|---|---|
| Jan | Feb | Mar | Apr | May | June | July | Aug | Sept | Oct | Nov | Dec |
| **Budapest** | | | | | | | | | | | |
| °F 29 | 32 | 42 | 53 | 61 | 68 | 72 | 70 | 63 | 52 | 42 | 34 |
| °C -2 | 0 | 6 | 12 | 16 | 20 | 22 | 21 | 17 | 11 | 6 | 1 |
| **Debrecen** | | | | | | | | | | | |
| °F 27 | 31 | 41 | 51 | 60 | 66 | 70 | 68 | 61 | 51 | 41 | 32 |
| °C -3 | -1 | 5 | 10 | 16 | 19 | 21 | 20 | 16 | 11 | 5 | 0 |

## GETTING THERE FROM BRITAIN

**Hungary is easily accessible from Britain by air, rail or road. Flying is the easiest option, with direct access from London and connections from most other British airports. Going by land involves rather a long haul, and you'll save little, if anything, by taking the train, although with an InterRail or Eurail pass you can take in Hungary as part of a wider European trip. Buses, on the other hand, can cost less than half the price of the plane. Other possible options include picking up discounted flights to Frankfurt or Vienna and continuing by land; or driving, a journey of over 1700km, best covered over a couple of days or more.**

### BY PLANE

Both British Airways and the Hungarian national airline, Malév, run two daily **direct scheduled flights from London Heathrow to Budapest**, taking around 2hr 20min, as well as a joint flight from London Gatwick four times a week. Both airlines offer APEX fares of around £202–290: Malév is usually cheaper, but BA operates special offers out of season. APEX tickets must be booked and paid for at least fourteen days in advance, you are required to stay at least one Saturday night, and confirmed bookings can't be changed. **Indirect flights** with other airlines (including Air France, Austrian Airlines, CSA, KLM, LOT, Lufthansa, Swissair and Sabena) are worth looking into – they take longer, but can be very competitive in price (£210 including airport tax).

There are no direct scheduled services from any **other British airports**, but most offer connecting flights to Heathrow. BA has add-on fares of £110–160 on top of the return fare from London, but it may be worth taking advantage of special offers to London, and getting a regular ticket from there. From Edinburgh, Glasgow, Leeds and Teesside, you can buy a through ticket with British Midland and Malév for an add-on fare of just over £70, though this is not available from the airlines and must be bought from an agent such as Regent Holidays or Intra Travel (see p.5). From regional airports served by Air France, Air UK, KLM, Lufthansa or Sabena, you can avoid London completely, changing planes in Europe instead (indeed, from Birmingham, which has no flights to London, this is your only option). Tickets to Budapest cost upwards of £240 return, and can be bought direct from the airlines or through specialist agents (see overleaf).

A number of **specialist tour operators** handle flights from the UK to Hungary, and you can save a lot of time, effort and money by calling these first. Hungarian Air Tours sometimes has winter special offers at around £150 return, in addition to selling regular Malév tickets; they also sell one-way tickets from £130. Danube Travel has APEX returns with Malév at £145–210, depending on season. Bridgwater Travel also offers good-value tickets with European airlines from regional UK airports, as do Regent Holidays and Intra Travel. For addresses, phone numbers and more details of all these companies, see the box on p.5.

For the very cheapest deals, STA Travel and Usit Campus, both with branches around the country, are highly reliable, and offer special discount deals for **students and under-26s**. Although **charter flights** to Hungary are not common, STA and Bridgwater Travel do occasionally offer them, usually in summer, out of London Gatwick, at prices of around £150 return.

Another possibility is to buy a bargain **flight to Frankfurt or Vienna** and continue from there, but of course you'll still have the expense of travelling to and from Hungary. In London, check the ads in the *Evening Standard* and *Time Out*; in Manchester try *City Life*, and elsewhere look in local listings magazines or the classified sections of the Sunday newspapers. The German Travel

## AIRLINES

**Air France**, 10 Warwick St, 1st Floor, London W1R 5RA (☎0181/742 6600).

**Air UK**, Stansted Airport (☎0345/666 777).

**Austrian Airlines**, 10 Wardour St, London W1V 4BJ (☎0171/434 7350).

**British Airways**, 156 Regent St, London W1R 5TA (☎0171/434 4700 or 0345/222 111).

**British Midland Airways**, Donington Hall, Castle Donington, Derby DE74 2SB (☎0345/554 554).

**DSA**, 72-73 Margaret St, London W1N 8HA (☎0171/255 1898).

**KLM**, Ticket office, Heathrow Airport, Terminal 4 (☎0990/750 900).

**LOT**, 313 Regent St, London W1R 7PE (☎0171/580 5037).

**Lufthansa**, 7–8 Conduit St, London W1R 9TG (☎0345/737 747).

**Malév**, 10 Vigo St, London W1X 1AJ (☎0171/439 0577).

**Sabena**, 10/18 Putney Hill, London SW15 6AA (☎0345/581 291).

**Swissair**, Swiss Centre, 10 Wardour St, London W1V 4BJ (☎0171/434 7300).

## INDEPENDENT TRAVEL SPECIALISTS

**Council Travel**, 28a Poland St, London W1 (☎0171/437 7767). *Flights and student discounts.*

**Usit Campus**, 52 Grosvenor Gardens, London SW1W 0AG (☎0171/730 3402); 541 Bristol Rd, Selly Oak, Birmingham B29 6AU (☎0121/414 1848); 61 Ditchling Rd, Brighton BN1 4SP (☎01273/570 226); 39 Queen's Rd, Bristol BS8 1QE (☎0117/929 2494); 5 Emmanuel St, Cambridge CB1 1NE (☎01223/324 283); 53 Forest Rd, Edinburgh EH1 2QP (☎0131/225 6111); 166 Deansgate, Manchester M3 3FE (☎0161/833 2046); 105–106 St Aldates, Oxford OX1 1DD (☎01865/242 067). *Student/youth travel specialists, with branches also in YHA shops and on university campuses all over Britain.*

**STA Travel**, 86 Old Brompton Rd, London SW7 3LH (☎0171/361 6161); 117 Euston Rd, London NW1 2SX; 25 Queen's Rd, Bristol BS8 1QE (☎0117/929 4399); 38 Sidney St, Cambridge CB2 3HX (☎01223/366 966); 75 Deansgate, Manchester M3 2BW (☎0161/834 0668); 36 George St, Oxford OX1 2AQ (☎01865/792 800); and 88 Vicar Lane, Leeds LS1 7HJ (☎0113/244 9212); and offices at the universities of Birmingham, Kent, Loughborough, etc. *Discount fares, with particularly good deals for students and young people.*

**Travel Bug**, 125a Gloucester Rd, London SW7 4SF (☎0171/835 2000); 597 Cheetham Hill Rd, Manchester M8 5EJ (☎0161/721 4000). *Large range of discounted tickets.*

Centre, 403–409 Rayners Lane, Harrow, Middlesex HA5 5ER (☎0181/429 2900), has round trips from London to Frankfurt starting at £115 in winter, and, while flights to Vienna are likely to be pricier, you may find a special offer or last-minute deal. There are also direct flights to either city from other UK airports.

Finally, note that you will have to add **airport departure tax** to most of these prices, currently £10 in the UK, and around £17 in Hungary.

### PACKAGE HOLIDAYS

The list of addresses and sample **package holidays** given opposite is merely a small selection of what's available. Send off for brochures if you're interested, and compare the various deals carefully, since season and type of accommodation can affect prices among the various companies. Unless stated

otherwise, prices detailed opposite are per person sharing the cheapest available double room during the high season, and include return flights and airport tax. Expect add-ons of upwards of £40 if flying from UK airports other than London.

### BY TRAIN

Travelling **by train**, the shortest journey from London's Victoria Station takes about 25 hours, including the ferry crossing, and fares are generally more expensive than flights. However, stopovers on the way are possible – in the Netherlands, Germany, the Czech Republic or Slovakia – and prices are more attractive if you're a student, under 26 or over 60. If you have an InterRail (see opposite) or Eurail (p.11) train pass, you can take in Hungary as part of a wider rail trip around Europe.

Canadian, Australian and New Zealand passport holders considering this journey should be aware that they will need **transit visas** in order to get through the Czech Republic and Slovakia, which are best obtained in advance.

## TICKETS AND PASSES

A standard second-class London to Budapest **return ticket** costs £260–278 (depending on whether you go via Ostend or Paris), or from £284 if you take the Eurotunnel via Brussels, on top of which you'll probably want to reserve a couchette (just over £16). If you are **under 26**, a BIJ ticket to Budapest, available through Eurotrain or Wasteels (see box overleaf), costs £212–219, depending on your route. Wasteels also offers reduced tickets for over-26s starting at £222

return. Both regular and BIJ tickets have two to three months' return validity; stopovers are allowed as long as you stick to the prescribed route.

Better value by far is to buy an **InterRail pass**, available to anyone resident in participating European countries for six months (the North American equivalent is called Eurail, for details of which see p.11). You can buy InterRail passes at train stations (or some travel agents) and the pass offers unlimited travel on a zonal basis on up to 25 European rail networks. The only extras you pay are supplements on certain express trains, plus half-price fares in Britain (or the country of issue) and on the cross-Channel ferries. To reach Hungary from the UK you'll need a pass valid for at least three zones; Hungary is zoned with

---

### SPECIALIST TOUR OPERATORS

**Attila Tours**, 36a Kilburn High Rd, London NW6 5UA (☎0171/372 0470). Bargain holidays: bus travel to and from Hungary plus a week's accommodation in chalets on the western outskirts of Budapest for around £150. Buses run all year, once a week, leaving London on Thursday and Budapest on Sunday; a return ticket excluding accommodation costs £60–110.

**Bike Tours**, PO Box 75, Bath BA1 1BX (☎01225/310 859). Well-run cycling tours, sometimes covering Hungary.

**Bridgwater Travel**, 217 Monton St, Manchester M30 9PN (☎0161/707 8547). Packages – city breaks and bus tours – and flight-only deals from London.

**Danube Travel**, 6 Conduit St, London W1R 9TG (☎0171/724 7577). Budapest city breaks for around £330 for three nights in a hotel, £290 in a pension, and slightly less if you are staying with a Hungarian family; plus fly-drive holidays from £245 for three days, seven-night spa holidays from £545, and city breaks combining Budapest with Vienna or Prague from £560.

**Hungarian Air Tours**, 3 Heddon St, London W1R 7LE (☎0171/437 9405). Three-night Budapest city breaks for £234–331, seven-night breaks for £323–400, and week-long spa holidays from around £640.

**Intra Travel**, 27 King's Exchange, Tileyard Road, London N7 9AH (☎0171/619 6700). Full range of holidays, including three- to seven-night Budapest city breaks from £273; fly-drive from around £250 for three nights; seven-night two-centre holidays

(Budapest with Pécs, Sopron, Eger or Lake Balaton) from under £400; and seven-night combinations of Budapest with Vienna (£605), Prague (under £400), or both (£695).

**Martin Randall Travel**, 10 Barley Mow Passage, London W4 4PH (☎0181/742 3355). Art and architecture tours on specific summer dates with expert guides: five nights in Budapest from £830, an eight-day tour for around £990, and an eight-day Spring Festival Break for £970. Prices include all taxes and tickets.

**New Millennium Holidays**, 20 High St, Solihull, West Midlands B91 3TB (☎0121/711 2232). Eight-day holidays, including bus travel, near Hévíz in the Balaton region from £139 (£299 by plane), in Budapest from £164, and two-centre holidays from £159.

**Prospect Music and Art Tours**, 454 Chiswick High St, London W4 5TT (☎0181/995 2151). Three-night opera breaks in a four-star hotel and tickets to two operas for £575.

**Regent Holidays**, 15 John St, Bristol BS1 2HR (☎0117/921 1711). Eastern European specialists offering tailor-made touring itineraries.

**Thermalia Travel**, 12 New College Parade, Finchley Rd, London NW3 5EP (☎0171/483 1898). Spa holiday specialists offering holidays at thermal resorts in Budapest and around the country from about £650 for seven nights, plus beauty, fitness and slimming courses, tennis for beginners, golf, and sailing. Also, three-night Christmas breaks for £299.

## TRAIN INFORMATION

**Eurostar**, Waterloo International Station, London SE1 (☎0345/303 030).

**Eurotrain**, 52 Grosvenor Gardens, London SW1 (☎0171/730 3402).

**International Rail Centre**, Victoria Station, London SW1 (☎0990/848 848).

**Wasteels**, Victoria Station, London SW1 (☎0171/834 7066).

## BUS INFORMATION

**Attila Travel**, 36a Kilburn High Rd, London NW6 (☎0171/372 0470).

**National Express Eurolines**, 164 Buckingham Palace Rd, London SW1 (☎0990/143 219).

Poland, the Czech Republic, Slovakia, Croatia, Romania, Bulgaria, Macedonia and Yugoslavia. Prices are currently £249 for a three-zone one-month pass if you're under 26 (£279 for all zones) and £275 for the over-26 version which, due to restrictions, is only valid in certain countries (the Netherlands, Germany and points east).

Finally, anyone over 60 and holding a Senior Citizen Railcard can buy a **Rail Europe Senior Card** (£5), which grants reductions of approximately 30 percent on European rail fares and sea crossings. Ask at any train station or some travel agents for details.

## BY BUS

Buses are an economical alternative to taking the train from **London to Budapest**, particularly if you're over 26. The cheapest deals are offered by Attila Travel (see also "Specialist Tour Operators", p.5), which charges around £100 for a return ticket, though special offers can be as low as £60; journey time is around 26 hours. The only other company plying the route is Eurolines, which runs three buses a week from Victoria Coach Station direct to Győr and Budapest (around 27hr).

## BY CAR: THE FERRIES AND LE SHUTTLE

If you have the time and inclination, **driving to Hungary** can be a pleasant proposition. Realistically, though, it's only worth considering if you are going to travel in Hungary for an extended period, or want to take advantage of various stopovers en route. If Budapest is your main goal, you'd be better off flying and renting a car once you're there.

It's important to plan ahead. The Automobile Association (AA) provides a comprehensive service offering general advice on all facets of driving

to Hungary; their European Route Service (☎0990/448 866) can provide a detailed printout of a route to follow. Driving licence, vehicle registration documents and insurance are essential; a Green Card is recommended.

## CROSSING THE CHANNEL

The Shuttle service through the **Channel Tunnel** doesn't significantly affect travel times for drivers to Hungary, though it does of course speed up the cross-Channel section. There are trains 24 hours a day, carrying cars, motorcycles, buses and their passengers, and taking 35 minutes between Folkestone and Calais. The Channel Tunnel entrance is off the M20 at junction 11A, just outside Folkestone. At peak times there are four departures hourly, making it possible to just turn up and buy

## CROSS-CHANNEL/NORTH SEA INFORMATION

**Holyman Sally Ferries**, (☎0990/595 522). Ramsgate–Ostend/ Dunkerque.

**Hoverspeed**, Dover (☎01304/240241). Dover and Folkestone to Boulogne and Calais by hovercraft or catamaran.

**Le Shuttle,** Customer Services Centre, PO Box 300, Folkestone, Kent (☎0990/353 535). Information and ticket sales.

**P&O European Ferries**, Dover (☎0990/980 980). Dover–Calais, Portsmouth–Cherbourg/Le Havre.

**P&O North Sea Ferries**, Hull (☎01482/377 177). Hull–Zeebrugge/Rotterdam.

**Stena Line**, Ashford (☎0990/707 070). Dover–Calais, Newhaven–Dieppe, Harwich–Hoek van Holland.

## CONNECTIONS FROM CONTINENTAL EUROPE

### Flights

The cost of direct **flights from other European cities** to Budapest isn't always proportionate to their proximity to Hungary. However, it's certainly worthwhile checking out flight prices with Malév, Air France, KLM, Alitalia or Lufthansa in any country.

### Trains

Timetables often use Hungarian names for destinations, which are given below. Canadians, Australians and New Zealanders are among those requiring transit visas for Slovakia.

There are two daily trains **from Paris** (Gare de l'Est), both taking roughly eighteen hours to reach Keleti Station in Budapest. Munich, Frankfurt and Berlin are the main points of departure **from Germany**; Frankfurt to Budapest (two trains a day) takes around eleven hours. Travellers coming **from the Czech Republic** have a choice of half a dozen trains from Prague via Bratislava (Pozsony), some of which come to Nyugati Station in Budapest, while Warsaw and Kraków are the points of departure **from Poland**. Most of the dozen or so services **from Vienna** leave from the Westbahnhof (except for the *Lehár* express which

leaves early in the morning from the Südbahnhof, returning there late in the evening), arriving at Keleti Station three to four hours later. If you're coming back the same way, it's worth buying a return ticket in Vienna, as one-way tickets cost more in Hungary. On some trains from Austria you can exchange money or travellers' cheques after crossing the Hungarian border, saving you from queuing at an exchange desk in one of the main Budapest stations.

### Hydrofoils

Although the frequency of **hydrofoils from Vienna** varies seasonally, the journey to Budapest always takes around four and a half hours. Departures are at 9am daily during the low season (mid-April to June & early Sept to Oct), and 8am and 2.30pm daily from early July to early September, but it's worth checking in Vienna as schedules may change. In Vienna, tickets are available from Riva Tours at I Krugerstrasse 26 (☎43 1/515-55) and Mahart Wien at Handelskai 265 (☎43 1/729 2162). A one-way ticket costs about 750 schillings/£45/US$68, and a return is 1100 schillings. Bookings should be made at least 24 hours in advance.

your ticket at the toll booth. Fares are calculated per car, regardless of the number of passengers, and vary according to time of year and time of day: the one-way fare is currently £74.50 in low season or £99.50 in peak season – July and August.

The alternative cross-Channel options for most travellers are the conventional **ferry or hovercraft links** between Ramsgate and Ostend (the most direct route); or from Dover, Folkestone, Ramsgate, Newhaven and Portsmouth to France; Felixstowe to Zeebrugge; Harwich to Holland; or Hull to Zeebrugge and Rotterdam. Ferry prices vary according to the time of year and, for motorists, the size of your car. The Ramsgate–Ostend run, for example, starts at about £151 standard return low season, for a car carrying three to five passengers. Foot passengers should be able to cross the Channel for about £25 each way year-round; taking a motorbike costs from £35 each way.

### THE DRIVING ROUTE

The most direct **route** from Ostend to Budapest runs via Brussels, Aachen, Cologne, Frankfurt, Nürnberg, Linz and Vienna. It's a distance of 1500km, which, driving non-stop, can be covered in 24 hours, but you shouldn't bank on driving it in under 36 hours. To avoid the long queues at Hegyeshalom and other main border crossings over summer, consider entering Hungary instead from Deutsch-Kreutz, just south of Eisenstadt. See under "Driving", p.22, for information about licences, insurance and driving inside Hungary.

**Hitching** along the same route can take up to three days, so you'd be wise to pack rainwear, a tent, a good road map, some Deutschmarks and/or food. There is currently no organized lift share agency in the UK, so you might try arranging a lift by putting up a notice in your local bookshop.

# GETTING THERE FROM IRELAND

There are no direct flights from Ireland to Hungary, and all air journeys involve changing planes, so it's a case of finding the cheapest and most convenient route.

**From Dublin** to Budapest, you can take Aer Lingus to Heathrow and then a BA flight from there, or British Midland and then Malév, or one of the Continental airlines such as Sabena or Swissair – ask at travel agents which company offers the cheapest prices. Standard APEX return fares start at around IR£270 from Dublin, IR£340 from Shannon, plus IR£15 or so airport tax.

**From Belfast**, flights also go via London, either with BA all the way, or British Midland to Heathrow, then Malév. A through ticket to Budapest, bought from BA, costs £300–380, but lower prices are generally available from Usit in Belfast, STA Travel or Danube Travel in London, or possibly (flying via Europe) with Intra Travel in London. British-based package tour operators also usually offer the option of flying from Belfast, with an add-on fare of around £106.

For **youth and student discount fares** in both the Republic and the North, the best first stop is Usit (see below for address). From Dublin, you can expect to pay IR£235–260, depending on the season, around IR£15 more from Shannon. From Belfast, prices are around £265–305 with BA, with occasional special winter offers for around £240 return.

**Travelling to London** by land and sea may save you a little money, but on the whole it's rarely worth the time and effort. Buying a Eurotrain boat-and-train ticket to London will slightly undercut the plane fares, but by this time you're starting to talk about a journey of days not hours to reach Budapest.

## FLIGHTS, PACKAGES AND TOURS FROM IRELAND

**Delta Travel**, 10 Malahide Rd, Artana, Dublin 5 (☎01/874 7666). *Occasional one-off packages.*

**Go Holidays**, 12 Upper O'Connell St, Dublin 1 (☎01/874 4126). *City breaks in Budapest and other holidays.*

**Terry Flynn Travel**, 47 The Quay, Waterford (☎051/72 126). *Packages and flights.*

**Thomas Cook**, 118 Grafton St, Dublin (☎01/677 1721). *Mainstream package holiday and flight agent, with occasional discount offers.*

**Usit**. Branches at: Aston Quay, O'Connell Bridge, Dublin 2 (☎01/602 1777); 10–11 Market Parade, Cork (☎021/270 900); Fountain Centre, College St, Belfast (☎01232/324 073). *Student and youth travel specialist.*

## AIRLINES

**Aer Lingus**, 40–41 O'Connell St, Dublin 1 (central reservations at Dublin airport on ☎01/705 3333); 2 Academy St, Cork (☎021/327 155); Northern Ireland reservations on ☎0645/737 747.

**British Airways**, Fountain Centre, College St, Belfast (☎0345/222 111); no Dublin office: contact Aer Lingus. Reservations: ☎1800/626 747.

## GETTING THERE FROM NORTH AMERICA

Some major airlines are beginning to offer direct flights from New York to Budapest, including Malév Hungarian Airlines, which makes daily non-stop flights from New York to Budapest. With other airlines you may fly on a one- or two-stop direct flight via London, Paris, or Frankfurt, or you might be better off flying to London (or Paris, Frankfurt or Vienna) and making your way overland from there (see "Getting There from Britain" for details). If you're planning to see Hungary as part of a wider European rail tour, you should consider buying a Eurail pass before you leave home.

### SHOPPING FOR TICKETS

Barring special offers, the cheapest fare is usually an **APEX** ticket, although with these you have to book – and pay – at least 21 days before departure, spend at least 7 days abroad (maximum stay 3 months), and you tend to get penalized if you change your schedule. There are also winter **Super Apex** tickets, sometimes known as "Eurosavers", which are slightly cheaper than an ordinary Apex, but limit your stay to between 7 and 21 days. Some airlines also issue **Special Apex** tickets to those under 24, often extending the maximum stay to a year, and many airlines offer youth or student fares to **under-25s**. It's worth remembering that most cheap return fares involve spending at least one Saturday night away and that many will only give a percentage

refund if you need to cancel or alter your journey; check the restrictions carefully before buying a ticket.

You can normally cut costs further by going through a **specialist flight agent** – either a **consolidator**, who buys up blocks of tickets from the airlines and sells them at a discount, or a **discount agent**, who wheels and deals in blocks of tickets offloaded by the airlines, and often offers special student and youth fares and a range of other travel-related services such as travel insurance, rail passes, car rentals, tours and the like. Bear in mind, though, that penalties for changing your plans can be stiff. Some agents specialize in **charter flights**, which may be cheaper than anything available on a scheduled flight, but again departure dates are fixed and withdrawal penalties are high; check the refund policy. If you travel a lot, **discount travel clubs** are another option – the annual membership fee may be worth it for benefits such as cut-price air tickets and car rental.

Don't automatically assume that tickets purchased through a travel specialist will be the cheapest: once you get a quote, check with the airlines and you may turn up an even better deal. Be advised also that the pool of travel companies is swimming with sharks – exercise caution and *never* deal with a company that demands cash upfront or refuses to accept payment by credit card.

Regardless of where you buy your ticket, the **fare** will depend on the season, and will be highest from around June to September. Note also that flying on weekends ordinarily adds $50 to the round-trip fare; **prices quoted below assume midweek travel**.

### FLIGHTS FROM THE US

If saving time is more important than finding the cheapest fare, you can get to Budapest on Malév, the Hungarian national airline, which flies direct to Budapest from New York. Otherwise, schedules and routeings are subject to change, but the last leg of the journey is likely to be on Malév no matter which airline you buy your ticket from.

**APEX fares** are virtually identical on all carriers. Low-season midweek return fares to Budapest start at around $600 from New York and $820 from West Coast cities, rising to $860 and $1100 respectively

## AIRLINES IN NORTH AMERICA

**Air France** in US ☎1-800/237-2747; in Canada ☎1-800/667-2747; www.airfrance.fr

**American Airlines** ☎1-800/433-7300 (domestic); ☎1-800/624-6262 (international); www.americanair.com

**British Airways** in US ☎1-800/247-9297; in Canada ☎1-800/668-1059; www.british-airways.com

**CSA Czech Airlines** ☎1-800/223-2365 or ☎1-800/628-6107; www.csa.cz

**Delta Airlines** ☎1-800/221-1212 (domestic); ☎1-800/241-4141 (international); in Canada, call directory inquiries ☎1-800/555-1212 for local toll-free number; www.delta-air.com

**KLM** in US ☎1-800/374-7747; in Canada ☎1-800/361-5073; www.klm.nl

**LOT Polish Airlines** in US ☎1-800/223-0593; in Canada ☎1-800/361-1017; www.poland.net/LOT

**Lufthansa** in US ☎1-800/645-3880; in Canada ☎1-800/563-5954; www.lufthansa-usa.com

**Malév Hungarian Airlines** East Coast ☎1-800/223-6884; West Coast ☎1-800/262-5380; www.malev.hu

**SAS** ☎1-800/221-2350; www.sas.se

**Swissair** in US ☎1-800/221-4750; in Canada ☎1-800/267-9477; www.swissair.com

**TWA** ☎1-800/221-2000 (domestic), ☎1-800/892-4141 (international); www.twa.com

**United Airlines** ☎1-800/241-6522 (domestic); ☎1-800/538-2929 (international); www.ual.com

## DISCOUNT TRAVEL COMPANIES IN NORTH AMERICA

**Air Brokers International**, 150 Post St, Suite 620, San Francisco, CA 94108 (☎1-800/883-3273; www.airbrokers.com). Consolidator.

**Air Courier Association**, 191 University Blvd, Suite 300, Denver, CO 80206 (☎1-800/282-1202 or ☎303/278-8810; www.aircourier.org). Courier flight broker.

**Council Travel**, head office: 205 E 42nd St, New York, NY 10017 (☎1-800/226-8624; www.ciee.org). Student travel organization with branches in many US cities. A sister company, Council Charter (☎1-800/223-7402), specializes in charter flights.

**Educational Travel Center**, 438 N Frances St, Madison, WI 53703 (☎1-800/747-5551; www.edtrav.com). Student/youth discount agent.

**Encore Travel Club**, 4501 Forbes Blvd, Lanham, MD 20706 (☎1-800/444-9800; www.emitravel.com). Discount travel club.

**Interworld Travel**, 800 Douglass Rd, Miami, FL 33134 (☎1-800/468-3796 or ☎305/443-4929; www.interworld.com). Consolidator.

**Last Minute Travel Club**, 100 Sylvan Rd, Woburn, MA 01801 (☎1-800/LAST MIN). Travel club specializing in standby deals.

**Moment's Notice**, 425 Madison Ave, New York, NY 10017 (☎212/486-0503). Discount travel club.

**New Frontiers/Nouvelles Frontières**, head offices: 12 E 33rd St, New York, NY 10016 (☎1-800/366-6387); 122 Rue St Hebert, Montréal, H2L 3Y8 (☎514/526-6774). Discount travel firm. Branches in LA, San Francisco and all over Canada.

**Now Voyager**, 74 Varick St, Suite 307, New York, NY 10013 (☎212/431-1616; www.nowvoyagertravel.com). Courier flight broker.

**STA Travel**, head office: ☎10 Downing St, New York, NY 10014 (☎1-800/781-4040; www.sta-travel.com). Worldwide specialist in independent travel with branches in the Los Angeles, San Francisco and Boston areas.

**TFI Tours International**, head office: 34 W 32nd St, New York, NY 10001 (☎1-800/745-8000). Consolidator; other offices in Las Vegas, San Francisco and Los Angeles.

**Travac**, head office: 989 6th Ave, New York NY 10018 (☎1-800/872-8800; www.travac.com). Consolidator and charter broker; has another branch in Orlando.

**Travel Avenue**, 10 S Riverside, Suite 1404, Chicago, IL 60606 (☎1-800/333-3335; www.travelavenue.com). Discount travel agent.

**Travel Cuts**, head office: 187 College St, Toronto, ON M5T 1P7 (☎416/979-2406 or ☎1-800/667-2887 (Canada only)). Canadian student travel organization with branches all over the country.

**Travelers Advantage**, 3033 S Parker Rd, Suite 900, Aurora, CO 80014 (☎1-800/548-1116; www.travelersadvantage.com). Discount travel club.

**UniTravel**, 11737 Administration Dr, St Louis, MO 63146 (☎1-800/325-2222; www.unitravel.com). Consolidator.

**Worldtek Travel**, 111 Water St, New Haven, CT 06511 (☎1-800/243-1723; www.worldtek.com). Discount travel agency.

**Worldwide Discount Travel Club**, 1674 Meridian Ave, Miami Beach, FL 33139 (☎305/534-2082). Discount travel club.

during high season. If you want to stay longer, you'll have to upgrade your ticket to a much more expensive, one-year return. You can sometimes cut the cost of high-season travel by buying a ticket from **travel agencies specializing in Eastern Europe**, such as Lotus Travel. Both agencies are excellent sources of advice on travelling in Hungary, and your best bet for finding out about any bargains that might be available.

Full-time students and anyone under 26 can take advantage of the excellent deals offered by **student/youth travel agencies** such as Council Travel, STA Travel and Nouvelles Frontières. Their flights go for around $800 from the East Coast, $1000 from the West Coast, even in high season, and an added advantage is their flexibility: there are low penalties for changes or cancellations, and the tickets are valid for six months to a year. Those who don't meet the student/youth requirements can still save some money by buying tickets through **discount agencies** such as those listed in the box opposite.

### FLIGHTS FROM CANADA

The only airlines to fly **from Canada to Budapest** are Lufthansa (via Frankfurt) and KLM (via Amsterdam). APEX fares start at CDN$1100 from Toronto (with Lufthansa or KLM) and CDN$1500 from Vancouver (Lufthansa only) during the low season, rising to CDN$1500 and CDN$1800 over summer. The alternatives are to travel to the US and then fly on from there (see above), or fly to a European city and then reach Hungary by air or overland. Although London is the cheapest "gateway" city, a bargain flight to Frankfurt or Vienna might prove less expensive in the long run.

### PACKAGE TOURS

**Package tours** can save you time and effort, and the hassle of finding your way around an unfamiliar country. Fully fledged guided tours are offered by Fugazy International, and the Hungarian tourist organization, IBUSZ (see p.19), which has a range of packages focusing on various aspects of Hungarian culture, plus horse-riding, walking and cycling tours. Forum Travel also offer tours, including escorted and independent bicycling tours; expect to pay $2000–2900 per person for a ten- to fourteen-day holiday, including return flights, accommodation and most meals. Forum Travel's escorted bicycle tours operate from May to September and start at $945 per person for a

---

### HUNGARIAN TRAVEL SPECIALISTS

**ETT Tours**, 198 Boston Post Rd, Mamaroneck, NY 10543 (☎1-800/551-2085).

**Forum Travel**, 91 Gregory Lane, Pleasant Hill, CA (☎925/671-2900, 1-800/252-4475; *www.foruminternational.com*).

**Fugazy International**, 770 US-1, North Brunswick, NJ (☎1-800/828-4488).

**Lotus Travel**, 3108 Lincoln Way, Costa Mesa, CA 92626 (☎1-800/675-0559; *www.pacbell.net/european*).

---

seven-night holiday out of Vienna (excluding flights from the US).

If you're simply interested in **booking accommodation** and transport within Hungary, contact Lotus Travel. Information on accommodation can also be obtained through Tradesco Tours and Hungarian Hotels (6033 W Century Blvd, Suite 670, Los Angeles, CA; ☎1-800/448-4321; *www. tradescotours.com*), but bookings must be made through one of the agencies mentioned above.

### TRAIN PASSES

If you're planning to do a lot of train travel in Europe, then consider buying a **Eurail pass**, which comes in various forms and must be bought before you leave home. Although it's not likely to pay for itself if you're planning to stick to Hungary, the pass also allows unlimited free train travel in sixteen other countries. The **Eurail Youthpass**

---

### RAIL CONTACTS IN NORTH AMERICA

**CIT Tours**, 342 Madison Ave, Suite 207, New York, NY 10173 (☎1-800/223-7987). *Eurail passes.*

**DER Tours/GermanRail**, 9501 W Divon Ave, Suite 400, Rosemont, IL 60018 (☎1-800/421-2929; *www.dertravel.com*). *Eurail passes.*

**Orbis Polish Travel Bureau**, 342 Madison Ave, New York, NY 10173 (☎1-800/223-6037; *www.orbis/usa.com*). *Passes for Hungary.*

**Rail Europe**, 226 Westchester Ave, White Plains, NY 10604 (☎1-800/848-7245). *Official Eurail pass agent in North America.*

**ScanTours**, 1535 6th St, Suite 205, Santa Monica, CA 90401 (☎1-800/223-7226; *www.scantours.com*). *Eurail passes.*

(for under-26s) costs US$398 for fifteen days, $578 for one month and $768 for two months; if you're 26 or over you'll have to buy a first-class pass, available in fifteen-day ($498), 21-day ($648), one-month ($798), two-month ($1098) and three-month ($1398) increments. You stand a better chance of getting your money's worth out of a **Eurail Flexipass**, which is good for a certain number of travel days in a two-month period. This, too, comes in under-26/first-class versions: five days cost $255/$348; ten days, $398/$560; and fifteen

days, $540/$740. A further alternative is to attempt to buy an InterRail Pass in Europe (see "Getting There from Britain", above). Most agents don't check residential qualifications, but once you're in Europe it'll be too late to buy a Eurail Pass if you have problems. You can purchase Eurail passes from any of the agents listed on p.11.

North Americans are also eligible to purchase a more specific pass valid for travel in Hungary only, for details of which see "Getting Around", p.21.

# GETTING THERE FROM AUSTRALIA & NEW ZEALAND

The cheapest flight to Budapest is from Aeroflot/Qantas, who charge A$1374 in the low period and A$1704 in peak season. Alitalia, Qantas and Ansett combine to charge A$1407/A$1957 repectively. Swissair, Olympic Airways, Qantas and KLM charge around A$1530 in low season and A$1900-2100 in the peak period. Round-the-world fares, which usually include six stopovers in one direction, start at A$2200.

There are no really cheap flights from **New Zealand**. Lufthansa/Lauda Air and Air New

## AIRLINES

**Aeroflot**, 388 George St, Sydney (☎02/233 7911). No NZ office.

**Air France**, 12 Castlereagh St, Sydney (☎02/321 1030); 57 Fort St, Auckland (☎09/303 1229).

**Air New Zealand**, 5 Elizabeth St, Sydney (☎02/9937 5111); Cnr. Customs and Queen Streets, Auckland (☎09/366 2424).

**Alitalia**, 118 Alfred St (Sth), Milsons Point (☎1300 653 747 or 9922 1555); 6th Floor, Trustbank Building, 229 Queen St, Auckland (☎09/379 4457).

**British Airways**, Level 26, 201 Kent St, Sydney (☎02/9258 3300); 154 Queen St, Auckland (☎09/356 8690).

**Garuda**, 55 Hunter St, Sydney (☎1300 365 330); 120 Albert St, Auckland (☎09/366 1855).

**KLM**, 5 Elizabeth St, Sydney (☎02/9231 6333 or 1800 505 747). No NZ office.

**Lauda Air**, 11/143 Macquarie St, Sydney (☎02/9241 4277); Trustbank Building, 229 Queen St, Auckland (☎09/379 4455).

**Lufthansa**, 12/143 Macquarie St, Sydney (☎02/9367 3888); 36 Kitchener St, Auckland (☎09/303 1529).

**MAS**, 16 Spring St, Sydney (☎02/9352 7878, 13 2627); Floor 12, Swanson Centre, 12–26 Swanson St, Auckland (☎09/373 2741).

**Olympic Airways**, Floor 3, 37–49 Pitt St, Sydney (☎02/9251 2044).

**Qantas**, 70 Hunter St, Sydney (☎13/1211); Qantas House, 154 Queen St, Auckland (☎09/357 8700 or ☎0800 808 767).

**United**, 10 Barrack St, Sydney (☎02/237 8888); 7 City Road, Auckland (☎09/307 9500).

NOTE: ☎1800 numbers are toll-free, but only apply if dialled outside the city in the address.

---

## DISCOUNT TRAVEL AGENTS

**Anywhere Travel**, 345 Anzac Pde, Kingsford, Sydney (☎02/9663 0411).

**Brisbane Flight Centre**, 260 Queen St, Brisbane (☎07/3229 9211).

**Budget Travel**, 16 Fort St, Auckland; other branches around the city (☎09/366 0061 or ☎0800/808 040).

**Destinations Unlimited**, 3 Milford Rd, Milford, Auckland (☎09/373 4033).

**Flight Centres Australia**, Level 11, 33 Berry St, North Sydney (☎131 600, 02/9460 0555); 19 Bourke St, Melbourne (☎03/9650 2899); plus other branches nationwide; National Bank Towers, 205–225 Queen St, Auckland (☎09/209 6171); Shop 1M, National Mutual Arcade, 152 Hereford St, Christchurch (☎03/379 7145); 50–52 Willis St, Wellington (☎04/472 8101).

**Northern Gateway**, 22 Cavenagh St, Darwin (☎08/8941 1394).

**Passport Travel**, Kings Cross Plaza, Ste 11/401 St Kilda Rd, Melbourne (☎03/9867 3888).

**STA Travel**. Australia: 855 George St, Sydney (☎02/9212 1255 or ☎1300 360 960); 256 Flinders St, Melbourne (☎03/9654 7266); other offices in state capitals and major universities. New Zealand: Travellers' Centre, 10 High St, Auckland (☎09/309 0458); 233 Cuba St, Wellington (☎04/385 0561); 90 Cashel St, Christchurch (☎03/379 9098); other offices in Dunedin, Palmerston North, Hamilton and major universities.

**Thomas Cook**. Australia: 321 Kent St, Sydney (☎02/9248 6100); 257 Collins St, Melbourne (☎03/9282 0222); branches in other state capitals. New Zealand: Shop 250a, St Luke's Square, Auckland (☎09/849 2071).

**Topdeck Travel**, 65 Glenfell St, Adelaide (☎08/8232 7222).

**Tymtro Travel** (☎02/9223 2211).

---

Zealand charge around NZ$2799 to Vienna or Frankfurt, but you'll possibly be better off buying a discounted fare to Australia (NZ$650 or less) and proceeding from there.

**Discount flight agents**, and specialist operators like Danube Travel (see above for contact numbers), should be able to get ten percent off the mid-season fares quoted above.

## VISAS AND RED TAPE

Citizens of the EU, United States and Canada no longer require visas for Hungary, simply receiving a stamp in their passport at the border, which allows a stay of up to ninety days. Citizens of France and Germany do not need a passport, only an identity card. New Zealanders and other nationalities, however, must still obtain a visa – either from a Hungarian consulate abroad, or on arrival at Budapest airport or any road crossing along the border – although if you are arriving by land, you are advised to get your visa in advance. Visas are not issued at rail crossings or the passenger dock for hydrofoils from Vienna.

Assuming that you require a visa, applications can be made to any Hungarian consulate abroad in person, or by post. **Tourist visas** are valid for thirty days' stay, with the option of single, double or multiple entries, while **transit visas** entitle you to 48 hours' stay. Besides two passport photos, you will need to submit your passport and the requisite fee (currently £26–42 for a single-entry

## HUNGARIAN EMBASSIES AND CONSULATES ABROAD

**AUSTRALIA** Embassy: 17 Beale Crescent, Deakin Canberra, ACT. 2600 (☎02/6282 3226 or ☎02/6285 3484); Consulate: Suite 405 Edgecliffe Centre 203-233, New South Head Rd, Edgecliffe Sydney, NSW 2027 (☎02/9328 7859 or ☎02/9328 7860).

**AUSTRIA** 1, Bankgasse 4–6, A–1010, Vienna (☎01/533-2631).

**BRITAIN** 35b Eaton Place, London SW1X 8BY (☎0171/235 2664; Mon–Fri 10am–12.30pm).

**CANADA** Embassy: 299 Waverley St, Ottawa, Ontario, K2P 0V9 (☎613/230-9614); Consulates: 1200 McGill College Ave, Suite 2040, Montréal, Québec H3B 4G7 (☎514/393-3302); 121 Bloor St, East Suite 1115, Toronto (☎416/923-8981).

**DENMARK** Strandvejen 170, 2920 Charlottenlund, Copenhagen (☎39-63-1688 or ☎31-63-1929).

**FRANCE** Embassy: 5 Bis, Square de l'Avenue Foch, 75116 Paris (☎1/45-00-00-29 or ☎1/45-00-41-59); Consulate: 92 Rue Bonaparte, 75006 Paris (☎1/43-54-66-96).

**GERMANY** Embassy: Turmstrasse 30 (Plittersdorf), 53175 Bonn 2 (☎228/37-11-12); Unter den Linden 76, 10177 Berlin (☎30/220-25-51).

**NETHERLANDS** Hogeweg 14, 2585 JD, Den Haag (☎070/350-0404 or ☎070/350-0956).

**NORWAY** Sophus Lies gt 3, Oslo 2 (☎255-2418 or ☎255-2419).

**SWEDEN** Strandvägen 74, 115.27 Stockholm (☎08/661-6762 or ☎08/662-5675).

**USA** Embassy: 3910 Shoemakers St NW, Washington DC 20008 (☎202/362-6730; visa enquiries ☎202/362-6737); 223 East 52nd St, New York, NY 10022 (☎212/752-0669); Consulate: 11766 Wilshire Blvd, Suite 410, Los Angeles, CA 90025 (☎310/473-9344).

---

visa obtained in Britain; consulates in Eastern Europe require payment in US$).

**Applications** in person are generally processed within 24 hours, though some consulates will issue visas the same day for a surcharge. To apply by post, obtain an application form from the consulate, then send the completed form and your passport by registered post, including a postal order (in Britain) or certified cheque (in the US), plus a stamped addressed envelope for return. Applications can also be made through IBUSZ at 1 Parker Plaza, Suite 1004, Fort Lee, NJ 07024 (☎1-800/367-7878) in the US, or Danube Travel at 6 Conduit St, London W1R 9TG (☎0171/493 0263) in Britain, which levies a surcharge.

### VISA EXTENSIONS AND REGISTRATION

Visitors can stay up to three months, after which they are required to register with the police. **Applications for extensions** must be made 48 hours before the visa expires, and you may be asked to show evidence of funds or proof of having exchanged money. In Budapest, go to the district police station (*kerületi rendőrség*) nearest to your place of residence; in provincial towns, apply to police headquarters (*főkapitányság*). The process usually takes about fifteen minutes. A simpler method of extending your stay, whether you need a visa or not, is to leave the country, either by taking the bus to Vienna and spending the day there, or taking the train to Komárom, walking across the bridge to Slovakia, and then back again.

After three months' stay, all visitors are required to register their address (and any subsequent changes of address) with the local police. In practice, however, **registration** need only concern those staying in "unofficial" accommodation (for example, with friends), since residents in hotels, hostels, pensions, guesthouses and campsites are automatically registered. Should you need to register, get an Alien's Registration Form (*Lakcímbejelentő lap külföldiek részére*) from any post office and have it countersigned by your host before taking it to the police station.

**Lost passports** must be reported to the local police station. You then take the police report to your consulate, which can sort out your papers to leave the country or issue a new passport. You may need to go back to the police for an exit stamp in order to leave the country. Your consulate should be notified by the police if your passport is found.

### CUSTOMS

**Customs** formalities are normally painless, though visitors arriving from Austria or Romania by road may get stuck in long queues at the border crossings. Visitors over the age of 16 are allowed 250 cigarettes (or 250g of tobacco or fifty cigars), two litres of wine and one litre of spirits as travel luggage. In addition there is a duty-free allowance of one litre of wine, one litre of spirits, five litres of beer, 500 cigarettes (or 100 cigars or 500g tobacco), and one kilogramme of coffee, tea and cocoa. Up to five kilogrammes of food is allowed, but it may not contain raw meat. There is no **import duty** on personal effects such as bicycles, cameras, portable cassette recorders and TV sets, but items with a high resale value (like laptop computers and video cameras) are liable to customs duty and 25 percent VAT unless you can prove that they are for personal use.

These customs regulations change fairly frequently, so it's worth checking the latest rules at a Hungarian consulate or tourist office before leaving home. You can **export** five kilos of foodstuffs which may include two kilos of processed meat products (for example, salami and canned meats). Duty-free export limits for tobacco and alcohol are the same as the import limits.

## HEALTH AND INSURANCE

No inoculations are required for Hungary, and standards of public health are good. Tap water is safe everywhere, while potable springs (*forrás*) and streams are designated on maps, and with signs, as *ivóvíz*. The national health service (OTBF) will provide free emergency treatment in any hospital or doctor's office for citizens of Britain, Finland, Norway, Sweden, the countries of the former Soviet Union, and former Eastern Bloc countries, but there is a charge for drugs and non-emergency care.

Even so, it's a very good idea to have some kind of **travel insurance**, since with this you're covered for loss of possessions and money, as well as the cost of all medical and dental treatment. Remember that certain activities classified as hazardous sports are unlikely to be covered by most policies, although by paying an extra premium you can usually get added cover for the period in which these activities are taking place.

With all policies you have to pay upfront and **reclaim the money** when you get home, producing hospital receipts or a police report to verify your claim.

### UK INSURANCE

**UK citizens** can ask about policies at any bank or travel agent, or use a policy issued by a specialist travel company like Usit Campus or STA Travel (see p.4 for address), or by the low-cost **insurers** Endsleigh Insurance (97–107 Southampton Row, London WC1; ☎0171/436 4451) or Columbus Travel Insurance (17 Devonshire Square, London EC2; ☎0171/375 0011). Two weeks' cover starts at around £13; a month from £19.

### NORTH AMERICAN INSURANCE

Before buying an insurance policy, check that you're not already covered. **Canadians** are usually covered for medical mishaps overseas by their provincial health plans. Holders of official **student/teacher/youth cards** are entitled to accident coverage and hospital in-patient benefits. **Students** will often find that their student health coverage extends during the vacations and for one term beyond the date of last enrolment. Bank and credit cards (particularly American Express) often have certain levels of medical or other insurance included, and travel insurance may also be included if you use a major credit or charge card to pay for your trip. **Homeowners' or renters'** insurance often covers theft or loss of documents, money and valuables while overseas, though conditions and maximum amounts vary from company to company.

After exhausting the possibilities above, you might want to contact a specialist **travel insurance** company; your travel agent can usually recommend one, or see the box above. Policies are comprehensive (accidents, illnesses, delayed or lost luggage, cancelled flights, etc), but maximum payouts tend to be meagre. The best deals are usually to be had through student/youth travel agencies.

Most North American travel policies apply only to items lost, stolen or damaged while in the custody of an identifiable, responsible third party – hotel porter, airline, luggage consignment, etc. Even in these cases you will have to contact the local police within a certain time limit to have a complete report made out so that your insurer can process the claim.

### AUSTRALIAN INSURANCE

In **Australia**, CIC Insurance, offered by Cover-More Insurance Services, Level 9, 32 Walker St, North Sydney (☎02/202 8000), has some of the widest cover available and can be arranged through most travel agents; there are branches in Victoria and Queensland too. It costs from A$140 for 31 days.

### HEALTH CARE, PHARMACIES AND HOSPITALS

Sunburn (*napszúrás*) and insect bites (*rovarcsípés*) are the most common **minor complaints**: suntan lotion is sold in supermarkets, and pharmacists stock *Vietnámi balzsam* (Vietnamese-made "Tiger Balm" – the best bug-repellent going) and bite ointment. Mosquitoes are pesky, but the bug to beware of in forests is the *kullancs*, which bites and then burrows into human skin, causing inflammation of the brain. The risk seems fairly small, but if you get a bite which seems particu-

larly painful, or are suffering from a high temperature and stiff neck following a bite, it's worth having it checked out as quickly as possible.

All towns and some villages have a **pharmacy** (*gyógyszertár* or *patika*), with staff (who are most likely to understand German) authorized to issue a wide range of drugs. However, pharmaceutical products are mainly of East European origin, so anyone requiring specific medication should bring a supply with them. Opening hours are normally Monday–Friday 9am–6pm, Saturday 9am–noon or 1pm; signs in the window give the location or telephone number of the nearest all-night (*éjjeli* or *ügyeleti szolgálat*) pharmacy.

In more serious cases, provincial tourist offices can direct you to local **medical centres** or doctors' offices (*orvosi rendelő*), while your embassy in Budapest will have the addresses of foreign-language-speaking **doctors** and **dentists**, who will probably be in private (*magán*) practice. Private medicine is much cheaper than in the West, as attested to by the thousands of Austrians who come here for treatment. (See the hospitals and dentistry listings at the end of the Budapest chapter on p.125 for details of some private clinics in the capital.) For muscular, skin or gynaecological complaints, doctors often prescribe a soak at one of Hungary's numerous **medicinal baths** (*gyógyfürdő*).

In **emergencies**, dial ☎104 for the *Mentők* ambulance service, or catch a taxi to the nearest *Kórház*. The standard of **hospitals** varies enormously, but low morale and shortages of beds testify to poor wages and the general underfunding of the health service. Depending on local conditions, Westerners might get the best available treatment, or be cold-shouldered; in the event of the latter, it's worth trying to bribe the staff as a last resort.

There is an Anonymous **AIDS** Advisory Service in Budapest at Budapest VIII, Joszef út 46 (Mon–Thurs 8am–4pm, Fri 8am–12 noon.) You can also call *Háttér* (Background), a gay helpline on health and other issues (6–11pm; English is generally spoken), on ☎1/329 3380. Two AIDS helplines in the regions are in Pécs (☎72/413 303) and Sopron (☎99/333 399).

## COSTS, MONEY AND BANKS

**Most Hungarians complain of "paying Swedish taxes on an Ethiopian wage" and of the rising cost of living, which has badly hit much of the population – though the comforts and wealth of Budapest might give a different impression. With inflation running at just under twenty percent, Hungarian forint prices quoted in this guide will inevitably become outdated, but, unless your own currency slips badly, real costs should remain fairly stable, due to the monthly devaluation of the forint. For this reason, many prices given in this guide are either expressed in US dollars or Deutschmarks (DM). Many hotels will quote Deutschmark prices, which are more stable.**

### AVERAGE COSTS

Although foreigners no longer find Hungary a really cheap place to visit, it's still good value on the whole. Depending on the exchange rate (see below) and where you go, most **costs** are two-thirds to three-quarters of what you'd pay at home, except in Budapest and the Lake Balaton resorts, which are more expensive than other parts of Hungary. Wherever you are, your biggest expenditure will be on **accommodation**. Outside Budapest and the Balaton, the average three-star hotel charges £35–40 (US$53–60) for a double room with bath, while the same in a private guesthouse costs about £10/$15. Although you can get stung for more in some **restaurants**, a three-course meal with wine can generally be had for around £5–10/$8–15. With flat fares (roughly 20p/30¢) in urban areas, and cheap inter-city trains and buses (averaging under £2–3/$3–5), **transport** will be the least of your expenses. Museums cost between 50 and 300 Ft.

If you're keeping to a tight budget, remember that some campsites and hostels give discounts to holders of IUS (student) cards (see "Directory" p.45). Further **savings** can be made by hitching, making or buying your own food, or eating in public canteens.

### CURRENCY AND EXCHANGE RATE

The Hungarian unit of currency is the **forint** (Ft or HUF), which comprises 100 **fillér**. The **exchange rate** is currently 370Ft to the pound sterling, 220Ft to the US$.

The forint comes in **notes** of 100, 500, 1000, 5000 and 10,000 Ft, with 50 *fillér*, 1, 2, 5, 10, 20, 50 and 100 Ft coins, together with the occasional 200Ft coin; there are older versions of the 1, 2, 5, 10 and 20 coins which are no longer valid currency, but you may get them palmed off on you occasionally. Restrictions on importing or exporting banknotes now only apply to sums of over 300,000Ft. There's no restriction on bringing in convertible currency, but there is a limit on sums more than the equivalent of 50,000Ft being taken out. If you enter the country with more, or with all your cash in small denominations, you should declare this on entry.

### TRAVELLERS' CHEQUES AND CREDIT CARDS

Although a modest amount of low-denomination US dollar bills or Deutschmarks and travellers' cheques is advisable, the safest and easiest way to carry your money is in your **bank card**. The number of **ATM**s (Automatic Teller Machines) is fast rising, especially in Budapest, but you can get money out of the wall in most regional towns too. Amex, Visa, Mastercard, Diners' Club, Carte Blanche and Eurocard **credit and charge cards** can be used to rent cars, buy airline tickets or pay your bills directly in hotels and restaurants and many shops. Outside the main tourist centres their usefulness is more restricted. **Travellers' cheques** issued by American, Australian, British, Dutch, Norwegian and German banks are all accepted, but for speedy refunds in case of loss, American Express (represented in Budapest at Deák Ferenc utca 10; ☎267-8680) is much the most reliable brand. You can cash **Eurocheques** up to the value of 30,000Ft at places displaying the Eurocheque logo.

### BANKS AND CHANGING MONEY

Exchange rates vary somewhat from place to place, and it's best to use the main tourist offices and banks when you want to change money. American Express in Budapest offers low rates, while the private exchange offices, whose top rate is for exchanges of large sums only, charge a high commission.

Providing you produce your passport, **changing money or travellers' cheques** is a painless operation, and can be done at any bank or regional tourist office, or at the majority of large hotels and campsites. Note that banks often close quite early, however, before 3pm on weekdays and even earlier on Fridays. Keep the **receipts** if you want to engage in the expensive process of exchanging forints back into hard currency when you leave Hungary: at road checkpoints, fifty percent of any remaining forints can be re-exchanged up to the value of US$50. The advantages of changing money on the illegal **black market** are minimal (ten percent above the official rate), and scalpers are skilled at cheating.

If you want to open a **foreign currency bank account** (*devizaszámla*), ask around to find the best conditions – some require a high minimum deposit, but money transferred from abroad takes days to come through here rather than weeks. Inter-bank money transfers are fastest through the SWIFT system, to which most Hungarian banks and some British banks are linked. However, funds can still take a long time to reach your Hungarian branch, especially if your account is not with the bank's main branch. You can also use the American Express office for **money transfers**, which might prove quicker and cheaper.

# INFORMATION AND MAPS

A large number of photo-packed brochures, maps and special-interest leaflets are available free from the Hungarian National Tourist Office, and distributed by their offices abroad and by the offices of the travel organization Tourinform. The most useful things to pick up are the large road map (which is perfectly adequate for travelling around Hungary); a pamphlet detailing the year's festivals and events; and the *Hotels* and *Camping* booklets,

---

**INFORMATION OFFICES ABROAD**

**Britain**: Hungarian National Tourist Office, PO Box 4336, London SW18 4XE (☎0171/823 1032, fax 823 1459).

**USA**: Hungarian National Tourist Office, c/o Embassy of the Republic of Hungary, Commercial Counsellor's Office, New York, NY 10155-3398 150 E 58th St, 33rd Floor (☎212/355-0240, fax 207-4103; *Huntour@Gramercy.ios.com*).

## IBUSZ AGENTS ABROAD

**Australia**: Suite 401, 115 Pitt St, Sydney NSW (☎02/223-41-97).

**Britain**: Danube Travel Ltd, 6 Conduit St, London W1R 9TG (☎0171/493 0263).

**USA**: 1 Parker Plaza, Suite 1104, Fort Lee, NJ 07024 (☎201/592-8585 or ☎1-800/367-7878); M/C79/50 5000 Airport Plaza Drive, Long Beach, Los Angeles CA (☎213/593-2952).

which list accommodation on a town-by-town basis, together with the tourist offices that handle bookings. There are also brochures on village tourism, listing farmsteads and country pensions; on religious sights; cycling tours, riding holidays and walking tours.

### TOURIST AGENCIES IN HUNGARY

In Hungary itself you'll find **local tourist agencies** in most larger towns (called, variously, Savaria Tourist, Komturist, etc) and a growing net-

### MAP OUTLETS

**UK**
**London**
Daunt Books, 83 Marylebone High St, W1 (☎0171/224 2295).

National Map Centre, 22–24 Caxton St, SW1 (☎0171/222 2466).

Stanfords, 12–14 Long Acre, WC2 (☎0171/836 1321).

**Glasgow**
John Smith and Sons, 57–61 St Vincent St, G2 5TB (☎0141/221 7472).

Maps by **mail or phone order** are available from Stanfords (☎0171/836 1321).

**NORTH AMERICA**
**Chicago**
Rand McNally, 444 N Michigan Ave, IL 60611 (☎312/321-1751).

**Montréal**
Ulysses Travel Bookshop, 4176 St-Denis (☎514/289-0993).

**New York**
British Travel Bookshop, 551 5th Ave, NY 10176 (☎1-800/448-3039 or ☎212/490-6688).

The Complete Traveler Bookstore, 199 Madison Ave, NY 10016 (☎212/685-9007).

Rand McNally, 150 E 52nd St, NY 10022 (☎212/758-7488).

Traveler's Bookstore, 22 W 52nd St, NY 10019 (☎212/664-0995).

**San Francisco**
The Complete Traveler Bookstore, 3207 Fillmore St, CA 92123 (☎415/923-1511).

Rand McNally, 595 Market St, CA 94105 (☎415/777-3131).

**Santa Barbara**
Pacific Traveler Supply, 25 E Mason St, 93101 (☎805/963-4438; phone orders: ☎805/968-4402).

**Seattle**
Elliot Bay Book Company, 101 South Main St, WA 98104 (☎206/624-6600).

**Toronto**
Open Air Books and Maps, 25 Toronto St, M5R 2C1 (☎416/363-0719).

**Vancouver**
World Wide Books and Maps, 736a Granville St, V6Z 1G3 (☎604/687-3320).

**Washington DC**
Rand McNally, 1201 Connecticut Ave NW, 20036 (☎202/223-6751).

**Note** that Rand McNally now have twenty stores across the US; phone ☎1-800/333-0136, ext 2111, for the address of your nearest store, or for **direct mail** maps.

**AUSTRALIA**
**Adelaide**
The Map Shop, 16a Peel St, SA 5000 (☎08/231 2033).

**Brisbane**
Hema, 239 George St, QLD 4000 (☎07/221 4330).

**Melbourne**
Bowyangs, 372 Little Bourke St, VIC 3000 (☎03/670 4383).

**Perth**
Perth Map Centre, 891 Hay St, WA 6000 (☎09/322 5733).

**Sydney**
Travel Bookshop, 20 Bridge St, NSW 2000 (☎02/241 3554).

work of **Tourinform** offices, set up by the Hungarian National Tourist Office, which have excellent information on accommodation and activities, although only a few of them will book rooms. Generally, Tourinform office staff are very friendly, and hand out free publications on the city or region you are in. IBUSZ and Express are two nationwide agencies, though both have reduced their activities in local accommodation sharply in recent years. Addresses, opening hours and phone numbers for the local agencies are given throughout the guide.

## MAPS

You may want to supplement the maps in this book with Hungarian town plans (*városi-térkép*), which also detail main sights and tram and bus routes.

These maps cost between 150Ft and 250Ft and are available from local tourist offices or, failing that, from bookshops (*könyvesbolt*). If you are travelling by car, the *Magyar Auto Atlasz* is a must. Available from bookshops, it contains plans of most towns (though some of the street names may be out of date) and road maps. Bookshops also stock **hiking maps** (*turistatérkép*) covering the highland regions, which should be purchased in advance wherever possible, as they may not be available on the spot; see p.41 for more on hiking. Tourinform issues a variety of useful, free **road maps**, including one showing Budapest's one-way streets and bypasses.

If you want to buy Hungarian maps in advance of your trip, try one of the specialist map suppliers listed in the box on p.19.

# GETTING AROUND

**Although it doesn't break any speed records, public transport reaches most parts of Hungary and, despite recent price increases, remains remarkably cheap. Regional transport schedules are summarized under "Travel Details" at the end of each chapter.**

## TRAINS

The centralization of the **MÁV** rail network means that many cross-country journeys are easier if you travel via Budapest rather than on branch lines where services are slower and less frequent. Timetables displayed in stations are in yellow (for departures) or white (for arrivals), with

the different types of fast **trains** picked out in red. By far the fastest are the Intercity ("IC" on the timetable) trains, which run express services between Budapest and Miskolc, Szeged and other larger towns; don't be mislead by Express trains (marked "Ex" on timetables), as although they stop at major centres only, and cost ten percent more than *gyorsvonat* and *sebesvonat* services, which stop more regularly, they are still pretty slow. The slowest trains (*személyvonat*) halt at every hamlet along the way, and since the fare is the same as on a *gyorsvonat*, you might as well opt for the latter. It's not worth using international trains for journeys within Hungary, since they are expensive and not always faster.

Most trains have first- and second-class sections, and many also feature a buffet car (indicated on timetables). Second-class trains have PVC seats and can be uncomfortable and crowded. First class offers slightly more comfort. International services routed through Budapest have **sleeping cars** and **couchettes** (*hálókocsi* and *kusett*), for which tickets can be bought at MÁV offices in advance, or sometimes on the train itself. There's also a **car train** on the Budapest–Dresden line in the summer, which travellers to Germany might find useful, although it doesn't carry camper vans or minibuses. **Bicycles** (*bicikli*) can be carried on most passenger trains (you have to buy a bicycle ticket too), although some Intercity trains might not let you on; look for the bicycle pictogram on the timetable. At the weekends and holidays you can get on anywhere where there is space in the corridor, while in rush hour during the week (6–8am and 2–3.30pm), you must use the last carriage. Special carriages with stands for bikes have recently been introduced on some trains; ask at the ticket office for details.

If you're planning to travel by rail extensively, it's worth investing in the **timetables** available from the MÁV office in Budapest at VI, Andrássy út 35 (☎322-8049), or large train stations. Train services (domestic and international) are covered by the chunky *Hivatalos Menetrend* (500Ft; note that the larger format version has no extra information), which also details boat and ferry services on the Danube and the Balaton; an English-language section at the front explains the symbols used.

### TICKETS AND PASSES

**Tickets** (*jegy*) for domestic train services can be bought at the station (*pályaudvar* or *vasútállomás*) on the day of departure, although it's possible to reserve them up to sixty days in advance. You can break your journey once between the point of departure and the final destination, but must get your ticket validated within an hour of arrival at the interim station. Most Hungarians purchase one-way tickets (*egy útra*), so specify a *retur* or *oda-vissza* if you want a **return ticket**. If you're found travelling without a ticket you have to buy one at many times the normal price.

**Seat bookings** (*helyjegy*), in the form of a separate numbered bit of card, are obligatory for

services marked ® on timetables (mostly international or express trains), and optional on those designated by an R. It is advisable to book a seat on Intercity trains, especially those going to Lake Balaton in the summer, but otherwise it is not necessary. Bookings can be made up to two months in advance at any MÁV office, and will add a few hundred forints to the total ticket price.

It's best to buy tickets for **international trains** (*nemzetközi gyorsvonat*) at least 36 hours in advance, since demand is heavy. The central MÁV ticket office in Budapest, which handles bookings, gets very crowded during summer; and staff and customers won't thank anybody who tries to pay by cheque or credit card. Note that student card holders are entitled to a 33 percent reduction.

**Concessionary fares** on domestic services are also available: there's a 33 percent discount for groups of ten to nineteen people, and 50 percent for groups of over twenty people; BIJ/Euro Domino ticket holders get 25 to 50 percent off, and pensioners (women over 55 and men over 60) get a twenty percent reduction if they show a passport. Children under four travel **free** if they don't occupy a separate seat, while children up to the age of fourteen pay 50 percent of the fare. InterRail/Eurail passes also allow free travel.

MÁV itself issues various **train passes**, valid on MÁV lines nationwide for a week or ten days, but you'd need to travel fairly extensively to make savings. A seven-day pass costs 10,230Ft first class, 6820Ft second class, and a ten-day pass 14,730/9820Ft. There's also a short-term **Hungarian Flexipass**, which you have to buy in your own country before departure (available from any agent selling InterRail/Eurail passes): a pass

valid for any five days in fifteen costs around
£35/$55 (first class); any ten days in one month,
£45/$69.

## BUSES

Buses from Budapest are generally comfortable,
though the stock in the rest of the country can be
quite ropey. Regional **Volán** companies run the
bulk of Hungary's **buses**, which are called *busz*
(pronounced "boose" as in "loose", *not* "bus",
which means "fuck" in Hungarian). Buses are often
the quickest way to travel between towns, and
while fares are higher than on the trains they're
still good value. Schedules are clearly displayed in
bus stations (*autóbuszállomás* or *autóbusz
pályaudvar*) in every Hungarian town. Arrive early
to confirm the departure bay (*kocsiállás*) and to be
sure of getting a seat. For long-distance services
originating in Budapest or major towns, you can
buy tickets with a seat booking up to half an hour
before departure; after that you get them from the
driver, but you risk standing throughout the journey.
Services **in rural areas** may be limited to one or
two a day, and tickets are only available on board
the bus. As on trains, children under four travel free
unless they occupy a separate seat, and at half-
fare up to the age of ten; otherwise there are no
concessions.

Volán also operates **international services**
to neighbouring countries and a few points further
west. The main depot for these is Erzsébet tér in
Budapest (see p.54), but services also run from
provincial towns like Siófok, Szombathely, Győr,
Miskolc, Szeged, Baja, Mohács and Debrecen. It's
fractionally cheaper to travel from Budapest to
Vienna by bus, but other destinations may cost
less by train.

## URBAN PUBLIC TRANSPORT

Public transport **within towns** is generally excellent, with buses, trolleybuses (*trolibusz*) and
trams (*villamos*) running from dawn until around
10.30 or 11pm. Express buses (numbered in red)
halt only at main stops, while express buses
whose number is accompanied by a red "E" run
almost non-stop between termini, so be careful
about boarding these. However, in Budapest a
black "E" signifies a night bus or *éjszakai járatok*,
which runs all night on main bus and tram routes.

**Tickets** for all services are sold in strips at
tobacconists and street stands, and should be
punched on board the vehicle. Municipalities set

their own flat rates, causing some variation in
prices nationwide. Generally, the local fare for all
transport is identical, so the same kind of ticket
can be used on all services, but tickets from one
town aren't supposed to be used in another. In
Budapest, various types of **passes** are available
(see p.58).

## DRIVING

To drive in Hungary you'll need an **international
driving permit** (issued by national motoring
organizations for a small fee; contact the AA in
Britain, AAA in the US) and **third-party insurance**. If you're taking your own car, check with
your insurance company to see if you're covered;
you'll probably need a **Green Card**. You can also
purchase insurance at the border, but this only
covers damage to third parties in Hungary and
pays out in forints, so it's wiser to fix it up before
leaving home.

*Autostop* or **hitchhiking** is widely practised
by young Magyars, and only forbidden on motorways. A fair number of drivers seem willing to
give lifts although communicating may be a problem. Hitching is considered pretty safe; use your
common sense.

### ROADS AND SERVICES

Hungary's roads fall into four categories.
Hungary's small **motorway** network consists of
the M1 to the border at Hegyeshalom (currently
the most expensive road in Europe, a toll of
1500Ft being charged for the 38-odd kilometres
between Győr and the border), the M3 towards
Miskolc, which stops after 120km at Füzesabony
(1000Ft); the M5 to Kecskemét and
Kiskunfélegyháza (1700Ft for the last 60km of the
motorway), and the M7 to Balaton. The M0 is the
ring motorway around the capital, of which the
stretch between the M5 and the M1 is complete.

Lesser **highways** (numbered with a single
digit from one to eight) radiate from Budapest like
spokes in a wheel, linked by **secondary roads**
identified by two or three digits (the first one
indicates the highway which the road joins; for
example, roads 82 and 811 both meet Route 8 at
some point). Lastly, there are unnumbered, bumpy
**back-country roads**, which tourists seldom use.
**Pedestrian zones** (found in many towns and
shaded light blue on maps) are indicated by
"Restricted Access" signs – *kivéve célforgalom*.
Information on nationwide **driving conditions** in

Hungarian can be obtained from ÚTINFORM (☎1/322-7643); conditions in Budapest are monitored by FŐVINFORM (☎1/317-1173).

Most **service stations** (*benzinkút*) stock 98 octane *extra*; 92 octane *szuper*, 86 octane *normál*, and diesel. **Lead-free** fuel (*olómmentes benzin*) is available everywhere now and even in deepest Hungary you should not have problems finding petrol.

## RULES AND REGULATIONS

**Speed limits** for vehicles are 120kph on motorways, 100kph on highways, 80kph on other roads and 50kph in built-up areas. Offenders can expect to be fined on the spot, this being a favourite activity of the police. In rural areas, wagons, cyclists, livestock and pedestrians are potential **traffic hazards**, so you should drive slowly, especially at night. Besides driving on the right, the most important **rules** are the prohibitions against repeatedly switching from lane to lane on highways; overtaking near pedestrian crossings; and sounding the horn in built-up areas unless to avert accidents. At crossroads, vehicles coming from the right have right of way, unless otherwise indicated by signs, and pedestrians have priority over cars turning onto the road. Remember that trams *always* have right of way, and that some traffic islands serve as bus or tram stops. On highways and secondary roads it's illegal to reverse, make U-turns, or stop at islands.

**Drinking and driving** is totally prohibited, and offenders with in excess of eight milligrams of alcohol are liable to felony charges. The state requires cars to be roadworthy (steering, brakes and all lights must work); and carry certain **mandatory equipment** – a triangular breakdown sign; spare bulbs for the indicators, head-, rear- and brake-lights; a first-aid box; and a supplementary mudguard made of a non-rigid material, attached to rear bumpers. Passengers must wear three-point safety belts in the front seats, where children are forbidden to travel.

A note for **pedestrians**: never assume that a car will stop for you on a pedestrian crossing. Drivers in Hungary will often do anything to avoid having to slow down and make way for pedestrians, swerving around them instead or screeching to a sudden halt. One judge even ruled that a pedestrian who got run over on a zebra crossing should have seen the car coming and was therefore not entitled to press charges on the motorist.

## ACCIDENTS AND EMERGENCIES

**Accidents** should be reported to the Hungaria Biztositó international motoring department at Budapest XI, Hamzsabégi út 60 (☎1/466-8830 or 466-5410 or 466-0247; Mon–Thurs 7.30am–4pm, Fri 7.30am–1.30pm) within 24 hours; if someone is injured the police must also be notified (☎107).

For breakdowns call the Autóklub Segélyhívó **24-hour breakdown service** (☎088) anywhere in the country, run by the **Hungarian Automobile Club**, MAK. MAK's national headquarters is at Budapest II, Rómer Floris utca 4A (☎1/ 212-2938); but they have several **repair shops** in the capital including Boldizsár utca 2 in the XI district (☎1/385-0722), and Nefelejcs utca 4 in the VII district (☎1/295-0419). **Spare parts** for foreign cars and other repair outlets are easiest to find in Budapest (see "Listings" in the Budapest chapter).

## CAR RENTAL

**Renting a car** is easy provided you're 21 or older, and hold a valid national driving licence that's at least one year old. You can order a car through rental agencies in your own country (see box below), and from hotel reception desks or certain travel agencies within Hungary, using cash or credit cards. In Budapest you can rent a car at the airport from numerous car rental companies (see "Listings" in the Budapest chapter).

Rental **costs** vary from £9/$15 per day for a Skoda Felicia to £15–25/$23–40 per day for an VW Golf and £20–40/$34–60 for a Ford Transit – not to mention the cost of fuel and the kilometre charge. You might find you get a better deal if you arrange a package **fly-drive** holiday in your own country. There are charges of 30p/45¢ per

---

### CAR RENTAL AGENCIES

**UK**
Avis ☎0181/848 8733.
Budget ☎0800/181 181.
Europcar/InterRent ☎0345/222 525.
Hertz ☎0181/679 1799.
Holiday Autos ☎0171/491 1111.

**North America**
Avis ☎1-800/331-1084.
Hertz ☎1-800/654-3001; in Canada ☎1-800/263-0600.
Holiday Autos ☎1-800/422-7737.

kilometre and £9–11/$13–16 insurance per day; credit cards are usually accepted for a deposit.

## PLANES AND BOATS

**Malév** doesn't operate any **domestic flights**, but many of their **flights abroad** (departing from Budapest's Ferihegy airport) are a good deal. If you're heading on to Greece or Turkey, they may prove an attractive alternative to travelling by train – especially for holders of student cards, who sometimes qualify for substantial discounts.

The Mahart company operates **passenger boats** in Hungary, with services on Lake Balaton, between Budapest and Esztergom, and on the section of the Danube running through the capital.

## BIKES AND MOTORBIKES

The only potential drawback to **motorcycling** is that spare parts may be problematic should you have a breakdown. Motorcyclists must be over 18, wear a helmet, and have a log book or other registration document, plus a Green Card for insurance. Aside from being required to use dimmed headlights by day, the rules of the road (and speed limits) are the same as for cars.

Given the generally flat terrain, and the light winds and low rainfall from July until the end of September, **cycling** is also a good way to see Hungary. There's also a growing number of cycle paths in the country, stretching over 200km to date, indicating an increasing awareness of the cycling community. However, there are several caveats for cyclists. They are not allowed on main roads (with single-digit numbers), and on some secondary roads between "peak hours" (7–9.30am and 4–6pm). Bikes can be carried on all passenger trains except some Intercity expresses and international trains, though in practice railway officials are not always that helpful. In towns, there are sunken tramlines and slippery cobbled streets to contend with. The Bicycle Tour Map produced by Tourinform has all cycle paths marked, as well as eight suggested tours. The most scenic areas are the Northern Uplands, the Danube Bend and parts of Transdanubia and the Bakony, where you'll find a few stiff climbs and lots of rolling hills. Conversely, the easiest cycling terrain, the Great Plain, tends to be rather monotonous visually.

It is possible **to rent bikes** (by the day or week) in most large towns and the Balaton resorts from MÁV, private operators and certain campsites (details are given where appropriate in the guide). Unfortunately, most machines are low-slung and heavy, with limited gears, although superior models are becoming more available. Bike shops are much more frequent than they used to be, with repair shops in most larger towns, including several in Budapest.

# ACCOMMODATION

The range of places to stay has changed radically in recent years, with plenty of new de luxe accommodation springing up. However, competitively priced pensions and guesthouses are also appearing, and tourists can now stay in holiday complexes formerly reserved for trade unionists, or in hostels attached to colleges. All in all, it shouldn't prove difficult to find somewhere that suits your tastes and budget.

Most towns have several hotels, pensions, and private lodgings, and quite often a campsite or hostel within easy reach of the centre. Even so, the cheapest places tend to fill up quickly during high season (June–Sept), so it's wise to make **reservations** if you're on a tight budget or bound for somewhere with limited possibilities. This can be done **from abroad** either through specialist travel agents (Danube Travel in Britain charges £10 for any number of bookings) or by telexing places yourself. The telex numbers for hotels, campsites and pensions appear in the *Hotels* and *Camping* booklets (see opposite).

## ACCOMMODATION PRICE CODES

All accommodation in this guide is graded according to the price bands given below. Note that prices refer to the **cheapest available double room in high season** or the price of **two people sharing a tent** in a campsite. 100Ft is roughly equivalent to $0.45 or DM1.

| | | |
|---|---|---|
| ① Under 2000Ft | ④ 6000–8500Ft | ⑦ 20,000–27,000Ft |
| ② 2000–4000Ft | ⑤ 8500–13,000Ft | ⑧ 27,000–40,000Ft |
| ③ 4000–6000Ft | ⑥ 13,000–20,000Ft | ⑨ over 40,000Ft |

**In Hungary**, bookings for the largest nation-wide upmarket hotel chain are handled through its head office in Budapest: Danubius/HungarHotels, V, Petőfi utca 16 (☎1/318-3018), and V, Szervita tér 8 (☎1/317-3652). Less expensive hotels and private lodgings in the provinces can be reserved through regional tourist offices or local branches of IBUSZ.

The chain of Tourinform offices in Budapest and the provinces is the best source of up-to-date information on accommodation of all kinds, although you cannot usually book accommodation through them. In the absence of any single, comprehensive **guide to accommodation** in Hungary, you'll have to make do with the free *Camping* and *Hotels* booklets stocked by most tourist offices.

A point to remember: many places have different prices for Hungarians and for foreigners, and some travellers have been quoted one price and found themselves facing a twenty percent higher bill when they arrive at the hotel.

### HOTELS

Although the Hungarian for **hotel** is *szálló* or *szállóda*, everyone understands the English term. Aside from smaller places in the provinces and a number of "international" hotels in Budapest, the largest hotel chain is Danubius/HungarHotels, the privatized state chain. For the moment, all hotels still have an official three- or four-**star rating** (five-star establishments are restricted to Budapest), although this gives only a vague idea of **prices**, which vary according to the locality and the time of year; **high season** is June to September. The star ratings are also a poor guide to standards, as some places officially meet the basic criteria in terms of facilities, but are in fact awful. This is especially the case in rural areas. As an indication of the way pricing policy is going, many places now simply post current room rates

in Deutschmarks (although you pay in forints). More predictably, prices in Budapest and the Balaton region are 15–35 percent higher than in other areas, though rates can drop by as much as thirty percent over **winter**. Breakfast is usually, but not always, included in the price.

As with prices, **standards** vary. While four- and five-star establishments are reliably comfortable, with private bathrooms, TV and central heating, three-star places can be soulless in gone-to-seed seventies fashion, or redolent of "old" Central Europe (a few are ensconced in former stately homes or castles). One- and two-star hotels probably won't have private bathrooms, but might have a sink in the room. Single rooms are rare and **solo travellers** will generally have to pay for a double.

Although the rating system bears some relation to **prices**, it is more of a reflection on location – and the trade-off between cost and convenience. In some towns, a centrally located pension might cost more than an older one- or two-star hotel, whereas elsewhere it could be the best alternative to a pricey three-star establishment. Similarly, some motels are very cheap, and others on a par with equivalently rated hotels in a better location. Even the rule of thumb that places get cheaper the further you are from Austria or Budapest doesn't always hold, since a pension in a remote village might exploit its monopoly to the hilt.

### PENSIONS, INNS AND MOTELS

Other types of accommodation are also categorized, by one to three stars. Private (often family-owned) **pensions** are appearing in all the towns and villages frequented by tourists, where they often undercut hotels with the same star rating. While some are purpose-built, with a restaurant on the premises, others are simply someone's house with a TV in the living room and a few rooms upstairs. There's no correlation between their appearance and title — some style themselves *panzió* (or *penzió*), others as *fogadó*. Places that describe themselves as **motels** are usually on the edge of town, or further out along the highway. Some coexist with bungalows and a campsite to form a tourist complex, and quite a few are near a thermal bath or swimming pool, with restaurants and sports facilities, too.

## PRIVATE ROOMS AND FARMSTEAD ACCOMMODATION

In Budapest and many other towns, **private rooms** in households are often the cheapest options. This type of accommodation (termed *Fiz*, short for *fizet vendégszolgálat*) can be arranged by local tourist offices for a fee, or by knocking on the door of places displaying *szoba kiadó* or *Zimmer frei* signs, which abound along the west bank of the Danube Bend, both shores of Lake Balaton, and in thermal spas throughout Hungary. There is a tendency to rent out apartments rather than rooms, which can push up prices.

In Budapest and the Balaton region, the **price** of a private double room is well below hotel and pension rates, although places accustomed to an influx of Germans and Austrians sometimes charge premium prices. Unfortunately, many landlords also charge thirty percent extra if you stay fewer than three nights, and a general lack of single rooms means that solo travellers have to pay for a double.

Although tourist offices rent sight unseen, you can still exercise judgement when **choosing a room** by rejecting dubious-sounding locations. As a rule of thumb, a town's Belváros (inner sector) is likely to hold spacious apartments with parquet floors, high ceilings and a balcony overlooking a courtyard, whereas in the outlying zones you'll probably be housed in a charmless, high-rise modern development. Either way, your hostess (widows and divorcées are the biggest renters) will probably be helpful, but a few words of Hungarian will make you seem less of a stranger. Use of the washing machine usually comes free, and some landladies will provide breakfast for a fee, although most leave early for work. For this reason, it's usually impossible to take possession of the room before 5pm; after that you can come and go with a key.

It's possible to rent whole **apartments** in some towns and resorts, while Tourinform and the regional tourist offices can give details of the

**Village Tourism** network — rooms in private houses in villages.

## HOSTELS AND DORMITORIES

Although many have closed or become private pensions, hostels are currently the cheapest available lodgings in Hungary. There are two kinds of official **tourist hostels**: *Túristaszálló*, generally found in provincial towns, and *Túristaház*, located in highland areas favoured by hikers. Both are graded "A" or "B" depending on the availability of hot water and the number of beds per room. *Túristaszálló* rates range from £2 to £8/$3 to $12: the former for a bed, the latter for a double or triple room. In *Túristaház*, which rarely have separate rooms, a dormitory bed goes for £2–3/$3–5. It's generally advisable to make bookings through the regional tourist office. Some hostels are official IYHF hostels, for which you'll need a membership card issued by the national hostel organization in your own country, though, in practice, many hostels in Hungary don't insist on one.

In many towns, you can also stay in vacant **college dormitories** for about £4/$6 a night. Generally, these accept tourists over the whole of the summer vacation (roughly July to mid-Aug) and in some cases at weekends throughout the year. It is usually possible to make bookings through the local Express agency or the regional tourist office, but otherwise you can just turn up at the designated college (*kollégium*) and ask if there are any beds available.

## BUNGALOWS AND CAMPSITES

Bungalows and campsites can be found in complexes throughout Hungary, where tourists of the world unite. Holiday homes (*üdül ház*) proliferate around resorts, where many were previously reserved for trade union members, but now take anyone to balance their books. Rates for renting **bungalows** or *faház*, literally "wooden houses", are £4–15/$6–23, depending on amenities and size (they usually sleep 2–4 persons). The first-class bungalows — with well-equipped kitchens, hot water and a sitting room or terrace — are excellent, while the most primitive at least have clean bedding and don't leak.

**Campsites** — *Kemping* — similarly range across the spectrum from "de luxe" to third class. The more elaborate places boast a restaurant and shops (sometimes even a disco)

and tend to be overcrowded; second- or third-class sites often have a nicer ambience, with lots of old trees rather than a manicured lawn ineffectually shaded by saplings, and acres of campers and trailers. Expect to pay at least £2/$3, or twice that around Lake Balaton, which has the most expensive sites in Hungary. Fees are calculated on a basic ground rent, plus a charge per person and a charge for any vehicle, and, for non-students, an obligatory local tax (*kurtaxe*). There are **reductions** of 25–30 per-cent during "low" season (Oct–May) when fewer sites are open, and during the high season for members of the FICC (International Camping and Caravanning Club). Children up to the age of 14 also qualify for 50 percent reductions on the cost of camping. While a few resorts and towns have semi-official **free campsites** (*szabad kemping*), **camping rough** is illegal, although young Hungarians sometimes do it in highland areas where there are "rain shelters" (*esőház*).

## EATING AND DRINKING

**Even under Communism, Hungary was renowned for its abundance of food: material proof of the "goulash socialism" that amazed visitors from Romania and the Soviet Union. Nowadays, there is more choice than ever, particularly in Budapest, where almost every cuisine in the world is available.**

For foreigners the archetypal Magyar dish is "goulash" – historically the basis of much Hungarian cooking. The ancient Magyars relished cauldrons of *gulyás* (pronounced "gou-yash"), a soup made of potatoes and whatever meat was available, which was later flavoured with paprika and beefed up into a variety of stews, modified over the centuries by various foreign influences. Hungary's Slav neighbours probably introduced native cooks to yogurt and sour cream – vital ingredients in many dishes – while the influence of the Turks, Austrians and Germans is apparent in a variety of sticky pastries and strudels, as well as recipes featuring sauerkraut or dumplings. Another influence was that of France, which revolutionized Hungarian cooking in the Middle Ages and again in the nineteenth century. Today, the influences are "international", with fast food such as pizzas, hamburgers and kebabs spreading from the capital to provincial towns, and even signs of vegetarian food and *nouvelle cuisine*.

### BREAKFAST, SNACKS AND TAKEAWAY FOOD

As a nation of early risers, Hungarians like to have a calorific **breakfast** (*reggeli*). Commonly, this includes cheese, eggs or salami together with bread and jam, and in rural areas is often accompanied by a shot of *pálinka* (brandy) to "clear the palate" or "aid digestion". Everyone is addicted to **coffee**. At intervals throughout the day, people consume tiny glasses of *kávé*: super-strong, served black and sweetened to taste, this is a brew that can double your heart beat. **Coffee houses** were once the centres of Budapest's cultural and political life – hotbeds of gossip where penurious writers got credit and the clientele dawdled for hours over the free newspapers. Sadly this is no longer the case, but you'll find plenty of unpretentious *kávéház* serving the beverage with milk (*tejeskávé*) or whipped cream (*tejszínhabbal*), should you request it. Cappuccinos vary in quality across the country, although in some smaller places you will still be met by blank looks as it is a relatively new discovery in Hungary. Most coffee houses have some pastries on offer, although you'll find much more choice in the patisseries (see "Cakes and Ice Cream", below) which, of course, also serve coffee. Tea-drinkers are in a minority here, perhaps because Hungarian **tea** with milk (*tejes tea*) is so insipid ; *tea citrommal* (with lemon) is quite good, however.

A whole range of places purvey **snacks**, notably *csemege* or **delicatessens**, which display a tempting spread of salads, open sandwiches, pickles and cold meats; in a few, you can eat on the premises. Some delis still use the system whereby customers order and pay at the cash desk (*kassza*) in return for a receipt to be exchanged at the food counter. If your Hungarian is minimal, this can throw up a few misunderstandings.

For sit-down nibbles, people patronize either *bisztró*, which tend to offer a couple of hot dishes besides the inevitable salami rolls; *snackbár*, which are superior versions of the same, with leanings in the direction of being a patisserie; or *büfé*. These last are found in department stores and stations, and are sometimes open around the clock. The food on offer, though, is often limited to tired sandwiches (*hurka*) and greasy sausages filled with rice (*kolbász*).

**On the streets**, according to season, vendors preside over tables of *kukorica* (corn on the cob) or trays of *gesztenye* (roasted chestnuts); while fried-fish (*sült hal*) shops are common in towns near rivers or lakes. *Szendvics, hamburger* and *gofri* (waffle) stands are mushrooming in the larger towns, while *Pizza Hut, McDonald's* and *Burger King* are spreading across the country. Another popular munch is *lángos*: the native, mega-size equivalent of doughnuts, often sold with a sprinkling of cheese and soured cream. If they are cooked in oil (*olaj*) then vegetarians can also partake of their delights. Fruit, too, is sold by street vendors and **in markets**, where you'll also find various greasy-spoon cafés forking out *hurka* and the like. Outdoor markets (*piac*) are colourful affairs, sometimes with the bizarre sight of rows of poultry sheltered beneath sunshades. In market halls (*vásárcsarnok*), people select their fish fresh from glass tanks, and their mushrooms from a staggering array of *gomba*, which are displayed alongside toxic fungi in a "mushroom parade" to enable shoppers to recognize the difference.

No list of snacks is complete without mentioning **bread** (*kenyér*), which is so popular that "Hungarians will even eat bread with bread", as

the old saying has it. White bread remains the staple of the nation, but in many supermarkets, especially in Budapest, you can usually get a range of brown (*barna*) and rye (*rozs*) breads.

## MAIN MEALS

Traditionally, Hungarians take their main meal at **midday**, although the old tendency for restaurants to have fewer dishes available in the evenings has now disappeared. However, it is worth remembering that many places still close early, around 10pm, especially outside of the capital. There's some compensation, though, in the bands of musicians that play in many restaurants at lunchtime and in the evening, their violin airs and melodic plonkings of the cimbalom (see p.38), an essential element of the "scene".

Places used to tourists often have **menus** in German (and sometimes English), a language of which most waiters and waitresses have a smattering. Particularly in Budapest, tourist-oriented establishments may give you a menu without prices – a sure sign that they're expensive, or plan to rip you off. Unfortunately, **overcharging** is on the increase, and even fluent Hungarian speakers can get burned if they don't check the bill carefully. While some restaurants offer a bargain set menu (*napi menü*) of basic dishes, the majority of places are strictly *à la carte*. For a three-course meal with wine, expect to pay £5–10/$8–15 in an average restaurant, twice that in downtown Budapest. A service charge isn't usually included in the bill and the staff depend on customers **tipping** (ten percent of the total is customary). Be warned that if you say "thank you" as you hand the money over, this implies that they can keep the change.

Hungarians have a variety of words for their finely distinguished **restaurants**. In theory an **étterem** is a proper restaurant, while a **vendéglő** approximates to the Western notion of a bistro, though in practice the terms are often used interchangeably. The old word for an inn, **csárda**, applies to posh places specializing in certain dishes (for example, a "Fishermen's inn" or **halászcsárda**), restaurants alongside roads or with rustic pretensions, as well as to the humbler rural establishments that the name originally signified.

When they can afford to be, Hungarians are enthusiastic eaters, so as a (presumably rich) Westerner you'll be asked if you want a **starter** (*előételek*) – generally a soup or salad. Nobody will mind, however, if you just have one of the dishes offered as the **main course** (*főételek*) or, alternatively, order just a soup and a starter. Bread is supplied almost automatically, on the grounds that "a meal without bread is no meal". **Drinks** are normally listed on the menu under the heading *italok*.

## VEGETARIANS

Despite the emergence of *vegetarianus* restaurants in Budapest, and a growing understanding of the concept, the outlook for **vegetarians** remains poor: most Hungarians are amazed that anyone might forgo meat willingly. You can find yourself on a diet of vegetables or cheese fried in breadcrumbs: *rántott gomba* (mushrooms), *rántott karfiol* (cauli-

---

## A FOOD AND DRINK GLOSSARY

What follows is by no means a comprehensive list of Hungarian dishes, but by combining names and terms it should be possible to decipher anything that you're likely to see on the menu. Alcoholic and soft drinks are covered in the main text, as are desserts and pastries, which are best sampled in the ubiquitous *cukrászda*.

### Basics

| | | | | | |
|---|---|---|---|---|---|
| *bors* | pepper | *kifli* | croissant-shaped roll | *tejföl* | sour cream |
| *cukor* | sugar | | | *tejszín* | cream |
| *ecet* | vinegar | *méz* | honey | *vaj* | butter |
| *egészségedre!* | Cheers! | *mustár* | mustard | *zsemle* or | bread rolls |
| *jó étvágyat!* | Bon appétit! | *rizs* | rice | *péksütemeny* | |
| *kenyér* | bread | *só* | salt | | |

The categories below refer to the general divisions used in menus. In cheaper places you will also find a further division of meat dishes: ready-made dishes like stews (*készételek*) and freshly cooked (in theory) dishes such as those cooked in breadcrumbs or grilled (*frissensültek*).

*Tészták* is a rogue pasta-doughy category that includes savoury dishes such as *turoscsusza* (pasta served with cottage cheese and a sprinkling of bacon), as well as sweet ones like *somlói galuska* (cream and chocolate covered sponge).

### Soups (*levesek*)

| | | | |
|---|---|---|---|
| *bakonyi betyárleves* | "Outlaw soup" of chicken, beef, noodles and vegetables, richly spiced | *husleves* | meat consommé |
| | | *jókai bableves* | bean soup flavoured with smoked meat – a meal in itself |
| *csirke-aprólék leves* | mixed vegetable and giblet soup | | |
| | | *kunsági pandúrleves* | chicken soup seasoned with nutmeg, paprika, and garlic |
| *erőleves* | meat consommé often served with noodles (*tésztával* or *metélttel*), liver dumplings (*májgombóccal*), or an egg placed raw into the soup (*tojással*) | | |
| | | *lencseleves* | lentil soup |
| | | *hideg meggyleves* | delicious chilled sour cherry soup |
| | | *palócleves* | mutton, bean and sour cream soup |
| *gombaleves* | mushroom soup | *paradicsomleves* | tomato soup |
| *gulyásleves* | goulash in its original Hungarian form as a soup, sometimes served in a small kettle pot (*bográcsgulyás*) | *tarkonyos borjúraguleves* | lamb soup flavoured with tarragon |
| | | *Újházi tyúkleves* | chicken soup with noodles, vegetables and meat |
| | | *zöldségleves* | vegetable soup |
| *halászlé* | a rich paprika fish soup often served with hot paprika | | |

*continued overleaf . . .*

# A FOOD AND DRINK GLOSSARY contd.

## Appetizers (*előételek*)

These can be served cold (*hideg*) or hot (*meleg*).

| | | | |
|---|---|---|---|
| *füstölt csülök tormával* | smoked knuckle of pork with horseradish | | with sheep's cheese (*juhtúróval töltött*) |
| *hortobágyi palacsinta* | pancake stuffed with minced meat and served with creamy paprika sauce | *rántott sajt, Camembert, karfiol* | Camembert or cauliflower fried in breadcrumbs |
| *körözött* | a paprika-flavoured spread made with sheep's cheese and served wth toast | *tatárbeefsteak* | raw mince that you mix with an egg, salt, pepper, butter, paprika and mustard and spread on toast |
| *libamáj* | goose liver | *velőcsont fokhagymás pirítóssal* | bone marrow spread on toast rubbed with garlic, a special delicacy associated with the gourmet Gyula Krudy |
| *rakott krumpli* | layered potato casserole with sausage and eggs | | |
| *rántott gomba* | mushrooms fried in breadcrumbs, sometimes stuffed | | |

## Salads (*saláták*)

Salads are often served in a vinegary dressing, although other dressings include blue cheese (*rokfortos*), yogurt (*joghurtos*) or French (*francia*).

| | | | |
|---|---|---|---|
| *csalamádé* | mixed pickled salad | *paradicsom saláta* | tomato salad |
| *fejes saláta* | lettuce | *uborka saláta* | cucumber which can be gherkins (*csemege* or *kovászos*) or the fresh variety (*friss*) |
| *idénysaláta* | fresh salad of whatever is in season | | |
| *jércesaláta* | chicken salad | | |

## Fish dishes (*halételek*)

| | | | |
|---|---|---|---|
| *csuka tejfölben sütve* | fried pike with sour cream | *pisztráng tejszínes mártásban* | trout baked in cream |
| *fogas* | a local fish of the pike-perch family | *ponty* | carp |
| *fogasszeletek Gundel modra* | breaded fillet of *fogas* | *ponty filé gombával* | carp fillet in mushroom sauce |
| *harcsa* | catfish | *rántott pontyfilé* | carp fillet fried in bread crumbs |
| *kecsege* | sterlet (small sturgeon) | *rostélyos töltött ponty* | carp stuffed with bread, egg, herbs and fish liver or roe |
| *nyelvhal* | sole | *süllő* | another pike-perch relative |
| *paprikás ponty* | carp in paprika sauce | *sült hal* | fried fish |
| *pisztráng* | trout | *tonhal* | tuna |

## Meat dishes (*húsételek*)

| | | | | | |
|---|---|---|---|---|---|
| *baromfi* | poultry | *hátszin* | rumpsteak | *őz* | venison |
| *bécsi szelet* | Wiener schnitzel | *kacsa* | duck | *pulyka* | turkey |
| *bélszin* | sirloin | *kolbász* | spicy sausage | *sertés* | pork |
| *bélszinjava* | tenderloin | *liba* | goose | *sonka* | ham |
| *csirke* | chicken | *máj* | liver | *vaddisznó* | wild boar |
| *fácán* | pheasant | *marha* | beef | *vadételek* | game |
| *fasírt* | meatballs | *nyúl* | rabbit | *virsli* | frankfurter |

*continued opposite . . .*

| | | | |
|---|---|---|---|
| *borjúpörkölt* | closer to what foreigners mean by "goulash", veal stew seasoned with garlic | *rablóhús nyárson* | kebab of pork, veal and bacon |
| *cigányrostélyos* | "gypsy-style" steak with brown sauce | *sertésborda* | pork chop |
| *csikós tokány* | strips of beef braised in bacon, onion rings, sour cream and tomato sauce | *sült libacomb tört burgonyával és párolt káposztával* | grilled goose leg with potatoes, onions and steamed cabbage |
| *csülök Pékné módra* | knuckle of pork | *töltött-káposzta* | cabbage stuffed with meat and rice, in a tomato sauce |
| *erdélyi rakott-káposzta* | layers of cabbage, rice and ground pork baked in sour cream – a Transylvanian speciality | *töltött-paprika* | peppers stuffed with meat and rice, in a tomato sauce |
| *hagymás rostélyos* | braised steak piled high with fried onions | *vaddisznó borók amártással* | wild boar in juniper sauce |
| *pacal* | tripe in a paprika sauce | *vasi pecsenye* | fried pork marinaded in milk and garlic |
| *paprikás csirke* | chicken in paprika sauce | | |

## Cooking terms

| | | | | | |
|---|---|---|---|---|---|
| *comb* | leg | *főzelék* | basic vegetable stews | *rántott* | deep fried in breadcrumbs |
| *mell* | breast | | | | |
| *angolosan* | (English-style) underdone/rare | *jól megsütve* | well done (fried) | *roston sütve* | grilled |
| | | *jól megfőzve* | well done (boiled) | *sülve* | roasted |
| *főtt* | boiled | *pörkölt* | stewed slowly | *sült/sütve* | fried |

## Sauces (*mártásban*)

Many restaurants serve meat or fish dishes in rich sauces – a legacy of the French influence.

| | | | |
|---|---|---|---|
| *bormártásban* | in a wine sauce | *tejszínes paprikás mártásban* | in a cream and paprika sauce |
| *ecetes tormával* | with horseradish | | |
| *fokhagymás mártásban* | in a garlic sauce | *vadasmártásban* | in a brown sauce (made of mushrooms, almonds, herbs and brandy) |
| *gombamártásban* | in a mushroom sauce | | |
| *kapormártásban* | in a dill sauce | | |
| *meggymártásban* | in a morello cherry sauce | | |
| | | *zöldborsós* | in a green pea sauce |
| *paprikás mártásban* | in a paprika sauce | *zöldborsosmártásban* | in a green peppercorn sauce |
| *tárkonyos mártásban* | in a tarragon sauce | | |

## Accompaniments (*köretek*)

| | | | |
|---|---|---|---|
| *galuska* | noodles | *rizs* | rice |
| *hasábburgonya* | chips – french fries | *zöldköret* | mixed vegetables (often of frozen origin) |
| *krokett* | potato croquettes | | |
| *petrezselymes burgonya* | boiled potatoes served with parsley | | |

## Vegetables (*zöldségek*)

| | | | | | |
|---|---|---|---|---|---|
| *bab* | beans | *kelkáposzta* | savoy cabbage | *paradicsom* | tomatoes |
| *borsó* | peas | *kukorica* | sweetcorn | *sárgarépa* | carrots |
| *burgonya/ krumpli* | potatoes | *lecsó* | a tomato-green pepper stew, a popular ingredient in Hungarian cooking | *spárga* | asparagus |
| | | | | *spenot* | spinach |
| *fokhagyma* | garlic | | | *uborka* | cucumber |
| *gomba* | mushrooms | | | *zöldbab* | green beans |
| *hagyma* | onions | *padlizsán* | aubergine/eggplant | *zöldborsó* | peas |
| *káposzta* | cabbage | *paprika –* | peppers – | *zukkini* | courgette |
| *karfiol* | cauliflower | *édes/erős* | sweet/hot | | |

*continued overleaf . . .*

## A FOOD AND DRINK GLOSSARY contd.

### Fruit (gyümölcs)

| | | | | | |
|---|---|---|---|---|---|
| alma | apple | körte | pear | őszibarack | peach |
| citrom | lemon | málna | raspberry | sárgabarack | apricot |
| dió | walnut | mandula | almond | szilva | plum |
| eper | strawberry | meggy | morello cherry | sző | grape |
| füge | fig | mogyoró | hazelnut | tök | marrow or |
| (görög) dinnye | (water) melon | narancs | orange | | pumpkin/squash |

### Cheese (sajt)

| | | | |
|---|---|---|---|
| füstölt sajt | smoked cheese | trappista | rubbery, Edam-type cheese |
| juhtúró | sheep's cheese | túró | curd cheese |
| márvány | Danish blue cheese | | |

flower), or *rántott sajt* (cheese), or if you are lucky, *padlizsán* (aubergine), *zukkini* (courgette), or *tök* (pumpkin). *Gomba paprikás* (mushroom paprika stew) is also OK if it is cooked in oil (*olaj*) rather than in fat (*zsír*). Alternatively there are **eggs** – fried (literally "mirror" – *tükörtojás*), soft-boiled (*lágy tojás*), scrambled (*tojásrántotta*), or in mayonnaise (*kaszínótojás*) – or salads, though in winter these are often of the pickled vegetable variety. Even innocuous vegetable soups may contain meat stock, and the pervasive use of sour cream and animal fat in cooking means that avoiding animal products or by-products is difficult. However, greengrocers (*zöldségbolt*) and markets sell excellent produce which, combined with judicious shopping in supermarkets (for pulses, grains, etc), should see you through.

### CAKES AND ICE CREAM

Numerous **patisseries** (*cukrászda*) pander to the Magyar fondness for sweet things. **Pancakes** (*palacsinta*) **with fillings** – *almás* (apple), *diós* (walnuts), *fahéjas* (cinnamon), *mákos* (poppy seeds), *mandulás* (almonds) or *Gundel*-style, with nuts, chocolate sauce, cream and raisins – are very popular, as are **strudels** (*rétes*) made with curds and dill (*kapros túrós rétes*), poppy seeds (*mákosrétes*) or plums (*szilvás rétes*). Even the humble dumpling is transformed into a *somlói galuska*, flavoured with vanilla, nuts and chocolate. But the frontrunners in the rich 'n' sticky stakes have to be chestnut pureé with whipped cream (*gesztenyepüré*); coffee soufflé (*kapucineres felfújt*); baked apple with vanilla, raisins and cream (*töltött alma*); and the staggering array of **cakes**. The average *cukrászda* dis-

plays a dozen or more types, including *dobostorta* (chocolate cream cake topped with caramel) and the pineapple-laden *ananásztorta*.

If you're still not satiated, there's **ice cream** (*fagylalt*), the opium of the masses, sold by the scoop (*gombóc*) and priced low enough so that anyone can afford a cone. The most common flavours are *vanília, csokoládé, puncs* (fruit punch), *citrom* and *kávé*, though mango, pistachio, and various nutty flavours can be found too – see the fruit section of the food glossary for the Magyar names. And finally there's *metélt or tészta* – a rather unlikely-sounding but quite tasty dessert of chopped sweet noodles, served cold with poppy seeds or some other topping.

### DRINKING: WINES, BEERS, SPIRITS AND SOFT DRINKS

Hungary's climate and diversity of soils are perfect for **wine** (*bor*), though cold winters mean that reds are usually on the light side. In the last couple of years the wine market has really begun to take off, and, though good vintages are still cheap by Western standards, prices are rising steadily. In bars and most restaurants you can either buy it by the bottle (*üveg*) or the glass (*pohár*). There are twenty wine-growing regions in the country, of which the best are Villány, Eger, Tokaj, Szekszárd and the Balaton. They even manage to grow grapes on the sandy soils around Kecskemét, at the edge of the Great Plain, but the wines from there are pretty vile. Overall, though, standards are constantly rising as more vineyards try to win the right to label their bottles *minőségi bor* (quality wine), the equivalent of *appellation contrôlée*. In recent years, Hungary's wines have improved dramatically, as private vineyards have recovered their old skills in making and selling their own wine. Experts predict that demand for good wine will quite soon begin to outstrip supply.

**Wine bars** (*borozó*) are ubiquitous and far less pretentious than in the West: the wine served is often pretty rough stuff, and there's usually a cluster of interesting characters round the bar. True devotees of the grape make pilgrimages to the extensive **wine cellars** (*borpince*) that honeycomb towns like Tokaj and Eger. By day, people often drink wine with water or soda water, specifying a *fröccs* or a yet more diluted *hosszú lépés* (literally, a "long step"). Wine can be sweet (*édes*), dry (*száraz*), semi-sweet (*félédes*) or semi-dry (*félszáraz*). Hungarians enjoy the ritual of **toasting**, so the first word to get your tongue around is *egészségedre* ("EGG-aish-shaig-edreh") – cheers! When toasting more than one other person, it's grammatically correct to change this to *egészségünkre* (cheers to us!). Hungarians only consider it appropriate to toast with wine or spirits. A simpler version that will get you by is *szia* (see-ya) for one person, and *sziasztok* (see-ya-stock) for more people.

## SPIRITS

As long as you stick to native brands, **spirits** are also cheap. The best-known type of *pálinka* – brandy – is distilled from apricots (*barack*), and is a speciality of the Kecskemét region, but spirits are also produced from peaches (*őszibarack*),

pears (*körte*), and any other fruits available. This is particularly true of *szilva* – a lethal spirit produced on cottage stills in rural areas, allegedly based on plums. Hungarians with money to burn order whisky (*viszki*) to impress, but most people find its cost prohibitive.

## BEER

Bottled **beer** (*sör*) of the lager type (*világos*) predominates, although you might come across brown ale (*barna sör*) and draught beer (*csapolt sör*). Hungarian beer production is almost totally in the hands of the big international breweries. Western brands like Tuborg, HB, Wernesgrünner and Gold Fassel are mostly brewed under licence in Hungary, while you can also find imported Czech brands like Urquell Pilsen. The old Austro-Hungarian beer Dreher has made a comeback in the hands of South African Breweries. Other brands to try are Arany Ászok, a very cheap light beer, and Pannonia Sör, a pleasant hoppy beer from Pécs.

**Beer halls** (*söröző*) range from plush establishments sponsored by foreign breweries to humble stand-up joints where you order either a small glass (*pohár*) or a half-litre mug (*korsó*).

## SOFT DRINKS

Pepsi and Coke and various sugary, fruit-flavoured **soft drinks** are sold everywhere. Several brands of unsweetened fruit juices can be found in supermarkets and greengrocers. Most food stores also stock bottled *limonádé*, mineral water (*ásványvíz*), soda water (*szódavíz*) and a range of fruit juices.

## POST AND PHONES

**There has been a massive improvement in communication services, especially in telephones, in recent years. Postal services, however, can still cause headaches.**

### POST OFFICES

**Post offices** (*posta*) are usually open Monday to Friday 8am to 6pm and until noon on Saturday, although in Budapest you'll find several offices functioning around the clock, while smaller post offices close at 3pm. Mail from abroad should be addressed "poste restante, posta" followed by the name of the town; tell your friends to write your surname first, Hungarian-style, and underline it; even this may not prevent your mail being misfiled, so ask them to check under all your names. To collect mail, show your passport and ask "Van posta a részemre?" It's probably safest to send mail to the American Express office in Budapest at V, Deák Ferenc utca 10.

It's quicker to buy **stamps** (*bélyeg*) at tobacconists: post offices are usually full of people making complicated transactions, and staff are rude and unfriendly. NB: letters and postcards have different rates, so don't buy a job lot of stamps — show your letter first. If you need to send a telegram (*távirat*), your best bet is the post office. In theory you can dictate them by dialling ☎192, but the line is often engaged and it's difficult to make yourself understood.

### TELEPHONES, FAXES, EMAIL AND THE INTERNET

Hungary's **telephone network** is being improved and expanded all the time, but improvements have sadly meant a rise in cost and international calls are now pretty expensive. In towns and cities, calls can be made from public phones with 10 or 20Ft coins (minimum call 20Ft), though cardphones have really taken off and are now common everywhere. It's worth having a phonecard to hand, since card phones are often more reliable than coin ones. Cards valid for 50 or 120 units are available at post offices and tobacconists, at a price which is going up all the time, but currently stands at around 750Ft for the cheaper type. To make a direct call outside the area you are in, dial ☎06 (which gives a burring tone), followed by the area code and the subscriber's number. To make international calls, dial ☎00, wait for the burr, then dial the country code and subscriber's number minus the first digit. The number for the international operator is ☎190.

The earlier poverty of the telephone system meant that mobile phones spread like wildfire across the country when they became available. Mobile phone numbers run ☎06-309 (or -509 or -209) followed by six digits. You have to dial all

| TELEPHONE CODES | |
|---|---|
| **Phoning abroad from Hungary** | **Phoning Hungary from abroad** |
| *Dial the following numbers + area code + subscriber number* | *Dial the following numbers + Hungarian area code + subscriber number* |
| Australia ☎00 61 | Australia ☎0011 36 |
| Ireland ☎00 353 | Ireland ☎00 36 |
| New Zealand ☎00 64 | New Zealand ☎00 36 |
| UK ☎00 44 | UK ☎00 36 |
| USA and Canada ☎00 1 | USA and Canada ☎011 36 |

the numbers, unless you are using a mobile phone with the same code yourself.

Faxes can be found everywhere, and email is spreading fast. There are several cybercafés in Budapest, as well as some others in the provinces. Matáv, the national telephone company, have Internet links you can use in many of their offices.

## THE MEDIA

**Without a knowledge of Hungarian you can only appreciate certain aspects of the media. Foreign cable and satellite television have made huge inroads, and there is a rash of tabloids and magazines devoted to soft porn and celebrity trivia.**

Western programmes are much in evidence on the two national **television** stations, which many Hungarians augment by subscribing to satellite channels like Sky, MTV or Super Channel, with whole apartment blocks sharing the cost of installation. Many hotels have access to foreign channels, though in some cases they will be German channels only. Television has been the scene of political battles in recent years as the newly elected democratic governments try to retain control of the medium. Parliament has finally, after much wrangling, passed a media law, which has led to the formation of two new Hungarian TV channels, TV2 and TV3. These are indistinguishable, both screening gameshows and low-budget soaps from morning to night.

The serious **press** suffers from being strictly partisan, with *Magyar Nemzet* supporting the liberal-conservative government, while *Népszabadság* (formerly Communist, but now avowedly socialist) and *Magyar Hirlap* see every move of the incumbent coalition as a threat to democracy.

In Budapest you can buy papers and magazines **in English** and other languages, notably *The Times*, *Financial Times*, *Guardian*, *Herald Tribune*, *Newsweek* and *Time*. German publications are also in plentiful supply. There is a wealth of English-language weeklies: *Budapest Week* is an (admittedly rather poor) arts weekly with good cinema listings, and *Budapest Sun* has entertainment and events listings as well as news coverage that is occasionally informative. The *Budapest Business Journal* covers mainly business and politics.

You could also drop into the British or American cultural centres in Budapest, or try the **radio**. A German-language station, *Radio Danubius*, lets rip with pop, rap and ads, broadcasting on a daily basis from 6.30am to 10pm throughout the summer until October 31 (100.5, 103.3, or 102 MHz VHF); while *Radio Petőfi* broadcasts news in English once daily from June to August. Alternatively, you can tune into the BBC World Service.

## OPENING HOURS AND HOLIDAYS

During the week, general office hours are from 8am to 4pm, but it's worth remembering that the staff at lesser institutions usually take an hour off around noon for lunch and leave early on Fridays. Aside from shops (see below) and tourist offices, the most obvious exceptions are museums, which are almost always closed on Monday. Otherwise, opening times are affected by public holidays, when most things shut down – museums have opening times that vary according to the holiday, and are not reliably open; there's a list of holidays in the box below. For the opening hours of pharmacies and banks see p.16 and p.18.

### SHOPS

Shops are open Monday to Friday from 10am to 6pm, with supermarkets and grocery stores open 8am to 6pm or until 7pm in larger towns. On Saturday most places close at 1pm in Budapest

and at noon in the countryside, and you cannot rely on finding shops open after that. There are exceptions: some shops in Budapest have caught on to the idea of extending their Saturday opening hours; and in Budapest and other larger centres there are numerous 24-hour shops – the signs to look for are Non-Stop, 0-24 or Ejjel-Nappali.

### MUSEUMS

Museums are generally open Tuesday to Sunday 10am to 6pm (winter 9am to 4pm, or earlier), but there are many exceptions; current hours are detailed in the guide. As public subsidies are withdrawn, many of the smaller museums may close down altogether over winter.

### PLACES OF WORSHIP

Hungary's few remaining mosques (*djami*) now qualify as museums rather than places of worship, but getting into **churches** (*templom*) may pose problems. The really important ones charge a small fee to see their crypts and treasures, and may prohibit sightseeing during services (*mise* or *istentisztelet*, or *Gottesdienst* in German). In small towns and villages, however, churches are usually kept locked except for worship in the early morning and/or the evening (between around 6pm and 9pm). A small tip is in order if you rouse the verger to unlock the building during the day; he normally lives nearby in a house marked *plébánia*. Visitors are expected to wear "decorous" dress – that is, no shorts or sleeveless tops.

Most of Hungary's **synagogues** were ransacked during World War II and subsequently left derelict or given over to other functions. A fair number have been reopened and restored since the late 1980s, though you may have to ask around for the key. Only Budapest retains a sizeable Jewish community, but in most places with a synagogue or Jewish cemetery, it is easy to get directions.

The Hungarian terms for the main **religious denominations** are: *Katolikus* (Catholic), *Református* (Calvinist), *Evangélikus* (Lutheran), *Görög* (Greek Orthodox), *Görög-Katolikus* (Uniate) and *Zsidó* (Jewish).

---

**PUBLIC HOLIDAYS**

On the following days, most things in Hungary shut down. Also, when these holidays fall on a Tuesday or Thursday, the day between it and the weekend may also become a holiday, and the previous or next Saturday a working day to make up the lost day.

**January 1** New Year's Day
**March 15** Independence Day
**Easter Monday**
**May 1** Labour Day
**August 20** St Stephen's Day
**October 23** National holiday
**December 25** (Since Christmas celebrations start on the 24th, many shops will be closed the whole day, and by the afternoon everything closes down.)
**December 26**

*For the dates of other major festivals and celebrations, not all of which are public holidays, see "Festivals", p.40.*

# POLICE, TROUBLE AND SEXUAL HARASSMENT

The Hungarian police (*Rendőrség*) always had a milder reputation than their counterparts in other Eastern Bloc states, and are keen to present a favourable image. White foreign tourists are generally handled with kid gloves unless suspected of black-marketeering, drug-smuggling, driving under the influence of alcohol, or of being illegal immigrants (who, like Hungary's Roma minority, are roughly treated).

## PAPERWORK, EMERGENCIES AND TROUBLE

Since police in towns occasionally ask to inspect **passports and visas**, you should make sure that everything's in order. In border regions, solo travellers may be (politely and briefly) questioned by plain-clothes officers; but here too, if your stamps are in order, there shouldn't be any problem. Most police officers have at least a smattering of German, but rarely any other foreign language. If you need the police, dial ☎107 in **emergencies**; should you be arrested or need legal advice, ask to contact your embassy or consulate (see the Budapest chapter Listings for addresses).

Although **theft** and violent crime are rare, their incidence is growing, not least because of the widening gap between rich and poor. Budapest in particular is no longer utterly safe at night, though still far less risky than most Western capitals. There has also been a worrying upsurge in **racist attacks** on Chinese, Africans, Asians and Arabs, in some cases encouraged by foreign neo-Nazis. That said, most **trouble** can be avoided: if you don't sunbathe nude or topless unless everyone else does, or deal on the black market, you've eliminated the likeliest causes.

## SEXUAL HARASSMENT

As anywhere in the world, sexual harassment can occur, though Hungary is one of the safest countries in Europe, and although you might get ogled you are unlikely to get physically molested. Walking around the city at night is one the great pleasures for single women after the hassle of Western Europe or the States. Prostitution is rife in the VIII district so you might feel uncomfortable about walking around there. Otherwise, you should take the usual precautions.

# ENTERTAINMENT AND FESTIVALS

**Music and dance are probably the easiest paths through the thicket of language that surrounds Hungarian culture, but they're not the only accessible forms of entertainment. During the summer in particular, you'll find plays or films in foreign languages, or festivals where language is a minor obstacle, in many of the main towns and resorts.**

## GYPSY AND FOLK MUSIC

In recent years gypsy or Roma music has really made a mark in the music scene in Hungary. Groups like Kalyi Jag, Andro Drom, and Ternipe tour extensively and are the focal point of most Roma festivals. A younger ensemble who have made no recordings as yet, the Szilvási Folk Band, are also worth looking out for. This music has little in common with the "Gypsy Music" which you will see advertised at touristy restaurants. This is known in Hungarian as *Magyar nóta*, and consists of a series of mid-nineteenth-century Hungarian ballads traditionally played by Roma musicians. Proper Roma music can be played on anything from spoons and milk jugs to guitars, and ranges from haunting laments to playful wedding songs, as you can see in French director Tony Gatliff's excellent film *Latcho Drom* about Roma music from India to Spain. Look out for concerts by any of the above groups, especially at the Almássy tér Cultural Centre in Budapest, which often organizes Roma evenings. Cassettes and CDs are also readily available.

That is not to say that *Magyar nóta* should be avoided. It is usually performed by one or two violinists, a bass player and a guy on the **cimbalom** – a stringed instrument played with little hammers. The more famous restaurants boast their own musical dynasties, such as the Lakatos family, who have been performing this sort of music for over a century. In the past, wandering self-taught artists like János Bihari, Czinka Panna and Czermak (a nobleman turned vagabond) were legendary figures.

Hungarian diners are usually keen to make requests or sing along when the *prímás* (band leader) comes to the table, soliciting tips. If approached yourself, it is acceptable (though rather awkward) to decline with a *nem köszönöm*, but if you signal a request to the band, you have to pay for it.

**Hungarian folk music** (*Magyar népzene*) is different again, having originated around the Urals and the Turkic steppes over a millennium ago. The haunting rhythms and pentatonic scale of this "Old Style" music (to use Bartók's terminology) were subsequently overlaid by "New Style" European influences – which have been discarded by twentieth-century enthusiasts in the folk revival centred around **Táncház**. These "Dance Houses" encourage people to learn traditional dances – with much shouting, whistling, and slapping of boots and thighs. Aside from Dance Houses, you can hear folk music at various festivals (see p.40), and at concerts by **groups** like Muzsikás and Téka.

## POPULAR MUSIC AND JAZZ

Budapest has undergone a **popular music** revival in the last few years: radio stations and music magazines have taken off and the city has become part of the international tour circuit. This has all had a knock-on effect on local music, which ranges from instrumental groups (*Korai Öröm* and *Másfél*) to techno-inspired performers like Anima Sound System. Heaven Street Seven call their version of guitar pop Dunabeat, while Quimby is the Hungarian equivalent to Tom Waits. Local radio station **Tilos Rádió** has done much to promote **DJs**, and there are now a host of them round the country. Some like Tommy Boy and Schultz play run-of-the-mill **techno**, while others like Palotai and Mango do a lot of wild mixing using a mass of sources and sounds. Bestiák are a sort of Magyar Spice Girls and Ganszta Zoli looks to LA gangster rap for his inspiration. The *Z* concert guide is issued free all over the country in record shops and lists concerts, parties and raves nationwide.

**Jazz** has always had a devout, but small, following in the country and more and more clubs and bars offer live jazz as an incentive. There are jazz **festivals** at Debrecen, Tatabánya, Székesfehérvár, Salgotarján, Nagykanizsa and Zalaegerszeg – usually over summer. Dés, Dresch, Aladár Pege and the Benkó Dixieland Band have all achieved success outside Hungary, but foreign jazz fans have yet to cotton on to pianist György Szabados, who works on the interface between jazz and classical music.

## CLASSICAL AND CONTEMPORARY MUSIC AND DANCE

Bartók, Kodály and Liszt spring to mind as the leading Hungarian composers, and there are several festivals annually to celebrate their work. The **Budapest Spring Festival** has become a major event, with classical music, contemporary dance, film and other arts represented. Smaller spring festivals take place at the same time in Szeged, Debrecen, Szombathely, Kecskemét and other towns; there are also similar festivals over **summer** (in Szeged) and **autumn** (in Budapest and Nyíregyháza).

Aside from these landmarks, the concert year features Haydn's and Beethoven's works (performed in the palatial surroundings of the Esterházy and Brunswick mansions); orchestral concerts at Veszprém and Diósgyőr castles; organ recitals in the main churches of Pécs, Buda, Debrecen, Eger, Miskolc, Szeged and Tihany; and chorales in the Gothic churches at Köröshegy and Nyírbátor (mainly over summer). Many great Hungarian performers like the pianist András Schiff and the violinist György Pauk live abroad, but pianist Dezső Ránki and cellist Miklós Perényi still work in Budapest and perform regularly. Orchestras and ensembles to watch for are the Budapest Festival Orchestra, the Liszt Chamber Orchestra and the Hungarian Radio and TV Symphony Orchestra.

Modern composers like György Kurtág, Tibor Szemző and László Sáry are internationally recognized and perform their music regularly in Budapest. The **Autumn Festival** has a special section dedicated to modern works and the Music Academy often stages modern concerts in its *kisterem* or small hall.

The state **opera** produces some good performances, but suffers from a lack of money which means that staging, lighting and costumes are old-fashioned. However, the singing and music is generally good. Smaller ensembles such as the Chamber Opera (*Kamaraopera*) are worth watching out for, as staging is usually more imaginative. The Budapest Opera's **ballet** company is classically oriented, but young performers like Yvette Bozsik have given **modern dance** a push and encouraged a lot of smaller companies like Artus and Transz Dansz to experiment further.

## CINEMA

What the Hungarian film industry lacks in funds it makes up for in ideas. In recent years some really great films have been released, which unfortunately probably never make it beyond the art film festivals in the West, making a visit to the cinema a must for film buffs while they are here. The annual **Hungarian Film Festival** in Budapest (*Magyar Filmszemle*) is held every February, when films (including documentary films) made in the past year are given a showing. You can usually find some films simultaneously translated into English during the festival – check their press centre at Rákóczi út 15 (*magyarfi@mail.datanet.hu*). During the **Budapest Spring Festival** at the end of March Hungarian feature films with English subtitles are shown. The **Media Wave** film festival held in Győr in late April shows alternative films from all over the world including the latest Hungarian offerings.

Older directors include István Szabó (*Mephisto, Colonel Redl*), Márta Mészáros (*Diary for My Children, Nine Months*) and Károly Makk (*Another Way about 1956, The Gambler*). However, they are currently struggling to hold their own as a new generation comes up behind them, including Peter Gothár, with his absurd humour and love of the fantastic (*Time Stands Still, Let Me Hang Vaska*), Ildikó Enyedi's sly look at history (*My Twentieth Century, The Magic Hunter*) and János Szász, whose latest film *The Witman Boys* won the best international film at Cannes. So-called art films are generally not dubbed, but there are films in English, French and

German advertised in the listings magazine **Pesti Est**. Dubbed films are indicated by m.b. or *Magyarul bészelő* on posters; the Hungarian for cinema is *filmszínház* or *mozi*.

## FESTIVALS

The **festival year** kicks off with the **Mohács Carnival** of masked revellers re-enacting ancient spring rites and ritual abomination of the Turks on March 1, followed later in the month by the **Spring Festivals** (*Tavaszi Fesztival*) of music and drama in Budapest, Szeged, Kecskemét, Debrecen and other towns. On **March 15**, wreaths are laid at monuments to commemorate the anniversary of the 1848 Revolution against the Habsburgs. Nowadays, **May 1** is just a public holiday, shorn of the Soviet-style parades that characterized it during the Communist period.

With the onset of tourists and fine weather, the summer months soon get crowded with events. Most of them are listed in *Where Budapest* and *Programme* magazines, or you can get information at Tourinform offices in Budapest.

You can see **historical pageants** at Veszprém, Tihany, Visegrád, Gyula or Esztergom; and **equestrian shows** with a "rodeo" atmosphere and amazing displays of horsemanship at Nagyvázsony, Apajpuszta, Tamási, Kisbér, Szántódpuszta and Hortobágy. The two-day Hortobágy Bridge Fair and the **Szeged Weeks** of music and drama reach their climax on **St Stephen's Day** (Aug 20), which honours the death of Hungary's patron saint and "founding father", with parades and fireworks in Budapest, a **Flower Carnival** in Debrecen and lesser displays in provincial towns.

Budapest's **Autumn Music Weeks** (late Sept to late Nov) more or less round off the year. **October 23**, the anniversary of the 1956 Uprising, has lost the emotional potency it had as a "forbidden anniversary" under Communism, and is now more of an excuse for each political party to outdo the other with displays of national emotion, especially from those politicians who faithfully toed the party line about "counter-revolution" that prevailed for forty years.

**Religious festivals** have been busily revived by the churches' believers in recent years. The biggest event is the August 20 procession of St Stephen's relic around the great Basilica in Pest. At Christmas and, more so, at Easter, the churches and cathedrals are packed – particularly in Esztergom, the seat of Hungarian Catholicism. Another, more remote focus for religious fervour is the village of **Máriapócs** in eastern Hungary, which draws thousands of pilgrims on August 15 and September 8 (see p.363).

It is also worth knowing about the tradition of **name-day celebrations**, which are as important to Hungarians as birthdays are in other countries. Customarily, the celebrant invites relatives and friends to a party, and receives gifts and salutations. Lest you forget someone's name-day, tradition allows congratulations to be rendered up to a week afterwards.

# SPORTS

Hungary is now on the circuit as a host for major sporting events, such as the Grand Prix. Full details of these, and national championships in everything from parachuting to canoeing, are available from **Tourinform, regional tourist offices** and *Programme* magazine.

Several pages of the weekly paper *Nemzeti Sport* are devoted to **football** (*labdarúgás*), Hungary's most popular sport. Current first-division contenders include the Budapest teams MTK, Ferencváros (aka "Fradi") and Újpest; and Győr, Diósgyőr and Vác from the provinces. Tickets for matches are cheap, as are facilities at local **sports halls** (*sportcsarnok*).

**Windsurfing** (*szörf*) and **sailing** equipment can be rented from the *kölcsönzo* at the main Balaton boat stations and Lake Velence, and **tennis** (*tenisz*) courts are often attached to more upmarket hotels in Budapest and main resorts. **Squash** (*fallabda*) courts have also begun to appear in Budapest. Hungary's topography rules out any dramatic or lengthy slopes, but that doesn't stop enthusiasts from **skiing** in the Mátra Mountains and the Buda Hills. Visitors into **hiking** can avail themselves of detailed maps of the highland regions.

## HORSE-RIDING

Hungarians profess a lingering attachment to the horse – their equestrian ally since the time of the great migration and the Magyar conquest – and the horse herds or *csikós* of the Plain are romantic figures of national folklore. Most native **horses** are mixed breeds descended from Arab and English thoroughbreds, crossed in recent years with Hanoverian and Holstein stock. The adjective most commonly used to describe their character is "spirited".

**Horse-riding tours** come in various forms. There are several itineraries around the Balaton, the Northern Uplands and the Great Plain, lasting from a week to ten days, with meals, lodgings and guide included; and somewhat bizarre expeditions by **covered wagons**, which tourists drive and navigate across the *puszta*. To give you an idea of prices, an eight-day tour starts at around 1200DM; ask for details at travel agencies in Budapest. Pegazus at Budapest V, Ferenciek tere

5, in the office facing you as you walk into the courtyard rather than the office on the street front (☎317-1552), organize riding at venues all over the country.

Regional tourist offices and local enterprises offer equestrian programmes and instruction at **riding schools** (*lovarda*), namely: Isaszeg, Üllő-Tornyoslöb and Ady-liget **near Budapest**; Taliándorog, Nagyvázsony, Nagyberek, Szentbékkálla, Szántódpuszta, Siófok and Keszthely **around the Balaton**; Tata, Szombathely, Sárvár, Radiháza, Nagycenk and Dunakiliti **in Transdanubia**; Visegrád on the **Danube Bend**; Szilvásvárad in the **Northern Uplands**; and Hortobágy, Bugac, Tiszafüred, Makó and Szatymaz on the **Great Plain**. Tourinform at Budapest V, Sütő utca 2 (☎317-9800), has the most comprehensive file on riding schools in Hungary and a map indicating where accommodation is also provided by the school. The schools provide saddlery, but you'll need your own riding clothes.

## HIKING

The most beautiful areas for **walking** are the Börzsöny, the Bükk, the Bakony and the Pilis, though all the wooded hill regions in Hungary are crisscrossed with walking **trails**, which are signed with coloured stripes and symbols on trees, stones and buildings. **Maps** (*turistatérkép*) are available in most bookshops, and it's worth working out how to use them. Walking paths on maps are shown as red lines, with a letter above them to tell you what colour the stripes on the trees or boulders are: Z = green, K = blue, S = yellow and P = red. Most paths are marked with stripes or crosses, but some are marked with a coloured circle (circular routes), a square (leading to a building or village), a triangle (leading to a peak), or an L-shape (leading to a ruin). Most villages in Hungary have a pub or bar, where you can get a drink, but not all have food, so if you're thinking of a longish hike it might be an idea to take a picnic. Some of the more popular areas, such as the Börzsöny, to the east of the Danube, north of Budapest, have basic **accommodation** called *turistaház* or *kulcsosház*, but you have to book in advance; tourist offices carry a list of phone numbers.

# WORK AND STUDY

Teaching English has traditionally been the main opportunity for work in Hungary, though the sector is much more professional now than it was five or six years ago, and it isn't so easy just to walk into a job without qualifications. Nevertheless, language teaching is a big business, and native speakers are scarce, particularly outside Budapest. You might find that state schools are willing to take you on just by virtue of the fact that English is your mother tongue.

## TEACHING

Assuming you can get enough clients, the most profitable option is **giving private lessons**. Qualified teachers can often charge up to 2000Ft an hour for a business client, but few private individuals can afford this; it's more realistic to stick to the going rate of around 1000–1500Ft. This often ends up being more than what you'd get **working in a language school**, where monthly salaries average 40,000–50,000Ft for around 24 lessons a week.

Naturally, language schools are good business and consequently attract their share of cowboys, though stories of schools employing teachers and then not paying them are fortunately now a rarity. The most reputable schools in Budapest are International House at II, Bimbó út 7 (☎212-4010), and the Bell School at II, Tulipán utca 8 (☎212-4190), both requiring TEFL certificates. Some employers will arrange **work permits**, but others leave it up to you. The process involves a lot of

paperwork, medical examinations and general humiliation.

Although **teaching in primary or secondary schools** pays much less (around 18,000–25,000Ft per month), the deal usually includes subsidized or free accommodation. Expect to teach around sixteen periods a week, mostly in the morning. Your timetable may also include exam preparation, marking, invigilation etc. Primary school work is not exam-oriented and largely involves playing games with pupils aged 6 to 14. Hungarian children learn to read later than children in Britain or the US, usually not until the age of 8, so unless you're experienced with kids it's probably not a good idea to take on a very young class. Secondary school classes are smaller, but teachers will need at least basic Hungarian, since the exam contains translation, and a lot of students will be preparing for the state language exam, which also has a translation component. Primary schools take anyone who seems capable and enthusiastic, though you are likely to require at least a certificate in TEFL and/or a PGCE.

**Recruitment** for state schools is handled by several agencies abroad (see below). In Hungary itself, your best bet is probably to contact IATEFL at the offices of ELTE/CETT, Ajtosi Dürer sor 19–21, who should be able to point you in the right direction. Better still you can make arrangements abroad. Qualified teachers (with a degree or TEFL certificate) are currently being recruited **in Britain** by the Eastern European Partnership, 15 Princeton Court, 53–55 Felsham Road, London SW15 1AZ (☎0181/780 2841). The two-year contract includes travel, accommodation and medical expenses. Other agencies such as the British Council may also advertise for teachers (usually in the *TES* or *Guardian* between April and June).

Native-speaking sixth-formers, students or teachers (up to the age of 45) can apply for jobs at English-language **summer camps** (generally three weeks during July/Aug). Besides giving Hungarian 15- to 17-year-olds the chance to practise their English, you're expected to organize sports and/or drama and musical activities – so previous experience in these areas is desirable. Board and accommodation is provided but applicants must pay for their own travel to Hungary; applications should be made to the Youth

Exchange Centre, Seymour Mews House, Seymour Mews, London W1H 9PE (☎0171/486 5101, ext 24) by the end of March.

In the **United States** volunteer teachers can apply to the Peace Corps at 1990 K St NW, Washington DC 20526, for two-year assignments; the Fulbright Program, which offers a round-trip fare, salary and housing; or George Washington University, PO Box 2798, Washington DC 20057.

## SUMMER COURSES

Eager to publicize their cultural achievements and earn foreign exchange, the Hungarians also organize **summer courses** in everything from folk art to environmental studies. Full details are contained in a booklet published in the spring, which can be obtained by writing to TIT (the Society for the Dissemination of Scientific Knowledge), H-1088 Budapest, VIII, Bródy Sándor utca 16. The deadline for most applications is May 1, so it's advisable to write some months in advance. Students are of all ages and come from countries as diverse as Switzerland and Venezuela, so the chance to meet people can be as much an attraction as the subject to be studied. These include photography (at Vác), Hungarian language and culture (Debrecen), fine arts (Zebegény), Esperanto (Gyula), Baroque recorder music (Sopron), jazz (Tatabánya), orchestral music (Pécs and Kecskemét), music-teaching by the Kodály method (Esztergom and Kecskemét), folk art (Zalaegerszeg) and nature studies (Keszthely). Fees include room and board and various excursions and entertainments.

# DIRECTORY

**ADDRESSES** These usually begin with the postcode, which indicates the town or city and locality. The most common terms are *utca* (street, abbreviated to *u.*), *út* (or *útja*, avenue), *tér* (or *tere*, square) and *körút* (ring boulevard). You may also encounter *rakpart* (embankment), *sétány* (promenade), *híd* (bridge), *köz* (lane), *hegy* (hill) and *liget* (park). Town centres are signposted *Belváros*, *Városközpont* or *Centrum*. A *lakótelep* is a high-rise housing estate.

**BRING** Any specific medication or contact lens sundries that you might need. Western fashion and pop magazines are much appreciated in trendy (*divatos*) circles. Passport-sized photos come in handy for season tickets, student cards, etc.

**CHILDREN** Children (*gyerek*) qualify for reductions on most forms of public transport (see "Getting Around"), and under-14s receive a 50 percent discount on the cost of camping. Separate visas aren't required for children under 14 who are included on a parent's passport (assuming they need one at all). The best facilities and entertainments for kids are in Budapest and the Balaton resorts. Children are forbidden to ride in the front seat of a car. Most supermarkets stock baby food and Libero disposable nappies.

**CIGARETTES** Sold in tobacconists (*dohánybolt*), supermarkets, bars and restaurants. Marlboro and Camel made under licence are cheaper than imports, but still more expensive than native brands like Helikon, Sopianae, and Symphonia. Even these local brands are not what they were, though, as all the tobacco factories have been bought up by Western companies and the native cigarette brands now appear in light and menthol varieties. Hardcore smokers might like to try the last bastion of the Hungarian tobacco industry, filterless, throat-rasping Munkás. Matches are *gyufa. Tilos a dohányzás* means "no smoking", and applies to cinemas, the metro, all buses, trams and trolleybuses, and all Malév Hungarian Airlines flights.

**CONTRACEPTIVES** Condoms (*óvszer, gumi* or *kondom*) are available at the cash tills in chemists, and in food stores. Reliable, locally manufactured contraceptive pills are available on prescription, although it's always more sensible to bring your own.

**ELECTRIC POWER** 220 volts. Round, two-pin plugs are used. A standard Continental adaptor allows the use of 13 amp, square-pin plugs.

**FILM** Kodak, Fuji, Agfa and Konica film is readily available, and most towns offer colour processing services. Mini-labs in Budapest and major towns can process and print films in a couple of hours.

**GAY AND LESBIAN LIFE** Although the age of consent for lesbians and gay men is 18, police harassment and public disapproval still occur. The organization HOMEROS-Lambda, founded in 1988, maintains a low profile, fearful of antagonizing the newly powerful Catholic Church, which allegedly pressured the government into halting advertisments for condoms and safer sex. A law passed under the Communists permits the compulsory blood-testing of "suspected" HIV-carriers. Given this, and public homophobia, it's hardly surprising that visible manifestations of gay life are limited to Budapest.

**LAUNDRY** Self-service launderettes (*mosoda*) are very rare, and since Patyolat (the local dry cleaning chain) went bust you will have to rely on the competent but expensive Hungarian-American Ametiszt. Staying in private lodgings, you may be allowed to use your host's washing machine. All supermarkets sell detergent.

**LEFT LUGGAGE** Most train stations have a left-luggage office (*ruhatár*), which has a daily charge (calculated on the size of your bags) for each item deposited, and sometimes includes "each item" strapped to your backpack. Beware of huge queues for baggage at Budapest's main stations (and some Balaton termini) during the summer, and keep *all* of the scrappy little receipts, or you'll never get your gear back. A few main stations have automatic luggage lockers, which take specific coins (you might have to go and buy something in order to get the right change, as officials are often very unhelpful in this area) and store your baggage for up to 24 hours.

**LOST PROPERTY** Anything left on a train is kept for one to three weeks at the destination of the train, or where it was handed in, and then stored at Váci út 3 by Budapest's Nyugati Station (Mon–Fri 8am–3pm). Passports are first sent to the police and then forwarded to embassies. For property lost on Budapest city transport see the Budapest Listings.

**MUSEUMS** Most of Hungary's museums have captions in Hungarian only, although important museums in provincial centres and the capital might sell catalogues in German, French or English. Skanzens or Village Museums are probably the most effective for surmounting the language barrier – fascinating ensembles of buildings and domestic objects culled from old settlements around the country, assembled on the outskirts of Szentendre, Nyíregyháza, Zalaegerszeg and Szombathely, or preserved *in situ* at Szalafő and Hollókő. Museum admission charges vary from 50Ft to 300Ft, while student cards (see opposite) secure reductions, or free entry in many cases. Some places have free admission on certain days, and most are closed on Mondays. Some museums insist you tie on slippers while inside the building; you ignore the order at your peril.

**NAMES** Surnames precede forenames in Hungary, to the confusion of foreigners. In this book, the names of historical personages are rendered in the Western fashion, for instance, Lajos Kossuth rather than Kossuth Lajos (Hungarian-style), except when referring to buildings, streets, etc.

**NUDISM** Often known by the German initials FKK, nudism is gaining ground, with nudist camps outside Budapest, Szeged, Mohács and Balatonberény, and nude sunbathing on segregated terraces at some pools, though you shouldn't assume that it's permitted. For more information, contact the

Naturisták Egyesülete (Naturist Union) at Budapest XIII, Kárpát utca 8.

**STUDENT CARDS** These entitle you to small reductions at some hostels and campsites, free or reduced admission to museums, and significant discounts on certain international train tickets and Malév flights. The East European student organization, IUS, produces its own card, which in the past has been the only one to give discounts; it may, however, be superseded by the ISIC card in the future. It's best to bring an ISIC card with you and then get an IUS card in Hungary from an Express office or train station.

**TAXES** Prices often include a sales tax (ÁFA), which ranges from 12 to 25 percent, so that any prices quoted are likely to jump sharply when it comes to paying. Check on whether ÁFA is included

(*Árak nem tartalmaznak ÁFA-t* is Hungarian for "Prices do not include tax"). If you make a purchase over 25,000Ft, it's worth filling in the form that enables you to claim tax back when you leave the country. Two companies who offer help in getting refunds are Inteltrade, Budapest I, Csalogány utca 6–10 (☎356-9800) and Europe Tax Free Shopping (☎212-4734).

**TIME** Hungary is one hour ahead of GMT, six hours ahead of Eastern Standard Time and nine ahead of Pacific Standard Time in North America. A word of caution: Hungarians express time in a way that might confuse the anglophone traveller. For example, 10.30am is expressed as "half eleven" (written 1/2 11 or f11), 10.45am is "three-quarter-eleven" (3/4 11 or h11), and 10.15am is "a quarter of the next hour" (1/4 11 or n11).

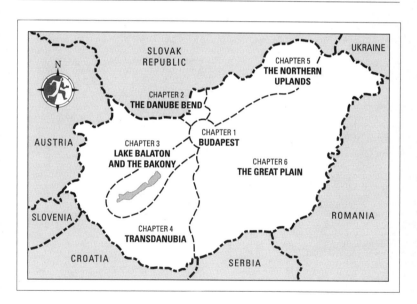

# CHAPTER ONE

# BUDAPEST

The importance of **BUDAPEST** to Hungary is difficult to overestimate. More than two million people live in the capital – one fifth of the population – and everything converges here: roads and rail lines; air travel (Ferihegy is the country's only civilian airport); industry, commerce and culture; opportunities, wealth and power. Like Paris, the city has a history of revolutions – in 1849, 1918 and 1956 – buildings, parks and avenues on a monumental scale, and a reputation for hedonism, style and parochial pride. In short, Budapest is a city worthy of comparison with other great European capitals.

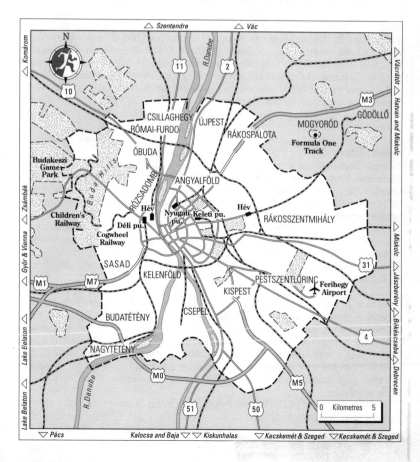

Surveying Budapest from the embankments or the bastions of Várhegy (Castle Hill), it's easy to see why the city was dubbed the "Pearl of the Danube". Its grand buildings and sweeping bridges look magnificent, especially when floodlit or illuminated by the barrage of fireworks launched from Gellért-hegy (Gellért Hill) every August 20, St Stephen's Day. The eclectic inner-city and radial boulevards combine brash commercialism with a *fin-de-siècle* sophistication, while a distinctively Hungarian character is highlighted by the sounds and appearance of the Magyar language at every turn.

Long known as the liveliest city in the former Eastern Bloc, Budapest has experienced a new surge of energy since the collapse of the Communist system. The choice of restaurants, bars and entertainment has never been so great – and there's a sleazy side to the city too, that accounts for its reputation as the "Bangkok of Europe". While some Hungarians fear the corruption and ultimate erosion of their culture by foreign influences, others herald the start of a new golden age with Budapest the foremost city in Mitteleuropa.

The River Danube – which is never blue – determines basic **orientation**, with Buda on the hilly west bank and Pest covering the plain across the river. More precisely, Budapest is divided into 23 districts (*kerület*), designated on maps and street signs by Roman numerals; some of the quarters' historic names have only recently been restored after decades of official disfavour. In **Buda**, the focus of attention is the I district, comprising the Várhegy and the Víziváros (Watertown); the XI, XII, II and III districts are worth visiting for Gellért Hill, Buda Hill, Óbuda and Római-Fürdő. **Pest** is centred on the downtown Belváros (V district), while beyond the Kiskörút (Small Boulevard) lie the VI, VII, VIII and IX districts, respectively known as the Terézváros, Erzsébetváros, Józsefváros and Ferencváros.

## Some history

Though Budapest has formally existed only since 1873 – when the twin cities of Buda and Pest were united in a single municipality, together with the smaller Óbuda – the history of settlement here goes back as far as the second millennium BC. During the first Age of Migrations, the area was settled by waves of peoples, notably Scythians from the Caucasus and Celts from what is now France.

During the first century BC, the Celtic Eravisci tribe was absorbed into Pannonia, a vast province of the Roman Empire. This was subsequently divided into two regions, one of which, Pannonia Inferior, was governed from the garrison town of **Aquincum** on the west bank of the Danube; ruins of a camp, villas, baths and an amphitheatre can still be seen today.

The Romans withdrew in the fifth century AD to be succeeded by the Huns. Germanic tribes, Lombards, Avars and Slavs all followed each other during the second Age of Migrations, until the arrival of the **Magyars** in about 896. According to the medieval chronicler, Anonymous, while other tribes spread out across the Carpathian basin, the clan of Árpád settled on Csepel sziget (Csepel Island), and it was Árpád's brother, Buda, who purportedly gave his name to the west bank of the new settlement. It was under the Árpád dynasty that Hungary became a Christian state, ruled first from Esztergom and later from Székesfehérvár.

The **development of Buda and Pest** did not begin in earnest until the twelfth century, and was largely thanks to French, Walloon and German settlers who worked and traded here under royal protection. Both towns were devastated by the Mongols in 1241 and subsequently rebuilt by colonists from Germany, who named Buda *"Ofen"*, after its numerous lime-kilns. (The name Pest, which is of Slav origin, also means "oven".) During the fourteenth century, the Angevin kings from France established Buda as a **royal seat**, building a succession of palaces on the Várhegy. It reached its apogee in Renaissance times under the reign of "Good King" Mátyás (1458–90) and his Italian-born wife, Queen Beatrice, with a golden age of prosperity and a flourishing of the arts.

Hungary's catastrophic defeat at Mohács in 1526 paved the way for the **Turkish occupation** of Buda and Pest, which lasted 160 years until a pan-European army besieged Buda Castle for six weeks, finally recapturing it at the twelfth attempt. Under **Habsburg rule**, with control exerted from Vienna or Bratislava, recovery was followed by a period of intensive growth during the second half of the eighteenth century. In the first decades of the following century, Pest became the centre of the **Reform movement** led by Count Széchenyi, whose vision of progress was embodied in the construction of the **Lánchíd** (Chain Bridge), the first permanent link between Buda and Pest, which had hitherto relied on pontoon bridges or barges.

When the Habsburg empire was shaken by revolutions which broke out across Europe in **March 1848**, local reformists and radicals seized the moment. While Lajos Kossuth (1802–94) dominated parliament, Sándor Petőfi (1823–49) and his fellow revolutionaries plotted the downfall of the Habsburgs in the *Café Pilvax* (which exists today in a sanitized restaurant-form in central Pest), from where they mobilized crowds on the streets of Pest. After the War of Independence ended in defeat for the Hungarians, Habsburg repression was epitomized by the hilltop Citadella on Gellért-hegy, built to cow the citizenry with its guns.

Following the Compromise of 1867, which established the Dual Monarchy familiarly known to its subjects as the K & K (from the German for "Emperor and King"), the twin cities underwent rapid **expansion** and formally merged. Pest was extensively remodelled, acquiring the Nagykörút (Great Boulevard) and Andrássy út, the grand thoroughfare that runs from the Belváros to the Városliget (City Park). Hungary's **millennial anniversary celebrations** in 1896 brought a fresh rush of construction, and Hősök tere (Heroes' Square) and Vajdahunyad Castle at the far end of Andrássy út are just two examples of the monumental style that encapsulated the age. New suburbs were created to house the burgeoning population, which was by now predominantly Magyar, although there were still large German and Jewish communities. A t the beginning of the twentieth century the **cultural efflorescence** in Budapest rivalled that of Vienna and its café society that of Paris – a *belle époque* doomed by World War I.

In the aftermath of defeat, Budapest experienced the Soviet-ruled **Republic of Councils** under Béla Kun, and occupation by the Romanian army. The status quo ante was restored by **Admiral Horthy**, self-appointed regent for the exiled Karl IV –the "Admiral without a fleet, for the king without a kingdom" – whose regency was characterized by gala balls and hunger marches, bombastic nationalism and anti-Semitism. Yet Horthy was a moderate compared to the Arrow Cross Fascists, whose power grew as **World War II** raged.

Anticipating Horthy's defection from the Axis in 1944, Nazi Germany staged a coup, installing an Arrow Cross government, which enabled them to begin the massacre of the **Jews** of Budapest; they also blew up the Danube bridges as a way of hampering the advancement of the Red Army. The six-month-long **siege of Budapest** reduced the Vár (Castle District) to rubble and severely damaged much of the rest of the city, making **reconstruction** the first priority for the post-war coalition government.

As the **Communists** gained ascendancy, the former Arrow Cross torture chambers filled up once again. A huge statue of the Soviet dictator (whose name was bestowed upon Budapest's premier boulevard) symbolized the reign of terror carried out by **Mátyás Rákosi**, Hungary's "Little Stalin". However, his liberally inclined successor, Imre Nagy, gave hope to the people, who refused to tolerate a comeback by the hardliners in 1956. In Budapest, peaceful protests turned into a city-wide **uprising** literally overnight: men, women and children defying Soviet tanks on the streets.

After Soviet power had been bloodily restored, **János Kádár** – initially reviled as a quisling – gradually normalized conditions, embarking on cautious reforms to create a **"goulash socialism"** that made Hungary the envy of its Warsaw Pact neighbours and the West's favourite Communist state during the late 1970s. A decade later, the regime saw the writing on the wall and anticipated Gorbachev by promising **free elections**, hoping to reap public gratitude. Instead – as Communism was toppled in Berlin and Prague – the party was simply voted out of power in Hungary.

The removal of the red star from Budapest's parliament building and the restoration of old street names throughout the city were symbolic of a desire to go back to **the future.** Since the election in 1990, the city administration has been run by the Free Democrat mayor, Gabor Demszky, a leading dissident under the old regime, and now making an impressive job of running the city – at least that is what the voters think, who have re-elected him twice, even as his party's fortunes have slumped in national elections.

# Arrival and information

Other than the airport, all **points of arrival** are fairly central and most within walking distance or just a few stops by metro from downtown Pest. The city's three metro lines and three major roads meet at the major junction of Deák tér in Pest, making this the main transport hub of the city. Depending on when and where you arrive, it's definitely worth considering either arranging somewhere to stay before leaving the terminal (there are reservation services at all of them), or stashing your luggage before setting out to look for a room. For all **departure** information, see the relevant sections of "Listings", pp.124–125.

> The telephone code for Budapest is ☎1

## By air
**Ferihegy Airport**, 20km from the centre, has two terminals: Ferihegy 2A, which is used by most airlines, and Ferihegy 2B, serving Malév and Malév's joint flights with other airlines: Aeroflot, Alitalia, Air France, CSA, Delta, Swissair and Lufthansa. A shuttle bus (Airport-Centrum Minibusz; every 30min, 5.30am–9pm; 600Ft) runs from outside the terminal buildings to Erzsebet tér in downtown Pest; tickets can be purchased on board. There is also the Airport Minibus, which takes you directly to your destination. Tickets (1200Ft) can be bought in the luggage claim hall while you are waiting for your luggage, or in the main concourse; you give your address and then

### BUDAPEST ADDRESSES

Finding your way around Budapest is easier than the welter of names might suggest. Districts and streets are well signposted, and those in Pest conform to an overall plan based on radial avenues and semicircular boulevards.

**Budapest addresses** begin with the number of the district – for example, V, Petőfi tér 3 – a system used throughout this chapter. When addressing letters, however, a four-digit postal code is used instead, the middle digits indicating the district (so that 1054 refers to a place in the V district). A potential source of confusion to visitors is the wholesale **renaming of streets** that took place in the early 1990s, when the Lenin körút was restored to Teréz and Erzsébet körút, and Népköztársaság útja to Andrássy út. Although references to the old names are rare, you'll still find many of the old signs on the walls, though they've been crossed out in red.

As a rule of thumb, **street numbers** ascend away from the north–south axis of the River Danube and the east–west axis of Rákóczi út/Kossuth utca/Hegyalja út. Even numbers are generally on the left-hand side, odd numbers on the right. One number may refer to several premises or an entire apartment building, while an additional combination of numerals denotes the floor and number of individual **apartments** (eg Kossuth utca 14/III/24). Confusingly, some old buildings in Pest are designated as having a half-floor (*félemelet*) or upper ground floor (*magas földszint*) between the ground (*földszint*) and first floor (*elsőemelet*) proper – so that what the British would call the second floor, and Americans the third, Hungarians might describe as the first. This stems from a nineteenth-century taxation fiddle, whereby landlords avoided the higher tax on buildings with more than three floors.

have to wait five to twenty minutes until the driver calls your destination. A slower but cheaper way to get to the centre is to go by public transport: take the red #93 (not to be confused with the black #93) from outside the terminal to the final stop, the faded, red and yellow metro station at Kőbánya Kispest, switching to the blue metro line (3), and alighting ten stops later at Deák tér. It takes about 45 minutes and costs 140Ft for the two tickets. You'll have to get the bus ticket before boarding; there is a machine by the stop, or ask at the airport information desk. Airport taxis are mafia-controlled and known to physically threaten other cabs that enter their patch. They charge way above the odds, with fixed rates of 3000–5000Ft, depending on your destination – almost twice the rate of other cabs – though they will charge unsuspecting foreigners many times that. You can order normal city cabs at Ferihegy's **tourist offices**, who can also can reserve accommodation in Budapest for you.

### By train

The Hungarian word *pályaudvar* (abbreviated to *pu.* in writing only) is used to designate the seven Budapest **train stations**, only three of which are on the metro and of any use to tourists. Translated into English, their names refer to the direction of services handled rather than location, so that Western Station (*Nyugati pu.*) is north of downtown Pest, and Southern Station (*Déli pu.*) is in the west of the city; Eastern Station (*Keleti pu.*), however, is to the east of the city centre.

On the northern edge of Pest's Great Boulevard, **Nyugati Station** has a 24-hour left-luggage office (120Ft or 240Ft depending on size) next to the ticket office beside platform 13. You can change money at Cooptourist (Mon–Fri

9am–4.30pm) or Budapest Tourist (Mon–Fri 9am–5.30pm, Sat 9am–noon), down in the underpass in front of the station near the entrance to the metro, where you can also book rooms. The Budapest Tourist Information Office, by the police office (*Rendőrség*) to the left of the main entrance of the station (daily 7am–8pm; ☎302-8580), can provide information on the city and accommodation. To reach Deák tér, ride the blue metro line two stops in the direction of Kőbánya-Kispest.

Trains from Vienna's Westbahnhof terminate at Pest's **Keleti Station** on Baross tér in the VIII district. This station is even worse for thieves and hustlers – especially at night, when it's taken over by prostitutes and the homeless. In summer there are long queues at the 24-hour left-luggage office (120Ft or 240Ft), and there are also long waits at the tourist offices in the Lotz Hall, IBUSZ (Mon–Fri 8am–4pm) and Traveller's Youth Hostels (7am–11pm), at the side exit of the station down platform 6. Keleti is three stops from Deák tér by the Déli pu.-bound red metro line.

A warning about taxis at Keleti Station: the unmarked taxis lining the road outside the doors of the station are worth avoiding, despite their drivers wearing badges saying "official taxi". Instead, look out for taxis from the companies listed on p.58, such as Főtaxi, which you can find by going out the main doors and turning right.

**Déli Station** is 500m behind the Várhegy in Buda. Accommodation and exchange are handled by Budapest Tourist, in the row of shops down the steps past the metro entrance (left-luggage is around the corner), or you can cross the park towards the Vár to deal with Cooptourist at Attila út 107. Déli Station is four stops from Deák tér on the red metro line.

## By bus

The majority of **international bus services** wind up at the **Erzsébet tér bus station**, just by Deák tér on the edge of downtown Pest. However, the planned building of the National Theatre in Erzsébet tér means the bus station may move to a new site in outer Pest in 1999. The bus station's left-luggage office is small but rarely busy, and there are several tourist offices in the vicinity – you'll find Dunatours and Cooptourist at Bajcsy-Zsilinszky út 17, 150m north of the bus station, and IBUSZ at Dob utca 1, slightly further in the other direction. Tourinform (see below) is just around the corner and the 24-hour IBUSZ bureau near the Pest embankment is less than ten minutes' walk away.

Some international services come to the **Népstadion bus station** in the XIV district, but this is mainly used by services coming from other parts of Hungary, as is the **Árpád híd bus station** in the XIII district. Neither has any tourist facilities, but they're both just four or five metro stops from the centre of Pest.

## By hydrofoil

Hydrofoils from Vienna (April–Oct) dock at the **international landing stage**, on the Belgrád rakpart (embankment), near downtown Pest. Volántourist is just outside the terminal and there are two IBUSZ offices five minutes' walk north, on Ferenciek tere, inland of the Erzsébet Bridge, and on Petőfi tér, on the road leading up to the *Marriott Hotel*.

# Information, maps and tours

Leaving aside the business of finding accommodation, the best source of **information** is the National Tourist Office's **Tourinform** at V, Sütő utca 2, just around the corner from Deák tér metro (May–Oct daily 9am–7pm; Nov–April Mon–Fri

9am–7pm, Sat & Sun 9am–4pm; ☎317-9800). Their friendly polyglot staff can answer just about any question on Budapest, or travel elsewhere in Hungary.

It's a good idea to get hold of a proper **map** of the city at the earliest opportunity. The small freebies supplied by tourist offices give an idea of Budapest's layout and principal monuments, but lack detail. Larger, folding maps are sold all over the place, but their size makes them cumbersome. For total coverage you can't beat the *Budapest Atlasz*, available in bookshops for 1200Ft, which shows every street, bus and tram route, and the location of restaurants, museums and suchlike. It also contains enlarged maps of the Vár, central Pest, Margit sziget (Margit Island) and the Városliget (City Park), plus a comprehensive index.

Details of **what's on** can be found in the magazines *Where Budapest* and *Panoráma* (both free in hotels), the weeklies *Budapest Week* and *Budapest Sun* (around 150Ft), and the Hungarian-language listings weeklies, *Pesti Est* (free in cinema foyers) and *Pesti Müsor* (available at newsagents for 70Ft).

Although Budapest can easily be explored without a guide, if you're hard-pressed for time, you might appreciate a **city tour** for two to three hours. These range in price from 2400Ft to 3600Ft and can be arranged through Tourinform (see opposite), Budapest Tourist (☎318-6600), leaving from their office at V, Roosevelt tér 5, or Buda Tours (☎302-6278), leaving from in front of the Gresham Casino next door to Budapest Tourist. IBUSZ and Budapest Tourist also organize **guided tours** of the parliament building, combined with visits to the Ethnographic Museum or the National Gallery (see p.98 for details).

# City transport

Most of Budapest's backstreets and historic quarters are eminently suited to **walking** – and this is much the best way to appreciate their character. Traffic is restricted in downtown Pest and around the Várhegy in Buda, and fairly light in the residential backstreets off the main boulevards, which are the nicest areas to wander around.

However, if you do need to make use of **public transport**, Budapest has an excellent system, which ensures that few parts of the city are more than thirty minutes' journey from the centre; many places can be reached in half that time. It doesn't take long to pick up the basics and it's also much better value than **taxis**, which sometimes overcharge tourists, and preferable to **driving** or **cycling** amidst the traffic jams and exhaust fumes that afflict the main thoroughfares. Budapest's outer suburbs are well served by the overground **HÉV train** network, while Danube **ferries** and the **Children's Railway** in the Buda Hills offer fun excursions.

### The metro, buses, trams and trolley buses

Running at two- to twelve-minute intervals between 4.30am and 11.10pm, Budapest's **metro** reaches most areas of interest to tourists, its three lines intersecting at Deák tér in downtown Pest (see map overleaf). From nearby Vörösmarty tér, the **yellow line** (line 1) runs out beneath Andrássy út to Mexikoi út, beyond the Városliget. The **red line** (line 2) connects Déli Station in Buda with Keleti Station and Örs vezér tere in Pest; and the **blue line** (line 3) describes an arc from Kőbánya-Kispest to Újpest-Központ, via Ferenciek tere and Nyugati Station. There's little risk of going astray once you've learned to recognize the

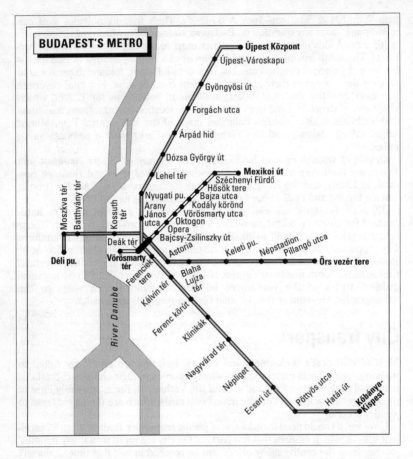

**BUDAPEST'S METRO**

- Újpest Központ
- Újpest-Városkapu
- Gyöngyösi út
- Forgách utca
- Árpád hid
- Dózsa György út
- Lehel tér
- **Mexikoi út**
- Széchenyi Fürdő
- Hősök tere
- Nyugati pu.
- Bajza utca
- Kodály körönd
- Arany
- Vörösmarty utca
- János
- Oktogon
- utca
- Opera
- Bajcsy-Zsilinszky út
- Deák tér
- Moszkva tér
- Batthyány tér
- Kossuth tér
- Déli pu.
- Vörösmarty tér
- Ferenciek tere
- Astoria
- Keleti pu.
- Népstadion
- Pillangó utca
- Örs vezér tere
- Blaha Lujza tér
- Kálvin tér
- River Danube
- Ferenc körut
- Klinikák
- Nagyvárad tér
- Népliget
- Ecseri út
- Pöttyös utca
- Határ út
- Kőbánya-Kispest

signs *bejárat* (entrance), *kijárat* (exit), *vonal* (line) and *felé* (towards). Drivers announce the next stop between stations and the train's direction is indicated by the name of the station at the end of the line.

A word of warning: there's an active **pickpocket** battalion on both the metro (especially the yellow line) and the city buses. Gangs distract their victims by pushing them or blocking their way, and empty their pockets or bags at the same time.

**Buses** (*autóbusz*) are useful for journeys that can't be made by metro – especially around Buda, where Moszkva tér (on the red line) and Móricz Zsigmond körtér (southwest of Gellért-hegy) are the main bus terminals. Bus stops are marked by a blue sign with a picture of a bus in the centre, and have timetables underneath; most buses run every ten to twenty minutes from 5am to 11pm (*Utolsó kocsi indul . . .* means "the last one leaves . . ."). Regular services are numbered in black, buses with red numbers make fewer stops en route, and those with a red "E" suffix run non-stop between terminals. You should punch your own ticket on board; to get the bus to stop, push the button above the door or on the

### USEFUL BUS AND TRAM ROUTES

*BUSES*

**#7** Bosnyák tér–Keleti Station–Móricz Zsigmond körtér (via Rákóczi út, Ferenciek tere, the Hotel Gellért, Rác and Rudas Baths). Red #7 continues on to Kelenföld Station.

**#16** Erzsébet tér–Dísz tér (Vár).

**#22** Moszkva tér–Budakeszi.

**#26** Nyugati tér–Szent István körút–Margit sziget–Árpád híd metro station.

**#27** Móricz Zsigmond körtér–near the top of Gellért-hegy.

**#56** Moszkva tér–Szilágyi Erzsébet fasor–Hűvösvölgy with the red #56E going almost without stopping.

**#65** Kolosy tér–Pálvölgyi Caves–halfway up Hármashatár-hegy.

**#86** Southern Buda–Gellért tér–the Víziváros–Flórián tér (Óbuda).

**#105** Apor Vilmos tér–Lánchíd–Deák tér.

**Várbusz Minibus** Moszkva tér–Royal Palace and back.

*NIGHT BUSES*

**#6É** Moszkva tér–Margit sziget–Nyugati Station–Great Boulevard–Móricz Zsigmond körtér.

**#78É** Örs vezér tere–Bosnyák tér–Keleti Station–Buda side of Erzsébet Bridge.

**#14É** and **#50É** both run along Kispest (Határ út metro station)–Deák tér–Lehel tér along the route of the blue metro and on to the north and south.

**#49É** Moszkva tér–Erzsébet Bridge–Hotel Gellért–Móricz Zsigmond körtér.

*TRAMS*

**#2** Margit Bridge–Petőfi Bridge along embankment–HÉV station at Közvágóhíd.

**#4** Moszkva tér–Margit sziget–Nyugati Station–Great Boulevard–Petőfi Bridge –Október 23. utca.

**#6** Moszkva tér–Margit sziget–Nyugati Station–Great Boulevard–Petőfi Bridge–Móricz Zsigmond körtér.

**#19** Batthyány tér–Víziváros–Kelenföld Station.

**#47** Deák tér–Szabadság Bridge–Hotel Gellért–Móricz Zsigmond körtér–Budafok.

**#49** Deák tér–Szabadság Bridge–Hotel Gellért–Móricz Zsigmond körtér–Kelenföld Station.

**#56** Moszkva tér–Szilágyi Erzsébet fasor–Hűvösvölgy.

*TROLLEY BUSES*

**#72** Arany Janos utca metro station–Nyugati Station-Széchenyi Baths-Petőfi Csarnok–Thököly út.
**#74** Dohány utca (outside the Main Synagogue)–Városliget.

handrail beside the door. After 8pm, you may have to enter by the first door and show your ticket or pass to the driver as you board, although in practice drivers are not always that strict. Busy routes are also served by **night buses** (up to four every hour), with black numbers and an "É" suffix.

Yellow **trams** (*villamos*) are chiefly good for travelling around the Great Boulevard or along the embankments. Services run from early in the morning to 11pm. **Trolley buses** (*trolibusz*) mostly operate northeast of the centre near the Városliget. The reason route numbers start at 70 is that the first trolley bus line was inaugurated on Stalin's seventieth birthday in 1949. Trolley bus #83 was started in 1961, when Stalin would have been 83.

*TICKETS AND PASSES*

**Tickets** valid for the metro, buses, trams, trolley buses and suburban HÉV lines (see opposite) are sold at metro stations, newspaper kiosks and tobacconists, and currently cost 75Ft. You can also buy **day passes** (*napijegy*) costing 600Ft, which are valid for unlimited travel until midnight, or three-day passes for 1300Ft. **Season tickets** are available from metro stations, covering trams, trolley buses, the metro, HÉV and cogwheel trains, and buses. These cost around 1450Ft for a week (there is also a 1550Ft weekly pass if you do not have a season ticket), 2000Ft for two weeks and 3000Ft for a month. Bring a passport photo along as you'll need a photocard for your passholder. Tickets valid only on the **metro** come in a variety of types, depending on how many lines you want to use, and how many stops you want to go. A metro section ticket (50Ft) takes you three stops on the same line, a metro transfer ticket (120Ft) is valid for as many stops as you like with one line change, and a metro section transfer ticket (80Ft) takes you five stops with one line change.

There is a 1000Ft **fine** for travelling without a ticket. If you have a season ticket but are not carrying it, the fine is even higher, though most of it is refunded upon presentation of the season ticket within three days at the Budapest Transport Company (BKV) office at VII, Akácfa utca 15, near Blaha Lujza tér metro. **Children** up to the age of 6 travel free.

## Taxis

Budapest has over 15,000 registered **taxis**, whose drivers have gained themselves a reputation for ripping off foreigners – the best advice is to use one of the following established companies: Főtaxi (☎222-2222) and Citytaxi (☎211-1111), the most reliable; Tele-5-taxi (☎355-5555); and Volántaxi (☎466-6666). The taxis to avoid are the unmarked private cars and those hanging around the stations and airport – the latter often charge a far higher rate than the official one from the airport into town. There are also fake Fő and City taxis, sporting copies of the red-and-white chequerboard or yellow shield logos, which will charge you a vastly inflated price.

Taxis can be flagged down on the street or, for a cheaper rate, ordered by phone. There are ranks throughout the city and you can hop into whichever cab you choose – don't feel you have to opt for the one at the front of the line if it looks at all dodgy. Be sure your taxi has a meter that is visible, and that it is switched on when you get in; rates should also be clearly displayed. **Fares** begin at 50Ft, and the price per kilometre is around 150Ft.

## Driving and cycling

All things considered, **driving** in Budapest can't be recommended. Road manners are nonexistent, parking space is scarce and traffic jams are frequent. The Pest side of the Lánchíd (Chain Bridge) and the roundabout before the tunnel under Várhegy are notorious for collisions. Careering trams, bumpy cobbles and unexpected one-way systems make things worse. If you do have a car, you might be better off parking it somewhere outside the centre and using public transport to get in and out. It's best not to leave it unattended for too long, though.

If you want to **rent a car**, choose one of the Western models offered by most companies (in the region of $60 a day, with special weekly rates) – old Russian Ladas, though cheaper, should be avoided. It's worth checking whether mileage and insurance are included in the price, and if there's a surcharge. Most places accept a credit card as a deposit; if you don't have one, you can expect to pay upwards of $1000. See "Listings", p.124, for agency addresses.

**Cyclists** must contend with the same hazards as drivers, as well as sunken tram-lines, and they are also banned from most major thoroughfares. However, cycle routes are beginning to appear, for example, up Andrássy út and along the Buda bank of the Danube to Szentendre and beyond. Budapest is the best place in Hungary for repairs or to buy a bike for use elsewhere; see p.124 for details of bike shops and rental outlets. Bicycles can be carried on HÉV trains and the Cogwheel Railway for the price of a single ticket, but not on buses or trams.

## HÉV trains

Overground **HÉV trains** provide easy access to Budapest's suburbs, running at least four times an hour between 6.30am and 11pm. As far as tourists are concerned, the most useful line is the one from **Batthyány tér** (on the red metro line) out to **Szentendre** (see p.129), north of Budapest, which passes through Óbuda, Aquincum and Római-Fürdő. The other lines originate in Pest, with one running northeast from **Örs vezér tere** (also on red metro line 2) to **Gödöllő** via the Formula One racing track at Mogyoród; the other southwards from **Soroksári út** (bus #23 or #54 from Boráros tér) to **Ráckeve**, on Csepel sziget. On all these routes, a normal city transport ticket will take you to the city limits, beyond which you must punch additional tickets according to the distance travelled. Alternatively, you can purchase a ticket that covers the whole journey at the ticket office in the station or from the conductor on board.

## Ferries and other rides

Although **ferries** play little useful part in the transport system, they do offer an enjoyable ride. From May to September there are regular excursion boats from the Vigadó tér dock on the Pest embankment, south to Boráros tér and north to Jászai Mari tér – both brief, scenic routes – running every fifteen to thirty minutes between 7am and 7pm and costing 100–300Ft. From May to August there is also a boat from the Jászai Mari tér dock to Pünkösdfürdő in northern Buda (1hr; check times on the board at the main dock), though you might prefer to disembark at Margit sziget, before the boat reaches dismal Békásmegyer. Ferry tickets can be obtained from kiosks (where timetables are posted) or machines at the docks.

Other pleasure rides can be found in the Buda Hills, on the **Cogwheel Railway** (**Fogaskerekű vasút**), the **Children's Railway** (**Gyermekvasút**) – largely staffed by kids – and the **Chairlift** (**Libegő**) between Zugliget and János-hegy. Details for all of these are given in the "Buda Hills" section (see p.86).

# Accommodation

The **accommodation** situation in Budapest has improved markedly in recent years. Predictably, the heaviest demand and highest prices occur over summer, when the city feels like it's bursting at the seams. Christmas and New Year, the Grand Prix and the Autumn Music Weeks are also busy periods, with higher rates in most hotels. Even so, it should always be possible to find somewhere that's reasonably priced, if not well sited.

Budget travellers will find most **hotels** expensive even during low season (Nov–March, excluding New Year); only a few are viable options. Though cheaper, **pensions** are often much the same as small hotels, with en-suite bathrooms and other mod cons. For both hotels and pensions, it's essential to **phone ahead** and

---

### ACCOMMODATION BOOKING AGENCIES

Of the city's four main booking agencies, both **Cooptourist** and **Budapest Tourist** specialize in private rooms and apartments, and the latter will also book bungalows. **IBUSZ** will make reservations in hotels, private rooms and apartments, while **Express** deal with the cheaper hostel and student-type accommodation.

**Budapest Tourist**

Nyugati Station, downstairs in the underpass in front of the station (Mon–Fri 9am–5.30pm, Sat 9am–noon; ☎332-6565).

VIII, Baross tér 3, across the square from Keleti Station (Mon–Fri 9am–4.30pm; ☎333-6587).

Déli Station, in the mall by the metro entrance (Mon–Thurs 9am–5pm, Fri 9am–4pm; ☎355-7167).

VII, Erzsébet körút 41 (Mon–Thurs 10am–6pm, Fri 10am–5pm, Sat 9am–1pm; ☎342-6521).

V, Roosevelt tér 5 (Mon–Thurs 9am–4.30pm, Fri 9am–4pm; ☎317-3555).

**Cooptourist**

Skála Métro department store, opposite Nyugati Station (Mon–Fri 9am–4.30pm; ☎312-3621).

V, Bajcsy-Zsilinszky út 17 (Mon–Fri 9am–5pm; ☎311-7034).

V, Kossuth tér 13 (Mon, Tues, Thurs & Fri 8am–4pm, Wed 8am–5pm; ☎332-6387).

**Danubius/HungarHotels**

V, Szervita tér 8 (Mon–Fri 8.30am–5pm; ☎317-3652).

V, Petőfi Sándor utca 16 (Mon–Fri 9am–5pm; July–Aug also Sat 9am–noon; ☎318-3018).

V, Magyar utca 3 (Mon–Fri 8am–5pm; July–Aug also Sat 9am–noon; ☎317-6227).

**Express**

VIII, Baross tér, Keleti Station (Mon–Fri 6am–6pm; ☎342-1772).

V, Semmelweiss utca 4 (Mon–Thurs 8.30am–noon & 12.45–4.30pm, Fri 8.30am–noon & 12.45–3pm; ☎317-8845 or 317-8600).

**IBUSZ**

Ferenciek tere 10, on the corner of Petőfi Sándor utca (Mon–Fri 8.15am–5pm; ☎318-1120).

V, Apáczai Csere Jánus utca 1 (24hr; ☎318-3925).

VII, Dob utca 1 (Mon–Fri 8am–6pm, Sat & Sun 8am–4pm; ☎322-7214).

---

**ACCOMMODATION PRICE CODES**

All accommodation in this guide is graded according to the price bands given below. Note that prices refer to the **cheapest available double room in high season** or the price of **two people sharing a tent** in a campsite. 100Ft is roughly equivalent to $0.45 or DM1. For more details, see p.24.

① Under 2000Ft      ④ 6000–8500Ft       ⑦ 20,000–27,000Ft
② 2000–4000Ft       ⑤ 8500–13,000Ft      ⑧ 27,000–40,000Ft
③ 4000–6000Ft       ⑥ 13,000–20,000Ft    ⑨ over 40,000Ft

---

book. If you're on a tight budget, your safest bet is a **private room**, arranged through a tourist agency. Though its location might not be perfect, the price should be reasonable and you can be sure of finding one at any time of year, day or night.

**Hostels** vary in price: some offer the cheapest accommodation in the city, while others are more expensive than private rooms, although you have the bonus of the helpful young staff who are around 24 hours a day. Another cheap option are **campsites**, where tent space can usually be found, even if all the **bungalows** are taken. The following recommendations are divided according to the type of accommodation, and subdivided by area.

# Hotels

Sadly, the days of budget breaks in luxury accommodation have long gone, with **hotel** prices rocketing in recent years. Hotels also get full up quickly so it's best to **book** before leaving home or, failing that, through an agency (see box opposite) or any airport tourist office on arrival.

Hotel star ratings give a fair idea of **standards**, though facilities at some of the older three-star places don't compare with their Western equivalents, even if prices are similar. Almost all hotels vary their **prices** according to season – the price codes given above are what you can expect to pay in high season. However, Hungary's hotel industry is still in the process of being privatized, so the following information is likely to change.

## Buda

**Buda** has fewer hotels than Pest, with less choice in the mid-range in particular, though there are some cheaper places in the northern suburbs. Broadly speaking, Buda's hotels are in four main areas: the historic but expensive Vár and Víziváros; around Tabán and Gellért-hegy, another pricey area (and if you're behind Várhegy and away from the river, not especially scenic); the Buda Hills, within easy reach of Moszkva tér; and out in Aquincum and Római Fürdő, where you'll find some of the cheapest places in Buda, mostly near stops on the HÉV line from Batthyány tér. If the best locations are beyond your means, you should also check out the section on hostels (see p.67), a few of which enjoy superb settings.

### THE VÁR AND VÍZIVÁROS

**Alba Hotel**, I, Apor Péter utca 3 (☎375-9244). Four-star hotel well situated by the Lánchíd, below Várhegy. Modern, comfy interior, but slightly lacking in atmosphere. Rooms have minibar and TV and there's car parking space. The Habsburg family stayed here for a wedding in the city in 1998. ⑥.

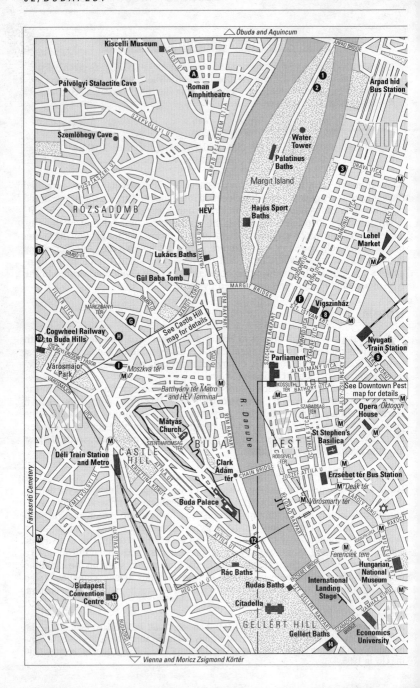

△ Óbuda and Aquincum

Kiscelli Museum

Pálvölgyi Stalactite Cave

Roman Amphitheatre

**A**

Árpád hid Bus Station

Szemlöhegy Cave

XIII

Water Tower

Palatinus Baths

Margit Island

Lehel Market

ROZSADOMB

II

HÉV

Hajós Sport Baths

Lukács Baths

B

BIMBO UT

Gül Baba Tomb

MARGIT BRIDGE

Vigszinház

F

Cogwheel Railway to Buda Hills

MARCZIBANYI TER

G

H

See Castle Hill map for details

Nyugati Train Station

Városmajor Park

I

Moszkva tér

Parliament

See Downtown Pest map for details

Batthyány tér Metro and HÉV Terminal

R. Danube

Opera House

Óktogon

Mátyás Church

BUDA

St Stephen's Basilica

Déli Train Station and Metro

CASTLE HILL

SZENTHAROMSAG

Clark Adám tér

PEST

V

Erzsébet tér Bus Station

XII

Deák tér

Buda Palace

Vörösmarty tér

Ferenciek tere

Rác Baths

Rudas Baths

International Landing Stage

Hungarian National Museum

Budapest Convention Centre

13

Citadella

GELLÉRT HILL

Gellért Baths

Economics University

14

▽ Vienna and Moricz Zsigmond Körtér

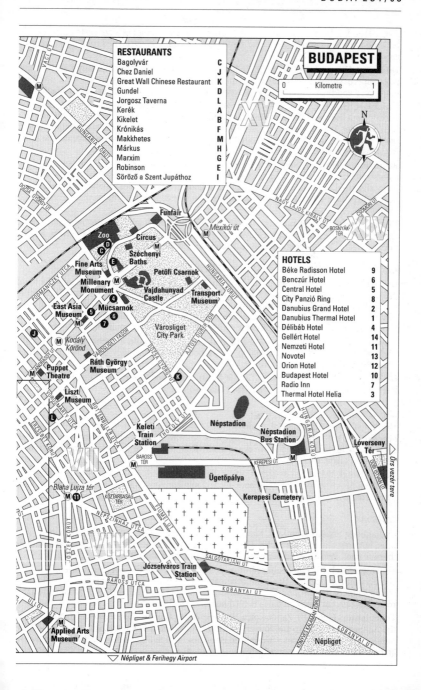

## RESTAURANTS

| | |
|---|---|
| Bagolyvár | C |
| Chez Daniel | J |
| Great Wall Chinese Restaurant | K |
| Gundel | D |
| Jorgosz Taverna | L |
| Kerék | A |
| Kikelet | B |
| Krónikás | F |
| Makkhetes | M |
| Márkus | H |
| Marxim | G |
| Robinson | E |
| Söröző a Szent Jupáthoz | I |

**BUDAPEST**

0     Kilometre     1

## HOTELS

| | |
|---|---|
| Béke Radisson Hotel | 9 |
| Benczúr Hotel | 6 |
| Central Hotel | 5 |
| City Panzió Ring | 8 |
| Danubius Grand Hotel | 2 |
| Danubius Thermal Hotel | 1 |
| Délibáb Hotel | 4 |
| Gellért Hotel | 14 |
| Nemzeti Hotel | 11 |
| Novotel | 13 |
| Orion Hotel | 12 |
| Budapest Hotel | 10 |
| Radio Inn | 7 |
| Thermal Hotel Helia | 3 |

Funfair

Mexikói út

Zoo

Circus

Széchenyi Baths

Fine Arts Museum

Petőfi Csarnok

Millenary Monument

Vajdahunyad Castle

Transport Museum

East Asia Museum

Mücsarnok

Városliget City Park

Kodály Körönd

Ráth György Museum

Puppet Theatre

Liszt Museum

Keleti Train Station

Népstadion

Népstadion Bus Station

Lóverseny Tér

Őrs vezér tere

Blaha Lujza tér

BAROSS TÉR

KEREPESI ÚT

Ügetőpálya

Kerepesi Cemetery

SALGÓTARJÁNI ÚT

Józsefváros Train Station

KŐBÁNYAI ÚT

KŐBÁNYAI ÚT

Applied Arts Museum

Népliget

Népliget & Ferihegy Airport

**Astra Hotel**, I, Vám utca 6 (☎214-1906). Brand-new small hotel in a converted 300-year-old building at the foot of the castle near Batthyány tér. Nine well-furnished rooms with minibar and air-conditioning. ⑥.

**Budapest Hilton**, I, Hess András tér 1–3 (☎214-3000). By the Mátyás Church on Várhegy, with superb views across the river, this hotel incorporates the remains of a medieval monastery and hosts summertime concerts in the former church. Luxurious to a fault. ⑨.

**Dunapart Hotel**, I, Szilágyi Dezső tér 33 (☎355-9244). A floating four-star hotel moored upriver from the Lánchíd, open year-round unless ice endangers the boat. Rooms on the river side are quiet, but the other side faces a busy road, though all are cramped, reminding you that you're on a boat. All have air-conditioning and TV, but only the suites have double beds. Breakfast is included. ⑥.

**Kulturinnov Hotel**, I, Szentháromság tér 6 (☎355-0122, fax 375-1886). Well positioned for sightseeing, in an extraordinary neo-Gothic building right by Mátyás Church. The hotel is badly signed in the main entrance on the first floor. Spacious quiet rooms with minibar, but no TV; breakfast included. The hotel also hosts Hungarian cultural events, concerts and exhibitions. ⑤.

**Victoria Hotel**, I, Bem rakpart 11 (☎457-8080). Pleasant, small hotel on the embankment directly below the Mátyás Church, with excellent views of the Lánchíd and the river. Rooms have minibar, TV and air-conditioning. Sauna and garage facilities. ⑥.

## AROUND THE TABÁN AND GELLÉRT-HEGY

**Gellért Hotel**, XI, Szent Gellért tér 1 (☎385-2200). Old hotel with large, light corridors and lots of character, which will hopefully survive the hotel's gradual refurbishment. The facade, especially when floodlit, is magnificent, and so is the thermal pool, which residents have their own lift down to (and free entry). Good food in the *söröző* (beer hall) and an excellent coffee shop. Rates rise by twenty percent during events such as the Formula One race. ⑨.

**Novotel**, XII, Alkotás utca 63–67, off Hegyalja út, 1km from the Erzsébet híd (☎209-1990). Eighties complex with air-conditioning, indoor pool and bowling alley. Children under 16 can share their parents' room for free. ⑨.

**Orion Hotel**, I, Döbrentei utca 13 (☎356-8583). Small, modern place in the Tabán district, just south of Várhegy. Rooms at the front can be noisy. ⑥.

## BUDA HILLS

**Budapest Hotel**, II, Szilágyi E. fasor 47 (☎202-0044). Cylindrical tower facing the Buda Hills, opposite the lower terminal of the Cogwheel Railway, 500m from Moszkva tér. Seventies decor in the lobby but good views over the city from the café at the top and from the rooms on the south side. ⑥.

**Panda Hotel**, II Pasaréti út 133 (☎394-1932). Pleasant, modern hotel only a ten-minute bus ride from Moszkva tér. All rooms have TV and minibar, most have showers, and three have baths. Sauna also available. ⑤.

## ÓBUDA

**Csillaghegy Strand Hotel**, III, Pusztakúti utca 3 (☎368-4012). Situated in the northern suburbs, but only ten minutes on the HÉV train to the centre. Attached to an excellent outdoor thermal pool. Prices include breakfast and entry to the baths. ③.

**Touring Hotel**, III, Pünkösdfürdő utca 38 (☎250-3184). On the northern edge of the city, about 11km from centre. Basic but acceptable one-star hotel with tennis court, pool tables and restaurant. Rooms have TV and minibar. Swimming pool facilities at the *strand* down the road. Ten percent discount for IYH card holders. ④.

**Tusculanum Hotel**, III, Záhony utca 10 (☎388-7673). Comfortable, new establishment, near the Aquincum HÉV stop and Roman ruins, though without much atmosphere. Rooms have minibar, TV and bathrooms with shower. Breakfast included. There's an ATM at the entrance and a tennis court next door, which you can use. ⑤.

## Margit sziget

Margit Island's hotels cater for wealthy tourists who come for the seclusion and fresh air – and for the thermal springs that made this a fashionable spa resort around the turn of the century.

**Danubius Grand Hotel**, XIII, Margit sziget (☎329-2300). The island's original, *fin-de-siècle* spa hotel, now totally refurbished with the full range of facilities. ⑧.

**Danubius Thermal Hotel**, XIII, Margit sziget (☎329-2300). Modern luxury hotel with thermal bath and pool, sauna, gym and other facilities. ⑧.

## Pest

Staying in **Pest** offers the greatest choice of hotels, and more in the way of restaurants and nightlife, but traffic noise and fumes are quite bad. Most of the outlying locations are easily accessible by metro. The prime spots are along the river bank with views across to the Royal Palace, although all the prewar grand hotels were destroyed during the war, and their replacements don't quite have the same elegance. The more expensive places tend to be in the downtown area, with prices falling as you go further out, though this is not always the case. Moving out of the centre, more hotels are grouped around the Nagykörút, the larger ring road, and the City Park.

*DOWNTOWN*

**Art Hotel**, V, Királyi Pál utca 12 (☎266-2166, fax 266-2170). Small hotel in quiet backstreets. Rooms are quite cramped, but have air-conditioning, minibar, phone and TV, though only Hungarian and German channels. Sauna, fitness room and laundry service. ⑥.

**Astoria Hotel**, V, Kossuth utca 19 (☎317-3411, fax 318-6798, email *astoria@hungary.net*). Completely refurbished, old hotel on a major junction in central Pest. Currently three-star, though there is talk of turning it into a five-star. Good-sized rooms have chairs and sofa, safe, minibar, phone and TV; half have baths, half showers. Very pleasant coffee house. ⑦.

**Atrium Hyatt**, V, Roosevelt tér 2 (☎266-1234, fax 266-9101, email *atriumhyatt@pannoniahotels. hu*). Overlooking the Lánchíd and the Danube, this five-star hotel has just undergone a big refurbishment. Dominating the atrium is a replica of one of the first Hungarian planes dating from 1911. Rooms are air-conditioned, and have the standard fittings for a top hotel, including safes, ISDN telephone lines and even a phone in the bathroom. The hotel also has a business centre, pool, gym, and sauna. Apartments available too. ⑨.

**Carmen Mini Hotel**, V, Károly körút 5/b (☎352-0798). Small hotel in the centre of town. Rooms have TV, bath and shower. Breakfast included. ⑤.

**ELTE Peregrinus Vendégház**, V, Szerb utca 3 (☎266-4911, fax 266-4913). Friendly elegant place in a quiet backstreet in central Pest with 25 rooms, complete with minibar and TV. Buffet breakfast included in the price. Rooms are spacious, unlike the bathrooms. It belongs to the university, and all rooms have writing tables to meet the needs of academic visitors. ⑤.

**Inter-Continental Hotel**, V, Apáczai Csere János utca 12–14 (☎327-6333, fax 327-6357, email *budapest@interconti.com*). Five-star hotel overlooking the Danube, where Richard Burton used to stay incognito. Recent purchase by the Inter-Continental chain is bringing a much needed refurbishment to the hotel. Rooms have usual luxury services, including trouser press. *Bécsi Kávéház*, the coffee house on the first floor, serves some of the best cakes in the city. ⑧.

**Kempinski Hotel Corvinus**, V, Erzsébet tér 7–8 (☎266-1000, fax 266-2000, email *hotel@kempinski.hungary.net*). Flashy five-star establishment in the centre of town, which seems to assume it is the best in town. Tastefully furnished rooms with all the usual luxuries as well as a writing table and three phones, including one in the bathroom. Swimming pool, sauna, solarium, fitness room and underground garage. Where Madonna, Michael Jackson and various Formula One Grand Prix stars have all stayed. ⑨.

**K&K Opera**, VI, Révay utca 24 (☎269-0222, fax 269-0230, email *kk.hotel.opera@kkhotel.hu*). Fully air-conditioned four-star hotel by the Opera House, with its own parking space. The rooms are pleasantly furnished and have minibar, TV, safe, and phone. Buffet breakfast included. ⑦–⑧.

**Marriott Budapest**, V, Apáczai Csere János utca 4 (☎266-7000, fax 266-5000). All rooms in this older five-star air-conditioned hotel overlook the Danube and have ISDN phone lines. Excellent buffet grill and an afternoon string quartet in lounge area. Sauna, squash court, parking facilities and baby-sitting service. ⑨.

*AROUND THE NAGYKÖRÚT*

**Béke Radisson Hotel**, VI, Teréz körút 43 (☎301-1600, fax 301-1615, email *beke@hungary.net*). Refurbished vintage hotel on the Nagykörút, 200m south of Nyugati Station. Rooms have minibar, TV, and safe. Sauna, pool, business centre, underground garage, restaurant and an excellent coffee house. ⑧.

**Medosz Hotel**, VI, Jókai tér 9 (☎374-3000). Ugly but comfortable hotel in a former trade union hostel overlooking a square near Oktogon. Small, light rooms with bath and TV. Good value for the location. ④.

**Nemzeti Hotel**, VIII, József körút 4 (☎269-9310, fax 314-0019, email *nemzeti@pannoniahotels.hu*). Small but elegant rooms with phone and minibar in this Art Nouveau-style place overlooking Blaha Lujza tér (metro line 2). Bar and restaurant have a decaying seventies magnificence about them. Breakfast included. ⑥.

*BEYOND THE NAGYKÖRÚT*

**Benczúr Hotel**, VI, Benczúr utca 35 (☎342-7970, fax 342-1558). Modern soulless hotel on a leafy street off Andrássy út, with nice garden at the back and parking in the yard (850Ft extra). Pleasant rooms with bath, TV, telephone and minibar. ⑥.

**Central Hotel**, VI, Munkácsy Mihály utca 5–7 (☎321-2000). Spacious rooms with balcony, TV and minibar in this former Communist Party hotel by Andrássy út. Pleasant wooden furniture and old wallpaper give the rooms a nice old-fashioned feel. Even the bathrooms are spacious. However, the rooms overlooking the main road are noisy. ①.

**Délibáb Hotel**, VI, Délibáb utca 35 (☎342-9301, fax 342-8153). A run-down former Esterházy mansion across from Hősök tere, overlooking a noisy main road, and offering basic accommodation. Some rooms have minibar. ④.

**Radio Inn**, VI, Benczúr utca 19 (☎322-8437, fax 322-8284). Spacious, but slightly dark rooms complete with kitchen and a spare second room and TV. Situated in nice leafy street, by the Chinese Embassy and opposite the Vietnamese Embassy. Pleasant garden. Buffet breakfast extra 896Ft. ⑤.

**Thermal Hotel Helia**, XIII, Kárpát utca 62–64 (☎270-3277). Finnish-owned modern four-star hotel with thermal baths. Located near the Danube in north Pest. ⑧.

# Pensions

There is little difference between the rates charged by hotels and **pensions** these days. The difference lies more in their characters, with pensions usually being smaller family-run places. However, pensions still fill up fast during summer, so reservations are pretty much essential. In most cases, you need to phone them direct.

**Beatrix Panzió**, II, Szehér út 3 (☎275-0550, fax 394-3730). Friendly eighteen-room pension with sauna in the Buda Hills; bar on ground floor. ⑤.

**Buda Villa Panzió**, XII, Kiss Áron utca 6 (☎275-0091, fax 275-1687, email *budapans@hungary.net*). Comfortable small pension in the hills just above Moszkva tér. Rooms have TV and there's a bar in the lounge on the first floor; breakfast is included. Small garden to relax in after a day's sightseeing. ⑤.

**Büro Panzió**, II, Dékán utca 3 (☎212-2928). Simple pension close to Moszkva tér. ④.

**City Panzió Mátyás**, V, Március 15. tér 8 (☎338-4700, fax 317-9086, email *matyas@taverna.hu*). Centrally located place offering simple, basic rooms with TV, minibar, and a buffet breakfast in the *Mátyás Pince* restaurant downstairs, which is painted inside a bit like the Mátyás Church. The pension overlooks a big road, so ask for a courtyard room if you want a quiet room, though the rooms on the corner have a great view of the river. ⑥.

**City Panzió Ring**, XIII, Szt. István körút 22 (☎342-5450, email *ring@taverna.hu*). Rooms have shower, TV, radio, phone and minibar. ⑥.

**Jäger–Trió Panzió**, XI, Ördögorom út 20D (☎246-4558). Friendly family-run place in the Sasad district in the hills; take bus #8 from Március 15. tér to the end of the line, then it's a ten-minute walk. Open March 15–Nov 15. ④.

**San Marcó Panzió**, III, San Marcó utca 6 (☎388-9997); take bus #60 from Batthyány tér. Small, friendly pension in Óbuda, run by Mrs Steininger. Shared bathrooms. ④.

# Private rooms and apartments

There are **private rooms** throughout the city, many in the sort of locations where a hotel would be unaffordable. Depending on location and amenities, **prices** for a double room range from 3000 to 4500Ft a night. On the downside, solo travellers will almost certainly have to pay for a double, and rates are thirty percent higher if you stay fewer than four nights (making pensions or hostels more economical for short-staying visitors). **Apartments**, from 5000Ft a night, are not as common as rooms, but you should be able to find an agency with one on its books.

It's easy enough to get a room from one of the **touts** at the train stations, but it's safer to go through a tourist agency, where you book and pay at the counter signposted *fizetővendég*. The three main **agencies** – Budapest Tourist, Cooptourist and Volántourist – have offices all over the city (see box on p.60 for details), but the ones at the stations and in central Pest are the most convenient for new arrivals.

Since rooms are rented unseen, it pays to take some trouble over your choice. Your host and the premises should give no cause for complaint (both are checked out), but the **location** or ambience might. For atmosphere and comfort you can't beat the nineteenth-century blocks where spacious, high-ceilinged apartments surround a courtyard with wrought-iron balconies – most common in Pest's V, VI and VII districts, and the parts of Buda nearest the Vár. Elsewhere – particularly in Újpest (IV district), Csepel (XXI) or Óbuda (III) – you're likely to end up in a box on the twelfth floor on a *lakótelep* (housing estate). The *Budapest Atlasz* is invaluable for checking the location of sites and access by public transport.

Because many proprietors go out to work, you might not be able to take possession of the room until 5pm. Some knowledge of Hungarian facilitates **settling in**; guests normally receive an explanation of the boiler system and multiple door keys (*kulcs*), and may have use of the washing machine (which requires another demonstration).

# Hostels

If you don't have a tent, a dormitory bed in a **hostel** is the cheapest alternative. Many also have rooms at much the same price as private accommodation, and with no surcharge for staying fewer than four nights. Prices are given per head, so that you can easily end up paying over 5000Ft for a double room. This includes 24-hour information from the English-speaking staff at the reception desk, but the rooms often have just very basic student furniture. Most hostels are open during July and August only, many of them located in the university area south of Gellért-hegy, though you can't always be sure of getting a bed in the hostel of your choice in summer without **booking** in advance (see box on p.60 for details). A Hostelling International card can be obtained from Express if needed, though in practice there don't seem to be any age or membership requirements.

If you arrive in the city on an international train, you will more than likely be given information about hostels even before the train pulls into the station. The competition between the private groups running the summer hostels is intense, but do not feel intimidated – you can afford to wait and choose. The larger organizations – Universum and More Than Ways – will also offer transport to the hostel, which can make arrival less daunting. The Tourist Information Centre office in Keleti Station (in the big side hall down by platform 6, on the left of the station as you face the trains) can give you information about more of the summer-only hostels and make bookings (daily 7am–11pm; ☎06-20/657-988). The main office of the More Than Ways, which runs the largest chain of hostels, is in the *Diáksport Hostel* at Dózsa Gy. út 152 (☎340-8585). The first six hostels listed below are open all the year round.

**Teréz Guest House**, VIII, Bezerédj utca 6 (☎333-2452). Cheapest of the cheap, with home cooking too. Two rooms in a private flat, jam-packed with beds and mattresses, ranging from 300 to 900Ft in price. On second floor of big old block near Blaha Lujza tér on red metro line. Parking available in courtyard. ①.

**Back Pack**, XI, Takács Menyhért utca 33 (☎385-5089). Tram #49 to "Tétényi út" stop out in Buda. Five- and eight-bed dorms. ①.

**Caterina Youth Hostel**, V, Andrássy ut 47 (☎291-9538 or 342 0804). Thirty-two beds crammed into every corner of this flat on the third floor of a grand Pest apartment block (note the fantastic entrance way). Laundry facilities. ①.

**Citadella**, I, Citadella sétány (☎466-5794). Romantically sited atop Gellért-hegy, with breath-taking views. Reservations can be made direct or through Budapest Tourist. Take bus #27 from Móricz Zsigmond körtér, and then it's a ten-minute walk from the last stop. Ten- and fourteen-bed dorms ① per person, doubles ④.

**Diáksport Hostel**, XIII, Dózsa György út 152 (☎340-8585). Near Dózsa György út metro on the blue line. Singles, doubles and triples, plus dorms with four, six, nine and twelve beds. 24-hour bar. ① per person, doubles ③.

**Express Hotel**, XII, Beethoven utca 7–9 (☎375-2528). In the backstreets south of Déli Station – two stops by tram #59. Ten percent discount for HI card holders. ③.

**KÉK Somogyi Kollégium**, XI, Szüret utca 2–18 (☎371-0066). Around the back of Gellért-hegy, two stops from Móricz Zsigmond körtér on bus #27. Open July & Aug. ③.

**Hostel Landler**, XI, Bartók Béla út 17 (☎463-3621). Near the Gellért Baths, housed in the Baross Gábor Kollégium; one of the older hostels, with high ceilings. Open July & Aug. ③.

**Strawberry Youth Hostel**, IX, Ráday utca 43–45 (☎218-4766, booking on 06-20/528-724). The older of two *Strawberry Hostels* near Kálvin tér, with basic student hostel furniture but tall spacious rooms, with rooms of two to six beds or dormitories. Internet access. Discount for HI card holders. Open July & Aug. ②.

# Campsites

Budapest's **campsites**, by far the best of which are located in the Buda Hills, gen-erally offer good facilities, and are pretty pleasant, with trees and grass and maybe even a pool, though they can become very crowded between June and September, and the smaller ones can run out of space. It is illegal to camp anywhere else, and the parks are patrolled to enforce this. The police usually tolerate people **sleeping rough** in train stations, but this is not to be recommended as there's a high risk of theft (or worse).

Budapest Tourist (see p.60 for details) can arrange detached **bungalows** of various sizes at several campsites and a number of other locations. Your best bet is to tell them more or less what you are looking for and let them handle the booking in the first instance, though if you decide to prolong your stay you can arrange this privately with the owners. Trying to sort it out for yourself over the phone can be a problem, as English is not always spoken, telephone numbers are liable to change, and opening times change from year to year depending on the weather. The campsites given below are all in Buda, since the Pest ones are far out and not very inviting. Tourinform can point you in their direction if you need them.

**Csillebérci Camping**, XII, Konkoly Thege M. út 21 (☎395-6537). Large, well-equipped site with space for 1000 campers. A range of bungalows also available. A short walk from the last stop of the #21 bus from Moszkva tér. Open year-round. 500Ft per person plus 600Ft tent fee, or 1000Ft for a car.

**Római-Fürdő Camping**, III, Szentendrei út 189 (☎368-6260). Huge site with space for 2500 campers beside the road to Szentendre in Római-Fürdő (25min by HÉV). Open year-round. Higher than average rates include use of the nearby swimming pool. 800Ft per person plus 700Ft tent fee or 1000Ft for a car.

**Tündérhegyi-Feeburg Camping**, XII, Szilassy út 8 (☎06-60-336-256). At the end of the #28 bus route, near the János-hegy chairlift and close to a nature reserve. Nice, tiny site accommodating 95 campers. Open March–Oct. 500Ft per person plus 500–600Ft tent fee; bungalows and camper vans also available.

**Zugligeti Niche Camping**, XII, Zugligeti út 101 (☎200-8346). At the end of the #158 bus route, opposite the chairlift up to János-hegy. Small, terraced ravine site in the woods, with space for 260 campers and good facilities including a restaurant occupying the former tram station at the far end. Open April–Oct. 600Ft per person plus 400Ft tent fee.

# Buda

Viewed from the embankments of the Danube, **Buda** forms a collage of palatial buildings, archaic spires and outsize statues, crowning craggy massifs. This glamorous image conceals more mundane aspects, but at times, in the right place, Buda can really live up to it. To experience the **Várhegy** (Castle Hill) at its best, come early in the morning to visit the **museums** before the crowds arrive, then wander off for lunch or a soak in one of the Turkish baths, and return to catch street life in full swing in the afternoon. The outlying **Buda Hills** – accessible by the **Libegő** (chairlift) and the **Children's Railway** – are obviously less visited during the week, while **Gellért-hegy**, with its superb views over the city, the **Rózsadomb** district and the **Roman ruins** of Óbuda and Római-Fürdő can be seen any time, but preferably when the weather's fine.

## The Várhegy

The **Várhegy** (Castle Hill), often referred to simply as the **Vár**, is Buda's most prominent feature, a long plateau laden with bastions, mansions and a huge palace, dominating the Víziváros (Watertown) below. The hill's grandiosity and strategic utility have long gone hand in hand: Hungarian kings built their palaces here because it was easy to defend, a fact appreciated by the Turks, Habsburgs

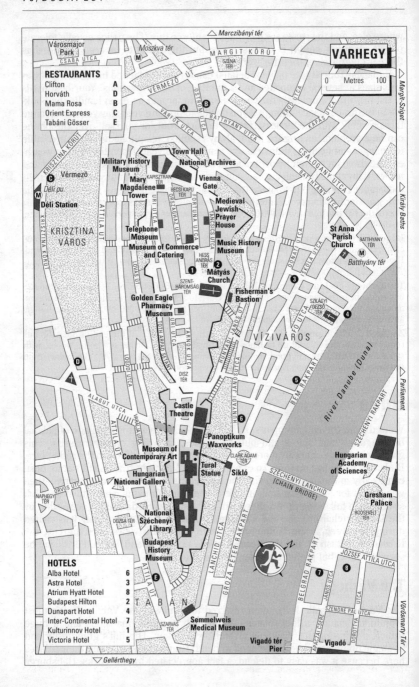

VÁRHEGY

0 Metres 100

RESTAURANTS
Clifton A
Horváth D
Mama Rosa B
Orient Express C
Tabáni Gösser E

HOTELS
Alba Hotel 6
Astra Hotel 3
Atrium Hyatt Hotel 8
Budapest Hilton 2
Dunapart Hotel 4
Inter-Continental Hotel 7
Kulturinnov Hotel 1
Victoria Hotel 5

and other occupiers. Its buildings, a legacy of bygone Magyar glories, have been almost wholly reconstructed from the rubble of 1945, when the Wehrmacht and the Red Army battled over the hill while Buda's inhabitants cowered underground – the eighty-sixth time that it was ravaged and rebuilt over seven centuries, rivalling the devastation caused by the recapture of Buda from the Turks in 1686.

Though the hill's appearance has changed much since building began in the thirteenth century, its main **streets** still follow their medieval courses, with Gothic arches and stone carvings in the courtyards and passages of eighteenth- and nineteenth-century Baroque **houses**, whose facades are embellished with fancy ironwork grilles. Practically every building displays a *Műemlék* plaque giving details of its history (in Hungarian only), and a surprising number are still homes rather than embassies or boutiques – there are even a couple of schools and corner shops. At dusk, when most of the tourists have left, pensioners walk their dogs and toddlers play in the long shadows of Hungarian history.

There are several **approaches** to Várhegy, mostly starting from the Víziváros (described on p.79). The simplest and most novel is to ride up to the palace by **Sikló** (see p.80) – a renovated nineteenth-century **funicular** that runs from Clark Ádám tér by the Lánchíd (daily 7.30am–10pm, closed second & fourth Mon of the month; 200Ft). Alternatively you can start from Moszkva tér (on metro line 2) and either take the **Várbusz** – a minibus leaving from the raised side of Moszkva tér, that terminates by the palace – or walk uphill to the Vienna Gate at the northern end of the Vár. Walking from Batthyány tér via the steep flights of steps (*lépcső*) off Fő utca involves more effort, and the stairway up to the Fishermen's Bastion is currently closed for repairs. The most direct approach **from Pest** is to ride bus #16 from Erzsébet tér across the Lánchíd to Clark Ádám tér – giving you the option of taking the Sikló or staying on the bus as far as Dísz tér, which is almost as close to the palace.

Restrictions on traffic in the Vár mean that private cars entering the district collect a ticket as they enter and pay as they leave – 240Ft per hour, or free if you leave within thirty minutes. Taxis, local residents, and guests of the *Hilton* do not have to pay, but hotel guests must get their card stamped by the reception desk.

## The Várnegyed

The **Várnegyed** (Castle District) is the residential area to the north of the palace where, for many centuries, residence was a privilege granted to religious or ethnic groups, each occupying a specific street. This pattern persisted though the 145-year-long Turkish occupation, when Armenians, Circassians and Sephardic Jews also established themselves under the relatively tolerant Ottomans. The liberation of Buda by a multinational Christian army under Habsburg command was followed by a pogrom and ordinances restricting the right of residence to Catholics and Germans, which remained in force for nearly a century. In 1944, the Swedish Red Cross established safe houses here for Jewish refugees, some of whom remained hidden in caves after the others were forced into the ghetto. By the time the Red Army finally took Buda on February 13, 1945, only four houses on the hill were habitable.

The obvious starting point is **Szentháromság tér** (Holy Trinity Square), the historic heart of the district, named after an ornate **Trinity Column** erected in 1713 in thanksgiving for the abatement of a plague. To the southwest stands the former **Town Hall** of Buda, which functioned as a municipality until the unification of Buda, Pest and Óbuda in 1873. Down the road at Szentháromság utca 7, the tiny **Ruszwurm patisserie** has been a pastry shop and café since 1827, and was a gingerbread shop in the Middle Ages. Its Empire-style decor looks much the same as it was under Vilmos Ruszwurm, who ran the patisserie for nearly four decades from 1884.

## THE MÁTYÁS CHURCH

At the heart of the Várhegy and Szentháromság tér's most prominent feature is the neo-Gothic **Mátyás Church** (*Mátyás templom*; daily April–Sept 8.30am–8pm, Oct–March 7am–7pm; free, crypt and treasures 100Ft), whose diamond-patterned roofs and toothy spires are wildly asymmetrical but nevertheless coherent in form. Officially dedicated to Our Lady, but popularly named after "Good King Mátyás", the building is a late nineteenth-century recreation by architect Frigyes Schulek, grafted onto those portions of the original thirteenth-century church that survived the siege of 1686. The frescoes and altars had been whitewashed over or removed when the Turks turned it into a mosque.

Entering the church through its twin-spired **Mary Portal**, the richness of the interior is overwhelming. Painted leaves and geometric motifs run up columns and under vaulting, while shafts of light fall through rose windows onto gilded altars and statues with stunning effect. Most of the **frescoes** were executed by Károly Lotz or Bertalan Székely, the foremost historical painters of the day. The **coat of arms of King Mátyás** can be seen on the wall to your left, just inside; his family name, Corvinus, comes from the raven (*corvus* in Latin) that appeared on his heraldry and on every volume in the famous Corvin Library.

Around the corner to the left, beneath the south tower, is the **Loreto Chapel**, containing a Baroque Madonna, while in the bay beneath the Béla Tower you can see two medieval capitals, one carved with monsters fighting a dragon, the other with two bearded figures reading a book. The tower is named after Béla IV, who founded the church, rather than his predecessor in the second chapel along, who shares a double sarcophagus with Anne of Chatillon. Originally located in the old capital, Székesfehérvár, the **tomb of Béla III** and his queen was moved here after its discovery in 1848. Although Hungary's medieval kings were crowned at Székesfehérvár, it was customary to make a prior appearance in Buda – hence yet another sobriquet, the "Coronation Church".

To the right of the pulpit is the entrance to the **crypt**, containing the red-marble tombstone of a nameless Árpád prince, and a small collection of **ecclesiastical treasures** and relics, including the right foot of St János. From here, stairs ascend to **St Stephen's Chapel**, decorated with a bust of the king and scenes from his life, whence another staircase leads to the **Royal Oratory**, exhibiting the coronation thrones of emperors Franz Josef and Karl IV, and a **replica of the Hungarian Crown Jewels**. The exhibition is more informative about the provenance of St Stephen's Crown than the Hungarian National Museum, where the originals are displayed (see p.106).

**Mass** is celebrated in the Mátyás Church every morning and several times on Sunday (7am, 8.30am, 10am, noon & 6pm). Its acoustics are superb, and evening **organ recitals** are regularly held throughout the year, with more **concerts** during the Spring Festival and summer season. Tickets are available on the spot or from any booking agency.

### THE FISHERMEN'S BASTION

After the Mátyás Church, the most transfixing sight is the **Fishermen's Bastion** (*Halászbástya*) just beyond, which frames the view of Pest across the river. Although fishermen from the Víziváros reputedly defended this part of the hill

---

### KING STEPHEN

If you commit just one figure from Hungarian history to memory, make it **King Stephen**, for it was he who welded the tribal Magyar fiefdoms into a state and won recognition from Christendom. Born Vajk, son of Prince Géza, he emulated his father's policy of trying to convert the pagan Magyars and develop Hungary with the help of foreign preachers, craftsmen and merchants. By marrying Gizella of Bavaria in 996, he was able to use her father's knights to crush a pagan revolt after Géza's death, and subsequently received an apostolic cross and crown from Pope Sylvester II for his coronation on Christmas Day, 1000 AD, when he took the name Stephen (István in Hungarian).

Though noted for his enlightened views (such as the need for tolerance and the desirability of multiracial nations), he could act ruthlessly when necessary. After his only son Imre died in an accident and a pagan seemed likely to inherit, Stephen had the man blinded and poured molten lead into his ears. Naming his successor, he symbolically offered his crown to the Virgin Mary rather than the Holy Roman Emperor or the Pope; she has since been considered the Patroness of Hungary. Swiftly canonized after his death in 1038, **St Stephen** became a national talisman, his mummified right hand a holy relic, and his coronation regalia the symbol of statehood. Despite playing down his cult for decades, even the Communists eventually embraced it in a bid for some legitimacy, while nobody in post-Communist Hungary thinks it odd that the symbol of the republic should be the crown and cross of King Stephen.

---

during the Middle Ages, the existing bastion is purely decorative. An undulating white rampart of cloisters and stairways intersecting at seven tent-like turrets symbolizing the Magyar tribes that conquered the Carpathian Basin, it was designed by Schulek as a foil to the church. Since an admission charge (100Ft; children 50Ft) was introduced, the upper level is no longer crowded with sightseers and vendors and has lost its spontaneous charm – but the view is as splendid as ever.

Between the bastion and the church, an equestrian **statue of King Stephen** honours the founder of the Hungarian nation, whose conversion to Christianity and coronation with a crown sent by the pope presaged the Magyars' integration into European civilization (see box above). The statue is reflected in the copper-glass facade of the **Budapest Hilton**, opposite, along with the church and the bastion. Incorporating chunks of a medieval Dominican church and monastery on the side facing the river, and an eighteenth-century Jesuit college on the other, the hotel bears a copy of the **Mátyás Relief** from Bautzen in Germany that's regarded as the only true likeness of Hungary's Renaissance monarch.

### North towards Kapisztrán tér

If you're not in a hurry to reach the palace, it's worth exploring the quieter, northern reaches of the Vár, whose streets abound in period details. A common medieval feature that's survived are the sedilia, rows of niches with seats, in the passageway to the inner courtyard. For an example, look no further than the *Fortuna* restaurant on Hess András tér, which occupies the site of Hungary's first printing press, set up by András Hess in 1473. Also notice the hedgehog relief above the door of the former *Red Hedgehog Inn* at no. 3, where Janissaries were billeted in Turkish times.

Don't miss the fascinating **Museum of Commerce and Catering** (*Kereskedelmi és Vendéglátóipari Múzeum*; Tues–Fri 10am–5pm, Sat & Sun 10am–6pm; 100Ft) at Fortuna utca 4, just off the square. In the Commerce section are antique shopfronts and interiors, and a model dog that raps on the glass with its paws, meant to attract passers-by into stores. The Catering part pays homage to the restaurateur Károly Gundel and the confectioner Emil Gerbeaud, while another section called "Hospitable Budapest" features furnishings from old coffee houses and a reconstructed bedroom from the *Hotel Gellért*. Waiters used such specialized items of cutlery as asparagus clippers, produced by the Budapest instrument-makers Ignácz Dreher & Son, whose 25-bladed pocket knife (anticipating the Swiss Army version) is also on display.

The **Music History Museum** at Táncsics Mihály utca 7 (*Zenetörténeti Múzeum*; April–Oct Tues–Sun 10am–6pm; Nov–March 10am–5pm; 100Ft) occupies the Baroque Erdödy Palace where Beethoven was a guest in 1800 and Bartók had his workshop before he emigrated. The museum displays scores of instruments representing three centuries of music, from a Holczman harp made for Marie Antoinette and a unique tongue-shaped violin in the Classical section to hurdy-gurdies, zithers, cowhorns and bagpipes in the Folk part. By the 1900s, homemade folk instruments were being replaced by factory products like the Schunda pedal-cimbalom. You can also see an exhibition of Bartók's scores and jottings, including bits of *The Wooden Prince* and *Violin Rhapsody No. 2*.

Next door, no. 9, was once a barracks where the Habsburgs jailed Hungarian radicals such as Mihály Táncsics – after whom the street is named – but in an earlier age it was home to both Ashkenazi and Sephardic Jews, and called Zsidó utca (Jewish Street). The Ashkenazi community was established in the reign of Béla IV and encouraged by King Mátyás. Though you wouldn't think so from the outside, no. 26 contains a **Medieval Jewish Prayer House** (*Középkori Zsidó Imaház*; May–Oct Tues–Sun 10am–5pm; 100Ft) once used by the Sephardis. All that remains of its original decor are two Cabbalistic symbols painted on a wall, though the museum does its best to flesh out the history of the community with maps and prints – all the real treasures are in the Jewish Museum in Pest (see p.104).

At the end of the street lies **Bécsi kapu tér**, named after the **Vienna Gate** that was erected on the 250th anniversary of the recapture of Buda. Beside it, the forbiddingly neo-Romanesque **National Archives** (no admission) guard the way to **Kapisztrán tér**, a larger square centred on the **Mary Magdalene Tower** (*Magdolna-torony*), whose accompanying church was wrecked in World War II. In medieval times this was where Hungarian residents worshipped; Germans used the Mátyás Church. Today the tower contains a private art gallery and boasts a peal of ornamental bells that jingles through a medley composed by the jazz pianist György Szabados, which includes Hungarian folk tunes, Chopin *Études* and the theme from *Bridge Over the River Kwai*.

Beyond is a **statue of Friar John Capistranus**, who exhorted the Hungarians to victory at the siege of Belgrade in 1456, which the pope hailed by ordering church bells to be rung at noon throughout Europe. It shows Capistranus bestriding a dead Turk and is aptly located outside the **Military History Museum**, located in a former barracks on the north of the square (*Hadtörténeti Múzeum*; April–Sept 10am–6pm, closed Tues; Oct–March 10am–4pm; 250Ft). This has gung-ho exhibitions on the history of hand-weapons from ancient times till the advent of firearms, and the birth and campaigns of the Honvéd (national army) during the 1848–49 War of Independence, but what sticks in the memory are the sections on the Hungarian Second Army that was decimated at Stalingrad, and the "Thirteen Days" of the 1956 Uprising (accompanied by newsreel footage at 11am & 2pm). The entrance to the museum is on the Tóth Árpád sétány, a promenade lined with cannons and chestnut trees, overlooking the Buda hills, which leads past a giant **flagpole** striped in Hungarian colours to the symbolic **grave of Abdurrahman**, the last Turkish Pasha of Buda, who died on the walls in 1686 – a "valient foe", according to the inscription.

*ORSZÁGHÁZ UTCA AND ÚRI UTCA*
Heading back towards Szentháromság tér, there's more to be seen on **Országház utca**, which was the district's main thoroughfare in the Middle Ages and known as the "street of baths" during Turkish times. Its present name, Parliament Street, recalls the sessions of the Diet held in the 1790s in a former Poor Clares' cloister at no. 28, where the Gestapo imprisoned 350 Hungarians and foreigners in 1945. No. 17, over the road, consists of two medieval houses joined together and has a relief of a croissant on its keystone from when it was a bakery. A few doors down from the former parliament building, Renaissance sgraffiti survive on the underside of the bay window of no. 22 and a Gothic trefoil-arched cornice on the house next door, while the one beyond has been rebuilt according to its original fifteenth-century form.

**Úri utca** (Gentleman Street) also boasts historic associations, for it was at the former Franciscan monastery at no. 51 that the five Hungarian Jacobins were held before being beheaded on the "Blood Meadow" below the hill in 1795. Next door is a wing of the Poor Clares' cloister that served as a postwar telephone exchange before being turned into a **Telephone Museum** (*Telefónia Múzeum*; Tues–Sun 10am–6pm; 50Ft). More hands-on than most Hungarian museums, it lets visitors dial up a Magyar pop song or an English-speaking guide on a vintage bakelite phone. Further down the street on either side, notice the statues of the four seasons in the first-floor niches at nos. 54–56, Gothic sedilia in the gateway of nos. 48–50, and three arched windows and two diamond-shaped ones from the fourteenth and fifteenth centuries at no. 31.

## South towards the palace
Heading south from Szentháromság tér towards the palace, you'll come to the intriguing **Golden Eagle Pharmacy Museum** (*Arany Sas Patikamúzeum*; Tues–Sun 10.30am–6.30pm; 60Ft) at Tárnok utca 18. The first pharmacy in Buda, established after the expulsion of the Turks, its original furnishings lend authenticity to dubious nostrums including the skull of a mummy used to make "Mumia" powder to treat epilepsy, and a reconstruction of an alchemist's laboratory, complete with dried bats and crocodiles. The *Tárnok* coffee house, next door but one, occupies one of the few buildings on the hill to have kept its Renaissance sgraffiti – a red and orange chequerboard pattern covering the facade.

A weirder attraction is the **Labyrinth of Buda Castle**, better known as the *Várbarlang* (Castle caves). Cavities created by hot springs and cellars dug since medieval times form 10km of galleries, which were converted into an air-raid shelter in the 1930s and used as such in World War II. Having remained in military hands till the 1980s, it is now marketed as a New Age experience of shamanism and history. One section features copies of the cave paintings of Lascaux, while masked figures and a giant head sunken into the floor enliven other dank chambers. If you want to understand more about their meaning, you can go on one of the guided tours, which leave from the main entrance at Úri utca 9 (daily

9.30am–7.30pm; 600Ft). There's another entrance beyond the castle walls at Lovas út 4, which is accessible by wheelchair for some of the way.

Both Tárnok utca and Úri utca end in **Dísz tér** (Parade Square), whose cobbled expanses are guarded by a **statue of a hussar**. From here on, ramparts and gateways buttress the hillside, controling access to the palace grounds. Ahead lies the scarred hulk of the old **Ministry of Defence**, while to your left is the **Castle Theatre** (*Várszínház*), where the first-ever play in Hungarian was staged in 1790 and Beethoven performed in 1808. The last building in the row is the **Sándor Palace** (*Sándor Palota*), formerly the prime minister's residence, where Premier Teleki shot himself in protest at Hungary joining the Nazi invasion of Yugoslavia. It now houses the **Panoptikum Waxworks** (March–Oct daily 10am–6pm; tours every 15min; 450Ft) – a lame romp through Hungarian history in all its gory glory.

Next door, the upper terminal of the **Sikló** funicular is separated from the terrace of Buda Palace by a stately gateway and the ferocious-looking **Turul statue**, a giant bronze eagle clasping a sword in its talons. In Magyar mythology the Turul sired the first dynasty of Hungarian kings by raping the grandmother of Árpád, who led the tribes into Europe. During the nineteenth century it became a symbol of Hungarian identity in the face of Austrian culture, but wound up being co-opted by the Habsburgs. More recently, it has been adopted as a symbol by Hungary's skinheads.

From here, you can descend a staircase to the **terrace** of the palace, commanding a sweeping **view** of Pest. Beyond the souvenir stalls prances an equestrian **statue of Prince Eugene of Savoy**, the liberator of Buda. The bronze statues nearby represent **Csongor** and **Tünde**, the lovers in Vörösmarty's drama of the same name.

## Buda Palace

As befits a former royal residence, the lineage of **Buda Palace** (*Budavári palota*) can be traced back to medieval times, with the rise and fall of various palaces on the hill reflecting the changing fortunes of the Hungarian state. The first fortifications and dwellings, hastily erected by Béla IV after the Mongol invasion of 1241–42, were replaced by the grander palaces of the Angevin kings, who ruled in more prosperous and stable times. This process reached its zenith in the reign of Mátyás Corvinus (1458–90), whose palace was a Renaissance extravaganza to which artists and scholars from all over Europe were drawn by the blandishments of Queen Beatrice and the prospect of lavish hospitality; the rooms had hot and cold running water and during celebrations the fountains and gargoyles flowed with wine. After the Turkish occupation, and the long siege that ended it, only ruins were left – which the Habsburgs, Hungary's new rulers, levelled to build a palace of their own.

From Empress Maria Theresa's modest beginnings (a mere 203 rooms, which she never saw completed), the Royal Palace expanded inexorably throughout the nineteenth century, though no monarch ever dwelt here, only the Habsburg Palatine (viceroy). After the collapse of the empire following World War I, Admiral Horthy inhabited the building with all the pomp of monarchy until he was deposed by a German coup in October 1944. The palace was left unoccupied, and it wasn't long before the siege of Buda once again resulted in total devastation. Reconstruction work began in the 1950s in tandem with excavations of the medieval sub-strata beneath the rubble, which were incorporated in the new building, whose interior is far less elegant than the prewar version, being designed to accommodate cultural institutions.

Today, the complex houses the **Museum of Contemporary Art** (Wing A), the **Hungarian National Gallery** (Wings B, C and D), the **Budapest History Museum** (E) and the **National Széchényi Library** (F) – of which the first three are definitely worth seeing and could easily take an afternoon. Each has its own separate entrance.

*THE HUNGARIAN NATIONAL GALLERY*

Most people's first port of call is the **Hungarian National Gallery** (*Magyar Nemzeti Galéria*; daily April–Nov 10am–6pm; Dec–March 10am–4pm; 105Ft, free Wed), devoted to Hungarian art from the Middle Ages to the present. It contains much that's superb, but the vastness of the collection and the fusty layout can make a visit tiring. The main entrance is on the eastern side of Wing C, overlooking the river, behind the statue of Eugene of Savoy. Though all the paintings are labelled in English, other details, even those in Hungarian, are scanty.

On the **ground floor**, marble reliefs of Beatrice and Mátyás and a wooden ceiling from a sixteenth-century church are the highlights of a **Medieval and Renaissance Lapidarium**, which you need to pass through to reach the fantastic collection of fifteenth-century **Gothic altarpieces** at the rear of Wing D. Notice the varied reactions to the *Death of the Virgin* from Kassa and the gloating of the mob in the Jánosrét *Passion*. From the same church comes a *St Nicholas* altar as long as a limo and lurid as a comic strip. The pointed finials on the high altar from Liptószentmária anticipate the winged altarpieces of the sixteenth century on the floor above. To get there without returning to the foyer, use the small staircase near the altarpieces and turn left, left and left again at the top.

The **first floor** picks up where downstairs left off by displaying **late Gothic altarpieces** with soaring pinnacles. Much of the **Baroque** art in the adjacent section once belonged to Prince Miklós Esterházy or was confiscated from private owners in the 1950s. Don't miss Ádám Mányoki's portrait of Ferenc Rákóczi II, a sober look at a national hero that foreshadowed a whole artistic genre in the nineteenth century. This and other **National Historical** art fills the central block, where you'll be confronted by two vast canvases as you come up the staircase: *Zrínyi's Sortie* by Peter Krafft depicting the suicidal sally of the defenders of Szigetvár, and the *Recapture of Buda Castle* by Gyula Benczúr. In Wing B, Benczúr's *The Baptism of Vajk* portrays St Stephen's conversion to Christianity, while Bertalan Székely's *Recovering the Corpse of the King* depicts the aftermath of the catastrophic defeat at Mohács. The rest of Wing B covers other trends in nineteenth-century art, with sections devoted to **Mihály Munkácsy** and **László Paál** – exhibited together since both painted landscapes, though Paál did little else whereas Munkácsy was internationally renowned for pictures with a social message – and **Pál Szinyei Merse**, the "father of Hungarian Impressionism", whose models and subjects were cheerfully bourgeois.

Walking upstairs to the **second floor**, you come face to face with three huge canvases by the visionary artist **Tivadar Kosztka Csontváry**, whose obsession with the Holy Land and the "path of the sun" inspired scenes like *Look Down on the Red Sea* and *Ruins of the Greek Theatre at Taormina*. When Picasso saw an exhibition of his works years later, he remarked: "And I thought I was the only great painter of our century." There are four more, smaller Csontvárys amongst the **twentieth-century art** in Wing C, which is largely attributable to members of the Gödöllő and Nagybánya artists colonies. The chief exponent of Art

Nouveau in Hungary was **József Rippl-Rónai**, whose portraits were little recognized in his lifetime but are now regarded as classics. Other trends such as Post-Impressionism are represented by works like Ödön Márffy's Cézanne-like *The Old Toll House at Vác*, but there's less abstract art than you'd expect from the 1930s and 40s. When open, the **third floor** exhibits art from the 1960s and 70s that has survived the post-Communist purge of works by socialist artists who were favoured under the old system.

## THE MUSEUM OF CONTEMPORARY ART

The stylish **Museum of Contemporary Art** (*Kortárs Művészti Múzeum*; Tues–Sun 10am–6pm; 100Ft) is a joint venture by the Ministry of Culture and corporate sponsors, established in 1996 to build upon an earlier bequest by the late German industrialist Peter Ludwig, in the year of Hungary's transition to democracy. Before then, Wing A of the palace had contained the Museum of the Working Class Movement, whose staff made amends for decades of misinformation by organizing an exhibition on the Stalinist era before moving out – hence the lavish use of red marble in the atrium. Although the **Ludwig Collection** includes US pop art such as Warhol's *Single Elvis* and Lichtenstein's *Vicky*, and a Hockney room-with-a-view from his Pointillist period, most of the museum's acquisitions are work by lesser-known Europeans, in veins from Hyper-Realism to neo-Primitivism. The museum has a pleasant **café** with a view of the Buda Hills.

## THE MÁTYÁS FOUNTAIN AND NATIONAL SZÉCHÉNYI LIBRARY

The courtyard outside is flanked on three sides by the palace, and overlooks Buda to the west. In the corner stands the flamboyant **Mátyás Fountain**, whose bronze figures recall the legend of Szép Ilonka. This beautiful peasant girl met the king while he was hunting incognito, fell in love with him, and died of a broken heart after discovering his identity and realizing the futility of her hopes. The man with a falcon is the king's Italian chronicler, who recorded the story for posterity. It is also enshrined in a poem by Vörösmarty.

A lofty gateway guarded by lions leads into the **Lion Courtyard**, flanked on the right by the **National Széchényi Library** (*Országos Széchényi Könyvtár*), whose full size is only apparent from the far side of the hill, where it looms over Dózsa tér like a mountain. Founded in 1802 on the initiative of Count Ferenc Széchényi (the father of István who spearheaded the Reform era), it is a repository for publications in Hungarian and material relating to the country from around the world and receives a copy of every book and newspaper published in Hungary. Its reading room is open to the public (Mon 1–9pm, Tues–Sat 9am–9pm; free) and there are temporary exhibitions on diverse subjects. During library hours, a passenger **lift** (10Ft) beside the building provides direct access to and from Dózsa tér, at the foot of Várhegy.

## THE BUDAPEST HISTORY MUSEUM

On the far side of the courtyard, the **Budapest History Museum** (*Budapest Történeti Múzeum*; mid-May to mid-Sept daily 10am–6pm; Nov–Feb daily 10am–4pm; March & Oct 10am–6pm, closed Tues; 250Ft, free Wed) covers two millennia on three floors before descending into the vaulted, flagstoned halls of palaces of old. Due to the ravages inflicted by the Mongols and the Turks there's little to show from the time of the Conquest or Hungary's medieval civilization, so most of the second floor is occupied by **Budapest in Modern Times**, an exhibition that gives an insight into urban planning, fashions, trade and vices from 1686 onwards, with items ranging from an 1880s barrel organ to one of the Swedish Red Cross notices affixed to Jewish safe houses by Wallenberg (see p.84). The **remains of the medieval palace** are reached from the basement via an eighteenth-century cellar. A wing of the ground floor of King Sigismund's palace and the cellars beneath the Corvin Library form a stratum overlaying the **Royal Chapel** and a **Gothic Hall** displaying statues found in 1974. In another chamber are portions of red marble fireplaces and a massive portal carved with cherubs and flowers, from the palace of King Mátyás. Emerging into daylight, bear left and up the stairs to reach another imposing hall, with a view over the castle ramparts.

If you feel like walking down the hillside into the Víziváros or Tabán (see p.81), the river-facing route switchbacks past a Rondella and the former **Palace Gardens** (whose crumbling statues and terraces are on the World Monument Fund's list of endangered sites) to end up at the lower terminal of the Sikló. Aiming for the Tabán, it's better to leave the castle grounds by the **Ferdinánd Gate** near the Mace Tower, from which steps run directly down to Szarvas tér.

# The Víziváros

Originally a poor quarter where fishermen, craftsmen and their families lived, the **Víziváros** (Watertown) between Várhegy and the Danube was repopulated after the expulsion of the Turks by Croatian and Serbian mercenaries and their camp-followers. Today it's a reclusive neighbourhood of mansions and old buildings meeting at odd angles on the hillside, reached by alleys which mostly consist of steps rising from the main street, **Fő utca**. Some of these are still lit by gas lamps and look quite Dickensian on misty evenings.

### Batthyány tér

The Víziváros's main square, named **Batthyány tér** after the nineteenth-century prime minister, was originally called Bomba tér after the ammunition depot sited here for the defence of the Danube waterway. Now home to a long-established market and the underground interchange between the red metro line and the HÉV rail line to Szentendre, it's always busy with shoppers and commuters. To the right of the market is a sunken, two-storey building that used to be the *White Cross Inn*, where Casanova reputedly once stayed. Many of the older buildings in this area are sunken in this way: ground level was raised several feet in the last century to combat flooding. The twin-towered **St Anna Parish Church**, on the corner of the square, sports the Buda coat of arms on its tympanum.

Heading south along Fő utca, you'll see a spiky polychrome-tiled church on **Szilágyi Desző tér**, and a floating hotel moored alongside the embankment. It was here that the Arrow Cross massacred hundreds of Jews, shooting them into the river in January of 1945, when Eichmann and the SS had already fled the city, which was by then encircled by the Red Army. An inconspicuous plaque commemorates the victims. Further on, you can see the old Capuchin Church featuring Turkish window arches, at no. 30 on the left-hand side. A couple of blocks later you emerge onto Clark Ádám tér, facing the Lánchíd.

### The Lánchíd, Sikló and Kilometre Zero

As the first permanent link between Buda and Pest, the majestic **Széchenyi Lánchíd** (Széchenyi Chain Bridge) has a special place in the hearts of locals, for whom it is a symbol of civic endurance. Austrian troops tried and failed to destroy it in 1849, but in 1945 the bridge fell victim to the Wehrmacht, who dynamited all of Budapest's bridges in a bid to check the Red Army. Their reconstruction was one of the first tasks of the postwar era; the Lánchíd reopened on November 21, 1949, on the centenary of its inauguration.

The bridge was the brainchild of **Count István Széchenyi**, a horse-fancying Anglophile with a passion for innovation, who founded the Academy of Sciences and brought steam engines to Hungary, amongst other achievements. Designed by **William Tierney Clark**, it was constructed under the supervision of a Scottish engineer, **Adam Clark** (no relation), who personally thwarted the Austrian attempts to destroy it by flooding the chain-lockers. Whereas Széchenyi later died in an asylum, having witnessed the triumph (and subsequent defeat) of Kossuth and the 1848 Revolution, Adam Clark settled happily in Budapest with his Hungarian wife.

During his time in Budapest, Clark also built the **tunnel** (*alagút*) under the Várhegy which, Budapesters joked, could be used to store the new bridge when it rained. Next to the tunnel entrance on the river end is the lower terminal of the **Sikló**, a nineteenth-century **funicular** running up to the palace (daily 7.30am–10pm; closed every second & fourth Mon of the month; 200Ft). Constructed on the initiative of Ödön, Széchenyi's son, it was only the second funicular in the world when it was inaugurated in 1870, and functioned without a hitch until wrecked by a shell in 1945. The yellow carriages are exact replicas of the originals, but are now lifted by an electric winch rather than a steam engine. In the small park at its foot stands **Kilometre Zero**, a zero-shaped monument from which all distances from Budapest are measured.

## Around the Király Baths and Bem tér

The area **north from Batthyány tér** to the Király Baths (strictly speaking part of the Víziváros) can be reached by heading up Fő utca. You'll pass the gloomy premises of the **Military Court of Justice** (nos. 70–72), where Imre Nagy and other leaders of the 1956 Uprising were tried and executed in 1958. The square outside has recently been renamed after Nagy, whose body lay in an unmarked grave in the Kerepesi Cemetery for over thirty years. The brand-new brick building at the far side of the square is the new Foreign Ministry.

You can identify the **Király Fürdő** (men: Mon, Wed & Fri 6.30am–7pm; women Tues, Thurs same hours, Sat 6.30am–noon; 250Ft) at Fő utca 82–86 by the four copper cupolas, shaped like tortoise shells, poking from its eighteenth-century facade. The octagonal pool – lit by star-shaped apertures in the dome – was built by the Turks in 1570 for the Buda garrison. The baths' name, meaning "king", comes from that of the König family who owned them in the eighteenth century. The baths have become a major meeting place for Budapest's **gay men**. It is now compulsory to wear swimming gear at this bath.

A couple of blocks further north, **Bem tér** was named after the Polish general Joseph Bem, who fought for the Hungarians in the 1849 War of Independence. Traditionally a site for demonstrations, it was here that crowds assembled on October 23, 1956, prior to marching on parliament, bearing Hungarian flags with the hammer and sickle cut out, hours before the Uprising. The square was also the focus for peace demonstrations and protests against the Nagymaros Dam (see p.154) during the 1980s.

At Bem utca 20, 200m up the hill west from the square, the **Foundry Museum** (*Öntödei Múzeum*; Tues–Sun 9am–4pm; 100Ft) is housed in the ironworks founded by Abrahám Ganz in 1844, which grew into a massive industrial complex. The huge ladles and jib-cranes are still in their original setting, while the museum's collection includes some fine cast-iron stoves.

# The Tabán, Gellért-hegy and beyond

South of the Várhegy lies the **Tabán** district, once Buda's artisan quarter, largely inhabited by Serbs (known as *Rác* in Hungarian), but almost totally demolished in the 1930s because of its unhygienic narrow streets and open sewers, and subsequently turned into a public park. There are, however, a few surviving buildings worth seeking out.

## The Tabán and the Rác and Rudas baths
At the northern end of the Tabán, the **Semmelweis Medical Museum** at Apród utca 1–3 (Tues–Sun 9.30am–5.30pm; 100Ft) honours the "saviour of mothers", Ignác Semmelweis (1815–65). He discovered the cause of puerperal fever (a form of blood poisoning contracted in childbirth) and a simple method for preventing the disease, which until then was usually fatal: the sterilization of instruments and the washing of hands with carbolic soap. Inside are displayed medical instruments through the ages, including such curios as a chastity belt. The small insignificant stones in the park behind the museum are in fact Turkish burial markers.

An even better reason to come to the Tabán, though, is the Turkish baths – the place to immerse yourself in history. The relaxing and curative effects of Buda's **mineral springs** have been appreciated for two thousand years. The Romans built splendid bathhouses at Aquincum, to the north of Buda, and, while these declined with the empire, interest revived after the Knights of St John built a hospice on the site of the present Rudas Baths, near where St Elizabeth cured lepers in the springs below Gellért-hegy. However, it was the Turks who consolidated the habit of bathing – as Muslims, they were obliged to wash five times daily in preparation for prayer – and constructed proper bathhouses which function to this day.

Two thermal baths lie at the southern end of the Tabán by the Buda bridgehead of the Erzsébet híd. Tucked under the main road that leads up the hill away from the bridge, Hegyalja út, the bright yellow **Rác Fürdő** (Mon–Sat 6.30am–6pm; 350Ft) retain an octagonal stone pool from Turkish times, but were otherwise rebuilt in the last century. The sulphurous water (40°C) is considered good for skin complaints and conditions affecting the joints. There are separate admission days for women (Mon, Wed & Fri) and men (Tues, Thurs & Sat). Heading on towards the Rudas Baths, you pass the **Ivócsarnok** (Water Hall) below the road to the Erzsébet Bridge – drinking water from three nearby springs is sold here (Mon, Wed & Fri 11am–6pm, Tues & Thurs 7am–2pm).

The **Rudas Fürdő** (Men only, Mon–Fri 6am–5pm, Sat & Sun 6am–noon; 350Ft), south of the Erzsébet híd, are outwardly nondescript, but the interior has hardly changed since it was constructed in 1556 on the orders of Pasha Sokoli Mustapha. Tselebi called this place the "bath with green pillars", and these columns can still be seen today. Bathers wallow in an octagonal stone pool with steam billowing around the shadowy recesses and shafts of light pouring in from the star-shaped apertures in the domed ceiling. To the left of the entrance is a swimming pool, open to both sexes.

## BATHING MATTERS

Most bathhouses are divided into a **swimming** area and a separate section for **thermal baths** (*gyógyfürdő*), sauna, steamrooms and sometimes even mud baths. To enter this latter section, you usually have to exchange your swimsuit for an apron (for women) or loincloth (for men) – although swimsuits are becoming acceptable in the steam baths. A basic ticket covers three hours in the pools, *szauna* and steamrooms (*gőzfürdő*); and supplementary tickets will buy you a massage (*masszázs*), tub (*kádfürdő*) or mud bath (*iszapfürdő*). In many pools swimmers are required to wear a bathing cap, which can be rented if necessary (as can swimsuits and towels).

## Gellért-hegy

**Gellért-hegy** is as much a feature of the waterfront panorama as the Várhegy and the parliament building: a craggy dolomite cliff rearing 130m above the embankment of the Danube, surmounted by the Liberation Monument and the Citadella. The hill is named after Bishop Ghirardus (Gellért in Hungarian), who converted pagan Magyars to Christianity at the behest of King Stephen. After his royal protector's demise, vengeful heathens strapped Gellért to a barrow and toppled him off the cliff, where a **statue of St Gellért** now stands astride a waterfall facing the Erzsébet híd.

Before ascending the hill, take a look at the **Gellért Hotel**, at the southern end of the hill by the green Szabadság híd, a famous Art Nouveau establishment opened in 1918, which Admiral Horthy commandeered following his triumphal entry into "sinful Budapest" in 1920. During the 1930s and 1940s, its balls were the highlight of Budapest's social calendar, when debutantes danced on a glass floor laid over its pool. The **Gellért Baths** (entered on the right-hand side of the hotel building on Kelenhegyi út) are magnificently appointed with majolica tiles and columns, and lion-headed spouts gushing into its mixed sex thermal pool (May–Sept daily 6am–7pm; Oct–April Mon–Fri 6am–7pm, Sat & Sun 6am–5pm; June–Sept evening swimming Fri & Sat; 1200Ft). You get to the changing rooms through a labyrinth of passages – staff are generally helpful and can direct you. There's also an outdoor summer pool with a wave machine and terraces for nude sunbathing. At the far end of the indoor pool, stairs lead down to the Turkish baths (which you can also enter separately May–Sept Mon–Fri 6am–7pm, Sat & Sun 6am–5pm, Oct–April Mon–Fri 6am–5pm, Sat & Sun 6am–2pm; 700Ft) with separate areas and ornate plunge pools for men and women. The baths' high prices increase over summer (bring a cap and towel to save money), but even if you don't plan on taking a dip you should take a peek into the foyer, entered via a portal carved with writhing figures.

In a cave on the river side of the hill, just opposite the entrance to the baths, you'll find a set of **chapels** which were blocked up during the Communist regime and only recently returned to the Paulines, Hungary's one indigenous religious order (founded 1256), who served as confessors to the Hungarian kings. To reach the **top of the hill** you can either travel to Móricz Zsigmond körtér and catch bus #27 to the last stop, from where it's a ten-minute walk; or you can climb one of the paths from the Gellért statue or the *Gellért Hotel* (see above) in about twenty minutes. The **panoramic view** from the top of the hill is stunning, drawing one's eye slowly along the curving river, past bridges and monumental landmarks, and then on to the Buda hills and Pest's suburbs, merging hazily with the distant plain.

*THE CITADELLA AND LIBERATION MONUMENT*
The hilltop **Citadella** was built by the Habsburgs in the aftermath of the 1848–49 Revolution to dominate the city with its cannons. When the historic Compromise was reached in 1867, citizens breached the walls to affirm that it no longer posed a threat to them. Since World War II, when an SS regiment holed up in the fortress, nothing more sinister than fireworks have been launched from the citadel. Today, it contains a casino and a tourist hostel, plus a museum comprising a few displays of archeological remains and old pots, but the 100Ft entrance fee is worth it for the view.

From the ramparts you get a fine view of the towering **Liberation Monument** beside the citadel – a female figure brandishing the palm of victory over 30m aloft; it's too large to be properly appreciated at ground level. The monument's history is ironic, since it was originally commissioned by Admiral Horthy in memory of his son – killed in the "Crusade against Bolshevism" – but was ultimately dedicated to the Soviet soldiers who died liberating Budapest from the Nazis. Its sculptor, Zsigmond Kisfaludi-Strobl, simply added smaller figures of Soviet soldiers around the base to gain approval as a "Proletarian Artist". Having previously specialized in busts of the aristocracy, he was henceforth known by his compatriots as "Kisfaludi-Strébel" (*strébel* meaning "to climb" or "step from side to side"). The statue survived calls for its removal following the fall of the Communist regime, though the soldiers around the base have been taken away.

## Farkasréti temető and the statue park
Further out of the city are two sites that recall the past in very different ways. Up in the hills, 2km from the centre, is the Wolf's Meadow Cemetery (*Farkasréti temető*; tram #59 from Moszkva tér to the end of the line), containing the **tomb of Béla Bartók**, whose remains were ceremonially reinterred here in July 1988 following their return from America, where the composer died in exile in 1945. His will forbade reburial in Hungary so long as there were streets named after Hitler or Mussolini, but the return of his body was delayed for decades to prevent the Communists from capitalizing on the event. Another giant of the musical world was buried next to him in 1998: **Sir Georg Solti**, who left Hungary in 1939 to meet Toscanini, and was saved by the outbreak of war from the fate of his Jewish parents. He returned to Hungary only in 1978, having built his reputation as a top conductor, and then made regular visits to conduct Hungarian orchestras. The amazing **crypt** in the cemetery chapel is even more impressive, with a wooden vault resembling the belly of a beast – a typically striking early design by **Imre Makovecz**.

On the southwest edge of the city, about 10km from the centre, stands the Statue Park (*Szoborpark*), which brings together many of the monuments that were damaged when the Communist regime fell (April–Oct daily 10am–6pm; Nov–March Sat & Sun only 10am–4pm; 200Ft). Here you'll find Lenin standing proud, countless proletarians, and the interesting work commemorating the 1919 Hungarian Soviet of Béla Kun, in which umbrella-bearing figures bring up the rear of the revolutionary crowd. The park is on the edge of the city on Route 70. Best access is by long-distance yellow **bus** from Kosztolányi Dezső tér – ask at the ticket desk for the Szoborpark.

# Around Moszkva tér and the Rózsadomb

The area immediately north of the Várhegy is largely defined by the transport hub of **Moszkva tér** and the reclusive residential quarter covering the **Rózsadomb** (Rose Hill). The interest here lies in the ambience of the latter, a couple of minor sights in the backstreets, and easy access to the Buda Hills.

## Moszkva tér and Szilágyi Erzsébet fasor

Once a quarry, and subsequently an ice rink and tennis courts, the busy transport nexus of **Moszkva tér** (Moscow Square) has succeeded in keeping its name despite political changes. Among the useful services that run from here are the red metro; bus #22 to Budakeszi; bus or tram #56 to Hűvösvölgy; and trams #4 and #6 to Margit sziget and Pest's Nagykörút. Aside from transport, Moszkva tér is only notable for the flower and vegetable **market** in the side streets to the north, and **Városmajor Park** to the west, where chess fans play beneath the elms behind the church and the tall bell-tower.

**Szilágyi Erzsébet fasor** runs alongside the park, past the cylindrical *Hotel Budapest* – nicknamed "the dustbin" for its shape – and the terminal of the **Cogwheel Railway** (see p.87), across the road. One kilometre on, you can glimpse on the right of the avenue of chestnuts a red marble **monument to Raoul Wallenberg**, the "Righteous Gentile", who gave up a playboy life in neutral Sweden to help the Jews of Hungary in 1944. Following the example of the Swiss diplomat Carl Lutz, and armed with diplomatic status and money for bribing officials, Wallenberg and his assistants plucked thousands from the cattle trucks and lodged them in "safe houses", manoeuvring to buy time until the Russians arrived. Shortly after they did, Wallenberg was arrested as a spy and vanished into the Gulag, where he is thought to have died in 1953. The monument was only set up in 1987, just before Budapest hosted the World Jewish Congress, marking another milestone in *perestroika*. But even then, the monument was tucked away far from the centre.

## The Rózsadomb

Budapest's most exclusive neighbourhood lies beyond smog-ridden **Margit körút** and the backstreets off Moszkva tér. If you're coming from Bem tér, consider a preliminary detour to the rather over-restored **tomb of Gül Baba** on Mecset utca, just above Margit körút (May–Oct Tues–Sun 10am–6pm; 200Ft). This small octagonal building is a shrine to the "Father of the Roses", a Sufi Dervish who participated in the Turkish capture of Buda but died during the thanksgiving service afterwards. Until recently the tomb stood solitary and forgotten, but the Turkish government donated funds for its restoration, and it now stands in a pristine little park with marble fountains and ceramic tiles. Carpets and examples of calligraphy adorn the shrine, which fittingly stands in a rose garden, surrounded by a colonnaded parapet with good views. At one time you had to remove your shoes before entering as a mark of respect, but now you can just clump into it in your walking boots.

The **Rózsadomb** (Rose Hill) itself is as much a social category as a neighbourhood, for a list of residents would read like a Hungarian *Who's Who*. During the Communist era this included the top Party *funcionárusok*, whose homes featured secret exits that enabled several ÁVO chiefs to escape lynching during the Uprising. Nowadays, wealthy film directors and entrepreneurs predominate, and the sloping streets are lined with spacious villas and flashy cars.

GREG EVANS

Mátyás Church, Budapest

CHARLES BOWMAN

The Parliament building from the Fishermen's Bastion, Budapest

The Dohány utca Synagogue, Budapest

The Blessing of the Grapes at the Serbian Church, Szentendre

Gellert Baths, Budapest

Streetlamp, Budapest

The Danube Bend at Visegrád

Margit Kovács Gallery, Szentendre

Heart-shaped gravestones, Balatonudvari

The Mátyás Fountain, Buda Palace, Budapest

PETER WILSON
PETER WILSON
PETER WILSON
PETER WILSON
W. JACOBS, TRIP

The abbey at Tihany, Lake Balaton

The ruined castle above Sirok

Heading down the hill to the riverbank, just north of the Margit híd, you can find the Neoclassical **Lukács Fürdő**, where there's both a thermal pool (men: Tues, Thurs, Sat & Sun, 6.30am–8pm; women: Mon, Wed & Fri same hours; 200Ft) and a small mixed swimming pool (Mon–Sat 6am–8pm, Sun 6am–7pm). To get to the baths you walk through the ticket hall, a folly-like structure that would not be out of place in a country mansion, and into the courtyard lined with plaques of gratitude in different languages from those who have benefited from the medicinal waters. The adjacent **Császár Komjádi Pool** has a Turkish bath-hall dating from the sixteenth century and still in use, plus an excellent modern outdoor swimming pool (covered in winter) that has just been renovated (Mon–Sat 6am–9pm, Sun 6am–7pm; 200Ft; hats compulsory in the pool). The entrances to both are on the embankment side of the building.

# Óbuda and Római-Fürdő

The district of **Óbuda**, up the river bank to the north, is the oldest part of Budapest, though that's hardly the impression given by the factories and high-rises that dominate the area today, hiding such ancient ruins as remain. Nonetheless it was here that the Romans built a legionary camp and a civilian town, later taken over by the Huns. This developed into an important town under the Hungarian Árpád dynasty, but after the fourteenth century it was eclipsed by the Vár. The original settlement became known as Óbuda (Old Buda) and was incorporated into the newly formed Budapest in 1873. The best-preserved ruins lie further north, in the **Római-Fürdő** district, accessible by HÉV train from Batthyány tér or the Margit híd.

## Roman ruins in Óbuda

The section of Óbuda **around Fő tér** blends gaudy Baroque with modern art and overpriced gastronomy, all within a minute's walk of the Árpád híd HÉV stop. At Szentlélek tér 1, the former Zichy mansion now contains the **Kassák Museum** (Tues–Sun 10am–6pm; 100Ft), dedicated to the Hungarian constructionist Lajos Kassák. Next door is the **Vasarely Museum** (Tues–Sun 10am–6pm; 100Ft), displaying eyeball-throbbing Op Art paintings by Viktor Vasarely, one of the founders of the genre. On cobbled Fő tér, just around the corner, you'll find the touristy *Sipos Halászkert* and *Postakocsi* restaurants. Whatever the weather, there are always several figures sheltering beneath umbrellas here: life-sized sculptures by Imre Varga, whose oeuvre is the subject of the nearby **Varga Museum** at Laktanya utca 7 (Tues–Sun 10am–6pm; 100Ft). A sense of humour pervades his sheet-metal, iron and bronze effigies of famous personages.

Although the largest site lies further out in the Római-Fürdő district, Óbuda does have several excavated ruins to show for its past. The finest of them is the weed-choked, crumbling **amphitheatre** (*amfiteátrum*) at the junction of Nagyszombat and Pacsirtamező utca, which is even larger than that of the Colosseum in Rome, seating up to 16,000 spectators. The amphitheatre can be reached by bus #86 (from Batthyány tér or anywhere along the embankment), or by walking 400m north from Kolosy tér (near the Szépvölgyi út HÉV stop). Having seen it, you can continue to the next collection of ruins by bus #6 or #86. While you're in the area, check out a couple of good patisseries renowned for their ice creams: the *Veress*, on the corner of Bokor utca leading south from the amphitheatre, and the *Daubner*, which attracts long queues up on Szépvölgyi út, leading towards the hills and caves (see opposite).

The **Camp Museum** (*Táborvárosi Múzeum*; May–Oct Tues–Fri 10am–2pm, Sat & Sun 10am–6pm; 150Ft), a modern edifice at Pacsirtamező utca 63, displays sarcophagi, the ruins of a bathhouse, fragmented murals and other relics of the legionary camp. This was situated near modern-day Flórián tér, where graceful columns now stand incongruously amid a shopping plaza, while the old **military baths** and other finds are huddled beneath the Szentendrei út flyover.

Ten minutes' walk to the northwest, behind the apartment building at nos. 19–21 on Meggyfa utca, three blue canopies shelter the remains of the **Hercules Villa** (April–Oct Tues–Fri 10am–2pm, Sat & Sun 10am–6pm; 150Ft), whose name derives from the third-century **mosaic floor** beneath the largest canopy. This mosaic, originally composed of 60,000 stones carefully selected and arranged in Alexandria, depicts Hercules about to vomit at a wine festival. Another mosaic portrays the centaur Nessus abducting Deianeira, whom Hercules had to rescue as one of his twelve labours.

### Aquincum

The legionary garrison of six thousand spawned a settlement of camp-followers – Aquincum – which, over time, became a *Municipium* and later a *Colonia*, the provincial capital of Pannonia Inferior. The **ruins of Aquincum** (May–Oct Tues–Sun 10am–6pm; 200Ft), easily visible from the Aquincum HÉV stop, lie along the Szentendre road a couple of kilometres north of Flórián tér; further on are the remains of an **aqueduct** and another **amphitheatre**, near the next HÉV stop, Római-Fürdő (Roman Bath).

Enough foundation walls and underground piping survive to give a fair idea of the **layout** of Aquincum, although you'll need to pay a visit to the museum and use considerable imagination to envisage the town during its heyday in the second to third centuries AD. A great concourse of people would have filled the main street, doing business in the forum and law courts (near the site entrance), and steaming in the public baths. Herbs and wine were burned before altars in sanctuaries holy to the goddesses Epona and Fortuna Augusta, while fraternal societies met in the collegia and bathhouses further east. The **museum** (same hours and prices as the site) contains oddments of the imperium – cake moulds, a bronze military diploma, buttons used as admission tickets to the theatre – and statues of gods and goddesses.

# The Buda Hills

Thirty minutes' journey by bus from Moszkva tér, the **Buda Hills** provide a welcome respite from Budapest's summertime heat. While some parts can be crowded at the weekend with walkers and mountain-bikers, it's possible to ramble through the woods for hours and see hardly a soul during the week. If your time is limited, the most rewarding options are the "**railway circuit**" or a visit to **Budakeszi Game Park** (daily 9am–5pm), reached by taking bus #22 from Moszkva tér to the Korányi Sanatorium stop, and then following the "Vadaspark" signs for a couple of kilometres. Beyond the park's exhibition centre lie woods and fields inhabited by red, roe and shovel-antlered fallow deer, wild boar, mallards, pheasants and other birds. Unrepentant carnivores have the opportunity of savouring these delicacies at the *Vadaspark* restaurant by the entrance.

## The "railway circuit"

The "railway circuit" begins with a short ride on tram #18 or #56 or bus #56 from Moszkva tér, out along Szilágyi Erzsébet fasor, to the lower terminal of the **Fogaskerekű vasút** (Cogwheel Railway). From here a small train clicks up through the **Svábhegy** suburb every ten minutes or so, past the world-famous **Pető Institute** for conductive therapy, to the summit of Széchenyi-hegy.

The terminal of the **Gyermekvasút** (Children's Railway), a narrow-gauge line that's almost entirely run by 13- to 17-year-olds, is a short walk across the park. Built by youth brigades in 1948, it enables kids who fancy a career with MÁV, the Hungarian Railways company, to get hands-on experience. Watching them wave flags, collect tickets and salute departures with solemnity, you can see why it appealed to the Communists. Until a few years ago, it was known as the Pioneers' Railway after the organization that replaced the disbanded Scouts and Guides movements (now re-formed). The railway has been through lean times, for a while operating at weekends only, but it now runs almost every day (every 45min–1hr; June–Aug daily 9am–5pm; Sept–May Tues–Sun same hours), stopping at various points en route to Hűvösvölgy (Cool Valley). The eleven-kilometre journey takes about 45 minutes.

The first stop, **Normafa**, is a popular excursion centre with a modest **ski-run**. Its name comes from a performance of the aria from Bellini's *Norma* given here by the actress Rozália Klein in 1840. Across the road, in a wooden hut, is *Rétes büfé*, a stall where you can get delicious strudel and coffee every day of the year including holidays. **János-hegy**, three stops on, is the highest point in Budapest. On the 527-metre-high summit, fifteen minutes' climb from the station, the **Erzsébet lookout tower**, soon to be restored as a restaurant/bar, offers a panoramic view of the city and the Buda Hills. By the buffet below the summit is the upper terminal of the **chairlift** (May–Sept 9.30am–5pm; off-season Oct–April 9.30am–4pm; closed every other Mon; 150Ft) down to Zugliget, whence #158 buses return to Moszkva tér.

From the main road by the next stop, **Szépjuhászné**, you can catch bus #22 to **Budakeszi Vadaspark** (Game Park). **Wild boars** – which prefer to roam during the evening and sleep by day – are occasionally sighted in the forests above **Hárshegy**, one stop before Hűvösvölgy. Also linked directly to Moszkva tér by #56 and #56E (nonstop) buses, **Hűvösvölgy** is the site of the popular *Náncsi Néni* restaurant (see p.112).

## Stalactite caves and other sights

The more northerly Buda Hills harbour a second clutch of attractions, best reached in a separate excursion from Kolosy tér in Óbuda (near Szépvölgyi út HÉV stop). From here, ride bus #65 for five stops out to Szépvölgyi út 162 to find the **Pálvölgyi cseppkőbarlang** (Stalactite Caves; guided tours in Hungarian only Wed–Sun hourly 10am–4pm; 40min; 160Ft). The tour of this spectacular labyrinth starts on the lowest level, which boasts rock formations such as the "Organ Pipes" and "Beehive". From "John's Lookout" in the largest chamber, you ascend a crevice onto the upper level, there to enter "Fairyland" and finally "Paradise", overlooking the hellish "Radium Hall" 50m below.

From the Pálvölgyi cave, another stalactite labyrinth and the Kiscelli Museum are each just twenty minutes' walk away – in opposite directions; buses run to both from Kolosy tér. The **Szemlőhegyi barlang** (caves) at Pusztaszeri út 35 (April–Oct Wed–Fri 10am–3pm, Sat & Sun 10am–4pm; 160Ft) abound in pea-shaped formations and aragonite crystals resembling bunches of grapes. Coming from Kolosy tér by bus #29, alight at the fourth stop near the Pusztaszeri út turn-off. You can buy a joint ticket for 240Ft to see both the caves. The **Kiscelli Museum** (April–Oct Tues–Sun 10am–6pm; Nov–March Tues–Sun 10am–4pm; 150Ft) occupies a former Trinitarian monastery in a beautiful setting at Kiscelli utca 108. Its collection includes antique printing presses and the 1830 Biedermeier furnishings of the Golden Lion pharmacy, which used to stand on Kalvin tér. The picturesque shell of the monastery's Gothic church makes a marvellous backdrop for operas, fashion shows and performances, definitely worth looking out for. Bus #165 from Kolosy tér turns around to begin its return journey near the museum, or you can take bus #60 from Batthyány tér to the stop by the Margit korház (hospital) and walk up the very steep Kiscelli utca.

A pleasant alternative is to ride bus #65 from Pálvölgyi caves to the end of the line at the foot of **Hármashatár-hegy**; it's a long hike up, so you might want to take a taxi up from Kolosy tér. This hill provides a fabulous **view** of Budapest to the southeast, while hang-gliders launch themselves off from the western side. It is also the one of best spots in the hills for **mushroom hunting**, a pastime that's almost as popular amongst Budapesters as it is with city folk in Russia and Poland. People can take their fungi to special *gomba* stalls (there's one on Lövőház utca by the market near Moszkva tér), where experts distinguish the edible from the poisonous.

# Margit sziget

A saying has it that "love begins and ends" on **Margit sziget** (Margaret Island), for this verdant expanse just upriver from the city centre has been a favourite spot for lovers since the nineteenth century, though until 1945 a stiff admission charge deterred the poor. Today it is one of Budapest's most popular recreation grounds, its thermal springs feeding outdoor pools and ritzy spa hotels. The easiest way of **getting there** is to catch bus #26 (which runs all the way along the island) from either the Nyugati pu. or Árpád híd metro stations in Pest. Alternatively, you can take tram #4 or #6 from Moszkva tér or the Nagykörút to the stop midway across the Margit híd, and walk onto the island via the short linking bridge. Motorists can only approach from the north, via the Árpád híd, at which point they must abandon their vehicles at a paying car park. You can **rent bikes** at the southern entrance to the island, on the left-hand side – they tend to be rather battered but are good enough to get around the 5km circuit.

The southern part of the island is for chilling out and improving your tan. A huge circular fountain presages the **Hajós Alfréd Pool** (popularly known as the "Sport"), named after the winner of the 100m and 1200m swimming races at the 1896 Olympics, who was also the architect who designed the indoor pool – though the main attractions are the all-season outdoor 50m pool and the fresh pastries at the buffet. Ten minutes' walk further on, a ruined thirteenth-century **Franciscan church** and a rose garden lie across the road from the **Palatinus Strand** (daily May–Sept), which can hold as many as ten thousand people at a time in seven open-air thermal pools, complete with a water chute, wave machine and segregated terraces for nude sunbathing.

Further north, an **outdoor theatre**, by a conspicuous water tower, hosts plays, operas, concerts and fashion shows over summer, and is a handy spot for a beer or snack. To the east stands a **ruined Dominican church and convent**; Béla IV vowed to bring his daughter up as a nun here if Hungary survived the Mongol invasion, and duly confined 9-year-old Princess Margit when it did. She apparently made the best of it, acquiring a reputation for curing lepers and other saintly deeds, as well as for not washing above her ankles. Beatification followed her death in 1271, and a belated canonization in 1943. The convent fell into ruin during the Turkish occupation, when the island was turned into a harem.

A short way northeast of the water tower is a **Premonstratensian Chapel** whose Romanesque tower dates back to the twelfth century, when the order first established a monastery on the island; its fifteenth-century bell is one of the oldest in Hungary. Beyond lie two **spa hotels** catering to wealthy northern Europeans with a yen to be pampered: the *Ramada Grand*, a refurbished *fin-de-siècle* pile, and the equally well-equipped *Thermal Hotel*, built in the 1970s. If it's **sport** you're after, **Euro Gym** on the eastern side of the island offers aerobics, tennis courts and a sauna, while the pleasant beer garden next door serves wood-grilled meats, Austrian lager and imported Kentish bitter.

# Pest

**Pest** is busier, more populous and vital than Buda: the place where things are decided, made and sold. While Buda grew up around the royal court, the east bank was settled by merchants and artisans, and commerce has always been its lifeblood. Much of its architecture and layout dates from the late nineteenth century, giving Pest a homogenous appearance compared to other European capitals. Boulevards, public buildings and apartment houses were built on a scale appropriate to the Habsburg empire's second city, and the capital of a nation which celebrated its millennial anniversary in 1896. Now bullet-scarred and grimy – or in the throes of restoration – these grand edifices form the backdrop to life in the **Belváros** (inner city) and the residential districts, hulking gloomily above the cafés, wine cellars and courtyards where people socialize. While there's plenty to see and do, it's the less tangible ambience that sticks in one's memory.

Away from the waterfront, you'll find that two semicircular boulevards are fundamental to **orientation**. The inner city lies within the **Kiskörút** (Small Boulevard), made up of Károly körút, Múzeum körút and Vámház körút. Further out, the **Nagykörút** (Great Boulevard) sweeps through the VI, VII, VIII and IX districts, where it is called Szent István körút, Teréz körút, Erzsébet körút, József körút and Ferenc körút respectively. Pest is also defined by **avenues** (*út*) radiating out beyond the Nagykörút – notably Bajcsy-Zsilinszky út (for Nyugati Station); Andrássy út, leading to the **Városliget** (City Park); Rákóczi út, for Keleti Station; and Üllői út, leading out towards the airport. As the meeting point of three metro lines and several main avenues, **Deák tér** makes a good jumping-off point for explorations.

## The Belváros

The **Belváros**, or Inner City, is the hub of Pest and – for tourists at least – the epicentre of what's happening – abuzz with pavement cafés, buskers, boutiques and nightclubs. Commerce and pleasure have been its lifeblood as long as Pest has existed, as a medieval market town or the kernel of a city whose *belle époque* rivalled Vienna's. Since their fates diverged, the Belváros has lagged far behind Vienna's Centrum in prosperity, though the last decade has narrowed the gap, at

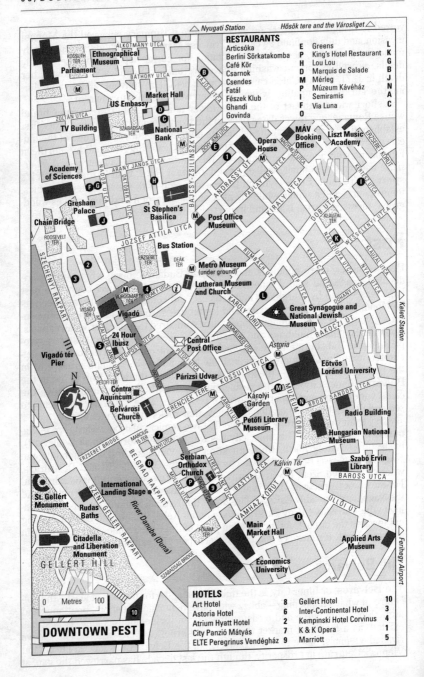

△ Nyugati Station     Hősök tere and the Városliget △

**RESTAURANTS**

| | | | |
|---|---|---|---|
| Articsóka | E | Greens | L |
| Berlini Sörkatakomba | P | King's Hotel Restaurant | K |
| Café Kör | H | Lou Lou | G |
| Csarnok | D | Marquis de Salade | B |
| Csendes | M | Mérleg | J |
| Fatál | P | Múzeum Kávéház | N |
| Fészek Klub | I | Semiramis | A |
| Ghandi | F | Via Luna | C |
| Govinda | O | | |

**DOWNTOWN PEST**

**HOTELS**

| | | | |
|---|---|---|---|
| Art Hotel | 8 | Gellért Hotel | 10 |
| Astoria Hotel | 6 | Inter-Continental Hotel | 3 |
| Atrium Hyatt Hotel | 2 | Kempinski Hotel Corvinus | 4 |
| City Panzió Mátyás | 7 | K & K Opera | 1 |
| ELTE Peregrinus Vendégház | 9 | Marriott | 5 |

least superficially. Though increasingly like any other Western city in its consumer culture, you can still get a sense of the old atmosphere, especially in the quieter backstreets south of Kossuth utca.

The **Kiskörút** (Small Boulevard) that surrounds the Belváros follows the course of the medieval walls of Pest, showing how compact it was before the phenomenal expansion of the nineteenth century swept the city far beyond its original boundaries. Within the Belváros there's little that's older than the eighteenth century, as the "liberation" of Pest by the Habsburgs left it in ruins. First-time visitors are struck by the statues, domes and mosaics on the skyline of Neoclassical and Art Nouveau piles, reflected in the mirrored banks and luxury hotels that symbolize the post-Communist era.

## Vörösmarty tér and Váci utca

The starting point for exploring the Belváros is **Vörösmarty tér**, the leafy centre of the district where crowds eddy around the portraitists, café tables and craft stalls that set up here over summer, Christmas and the wine festival. While children play in the fountains, teenagers lounge around the **statue of Mihály Vörösmarty** (1800–50), a poet and translator whose hymn to Magyar identity, *Szózat* (Appeal), is publicly declaimed at moments of national crisis. Its opening line – "Be faithful to your land forever, Oh Hungarians" – is carved on the pedestal. Made of Carrara marble, it has to be wrapped in plastic sheeting each winter to prevent it from cracking.

On the north side of the square is the **Gerbeaud patisserie**, Budapest's most famous confectioners. Founded in 1858 by Henrik Kugler, it was bought in 1884 by the Swiss confectioner Emile Gerbeaud, who invented the *konyakos meggy* (cognac-cherry bonbon) and sold top-class cakes at reasonable prices, making *Gerbeaud* a popular rendezvous for the middle classes. His portrait hangs in one of the rooms whose gilded ceilings and china recall the *belle époque*.

Beside *Gerbeaud*'s terrace is the entrance to the **Underground Railway** (*Földalatti Vasút*), whose vaguely Art Nouveau cast-iron fixtures and elegant tilework stamp it as decades older than the other metro lines. Indeed, it was the first on the European continent and the second in the world (after London's Metropolitan line) when it was inaugurated in 1896. Visit the Underground Railway Museum at Deák tér (see p.94) to learn more about its history.

At the lower end of the square, the **Bank Palace** was built (1913–15) in the heyday of Hungarian self-confidence by Ignác Alpár, and now houses the **Budapest Stock Exchange**, which was reborn in 1990, and allows visitors to observe its trading floor (Mon–Fri 10.30am–1.30pm; free).

*VÁCI UTCA*

**Váci utca** has been famous for its shops and **korzó** (promenade) since the eighteenth century, and the banning of cars along its length some years back has restored some of its former tranquillity. Until it was pulled down in the 1870s, the northern Vác Gate in the medieval walls of Pest stood near the corner of what is now Türr István utca; like Váci utca, its name came from the town of Vác on the Danube Bend, to which it led. Though the shopfronts and fashions have changed, its parade of dressed-to-kill babes and their moneyed escorts would be familiar to a time-traveller from the Reform Era. During the 1980s, its vivid **streetlife** became a symbol of the "consumer socialism" that distinguished Hungary from other Eastern Bloc states. Dreadlocked rollerbladers heralded its assimilation into the global village a year before the Wall came down, and its nightclubs were among the first to be taken over by foreign Mafia gangs, whose turf wars were blamed for a car-bomb that killed four bystanders just off Váci utca in 1998.

Immediately to your left stands **Kristóf tér**, a small plaza running across to Szervita tér and Petőfi Sándor utca (see below), adorned by the **fisher-girl statue**, while a few metres down to the right, today's **Pest Theatre** (no. 9) occupies the site of the *Inn of the Seven Electors*, where the 12-year-old Liszt performed in 1823. From the postmodernist *Taverna Hotel* onwards, every other shop sells souvenirs, clothes or jewellery. Besides designer-label stores, there are all kinds of small **shops** in the yards off the street, some of them reached by spiral staircases. On Váci utca itself, you'll see lines of women selling embroidered quilts and table-cloths; the ones in country dress are from ethnically Hungarian regions of Romania.

Making your way on down **Váci utca**, you pass the back of Ferenciek tere (see below), to the quieter part of the street. The stretch down to Fővám tér has become an **alternative korzó** since it was pedestrianized in 1997, with lots of options for eating and drinking in the cobbled side streets. Notice the beautifully restored prewar **Officers' Casino** on the corner of Ferenciek tere (now a bank's headquarters) and the pictorial **plaque** on the wall of no. 47, commemorating the fact that the Swedish King Carl XII stayed here during his lightning fourteen-day horse-ride from Turkey to Sweden, in 1714. Further down at nos. 62–64 is the **Old Budapest City Hall**, a dramatic nineteenth-century hulk, where the city council still meets, while at the far end is the popular tourist destination, the Great Market Hall (see p.108).

## SZERVITA TÉR AND PETŐFI UTCA

If the crowds in Váci utca put you off, you can head down Kristóf tér towards Szervita tér – named after the eighteenth-century **Servite Church**, but mainly distinguished by two buildings on the left-hand side of the street. No. 3 has a gable adorned with a superb **Secessionist mosaic** of *Patrona Hungaria* (Our Lady of Hungary) flanked by shepherds and angels, one of the finest works of Miksa Róth, while the **Rózsavölgyi Building**, next door, was built a few years later by the "father" of Hungarian Modernism, Béla Lajtha; his earlier association with the National Romantic school is evident from the majolica decorations on its upper storeys. On the ground floor is the Rózsavölgyi music shop, one of the best in the city. Equally striking, but rather less attractive, is the **MATÁV** phone, fax and email centre at the top of **Petőfi utca**, which runs down to Ferenciek tere parallel to Váci utca. This has none of the glamour and all the traffic, but you may be lured by its array of **music shops** or need to visit the **Central Post Office** (no.13).

At the corner of Ferenciek tere, you'll find the **Párisi Udvar**, a flamboyantly eclectic shopping arcade on the corner of Petőfi utca. Completed in 1915, its fifty naked figures above the third floor were deemed incompatible with its intended role as a savings bank. The old deposit hall now houses an IBUSZ office, while the arcade is as dark as an Andalucian mosque and twice as ornate.

## Ferenciek tere and further south

The Párisi Udvar is just one of several impressive buildings round Ferenciek tere, although none can offset the fact that the square is dominated by a three-lane highway running from the Erzsébet híd due east to Keleti Station. The road coming off the bridge runs down between twin *fin-de-siècle* office buildings known as the **Klotild Palaces**.

The square is named after the **Franciscan Church** on the corner of Kossuth utca, whose facade bears a relief recalling the Great Flood of 1838, which killed over 400 citizens. More would have died were it not for Baron Miklós Wesselényi, who rescued scores of people in his boat, as depicted on the plaque.

Heading south from the church, past the *Kárpátia* restaurant, you come to another thoroughfare, initially named after Count Mihály Károlyi, the liberal politician whose birthplace at no. 16 now houses the **Petőfi Literary Museum** (*Petőfi Irodalmi Múzeum*; Tues–Sun April–Oct 10am–6pm, Nov–March 10am–4pm; 80Ft), showcasing the personal effects of Petőfi and other Hungarian writers.

Heading on along Kecskeméti utca, past the law faculty and right into Szerb utca, you'll reach the **Serbian Orthodox Church**, built by Serbian artisans and merchants who settled here after the Turks were driven out. Secluded in a garden, it is only open for High Mass (Sun 10.30–11.45am), when the singing of the liturgy, the clouds of incense and flickering candles create a powerful atmosphere. A block or so south, part of the **medieval wall of Pest** can be seen on the corner of Bástya utca and Veres Pálné utca.

## Along the embankment

The **Belgrád rakpart** (Belgrade Embankment) bore the brunt of the fighting in 1944–45, when the Nazis and the Reds exchanged salvos across the Danube. Like the Várhegy in Buda, postwar clearances exposed historic sites and provided an opportunity to integrate them into the environment – but the magnificent **view** of Buda Palace and Gellért-hegy is hardly matched by two colossal eyesores on the Pest side. While such historic architecture as remains can be seen in a fifteen-minute stroll between the Erzsébet híd and the Lánchíd, **tram #2** enables you to see a longer stretch of the waterfront between Fővám tér and Kossuth tér, periodically interrupted by a tunnel.

Heading north from Fővám tér, the riverscape is dominated by the bold white pylons and cables of the **Erzsébet híd** (Elizabeth Bridge), the only one of the Danube bridges blown up by the Germans in 1945 that was not rebuilt in its original form. In the shadow of the approach road, the grimy facade of the **Belváros Parish Church** (Mon–Sat 9am–12.30pm & 6–7pm, Sun 10am–noon) masks its origins as the oldest church in Pest. Founded in 1046 as the burial place of St Gellért, it was rebuilt as a Gothic hall church, turned into a mosque by the Turks and reconstructed in the eighteenth century. By coming after Latin Mass on Sunday you can see Gothic sedilia and a Muslim *mihrab* (prayer niche) behind the high altar that are otherwise out of bounds; the nave and side chapels are Baroque.

On the square beside the church, a sunken enclosure exposes the remains of **Contra-Aquincum**, a Roman fort that was an outpost of their settlement in Óbuda. More pertinently to modern-day Hungary, the name of the square, **Március 15 tér**, refers to March 15, 1848, when the anti-Habsburg Revolution began, while the adjacent **Petőfi tér** is named after Sándor Petőfi, the poet whose *National Song* – the anthem of 1848 – and romantic death in battle made him a patriotic icon. The **Petőfi statue** has long been a focus for demonstrations as well as patriotic displays – especially on March 15, when it is bedecked with flags and flowers. Behind is the Baroque **Greek Orthodox Church**, the largest church in Hungary, reflecting the importance of the Greek community in the 1790s. Today, services (Sat 6pm, Sun 10am) are in Hungarian, but accompanied by singing in the Orthodox fashion.

North of Petőfi tér is a **24-hour IBUSZ** office, which lies in the shadow of the gigantic **Marriott Hotel**. The concrete esplanade on the Danube side of the hotel is a sterile attempt to recreate the prewar **Duna-korzó** – the most informal of Budapest's promenades, where it was socially acceptable for strangers to approach celebrities. Since the 1960s it has been a **gay cruising** area – not that you'd notice if you're not in the market. The outdoor cafés here are as expensive as the view is wonderful.

*THE VIGADÓ*

Like Váci utca, the Duna-korzó opens onto an elegant square full of stalls and buskers, named after the **Vigadó** concert hall, whose name translates as "having a ball" or "making merry". Inaugurated in 1865, this splendidly Romantic pile by Frigyes Feszl has hosted performances by Liszt, Mahler, Wagner and Von Karajan. Badly damaged in wartime, it didn't reopen until 1980, such was the care taken in recreating its sumptuous decor. Its Large Hall and grand staircase can only be seen by concert-goers, though the foyer is accessible from 1pm, when the box office opens. The modern building on the right occupies the site of the *Angol királynő* (English Queen) hotel, where the likes of the Shah of Persia and Emperor Dom Pedro of Brazil used to stay during the city's *belle époque*.

From Vigadó tér, the Duna-korzó continues past the *Inter-Continental Hotel* (as it has been since 1997) to end in a swirl of traffic at Roosevelt tér, on the edge of József Attila utca and the Lipótváros.

## Deák tér and Erzsébet tér

Three metro lines, two segments of the Kiskörút and several important avenues meet at **Deák tér** and **Erzsébet tér** – two squares that merge into one another (making local addresses extremely confusing) to form a jumping-off point for the V, VI and VII districts. You'll recognize the area by two landmarks: the enormous mustard-coloured **Anker Palace** on the Kiskörút, and the **Lutheran Church** by the metro pavilion on the edge of the Belváros, which regularly hosts free concerts, including Bach's *St John Passion* over the fortnight before Easter. Next door, the **Lutheran Museum** (*Evangélikus Múzeum*; Tues–Sun 10am–6pm; 200Ft) displays a facsimile of Martin Luther's last will and testament, and a copy of the first book printed in Hungarian, a New Testament from 1541. Across the way is a Porsche showroom, occupying what used to be a propaganda bureau for the old German Democratic Republic – one of those jokes played by history that Marx was keen on.

Accessible via the upper sub-level of Deák tér metro, the **Underground Railway Museum** (*Földalattivasút Múzeum*; Tues–Sun 10am–6pm; 70Ft or one BKV ticket) extols the history of Budapest's original metro. Its genesis was a treatise proposing a steam-driven tram network starting with a route along Andrássy út; an underground line was suggested as a fallback in case the overground option was rejected. Completed in under two years, in time for the Millennial Exhibition, it was inaugurated by Emperor Franz Josef and bore his name until 1918. The exhibits include two elegant wooden carriages (one used up until 1973) and period fixtures and posters that enhance the museum's nostalgic appeal. To the north lies a huge building site where the **new national theatre** is under way, beside the **Erzsébet tér bus station**. This is due to be relocated once

the theatre is finished, but depending on how things go it may be the place to board international services or embark on tours of the city for some time yet.

# Lipótváros

The **Lipótváros** (Leopold Town) started to develop in the late eighteenth century, first as a financial centre and later as the seat of government and bureaucracy. Though part of the V district, its ambience is quite different from that of the Belváros, with sombre streets of ponderously Neoclassical buildings interrupted by squares flanked by monumental Art Nouveau or neo-Renaissance piles. Busy with office workers by day, it was dead in the evenings and at weekends till a few years ago, when new restaurants like *Gandhi* and *Lou Lou* brought some life to the area after dark. Another new source of vitality is the Central European University, funded by the Hungarian-born billionaire financier George Soros.

Depending on where you're coming from, it makes sense to start with Roosevelt tér, just inland of the Lánchíd, or St Stephen's Basilica, two minutes' walk from Erzsébet tér. Most of the streets between them lead northwards to Szabadság tér, whence you can head on towards Kossuth tér – though the like-named metro station or tram #2 from the Belgrád rakpart will provide quicker access to parliament.

## Roosevelt tér

At the Pest end of the Lánchíd, **Roosevelt tér** is blitzed by traffic, making it difficult to stand back and get a good view of the **Gresham Palace** on the eastern side of the square. This decrepitly splendid example of Art Nouveau was commissioned by a British insurance company in 1904; high up on the facade is a relief of a man wearing a ruff, representing Sir Thomas Gresham, the originator of Gresham's law, that bad money drives out good. Through the tall wrought-iron gates patterned with peacocks is a T-shaped, glass-roofed arcade with three staircases leading to stained-glass windows of Hungarian heroes designed by the Art Nouveau master Miksa Róth.

Statues of Count Széchenyi and Ferenc Deák stand at opposite ends of the square, the former not far from the **Hungarian Academy of Sciences** (*Magyar Tudományos Akadémia*; no admission), which was founded after Széchenyi pledged a year's income from his estates towards its establishment in 1825 – as depicted in a relief on the wall facing Akadémia utca. The Nobel Prize-winning scientist György Hevesy – discoverer of the element hafnium – was born at Akadémia utca 3, across the road.

While the Lánchíd and the Academy are tangible reminders of Széchenyi's enterprise, Deák's achievement in forging an *Ausgleich* (Compromise) with the Habsburgs was symbolized by the crowning of Emperor Franz Josef as King of Hungary in 1867. Soil from every corner of the nation was piled into a Coronation Hill, atop which he flourished the sword of St Stephen and promised to defend Hungary against all its enemies – a pledge that proved almost as ephemeral as the hill itself. Eighty years later, the square was renamed Roosevelt tér in honour of the late US president – a rare example of Cold War courtesy that was never revoked.

## St Stephen's Basilica and Bajcsy-Zsilinszky út

The restoration of **St Stephen's Basilica** (*Szent István-bazilika*; Tues–Sun 10am–6pm; free) on Bajcsy-Zsilinszky út is proceeding almost as slowly as its construction did. Building began in 1851 under the supervision of József Hild, continued after his death under Miklós Ybl, and was finally completed by Joseph Krauser in 1905. At the inaugural ceremony, Emperor Franz Josef was seen to glance anxiously at the dome, whose collapse during a storm in 1868 had naturally set progress back. At 96m it is exactly the same height as the dome of parliament – both allude to the putative date of the Magyars' arrival in Hungary.

The Basilica is best visited at the weekend as the interior is often closed during the week, though its portal is left open to allow a limited view. However, its glory lies in the carvings, frescoes and chapels, the variegated marble, gilded stucco and bronze mouldings, and the splendid organ above the doorway. In a chapel to the left at the back is the **mummified hand of St Stephen**, Hungary's holiest relic, whose custodian solicits 100Ft coins to illuminate the casket holding the *Szent Jobb* (literally, "holy right"), which is paraded around the church on August 20, the anniversary of Stephen's death. Although the **treasury** (May–Sept Mon–Sat 9am–5pm, Sun 1–5pm; Oct–April daily 10am–6pm; 100 Ft) is nothing special, don't miss the **Panorama Tower** (daily April & May 10am–5pm, June–Aug 10am–7pm, Sept & Oct 10am–6pm; 300Ft), offering a grand **view** of Pest; it's accessible by lift, or by climbing the 302 steps.

While Stephen is revered as the founder and patron saint of Hungary, the pantheon of national heroes includes a niche for Endre Bajcsy-Zsilinszky (1866–1944). Originally a right-winger, he ended up an outspoken critic of Fascism, was arrested in parliament (a statue on Deák tér captures the moment) and shot as the Russians neared Sopron. **Bajcsy-Zsilinszky út** runs northwards to **Nyugati tér**, where the Skála-Metró department store faces **Nyugati Station**, an elegant, iron-beamed terminal built in 1874–77 by the Eiffel Company of Paris that contains probably the ritziest *McDonald's* in the world.

## Szabadság tér and around

For over a century the Lipótváros was dominated by a gigantic barracks where scores of Hungarians were imprisoned or executed, until this symbol of Habsburg tyranny was demolished in 1897 and the site redeveloped as **Szabadság tér** (Liberty Square). Invested with significance from the outset, it became a record of the vicissitudes of modern Hungarian history, where each regime added or removed monuments, according to their political complexion.

In the early years of this century, Hungary's burgeoning prosperity was expressed by two monumental temples to capitalism: the Stock Exchange, whose designer, Ignác Alpár, blended motifs from Greek and Assyrian architecture and crowned it with twin towers resembling Khmer temples; and the **National Bank** across the square, its facade encrusted with reliefs symbolizing honest toil and profit. While the former became the headquarters of Hungarian Television (*Magyar Televizió*, or *MTV*) after the Communists abolished the stock market, the latter still functions as intended and contains a small **Museum of Banknotes** (Thurs 9am–2pm; free), featuring such curiosities as the "Kossuth" banknotes that were issued in America during his exile and notes denominated in billions of forints from the period of hyper-inflation in 1946. Today's capitalists have commissioned the postmodernist International Bank Centre at the southern end of the square.

Turning from money to politics, notice the **statue of General Harry Bandholtz** of the US Army, who intervened with a dogwhip to stop Romanian troops from looting the Hungarian National Museum in 1919. The statue was erected in the 1930s, when Hungary was still smarting from the Treaty of Trianon that gave away two-thirds of its territory and a third of its Magyar population to

Romania, Czechoslovakia and Yugoslavia. This deeply felt injustice inspired several other monuments on Szabadság ter, namely the Monument to Hungarian Grief – featuring a flag at half-mast and a quotation from Lord Rothermere (the proprietor of the *Daily Mail*, whose campaign against Trianon was so appreciated that he was offered the Hungarian crown) – and four statues called North, South, East and West, whose inauguration was attended by 50,000 people.

After 1945 all of these monuments were removed by the Communists, who converted the base of the Monument to Hungarian Grief into the **Soviet Army Memorial**, commemorating the liberation of Budapest from the Nazis. When the Socialists got the boot in 1990, there were calls to remove the Soviet memorial and restore all the old nationalist ones (Bandholtz had already been reinstated prior to President Bush's visit in 1989), but wiser counsels prevailed. There was once even a monument called "Gratitude", erected in 1949 in honour of Stalin's seventieth birthday – but of course nobody has proposed restoring that one.

To compound the irony, the Soviet memorial stands near the former headquarters of the Fascist Arrow Cross, and directly in front of the **US Embassy**, which for fifteen years gave shelter to Cardinal Mindszenty, the Primate of Hungary's Catholic Church. Though the US government was pleased to do so in the aftermath of the 1956 Uprising (when Mindszenty was freed from jail by insurgents), his presence later became an embarrassment to both the US government and the Vatican, which finally persuaded him to leave for Austria in 1971.

Behind the US embassy, the **former Post Office Savings Bank** on Hold utca is a classic example of Hungarian Art Nouveau – its facade patterned like a quilt, with swarms of bees (symbolizing savings) ascending to the polychromatic roof, which is the wildest part of the building. Its architect, Ödön Lechner, once asked why birds shouldn't enjoy his buildings, and amazing roofs are also a feature of his other masterpieces in Budapest, the Applied Arts and Geological museums. The bank's interior is open to the public on only one day a year – European Heritage Day, in September (ask Tourinform for details). Across the street is a wrought-iron **market hall**, one of five opened on a single day in 1896, which continue to serve the centre of Budapest to this day.

At the junction of Hold and Báthory utca, a lantern on a plinth flickers with an **Eternal Flame** commemorating Count Lajos Batthyány, the prime minister of the short-lived republic declared after the 1848 War of Independence, whom the Habsburgs executed on this spot on October 6, 1849. As a staunch patriot – but not a revolutionary – Batthyány is a hero for conservative nationalists, and his monument the destination of annual marches on October 6 or other public holidays.

The refrains and paradoxes of Hungarian history are echoed on **Vértanuk tér** (Martyrs' Square), between Szabadság tér and Kossuth tér, where a **statue of Imre Nagy** – the reform Communist who became prime minister during the 1956 Uprising and was shot in secret afterwards – stands on a footbridge, gazing towards Parliament. With his raincoat, trilby and umbrella hooked over his arm, Nagy cuts an all too human, flawed figure, and is scorned by those who pay their respects to Batthyány.

## Kossuth tér

The Lipótváros reaches its monumental climax at **Kossuth tér**, named after the leader of the 1848 Revolution, Lajos Kossuth, but also featuring a statue of an earlier hero of the struggle for Hungarian independence, Prince Ferenc Rákóczi II. The quote inscribed on the latter's plinth – "The wounds of the noble

Hungarian nation burst open!" – refers to the anti-Habsburg war of 1703–11, but could just as well describe the evening of October 23, 1956, when crowds filled the square, chanting anti-Stalinist slogans at Parliament and calling for the appearance of Nagy – the prelude to the Uprising that night. An eternal flame burns in memory of those who died here on October 25, when ÁVO snipers opened fire on a peaceful crowd that was fraternizing with Soviet tank-crews. Thirty-three years later, the wheel turned full circle as the Republic of Hungary was proclaimed to an enthusiastic crowd from the same balcony that Nagy had spoken from, and the People's Republic of Hungary was officially consigned to the dustbin of history – a watershed symbolized by the removal of the red star from Parliament's dome, and the replacement of Communist emblems by the traditional coat of arms, featuring the double cross of King Stephen.

### PARLIAMENT AND THE MUSEUM OF ETHNOGRAPHY

Budapest's stupendous **Parliament building** (*Országház*) sprawls for 268m along the embankment, a grander version of the Houses of Parliament in London in an Eclectic or neo-Gothic style, scornfully described by the writer Gyula Illyés as "No more than a Turkish bath crossed with a Gothic chapel". Scores of flying buttresses and 88 statues of Hungarian rulers lift one's eyes towards the 96-metre-high cupola that straddles its symmetrical wings; the height of the dome is an allusion to the date of the Magyar conquest of Hungary. Although the nobility had maintained a Diet for centuries, which became a force for change during the Reform Era, it had no permanent home until work began on the building in 1885, and had grown sluggish by the time its grandiose seat was completed in 1902. Under Fascism, opposition MPs learned to fear for their lives, while after the Communists took over debates became a mere echo of decisions taken at Party headquarters on Akadémia utca, till Parliament began to recover its authority in the late 1980s. When not in session, there are **guided tours** in English of its magnificent interior (July–Sept Mon–Fri at 10am & 2pm from Gate XII, Sat & Sun 10am from Gate VI; Oct–June Wed–Fri 10am from Gate XII, Sat & Sun 10am from Gate VI; 750Ft). Tickets are sold from Gate X; come early, as they sell out fast.

Across the road at no. 12 stands a neo-Renaissance pile housing the **Museum of Ethnography** (*Néprajzi Múzeum*; Tues–Sun 10am–6pm; 200Ft, free on Tues), one of the finest museums in Budapest. Its permanent exhibition on **Hungarian folk culture** (on the second floor) is fully captioned in English, and arranged under headings such as "Institutions" and "Peasant Work". Though the beautiful costumes and objects on display are no longer part of everyday life in Hungary, you can still see them in parts of Romania such as Maramures and the Kalotaszeg, which belonged to Hungary before 1920. Temporary exhibitions (on the first and third floors) can cover anything from Bedouin life to Hindu rituals, while over Easter and Christmas the museum puts on **concerts** of Hungarian folk music and dancing, and **craft fairs**.

# The Terézváros

The **Terézváros** (Theresa Town), or VI district, bordered by Bajcsy-Zsilinszky út and Andrássy út, was laid out in the late nineteenth century and heavily influenced by Haussmann's redevelopment of Paris. At that time it was one of the smartest districts in the city – especially around the Városliget – but today much of the area is run-down and deprived. One step towards its revival is the plan for

a "Hungarian Broadway" on Nagymező utca, which cuts across the main thoroughfare, Andrássy út, just below the Oktogon intersection.

## Andrássy út

Running in a perfect straight line for two and a half kilometres up to Hősök tere on the edge of the Városliget, Budapest's longest, grandest avenue was inaugurated in 1884 as the Sugár (Radial) út but soon renamed **Andrássy út** after the statesman Count Gyula Andrássy. The name stayed in popular use throughout the years when this was officially Stalin Avenue (1949–56) or the Avenue of the People's Republic (1957–89), until it was formally restored. With its greystone edifices laden with dryads, its Opera House and coffee houses, the avenue retains something of the style that made it so fashionable in the 1890s, when "Bertie", the Prince of Wales, drove its length in a landau, offering flowers to women as he passed. The initial stretch up to the Oktogon is within walking distance of Erzsébet tér, but if you're going any further it's best to travel from sight to sight by the yellow metro beneath the avenue, or bus #4.

At Andrássy út 3 the **Post Office Museum** (*Posta Múzeum*; Tues–Sun 10am–6pm; 150Ft) occupies a fabulous old apartment complete with parquet floors, marble fireplaces, Venetian mirrors and frescoes by Károly Lotz. Exhibits include a compressed-air mail tube, vintage delivery vehicles, and a display on the inventor Tivadar Puskás, a colleague of Thomas Edison, who set up the world's first switchboard and telephonic news service in Budapest in the early 1900s.

The **State Opera** (*Állami Operaház*) was founded by Ferenc Erkel, the composer of Hungary's national anthem, and occupies a magnificent neo-Renaissance pile built in 1875–84 by Miklós Ybl. It can boast of being directed by Mahler (who complained about the anti-Semitism in Hungary), hosting performances conducted by Otto Klemperer and Antal Doráti, and sheltering hundreds of local residents in its huge cellars during the siege of Budapest. Tours of the grand interior (daily at 3 & 4pm; 100Ft) leave from the side entrances, performances permitting. The productions might be dated, but it's still a cheap night out at the opera – and worth it for the decor alone. In a similar vein, don't miss the **New Theatre** (*Új Színház*) on Paulay Ede utca, off the other side of Andrássy út, whose blue and gold Art Nouveau facade and foyer (by Béla Lajta) have recently been restored to their original splendour.

One block north of the Opera, Andrássy út is crossed by **Nagymező utca** – nicknamed "**Broadway**" after the clubs and theatres on either side. During the interwar years the most famous was the *Arizona* club run by Sándor Rozsnyai and his wife Miss Arizona, which inspired Pal Sándor's film of the same name, starring Hanna Schygulla and Marcello Mastroianni; the Rozsnyais were murdered by the Arrow Cross in 1944. Their club was at Nagymező utca 20, in a building where you'll now find the **Mai Manó Photography Museum** (Mon–Fri 2–6pm) on the first floor.

Further up Andrássy út, two squares with pavement cafés provide a leafy interlude. To the left is Jókai tér, with a large statue of Jókai himself; to the right, past the excellent Writers' Bookshop (*Írók Boltija*) is Liszt Ferenc Tér, although the statue nearest the road is that of the poet Endre Ady; Liszt is set further back, hammering an imaginary keyboard with his vast hands. The square runs on past cafés and restaurants to the Music Academy at the far end that bears Liszt's name. Continuing along Andrássy ut brings you shortly to the intersection with the Nagykörút at the **Oktogon**, an eight-sided square flanked by Eclectic buildings. With 24-hour fast-food chains ensconced in three of them, and trams and taxis running along Nagykörút (the Great Boulevard) through the small hours, the Oktogon never sleeps. During the Horthy period it rejoiced in the name of Mussolini tér, while under the Communists it was called November 7 tér after the date of the Bolshevik revolution.

## BEYOND THE OKTOGON

A minute's walk past the Oktogon on the left-hand side, Andrássy út 60 was once the most terrifying address in Budapest – the **headquarters of the secret police**. Jews and other victims of the Arrow Cross were tortured here during World War II, and the ÁVO (see box below) later used the building for the same purpose. When it was captured by insurgents in 1956, no trace was found of the giant meat-grinder rumoured to have been used to dispose of corpses. The memorial plaques on the exterior were affixed in the 1990s; the one for Cardinal Mindszenty, sponsored by nationalists who mourn the decline of the Hungarian language, contains several grammatical errors.

A little further on the opposite side, the Old Music Academy at no. 67 harbours the **Liszt Memorial Museum** (*Liszt Ferenc Emlékmúzeum*; Mon–Fri 10am–6pm, Sat 9am–5pm; 100Ft), where the composer lived from 1881 until his death in 1886. His glass piano and travelling keyboard are the highlights of an extensive collection of memorabilia and scores. Concerts are performed here by young pianists every Sunday at 11am (free with admission to museum).

Another great Hungarian composer lends his name to the **Kodály körönd**, one of Budapest's most elegant squares, flanked by four neo-Renaissance mansions (one with gilt sgraffiti). At no. 1, the flat where Kodály lived until his death in 1967, is a **Kodály Memorial Museum** (Wed 10am–4pm, Thurs–Sat 10am–6pm, Sun 10am–2pm; 80Ft), preserving his library, salon, dining room and folk-art collection. During World War II the körönd was named Hitler tér, prompting Bartók (who emigrated) to vow that he would not be buried in Hungary so long as anywhere in the country was named after Hitler or Mussolini.

Just beyond the körönd are two fine collections of Asian art, worth seeing if you're in the mood. Left along Bajza utca, the **György Ráth Museum** (Tues–Sun 10am–6pm; Nov–March until 5pm; 100Ft, free Tues), in an Art Nouveau villa at Városligeti fasor 12, is an art historian's bequest of Chinese snuff bottles and painted scrolls, Samurai armour and lacquer combs, while the nearby **Museum of Eastern Asiatic Art** (*Kelet-ázsiai Múzeum*; same hours & prices) at Andrássy út 103 exhibits Tibetan scrolls and Indian sculptures trawled by businessman Ferenc Hopp on five voyages to the Far East. From here, the final stretch of Andrássy út up to Hősök tere is lined by large villas, set back from the avenue.

### THE ÁVO

The **Communist secret police** began as the party's private security section during the Horthy era, when it betrayed Trotskyites to the police to take the heat off their Stalinist comrades. After World War II it became the Államvédelmi Osztály or **ÁVO** (State Security Department), its growing power implicit in a change of name in 1948 – to the State Security Authority or **ÁVH** (though the old acronym stuck). Ex-Nazi torturers were easily persuaded to apply their skills on its behalf, and its network of spies permeated society. So hated was the ÁVO that any members caught during the Uprising were summarily killed, and their mouths stuffed with banknotes (secret policemen earned more than anyone else).

# Hősök tere and around

Laid out in 1896 to mark the thousandth anniversary of the Magyar conquest, **Hősök tere** (Heroes' Square) is appropriately grand. The **Millenniary Monument** at its centre consists of a 36-metre-high column topped by the figure of Archangel Gabriel who, according to legend, appeared to Stephen in a dream and offered him the crown of Hungary. Around the base are Prince Árpád and his chieftains, who led the Magyar tribes into the Carpathian Basin. As a backdrop to this, a semicircular colonnade displays statues of Hungary's most illustrious leaders, from King Stephen to Kossuth. During the brief Republic of Councils in 1919, when Hungary was ruled by revolutionary soviets, the square was decked out in red banners and the column enclosed in a red obelisk. More recently, it was the setting for the ceremonial reburial of Imre Nagy and other murdered leaders of the Uprising (including an empty coffin to represent the "unknown insurgent") on June 16, 1989 – an event which symbolized the dawning of a new era in Hungary. Today it's more likely to be filled with rollerbladers and skateboarders who make use of this huge space on summer evenings.

## Museum of Fine Arts

To the left of the square stands the **Museum of Fine Arts** (*Szépmsvészeti Múzeum*; Tues–Sun 10am–5.30pm; 500Ft), the international equivalent of the Hungarian National Gallery, housed in an imposing Neoclassical pile completed in 1906. Most of the collections have recently been reorganized, making the floor plans shown on the ticket out of date, but as all the exhibits are captioned in English there's no need to buy a catalogue or guide tape. On the lower ground floor there's an excellent art bookshop and the snazziest toilets in Budapest.

Also on the lower ground floor is a small **Egyptian Collection**, chiefly from the Late Period and Greco-Roman eras, whose highlights are four huge painted coffins and a child-sized one, a mummified crocodile, cat and falcon, and a tautly poised bronze of the cat-goddess Bastet. The **Twentieth-Century Art Collection** across the way features few artists you're likely to have heard of but is nonetheless stimulating. Look out for an Expressionist portrait by Oskar Kokoschka and Marc Chagall's *Village in Blue* in the Majakovskij Hall, **Victor Vasarely**'s Op Art view of the Giza pyramids, and cut-glass abstracts by Adolf Luther and Uli Pohl in the **Ionic Pyramid** room.

On the ground floor, most visitors make a beeline for the **Nineteenth-Century Art Collection**, where the drama of **Courbet**'s *Wrestlers* and the delight of **Monet**'s *Plum Trees in Blossom* or **Corot**'s *Remembrance of Coubrou* aren't sustained by weaker efforts by Manet, Cézanne and Toulouse-Lautrec. The hall at the end displays **historical** paintings like *Nero on the Ruins of Rome*, while **Symbolist and Decadent** pictures such as Franz von Stuck's *The Kiss of the Sphinx* adorn the last room. Don't spend long on the Mediterranean antiquities across the foyer, but do check if the **Prints and Drawings Room** has reopened, as it holds works by Raphael, Leonardo, Rembrandt, Rubens, Dürer, Picasso and Chagall.

Upstairs are the **Old Masters**, many once owned by Count Miklós Esterházy. The **Spanish Collection** of seventy works is perhaps the best in the world outside Spain, with seven **El Greco**s (most notably *Christ Stripped of His Garments* and *The Agony in the Garden*) in Room XV, and five Goyas, several Murillos (including *Ecce Homo*) and a Velásquez in Room XVI. The **Italian Collection** is almost as impressive, with **Raphael**'s "Esterházy Madonna" and portraits by

Giorgione and Titian in Room XVIII, Veroneses and Tintorettos in Room XXIII. The **German Collection** contains **Holbein**'s *Dormition of the Virgin*, Dürer's *Young Man* and works by **Altdorfer** and **Cranach** the Elder, while Room XXI exhibits such artists as **Canaletto**, Tiepolo and Kauffmann. Whereas the **Dutch Collection** has such gems as **Van Dyck**'s *St John the Evangelist* (Room B) and a whole room of fantastic **Brueghels**, the single room of **English art** can only muster a dull portrait apiece by Hogarth, Reynolds and Gainsborough.

### The Palace of Arts and bygone statues

On the other side of the square is the **Palace of Arts** (*Műcsarnok*; Tues–Sun 10am–5.30pm; 200Ft, free Tues), a Grecian pile with gilded columns and a mosaic of St Stephen as patron of the arts. Its magnificent facade and foyer are in contrast to the four austere rooms used for **temporary exhibitions** (two or three at a time) or thematic avant-garde shows, which are often first rate. Since the palace was inaugurated in 1896, its steps have been a stage for the state funeral of the painter Munkácsy, the reburial of Nagy, and other public ceremonies.

Before heading into the Városliget, spare a thought for two **bygone statues** on Dózsa György út, the wide avenue running off beside the palace. In Communist times it was here that Party leaders reviewed parades from a grandstand, like their masters on Red Square. The 25-metre-high **statue of Stalin** that towered above it was torn down during the Uprising and dragged to the Nagykörút, where it was hammered into bits for souvenirs. Later, a **statue of Lenin** was erected in its place, which remained until it was taken away "for structural repairs" in 1989. It can now be seen in the Statue Park (p.83).

## The Városliget

The leafy **Városliget** (City Park) starts just behind Hősök tere, where the fairy-tale towers of **Vajdahunyad Castle** rear above an island girdled by an artificial lake that's used for boating in the summer and is transformed into the most splendid ice rink in Europe in winter. Like the park, the castle was created for the Millenniary Anniversary celebrations of 1896, so dramatic effects were the order of the day. This "stone catalogue" of architectural styles incorporates a **replica of the Chapel at Ják** in western Hungary (see p.236) and parts of two Transylvanian castles (one of the originals, the Hunyadi Castle in Romania, gives its name to the building).

The main wing houses an **Agricultural Museum** (Tues–Sat 10am–5pm, Sun 10am–6pm; 100Ft) which is guaranteed to make vegetarians blanch and everybody else yawn, but children usually like the hooded **statue of Anonymous** outside. This nameless chronicler to King Béla is the prime source of information about early medieval Hungary, though the existence of several monarchs of that name during the twelfth and thirteenth centuries makes it hard to date him with any exactitude.

Leaving the island by the causeway at the rear, you're on course for the **Petőfi Csarnok**, an uninspiring-looking "Metropolitan Youth Centre" that regularly hosts good concerts (out of doors in summer), films, parties, and a good flea market at weekends (☎343-4327 for information in English). On the first floor is the Aviation and Space Flight Exhibition (*Repüléstörténeti és arhajózási kiállítás*; April–Nov Tues–Fri 10am–5pm, Sat & Sun 10am–6pm; 150Ft), whose vintage planes and genuine space capsule appeal to kids. The exhibition is part of the

Transport Museum (*Közlekedési Múzeum*; Tues–Sun 10am–6pm; 150Ft), about 100m away on the edge of the park, which contains antique cars, models galore, and mothballed steam trains.

## The Széchenyi Baths, Zoo, Circus and Vidám Park

On the other side of the park's central promenade, Kós Károly sétány, the **Széchenyi Baths** could be mistaken for a palace, so grand is its appearance. Outside is a statue of the geologist Zsigmondy Vilmos, who discovered the thermal spring that feeds its outdoor pool (daily: summer 6am–7pm; winter 6am–4pm; 350Ft) and Turkish baths (Mon–Sat 6am–7pm, Sun 6am–1pm; same ticket). Here you can enjoy the surreal spectacle of people playing chess while immersed up to their chests in steaming water – bring you own set if you wish to join in.

On the other side of Állatkerti körút lie three homes of very different entertainment. Directly across the road is the **Municipal Circus** (*Fővárosi Nagycirkusz*), which traces its origins back to 1783, when the Hetz Theatre played to spectators on what is now Deák tér (performances mid-April to end Aug: Wed 7.30pm, Thurs & Fri 3.30pm & 7.30pm, Sat 10am, 3.30pm & 7.30pm, Sun 10am & 3.30pm; ☎342-8300). To the right is the **Vidám Park**, an old-fashioned, rather shabby amusement park (daily: April–Sept 8am–8pm; Oct–March 10am–6pm; 50–80Ft per ride), known as the "English Park" before the war. It has all the usual rides, only a few of which operate over winter. The musical *Carousel* was adapted from Ferenc Molnár's play *Liliom*, set in and around this fairground, which was (and still is) a popular destination for country people coming to the city.

Down to the left of the circus stands the magnificent entrance of Budapest's **Zoo** (*Állatkert*; daily: April–Sept 9am–6pm; Oct–March 9am–4pm; 200Ft). When opened in 1866, its Art Nouveau pavilions by Károly Kós seemed the last word in zoological architecture. Renovations are currently under way, and there are also plans to restore the botanical strengths of the zoo. The children's corner is signposted "Állatóvoda". Right next to the entrance to the zoo stands one of the grandest restaurants in the city, *Gundel*'s (see p.113).

# The VII district: Erzsébetváros

The **Erzsébetváros** (Elizabeth Town) or VII district, between Andrássy and Rákóczi út, is mainly residential, composed of nineteenth-century buildings whose bullet-scarred facades, adorned with wrought-ironwork, conceal a warren of dwellings and leafy courtyards. It is also traditionally the **Jewish quarter** of the city, which was transformed into a ghetto during the Nazi occupation and almost wiped out in 1944–45, but has miraculously retained its cultural identity. There is no better part of Pest to wander around, savouring the atmosphere and discovering things for yourself. Approaching the area from Deák tér, as most people do, the first landmark is the Dohány utca (Tobacco Street) Synagogue, just off Károly körút.

## The Dohány utca Synagogue and Jewish Museum

The splendid **Dohány utca Synagogue** (*Dohány utcai Zsinagóga*; Mon–Fri 10am–3pm, Sun 10am–1pm; 400Ft) is one of the landmarks of Pest. Europe's largest synagogue and the second biggest in the world after the Temple Emmanuel in New York, it can hold 3000 worshippers of the Neolog community – a Hungarian denomination combining elements of Reform and Orthodox

Judaism. Its design epitomizes the Byzantine–Moorish style that was popular in the 1850s, and the colours of its brickwork (yellow, red and blue) are those of Budapest's coat of arms. During the past decade the synagogue has been restored at a cost of over $40 million, funded by the Hungarian government and the Hungarian-Jewish diaspora, notably the Emmanuel Foundation, fronted by the actor Tony Curtis, born of 1920s emigrants.

Having admired its gilded onion-domed towers and passed through a security check, you can marvel at its **interior** by Frigyes Feszl, the architect of the Vigadó. The layout reflects its Neolog identity, with the *bemah*, or Ark of the Torah, at one end in the Reform fashion, but men and women seated apart, according to Orthodox tradition. The ceiling is decorated with arabesques and Stars of David, the balconies surmounted by gilded arches and the floor inset with eight-pointed stars. On Jewish festivals it is filled to the rafters with Jews from all over Hungary. At other times, the hall is used for **concerts** of classical or klezmer music, as advertised outside.

Alongside is a courtyard full of simple headstones, marking the **mass grave** of 2281 Jews who died here during the winter of 1944, and a remnant of the brick **wall** that enclosed the ghetto, with a plaque commemorating its liberation by the Red Army. Behind looms the cuboid, domed **Heroes' Temple**, erected in honour of the 10,000 Jewish soldiers who died fighting for Hungary during World War I, which serves as an everyday synagogue and is not open to tourists.

To the left of the main entrance and up the stairs is the **Jewish Museum** (*Zsidó Múzeum*). Notice a relief of Tivadar (Theodor) Herzl, the founder of modern Zionism, who was born and taught on this spot. In the foyer is a gravestone from the third century AD – proof that there were Jews in Hungary six hundred years before the Magyars arrived. The first three rooms are devoted to Jewish festivals, with beautifully crafted objects such as Sabbath lamps and Seder bowls, while the final one covers the Holocaust, with chilling photos and examples of anti-Semitic propaganda. Oddly, the museum says nothing about the huge contribution that Jews have made to Hungarian society, in every field from medicine to poetry.

Upon leaving, turn the corner onto Wesselényi utca and enter the **Raoul Wallenberg Memorial Garden**, named after the Swedish diplomat who saved 20,000 Jews by lodging them in safe houses or plucking them from trains bound for Auschwitz. He was last seen alive the day before the Red Army liberated the ghetto; it's thought he was arrested by the Soviets on suspicion of espionage and died in the Gulag. The park's centrepiece is a **Holocaust Memorial** shaped like a weeping willow, each leaf engraved with the names of a family killed by the Nazis. Also within the grounds is the **Goldmark Hall**, named after Károly Goldmark, the composer of the opera *The Queen of Sheba*.

## Around the backstreets

Fanning out behind the synagogue is what was once the **Jewish ghetto**, created by the Nazis in April 1944. As their menfolk had already been conscripted into labour battalions intended to kill them from overwork, the 70,000 inhabitants of the ghetto were largely women, children and old folk, crammed into 162 blocks of flats; over 50,000 of them around Klauzál tér alone.

Directly across the road from the Wallenberg Garden, Rumbach Sebestyén utca leads westwards to the **Synagogue** of the so-called Status Quo or middling-conservative Jews, which is outwardly akin to the Dohány utca synagogue but inwardly conforms to Orthodox prescriptions, and isn't open to the public.

Returning in the same direction as far as Dob utca, you'll see a **monument to Carl Lutz**, the Swiss Consul who began issuing *schutzpässes* to Jews, attesting that they were Swiss or Swedish citizens, as Wallenberg did later. Lutz was a more ambiguous figure, who ceased issuing passes and tried to prevent others from doing so after being threatened by the Gestapo. His monument – a gilded angel swooping down to help a prostrate victim – is known locally as "the figure jumping out of a window".

Just beyond, a portal at no. 16 leads into the **Gozsdu udvar**, an eerie 200-metre-long passageway connecting seven courtyards that runs through to Király utca – a bustling centre of life until the Holocaust. It is now scheduled for redevelopment, which the remaining residents fear will result in it becoming an adjunct to a business centre opening onto Károly körút. However, Romanian claims to the building – due to an unsettled compensation deal between the two countries before the war – may delay any further action, and leave it hanging empty.

The kosher *Frölich* patisserie at Dob utca 22 presages a slew of Jewish businesses on **Kazinczy utca**, the centre of the 3000-strong Orthodox community. There's a butcher's in the yard of no. 41, up to the left of Dob utca, while down to the right is a wig-maker's (no. 36) and a kosher baker (no. 28), opposite the non-kosher Jewish *Carmel* restaurant (no. 31). Near the latter stands the **Orthodox Synagogue**, an Art Nouveau edifice that melds into the curve of the street. Though its interior is off limits to the public, the gate to the right leads into an L-shaped courtyard containing a Jewish school and the *Hanna* kosher restaurant – also accessible via an arcade on Dob utca.

For something quite different, visit the **Hungarian Museum of Electrotechnics** (*Magyar Elektrotechnikai Múzeum*; Tues–Sat 11am–5pm; free) in a former electricity sub-station at Kazinczy utca 21. Its curators demonstrate the world's first dynamo (invented in 1859 by Ányos Jedlik) and other devices in rooms devoted to such topics as the history of light bulbs, or the Hungarian section of the Iron Curtain. Though the current was too weak to kill and the minefields were removed in 1965, patrols kept it inviolate until 1989, when the Hungarians ceased shooting escapees, thereby spelling the end of the Iron Curtain as a whole.

# The VIII district: Józsefváros

The VIII district – otherwise known as **Józsefváros** (Joseph Town) – is separated from the VII district by Rákóczi út, which runs out to Keleti Station, and from the Belváros by Múzeum körút, part of the Kiskörút. Nicknamed "Chicago" during the 1920s and 1930s, this quarter has a mixed reputation – it's the site of prestigious institutions but also something of a red-light district and thieves' hang-out.

**Múzeum körút** resembles Andrássy út in miniature, lined with trees, shops and grandiose piles, as it curves around to meet Kálvin tér. Immediately below the Astoria junction stands the **natural sciences faculty** of the university (*Eötvös Loránd Tudományos-egyetem – ELTE*), whence a group of scientists who worked on the US atomic bombs graduated before World War II, including Edward Teller, the "Father of the Hydrogen Bomb". Further on and across the street, remnants of the medieval walls of Pest can be seen in the courtyards of nos. 17 and 21. The walls gradually disappeared as the city was built up on either side, but fragments remain here and there.

## The Hungarian National Museum, Bródy Sándor utca and Kálvin tér

Like so many other institutions in Budapest, the Hungarian National Museum (*Magyar Nemzeti Múzeum*; May–Sept Tues–Sun 10am–6pm; Oct–April Wed–Sun 10am–4pm; 250Ft) was the brainchild of Count Széchenyi, who donated thousands of prints and manuscripts to form the basis of its collection in 1802. Shortly after it opened, this Neoclassical edifice, designed by Mihály Pollack, became the stage for a famous event in the 1848 Revolution, when Sándor Petőfi first declaimed the *National Song* with its rousing refrain – "Choose! Now is the time! Shall we be slaves or shall we be free?" – from its steps. Ever since, March 15 has been commemorated here with flags and patriotic speeches.

The museum covers the history of Hungary since the Magyar conquest, with an excellent section on the twentieth century. There are captions and explanatory texts in English, as well as info-touch machines giving extra information on exhibits, also in English. Highlights include some beautiful pieces of seventeenth-century jewellery, Renaissance pews from Nyírbátor, and the **Coronation Regalia** – reputedly the very crown, orb and sceptre used by King Stephen. The Hungarian coat of arms faithfully reproduces the distinctive bent cross that surmounts the crown. As the symbol of Hungarian statehood for over a millennium, the regalia has endured endless trials to ensure its safety: buried in Transylvania to hide it from the Habsburgs, it was abducted to Germany by Hungarian Fascists in 1945, and thence taken to the US, where it reposed in Fort Knox until its return home in 1978.

**Bródy Sándor utca**, flanking the museum grounds, seems an unlikely place for a revolution to start – yet this is where the Uprising started, outside the nondescript **Radio Building** (no. 7), when ÁVO guards fired upon students demanding access to the airwaves, an act which turned the hitherto peaceful protests of October 23, 1956, into a revolt against the secret police and other manifestations of Stalinism.

Street fighting was especially fierce around **Kálvin tér**, on the far side of the museum at the junction of Üllői út and the Kiskörút, where insurgents battled tanks rumbling in from the Soviet base on Csepel sziget. It seems almost miraculous that the ornate reading room of the **Szabó Ervin Library** (Mon, Tues & Thurs 9am–9pm, Sat & Sun 9am–1pm; free), on the corner of Baross utca, survived unscathed. Walk up Reviczky utca behind the library and you reach Mikszáth Kálmán tér, an architectural wonderland, recently restored unlike many of the small squares in these backstreets.

### Beyond the Nagykörút

The József körút section of the Nagykörút marks the beginning of the **red-light district**, where topless bars vie with streetwalkers for custom around **Rákóczi**

---

### PROSTITUTION IN BUDAPEST

During the Habsburg and Horthy eras, **prostitution** was licensed – as it still is in Vienna – with fixed prices for each quarter of the city. In 1950, the Communists shut down the licensed brothels and compelled many of the prostitutes to undergo "re-education through labour" at Dunaújváros, but they gradually drifted back into Budapest in the 1960s, just as a wave "amateurs" was emerging to cater for tourists. Today the sex industry is booming, with Budapest currently the porn capital of Europe. Poor eastern Europeans are obviously willing to do more for less, though, fortunately, AIDS hasn't had much impact on the city as yet.

**tér** (see box opposite). The northwest corner of **Köztársaság tér** is slightly more respectable as this is where the **Erkel Theatre** draws crowds of respectable citizens most evenings. Some way northeast of here are **Keleti Station** on **Baross tér**. South of Keleti lies the Kerepesi Cemetery, while heading east are some of the city's major sports venues.

*KEREPESI CEMETERY*

**Kerepesi Cemetery**, between the Ügetőpálya racing track and Fiume út (daily 7am–8pm, but not reliable in winter), is the Père Lachaise of Budapest, where the famous, great and not-so-good are buried. From the main entrance (where maps and guides are available), one stop from Baross tér by tram #23 or #24, it's a ten-minute walk to the **Pantheon of the Working Class Movement**, where former Party leader János Kádár and other Communists are interred. This used to include the tomb of László Rajk – Kádár's predecessor as Minister of the Interior in 1949. Following a so-called "confession" extracted from him by Kádár, Rajk was executed. Though subsequently rehabilitated with full honours, his body was recently removed from the Pantheon by his son László (a leading 1980s dissident).

Further south lie the florid **nineteenth-century mausoleums** of Kossuth, leader of the 1848 Revolution against the Habsburgs; Count Batthyány, whom they executed for rebellion; and Ferenc Deák, who engineered the Compromise between Hungary and the empire. The great diva Lujza Blaha, the "Nation's Nightingale", is also buried in Kerepesi. At the far end, over the wall, you can see an overgrown Jewish cemetery (Mon–Fri & Sun 8.30am–2pm; ring at the gate). Access to this section, which includes some beautiful Art Nouveau tombs amidst the undergrowth, is from Salgotarján utca (two stops on from the main entrance on tram #37). The cemetery was in use until 1958, and contains the graves of politicians, artists and industrialists. Especially worthy of note are the gravestones of Gyula Sváb and Emil Guttman by Béla Lajta.

*NÉPSTADION*

The **Népstadion** district, north across Kerepesi út, is chiefly notable for the 76,000-seat **People's Stadium**, where league championship and international **football** matches, **concerts** by foreign rock stars and events such as the national dog show are held. Stalinist statues of healthy proletarian youth line the court that separates it from the smaller **Kisstadion** and the indoor **Sportcsarnok**, which also hosts occasional concerts. The **Népstadion bus station** completes this concrete ensemble. All are best reached by red metro (from Keleti Station or downtown) or by trolley bus #75 along Dózsa György út from the edge of the Városliget.

# Ferencváros and beyond

The **Ferencváros** (Francis Town), or IX district, was built to house workers in the 1880s and remains the most working-class of Budapest's inner suburbs. During the 1930s and 1940s its population confounded Marxist orthodoxy by voting for extreme right parties that returned the favour by supporting the local football team **FTC** (popularly known as *Fradi*), which became the unofficial team of the opposition under Communism and is nowadays noted for its skinhead following. The club's green and white colours can be seen throughout the district.

Initially, Ferencváros takes its tone from two institutions on **Vámház körút**, the section of the Kiskörút that separates it from the Belváros. The wrought-iron **Great Market Hall** (*Nagycsarnok*; Mon 6am–4pm, Tues–Fri 6am–6pm, Sat 6am–2pm) is as famous for its ambience as for its produce, with tanks of live fish downstairs and stalls festooned with strings of paprika at the back. Mrs Thatcher endeared herself to locals by haggling here during a visit in 1984. Nearer the Danube, the **Economics University** makes a fine sight at night, reflected in the river, and adds to the liveliness of the area by day. Until 1989 the university was named after Karl Marx, a statue of whom remains in its atrium. The building was originally Budapest's main Customs House (*Vámház*) – hence the name of the körút. On the Belváros side of the boulevard, a freestanding section of the **medieval walls** of Pest can be found in the courtyard of no. 16. Everything else of interest in the district is too far away to walk, but readily accessible by public transport.

## Along Üllői út

Don't bother with **Üllői út** unless you have a particular destination in mind, since this grimy thoroughfare of ponderous Neoclassical blocks runs for miles out to the airport. Fortunately, its principal attraction is only one block back from the Ferenc körút metro stop, at the junction with the Nagykörút.

The **Applied Arts Museum** (*Iparművészeti Múzeum*; Tues–Sun 10am–6pm; 200Ft) is worth a visit purely to see the building, one of the finest works of Ödön Lechner, who tried to create a uniquely Hungarian form of architecture emphasizing the Magyars' Ugric roots. Topped by a huge green and yellow dome, its portico adorned with Turkish motifs on a yolk-coloured background, the interior is pure white and reminiscent of Moghul architecture (it was thought at one time that the Magyars came from India). Though largely used for temporary exhibitions, there's a fine permanent show of **Arts and Crafts** since medieval times. A separate section entitled **Style 1900** is devoted to the movement known as Art Nouveau, Jugendstil or Secessionist, with examples ranging from William Morris wallpaper to stained-glass panels by Hungarian masters like József Rippl-Rónai and Miksa Róth. Owing to an enlightened purchasing policy, the museum owns one of the finest collections of this kind in the world, and the exhibition is set to run until the end of 1999.

Beyond the Nagykörút, on the right-hand side of Üllői út, stands the former **Kilián Barracks**, whose garrison was the first to join the 1956 insurgents. As the Uprising spread, it became the headquarters of Colonel Pál Maleter and teams of teenage guerrillas, who sallied forth from the passages surrounding the **Corvin Cinema** on the other side of the road to lob Molotov cocktails at Soviet tanks. Since the fall of Communism they have been honoured by a **statue of a young insurgent** outside the cinema.

## Further out: Népliget, FTC and Új köztemető Cemetery

Two and a half kilometres further out along Üllői út lies the **Népliget** or People's Park, which lacks the allure of the Városliget but does have a **Planetarium**, 100m from Népliget metro. Besides astronomical programmes, it also hosts Laser Shows with music by Michael Jackson, Genesis and others (☎265-0725 for details). For football fans, a bigger draw will be the **FTC Stadium** on the other side of Üllői út, where Hungary's premier team does its stuff (see p.121).

The only other attraction is way out in the X district, 15km from central Pest. The **Új köztemető Cemetery** (daily dawn to dusk; free) is the final resting place of Imre Nagy and 260 others executed for their part in the Uprising, who were buried in unmarked graves in 1958. Any flowers left at **Plot 301** were removed by the police until 1989, when the deceased received a state funeral on Hősök tere. The plot is 2km from the main gates, with minibuses running there every twenty minutes. Near the graves, an ornate wooden gateway and headposts mark a mass grave now designated as a National Pantheon.

Undoubtedly the finest tomb in the adjacent **Jewish cemetery**, where famous rabbis and Ernő Szép, author of *The Smell of Humans*, are buried, is the blue Art Nouveau tomb of Sándor Schmidl, designed by Ödön Lechner and Béla Lajta and presently under reconstruction, though you can peek in at it. Getting to the cemeteries entails a 35-minute ride by tram #37 or #28 from Népszínház utca (near Blaha Lujza tér metro), out past the breweries of Kőbánya, to the main gates on Kozma utca. Tram #37 runs on past the entrance to the Jewish cemetery, 700m up the road.

# Eating and drinking

Hungarians relish **eating and drinking**, and Budapest is great for both. Though Magyar cuisine naturally predominates, you can find everything from Middle Eastern to Japanese food, bagels to Big Macs. The diversity of cuisine is matched by the range of outlets and prices – from de luxe restaurants where a meal costs an average citizen's monthly wage, to backstreet diners that anyone can afford. Many restaurants and bars have live music in the evenings; places where the emphasis is on music and dancing are covered under "Entertainment and sports".

## Coffee houses and patisseries

Daily life in Budapest is still punctuated by the consumption of black coffee drunk from little glasses, though cappuccinos and white coffee are becoming ever more popular. These quintessentially Central European coffee breaks are less prolonged these days than before the war, when Budapest's **coffee houses** (*kávéház*) were social club, home and haven for their respective clientele. Free newspapers were available to the regulars – writers, journalists and lawyers (for whom the cafés were effectively "offices") or posing revolutionaries – with sympathy drinks or credit to those down on their luck. Today's coffee houses and **patisseries** (*cukrászda*) are less romantic but still full of character, whether fabulously opulent, with silver service, or homely and idiosyncratic.

### Buda

**Angelika**, I, Batthyány tér 7. Quiet, old-fashioned place next to the Szent Anna Church. Also does cocktails. Daily 10am–8pm.

**Ruszwurm**, I, Szentháromság tér 7. Diminutive Baroque coffee house near the Mátyás Church; almost impossible to get a seat in summer. Delicious cakes and ices. Daily 10am–8pm.

### Pest

**Astoria Kávéház**, V, Kossuth utca 19. Another famous turn-of-the-century coffee-house-cum-bar, in the *Astoria Hotel*. Daily 7am–11pm.

**Bécsi Kávéház**, V, Apáczai Csere János utca 12. Exquisite cakes and smooth service, on the first floor of the *Inter-Continental Hotel*. Daily 9am–9pm.

**Frölich**, VII, Dob utca 22. A kosher patisserie whose speciality is *flodni*, an apple, walnut and poppy-seed cake. Tues–Thurs 8am–5pm, Fri 8am–2pm, closed Jewish holidays.

**Gerbeaud**, V, Vörösmarty tér 7. A Budapest institution with a gilded salon and terrace. Pricey and full of tourists. The *Kis Gerbeaud* round the corner is a cheaper, stand-up version. Daily 9am–10pm.

**Ibolya**, V, Ferenciek tere. Iced coffee outside in the summer, sticky cakes, *Szalon sör*, beer from the southern Hungarian town of Pécs, and a smoky atmosphere indoors all year round. One of the old-school coffee shops. Daily 6am–10pm.

**Kaffee Károlyi**, V, Károlyi Mihály utca. Popular with the younger generation. Plays music from the seventies and serves good Italian coffee. Daily 9am–9pm.

**Király**, V, Király utca 19. Cosy café above a patisserie serving excellent cakes and ice cream. Daily 10am–midnight.

**Lukács**, VI, Andrássy út 70. One of the old coffee houses, recently restored to its full grandeur. Mon–Fri 8am–8pm, Sat & Sun 10am–8pm.

**Művész**, VI, Andrássy út 29. Another grand old coffee house, serving standard cakes. Most famous for its location, decor and clientele; frequented by writers and fur-hatted old ladies. Daily 8am–midnight.

**Múzeum Cukrászda**, VIII, Múzeum körút 10. Friendly hangout near the National Museum. Fresh pastries arrive early in the morning. Open 24hr.

**New York**, VII, Erzsébet körút 9–11. Wonderful Art Nouveau decor that's worth the price of a cappuccino or a cocktail. The restaurant downstairs is pricey and nothing special. Daily 9am–10pm.

**Szalay**, V, Balassi Bálint utca 4. Old-style cake shop, one of the few remaining in Budapest. Wed–Sun 8am–4pm.

**Zsolnay**, VI, Teréz körút 43. Elegant café on the first floor of the *Béke Radisson Hotel*; excellent cakes. Daily 10am–10pm.

# Fast food, self-service and snack bars

Budapest has taken to **fast food** in a big way, and new fast-food outlets and **snack bars** are opening all the time. A Hungarian peculiarity are the *étkezde* – small, lunch time diners where customers sit at shared tables to eat hearty home-cooked food.

**Falafel**, V, Paulay E. utca 53. Budapest's most popular falafel joint, where you stuff your own pitta breads. Seating upstairs. Mon–Fri 10am–8pm, Sat 10am–6pm.

**Gusto's**, II, Frankel Leo utca (☎316-3970). Near the Buda side of Margit Bridge, a tiny little bar serving the best tiramisu in town. Booking essential. Mon–Sat 10am–11pm.

**Izes Sarok**, V, Bajcsy-Zsilinszky út 1 (on the edge of Erzsébet tér). Good for open sandwiches, coffee and juices. Mon–Thurs 8am–7pm, Fri 8am–5pm.

**Kádár Étkezde**, VII, Klauzál utca 10. Cheap diner in Pest with delicious home cooking; traditional non-kosher Budapest Jewish food on Friday. Mon–Sat 11.30am–3.30pm; closed mid-July to mid-Aug.

**McDonald's**, V, Régiposta utca 2, just off Váci utca; many outlets throughout the city, including in Nyugati Station's magnificently decorated erstwhile restaurant. Daily 8am–9pm.

**Mini Étkezde**, Dob utca 45. A cheap lunchtime diner just off Klauzál tér in the Jewish quarter. Mon–Fri 11.30am–3pm; closed mid-July to mid-Aug.

**New York Bagels**, Bajcsy Zsilinszky út 21 (by the Arany János utca metro station); and at the top of the East-West Centre at Astoria (great views). A chain restaurant with outlets around the city serving New York-style bagels and fillings – and they have English-language papers to read. Mon–Fri 7am–10pm, Sat & Sun 9am–10pm.

**Zöldfaló Salad Bar**, XII, Csaba utca 8 (entrance in Hajnóczy utca). Good falafels and as much salad as you can stuff in. Mon–Fri 10am–6pm.

# Restaurants

The city's **culinary scene** has diversified enormously in recent years, with many new places offering Chinese and Japanese food, mainly to wealthy tourists and nouveau-riche natives. Restaurants with Hungarian gypsy bands tend to be touristy and expensive, and while you can still eat well and cheaply if you know where to look, **rip-offs** abound. Favoured tactics include issuing menus without prices, hiking up the bill or charging exorbitant amounts for the wine. Insist on a proper menu (including prices for drinks) and don't be shy about querying the total. It is also wise to **reserve** a table if you're determined to eat somewhere in particular, though you can usually find an alternative within a couple of blocks. We've included phone numbers where booking is advisable.

As forint **prices** rise continuously, we have classified restaurants in comparative terms. Expect to pay no more than $11 per head for a full meal with drinks in a **cheap** place; around $16 in an **inexpensive** one; $28 in a **moderate** restaurant; $40–55 in an **expensive** one; and upwards of $55 in a **very expensive** establishment. Some of the places listed below are rough-and-ready, others glittering citadels of *haute cuisine* – it's worth checking out both ends of the spectrum. A popular development with foreign residents in the city are the **Sunday brunches** now available in the city, giving you as much as you can eat for a fixed price. The *Marriott Hotel* in the centre of town and *Gundel's* by the Városliget are two of the best.

You can generally reckon that the places further from the Belváros or Várhegy are likely to be cheaper. If they don't have a menu (*étlap*) in German (which most waiters understand) or English, the food and drink vocabulary on pp.29–32 should help when **ordering meals**. Simply pointing to dishes on the menu or neighbouring tables is a bit risky.

## Buda

Despite the plethora of tourist traps in the Vár, **Buda** offers some excellent possibilities if you don't mind a bit of a journey. There is no typical style of Buda restaurant: they range from grand villas in the hills to small friendly locals. The **"historic" restaurants** in the Vár tend to charge exorbitant prices for mediocre food and so are not included in this list.

### VÁRHEGY AND THE VÍZIVÁROS

**Clifton**, I, Batthyány utca 63 (☎212-2494). Cellar restaurant and beer bar with peculiar decor but good food. Inexpensive. Booking is advisable. Open daily 10am–11pm.

**Horváth**, I, Krisztina tér 3. Friendly place just down from Déli Station near the tunnel under the castle, offering traditional cooking. Moderate. Daily noon–11pm.

**Mama Rosa**, I, Ostrom utca 31 (☎201-3456). Reasonable pizza and spaghetti place, with vegetarian options. Recommended mainly for its position close to the Vár and Moszkva tér. Inexpensive. Daily noon–9pm.

**Tabáni Gösser**, I, Attila út 19 (☎375-9482). Unpretentious place in the Tabán serving Hungarian food and Austrian beer. Inexpensive. Daily noon–midnight.

### MOSZKVA TÉR AND FURTHER OUT

**Borpatika**, XI, Bertalan Lajos utca. Drinking upstairs, checked tablecloths and home cooking downstairs. Often full. Inexpensive. Meals available daily until 9pm.

**Da Toto**, XII, Alkotás utca 31. Good pizzas and pasta within striking distance of Déli Station. Inexpensive. Daily 11am–1am.

**Ezüst Ponty**, XII, Németvölgyi út 96 (☎209-1715). Agreeable fish restaurant with tables in the garden in summer; catch tram #59 from Moszkva tér. Moderate. Daily noon–midnight.

**Kikelet Vendéglő**, II, Fillér utca 85 (☎212-5444). Situated up on a hill above Moszkva tér with a view over the city and a lovely shaded garden. Limited menu, but ask what else they have on offer – usually garlic chicken. Bus #49 from Moszkva tér. Moderate. Daily noon–midnight

**Makkhetes**, XII, Németvölgyi út 56. Typical Hungarian restaurant with a typically early closing time. Inexpensive. Daily 11am–10pm.

**Marcello**, XI, Bartók Béla út 40 (☎466-6231). Inconspicuous basement place serving good pizzas, near Móricz Zsigmond körtér. Inexpensive. Mon–Sat noon–10pm.

**Márkus Vendéglő**, II, Lövőház utca 17 (☎212-3153). Friendly Hungarian restaurant near Moszkva tér. Inexpensive. Daily 9am–1am.

**Marxim**, II, Kisrókus utca 23. Popular pizza restaurant, whose decor makes humorous digs at Stalin. Inexpensive. Mon–Fri noon–1am, Sat noon–2am, Sun 6pm–1am.

**Náncsi Néni**, II, Ördögárok út 80 (☎397-2742). Popular garden restaurant in the leafy Hűvösvölgy, ten minutes' walk from the terminus of bus #56. Live music and excellent food. Booking essential. Moderate to expensive. Mon–Sat noon–9pm, Sun noon–5pm.

**Orient Express**, I, Vérmező. In an old railway carriage on the edge of the park just opposite Déli Station. Hungarian and international dishes. Moderate. Daily 11am–1am.

**Söröző a Szent Jupáthoz**, II, Retek utca 16. Hungarian dishes served with the emphasis on quantity not quality. Good for the starving. Cheap. Open 24 hours a day.

**Udvarház**, III, Harmashatárhegy (☎388-8780). At the top of Harmashatár hill, a cool place to dine on hot summer days with the city shimmering in the distance. Bus #65 from Kolosy tér in Óbuda and then a long walk, or taxi right up. Expensive. Tues–Sun 11am–11pm.

*ÓBUDA*

**Gigler**, III, Föld utca 50/c. One of the few remaining old-style Óbuda restaurants frequented by locals. A family-run place with good wine from the barrel. Inexpensive. Tues–Sat noon–10pm, Sun noon–4pm.

**Kerék**, III, Bécsi út 103 (☎250-4261). A small place serving traditional Hungarian food with accompaniment provided by a couple of old musicians. Outside seating in summer. Moderate. Daily noon–11.30pm.

**Kisbuda Gyöngye**, III, Kenyeres utca 34 (☎368-6402). Good food in finely decorated turn-of-the-century-style surroundings. Booking essential. Expensive. Daily noon–midnight.

## Pest

There's a much wider range of places in **Pest**, particularly within the Nagykörút, where rip-offs await the unwary. It's also possible to find some excellent restaurants, especially if you're prepared to do a bit of exploring. Most of the following are easily accessible from downtown Pest, though you should reserve a table to avoid a wasted journey.

*WITHIN THE NAGYKÖRÚT*

**Articsóka**, VI, Zichy Jenő utca 17 (☎302-7757). Roof-terrace café and restaurant with a Mediterranean atmosphere. Good for vegetarians. Inexpensive. Daily 8am–10pm.

**Berlini Sörkatakomba** ("Beer Catacombs"), IX, Ráday utca 9 (☎217-6757). Smoky cellar restaurant by the Kálvin tér metro. Genial atmosphere; popular with the younger generation. Inexpensive. Daily 11am–4am.

**Café Kör**, V, Sas utca 12 (☎311-0053). Popular place near the basilica. Good grilled meats and salads. Best to book. Moderate. Mon–Sat 10am–10pm.

**Csarnok**, V, Hold utca 11, one block east of Szabadság tér (☎269-4906). Good, down-to-earth Hungarian restaurant specializing in mutton, lamb and bone-marrow dishes. Inexpensive. Mon–Fri 9am–11pm.

**Csendes**, V, Ferenczy István utca 7 (☎267-0218). Transylvanian restaurant near Astoria. Cheerful Hungarian atmosphere with specialities like *tócsni* – potato pancake. Inexpensive. Mon–Sat noon–10pm.

**Fatál** ("Wooden Dish"), V, Váci utca 67 (☎266-2607). Gargantuan servings, but avoid the "vegetable feast", which is mostly batter. Entrance is on Pintér utca, which runs between Váci utca and the *Fregatt* pub on Molnár utca. Inexpensive. Daily 11.30am–2am.

**Fészek Klub**, on the corner of Dob and Kertész utca (☎322-6043). A lovely courtyard for summer dining, and interesting decor, though the food and service can be a letdown. As an artists' club it charges 50Ft at the door (unless you book in advance). Moderate. Daily noon–2am.

**Gandhi**, V, Vigyázó Ferenc utca 4 (☎269-4944). New vegetarian restaurant with wide range of dishes and salads, plus 40 types of tea. Inexpensive. Daily noon–11pm.

**Govinda**, V, Belgrád rakpart 18. Hare Krishna vegetarian restaurant which does good set meals, accompanied by the whiff of soporific incense. Inexpensive. Tues–Sun noon–9pm.

**Greens**, VII, Dob utca 3 (☎352-8515). Cellar restaurant offering a range of vegetable stews. Inexpensive. Daily 11am–2am daily.

**King's Hotel**, VII, Nagydiófa utca 25–27 (☎352-7675). Mehadrin kosher food, in a popular lunch spot where kosher food is hard to find. Daily noon–9.30pm.

**Marquis de Salade**, VI, Hajós utca 43 (☎302-4086). Arany János utca metro, just off Bajcsy Zsilinszky út. Big portions of food from all round the world. Recently enlarged with big basement decorated with beautiful Persian carpets. Moderate. Daily 11am–midnight.

**Mérleg**, V, Mérleg utca 6 (☎317-5910). Small, popular place serving simple Hungarian food near the Lánchíd. Moderate. Daily 8am–11pm.

**Múzeum Kávéház**, VIII, Múzeum körút 12 (☎267-0375). Excellent food in grand setting with piano music in the background. Near Astoria metro. Booking essential. Expensive. Mon–Sat 10am–1am.

**Semiramis**, V, Alkotmány utca 20. Syrian place offering good lunchtime fare such as chicken with spinach and kofta, at tables covered with plastic cloths. Inexpensive. Mon–Sat noon–9pm.

**Via Luna**, V, Nagysándor József utca 1 (☎312-8058). Popular Italian restaurant in the heart of central Pest. Good filling salads. Moderate. Daily noon–11.30pm.

### BEYOND THE NAGYKÖRÚT

**Bagolyvár**, XIV, Állatkerti körút 20 (☎321-3550). Sister to the *Gundel* (see below), but offering traditional Hungarian family-style cooking at far lower prices. Moderate. Daily noon–11pm.

**Chez Daniel**, VI, Szív utca 32 (☎302-4039). Excellent French restaurant, the best in town, run by an idiosyncratic master chef. Booking recommended. Moderate to expensive. Daily noon–10.30pm.

**Great Wall (Nagy Fal)**, XIV, Ajtósi Dürer utca 1 (☎343-8895). Good Chinese restaurant on the southeastern corner of the Városliget. Moderate. Daily 11.30am–11.30pm.

**Gundel**, XIV, Állatkerti körút 2, near the zoo in the Városliget (☎321-3550). Budapest's most famous restaurant offers plush surroundings and a fantastically expensive menu. Bookings and smart dress required. Expensive. Daily noon–4pm & 7pm–midnight.

**Jorgosz Taverna**, VI, Csengery utca 24 (☎351-7725). Lively Greek place near Oktogon with bouzouki music in the evenings. Or try the sister restaurant next door serving Spanish food. Moderate. Daily noon–midnight.

**Krónikás**, XIII, Tátra utca 2 (☎269-5048). Caters for people coming out of the nearby Vígszínház theatre. Very good food. Moderate. Daily noon–midnight.

**Robinson**, XIV, Városligeti-tó sziget (☎343-3776). In the Városliget, behind the Museum of Fine Arts, beside the lake. This top-flight international restaurant offers superb food and service. Very expensive. Daily noon–midnight on the terrace; noon–3pm & 7pm–midnight indoors.

# Bars, wine bars and beer halls

It's hard to draw a firm line between places to eat and places to **drink** in Budapest, since some patisseries double as cocktail bars, and restaurants as beer halls (or vice versa), while the provision of live music or pool tables blurs the distinction between drinking spots and clubs. The scene is constantly changing as places open or close, revamp their image, become trendy or the pits.

Insofar as you can generalize, most places that style themselves "drinkbars" mainly serve cocktails. The majority of *borozó* or **wine bars** are nothing like their counterparts in the West, being mainly working men's watering holes, offering such humble snacks as *zsíros kenyér* (bread and pork dripping with onion and paprika). Conversely, **beer halls** (*söröz*) are often quite upmarket, striving to resemble an English pub or a German *bierkeller*, and serving full meals. The addition of *pince* to the name of an outlet for wine (*bor*) or beer (*sör*) signifies that it is in a cellar; many of the new places stink of mould until the crowds arrive. Most open around lunchtime and stay open until after midnight, unless otherwise stated. The following list is not exhaustive, since it excludes various **club-type places** (covered under "Entertainment and sports").

## Buda

**Bambi**, I, Frankel Leó utca 2–4. One of the few surviving socialist-realist bars, with red plastic covered seats and stern waitresses, serving breakfast, omelettes, snack lunches, cakes, and alcohol all day long. Mon–Fri 7am–9pm, Sat & Sun 9am–8pm.

**Belga Söröző**, I, Bem rakpart 12. Essentially a restaurant, but the emphasis is definitely on Belgian beer. Daily noon–11pm.

**Kecskeméti Borozó**, II, Széna tér. By Moszkva tér on the corner of Retek utca. Smoky, sweaty, crowded stand-up wine bar. A notice on the wall says: "We do not serve drunks", but you will have to shut your eyes to believe that one. However, they do serve that staple Hungarian bar fare, *zsíros kenyér*, bread with lard, paprika and onions. Mon–Sat 9am–11pm.

**Kisposta**, XII, Krisztina körút 6. The "Little Post Office" has preserved its sixties interior and unique atmosphere, with a collection of drunks and assorted others dancing to the sounds of Tibor and his drum machine playing Hungarian classics and foreign golden oldies you might struggle to recognize.

**Libella**, XI, Budafoki út 7. Small friendly bar near *Gellért Hotel* with chess and draughts.

**Miniatűr Eszpresszó**, II, Rózsahegy utca 1. Small bohemian bar with red velvet furnishings and piano music after 9pm. If you win approval from the woman who presides over the place, you get to sit in the inner room by the pianist. Mon–Sat 7pm–3am.

**Móri Borozó**, I, Fiáth János utca 16, just up from Moszkva tér, opposite the extraordinary "Swan House". Cheap and cheerful neighbourhood wine bar attracting a young crowd. Darts and bar billiards in the room at the far end. June–Aug daily 4–11pm; Sept–May Mon–Sat 2–11pm, Sun 2–9pm.

**Park Café**, XI, Kosztolányi Dezső tér 2. Trendy music bar in the middle of the park where the city's bright young things go to be seen. Daily noon till late.

**Teázó**, I, Attila út 27. Quiet, spacious place specializing in tea. Daily 11am–1am.

**Vinceller Borozó**, I, Fő utca 71. Agreeable wine cellar near the Király Baths. Daily 8am–10pm.

## Pest

**Café Mediterrán**, VI, Liszt Ferenc tér 11. Red walls, cane furniture and a relaxed atmosphere. English bitter on tap. Daily 10am–2pm.

**Café Pardon**, VI, Szondi utca 11. Fun for a post-dinner drink. If they have the ingredients, they'll mix you a cocktail, otherwise it's Czech beer. Live piano music. Open till 1 or 2am.

**Captain Cook**, VI, Bajcsy-Zsilinszky út 19/A. Popular café/pub with seats outside in summer. Daily till 2am.

**Crazy Café**, VI, Jókai utca 30. Lively place with a huge variety of beer and a karaoke machine. Daily till 1am.

**Paris-Texas**, IX, Ráday utca 22. Stylish café with good atmosphere near Kalvin tér. Daily 9am–dawn.

**Portside**, VII, Dohány utca 7. Large cellar offering beer and good food. Pool tables on the left of the entrance. Open till 4am at weekends.

**Sixtusi Kápolna**, VII, Nagydiófa utca 24. The "Sistine Chapel" is rather like the brown bars of Amsterdam, attracting a friendly crowd of non-business expats. Mon–Sat 6pm–1am.

**Talk-Talk Café**, V, Magyar utca 12–14. Bar with good atmosphere just behind the *Astoria Hotel*, though marred by slow service. Daily till 1am.

# Entertainment and sports

The range of **entertainment** available in Budapest includes everything from nightclubbing to opera-going, jazz to folk dancing and Formula One racing to foot-

## FESTIVALS AND EVENTS: THE BUDAPEST YEAR

The highlights of Budapest's cultural calendar are the **Spring Festival** in late March and the **Autumn Festival** from late September to late October, though these are less impressive than in the past, owing to cuts in funding. Both offer music, ballet and drama (including star acts from abroad). The ten-day **Budapest Film Festival** is usually in February, though its future is not certain at present. The **BudaFest opera festival** is held in the opera house during the summer recess.

On **March 15** Budapest decks itself out in flags and cockades in honour of the 1848 Revolution, and there are patriotic gatherings at the Petőfi statue and the National Museum. **Easter** is marked by church services and outbreaks of *locsolkodás* (splashing) – when men and boys visit their female friends to spray them with cologne and receive a painted egg or pocket money in return. The fall of Communism has put paid to grandiose parades on April 4 and May 1, but May Day remains a national holiday.

While many theatres close down for the season, there are plenty of concerts and two major sporting events over the **summer**. **St Stephen's Day** (August 20), honouring the founder of the Hungarian state, occasions day-long celebrations at the Basilica (see p.95), a craft fair and folk dancing at different venues in the Vár, and a spectacular display of fireworks at 9pm. Over a million people line the embankments to watch the latter fired off from Gellért-hegy, so prime vantage points like Erzsébet and Szabadság bridges are taken by 8pm, and the traffic jam that follows the display is equally mind-blowing. If you want to eat out that night, you should book a place well in advance, as all the restaurants are packed.

As the Autumn Festival winds down and trees in the parks turn russet and gold, it is nowadays permitted to honour the **anniversary of the 1956 Uprising**. October 23 was a taboo anniversary for decades, then suddenly accorded cathartic, televised recognition; however, interest now seems to be waning among the majority of Hungarians who are too young to have experienced the Uprising, while others find their memories too painful to want to reawaken them. On **December 6**, children hang up Christmas boots for "little Jesus" to fill, and people prepare for the Christmas Eve feast of jellied carp or turkey. Festivities build up towards **New Year's Eve**, when revellers gather on the Nagykörút, engaging in trumpet battles at the junction with Rákóczi út.

ball. To find out **what's on**, check out *Where Budapest*, a free magazine distributed in hotels; the listings in *Budapest Week* and *Budapest Sun*; or the Hungarian-language weekly *Pesti Est* (available free in cinemas) for its English-language film section. Another source of information is the monthly *Koncert Kalendárium* (free from Tourinform, and the National Philharmonic Ticket office at Mérleg utca 10), which lists classical music performances, plus **booking agencies**. A number of festivals and events which occur annually are described in the box on p.115.

# Rock concerts, clubs and discos

Budapest attracts every Hungarian band worth its amplifiers and a growing roll-call of international stars, making it the best place for **rock concerts** in Hungary. Major foreign acts appear at the vast Népstadion, the smaller Kisstadion or the nearby Budapest Sportcsarnok, and their appearances are well publicized in the media. Don't get too excited by flyposters advertising Michael Jackson or the Cure, however, as these usually refer to light shows or DJs at clubs and discos. Posters around town – particularly around Deák tér, Ferenciek tere and the Astoria underpass – also publicize concerts by Hungarian bands. Prices range from 1000Ft up to as much as 5000Ft for international superstars. For an authentically grim Magyar rock-opera, you can't beat *István a király* (Stephen the King) or the new *Attila Sword of God*, both of which are about the early heroes of the Hungarian nation. **Tickets** for most performances are available from Music Mix at V, Váci utca 33 (☎338-2237), and Publika at VII, Károly körút 9 (☎322-2010).

Some **clubs** and **discos** in the city are still run under the aegis of universities, though there are an increasing number of private ventures, some of which have a fairly strict entrance policy (entry is 200–1000Ft). Clubbers are fickle, so places open and close, lose their credibility or acquire cachet – most of the venues we've listed are located in Pest. The gay and jazz scenes are covered separately (see opposite and p.118).

### Live music venues

Local bands most often perform at the **Petőfi Csarnok**, a big youth centre near the Városliget (see p.102). The following cultural centres are also popular venues, as are many of the clubs and discos listed in the next section.

**Almássy téri Szabadidő Központ**, VII, Almássy tér 6 (☎267-8709). One of the city's main district cultural centres, located in downtown Pest.

**Fonó Budai Zeneház**, XI, Sztregova utca 3 (☎206-5300). Large, lively concert venue out past Móricz Zsigmond körtér. Tram #18 or #47.

**Fővárosi Művelődési Ház**, XI, Fehérvári út 47 (☎203-3868). Cultural centre in Buda, staging several rock concerts each month.

**I Kerületi Művelődesi Ház**, I, Bem rakpart 6 (☎201-0324). The I district cultural centre, between the Lánchíd and the *Hotel Victoria*.

### Clubs and discos

**E-Klub**, X, Népliget (at the Planetarium). Formerly in block E of the Technical University, this once-wild cattle market for engineering students has been exiled to outer Pest. Today a more mixed crowd packs in for the two discos on different floors and beer galore. Fri & Sat 8pm–5am. Live rock music on Fridays.

**E-Play**, VI, Teréz körút 55. Housed in the top of the magnificent Nyugati Station, this is a newly decked-out techno haunt for the fast and flashy. Daily 8pm–dawn.

**Franklin Trocadero Café**, V, Szent István körút 15. Excellent Latin music and dancing just up from Nyugati Station. Daily 9pm–5am.

**Közgáz DC**, IX, Fővám tér 8 (☎215-4373). Massive, sweaty party scene at the Economics University, with a live rock band and nonstop disco, two films and a karaoke show, plus a "tea house", ice cream bar and lots of beer. Fri 8.30pm–3am.

**Made Inn**, VI, Andrássy út 112 (☎111-3437). Ultra-trendy disco and hangout for jetsetters dressed (or barely dressed) in the flashiest MTV fashions. You can't miss the gleaming sports cars out front. Outdoor patio packed in summer; live bands most Fridays and a Greek band most Sundays. Good Greek food. Cover charge 500Ft. Daily noon–3am.

**Nincs Pardon**, VIII, Almássy tér 11. Bar/nightclub with a tiny dance floor and variable music, usually not techno; open sandwiches at the bar. Packed on Saturdays. Open daily.

**Petőfi Csarnok**, XIV, Zichy M. út 14 (☎342-4327). Huge purpose-built youth centre near the back of the Városliget, hosting concerts by local and big-name foreign bands, contemporary dance performances, Greek folk dancing (Sun in summer), the Madonna Club, the Pet Shop Boys Club and other band-specific DJ nights. Exhibitions are also held here, and there's a flea market on Saturday and Sunday mornings. Ring the above number for more details in English.

**Piaf**, VI, Nagymező utca 20. This fashionable bar on "Broadway" charges 300Ft to enter – unless you come with a regular. Basically a room and a cellar graced by the odd film star and lots of wannabes, with occasional jazz or rock sets. Daily from 10pm until well after dawn.

**SOTE Club**, IX, Nagyvárad tér 4 (in the Semmelweiss Orvosi Egyetem near Nagyvárad tér metro stop). A heaving disco plus sideshows including jazz gigs, rock concerts and movies.

**Süss fel nap**, on the corner of Honvéd utca and Szent István körút. Big club with mixed music and a young crowd. Daily 8pm–4am.

**Vox**, II, Márcibányi tér 5/a. Live acts and funky music in this popular dive on the Buda side. Daily 8pm–3am.

# Gay Budapest

Budapest's **gay scene** has taken wing in recent years, with new, overtly gay clubs replacing the old, covert meeting places, and the appearance of a trilingual month-ly listings magazine, *Mások* ("Outsiders"). However, gays must still tread warily and lesbians even more so. The Magyar euphemism for gay is *meleg* – "warm". Aside from places listed below, the Király Baths especially, and less so the Rudas Baths, as well as the sunbathing terrace of Palatinus pool on Margit sziget, are gay hangouts for men only. Restaurants with a particularly gay clientele include *Club 93* (V, Vas utca 2; 11am–midnight), a cheap pizzeria near Astoria that is pop-ular after 8pm, and *Kis Sün* (VI, Podmaniczky utca 29; 11am–11pm) near Nyugati Station. In this male-dominated town the *Angyál* and *Capella* are the best bars for women.

**Angyál Bár**, VII, Szövetség utca 33. Budapest's premier gay club. Looks like an airport lounge, but has an interesting crowd. Men-only on Saturdays, but popular with women on Fridays and Sundays.

**Art 44**, XI, Halmi utca 44. Out beyond Móricz Zsigmond körtér, this new place goes gay after midnight, when the door is locked and you have to ring to get in.

**Capella**, V, Belgrád rakpart 23. Drag queens, jungle music and lots of kitsch. Just the place for Friday night on the town. A very mixed joint, with men, women and a lot of straights too.

**Darling**, V, Szép utca 1. A beer-house and gallery that gets "warmer" after 9pm and stays open till late.

**Mystery Bar-klub**, V, Nagysándor József utca 3 (☎312-1436). Very small bar near the Arany József metro, for talking rather than dancing – there's no disco. If the door's locked you might have to wait to be let in. Mon–Sat 9pm–4am.

**No Limit**, V, Semmelweiss utca. Small bar with a mirror on the ceiling to make it appear bigger. No dancing. Fairly expensive drinks with names like "Boy Cocktail".

## Jazz

Although jazz is currently fashionable in Budapest, regular venues are few in number. Some bands appear at local cultural centres, others in some of the places listed above under "Clubs and discos", such as the Petőfi Csarnok.

**Hades Jazztaurant**, VI, Vörösmarty utca 31 (☎352-1503). Pleasant bar/restaurant with live music. Open till 2am (midnight on Sun).

**Jazz Café**, V, Balassi Bálint utca 25 (☎132-4377). Small underground club with blue neon lighting. One of the few places in town with live jazz every night from 8pm. Mon–Fri 3pm–3am, Sat & Sun 6pm–3am.

**Jazz Fél Tíz**, VIII, Baross utca 30. Slightly lugubrious interior and wideboys hanging around at the door, but the music, which starts at 9.30pm, is often good – including blues and blue grass.

**Kosztolányi Művelődési Ház**, IX, Török Pál utca 3. The world-famous Benkó Dixieland Band plays here every Wednesday evening when not touring abroad.

**Közgáz Jazz Klub**, IX, Kinizsi utca 2–4 (☎217-5110). Belongs to the Economics University and favours progressive jazz. Local ethno-jazz wizard Mihály Dresch and his quartet play here to a crowd of loyal fans most Fridays from 8pm. Ring before going, though, as days and times tend to vary.

## Folk music and táncház

Hungarian **folk music and dancing** underwent a revival in the 1970s, drawing inspiration from communities in Transylvania, regarded as pure wellsprings of Magyar culture. Enthusiasts formed "dance houses" or **táncház** to revive traditional instruments and dances, and get people involved. Visitors are welcome to attend the weekly gatherings (60–100Ft admission) and learn the steps. Muzsikás, Téka and Kalamajka groups play sounds from Transylvania, while other groups are inspired by South Slav music from Serbia, Croatia and Bulgaria.

Details of events are available from *Where Budapest*, *Budapest Sun* and *Budapest Week*. Bear in mind that many cultural centres close for summer, so check before you go.

**Almássy téri Szabadidő Központ**, VII, Almássy tér 6, north of Blaha Lujza tér (☎267-8709). The Rece Fice ensemble plays southern Slavic, Bulgarian and Greek music every Monday at 6pm, and there often big Hungarian or gypsy (Roma) gatherings too.

**Belvárosi Művelődési Ház**, V, Molnár utca 9 (☎317-5928). The Kalamajka ensemble plays to a packed dance floor on Saturday nights at this downtown Pest cultural centre. Instruction from 7pm. There is also music in the bar upstairs, and as the evening rolls on a jamming session often develops.

**Fonó Budai Zeneház**, XI, Sztregova utca 3 (☎206-5300). Large, lively concert venue out past Móricz Zsigmond körter. Transylvanian folk musicians play every Wednesday evening. Tram #18 or #47.

**Gyökér Club**, VI, Eötvös utca 46, near Nyugati Station (entrance round the corner in Szob utca). Dancing on Monday and Friday; pleasant atmosphere and good restaurant, but watch out for the watered-down wine.

**Marcibányi téri Szabadidő Központ**, II, Marcibányi tér 5/A. Muzsikás plays every Thursday night from 8pm. Not a dance house as such – the group just plays and people sit round in a very informal atmosphere.

**I Kerületi Művelődési Ház**, I, Bem rakpart 6 (☎201-0324). Hosts the Téka ensemble every Friday. Children 5–6pm, teenagers 6–7pm and adults from 7pm.

# Opera, ballet and classical music

**Opera** is highly esteemed in Hungary, a country whose composers and writers have created such works as *Bánk Bán, László Hunyadi, The Queen of Sheba* and *Blood Wedding*. Most productions are in Hungarian, a custom introduced by Mahler when he was director of the State Opera House in Budapest; fans prefer their opera "old style", with lavish sets and costumes, and they interrupt with ovations after particularly bravura passages. Operas by Mozart, Verdi, Puccini, Wagner and national composers are staged throughout the year, while several new productions are premiered during the Spring and Autumn festivals, when you can also catch performances by the State Opera **ballet** and visiting foreign companies.

The city excels in its variety of **classical music** performances, although pre-Baroque stuff is poorly represented. There are several concerts every night of the year, especially during the two festivals. Look out for performances by the Liszt Ferenc Chamber Orchestra and the Budapest Festival Orchestra, pianists Zoltán Kócsis and Desző Ránki, and cellist Miklós Perényi. The State Symphony Orchestra is conducted by Kobayashi Ken-Ichiro of Japan, who fills the house with his racing tempos and populist programmes. Over summer, smaller concerts take place outdoors on Margit sziget, and in historic buildings such as the **Mátyás Church**. Choral or organ recitals are also held at the church on Fridays and Saturdays between June and September (from 8pm), and less frequently the rest of the year. Bear in mind that many city venues – the opera, theatre and concert halls – **close for the summer** at the end of May, reopening in mid-September. There is a summer season of concerts at Martonvásár (see p.161) and Vácrátót, within commuting distance of Budapest. The big yellow church in central Pest, the **Deák téri Evangélikus templom**, has regular concerts including Bach Passions before Easter; information for these is posted by the church's entrance. **St Stephen's Basilica** and the Kálvín tér church in central Pest also host occasional concerts; consult Tourinform for details.

Weekly and monthly listings magazines cover all musical events, and **information** can also be obtained from Tourinform and the main ticket offices. **Tickets** for the Opera, Operetta and Erkel theatres are available from the Central Box Office at VI, Andrássy út 18 (*Központi Jegyiroda*; Mon–Thurs 9am–6pm, Fri 9am–5pm; ☎312-0000), the Filharmónia at V, Mérleg utca 10 (Mon–Fri 10am–6pm; ☎118-0281), and the Vigadó Jegyiroda at V, Vörösmarty tér 1 (Mon–Fri 9am–7pm, Sat & Sun 10am–3pm; ☎327-4322). The Opera House has its own box office on the left of the building for Opera and Erkel events (from 11am until performances start, lunch break 1.45–2.30pm, closed Mon). It also sells tickets for outdoor performances in and around Budapest (Martonvásár, Vácrátót, etc). Music Mix at V, Váci utca 33 (☎338-2237), and Publika at VII, Károly körút 9 (☎322-2010), also sell tickets to most classical concerts, as well as other events such as fashion shows and pop concerts.

**Budapest Kongresszusi Központ** (Budapest Convention Centre), XII, Jagelló út 1–3 (☎209-1990). Modern and uninspiring concert hall behind the *Novotel*, but a venue for big concerts.

**Erkel Színház**, VIII, Köztársaság tér 30 (☎333-0540). A modern venue for operas, ballet and musicals, on the edge of the red-light district near Keleti Station.

**Liszt Ferenc Zeneakadémia** (Music Academy), VI, Liszt Ferenc tér 8 (☎342-0179). Nightly concerts and recitals in the magnificent *Nagyterem* (Great Hall) or the smaller *Kisterem*. The former is usually shut during summer, as it gets too hot.

**Magyar Állami Operaház** (Hungarian State Opera), VI, Andrássy út 22 (☎302-4290). Budapest's grandest venue, with gilded frescoes and three-tonne chandeliers – a place to dress up for. Box office (Tues–Sat 11am–7pm, Sun 10am–1pm & 4–7pm) is on Dalszínház utca, round the corner; returns also sold at Andrássy út 18. Prices rise for performances on Friday and Saturday.

**Operetta Színház**, VI, Nagymező utca 17 (☎332-0535). Stages classical Hungarian operettas and modern musicals; located on "Broadway", a few blocks from the opera house.

**Vigadó**, V, Vigadó tér 1 (☎327-4322). Another fabulously decorated hall, though the acoustics are inferior. Box office opens 1pm.

## Theatre

If you're undeterred by the language barrier, **theatre** can be a rewarding experience, though mainstream Hungarian works tend to be rather melodramatic and unsubtle. The **Katona József Company** won plaudits at the Old Vic in London and the Odéon in Paris, and remains the most exciting company in town. Their permanent repertory includes *The Government Inspector*, *Ubu Roi* and *Twelfth Night*. The Katona Theatre is at Petőfi Sándor utca 6, next to the Párizsi Udvar. Its box office opens at 2pm, while tickets for any unoccupied seats are sold just before the show starts at 7pm. There is also a growing number of **alternative theatre** venues around town that do not necessarily rely on language. One of the best is the Mozgó haz (Moving House) group, who combine music and movement in very inventive ways. They won the top award at the International Theatre Festival in Sarajevo in 1998, and appear in different venues in town. Check out the **MU Színház**, XI, Körössy József utca 17; **RS9** at VII, Rumbach Sebestyén utca 9; **Szkéné Színház**, XI, Műegyetem rakpart 3; **Studio K**, IX, Mátyás utca 9; the Trafó, a new contemporary arts centre at IX, Lilom utca 41; and lastly the **Merlin Theatre** at V, Gerlóczy utca 4 (☎317-9338) in the centre of town, which often hosts visiting British companies. Look out for flyers and check out the theatre listings publication *Súgó* (published in English in July & Aug). During summer there are easy-to-understand performances at the outdoor theatre on Margit sziget. Puppet theatres are covered under "Children's Budapest" on p.122.

## Cinemas

Hollywood blockbusters and Euro soft-porn films currently dominate Budapest's mainstream **cinemas**, though the city has a chain of "arts cinemas", which specialize in the latest releases and obscure films from Eastern and Western Europe. Their provenance is indicated thus: *angol* (British), *lengyel* (Polish), *német* (German), *olasz* (Italian), and *orosz* (Russian). *Budapest Week* and *Budapest Sun* both run listings of all movies playing in English, with the latter covering films in other languages as well. If you understand Hungarian, the fullest **listings** appear in *Pesti Est* and *Pesti Műsor* (*PM*) under the heading *Budapesti mozik műsora*. Here, the times of shows are cryptically abbreviated to *n8* or *1/4 8* for 7.15pm; *f8* or *1/2 8* for 7.30pm; and *h8* or *3/4 8* for 7.45pm. "*Mb.*" indicates the film is dubbed, and "*fel.*" or "*feliratos*" means that it has Hungarian subtitles.

Budapest has some of the most beautiful movie houses around. It is worth checking out the Moorish interior of the **Uránia**, at VIII, Rákóczi út 21, and the coffered ceiling of the turn-of-the-century **Pushkin**, at V, Kossuth Lajos ucta 18, just for the interior decor, while the **Cirkógejzir**, at V, Balassi Bálint ucta 15–17 is an alternative joint complete with Chinese tea before showings. Cinema is still cheap, and sometimes films get to Budapest before they reach New York. In the summer there are also outdoor and drive-in cinemas on the edge of town.

# Sports

Apart from popular spectator sports such as soccer, horse-racing, and the Grand Prix, the city offers a range of **sports facilities** for participators. There's a **swimming pool** in the southern part of Margit sziget, the Hajós Alfréd uszoda (see p.88), as well as pools in many of the thermal baths, for example the Rudas, the Lukács and the Gellért. **Tennis** courts can be booked at the *Thermal Hotel Helia* in north Pest, XIII, Kárpát utca 62 (☎270-3277), and at the Euro-Gym on Margit sziget (☎269-3228). You can go **horse-riding** year-round at the Petneházy school at II, Feketefej utca 2–4 (Tues–Fri 9am–noon & 2–4pm, Sat & Sun 9am–1pm; ☎397-1208); alternatively, head out for the Great Plain, where there are many small riding schools. In winter, it's possible to **ski** at Normafa and Jánoshegy in the Buda Hills – equipment can be rented from Suli Sí in the Komjádi swimming complex at II, Árpád fejedelem utca 8 (☎212-2750). Skates can be rented at the **ice rink** in the Városliget between November and March.

## Soccer
While **international matches** are held at the 76,000-seater Népstadion, national football revolves around the turf of four **premier league teams**. Ferencvárosi Torna Club (aka FTC or Fradi) are based at IX, Üllői út 129, near the Népliget metro. Their colours are green and white and their fans try to pick fights with supporters of Újpesti Torna Egylet, whose ground is at IV, Megyeri út 13 (three stops on bus #30 from Újpest Központ metro station). Their main rivals are MTK, the 1997 champions, whose club is at VIII, Salgótarján utca 12–14, tram #37 from Blaha Lujza tér, and Honvéd-Kispest, based at XIX, Új temető út 1–3 (tram #42 from Határ út metro to the end of the line). Matches are played on Saturday afternoons and Monday evenings; see *Programme* or any Hungarian newspaper for details.

## Horse-racing
**Horse-racing** was introduced from England by Count Széchenyi in 1827 and flourished until 1949, when flat racing (*galopp*) was banned by the Communists. In the mid-1980s it resumed at the **Lóversenytér** (☎252-0888), north of the International Fair grounds at Kincsem Park, X, Albertirsai út 2 (Pillangó utca metro). Kincsem ("My Treasure") was the legendary mare that won all her 54 races at the end of the last century. Punters gather here every Sunday afternoon during the racing season, and the **Hungarian Derby** is held on the second or third Sunday in July. Devoted fans also attend **trotting races** at the **Ügetőpálya** at Kerepesi út 11 (bus #95 or trolley bus #80 from either Népstadion or Keleti Station), starting at 2pm on Saturday and 4pm on Wednesday. The atmosphere at both tracks is informal, but photographing the racegoers is frowned upon, since many attend unbeknownst to their spouses or employers. Races are advertised in *Fortuna* magazine. Betting

operates on a tote system, where your returns are affected by how the odds stood at the close of betting. The different types of bet you can make are *tét* (placing money on the winner); *hely* (on a horse coming in the first three); and the popular *befutó* (a bet on two horses to come in either first and second or first and third). Winnings are paid out about fifteen minutes after the end of the race.

## The Hungarian Grand Prix

First held in 1986, the **Hungarian Grand Prix** takes place every summer at the purpose-built **Formula One Racing** track at Mogyoród, 20km northeast of Budapest. It is usually scheduled for early August, and financial uncertainties surrounding the event spark off rumours every year that this is the last year it will be held. Details are available from Tourinform or any listings magazine. You can reach the track by special buses from the Árpád Bridge bus station; trains from Keleti Station to Fót, and then a bus from there; or by HÉV train from Örs vezér tere to the Szilasliget stop, which is 1800m northeast of Gate C. Tickets, available from Budapest Tourist, range from £5/$8 to £32/$50 for the first two days, from £8/$13 to £120/$190 for the final day, and from £10/$15 to £130/$200 for a three-day pass – the price being partly determined by the location, and whether you book in advance or risk disappointment on the day.

# Children's Budapest

Facilities for **children** in Budapest do leave something to be desired, though that is not a reflection of Hungarian attitudes to kids: Hungarians love children and will often talk to them on the bus, give up their seats for them, and roundly criticize you if they think your child is not sufficiently wrapped up in winter.

From Klauzál tér's scaled-down assault course to the folksy wooden see-saws and swings erected on Széchenyi-hegy, there are children's **playgrounds** all over Budapest. Adults could combine a visit to Jubileumi Park on the southwestern slope of Gellért-hegy with some sightseeing, or extract some childish diversions from the Városliget (see p.102), with its mock castle and old trains, its **amusement park**, **circus** and **zoo**. The "**railway circuit**" of the Buda Hills (p.87) should also appeal to all ages, while the stomach-churning exhibits at the **Waxworks** on Várhegy (p.76) could be just the thing for kids going through a gory phase.

If the Petőfi Csarnok, the cultural centre in the Városliget, has nothing suitable for children, you could take them to a dance club at one of the local cultural centres; alternatively visit one of Budapest's **puppet theatres** (*bábszínház*). Morning and matinée performances are for kids, while the evening's occasional masked grotesqueries or renditions of Bartók's *The Wooden Prince* and *The Miraculous Mandarin* are intended for adults. Tickets are available from the puppet theatre itself, at VI, Andrássy út 69 (☎342-2702), or the Central Box Office at Andrássy út 18 (☎312-0000). Children's entertainment is advertised in *Programme*, which you can pick up free from Tourinform or in large hotels. Last but not least, there is "**Kidstown**" (*Kölyökvár*), a play and activity centre open every Sunday (10am–1pm) at VII, Almássy tér 6. This offers all sorts of activities from face-painting to model-building – plus films, music and drama from mid-October to April (☎267-8709 for details).

Another popular destination for kids is the **Görzenál Skatepark** at III, Árpád fejedelem útja (Szentendre HÉV to Timár utca; daily 10am–8pm; ☎250-4800), where you can rollerblade, skateboard and cycle on ramps and jumps to your heart's content.

# Shopping

Budapest's range of **shops** has expanded massively in recent years, as big international names such as Marks & Spencer have appeared in its streets. The most popular things to bring home as souvenirs are wine, porcelain, foodstuffs, such as paprika, salami and goose liver, and CDs. Imported clothes and accessories are often expensive here. Most shops are open Monday to Friday 10am–6pm, and Saturday until 1pm, with most foodstores opening from 8am to 6 or 7pm. Recently some shops in the centre of the city have been staying open later on Saturdays. The new shopping malls on the edge of the city also tend to have longer opening hours. You can usually find a 24-hour – *non-stop* – shop serving alcohol, cigarettes and some food in the centre of town, though in the residential parts of Buda they may be harder to find.

Main **shopping areas** are located to south of Vörösmarty tér in central Pest, in particular in and around pedestrianized Váci utca and Petőfi Sándor utca, which have the biggest concentration of glamorous and expensive shops. The main streets radiating out from the centre – Bajcsy-Zsilinszky, Andrássy and Rákóczi út – are other major shopping focuses, as are the two ring boulevards, the Great Boulevard (especially from Margit Bridge to Blaha Lujza tér) and the Kiskörút, while the small streets inside the Nagykörút are also worth exploring.

The emergence of a thriving **wine industry** is reflected in the number of new wine shops in the city. The Budapest Wine Society at I, Batthyány utca 59, near Moszkva tér, has a good selection and the staff speak English (Mon–Fri 10am–8pm, Sat 10am–6pm, free wine tastings on Sat afternoons; ☎202-2569). Another good outlet is La Boutique des Vins at V, József Attila utca 12, near Deák tér (Mon–Fri 10am–8pm, Sat 10am–3pm; ☎317-5919).

Outlets for the main **porcelain** makers are Haas & Czjzek, at VI, Bajcsy-Zsilinszky út 23, opposite the Arany János metro station, which stocks all the main brands, or the shops of the producers, such as Herend at V, József nádor tér 11, or Zsolnay, at V, Kigyó utca 4. If you're interested in **clothes**, it is worth looking at the work of some of the young fashion designers in the city, such as the exotic, sometimes eccentric creations of Manier, at V, Váci utca 53.

Budapest's **Antiques Row** is Falk Miksa utca, at the Pest end of the Margit Bridge. Shops in the Vár are almost exclusively given over to providing foreign tourists with folksy souvenirs, embroidered tablecloths, hussar pots, fancy bottles of Tokaji wine and so forth. Another good source of presents are the **market halls** in Pest: the spectacular Central Market Hall (Nagycsarnok), or smaller ones on Hold utca (behind the American Embassy) and on Rákóczi tér (in the red-light district).

A recent development are the modern **shopping malls** outside the centre of town, combining major shopping centres with entertainment facilities under one roof. Two of the best are Duna Plaza, XIII, Váci út 178 (Gyöngyös utca metro), and Polus Center, XV, Szentmihályi út 131 (special buses run from Keleti Station). Budapest has two **flea markets**: the more expensive *Ecseri piac* where sellers are aware of the money they can make from rich foreign tourists, but where there also are bargains to be found, and Petőfi Csarnok in the Városliget (see p.102), a new antiques venue that has expanded fast.

For rock, pop and jazz **records** (including bootlegs), try DOB Records, VII, Dob utca 71, Lemezkucko, VI, Király utca 67, or WAVE Records, V, Bajcsy-Zsilinszky út 15. For **classical music**, try Hungaroton at V, Vörösmarty tér 1, Fotex Records at V, Szervita tér 2, or the Amadeus CD shop by the Danube behind the *Inter-Continental Hotel*. The friendly Rózsavölgyi at V, Szervita tér 5, has an excellent selection of classical music, with pop and folk downstairs, plus sheet music.

# Listings

**Airlines** Aeroflot, V, Váci utca 4 (☎318-5955); Air France, V, Kristóf tér 6 (☎318-0411); Alitalia, V, Ferenciek tere 2 (☎266-5913); Balkan, V, Párizsi utca 7 (☎317-1818); British Airways, V, East-West Business Centre, VIII, Rákóczi út 1–3 (☎266-6699); CSA, V, Vörösmarty tér 2 (☎318-3045); KLM, VIII, Rákóczi út 1–3 (☎373-7737); Lufthansa, V, Váci utca 19–21 (☎266-4511); Malév, V, Roosevelt tér 2 (☎266-5913); Sabena, V, Váci utca 1–3 (☎318-4111); SAS, V, Váci utca 1–3 (☎266-2633); Swissair, V, Kristóf ter 7–8 (☎267-2500); TAROM, Ferihegy airport, Terminal 2B (☎296-8661).

**Airport information** Terminal 2A ☎296-7000, for departures, ☎296 8000 for arrivals; Terminal 2B ☎296-5053 for departures; ☎296-5882 for arrivals. The Airport Minibus service can take you directly to your destination. Tickets (1200Ft) can be purchased while waiting in the luggage hall or when you come out into the main concourse. You can also return to the airport on the minibus – call a day in advance if you're on an early flight, and allow a couple of hours to get there.

**Banks and exchange** There is a 24-hour exchange service at branches of IBUSZ at V, Petőfi tér 3, and Apáczai Csere János utca 1. You can transfer money from abroad through the Magyar Külkereskedelmí Bank, V, Szent István tér 11; through Interchange, the regional agents for Western Union, which have branches at the main stations and in the city centre (☎266-4995); and through the American Express Moneygram service (minimum $100), V, Deák utca 10 (☎267-8680). Money transfers allegedly take only a few minutes. The Magyar Külkereskedelmí Bank also has safe-deposit boxes for storing valuables.

**Bike rental** Try Nella Bikes off Bajcsy-Zsilinszky út at V, Kálmán Imre utca 23 (Mon–Fri 10am–6pm, Sat 9am–1pm; ☎131-3184); Tura Mobil at VI, Nagymező utca 43 (☎312-5073); or Kerékvár at I, Hunyadi János utca 4 (☎201-0713) at the Buda end of the Lánchíd.

**Bookstores** English-language bookstores include Bestsellers at V, Október 6 utca 11 (☎312-1295); Akadémia at V, Váci ucta 18 (☎318-2718); The CEU Bookshop at Nádor utca 9; the Foreign Language Bookshop at V, Petőfi Sándor utca 2 (☎318-3136); Fókusz at VII, Rákóczi út 14–16 (☎267-9205); Litea at I, Hess András tér 4 (☎375-6987), and V, Vörösmarty tér 4. There are secondhand (*Antikvárium*) bookstores at V, Váci utca 28 & 75; V, Múzeum körút 15; the Stúdió at VI, Jókai tér 7; and Bibliotéka on the corner of Andrássy út and Bajcsy-Zsilinszky út.

**British Council**, VI, Benczúr utca 26 (☎321-4039). Library, newspapers and a noticeboard. Mon–Thurs 11am–6pm, Fri 11am–5pm. Closed Aug.

**Camping and Caravanning Club**, IX, Kálvin tér 9 (Mon–Fri 9am–5pm; ☎217-7248). Can supply canoeing maps of the Danube, advise on equipment and arrange reductions for FICC members.

**Car rental** Budget at the *Hotel Mercure Buda*, I, Krisztina körút 41–43 (☎356-6333); Főtaxi at VII, Kertész utca 24–28 (☎322-1471); Eurodollar, XI, Prielle Kornélia utca 45 and at the airport (☎204-2993 or 204-2994, airport 290-1990); Hertz at V, Aranykéz utca 4–8 (☎296-0999), and at both airport terminals; and Inka at V, Bajcsy-Zsilinszky út 16 (☎317-2150).

**Car repairs** Some makes of American cars at Americar Service Kft, XIII, Apály utca 1–3 (☎329-9084); BMW Special BMW Team, XIII, Kassák Lajos utca 75 (☎320-9986); Downtown Car Service IX, Ernő utca 30 (☎215-2917 or 216-0530); Ford Petrányi-Autó Kft, VI, Kerepesi út 105–113 (☎260-5050); Herceg Opel, XIV, Miskolci utca 93 (☎383-7849); Hungarian Volkswagen Service, XII, Vöröskő utca 13 (☎355-9213); Peugeot-Gablini, XIV, Fogarási út 195–197 (☎222-1210); the Magyar Autóklub runs a 24-hour breakdown assistance (☎088).

**Driving information** For motoring information contact Magyar Autóklub, II, Rómer Floris utca 4A (☎212-2938); Fővinform for traffic conditions in Budapest (☎317-1173); Útinform (☎322-2238 or 322-7052) for national conditions.

**Embassies** Australia, XII, Királyhágó tér 8–9 (☎201-8899); Austria, VI, Benczúr utca 16 (☎269-6700); Bulgaria, VI, Andrássy út 115 (☎322-0824); Canada, XII, Budakeszi út 32 (☎275-1200); Czech Republic, VI, Rózsa utca 6 (☎351-0539); Denmark, XII, Határőr út 37 (☎355-7320); Germany, XIV, Stefánia út 101–3 (☎467-3500); Israel, II, Fullánk utca 8 (☎200-0781); Netherlands, II Füge utca 5–7 (☎326-5301); Norway, I, Ostrom utca 13 (☎212-9400); Romania, XIV, Thököly út 72 (☎352-0271); Russian Federation, Bajza utca 35 (☎302-5230); Slovakia, XIV, Stefánia út 22 (☎251-1700); Slovenia, II Cseppkő utca 68 (☎325-9202); Sweden, XIV, Ajtósi sor 27A (☎352-2804); UK, V, Harmincad utca 6 (☎266-2888); USA, V, Szabadság tér 12 (☎267-4400).

**Emergencies** Ambulance ☎104; police ☎107; fire service ☎105.

**Hospitals and dentistry** There are 24-hour casualty departments at V, Hold utca 19, behind the US embassy (☎311-6816), and at II, Ganz utca 13–15 (☎202-1370). The Országos Baleseti Intézet VIII, Fiumei út 17 (☎333-7599), specializes in broken limbs and accidents; Profident, VII, Károly korut 1, is a round-the-clock dentist where they speak English. Private clinics with English-speaking personnel include the IMS (International Medical Services) at XIII, Váci út 202 (Mon-Fri 7.30am–8pm; ☎329-8423) and at III, Vihar utca 29 (8pm–8am; ☎250-3829 or 250-1899); and the R-Klinika at II, Felsőzöldmáli út 13 (☎325-9999 or 325-8942). Embassies can also recommend private, foreign-language-speaking doctors and dentists.

**International buses and trains** International train tickets should be purchased 24–36 hours in advance, at the stations or the MÁV booking office, VI, Andrássy út 35 (Mon–Fri 9am–5pm; ☎322-0856). Bookings are required on all international train routes but it may not be possible to obtain them on trains leaving from Kőbánya-Kispest. This also applies to services from Zugló Station, which sometimes handles international traffic. The Vienna-bound *Wiener Waltzer* often runs late, so reserve sleepers on from Austria in Budapest. Also bring drinks, as the buffet staff overcharge shamelessly. Tickets for international buses must be purchased at the bus station in hard currency, and should be booked 24 hours in advance.

**Lost property** For items left on public transport go to the office at VII, Akácfa utca 18 (Mon, Tues & Thurs 7.30am–3pm, Wed 7.30am–7pm, Fri 7.30am–2pm; ☎322-6613). Lost or stolen passports should be reported to the police station in the district where they were lost. Any found are handed to the relevant embassy.

**Pharmacies** The following are all open 24 hours: II, Frankel Leó út 22 (☎212-4406); VI, Teréz körút 41 (☎311-4439); VII, Rákóczi út 86, at Baross tér (☎322-9613); XI, Kosztolányi Dezső tér 11 (☎466-6494); XII, Alkotás utca 1B, opposite Déli Station (☎355-4691); XIV, Bosnyák utca 1/A (☎383-0391). For herbal remedies try Herbária, VIII, Rákóczi út 49, and V, Bajcsy-Zsilinszky út 58.

**Photo booths** Passport-sized photos are available from automatic booths in Deák tér, Kálvin tér, Nyugati tér and Moszkva tér metro stations (400Ft for 4 colour photos); Sooter's at V, Deák Ferenc. utca 22 (399Ft for 4 colour shots); and the third floor of the Corvin department store on Blaha Lujza tér.

**Post offices** Main office/poste restante at V, Petőfi Sándor utca 13 (Mon–Fri 8am–8pm & Sat 8am–2pm); 24-hour post office at VII, Baross tér 11C (by Keleti Station).

**Taxis** English-speaking taxi companies include: Volántaxi (☎466-6666), Főtaxi (☎222-2222), Citytaxi (☎211-1111), Buda-taxi (☎233-3333) and Tele-5-taxi (☎355-5555).

**Telephones** International calls can be made from the Telephone and Telegram Bureau, V, Petőfi Sándor utca 17–19 (Mon–Fri 8am–8pm & Sat 10am–4pm) or from any phone booth on the street; the international operator can be reached on ☎199.

## travel details

### Trains

**Déli Station** to: Balatonfüred (every 1–2hr; 2hr–2hr 15min); Balatonszentgyörgy (every 1–2hr; 3–3hr 30min); Dombóvár (every 1-2hr, including 5 intercity trains; 2hr or 1hr 30min if intercity); Pécs (5 intercity daily; 2hr 30 min); Siófok (every 1hr; 1 hr 45min); Székesfehérvár (every 60–90min; 1hr); Szekszárd (5 daily; 2hr 45min); Szombathely (6 daily; 3hr); Veszprém (6 daily; 2hr); Zalaegerszeg (3 daily; 4hr).

**Keleti Station** to: Békéscsaba (every 1-2hr; 2hr 45min); Eger (5 daily; 2hr); Győr (every 1hr; 1hr 30min–2hr); Miskolc (every 1hr; 1hr 45min–2hr 15min); Sopron (17 daily; 2hr 50min); Tata (every 2hr; 1hr).

**Nyugati Station** to: Debrecen (every 1hr; 2hr 30min–3hr); Kecskemét (every 1–2hr; 1hr 30min); Nyíregyháza (every 1–2hr; 3hr–3hr 30 min); Szeged (every 1–2hr; 2hr–2hr 30min).

### Intercity buses

**Árpád híd** to: the Danube Bend: Esztergom via the Bend (every 30–40min; 1hr 15min) or Dorog (every 30min; 55min); Szentendre (every 30–60min; 30min); Vác (every 30min; 30min); Visegrád (30–60min; 1hr).

**Erzsébet tér** to: Lake Balaton and Transdanubia: Balatonfüred (5 daily; 2hr 10-40min); Dunaújváros (hourly; 1hr 20min); Győr (every 30–60min; 1hr 50min); Harkány (2 daily; 4hr 30min); Hévíz (4 daily; 4hr); Keszthely (3 daily; 3hr 40min); Mohács (3 daily; 4hr); Nagyvázsony (2 daily except Sun; 3hr); Pécs (5 daily; 4hr); Siklós (1 daily; 4hr 50min); Siófok (8 daily; 1hr 35min–2hr 10min); Sopron (4 daily; 3hr 50min); Sümeg (3 daily; 3hr 40min); Székesfehérvár (every 40–60min; 1hr 15min); Szekszárd (hourly; 3hr); Szombathely (2 daily; 4hr 25min); Veszprém (every 60–90min; 2hr 10min); Zalaegerszeg (1 daily; 4hr 45min); Zirc (3 daily; 2hr 30min).

**Népstadion** to: Northern Hungary and the Great Plain: Aggtelek (2 daily; 5hr); Baja (every 1–2hr; 3hr 15min); Balassagyarmat (every 1–2hr; 2hr 10min); Békéscsaba (2 daily; 4hr); Eger (every 60min; 2hr); Gyöngyös (hourly; 1hr 35min); Kalocsa (every 1–2hr; 2hr 20min); Kecskemét (15–20 daily; 1hr 45min); Kiskunfélegyháza (8–10 daily; 2hr); Mátraháza (every 2–3hr; 1hr 50min); Szeged (5 daily; 3hr 25min).

### International trains

Bookings are required on all international routes. Some international trains may not have buffets so check and bring supplies if necessary.

**Déli Station** to: Vienna (1 daily; 3hr 30min); Zagreb (1 daily; 7hr).

**Keleti Station** to: Arad (7 daily; 5hr 30min); Basel (2 daily; 16hr); Belgrade (5 daily; 7hr); Berlin (3 daily; 12hr 30min); Brasov (5 daily; 11hr); Bratislava (7 daily; 3hr 30min); Bucharest (5 daily; 14hr); Cologne (2 daily; 13hr); Dresden (3 daily; 10hr 30min); Frankfurt (2 daily; 10hr); Istanbul (1 daily; 30hr); Katowice (2 daily; 8hr); Kosice (3 daily; 4hr); Kraków (1 daily; 11hr); Leipzig (3 daily; 12hr 30min); Munich (3 daily; 9hr); Novi Sad (5 daily; 6hr); Nürnberg (2 daily; 10hr 30min); Poprad Tatry (1 daily; 5hr 30min); Prague (5 daily; 11hr 30min); Salzburg (3 daily; 7hr); Sighisoara (5 daily; 9hr 30min); Timisoara (2 daily; 6hr 30min); Venice (2 daily; 13hr 30min); Vienna (6 daily; 3hr–3hr 30min); Warsaw (2 daily; 11hr 30min); Zagreb (1 daily; 6hr).

**Nyugati Station** to: Baia Mare (1 daily; 7hr 30min); Bratislava (4 daily; 3–6hr); Chop (1 daily; 7hr); Cluj (2 daily; 8hr); Oradea (3 daily; 5hr 30min); Satu Mare (1 daily; 7hr).

### International buses

Tickets should be booked 24 hours in advance.

**Erzsébet tér** to: Arad (1 weekly; 6hr 30min); Banská Bystrica (2 weekly; 4hr); Berlin (June–Sept 6 weekly, otherwise 2 weekly; 15hr); Bratislava (1 daily; 4hr); Cluj (June 3 weekly, otherwise 2 weekly; 9hr 30min); Dresden (June–Sept 4 weekly, otherwise 2 weekly; 12hr); Graz (June–Sept 2 weekly; 6hr); Kraków (2 weekly; 11hr); Levice (3 weekly; 3hr); Munich (June–Sept daily, otherwise 3 weekly; 10hr); Nürnberg (June–Sept daily, otherwise 3 weekly; 11hr); Oradea (June–Sept 3 weekly, otherwise 2 weekly; 6hr); Poprad Tatry (2 weekly; 6hr 30min); Prague (June–Sept 4 weekly, otherwise, 1 weekly; 8hr 30min); Subotica (1 daily; 4hr 30min); Timisoara (1 weekly; 8hr 10min); Tîrgu Mures (June–Sept 2 weekly, otherwise 1 weekly; 11hr 45min); Venice (June–Sept daily, otherwise 3 weekly; 12hr); Vienna (3–4 daily; 3hr 20min); Zakopane (2 weekly; 9hr).

### Hydrofoils and ferries

**Belgrád rakpart international landing stage** to Vienna (April–Oct 1–2 daily; 5hr).

**Vigadó tér pier** to: Esztergom (May–Sept 1–2 daily; 5hr); Szentendre (May–Sept 1 daily; 90min); Vác (May–Sept 1 daily; 2hr 45min); Visegrád (May–Sept 1–2 daily; 3hr).

# CHAPTER TWO

# THE DANUBE BEND

To escape Budapest's humid summers, many people flock north of the city to the **Danube Bend** (*Dunakanyar*), one of the grandest stretches of the river, outdone only by the Kazan Gorge in Romania. Entering the Carpathian Basin, the Danube widens dramatically, only to be forced by hills and mountains through a narrow, twisting valley, almost a U-turn – the "Bend" – before dividing for the length of Szentendre Sziget and flowing into Budapest. The **historic towns and ruins** of Szentendre, Esztergom and Visegrád on the west bank can be seen on a long day-trip from Budapest, but it would be a shame not to linger here and visit the quieter east side too, boasting the sedate town of Vác, the gardens of Váctrátót and the charms of Nagymaros and Zebegény, as well as the neighbouring Pilis and Börzsöny highlands, with opportunities for **hiking** or **horse-riding**.

The **Danube** is the second longest river in Europe after the Volga, flowing 2857km from the Black Forest to the Black Sea. Between the confluence of the Bereg and Briach streams at Donaueschingen and its shifting delta on the Black Sea, the Danube is fed by over three hundred tributaries from a catchment area of 816,000 square kilometres, and has ten nations along its banks. Known as the Donau in Germany and Austria, it becomes the Duna from the Czech Republic down through Slovakia, Slovenia, Croatia, Serbia, Bulgaria, Romania and Moldova, forming the frontier for much of the way. Used by armies and tribes since antiquity, this "dustless highway" deeply impressed the German poet Hölderlin who saw it as an allegory for the mythical voyage of the ancient German forefathers to the Black Sea, and for Hercules' journey from Greece to the land of the Hyperboreans. Attila Jószef described it as "cloudy, wise and great", its waters from many lands as intermingled as the peoples of the Carpathian Basin.

While the Danube's strategic value ended after World War II, economic and environmental concerns came to the fore in the 1980s, when the governments of Hungary, Austria and Czechoslovakia began to realize a plan to **dam** the river between Gabčikovo and Nagymaros. The public opposition that compelled Hungary to abandon the project was a milestone along the road to democracy,

## ACCOMMODATION PRICE CODES

All accommodation in this guide is graded according to the price bands given below. Note that prices refer to the **cheapest available double room in high season** or the price of **two people sharing a tent** in a campsite. 100Ft is roughly equivalent to $0.45 or DM1. For more details, see p.24.

| | | |
|---|---|---|
| ① Under 2000Ft | ④ 6000–8500Ft | ⑦ 20,000–27,000Ft |
| ② 2000–4000Ft | ⑤ 8500–13,000Ft | ⑧ 27,000–40,000Ft |
| ③ 4000–6000Ft | ⑥ 13,000–20,000Ft | ⑨ over 40,000Ft |

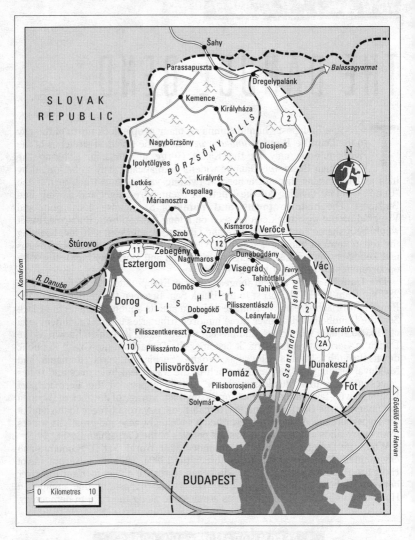

mobilizing society in a way no overtly political cause ever could have. The dam's tendency to stir up trouble has survived the changes of 1989, and it has now become a source of deep friction between Hungary and Slovakia. In the early 1990s, Slovakia pressed ahead and diverted the Danube on its own while Hungary was busy demolishing the work it had begun at Nagymaros. The controversy surrounding the dam now seems certain to survive into the next century, as both countries press their claim that the other must pay for breaking international law.

# THE WEST BANK

The natural defence presented by the broad river and the hilly western bank has long attracted the inhabitants of this region to build their castles here. The Romans built a camp to keep the barbarians at bay, unwittingly staking out the sites of the future castles of the Magyar kings, who, a thousand years later, had to repel the Mongols arriving from the east. **Esztergom**, the scene for the Hungarians' official conversion to Christianity in the tenth century, served as the royal seat for three hundred years, after which the kings moved their base down-river to the citadel of **Visegrád**. With the expulsion of the Turks in the seventeenth century, the fertility and beauty of the landscape became the main attractions. Baroque **Szentendre** was established in the eighteenth century when Serbs fleeing up the Danube from the Turks settled here. Later, in the 1920s, it became an artists' colony. If you want to explore the countryside, the **Pilis range** of mountains makes for excellent hiking.

Its proximity to Budapest makes Szentendre the logical place to start your trip. With frequent onward **bus** services, it's easy to move on to Visegrád and then continue westward to Esztergom. Both these towns are also accessible direct from Budapest: hourly buses from the Árpád híd terminus follow an anticlockwise route around the Bend – although Esztergom can be reached more directly by the less scenic clockwise route that goes via Dorog; this is also the route taken by **trains** to Esztergom from the capital's Nyugati Station. Train access is otherwise limited in the Bend: you can catch a train to Visegrád only by going up the east bank to Nagymaros via Vác and taking the ferry across the river, but there is no onward train to Esztergom.

In summer you can take the more leisurely option of travelling by **ferry** from Budapest's Vigadó tér pier to Visegrád (daily: May–Aug at 7.45am & 10am; Sept at 10am; 3hr) and Esztergom (mid-May to mid-Sept daily at 8am; 5hr). From June to August there is the faster hydrofoil operating to Visegrád (daily at 10.50am; 50min) and Esztergom (daily at 8am & 5pm; 1hr 20min). For further information, contact any Tourinform office or the Mahart shipping company by Vigadó tér pier. To make a day-trip from Budapest, you might want to combine transport, taking a boat up to Esztergom and then catching the bus round to Visegrád and back to Budapest.

# Szentendre and around

Visitors are seldom disappointed by the Baroque heart of **SZENTENDRE** (St Andrew), which, despite its rash of tourist boutiques, remains a delightful maze of houses painted in autumnal colours, with secretive gardens and lanes winding up to hilltop churches; Claudio Magris called it "the Montmartre of the Danube". The town's location on the lower slopes of the Pilis range is not only beautiful, but ensures that Szentendre enjoys more hours of sunlight than anywhere else in Hungary, making it a perfect spot for an artists' colony.

Before the artists moved in, Szentendre's character had been formed by waves of refugees from Serbia. The first influx followed the catastrophic Serb defeat at Kosovo in 1389, which foreshadowed the Turkish occupation of Hungary in the sixteenth century, when Szentendre fell into ruin. After Hungary had been liberated, the Turkish recapture of Belgrade in 1690 precipitated the flight of 30,000 Serbs and Bosnians led by Patriarch Crnojevic, six thousand of whom settled in Szentendre, which became the seat of the Serbian Orthodox Church in exile. Prospering through trade, they replaced their wooden churches with stone ones and built handsome town houses. However, as Habsburg toleration waned and phylloxera (vine-blight) and floods ruined the local economy, they began to trickle back to Serbia, so that by 1890 less than a quarter of the population was Serb. Today, only about seventy families of Serbian descent remain.

In 1928, thanks to its close proximity to Budapest and the excellent light conditions, Szentendre became a working artists' colony, and today its links with art are as strong as ever, with around 150 artists working here and the town's countless museums and galleries vying for the attention of the peak-season tourist crowds. The town is very popular and can get crowded as a result, but it's still possible to escape the tourists and enjoy the quieter side of the place.

The best times to visit are on weekdays in the summer, or at weekends during the winter months – between November and March most of Szentendre's museums are only open from Friday to Sunday. Another good time to visit is for Szentendre's **summer festival** (*Szentendrei Nyár*), which runs from late June to late August, culminating in a pop concert and fireworks on August 20. On the preceding day, a **Serbian festival** with *kolo* (circle) dancing takes place at the Preobraženska Church. All three tourist offices can furnish you with information on the festival's events.

# Arrival and accommodation

Szentendre's **bus and train (HÉV) stations** are next door to one another, ten to fifteen minutes' walk south of the town centre. Local buses run to the centre via Dunakanyar körút. There are two docks for **Danube ferries**: one for the boat to Szentendrei Sziget (Szentendre Island); the other, 500m further north, for services between Budapest and Esztergom.

The best place to go for **tourist information** and a free **map** is Tourinform at Dumsta Jenő utca 22 (March–Oct Mon–Fri 9.30am–4.30pm, Sat & Sun 10am–2pm; Nov–Feb Mon–Fri 10am–4pm; ☎26/317-965), where the staff are friendly and speak English. IBUSZ, at Bogdányi utca 11 (April–Oct Mon–Fri 9am–4pm, Sat & Sun 10am–2pm; Nov–March Mon–Fri 9am–4pm; ☎26/310-181), and Dunatours, at Bogdányi utca 1 (May–Sept Mon–Fri 9.30am–6pm, Sat & Sun 10am–2pm; Oct–April Mon–Fri 9.30am–6pm; ☎26/311-311), can book accommodation, but are less hot on information. Szentendre's main **post office** is at Rákóczi út 4, with another branch at Kossuth ucta 23–25, by the HÉV terminal. There's an **ATM** in the HÉV terminal.

## Accommodation

IBUSZ can arrange **private rooms**, though some are located in outlying suburbs such as Tyukos-Dűlő or Leányfalu. Alternatively look out for *Zimmer frei* signs advertising vacancies. Another budget option is to **camp** on Pap Sziget (Priest's Island), north of the centre. The *Pap Sziget* site (☎26/310-697; May–Sept) also has two- to four-person bungalows by the river (①), a pension (②), a motel (③), a restaurant and tennis courts. The camping fee includes use of the swimming pool on the island.

**Aradi Panzió**, Aradi utca 4 (☎26/314-274). Eight rooms with bathroom and television in a quiet street 500m from the HÉV station. ③.

**Bükkös Panzió**, Bükköspart 16 (☎26/312-021). Nice location by a stream lined with weeping willows, 100m west of the Požarevačka Church. Comfy rooms with TV, phone and minibar. Restaurant, laundry service and secure parking. ④.

**Hotel Cola**, Dunakanyar körút 50 (☎26/310-410). North of the centre, on the bus route to Pap Sziget and Leányfalu. Rooms have terrace and TV, but make sure you get one away from the busy main road. Run by a friendly and helpful proprietor. ④–⑤.

**Horváth Panzió**, Daru piac 2 (☎26/313-950). Small modern pension in the northern part of the old town; en-suite double rooms and a bar. ④.

**Ilona Panzió**, Rákóczi utca 11 (☎26/313-599). Small pension a couple of minutes' walk from the centre of town. Rooms have shower and toilet and there's a breakfast terrace. ③.

**Panzió No.100**, Ady Endre utca 100 (☎26/312-881). Situated 100m west of Route 11 in the suburb of Leányfalu. All rooms are en-suite with phone and air-conditioning. Secure parking. ④.

# The Town

Most of Szentendre's main tourist attractions are centred on the main square, Fő tér. On your way in from the station, along Kossuth utca, you can make a detour to examine a hoard of **Roman stonework** at Dunakanyar körút 1 (March–Oct Mon–Fri 10am–4pm); turn left up Római sánc köz and carry straight on up for five minutes. Its opening times are unreliable, however, and you may have to look at the stones from behind the wire fence. The eroded lintels and sarcophagi belonged to Ulcisia Castra, a military town named after the Eravisci, an Illyrian-Celtic tribe subdued by the Romans during the first century AD.

Back on Kossuth utca, another five minutes' walk up the street, just before the Bükkos stream, you'll encounter the first evidence of a Serbian presence – the **Požarevačka Church** (Fri–Sun 11am–5pm; 50Ft). Typical of the churches in Szentendre, this was built in the late eighteenth century to replace an older wooden church, although its Byzantine-style iconostasis was inherited rather than specially commissioned. Beyond the stream, Dumtsa Jenő utca continues past the Tourinform office on the corner at no. 22, and the **Marzipan Museum and Pastry Shop** at no. 12, where the marzipan creations include a model of the Hungarian parliament; a plaque on the wall opposite marks the birthplace of nineteenth-century Serbian novelist Jakov Ignjatovic, who created the Serb realist novel. Further up on the right is the **Barcsay Collection** (mid-March to Oct Tues–Sun 10am–4pm; Nov to mid-March Fri–Sun same hours; 90Ft), a museum housing drawings and paintings by Jenő Barcsay (1900–1988), who was born in Transylvania but lived and worked in Szentendre from 1928 His dark prewar canvases give way to more abstract works after the war, avoiding the strictures of the regime. His anatomical drawings at the end of the display confirm his skill as a draughtsman. During the summer festival, concerts are held in the courtyard of the museum.

A little further on, the road is crossed by Péter-Pál utca, where a left turn brings you to the **Peter-Paul Church**, a yellow and white Baroque church built in 1708. Its original furnishings were taken back to Serbia after World War I, and the church is now Roman Catholic. Organ recitals take place at the church regularly; ask at Tourinform for details. From here, or from the last uphill stretch of Dumtsa Jenő utca, it's just a block to the main square.

## Around Fő tér

Swarming with buskers and tourists during summertime, Szentendre's main square, **Fő tér**, is a place either to savour or avoid. At the centre of the square stands the Plague Cross, its triangular marble base decorated by icons, which was erected

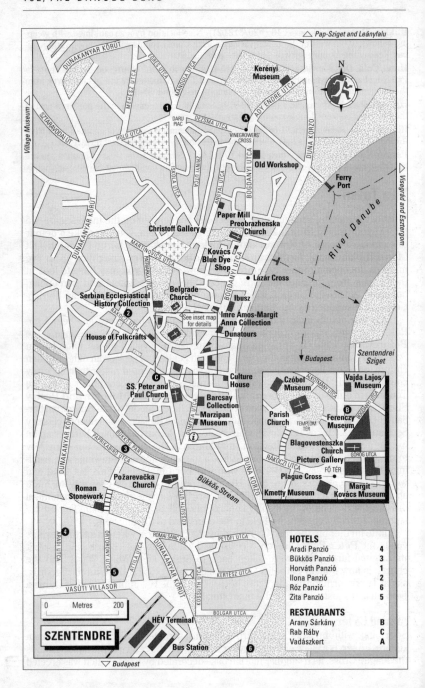

△ Pap-Sziget and Leányfalu

N

Kerényi
Museum

△ Village Museum

DARU
PIAC

❶

DEZSMA UTCA

Ⓐ

VINEGROWERS'
CROSS

DUNAKANYAR KÖRÚT

EGRES UTCA

MANDULA UTCA

MÉHÉSZ UTCA

HOLD UTCA

ISKOLA UTCA

ZRINYI UTCA

ANGAL UTCA

BOGDÁNYI UTCA

ADY ENDRE UTCA

DUNA KORZÓ

Old Workshop

Ferry
Port

△ Visegrád and Esztergom

Paper Mill
Preobrazhenska
Church

River Danube

Christoff Gallery

MARTINOVICS UTCA

PATRIARKA UTCA

Kovács
Blue Dye
Shop

• Lázár Cross

Serbian Ecclesiastical
History Collection

RÁKÓCZI UTCA

❷

Belgrade
Church

Ibusz

See inset map
for details

Imre Amos-Margit
Anna Collection

House of Folkcrafts

Dunatours

DUNAKANYAR KÖRÚT

Szentendrei
Sziget

▼ Budapest

Ⓒ

SS. Peter and
Paul Church

Culture
House

Czóbel
Museum

ALKOTMÁNY UTCA

Vajda Lajos
Museum

Barcsay
Collection

Parish
Church

TEMPLOM
TÉR

Ferenczy
Museum

Ⓑ

BOGDÁNYI UTCA

Marzipan
Museum

ⓘ

Blagovestenszka
Church

GÖRÖG UTCA

PAPRIKABÍRÓ UTCA

BÜKKÖS PART

❸

RÁKÓCZI UTCA

Picture Gallery

FŐ TÉR

Plague Cross •

Margit
Kovács Museum

Požarevačka
Church

Kmetty Museum

DUNAKANYAR KÖRÚT

Roman
Stonework

Bükkös Stream

DUNA KORZÓ

ARADI UTCA

❹

ORTORONY UTCA

RÓMAI SÁNC KÖZ

KOSSUTH LAJOS UTCA

PETŐFI UTCA

❺

ATTILA UTCA

DUNAKANYAR KÖRÚT

KERTÉSZ UTCA

KOSSUTH UTCA

VASÚTI VILLASOR

0    Metres    200

BOLGÁR UTCA

HÉV Terminal

SZENTENDRE

Bus Station

▽ Budapest

**HOTELS**

| Aradi Panzió | 4 |
| Bükkös Panzió | 3 |
| Horváth Panzió | 1 |
| Ilona Panzió | 2 |
| Róz Panzió | 6 |
| Zita Panzió | 5 |

**RESTAURANTS**

| Arany Sárkány | B |
| Rab Ráby | C |
| Vadászkert | A |

❻

by the merchants' guild after Szentendre escaped infection in 1763. From here, diverging streets and alleys lead to an assortment of galleries and museums around the square, as well as to the many tourist shops, especially down Bogdányi utca.

The **Kmetty Museum**, immediately on your left if entering the square from Dumsta Jenő utca (mid-March to Oct Wed–Sun 10am–4pm; Nov to mid-March Fri–Sun same hours; 90Ft), contains some delightful watercolours by János Kmetty (1889–1975), and, downstairs, his blue, cubist paintings from a later period. The entrance is drowned by a boutique in summer, with goods hanging all round the door.

On the south side of the square is the Church of the Annunciation, or **Blagovestenška Church**, the most accessible of the Orthodox churches in the town. Painted by Mikhail Zivkovia of Buda in the early eighteenth century, the icons evoke all the richness and tragedy of Serbian history. The building itself is thought to have been designed by András Mayerhoffer in the 1750s. Look out for the tomb of a Greek merchant of Macedonian origin to the left of the entrance, and the Rococo windows and gate facing Görög utca (Greek Street).

Just behind the church, at Vastagh György utca 1, is by far the most popular of the town's galleries, the **Margit Kovács museum** (mid-March to Oct Tues–Sun 10am–6pm, June–Sept also Mon 10am–4pm; Nov to mid-March Tues–Sun 10am–4pm; 250Ft). This is a wonderful collection that never fails to delight, the themes of legends, dreams, love and motherhood giving Kovács' graceful sculptures and reliefs universal appeal. Her expressive statues with their big eyes aren't particularly well known abroad, but in Hungary, Kovács, who died in 1977, is duly honoured as the nation's greatest ceramicist and sculptor. Because the museum is small, there is an inevitable wait at the entrance, but it is well worthwhile.

Back on the main square, next door to the church, a portal carved with emblems of science and learning provides the entrance to a former Serbian school, now the **Ferenczy Museum** (mid-March to Oct Tues–Sun 10am–4pm; Nov to mid-March Fri–Sun same hours; 90Ft). Károly Ferenczy (1862–1917) pioneered Impressionism and *plein air* painting in Hungary, while his eldest son Valér (1885–1954) swung towards Expressionism. His younger sons, twins Nóemi (1890–1957) and Béni (1890–1967) branched out into textiles and bronzeware, with diminishing returns.

Several of the square's buildings (nos. 8, 17, 19 and 22) are old Baroque **trading houses** with their dates and trades engraved above the gates. The former Pálffy House (no. 17) bears the sign of the merchants' guild, combining the patriarchal cross of Orthodoxy with an anchor and a number four to symbolize Danube trade and the percentage of profit deemed appropriate by the guild.

A short walk out of the top western end of the square brings you into Rákóczi utca with the Baroque **Town Hall** (*Városház*) on your left, which hosts summer concerts in its courtyard, while opposite at Rákóczi utca 1 is the **House of Folk Crafts** (mid-March to Oct Tues–Sun 10am–4pm; 60Ft), in an old bellhouse, with small temporary displays on blacksmithing and wine-making. The covered wooden steps leading up the hill behind are presently closed – the nearest stairs are just back along Rákóczi utca towards the main square.

## Templom tér and Bogdányi utca

From Fő tér or Rákóczi utca, you can ascend an alley of steps to gain a lovely view of Szentendre's rooftops and gardens from **Templom tér**, where **craft stalls** plying their wares are regularly set up under the acacia trees to help finance the restoration of the Catholic **parish church**. Of medieval origin, with Romanesque and Gothic features, it was rebuilt in the Baroque style after falling derelict in Turkish times; the frescoes in its sanctuary were collectively painted by the artists' colony. Across the square, the **Czóbel Museum** (mid-March to Oct Tues–Sun 10am–4pm; Nov to mid-March Fri–Sun same hours; 90Ft) exhibits paintings of brooding nudes by Béla Czóbel (1883–1976) and his wife Mária Modok (1896–1971), whose fierce brush strokes challenged the Neoclassical trend of the Horthy era.

A minute's walk north of Templom tér, the burgundy spire of the Orthodox episcopal cathedral or **Belgrade Church** rises above a walled garden off Alkotmány utca. The entrance to the grounds is from the corner of Alkotmány utca and Patriarka utca. The sexton is reluctant to open the church for tourists, so the only way to see its lavishly ornamented interior is to attend a service (Sat 5pm, 6pm in summer, Sun 10am & 4pm). Its icons, by Vasilije Ostoic, depict scenes from the New Testament and saints of the Orthodox Church. There are many old tombstones in the churchyard with Cyrillic inscriptions. This tale of demographic decline is echoed by the **Serbian Ecclesiastical History Collection** in the episcopal palace (mid-March to Oct Wed–Sun 10am–4pm; Nov to mid-March Fri–Sun same hours; 100Ft), whose icons, vestments and crosses come from churches in Hungary that fell empty after the Serbs returned to the Balkans and the last remaining parishioners died out.

From the Belgrade Church you can follow Alkotmány utca back down towards the main square. Just before you get there, you pass two more museums hiding in Hunyadi utca on your left. The **Vajda Lajos Museum** at no. 1 (mid-March to Oct Tues–Sun 10am–4pm; Nov to mid-March Fri–Sun 10am–4pm; 90Ft) commemorates the work of a Szentendre painter who died in the Holocaust. Vajda's early work reveals cubist and constructivist influences, while his later charcoal works seem to foretell the approaching torment. Although the museum is housed in a wealthy bourgeois villa, the artist himself was poor – as you can see from the materials he worked with. Downstairs is an excellent display of works by artists of the "European School", including Bálint Endre and Jenő Barcsay. This group formed after the war but was quickly stopped by the Communists. On the other side of Hunyadi utca, a few steps further along, is a new display, the **Szántó Jewish Memorial House and Synagogue** (May–Oct Tues–Sun 10am–5pm; donations accepted) set up by the grandson of a Holocaust victim, Lajos Szántó, who lived in the town. Most of Szentendre's Jewish community, which never numbered more that 250, were deported and killed during the Holocaust. The documents and relics are few, but they make a moving display.

Heading north from Fő tér, Bogdányi utca is packed with stalls, attended by shop assistants dressed up in folk gear. The **Wine Museum** at no. 10 (daily 10am–10pm; 100Ft) is really there to lure people into the *Labirintus* restaurant, but otherwise does a fair job of describing Hungary's wine-making regions using maps, wine-bottle labels and other artefacts. The sting in the tail is the invitation to sample half a dozen wines for an extra 700Ft – more than twice what you'd pay in a regular *bórozó*. Next door at no. 10b a painterly couple are commemorated by the **Imre Ámos–Margit Anna Collection** (mid-March to Oct Tues–Sun 10am–4pm; Nov to mid-March Fri–Sun 10am–4pm; 90Ft). Imre Ámos was sent to a Jewish labour camp in 1940, where he died in 1944. The museum contains works from the last years of his life, including *Self Portrait with Angel* from 1938 and the disturbing Apocalypse series of 1944. Downstairs, his wife Margit Anna's works are split into two periods: the warm, mellow pictures from before the Holocaust to the right of the entrance, and to the left the uncomfortably bright, sometimes grotesque images that she produced after the war.

A little further along, Bogdányi utca opens onto a square at the far corner of which stands the **Lázár Cross**, a small iron cross that's easy to miss behind the parked cars that fill the square. It honours King Lázár of Serbia, whom the Turks beheaded after the battle of Kosovo in revenge for the death of Sultan Murad. His body was brought here by the Serbs and buried in a wooden church. When the relic was taken back to Serbia in 1774, the place was marked by a cross in his memory. Horse-drawn carriages can be rented here for trips round the town; prices start at 3000Ft for half an hour, though it's possible to bargain them down. Bogdányi utca continues past the square; at no. 36, the **Kovács Blue Dye Shop** showcases a traditional style of folk dyeing: everything – pillow cases, skirts, oven cloths, you name it – is blue, and there's a small display to show how it is done.

The **Preobraženska Church**, a few steps further along Bogdányi utca, was erected by the tanners' guild in 1741–76, and its *embonpoint* enhanced by a Louis XVI gate the following century. Though its lavish iconostasis merits a look, the church is chiefly notable for its role in the Serbian festival on August 19, when it hosts the Blessing of the Grapes ceremony (recalling Szentendre's former role as a wine-producing centre). This is followed by a traditional procession round the church and further celebrations in the town square and elsewhere.

At the far end of Bogdányi utca, five minutes' walk further on, is another cross, the **Vinegrowers' Cross**, raised by a local guild and fittingly wreathed in grapevines. Having come this far, you might as well check out the hulking out-door creations of Jenő Kerényi in the **Sculpture Park**, a few minutes walk away at Ady utca 5, just past the *Vadászkert* restaurant (mid-March to Oct Wed–Sun noon–6pm).

## Eating and drinking

Like everything in Szentendre, **restaurants** tend to be pricey by Hungarian standards, and crowded during the summer. Tour groups tend to make for the ones on Fő tér, but just yards further up the hill is the small *Aranysárkány* ("Golden Dragon") at Alkotmány utca 1a, which serves excellent Hungarian food, despite its name; booking is advisable (☎26/311-670; daily noon–10pm). The menu is moderately priced, and the restaurant is air-conditioned – bliss on a hot day. *Rab Ráby Vendéglő* at Péter-Pál utca 1a (daily noon–11pm), just by the Peter-Paul Church, is more traditionally Hungarian in style, and a touch more expensive. North of the centre near the Kerényi Museum, you can sit outside and enjoy Hungarian food including game at a moderate price at the *Vadászkert* at Ady Endre út 6 (April–Sept noon–11pm; Oct–March noon–10pm). If you fancy a tasty snack, look out for a yellow sign in the main square pointing up a small alleyway saying *"lángos"* –deep-fried batter topped with cheese or sour cream.

## Szentendre Village Museum

The **Szentendre Village Museum** on Sztaravodai út, 4km to the west of town (April–Oct Tues–Sun 9am–5pm; 250Ft), is easily the most enjoyable local attraction. Hungary's largest open-air museum of rural architecture (termed a *Skanzen*, after the first such museum, founded in a Stockholm suburb in 1891), it will eventually include "samples" from ten different regions of the country – though only four have been finished so far – and the remains of a Roman villa. The museum is accessible by buses running roughly every hour from stand 8 of the bus terminal, by the HÉV station; get off when you see the spires in a field to the right; the entrance is 100m off the road. You can get an excellent book on the contents of the museum, which guides you round building by building, and has maps both of the layout of the museum and of the villages. Each building also has its warden, who can explain everything in great detail, though usually only in Hungarian.

Downhill to the right from the entrance is a composite village from the Upper Tisza region in northeast Hungary, culled from isolated settlements in the **Erdőhát** (see p.365). The guide points out the finer distinctions between the various humble peasant dwellings scattered among the barns and woven pigsties. As you walk towards the church, the houses move up the social scale, as even the fences show, going from rough wickerwork to a mart plank fence. The first house, a poor cottage from Kispalad, has mud floors, which the warden sprinkles in the traditional way to stop the dust rising, and a rough thatch. Further down is a house with wooden roof tiles and wooden floors. Rural carpenters produced highly skilled work, examples of which are the circular "dry mill" from Vámosoroszi, the wooden bell-tower from Nemesborzova, and the carving inside the church from Mándok (on a hilltop beyond).

As you walk up past the Calvinist graveyard, where the grave markers from four villages include the striking boat-shaped markers from Szatmárcseke in eastern Hungary, signs point you to the remains of the third-century Roman village, and on to the Western Transdanubia section. The thatched houses from the Őrség region (see p.239) are often constructed of wood and covered in adobe. The school from the village of Kondorfa has its old benches with slates for writing on, a towel and basin for washing, and behind the door the children's little home-spun bags. The teacher's living quarters are at the other end of the building, separated by a kitchen with an apron chimney, where the smoke goes out of a hole in the roof. At one end of the L-shaped house from Szentegyörgyvölgy dating from the nineteenth century, a small hen ladder runs up to the roof for the poultry, and in the open end of the attic you can see large woven straw baskets for storing grain. By contrast, the next section, originating from the ethnic German communities of the Kisalföld (Little Plain) in Northwest Transdanubia, seems far more regimented. Neatly aligned and whitewashed, the houses are filled with knick-knacks and embroidered samplers bearing homilies like "When the Hausfrau is capable, the clocks keep good time". The newest region is the Market Towns of the Great Hungarian Plain, which is in the process of being laid out. The house from Süsköd has a beautiful facade on the street, with the visitors' room or "clean room" laid out for Christmas celebrations with a nativity crib and a church-shaped box. Walking through the sections brings you back to the entrance of the museum.

**Demonstrations** of traditional crafts such as weaving, pottery and basket-making usually take place at the museum on the first and third Sunday of each month as well as on public holidays, but check at the museum (☎26/312-304) or at the Tourinform office in town for precise dates of events. Local festivals are also celebrated here, such as the grape harvest in October, when folkloric programmes and grape-pressing take place. Shops outside the museum entrance sell snacks and ice creams as well as local crafts, including beautiful handmade paper from the Vincze paper mill.

## Szentendre Sziget

Across the water from Szentendre is the sparsely populated **Szentendre Sziget** (Szentendre Island), stretching from below Szentendre up almost to Visegrád. Its open expanses have escaped the holiday home development seen on the road north of Szentendre, and the villages here give you the feeling that time has passed them by. Access to the island is poor, with only one bridge connecting it to the mainland at **Tahitótfalu**, 10km north of Szentendre. Buses run from the Budapest Árpád híd bus terminal to Tahitótfalu, and ferries from each main settlement on the bank go across to the island. There's also one car ferry connecting Vác on the east bank with the road to Tahitótfalu.

**KISOROSZI**, the small village near the northern tip of the island, is so quiet that it has no official accommodation, though if you ask around, you should be able to find a room. Ferries connect the village to the west bank hourly, linking with the bus from Budapest (Árpád híd terminal). Just up from the river bank is a *cukrászda* where locals sip their coffees. Up to the left at the crossroads, a half-hour walk brings you to the peaceful, sandy north tip of the island, with stunning views across to Visegrád, and a campsite amidst the trees (400Ft per tent). A couple of kilometres along the road to Tahitótfalu is a nine-hole **golf course**, one of the first in Hungary, created in 1984. The island also makes excellent terrain for riding, and one of the island's several **riding** schools is the Hubert Lovarda, 2km south of Tahitótfalu, on the road to Pócsmegyer (☎26/395-776 or 1/250-2263), which is well served by buses.

As you head north along the west bank, the land starts to rise and orchards and vineyards flourish around Dunabogdány, once a picturesque village but now a holiday home for Budapesters and a throughway for the busy Route 11. Its Germanic traditions are commemorated by a **local history collection** at Kossuth utca 93, but its unreliable opening times (ask at the offices in the courtyard if the woman is there to open up) and its collection of German memorabilia and household bits may not make it worth the stop. A few kilometres further on, the Danube Bend and Visegrád heave into sight.

# Visegrád and around

When the hillsides start to plunge and the river twists, keep your eyes fixed on the mountains to the west for a first glimpse of the citadel and ramparts of **VISEGRÁD**. The citadel is almost as it appeared to János Thuroczy in 1488, who described its "upper walls stretching to the clouds floating in the sky, and the lower bastions reaching down as far as the river". At that time, courtly life in Visegrád, the royal seat, was nearing its apogee, and the palace of King Mátyás and Queen Beatrice was famed throughout Europe. The papal legate Cardinal Castelli described it as a "paradiso terrestri", seemingly unperturbed by the presence of Vlad the Impaler, who resided here under duress between 1462 and 1475.

Tucked in between the hills and the river as the Danube flows north, Visegrád is a compact town, with most local activity centred around the ferry and the church. The three main **historical sites** all lie north of the centre: the Royal Palace and Solomon's Tower down near the river, and the citadel perching on top of the hill above. All the river sites are in easy walking distance, but you might

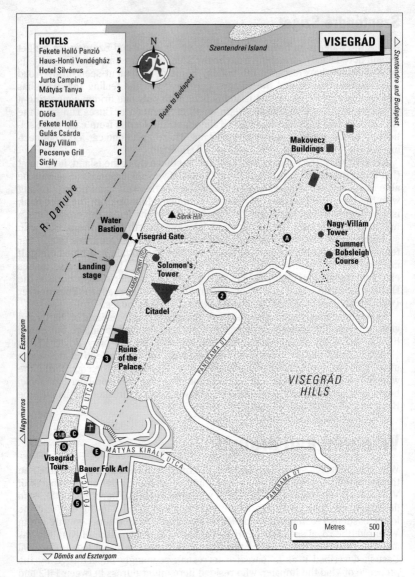

**HOTELS**
| | |
|---|---|
| Fekete Holló Panzió | 4 |
| Haus-Honti Vendégház | 5 |
| Hotel Silvánus | 2 |
| Jurta Camping | 1 |
| Mátyás Tanya | 3 |

**RESTAURANTS**
| | |
|---|---|
| Diófa | F |
| Fekete Holló | B |
| Gulás Csárda | E |
| Nagy Villám | A |
| Pecsenye Grill | C |
| Sirály | D |

VISEGRÁD

prefer taking a bus up to the citadel if the climb is too forbidding. While here, you can also visit the surrounding **Visegrád Hills**, boasting gorgeous views, and providing an unexpected but appropriate setting for several works by the visionary architect Imre Makovecz (see p.143). Though the ruins can be visited on a flying visit, the hills require a full day and a fair amount of walking, with the option of longer hikes or pony-trekking.

# Arrival and accommodation

**Boats** from Budapest and Esztergom land at Visegrád just below Solomon's Tower, twenty minutes' walk to the north of the centre. **Buses** make three stops in Visegrád – there is no bus station here – by the ferry and boat stations, and one in-between, near the palace. You can also travel by **train** from Nyugati Station to Nagymaros-Visegrád on the Szob line, and then catch a ferry across to Visegrád. For **information**, try Visegrád Tours by the *Sirály* restaurant down by the landing stage, who can also book accommodation (daily 9am–6pm; ☎26/398-160).

For such a popular destination, Visegrád is poorly equipped in terms of **accommodation**, and in the last year three of the cheaper hostels have closed, sharply reducing the options. At the top end of the scale, near the Royal Palace, the *Mátyás Tanya* at Fő utca 47 is elegantly set in the former journalist union's holiday home (☎26/398-309; ⑤); rooms have TV and bath. At the top of the hill, close to the citadel, is the modern *Hotel Silvanus*, Fekete-hegy (☎26/398-311; ④), with tennis courts, bowling green, sauna and an excellent view. Cheaper options are the *Haus-Honti Vendégház* in the centre of town overlooking a stream, at Fő utca 66 (☎26/398-120; ③), a small, charming pension where you can also rent bikes; and the *Fekete Holló Panzió* at Rév utca 12, next to the restaurant of the same name (☎26/397-290; ②), which offers rooms with bath right by the river.

Along Fő utca you'll see plenty of *Zimmer frei* signs advertising vacant **rooms**, though these can be quite expensive. Rooms are slightly cheaper on Széchenyi utca, parallel to Fő utca south of the centre; try no. 24 (☎26/398-298; ②) or no. 39 (☎26/398-354; ②). The nearest place to pitch a tent is at *Kék Duna Autós Camping* (☎26/398-102; May–Sept), which is well placed by the Danube, near the town centre along the main road to Esztergom. Not so easy to reach is *Jurta Camping* near Mogyoró-hegy (☎26/398-217; May–Sept), though it has a nice view; three buses a day go from the Nagymaros ferry station. Finally, if you get stuck, ask at Bauer Folk Art at Fő utca 46 (May–Sept daily 10am–5pm;☎26/316-469), who can help you in finding private rooms.

# The ruins of Visegrád

The layout of the **ruins of Visegrád** (whose Slavic name means "High Castle") dates back to the thirteenth century, when Béla IV began fortifying the north against a recurrence of the Mongol invasion. Its most prominent features are the citadel on the hill and Solomon's Tower near the riverside below, part of the fortification that forms a gate over the road that you pass through arriving from Budapest. The palace itself is inconspicuously sited, further inland and 500m south of Solomon's Tower. As Visegrád fell into dereliction after the Turkish occupation, mud washing down from the hillsides gradually buried the palace entirely, and later generations doubted its very existence. In 1934, however, the archeologist János Schulek made a breakthrough. While at a New Year's Eve party, after he had been in Visegrád for some time hunting for the lost palace without success, the wine ran out and Schulek was sent to get some more from the neighbours. An old woman told him to go down to the wine cellar, and there he found clues in the stones that convinced him the palace was here, later unearthing one of the palace vaults.

In July each year the ruins provide the setting for **medieval pageants** intended to recreate the splendour of Visegrád's Renaissance heyday, with jousting, displays of medieval crafts like blacksmithing, and much merriment – ask at Visegrád Tours (see p.139) for details.

## The palace

Now largely excavated and partially reconstructed, the **Royal Palace**, ten minutes' walk from the centre at Fő utca 27–29 (Tues–Sun: April–Oct 9am–5pm; Nov–March 8am–4pm; 100Ft) spreads over four levels or terraces. Originally founded in 1323 by the Angevin king Charles Robert, the palace was expanded by subsequent kings, the largest development occurring in the reign of Mátyás Corvinus.

Walking up from the entrance, you pass the *kőtár*, a collection of excavated stones from Roman to medieval times, before arriving at the palace proper. Here you enter at the second level, the **cour d'honneur**, which was constructed for Charles's successor, Louis, and provided the basis for subsequent building by Sigismund and, later, Mátyás Corvinus. Its chief features are the pillastered **Renaissance loggia** and a copy of a panel from the **Hercules Fountain** that stood in the middle of the courtyard. The original pieces are displayed in the museum in Solomon's Tower, but you can get an idea of what it looked like in the display to your left as you enter the courtyard.

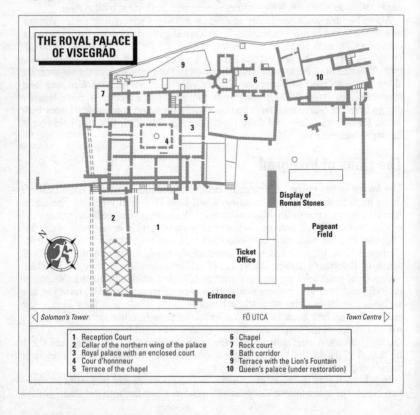

**THE ROYAL PALACE OF VISEGRÁD**

Display of Roman Stones

Pageant Field

Ticket Office

Entrance

◁ Solomon's Tower          FŐ UTCA          Town Centre ▷

1  Reception Court
2  Cellar of the northern wing of the palace
3  Royal palace with an enclosed court
4  Cour d'honnneur
5  Terrace of the chapel
6  Chapel
7  Rock court
8  Bath corridor
9  Terrace with the Lion's Fountain
10  Queen's palace (under restoration)

Down the steps in the exhibition room, you enter the **wine cellar**, where the Hungarian, Czech and Polish kings signed the closing document at the Visegrád Congress of 1335. Called to discuss the growing Habsburg threat, they failed to agree on any concrete steps, but nevertheless managed to consume 10,000 litres of wine and vast amounts of food in the process. In February 1991, Visegrád played host to another less extravagant summit, when the prime ministers of Hungary, Poland and Czechoslovakia met here to put together a joint strategy for trade and EC membership in the post-Communist era. Again the setting for signing the final document was the cellar, and again the concrete results were limited – although it did mean that the present display of stonework from the age of King Mátyás was put together so that the cellar would not be totally empty. Work has begun on creating an entrance at ground level into the cellar, but this may take a while to realize.

Legend has it that Mátyás was eventually poisoned by his wife Beatrice, who wanted to rule on her own. The chalice containing the fatal potion may well have passed between the **royal suites** that once stood beneath an overhang on the third terrace, separated by a magnificent **chapel**. Reportedly, the finest sight at this time was the garden on the fourth terrace, embellished by the **Lion Fountain**. A perfect copy of the original (carved by Ernő Szakál) bears Mátyás's raven crest and dozens of sleepy-looking lions, although, unlike the original, it's not fed by the gutters and pipes that channelled water down from the citadel. The original pieces are again in Solomon's Tower.

## Solomon's Tower

Five minutes' walk north along Fő utca, just after it rejoins the main highway, you can take a right onto Salamon torony utca, which climbs up through the Budapest Gate of the old castle fortifications to reach **Solomon's Tower**, a mighty hexagonal keep, buttressed on two sides by unsightly concrete slabs (May–Sept Tues–Sun 9am–5pm; 100Ft), and named after an eleventh-century Hungarian king. The **Mátyás Museum** on the ground and first floor of the tower exhibits finds from the palace, including the white Anjou Fountain of the Angevins; the original pieces of the Lion and Hercules fountains, together with a reconstruction of the child Hercules struggling with the hydra; and the red marble *Visegrád Madonna*, a renaissance masterpiece that shows many similarities to the works of Tomaso Fiamberti nearby. The next two floors present the history of Visegrád up to the Turkish occupation. It's worth climbing to the top for the view of the lines of fortification running down from the citadel on both sides, meeting at the Water Bastion by the river. However, neither this, nor the **ruined Roman fort** to the north, atop Sibrik Hill, are worth a special detour, so you might want to save your energy for the climb to Visegrád's citadel.

## The citadel

Dramatically sited on a crag directly above Solomon's Tower and commanding a superb view of Nagymaros and the Börzsöny Mountains on the east bank, Visegrád's triangular **citadel** (March 15–Nov 15 daily 9am–6pm; rest of the year Sat & Sun 10am–4pm; closed when it snows, as the battlements are too slippery; 180Ft including all displays) served as a repository for the Hungarian crown jewels until they were stolen by a treacherous maid of honour in the sixteenth century. Restoration of the castle began in the late nineteenth century, after an eager local priest brought the government's attention to the dire state of the place, and work still continues slowly. Its state before the work began in 1870 is shown inside in a photograph in the exhibition on the history of the castle, which includes a hologram of the crown and drawings of how the castle looked at different periods; you can see the same drawings in the Royal Palace and Solomon's Tower. The waxworks display on instruments of torture and execution in the Middle Ages is fairly gruesome, with careful descriptions – in Hungarian only – of how the different instruments were used; Vlad might have learnt a thing or two here. In the innermost courtyard is a display on hunting, fishing and quarrying, with mock-ups of medieval scenes showing hunters and their tools, a stuffed deer lying dead in a cart and an animal caught in a trap. Information is only in Hungarian and German, but you get the general idea from the displays.

You can reach the citadel from the centre of town via the "Calvary" footpath (signposted *Fellegvár* and marked by a red cross on the way), heading up to the left off Nagy Lajos utca, 50m behind the church. It takes its name from the calvary of reliefs that you follow on your way up. Alternatively, you can start from Solomon's Tower and walk through the gate and uphill, looking out for signs up to the right after ten to fifteen minutes. Both routes involve around forty minutes of steep walking. There are also three buses a day (April–Sept 9.30am, 12.30am & 3.30pm), which stop at both the boat and the ferry stations on the river side of the road, and follow the scenic Panorama Route into the hills.

## The Visegrád Hills

Thickly wooded and crisscrossed with paths, the **Visegrád Hills** are a popular rambling spot. From the car park near the citadel, you can follow the main road to a signposted path off to the left, which leads to the **Nagy-Villám observation tower** (*kilátó*; daily: March–Oct 10am–5pm; Nov–Feb 10am–3pm; 60Ft). Sited at the highest point on the Danube Bend, it offers a view that stretches as far as Slovakia. The *Nagy-Villám Vendéglő* on the way up offers a moderately priced meal with fine views. By the *kilátó* is the **Summer Bobsleigh Course** (*Nyári Bob*), where for 150Ft you can race down a one-kilometre run (April–Oct, except on rainy days when the brakes are rendered ineffective; ☎26/397-397). You can also visit the collection of wooden buildings designed by **Imre Makovecz** at Mogyoró-hegy (Hazelnut Hill), a kilometre north of the observation tower (see box opposite).

If you feel like **hiking**, you could try the twelve-kilometre trail marked with blue stripes running from the tower, via Paprét (Priest's Meadow), to Pilisszentlászló, which takes two to three hours. Although Visegrád itself has nowhere to swim, there is a salubrious terraced *strand* and natural warm-water **pool** 4km away at Lepence, at the Pilisszentlászló turn-off towards Dömös (May–Sept 9am–6pm; ☎26/398-208). A series of pools have been cut into the hillside overlooking the Danube, making it one of the most spectacular open-air pool complexes in Hungary.

## Eating, drinking and entertainment

Fried-fish and sausage stalls along the promenade offer basic options for eating out, which are augmented by several **restaurants**. Two of the best places are near the church in the centre of town: the *Gulás Csárda* in Nagy Lajos király utca 4 serving good Hungarian food at reasonable prices, and the *Diófa Étterem* at Fő

## IMRE MAKOVECZ AT VISEGRÁD

**Imre Makovecz** was a promising architect in the Kádár years, but was branded a troublemaker for his outspoken nationalism, banned from teaching, and "exiled" to the Visegrád forestry department in 1977. During this time he made many of the the wooden buildings which can be seen at Mogyoró-hegy in Visegrád. Over the next decade he refined his ideas, acquiring a group of student followers for whom he held summer schools. Employing cheap, low-technology methods in a way he branded as specifically Magyar, he taught his students how to construct temporary buildings using raw materials such as branches and twigs. The Cultural House near the *Jurta Camping* in Visegrád is an excellent example, with a turfed roof and a light homely interior that has worn well.

Now one of the most influential architects in Hungary, Makovecz's buildings can be found all over the country. They include the community centres in Sárospatak, Zalaszentlászló and Szigetvár, churches at Paks and Siófok, and the oesophagus-like crypt of the Farkasréti cemetery in Budapest. Makovecz also designed the much admired Hungarian Pavilion at the 1992 Expo in Seville, with its seven towers representing the seven Magyar tribes. He has won much praise abroad, with strong support from Prince Charles, for whom his anti-modernist, back-to-nature style has a strong appeal. However, his generous use of wood does not appeal to all environmentalists, and his dabbling in right-wing politics turns his whole idea of a return to the "real" Hungarian style of building, once a righteous tool against the old regime, into something less appealing.

utca 48, which is very agreeable, unpretentious, and modest in price, and even boasts a few Swedish specialities on its menu. For simple quick food, the self-service *Pecsenye Grill* opposite the church on Rév utca is the best place. Of the riverside restaurants, the *Sirály* at Rév utca 7 is quite pricey and caters for large parties; the *Fekete Holló* at Rév utca 10 across the road is quieter. The *Nagy-Villám Vendéglő* above the citadel, which offers fine views and a moderately priced meal, also caters for large groups. In summer there are **discos** at the *Sirály*, and sporadic disco **cruises** between Visegrád and Esztergom, which leave from the main landing stage as advertised.

# Esztergom

Beautifully situated in a crook of the Danube facing Slovakia, **ESZTERGOM** is dominated by its basilica, whose dome is visible for miles around. The sight is richly symbolic, since it was here that Prince Géza and his son Vajk (the future king and saint Stephen) brought Hungary into the fold of Roman Catholic (not Orthodox) Christendom, in the nation's first cathedral. Even after the court moved to Buda following the Mongol invasion, Esztergom remained the **centre of Catholicism** until the Turkish conquest, when the clergy dispersed to safer towns and it became an Ottoman stronghold, besieged by Christian armies. While the town recovered in the eighteenth century, it wasn't until the 1820s that it became the Primal See again, following a nationwide campaign. As part of the *ancien régime*, the Church was ruthlessly persecuted during the Rákosi era (though the basilica was well maintained, allegedly because the wife of the Soviet leader Khrushchev liked it). From the 1960s onwards, however, the Communists

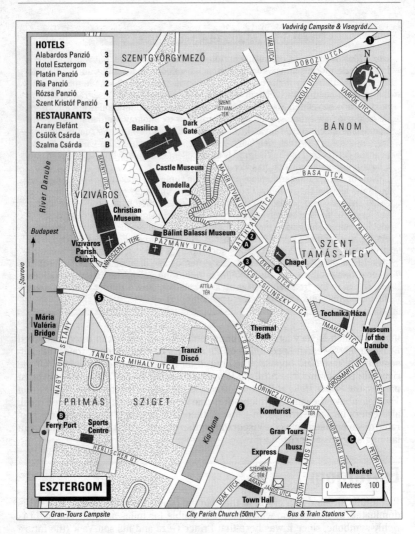

Vadvirág Campsite & Visegrád △ ➊
N

HOTELS
Alabardos Panzió       3
Hotel Esztergom        5
Platán Panzió          6
Ria Panzió             2
Rózsa Panzió           4
Szent Kristóf Panzió   1

RESTAURANTS
Arany Elefánt          C
Csülök Csárda          A
Szalma Csárda          B

SZENTGYÖRGYMEZŐ

DOBOZI UTCA

VÁR UTCA

ISKOLA UTCA

VARFŐK UTCA

BÁNOM

SZENT ISTVÁN TÉR

Basilica      Dark Gate

MÁJER ISTVÁN UTCA

BASA UTCA

VASVÁRI PÁL UTCA

Castle Museum

Rondella

River Danube

BERÉNYI UTCA

VÍZIVÁROS

Christian Museum

Bálint Balassí Museum

BATTHYÁNY UTCA

SZENT TAMÁS-HEGY

Budapest

Vízivaros Parish Church

MINDSZENTY TÉRE

PÁZMÁNY UTCA

➋
Ⓐ
➌     TŐRÖK UTCA     Chapel
BAJCSY-ZS. ILINSZKY UTCA     Ⓒ     ➍

Sturovo △

ATTILA TÉR

➎

KIS-DUNA SÉTÁNY

Thermal Bath

Technika Háza

IMAHÁZ UTCA

Museum of the Danube

Mária Valéria Bridge

TÁNCSICS MIHÁLY UTCA

Tranzit Disco

VÖRÖSMARTY UTCA

KÖLCSEY UTCA

NAGY DUNA SÉTÁNY

LŐRINCZ UTCA

PRÍMÁS     SZIGET

Kis-Duna

➏

Komturist

RÁKOCZI TÉR

SÁNDOR JÁNOS UTCA

Ⓑ   Ferry Port   Sports Centre

HERLISCHER ÚT

Gran Tours

Express   Ibusz

LAJOS UTCA

KOSSUTH

PETŐFI UTCA

Ⓒ

Market

SZÉCHENYI TÉR

ARANY JÁNOS UTCA

0  Metres  100

ESZTERGOM

DEÁK UTCA   Town Hall

▽ Gran-Tours Campsite          City Parish Church (50m) ▽          Bus & Train Stations ▽

settled for a modus vivendi, hoping to enlist the Church's help with social problems and to harness the patriotic spirit of the faithful. The avowedly Christian government elected in 1990 did its best to restore Church property and influence, and, while this process slowed down after the Communists returned to power, their concordat with the Vatican in 1997 eased fears of it going into reverse.

Esztergom combines historic monuments and small-town charm in just the right doses, with a summer festival as an inducement to linger. The town's layout is easily grasped and most of the restaurants and pensions are within walking distance of the centre. The only drawback is the infrequency of direct buses between Visegrád and Esztergom, which makes it difficult to see both towns in one day.

# Arrival and accommodation

If you arrive **by bus** from Visegrád, it's best to get off near the Basilica Hill or in the centre rather than travelling on to the bus station on Simor János utca, where services from Budapest terminate. From the **train** station, 1km further south, buses #1 and #5 run into the centre. **Ferries** from Budapest tie up on the Danube embankment of Prímás Sziget, fifteen minutes' walk from the centre.

For **information**, private rooms or concert bookings, Gran Tours, on the corner of Rákóczi tér (May–Sept Mon–Fri 8am–6pm, Sat 9am–noon; Oct–April Mon–Fri 8am–6pm; ☎33/417-052), has helpful English-speaking staff, and is streets ahead of Komtourist at Lőrincz utca 6 (June–Aug Mon–Fri 8am–4pm, Sat 8am–noon; Sept–May Mon–Fri 8am–noon; ☎33/312-082). Both places **change money**, as does the K&H bank opposite Gran Tours, which has an ATM outside.

## Accommodation

Though day-trippers are a year-round presence, relatively few tourists stay here outside of summer, when Slovaks and Germans descend in force, making it wise to book ahead. During July and August, the cheapest option is college **dormitory beds** (①), bookable through Gran Tours. The next best deal are **private rooms** (①–②), available year-round from Gran Tours or Komtourist. Of the two **campsites**, *Gran-Tours Camping*, 500m south of the ruined bridge on Prímás Sziget (☎33/311-329; ②–③; May to mid-Oct, bungalows until late Sept), has better facilities and is far more conveniently located than *Vadvirág Camping*, 3km along the road to Visegrád near the tail-end of the #6 bus route (☎33/312-234; mid-April to mid-Sept), with grassy tent-space and two-person bungalows (①) – but both sites are equally noisy.

### HOTELS AND PENSIONS

**Alabardos Panzió**, Bajcsy-Zsilinszky utca 49 (☎33/312-640). Decent pension with a dozen rooms and a small terrace on an alley off the main road, midway between the upper and lower town. ④.

**Hotel Esztergom**, Nagy Duna sétány, Prímás Sziget (☎33/312-883). Modernized 1970s three-star hotel in a pleasant setting in the lower town, with a restaurant, roof terrace and sports facilities. ⑤.

**Márta Panzió**, Bocskoroskuti út 1 (☎33/311-983). Quiet, modern pension twenty minutes' walk from town near the Visegrád road. Rooms have television and bathroom. Secure parking. ②.

**Platán Panzió**, Kis-Duna sétány 11 (☎33/311-355). Perhaps the cheapest of the pensions in Esztergom: a nice, basic place opposite Prímás Sziget, close to the centre of the lower town. ②.

**Ria Panzió**, Batthány utca 11 (☎33/313-115). A small, comfortable pension with a good location below Basilica Hill. Secure parking, a pocket-sized garden and beer terrace. ④.

**Rózsa Panzió**, Török Ignác utca 11, directly below Szent Tamás-hegy (☎33/317-250). Its old wing is shabby, but the upper rooms in the new annexe have a fine view that makes up for the somewhat spartan facilities. ②.

**St Kristóf Panzió**, Dobozi Mihály utca 11 (☎33/316-255). An attractive new pension on the Visegrád road, ten minutes from the basilica, with a garden and an excellent restaurant. If full, there are also rooms for rent opposite. ④.

# The Town

The main focal point of the town is **Basilica Hill**, whose landscaped slope appears on maps as Szent István tér. After seeing the basilica and the castle remains here, you'll probably want some refreshment before heading downhill to the **Víziváros**, where art buffs can get stuck into the Christian Museum and others will be drawn to the shady *korzó* beside the Kis-Duna, separating **Prímás Sziget** from the **lower town**. In the lower town, the emphasis is on enjoyment, with cafés, bars and discos and an outdoor thermal pool.

## The basilica

Built on the site of the first cathedral in Hungary, where Vajk was crowned as King Stephen by a papal envoy on Christmas Day, 1000 AD, Esztergom's Neoclassical **basilica** (daily: March–Sept 7am–6pm; Oct–Feb Tues–Sun 7am–5pm; free) is the largest in the country, measuring 118m in length and 40m in width, and capped by a dome 100m high. Representing a thousand years of faith and statehood, it was begun by Pál Kühneland and János Packh in 1822, and finally completed by József Hild in 1869, thirteen years after its consecration, once the dome was in place. Liszt's *Gran Mass* was composed for the occasion (*Gran* being the German name for Esztergom). In 1991, the church hosted two events symbolizing its triumph over Communism: the reburial of the exiled Cardinal Mindszenty and the first papal visit to Hungary.

The exterior of the basilica is unadorned except for the primates' coats of arms flanking the great bronze doors that are only used on special occasions. Its nave is on a massive scale, clad in marble, gilding and mosaics. To the left of the entrance is the lavish red and white marble **Bakócz Chapel**, whose Florentine altar was salvaged by Archbishop Tamás Bakócz from the original church. The basilica's main altarpiece was painted by the Venetian Michelangelo Grigoletti, based on Titian's *Assumption* in the Frari Church in Venice. To the right lies the **treasury** (*kincstár*; daily: May–Oct 9am–4.30pm; Feb–April, Nov & Dec 10am–4pm; 160Ft), an overpowering collection of bejewelled croziers and chalices and kitsch papal souvenirs.

---

### THE RETURN OF CARDINAL MINDSZENTY

When the much travelled body of **Cardinal József Mindszenty** was finally laid to rest with state honours in May 1991, it was a vindication of his uncompromising heroism – and the Vatican realpolitik that Mindszenty despised. As a conservative and monarchist, he had stubbornly opposed the postwar Communist takeover, warning that "cruel hands are reaching out to seize hold of our children, claws belonging to people who have nothing but evil to teach them". Arrested in 1948, tortured for 39 days and nights, and sentenced to life imprisonment for treason, Mindszenty was freed during the Uprising and took refuge in the US Embassy, where he remained for the next fifteen years, an exile in the heart of Budapest.

When the Vatican struck a deal with the Kádár regime in 1971, Mindszenty had to be pushed into resigning his position and going to Austria, where he died in 1975. Although his will stated that his body should not return home until "the red star of Moscow had fallen from Hungarian skies", his reburial occurred some weeks before the last Soviet soldier left, in preparation for the pope's visit in August of that year. Nowadays the Vatican proclaims his greatness, without any hint of apology for its past actions.

Towards the nave are two stairways, the first leading to a **crypt** (*krypta*; daily 9am–4.45pm; 50Ft), which is like a set from a Dracula film, with seventeen-metre thick walls to support the enormous weight of the basilica, and giant stone women flanking the stairway down to gloomy vaults full of entombed prelates. Though several other mausolea look more arresting, it is the **tomb of Cardinal Mindszenty** (see box opposite) that transfixes Hungarians. The other stairway ascends for over three hundred steps to the stiflingly hot interior of the **cupola** (*kupola*; May–Oct daily 9am–5pm; 80Ft), though any discomfort is forgotten the moment you step outside and see the magnificent **view** of Esztergom, with the Slovak town of Štúrovo across the water.

## The Castle Museum

On higher ground, thirty metres south of the basilica, are the red-roofed, recon-structed remains of the palace founded by Prince Géza, now presented as the **Castle Museum** (Tues–Sun: April–Oct 9am–5pm; Nov–March 10am–4pm; 160Ft). A royal seat for almost three hundred years, it was here that Béla III entertained Philip of France and Frederick Barbarossa on their way to the Third Crusade. After Buda became the capital, Hungary's primates lived here, and the Renaissance prelate János Vitéz made it a centre of humanist culture, where Queen Beatrice spent her widowhood. Although the palace was sacked by the Turks in 1543 and twice besieged before they were evicted in 1683, enough survived to be excavated by Leopold Antal in the 1930s – indeed, it is more impressive than the remains of Buda's royal palace.

Though foreigners are expected to join a tour in Hungarian, you can slip away to the rooms displaying visualizations of the palace in various epochs to reach the royal suite ahead of the crowd. Traces of the frescoes that once covered every wall in the palace can be seen in the vaulted living-hall from Béla III's reign, whence a narrow stairway ascends to the study of Archbishop Vitéz – known as the **Hall of Virtues** after its allegorical murals of Intelligence, Moderation, Strength and Justice. Beyond lies the **royal chapel**, whose Gothic rose window and Romanesque arches were executed by craftsmen brought over by Béla's two French wives; its frescoes of saints and the Tree of Life reflect his Byzantine upbringing. A spiral staircase leads to the palace rooftop, offering a panoramic view of Esztergom and the river, and a fresh perspective on the basilica.

During June and July, **plays** and **dances** are staged in the **Rondella** bastion, whose exit is guarded by a giant statue of a warrior. As you descend the hillside, notice the monumental **Dark Gate**: a tunnel built in the 1820s as a short cut between church buildings on either side of the hill and later exploited by the Soviet Army, which maintained a base there until 1989. The former primate's wine cellars, next door, have been converted into a restaurant.

## The Víziváros and Prímás Sziget

Below the castle ramparts lies the picturesque **Víziváros** (Watertown), a small dis-trict of Baroque churches and seminaries where practising choirs are audible along the streets. Turning into Pázmány utca, you come to the **Bálint Balassi Museum** at no. 63 (Tues–Sun 9am–5pm; 50Ft), which mounts temporary historical exhibi-tions rather than dwelling on the romantic poet Bálint Balassi (1554–94), who died trying to recapture Esztergom from the Turks. This half-crazed philanderer was famous for sexually assaulting women and then dedicating verses to them – behaviour that resulted in him being beaten unconscious on several occasions.

A couple of minutes further on you'll come to the Italianate Baroque **Víziváros Parish Church** and the old Primate's Palace at Berényi utca 2. The latter now houses the **Christian Museum** (Tues–Sun 10am–6pm; 150Ft), Hungary's richest hoard of religious art, which includes the largest collection of Italian prints outside Italy, Renaissance paintings and wood carvings by German and Austrian masters, and the unique "Lord's Coffin of Garamszentbenedek" – a wheeled, gilded structure used in Easter Week processions, from around 1480.

From the parish church you can cross a bridge onto **Prímás Sziget** (Primate's Island), a popular tourist spot with a hotel (see p.145), restaurant, campsite and tennis courts. A little way south of the landing stage for ferries to Štúrovo, you'll see the elegant stump of the Mária Valeria bridge that connected the two towns before it was blown up in 1945. Plans to restore it are stymied by the frosty state of Magyar–Slovak relations, though one still sees lots of Slovak cars driving from the ferry stage into the centre of town.

### The lower town and Szent Tamás-hegy

While Rákóczi tér, with its supermarkets and banks, is the de facto centre of the **lower town**, its most attractive feature is the **Kis-Duna sétány**, a riverside walk lined with weeping willows and villas, where people promenade. Inland, civic pride is manifest in the brightly painted public buildings on **Széchenyi tér**, including a town hall with Rococo windows that once belonged to Prince Rákóczi's general, János Bottyán, whose statue stands nearby. The old part of town extends as far south as the **City Parish Church**, built on the site of a medieval monastery where Béla IV and Queen Mária Lascaris were buried. To the right of its gateway is a plaque showing the level of the flood of 1832.

The taming of the river is one of the themes of the **Museum of the Danube** at Kölcsey utca 2 (March–Oct Tues–Sun 10am–5.30pm; 50Ft). Count Széchenyi was the prime mover of the plan to curb flooding and improve navigation on the Danube, using the labour of thousands of Hungarian navvies and technology imported from England – including the steam-dredger *Vidra*, a model of which can be seen. There is also an exhibition on the controversial Danube barrages at Nagymaros and Gabčíkovo, that have been a bone of contention between Hungary and Slovakia since 1989.

To end with an overview of the lower town, walk up Imház utca past a flamboyant, Moorish-style edifice that was once Esztergom's synagogue and is now a science club, or **Technika Háza**. Shortly afterwards you'll find a flight of steps leading to **Szent Tamás-hegy** (St Thomas's Hill), a rocky outcrop named after the English martyr Thomas à Becket. A **chapel** was built here in his honour by Margaret Capet, whose English father-in-law, Henry II, prompted Thomas's assassination by raging "Who will rid me of this turbulent priest?" Even after her husband died and Margaret married Béla III of Hungary, her conscience would not let her forget the saint. The existing chapel (postdating the Turkish occupation) is fronted by a trio of lifesize statues representing Golgotha.

# Eating, drinking and entertainment

As in Szentendre, Hungarian food rules the menus, and **restaurants** near the tourist sites are geared to coach parties and a fast turnover, though none of them is so bad or expensive that you feel compelled to look elsewhere. Indeed, it's hard to resist a meal in the cavernous cellars of the *Prímás Pince* (daily 10am–9.30pm), beneath Basilica Hill. On Prímás Sziget, the *Hotel Esztergom*'s restaurant is excellent, or there's the terraced rustic-style *Szálma Csárda* near the Budapest ferrydock serving fish and poultry. In the Víziváros, *Anonym* at Berényi utca 6 specializes in exotically sauced game dishes, while the *Csülök Csárda* (daily noon–midnight), serving up large portions of moderately priced Hungarian food, is popular with locals and tourists alike. Less touristy places in the lower town include the *Arany Elefánt* (daily 11am–10pm) at Petőfi utca 15; the *Kispipa Étterem* at Kossuth utca 19 (Mon–Thurs 11am–10pm, Sat till midnight, Sun till 9pm), devoted to chicken, turkey and goose liver recipes; and the restaurant in the *St Kristóf Panzió*, which delivers the best home-cooking in town. The only non-Magyar option is the *McAllenney Pizzeria* at Kossuth utca 11 (daily 10am–midnight, Sat till 2am), which offers some veggie choices and a variety of crepes. If you're catering for yourself, there's a daily outdoor **market** on Simor János utca.

Almost any of these restaurants are feasible **drinking** spots, as are the **pavement cafés** between Rákóczi and Széchenyi tér, which are also good for sandwiches, cakes and ices – though only the *Gambrinus Maláta Bar* at Vörösmarty utca 3 (Mon–Sat noon–midnight, Sun till 10pm) could be described as trendy, with dance music on the jukebox and varnished branches everywhere.

Summer is the time for **concerts** in Esztergom, with an annual programme of choral and organ music in the basilica and the Víziváros parish church, plus a **Guitar Festival** during the first half of August in odd-numbered years; details of both from Gran Tours. For livelier nocturnal entertainment there are two **discos** on Prímás Sziget – the daily *Tranzit* at Táncsics Mihály utca 11 and the Saturday-nighter in the sports centre on Herlischer út – plus fleeting events advertised on Rákóczi tér. By day, you can work up a sweat in the sports centre (daily 2–9pm) or the tennis courts near Gran Tours' campsite, or pass the time soaking in the large outdoor **thermal bath** (May–Sept daily 9am–6pm; 150Ft), behind the presently defunct *Hotel Fürdő* on Bajcsy-Zsilinszky utca.

# The Pilis range

Whether you describe them as mountains or hills, the **Pilis range** (*Pilis hegység*), behind the west bank, offers lots of scope for **hiking** amidst lovely scenery. The beech and oak woods on these limestone slopes are most beautiful in the autumn, but there's a possibility of sighting red deer or wild boars at any time of year. Ruined monasteries and lodges attest to the hermits of the Order of St Paul and the royal hunting parties who frequented the hills in medieval times.

The Pilis is directly accessible by bus from Esztergom, Pomáz (near Szentendre) or the Árpád híd terminus in Budapest, or you can hike up by various routes – from the Nagy-Villám Tower at Visegrád, or from Dömös, 6km west of Visegrád. If you're planning any walking, buy a **map** of the Pilis in Budapest or the Danube Bend towns, which shows the paths (*turistaút/földút*), caves (*barlang*), and rain shelters (*esőház*) throughout the highlands.

## Pomáz

**POMÁZ**, on the HÉV line between Budapest and Szentendre, is an excellent place from where to step off into the Pilis, with hourly buses leaving from the HÉV station, on the eastern edge of town, to Dobogókő, 18km northwest of Pomáz. Before doing so, though, it's worth exploring the town, most of which is fairly recent, though the Roman sarcophagus outside the town hall on the main street indicates that people have been living and dying here for a long time. Serbian immigrants fleeing from the Turks arrived in the late seventeenth century, and by the nineteenth century there was a flourishing German community here too. However, the first museum you come to as you walk up to the town from the HÉV station has nothing to do with either group: the **ethnographical collection** of folk costumes and embroidery, behind the colourful Transylvanian gate at József Attila utca 28/b (*Magyar Néprajzi Gyűjtemény*; Tues & Thurs 2–6pm, Sat & Sun 10am–noon & 1–6pm; 50Ft), was put together by private collector János Hamar, and covers four regions of Hungarian-speaking communities; every spare inch of furniture here is covered with decoration. The **Community History Collection** at Kossuth Lajos utca 48, a ten-minute walk up the road just past Hősök tere, on the left of the main road (*Község Történeti Gyűjtemény*; Sat & Sun 10am–noon & 2–6pm; closed Dec & Jan; 80Ft), offers something more local. It recreates homes in Pomáz belonging to the Serbian and German communities, and includes a very nice enamel stove which also served as a boiler, with a tap on one side to let out the hot water. Archeological finds from the area are housed to the left of the entrance. The Swabian community, originally from Germany, was mostly deported back there after World War II, and links with the deported families have only been officially re-established over the last ten years.

Pomáz's Serb community has been shrinking steadily this century, although you can still hear old ladies chatting to each other in Serbian on street corners, and the town is proud of its dance group which has won prizes in Belgrade. Five minutes further up Kossuth utca, at Szabadság tér, is a **Plague Cross** erected in 1792. Five minutes' walk up to the right along the suitably named Szerb utca stands the church of St George, which holds masses for the small community at 10am on the second and fourth Sundays of the month. Your best chance to look around the church is to go in just before the service starts. The church's main annual celebration is the feast of the church's patron saint on May 6. The square behind the church, Vujicsics tér, takes its name from the Serbian composer Tihamer Vujicsics (1929–75), who was born in the street beyond; a plaque on Plébánia utca marks the spot. The **Vujicsics Ensemble**, which preserves his memory, started in Pomáz and performs frequently there in the summer, although it's now based in Szentendre.

Pomáz has a couple of **pensions**: the *Rákos Panzió* at Beniczky utca 63 (☎26/325-355; ③), five minutes' walk up the main road past the Plague Cross, and the *Tutti Panzió*, ten minutes' walk from the station to the left along the main road at Budakalász út 14 (☎26/325 888; ①).

## Dobogókő and Dömös

Standing in the shadow of 756-metre-high Pilis-tető, **DOBOGÓKŐ** has been a hiking centre since the late nineteenth century, when one of Hungary's first hostels was established here, and is still the best base for walking in the Pilis. The most popular way to see the area is to take the bus up (buses leave hourly from just by the HÉV terminal at Pomáz, and twice daily from Budapest's Árpád híd terminal), and then to walk down the Rám precipice – a four- to five-hour hike that's not advisable in wet weather – to Dömös, which offers fabulous views down to the river.

The hostel building at Dobogókő, just up through the trees from where the buses turn round, is now home to the small **Museum of Rambling and Nature Tourism** (Thurs, Sat & Sun 9am–1.45pm; 15Ft). Exhibits include old photos of the area, showing that there was hardly a tree around the village a hundred years ago, and some old equipment, including skis with a strip of seal fur on the bottom to prevent the ski from slipping downhill. However, most of the information is in Hungarian, so you will probably want to pass quickly round and get back in the open air.

The *Eötvös Loránd Tourist House* next to the museum offers some of the cheapest **accommodation** around (☎26/347-534; ①), and also serves strudels and other snacks during the week, and lunch on Saturday from noon to around 6pm. Tents can be pitched between the bus terminus and the *Tourist House*; ask there for permission. Campers can use the *Tourist House*'s bathroom and weekend restaurant. Just down from here is the similarly cheap *Margit Tourist House*, with rooms of four to ten beds (①), and the more upmarket *Hotel Nimród* (☎26/347-527; ③), which handles reservations for both. If there are no rooms available at the top of the hill, there's the *Platán Panzió* (☎26/347-680; ②) and the *Pilis Hotel* (☎26/347-504; ③) on the main road leading up to Dobogókő about 1km from the top of the hill.

Aside from the hotels, for **food** there is the *Bohém Tanya* by the car park at the bus terminus, with red chequered tablecloths, serving solid Hungarian fare from noon to 5.30pm, or for a filling bean goulash or toasted sandwiches there is the *Zsindelyes Csárda*, 300m down past the *Hotel Nimród* (daily 10am–8pm, Oct–March till 6pm), a wooden construction by Imre Makovecz, which also houses the engine house of the ski lift.

Walking up to Dobogókő from the river, the best starting point is **DÖMÖS**, 7km west of Visegrád, where buses between Visegrád and Esztergom stop off. Inconspicuous wooden signposts near the stream in the centre of the village indicate the start of trails into the hills, which abound in raspberries during early summer. Follow the Malom tributary for 2.5km and you'll reach a path that forks right for the Rám precipice (3hr) and Dobogókő (4–5hr), and left for the Vadálló Rocks (3hr) beneath the towering "Pulpit Seat" – a 641-metre crag that only the experienced should attempt to climb.

# THE EAST BANK

Compared to its western counterpart, the Danube Bend's **east bank** has fewer monuments and, consequently, fewer visitors. **Vác**, the only sizeable town, has a monopoly on historic architecture, styling itself the "city of churches". Not far from the town is the beautiful botanical garden at **Vácrátót**, while further north you can view some of the finest scenery in the Danube Bend at **Zebegény** and **Nagymaros**, which, like other settlements beneath the **Börzsöny range**, mark the start of trails into the highlands.

Starting **from Budapest**, you can reach anywhere along the east bank within an hour or two by train from Nyugati Station, or by bus from the Árpád híd terminal. The slower alternative is to catch a boat from Budapest's Vigadó tér pier to Vác (2hr 30min), or on to Nagymaros and Zebegény. There are also regular ferries from the west bank.

# Vác

The small town of **VÁC**, 40km north of Budapest, has a worldlier past than its present sleepy atmosphere suggests, the result being that you can enjoy its architectural heritage in relative peace. Its bishops traditionally showed a flair for self-promotion, like the cardinals of Esztergom, endowing monuments and colleges. Under Turkish occupation (1544–1686), Vác assumed an oriental character, with seven mosques and a public *hammam*, while during the Reform Era it was linked to Budapest by Hungary's first rail line (the second continued to Bratislava). In 1849 two battles were fought at Vác, the first a victory for the town over the Austrian army, followed a few months later by a defeat in July 1849 when the town was captured; the battles are commemorated by a bright green **obelisk** by the main road from Budapest, shortly before you enter the town. More recently Vác became notorious for its prison, which has one of the toughest regimes in the country and was used to incarcerate leftists under Admiral Horthy and "counter-revolutionaries" under Communism. Though Vác's legacy of sights justifies a visit, it's not worth staying unless you're planning to visit Vácrátót (see p.154) or Zebegény (see p.155), or are coming specially for the annual festival at the end of July (see opposite).

# The Town

From the stately **Március 15 tér**, which rivals Szentendre for its handsome mélange of Baroque and Rococo, narrow streets and steps on one side lead down to the river, ferries and the riverside promenade, with the prison and Triumphal Arch to the north. To the south lie most of the main sights.

The Baroque style evolved into a fine art here, as evinced by the gorgeous decor of the **Dominican church** on the south side of the square. At no. 6 stands the original Bishop's Palace, converted into Hungary's first Institute for the Deaf and Dumb in 1802. It was Bishop Kristóf Migazzi (1714–1803) who erected Vac's Cathedral (see below) and the Baroque **Town Hall** across the square, its gable adorned with two prostrate females bearing the coats of arms of Hungary and of Migazzi himself. During his years as Bishop of Vác (1762–86), this ambitious prelate was the moving force behind Vác's eighteenth-century revival, impressing Empress Maria Theresa sufficiently to make him Archbishop of Vienna.

There's a small but lively **market** in the sidestreet behind the Dominican church, and further down on Káptalan utca the **Hincz Museum** (Tues–Sun 10am–6pm; 100Ft) gives a brief overview of the town's history, including some excellent photos. You will also find works by the local artist who gives his name to the museum upstairs on one side of the entrance way, and temporary displays on the other side.

### The Cathedral

A few minutes on down Káptalan utca brings you to the back of Vác's **Cathedral** on Konstantin tér. Chiefly impressive for its gigantic Corinthian columns, Migazzi's church is a temple to self-esteem more than anything else. Its Neoclassical design by Isidore Canevale was considered revolutionary in the 1770s, the style not becoming generally accepted in Hungary until the following century. Migazzi himself took umbrage at one of the frescoes by Franz Anton Maulbertsch, and ordered *The Meeting of Mary and Elizabeth*, above the altar, to be bricked over. His motives for this are unknown, but one theory is that it was because Mary was depicted as pregnant. The fresco was only discovered during restoration work in 1944. From the Cathedral you can head along Múzeum utca to Géza király tér, the centre of Vác in medieval times, where there's a Baroque **Franciscan church** with a magnificent organ, pulpits and altars.

### Along the waterfront to the prison

From the Dominican church you can follow the road down to the **riverside promenade**, József Attila sétány, where the townsfolk of Vác walk on summer weekends and evenings. On Ady Endre sétány, level with Március 15 tér, is the wharf for **ferries to Szentendre Sziget** (see p.137), which run every hour (80Ft for passengers, 420Ft for a car; last ferry leaves around 9pm). Since the ferry is now in private hands, it will turn round and pick up cars who have just missed it – you just have to sound your horn. From the ferry you can walk across the island to Tahitótfalu (4km), or take a bus.

The northern stretch of the promenade, named after Liszt, runs past the **Round Tower**, the only remnant of Vác's medieval fortifications. Beyond the dock for ferries to Budapest and Esztergom rises the forbidding hulk of the town's **prison**. Ironically, the building was originally an academy for noble youths, founded by Maria Theresa. Turned into a barracks in 1784 – you can still see part of the older building peering awkwardly above the blank white walls of the prison – it began its penal career a century later, achieving infamy during the Horthy era, when two Communists died here after being beaten for going on hunger strike to protest against maltreatment. Later, victims of the Stalinist period were imprisoned here, but in October 1956 a mass escape occured. Thrown into panic by reports from Budapest where their colleagues were being "hunted down like animals, hung on trees, or just beaten to death by passers-by", the ÁVO guards donned civilian clothing and mounted guns on the rooftop, fomenting rumours of the Uprising among prisoners whose hopes had been raised by snatches of patriotic songs overheard from the streets. A glimpse of national flags with the Soviet emblem cut from the centre provided the spark: a guard was overpowered, locks were shot off, and the prisoners burst free. Edith Bone was an inmate at the time, an English journalist who had been accused of spying and imprisoned for fifteen years in 1949. Robert Maxwell was also imprisoned here during World War II, accused of spying, then using his original name of Ludvik Hoch.

The **Triumphal Arch** flanking the prison was another venture by Migazzi and his architect Canevale, occasioned by Maria Theresa's visit in 1764. Migazzi initially planned theatrical facades to hide the town's dismal housing (perhaps inspired by Potemkin's fake villages in Russia, created around the same time), but settled for the Neoclassical arch, from which Habsburg heads grimace a stony welcome.

## Practicalities

**Arriving** by bus, train or ferry, you can walk into the centre in around ten minutes. From the train station, head 400m along Széchenyi utca to reach Március 15 tér, passing a couple of tourist offices en route. Coming from the bus station, cross over Dr Csányi László körút to get onto Széchenyi utca. Disembarking at the landing stage for ferries from Budapest, you can see the prison and triumphal arch to the north; head south along the promenade to the ferry and then up to the centre. Ferries from Szentendre Sziget dock only two blocks from Március 15 tér.

Vác has two **tourist information** offices: Tourinform, at Dr Csányi László körút 45 (Mon–Fri 9am–5pm; ☎27/316-160), which is, as usual, the best; and Dunatours at Széchenyi utca 14 (Mon–Fri 8am–4pm, Sat 8am–noon; ☎27/310-950). Both can fill you in on local events such as Vác's annual **festival**, the three-day Váci Világi Vigalom (literally, the Vác Secular Entertainment, though why secular no one seems able to say) at the end of July, which includes music, exhibitions and motorboat races.

## Accommodation, eating and drinking

For a large town, Vác has surprisingly little **accommodation**, with no big hotels at all. Private rooms can be rented through Dunatours; otherwise there's the *Tabán Panzió* at Corvin Iépcső 3, down one of the narrow alleyways by the river near the prison (☎27/315-607; ③), and the friendly *Fónagy és Walter Vendégház* at Budapest főút 36, ten minutes south of the main square (☎27/310-682; ②), which has its own wine cellar, where you can taste and buy Hungarian wines.

Whereas the medieval traveller Nicolaus Kleeman found Vác's innkeepers "the quintessence of innkeeperish incivility", modern visitors should find things have improved. The best **restaurants** in town are the *Halászkert* at Liszt sétány 9, overlooking the Danube, which specializes in fish, and the *Kőkapu Étterem* at Dózsa utca 5, just past the triumphal arch, which serves up standard Hungarian fare. Locals frequent the *Barlang Pizzéria,* which serves up good, large pizzas; you'll find it in an old cellar literally under Március 15 tér, reached by some steps right in the middle of the square. The *Pokol Csárda* by the ferry station on Szentendre Sziget (March to mid-Nov Tues–Sun; last ferry goes around 9pm) caters for tourist groups and can get quite rowdy.

### Vácrátót

**VÁCRÁTÓT**, 35km from the centre of Budapest in the hinterland of Vác, has one of Hungary's best-known **Botanical Gardens** (daily: April–Sept 7am–6pm; Oct–March 8am–4pm; 100Ft). Founded in the 1870s by Count Vigyázó, it was subsequently bequeathed by him to the Hungarian Academy of Sciences. Complete with waterfalls and mock ruins, the garden contains thousands of different trees and shrubs from around the world, covering 2.3 square kilometres and taking a good two hours to walk round. On some Saturday evenings in the summer, concerts are held on the lawns in front of the former manor house, with a backdrop of tall copper beeches on one side and a lake on the other. Tickets are available from the Filharmónia Ticket Office in Budapest (see p.119) or Dunatours in Vác.

Motorists can reach Vácrátót from Budapest by turning east off Route 2, north of Sződliget (about 5km before Vác). The village is otherwise accessible by train from Nyugati Station in Budapest, with a bus going from the station to the gardens (1hr 30min); by bus from the northern end of the blue metro (Újpest) in Budapest; or by bus or train from Vác. The nearest **accommodation** is the *Bell Hotel*, 4km down the road in the village of Őrbottyán at Rákóczi utca 1 (☎27/360-160; ③).

# Nagymaros, Zebegény and Szob

The north bank of the Danube gradually becomes more steep as you head towards two settlements, Nagymaros and Zebegény, both of which merit attention for their atmosphere and as starting points for reaching the Börzsöny hills. The main claim to fame of Szob, the last town on the Hungarian north bank of the river, is as a junction for buses from the Börzsöny hills and as the border crossing for trains to Slovakia, the Czech Republic and eastern Germany.

### Nagymaros

Twenty kilometres west from Vác along the bank of the Danube, **NAGYMAROS**, the home of nobles in the age of royal Visegrád, is a quietly prosperous village with an air of faded grandeur – an unlikely focus for years of environmental protest. The cause is not Nagymaros itself, where a drunk's ejection from an *italbolt* (local bar) counts as a major disturbance, but a short way upriver, where extensive environmental landscaping has been employed over the remains of the aborted **dam** (see box overleaf).

The village lies across the river from Visegrád, with a superb view of the latter's citadel: "Visegrád has the castle, but Nagymaros has the view", as the locals have always boasted. The railway line cuts the village firmly in two: above the line, whitewashed houses straggle up the hillside, while below is the main road, and beyond that the river and ferry to Visegrád. From the Nagymaros-Visegrád Station, duck under the bridge and walk up past the *Mátyás Király Restaurant* to the leafy main square, Fő tér. At the bottom of the square, across the main road, is the ferry, while at the top, on the other side of the rail line, is a Gothic church, parts of which date back to 1509. After 1500m, the path divides at a car park – one fork heads south to Hegyes-tető, where you can enjoy a **panoramic view of the Bend**, while the other heads up into **the Börzsöny**, towards Törökmező, a five-kilometre walk away along a footpath marked with red signs.

Private **accommodation** in Nagymaros is best found on the spot by wandering the streets in search of *Zimmer frei* signs. Alternatively, you can stay at the *Feketesas Udvarház* (☎27/354-045; ④), a magnificently kitsch hotel and restaurant complex just north of the ferry station, complete with garden gnomes, tinkling waterfalls and a view of the Visegrád Castle opposite, or you can head up through the beech woods to the *Törökmező Hostel* (☎27/350-63; 1400Ft per person). For **food**, try the *Feketesas* near the water, or the *Mátyás Király Restaurant* on Magyar utca, near the train station, where you can sit outside.

## Zebegény

At **ZEBEGÉNY**, 5km further along the bank of the river, where the Danube turns south, the excellent light and the magnificent view of the Bend have lured painters for years. Most of the village lies to the east of the rail tracks. From Route 12 you pass under the train station and immediately come to the distinctive **Catholic Church** (1908–14), the only one in Hungary to be built in the National Romantic style, an amalgam of Art Nouveau and folk art, designed by Károly Kós. Inside, frescoes by Aladár Körösfői Kriesch depict Emperor Constantine's vision of finding the Holy Cross in Jerusalem with his mother, St Helena. Five minutes' walk behind the church over the stream and down to the right brings you to one of Zebegény's curiosities, the so-called **Museum of Navigation and Seafaring People** at Szőnyi utca 9 (April–Oct Tues–Sun 9am–5pm; 220Ft), housing the bizarre private collection of Captain Vince Farkas, who has sailed the world and amassed some nifty carved figureheads in the process (though how tigers and totem poles fit in is a puzzle). Following Szőnyi utca for another ten minutes brings you to the **memorial house and studio** of one of Zebegény's best-known artists, István Szőnyi, who died in 1960, at Bartóky József utca 7 (Tues–Sun: March–Nov 9am–5pm; Dec–Feb 10am–6pm; 100Ft). Szőnyi first began to paint here, and the house hosts an international **art school** every summer.

**Accommodation** consists of several *Zimmer frei* five minutes' walk up from the church at Kossuth utca 29 (☎27/373-195); the *Malomkerék Vendégfogadó* at Malom utca 21, fifteen minutes further up and over the stream to the left (☎27/373-010; ②), where you can also rent bicycles and canoes; or the *Almáskert Pension* on Almáskert utca 13, twenty minutes' walk further on, at the edge of the village (☎27/373-037; ②). If the prospect of a room directly overlooking the river appeals, five minutes' walk from the church (under the railway, left on the main road, left and then first right) brings you to cheap rooms at Táncsics Mihály utca 2 (☎27/373-255; ①). There is a more luxurious option 1km to the south at the modern *Kenderes Hotel* on Dózsa György út 26 (☎27/373-444; *kenderes@dunaweb.hu*; ③–④)), where rooms have a bathroom, television and safe; you can also rent watersport equipment and use the sauna and swimming pool. Nagymaros and Szob are the nearest alternatives for accommodation, or you could take the **ferry** across to Pilismarót on the west bank to stay at Dömös, Esztergom or Visegrád.

## Szob

Depots, dust and *ennui* sum up most frontier posts, and **SZOB**, 5km west of Zebegény, is no exception. Motorists can't drive across to Slovakia, so few tourists come here. For chance visitors, however, the **Börzsöny Museum** at Hámán utca 14 (Tues–Sun 10am–5pm; 60Ft) is ready with peasant costumes, carved tombstones, and a piece of the petrified primeval tree found at Ipolytarnoc and now distributed among several provincial museums.

**Crossing into Slovakia by road** is absurdly difficult: you either take the ferry across the Danube, travel 12km up the road to Esztergom, and there catch another ferry back across to Slovakia; or you drive 30km north to **Parassapuszta** on the Ipoly River, which demarcates the frontier. The crossing at Letkés/Salka can be used only by Hungarians and Slovakians. The neighbouring village of

### THE GABČIKOVO-NAGYMAROS DAM

Controversy concerning the building of a **dam at Nagymaros** became a focus of opposition to the Communist regime in the 1980s and was even an element in hastening its demise. The dam was part of the Gabčikovo-Nagymaros Hydroelectric Barrage, a grandiose project dreamt up by Hungarian and Czechoslovak planners in 1978, and supported and partly financed by the Austrians, who hoped to gain access to a cheap source of electricity. The barrage was intended to make use of 200km of the River Danube, diverting it for 25km and tapping its energy with two dams. While work on the dam at Nagymaros was abandoned in 1989 after five years of opposition by *Duna Kör* (the Danube Circle), the dam at Gabčikovo was almost completed at the time of the Velvet Revolution. Having invested heavily in the project, the newly constituted Slovak government pressed ahead and diverted the Danube away from Hungary onto the Gabčikovo turbines, but, as an operating dam at Nagymaros had been an essential part of the original project, environmental havoc was wreaked on the stretch of the Danube above Győr (see p.212) for comparatively little energy gain.

In 1994 the Hungarian government began demolishing the unused dam at Nagymaros, and both sides turned to the International Court at The Hague for a ruling in the vain hope that this would end the dispute. When the judges finally spoke in early 1998, the Hungarian government promptly declared that the ruling compelled them to go ahead with a dam somewhere on the river. It seemed like Gyula Horn's sweet revenge: the man who had always advocated the dam and watched it destroy the old one-party system could now push the same line as leader of a democratically elected government. Horn was too cocky, however, and the elections later in 1998 swept him and the Socialists from power. The new government declared in one of their first statements that the dam would not be built and the issue now looks set to return to The Hague again.

Drégelypalánk, 7km away, is on the Vác–Diósjenő–Balassagyarmat train line (trains roughly every 2hr).

# Walking in the Börzsöny

The **Börzsöny range**, squeezed between the Danube and Slovakia, sees few visitors despite its scattering of hostels and forest footpaths, and the abundance of rabbits, pheasants and deer watched only by circling eagles. It's feasible to camp rough here, though most of the places covered below offer some form of accommodation. Would-be walkers should buy Cartographia's Börzsöny-hegység map of the hills (available at the Tourinform office in Vác or from map shops), which shows paths and the location of hostels (*túristaház*).

**Mount Csóványos** (939m) is the highest peak in the Börzsöny, and also the most challenging. Hikers usually approach it from the direction of **DIÓSJENŐ**, a sleepy mountain village that's accessible by bus or train from Vác. Diósjenő's **campsite** (☎35/364-134; ①; May–Sept) lies just over 1km from the village and 2km from the train halt, and its small stock of rooms (②)can be reserved direct or through Nógrád Tourist in Salgótarján, in the Northern Uplands (☎32/316-940). Six kilometres further up the road towards Kemence, there is riding and a pension (☎27/365-139; ③) at **Királyháza**; the road runs along a delightful wooded valley, but there is no bus from Diósjenő.

An alternative route into the mountains begins at Kismaros, 12km up the Danube from Vác. From here narrow-gauge trains trundle to **KIRÁLYRÉT** (April–Oct Mon–Fri 9.50am & 3.45pm, Sat & Sun 8.40am, 9.50am, 11.45am, 3.45pm, 5.45pm; Nov–March Sat & Sun only, same hours), with connecting trains to and from Budapest from the main line station across the road. Close to the station is the *Fővárosi Önkormányzat Üdülője*, a hostel with cheap beds (☎27/375-033; ①), and you can eat cheaply at the local restaurant. Supposedly once the hunting ground of Beatrice and Mátyás, this "Royal Meadow" has paths going in several directions. One trail, marked in green, goes across to the village of Nógrád with its ruined castle, 5km from Diósjenő on the Diósjenő–Vác railway line. Another, marked in red, leads to the Magas-Tax peak about one and a half hours' walk away, with another cheap hostel, the *Magas Tax Turistaház* (☎60/346-150; ①). The path goes on to the "Big Cold" peak, **Nagy Hideg Hegy**, which has excellent views, and branches out to Mount Csóványos and the villages of Nagybörzsöny and Kóspallag; use the Börzsöny-hegység map to guide you.

## Nagybörzsöny and Kóspallag

From Nagy Hideg Hegy, a trail marked by blue squares leads westwards to **NAGYBÖRZSÖNY**, 20km north from Szob. Alternatively you can get there by bus from Szob and make this your starting point for walking east. A wealthy town during the Middle Ages, Nagybörzsöny declined with the depletion of its copper, gold and iron mines in the eighteenth century, and is now a mere logging village with an overdose of churches – four in all. The walled thirteenth-century Romanesque **Church of St Stephen**, on the left as you enter the village, was left stranded as the cemetery chapel when the village moved closer to the mines in the fifteenth century. If you are walking from the centre of the village, stop in at Petőfi utca 17 en route to ask for the gigantic church key, as the church is normally closed. Just across the road from the house is the Gothic **Miners' Church**, some of whose features have survived later alterations; again, if the church is closed, ask at Petőfi utca 17. Just below the church, an exhibition of folk costumes, home furnishings, and mining accessories can be found at the **Mining Museum** at Petőfi utca 19 (Wed–Sun 10am–4pm; 40Ft), with explanations in Hungarian and German only, but you get the general feel anyway. Just up from the main square, where the bus terminus is located, you will find the village's still-working water-mill along to the left by the stream (Tues–Sun 9am–5pm). For **accommodation**, there are basic doubles (shared bathrooms) above the *Butella Borozó* (②) just above the main road near the Romanesque church; or a ten-minute walk along the track past the wine bar leads down to the *Nagybörzsöny Község Vendégháza*, by a fishing lake – a rather out-of-the-way site where you can get a room (②). Otherwise it is worth asking in the village about private rooms.

The other trail from Nagy Hideg Hegy (marked with a blue horizontal line) runs south down to **KÓSPALLAG**, another prosaic village, notable only as a place to catch **buses** to Vác (six daily until 9pm). However, pursuing the path onwards, things improve beyond the Vác–Szob road junction below the village, where the path wanders through beech woods to a lovely open meadow graced with a solitary tree and the first view of the Danube. Cutting southwest across the meadow puts you back on the path to the *Törökmező Hostel* (see p.155). The path divides by the exercise camp in the woods, and heading west along the path marked with green signs you come down to Zebegény (5km). Alternatively you can head on another 4km along the blue path, past the hostel, to a car park at the junction of paths to Hegyes-tető (Hilly Peak) and Nagymaros.

If you take the road from Kóspallag to Szob, you come to **MÁRIANOSZTRA**, a place of pilgrimage 9km from Szob and served by hourly buses. These pilgrimages take place on the second Sunday in May, and on the Sundays preceding August 15 and September 14. The Baroque church in the centre of the village (now in the courtyard at the entrance of a men's prison) dates from 1360, and retains some original fragments. One curiosity is the copy of the *Black Czestochowa Madonna*, the original of which was taken to Poland in 1382 by Hungarian monks sent to found the monastery there. An hour's walk north from the village takes you to **Kopasz hegy** (Bald Hill) which affords some of the best views in the region.

## travel details

### Trains

**Budapest** to: Esztergom (every 40min; 1hr 15min–1hr 40min); Szentendre (every 15–30min; 45min); Vác (every 30min; 45min); Vácrátót (7 daily; 1hr 20min).

**Esztergom** to: Budapest (every 40min; 1hr 15min–1hr 40min); Komárom (4 daily; 45min).

**Kismaros** to: Királyrét (5 daily; 45min).

**Vác** to: Balassagyarmat (7–9 daily; 2hr); Budapest (every 30min; 45min); Diósjenő (7–9 daily; 45min).

**Vácrátót** to: Aszód (3 daily; 1hr 30min); Budapest (1hr 20min); Vác (10 daily; 15min).

### Buses

**Budapest** (**Árpád híd**) to: Dobogókő (1–3 daily; 2hr 30min); Esztergom via the Bend (hourly; 2 hr) or via Dorog (every 30min; 1hr 15min); Vác (express bus hourly; 30min); Visegrád (30–60min; 1hr 15 min).

**Budapest** (**Népstadion**) to: Vác (hourly; 1hr).

**Esztergom** to: Budapest via the Bend (hourly; 2hr) or via Dorog (every 30min; 1hr 15min); Győr (2 daily; 2hr); Komárom (hourly; 90min); Sopron (2 daily; 4hr); Szentendre (hourly; 1hr 30min); Veszprém (2 daily; 2hr); Visegrád (hourly; 40min).

**Szentendre** to: Esztergom (hourly; 1hr 30min); Visegrád (hourly; 40min).

**Vác** to: Budapest (express bus hourly; 30min); Diósjenő (5–7 daily; 1hr); Kóspallag (every 90min; 90min); Szob (every 20–40min; 30min); Vácrátót (hourly; 45min).
**Visegrád** to: Budapest (30–60min; 1hr 15 min); Dömös (hourly; 15min); Esztergom (hourly; 40min).

**Ferries** (operating April to October)
**Basaharc** to: Szob (hourly; 10min).
**Budapest** (Vigadó tér) to: Esztergom (1–2 daily; 5hr 20min); Szentendre (1–3 daily; 1hr 40min); Vác (1 daily; 2hr 25min); Visegrád (1–4 daily; 3hr 30min); Zebegény (1–2 daily; 4hr 20min).
**Esztergom** to: Budapest (1–2 daily; 4hr); Štúrovo, Slovakia (hourly; 10min); Szentendre (mid-May to Aug 2 daily; 3hr 20min); Vác (1 daily; 2hr 15min); Visegrád (1–2 daily; 1hr 30min).
**Kismaros** to Kisoroszi (every 30min–1hr 30 min; 10min).
**Kisoroszi** to Kismaros (every 30min–1hr 30 min; 10min).

**Leányfalu** to: Pócsmegyer (every 20–60min; 10min).
**Nagymaros** to: Visegrád (hourly; 10min).
**Pilismarót** to: Zebegény (hourly; 10min).
**Szob** to: Basaharc (hourly; 10min).
**Tahitótfalu** to: Vác (hourly; 10min).
**Vác** to: Budapest (1 daily; 1hr 45min); Esztergom (mid-May to mid-Sept 1 daily; 3hr); Tahitótfalu (hourly; 10min).
**Visegrád** to: Budapest (1–4 daily; 2hr 30min); Esztergom (1–2 daily; 1hr 45min); Kisoroszi (2 daily; 20 min); Nagymaros (hourly; 10min); Vác (1 daily; 45min); Zebegény (1–2 daily; 45min).

**Hydrofoil** (June to August **weekends only**)
**Budapest** to: Esztergom (2 daily; 1hr 20min); Visegrád (1 daily; 50 min).
**Esztergom** to: Budapest (2 daily; 1hr 10min).
**Visegrád** to: Budapest (1 daily; 50 min).

# CHAPTER THREE

# LAKE BALATON AND THE BAKONY

L ake Balaton, affectionately known to Hungarians as "Balcsi", is the nation's substitute for a coastline. Millions of people come here every summer to enjoy the lake's milky green waters, which, with an average depth of only 3m, are warm enough to swim in from May to October. Though few would subscribe to the old romantic view of Balaton as the "Hungarian sea", it is still the largest freshwater lake in Europe – nearly 80km long and varying in width from 14km to a mere 1.5km at the point where the lake is almost cut in two by the Tihany peninsula – and all that remains of the ancient Pannonian Sea that once covered the region.

Balaton's low-lying **southern shore** is almost entirely built up with resorts. Modelled on brash and bustling **Siófok**, they are all fairly similar, and it can be quite hard to work out where one ends and another begins. The western end of the lake, however, is more peaceful – home to the reedy **Kis-Balaton** nature reserve. The **northern shore** is also crowded, but waterfront development here has been limited by reed beds and cooler, deeper water. **Tihany** and the wine-producing **Badacsony Hills** offer splendid scenery and sightseeing, while at the far end of Balaton the delightful university town of **Keszthely** is a short ride from the world's second-largest thermal lake at **Hévíz**.

Midway between Budapest and Balaton, **Lake Velence** is similar to Balaton but smaller, and is close to **Martonvásár**, where summer Beethoven concerts in the grounds of the Brunswick Mansion draw many visitors from the capital. While you're in the Balaton area, it would be a shame not to visit **Székesfehérvár**, situated between the two lakes, with its romantic Belváros and "Bory's Castle", and to see something of the wooded **Bakony** region north of Balaton, dotted with picturesque villages and ruined castles, and the setting for the historic towns of **Veszprém**, **Sümeg**, **Tapolca** and **Pápa**.

---

### ACCOMMODATION PRICE CODES

All accommodation in this guide is graded according to the price bands given below. Note that prices refer to the **cheapest available double room in high season** or the price of **two people sharing a tent** in a campsite. 100Ft is roughly equivalent to $0.45 or DM1. For more details, see p.24.

| | | |
|---|---|---|
| ① Under 2000Ft | ④ 6000–8500Ft | ⑦ 20,000–27,000Ft |
| ② 2000–4000Ft | ⑤ 8500–13,000Ft | ⑧ 27,000–40,000Ft |
| ③ 4000–6000Ft | ⑥ 13,000–20,000Ft | ⑨ over 40,000Ft |

Though its **history** is hardly writ large, the region was first settled in the Iron Age, and has been a wine-growing centre since Roman times. During the sixteenth century, it formed the front line between Turkish and Habsburg-ruled Hungary, with an Ottoman fleet based at Siófok and an Austrian one at Balatonfüred. Spas and villas began to appear from 1765 onwards, but catered largely to the wealthy until the Communists began promoting holidays for the masses after World War II. During the 1960s, footloose youths started flocking here, and in the 1970s and 1980s there was a boom in private holiday homes and room-letting, fuelled by an influx of tourists from Germany and Austria. Recent scares on water quality led to fears of a fall in visitors, but Balaton seems once again to be a popular destination, especially for east German visitors.

Lake Balaton is easily accessible from Budapest and Transdanubia. **Trains** from Budapest's Déli Station run to all the main resorts, with a daily intercity service providing the fastest access to Keszthely (2hr 30min) via the southern shore. **Buses** to Székesfehérvár, Veszprém and Balaton leave from the Erzsébet tér depot. If you're driving to Balaton, the M7 to Siófok is the quickest road; to get to the northern shore, turn off the M7 onto Route 71 for Balatonfüred. Over summer, however, you can expect long tailbacks on the M7 on Friday evenings and Saturday mornings, and also on the way back to Budapest on Sunday evenings.

From April to October, regular **passenger ferries** zigzag from Siófok to Balatonfüred on the opposite bank, then west to Tihany-rév and back across the lake to Balatonföldvár. During July and August, another service runs the length of the lake from Balatonkenese to Keszthely (5hr), making regular stops on both banks en route. Between early March and November, there is also a **car ferry** between Tihany-rév and Szántódrév.

# Budapest to Lake Velence

Just half an hour from Budapest, **Lake Velence** resembles a diminutive version of Balaton, with hills to the north and two contrasting shorelines. The southern shore, followed by Route 70 and the rail line, is awash with holiday homes and tourists, while the opposite bank is too reedy for swimming, but ideal for birds. Another reason to stop en route is the Brunswick Mansion at **Martonvásár**, where Beethoven stayed, and where outdoor concerts of his music are held in the summer.

## Martonvásár

Visiting **MARTONVÁSÁR** – about halfway between Budapest and Velence – you are transported into another era. A fifteen-minute walk down the road opposite the station leads to the neo-Gothic **Brunswick Mansion** (*Brunszvik Kastely*; daily 8am–6pm; 160Ft), set in a lovely park, where **Teréz Brunswick** founded Hungary's first nursery school in 1828. Beethoven came to the mansion several times in the early years of the nineteenth century, teaching music to Teréz and her sister, Josephine, who may have been the "immortal beloved" of **Beethoven's** love letters, and the inspiration for his *Moonlight* and *Appassionata* sonatas. Some reckon, though, that his muse was Giulietta Guiccardi, the "beautiful devil" whom he also met here between 1800 and 1806.

A small **Beethoven Museum** (May–Oct Tues–Fri 10am–noon & 2–6pm, Sat & Sun 10am–6pm; Nov–April Tues–Fri 10am–noon & 2–4pm, Sat & Sun 10am–4pm;

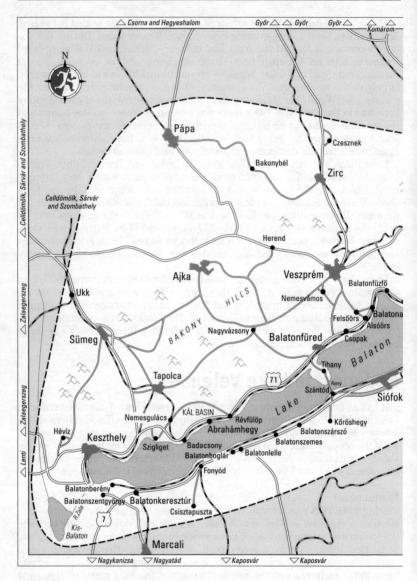

80Ft) presents the history of the mansion and Beethoven's stay there. The display includes a hammerklavier that Beethoven himself might have played, as well as some of his letters, though the only guidance you can get on the exhibits in English is a small leaflet sold at the entrance. Housed in a hut in the grounds to the left of the mansion, the **Nursery Museum** (*Óvodamúzeum*; Tues–Fri 10am–2pm, Sat & Sun 11am–3pm; 80Ft) offers a cramped display of artefacts,

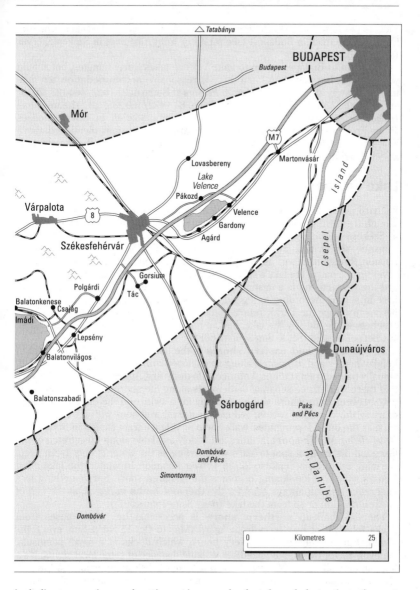

including a row of enamel potties set in a wooden bench, and photos from the past 150 years illustrating Hungary's pioneering role in nursery education.

A more compelling reason to come to the mansion is for the **summer evening concerts**, held on an island in the middle of the park beneath a great bower of beech and sycamore. Armed with mosquito repellent and a couple of bottles from the bar-buffet, you can listen to the music as the sun sets through the trees.

Tickets (sectors C and D offer the best views of the stage) are available from the Central Box Office in Budapest (see p.119) or from Albatours in Székesfehérvár (see p.168).

The **train** to Budapest or on to Lake Velence takes thirty minutes, but should you miss the last one at 11.15pm there is reasonable **accommodation** ten minutes' walk away at the friendly *Macska Pension* at Budai út 21 (☎22/460-127; ②), or at the *Tanne Fogadó*, 360m further up at no. 83 (☎22/460-285; ③). The town hall (*polgármesteri hivatal*) can help arrange accommodation in private houses (Mon–Fri 8am–4pm; ☎22/460-229). For **meals**, both pensions mentioned above have good restaurants, or closer to the mansion is the more basic *Postakocsi* eatery at Fehérvári utca 1, on the corner of Dósza György út, leading up to the park.

# Lake Velence

It's hard not to smile when told that Velence is the Hungarian name for Venice, though the town probably came by the name because Italian craftsmen working in Székesfehérvár lived here in the Middle Ages, rather than from any more romantic similarities. Today, **Lake Velence** (*Velencei-tó*) serves as a lesser Balaton, though its resort aspect is balanced by a strong wildlife presence. Reeds cover up to a half of the lake's surface, helping to maintain the quality of the water, and the western end is a nesting ground for some 30,000 **birds**, which migrate here in spring. According to legend, three sisters, who turned themselves into herons to escape the Turks, return home here every year. The best spot for bird-watchers is the hide by the lake, half an hour's walk west of Agárd train station, at Chernel utca 58 (Sat & Sun 3–6pm; 60Ft).

The **southern and eastern shores** of the lake are one continuous strip of holiday homes and campsites, along an enclosed *strand*. If it weren't for the individually named train stations, **Velence**, **Gárdony** and **Agárd**, you'd never realize that there were three separate settlements along the shore. The **beaches** alternate between ones where you have to pay for a swim and the dubious privilege of using the changing rooms, and *szabad strand*, free ones with fewer facilities, such as the one a few minutes' walk north of Velence train station in front of the *Hotel Helios*. **Water-sport** facilities are widely available along this stretch of the lake, and it's an ideal spot to learn windsurfing as the water is only 1–2m deep, warming up to an acceptable 22–26°C over summer. In winter, the lake often freezes solid and ice-skating becomes the favoured sport. For something less energetic, you can always head for the **thermal baths** in Agárd, at the end of Határ utca, 1km or so from the lake (daily 8am–7pm; 450Ft).

The less built-up **northern shore** is accessible by hourly buses from Székesfehérvár or by a ferry from Agárd (May to Oct 15 Sat & Sun, every 1hr 30min; June to Aug 20 daily every hour), which docks at a small peninsula, Szunyog Sziget (Mosquito Island), in walking distance of some local sights. It's a ten-minute walk up to **Mészeg Hill**, where an obelisk commemorates the first Hungarian victory in the 1848–49 Revolution. A further ten minutes uphill brings you to a memorial to the Hungarian soldiers who died in Russia during World War II, fighting on the side of the Nazis. This canopy-chapel is designed to ease an old wound for Hungarians, who lost over 100,000 men in Russia, mainly at the River Don, but were unable to mourn them during the Communist era.

The wooden tower peeking over the trees belongs to the **Pákozdi Arborétum**, 1km away and signposted up a road to the right, which displays local plants and rocks. You get an excellent view of the Velence hills from the tower, which are the oldest in Hungary, formed from magma and granite. There is more geology above the village of **PÁKOZD**, thirty minutes' walk under the motorway and left along the main road. Turning off the main road just past another 1848 monument, it's a stiff walk up the 241-metre-high **Pogány-kő** (Pagan Rock), where several colossal "rocking stones" (*ingókövek*) sway perceptibly in the wind.

## Practicalities

Orientation couldn't be easier: wherever you get off the train, simply head for the lake. The best place to stay is Velence, which has the most variety of accommodation, as well as being further from the railway. **Information** is available from Tourinform in the Velencetours office, Halász utca 37, ten minutes' walk north along Tópart utca from Velence Station (June–Aug Mon–Sat 8am–6pm, Sun 8am–2pm; Sept–May Mon–Fri 9am–5pm, Sat 9am–1pm; ☎22/472-029). If you want a tourist office (and accommodation) nearer to the train, Velencetours in Gárdony is just across the main road from Gárdony Station at Szabadság utca 16, behind a group of stalls (Mon–Fri 7.30am–5pm, Sat 7.30am–1pm; not reliable in winter; ☎22/355-099). At Pákozd, on the north shore, there is a tourist office at Budai utca 134, at the east end of the village (Tues–Sat 9am–5pm, Sun 9am–1pm; ☎22/458-722), which also deals with the cheapest accommodation in the area; you may have to ring the bell in winter to get attention.

Of the **restaurants**, locals at Gárdony go to the *Ponty* near the station, although it is sandwiched between the main road and the railway, and in Velence the *Juventus Hotel* on the shore has a reasonable restaurant. At Pákozd, on the north side of the lake, there's the friendly *Franci Söröző*, in the centre at Budai út 74, which does excellent savoury scones (*pogácsa*) and homestyle Hungarian food, and, almost opposite, the *Bella Betérő*.

*ACCOMMODATION*

Like Balaton, Lake Velence closes down from mid-September to April and is very busy the rest of the year, so it is worth phoning to check on places rather than just turning up. **Private rooms, flats and houses** (②–④) are bookable through all the tourist offices, and many householders also rent them directly (look for *Zimmer frei* signs), but they may not be any cheaper than the rest of the accommodation on offer. There's a huge **campsite**, *Panorama Camping*, on Kemping utca (☎22/472-043; ②; mid-March to mid-Oct), on the northeastern shore of the lake, roughly 2km from Velence Station, where you can also rent bungalows (②). It's not cheap, but there are tennis courts, a minigolf course, water-bikes, restaurants, and masseurs for post-beach relaxation. A couple of kilometres from the lakeside, but right beside Agárd's thermal baths, *Termál Camping* on Határ utca (☎22/370-294; ①–③) also has a pension, and guests qualify for reduced admission prices to the baths. Four buses run daily from the centre.

**Családi Panzió**, Templom köz 12 (☎22/472-710). Cheap modern pension with little character at north end of Velence near the church and 600m from the water. Rooms have TV and bathroom. ③.

**Helios Hotel**, Tópart utca 34 (☎22/472-941). Just ten minutes' walk from Velence Station and very near the lake, this small hotel has its own pool. There's a free beach opposite, but you can use the *strand* and facilities of the nearby *Juventus Hotel*, run by the same people. Rooms have fridge and bathroom. ④–⑤.

**István Panzió**, Templom köz 8–10 (☎22/472-702). Cheap but characterless pension at north end of Velence, 600m from the water. Rooms have TV and bathroom. ③.

**Juventus Hotel**, Kisköz 6 (☎22/472-159). Right on the lake, fifteen minutes' walk from Velence Station, with a sauna and tennis courts, and water-sports on its own bit of beach. ⑤.

**Touring Hotel**, Tópart utca 1 (☎22/370-019). Modern block on the lakeside twenty minutes' walk west of Agárd Station and beside the pier. Has advantage of not backing right onto the railway, unlike others here. Bikes and water-bikes can be rented here. May–Sept. ③.

# Székesfehérvár

Reputedly the site where Árpád pitched camp and founded his dynasty, **SZÉKESFEHÉRVÁR**, 60km southwest of Budapest, was probably the first Hungarian town. Its name (pronounced "*Saik*-esh-fehair-var") comes from the white castle (*fehérvár*) founded by Prince Géza, whose son Stephen made it his royal seat (*szék*). As the centre of his efforts to civilize the Magyars, it was named in Latin "Alba Civitas" or "Alba Regia". Since this medieval town was utterly destroyed by the Turks, Székesfehérvár today owes its Belváros to the Habsburgs, and its high-rise suburbs to the final German counter-attack in 1945, which levelled almost everywhere else. The town's principal attractions are its narrow winding streets and diverse galleries in the Belváros, and the wonderful suburban folly known as Bory's Castle.

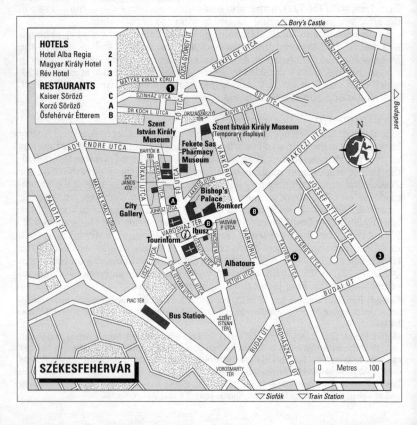

# The Town

Székesfehérvár's **Belváros** occupies approximately the same area as the great castle once did, as evinced by a section of the medieval walls alongside the **Romkert** (April–Oct Tues–Sun 9am–5pm; 110Ft). Among the stonework in this "Garden of Ruins" is a richly carved Roman sarcophagus found in 1803 and believed to hold the remains of King Stephen. Directly across the road are the excavated **foundations of the cathedral** where Stephen was buried. Designed for him by Italian architects in an attempt to rival St Mark's in Venice, it hosted the coronations of 38 Hungarian kings. After the town fell to the Turks in 1543, the cathedral was plundered of its gold and jewels, and then blown up.

**Városház tér**, the main square beside the ruins, recalls Székesfehérvár's revival under Maria Theresa, with its Baroque town hall, Franciscan church and Zopf-style **Bishop's Palace**, built with stones from the ruined cathedral by Bishop Milassin, whose coat of arms appears on the gable. Running off to the north, **Fő utca** is so perfectly preserved that you expect to see crinoline-clad ladies emerging from the **Fekete Sas Pharmacy Museum** at no. 9 (Tues–Sun 10am–6pm; 60Ft). This eighteenth-century pharmacy, called the Black Eagle, operated right up until 1971, and visitors can see the original fittings and fixtures, along with displays on traditional remedies. Like the Baroque church of St John across the street, it was founded by the Jesuits.

## The City Gallery and Szent István Király Museum

Around the back of the St John's Church, at Oskola utca 10, is the **City Gallery** (*Városi Képtár*; Tues–Sun: April–Oct 10am–6pm; Nov–March 9am–5pm; 100Ft), which has a brilliant display of nineteenth- and twentieth-century Hungarian art. The Deák Collection, which was bequeathed to the city by a local collector, is housed in three medieval houses that have been joined together, with a labyrinth of small rooms exhibiting works by top Hungarian artists, such as Victor Vasarely, Lajos Kassák, Endre Bálint and Rippl-Rónai. In the same block is a collection of sculptures by Erzsébet Schaár (same hours as the gallery; 100Ft); ask the people at the main desk to guide you through the labyrinth to get to the sculptures.

Back on Fő utca, at no. 6, next to the church, is the permanent collection of the **Szent István Király Museum** (Tues–Sun: May–Sept 10am–4pm; Oct–April 10am–2pm; 100Ft), a lively exhibition on local history containing archeological finds and domestic treasures. Especially notable are the eastern Celtic pottery and nineteenth-century court dress. The museum also puts on temporary shows of contemporary Hungarian art at Országzászló tér 3, at the top of Fő utca (Tues–Sun 10am–2pm; 100Ft).

## South of Városház tér

More of the historic architecture is clustered south of Városház tér. Walking south down Arany János utca, you'll pass the Baroque **St Stephen's Cathedral**, a much rebuilt edifice that dates back to the thirteenth century. The **Chapel of St Anna** alongside is the only remnant of medieval Székesfehérvár spared by the Turks, who put it to use as a mosque – notice the Koranic inscriptions and arabesque murals. Continuing south along Arany János utca, you'll come to the fanciful Zopf-style **Budenz House** at no. 12 (Tues–Sun: March–May & Oct 10am–2pm; June–Sept 10am–4pm; 100Ft), which has a collection of beautiful old furniture and Hungarian art belonging to the Ybl family. Architect Miklós Ybl was born in this house, and in one of the rooms downstairs you can see his drawing cabinet and photos of buildings he designed, including the Budapest Opera House. Further down the street, a right turn takes you into Petőfi utca; a plaque on the wall of the cinema marks the house where the ubiquitous Sándor Petőfi lived for a couple of months at the end of 1842 as a travelling actor. The **Carmelite Church** on the corner of Kossuth utca has Rococo carvings and frescoes by the Austrian painter Franz Anton Maulbertsch. Round to the left, at Megyeház utca 17, the **New Hungarian Gallery** (*Új Magyar Képtár*, Tues–Sun 10am–5pm; 100Ft) has an unimpressive display of twentieth-century Hungarian art, although younger artists like Attila Szűcs are worth seeing.

## Bory's Castle

The town's most curious sight is **Bory's Castle** (*Bory Vár*, March–Nov daily 9am–5pm; 100Ft), situated out in the eastern suburbs at Máriavölgy utca 54, beyond the microchip and TV factories. An eclectic structure combining features of Scottish, Romanesque and Gothic architecture, it was built between 1923 and 1959 in an ordinary suburban street by a group of students directed by the artist **Jenő Bory**. Its rooms and courtyards are filled with statues and paintings of Ilona Komocsin, Bory's wife and model, whose memory the castle enshrines. Although the overall effect of Ilona's multiple images is slightly morbid, the castle is a marvellous place to wander around and explore. **Buses** #26 from Piac tér, #32 from the train station, and #26A from the bus station run regularly to the castle.

# Practicalities

Székesfehérvár's **train station** is 1km south of the centre; catch any bus heading up Prohászka Ottakár út, which subsequently becomes Várkörút, and get off near the *Hotel Alba Regia*. The intercity **bus station** on Piac tér is a more convenient place to arrive, being just a few minutes' walk from the Belváros. **Information** is available from the helpful Tourinform at Városház tér 1 (Mon–Fri 9am–noon & 1–4pm; ☎22/312-818), IBUSZ at Vasvári Pál utca 3 (Mon–Fri 8am–4pm; ☎22/329-393), and Albatours at Kossuth utca 14/a (Mon–Fri 8.30am–4.30pm; ☎22/312-494). The main **post office** is on the corner of Kossuth utca and Petőfi utca, and there's an **ATM** at the top end of Fő utca.

Your choices are limited if you are looking for somewhere to **stay** in town. The *Hotel Alba Regia*, Rákóczi utca 1 (☎22/313-484; ④), is a three-star seventies establishment overlooking the Romkert, while at the northern end of the Belváros, the *Magyar Király* at Fő utca 10 (☎22/311-262; ④), a grand hotel built in the 1870s, has disappointingly ordinary rooms. Further out on the main ring road, 2km east of the centre, is the 28-room thatched pension *Fogadó a Két Góbéhoz*, at Gugásvölgyi út 4 (☎22/340-689; ②), accessible by buses #26 and #32. The *Rév Hotel*, just east of the centre at József Attila utca 42, claims it will be closed to tourists, but it is worth checking to see if it has rooms available, as they are cheap (☎22/314-441; ②). **Private rooms** (②) can be booked through Albatours and IBUSZ, while Tourinform can advise on hostel accommodation over the summer and at weekends throughout the year, though be warned that some hostels are on the outskirts of town. For **camping**, try *Autós Camping* at Bregyó köz 1 (☎22/313-433; ①; May–Sept), about ten minutes' walk north of the centre (or buses #12 and #14).

The town has several places that serve good Hungarian **meals** at a reasonable price, including the *Ősfehérvár Étterem* opposite the Romkert, the *Kaiser Söröző* at Távírda utca 14, which has an excellent lunch menu, and the *Fekete Holló* by the baths on Szabadharcos utca. You can also eat well at the *Korzó Söröző*, Fő utca 2, which serves Czech beer and has outdoor seating. There are several drinking holes on Fő utca, including the student hangout *Royal Darts* at Budai út 18.

# On from Székesfehérvár

Székesfehérvár is a major transport hub for cross-country and international routes to Leipzig and Vienna, but travellers staying within the confines of the Bakony and Balaton region are faced with a choice of only two routes. Travelling **west towards Veszprém** in the Bakony by bus or train, the first major town is **VÁRPALOTA**, 18km away. The grand name of the town "castle-palace" comes from the impressive hulk of the Thury Fortress, which dominates the town centre. In the 1950s a dinosaur power plant and aluminium foundry was built on the edge of town turning it into a major industrial centre, but now the wasteful industry is being closed down, leaving a very run-down place with lots of drab housing estates. Served by regular trains (twenty minutes' walk south of the centre) and buses running between Székesfehérvár and Veszprém, the centre of the town lies on the northern side of Route 8, with everything you might need around the main square, Szabadság tér, or Szent István út, leading off it to the east.

Dominating Szabadság tér, the Thury Fortress takes its name from György Thury, who warded off the besieging Turks in 1566, but it gained its present form in the eighteenth century. Now all it houses are the **Museum of the Chemical Industry** (*Vegyészeti Múzeum*) and the **Mining Museum** (*Bányászati Múzeum*) (April–Oct Tues–Sun 11am–5pm; both 70Ft), as well as fragments of Roman stonework and remains from the medieval fortress, together with hideous bright paintings of no clear relevance by the entrance. Up the stairs you come to rooms of old machinery, documents about Hungarian alchemy, lots of pictures of male scientists – about the only portrait of a woman shows her holding a rose – and information about the Hungarian workers' movement: the museum was founded in 1961, and its age shows. There is minimal information in English about this

## THE SEVSO TREASURE

Another as yet unexcavated Roman villa at Szabadbattyán, 7km southwest of Székesfehérvár, has been linked with the mysterious **Sevso treasure**, a large collection of Roman silver bearing the name of a Roman dignitary called Sevso. The treaure first appeared in 1990, when the Marquis of Northampton put the treasure up for sale at Sotheby's in New York. Twenty-three countries that were formerly part of the Roman Empire complained, and Sotheby's called off the sale on account of the uncertain origin of the goods. Lebanon, Croatia and Hungary all claimed the silver came from their territory, but none succeeded in pushing its claims through in court. The Hungarian government has conducted soil tests that would suggest that the treasure came from this villa, and it links its discovery with the death of a military conscript almost twenty years ago, who probably found the treasure and was murdered when he tried to sell it on. Now the other two countries seem to have dropped their claims, and Hungary hopes that the Marquis will soon sell the treasure to them to get it off his hands – once he has finished suing the lawyers who failed to push through the sale in New York.

museum or the mining museum, so you need to be an avid industry fan to enjoy this one. The only other major sight locally is the **Roman weir** constructed of gigantic stones, whose remains stretch for almost 1km near the suburban swimming resort of **Petfürdő**, 3km south of Várpalota, but you're unlikely to want to linger in these parts.

Driving to the **southern shore of Lake Balaton**, you can make a detour to TÁC, 5km off Route 70; by train, you'll need to get off at Szabadbattyán Station and catch a local bus, or take a bus from Székesfehérvár's bus terminal and get off in the centre of the village at the Soviet war memorial (a rare sight in Hungary now), where signs point towards the **Roman ruins of Gorsium**, fifteen minutes' walk away (daily: April–Sept 8am–6pm; Oct–March 8am–4pm; 100Ft including entry to the museum). Gorsium began life as a military camp, but by the beginning of the second century had become the religious centre of Pannonia. The site covers two square kilometres, and is still being excavated. The foundations so far uncovered include a palace, a temple, the forum, a theatre and a cemetery, with some well-preserved grave markers lining the paths of the site. It is worth getting a map at the entrance as it is hard to make sense of it otherwise. Carved stonework and other finds are displayed in a **museum** to the right of the entrance (April–Oct Tues–Sun 10am–5pm; Nov–March during site opening hours upon request). The ruins host an annual **festival** called the "Floralia" at the end of April, which celebrates the arrival of spring; its highlights are a flower show, craft stalls, Greek plays, and gladiatorial combat. Tickets are available from Tourinform in Székesfehérvár.

# Lake Balaton: the southern shore

The **southern shore** of Lake Balaton is almost entirely built up, with an endless procession of *strand* – the generic term for any kind of bathing place – which we've been obliged to call **beaches** for want of a better word, though most are grassy sunbathing areas with concrete embankments along the shoreline.

While the discerning head for **Balatonvilágos**, the masses plump for **Siófok**, which, as the largest resort, is the model for others such as **Fonyód**; the nightlife and drinking here are somewhat tamer, however. In **Koroshegy** and **Balatonszemes**, you can even find a touch of history or high-brow culture, while **Balatonlelle** and **Balatonboglár** are notable for their festivals, and **Kishegy** for its wine. Nature only reasserts itself at the western end of the lake, where the River Zala flows through the reeds into the **Kis-Balaton** (Little Balaton) bird reserve. All the resorts along the southern shore are accessible by train from Budapest or Székesfehérvár.

### Balatonvilágos

Approaching the southern shore by train, you'll catch your first glimpse of Balaton at **BALATONVILÁGOS**. One of the lushest, least commercialized resorts, built on wooded cliffs and along the shore, it was formerly reserved for Party officials, and boats were forbidden to dock in its harbour – even those seeking refuge from a storm. Moreover, unlike other resorts, it has what can properly be called a **beach**.

The Tourinform office at Dózsa Gy utca 1, next to the post office, in the upper part of the village, can give information on **accommodation** (June–Aug Mon–Sat 8am–4pm, Sun 8am–2pm; Sept–May Mon–Sat 8am–6pm; ☎88/446-034). Heading

---

### STORM WARNINGS

From May to September Balaton is prone to occasional storms. **Storm warnings** are given by flashing lights: thirty flashes per minute indicates winds of 40–60km per hour; sixty flashes per minute means winds of over 60km per hour. Windsurfers or sailors should head for land at once.

---

down the road that runs past the train station at the western end of the village, you'll find plenty of lakeside accommodation. The pleasant-looking *Napfény Szálló* is at Rákóczi út 12 (☎88/480-632; ②), and 500m further on is the modern and civilized *Dalma Panzió* at Rákóczi út 33 (☎88/380-883 or 446-015; ②). The *Hotel Balatonvilágos* is at Zrinyi utca 24 (☎88/380-934; ③), which is more charming than most of the modern blocks along the front. Another 500m further on is a paying beach (120Ft), while the free beach (*szabad strand*) is another 1km further on. If you are going to the latter from Tourinform, it is quicker to make your way down one of the stairways that go under the railway line.

# Siófok

**SIÓFOK** is the largest resort on Balaton: a plebeian, open-armed place that was the first to introduce strip bars and sex clubs to augment the traditional pleasures of boozing, guzzling, sunbathing and dancing. Though its vitality and tackiness might appeal for a while, you're unlikely to want to stay long – and the accommodation situation is dire.

### Arrival, information and accommodation

The bus and train **stations** are next to each other on Fő utca, the town's main axis, just across the road from the **post office** and **ATM**. **Ferries** to and from Balatonfüred on the northern shore dock to the west of the park, at the mouth of the Sió Canal. The best sources of **information** are Tourinform, housed in the water tower (May & June Mon–Sat 8am–6pm; July to Aug 20 Mon–Sat 8am–8pm, Sun 9am–noon; Aug 21–April Mon–Fri 9am–noon & 1–4pm, Sat 9am–noon; ☎84/310-117); Siótour at Szabadság tér 6 (May & June Mon–Sat 8am–6pm; July to Aug 20 Mon–Sat 8am–8pm, Sun 9am–noon & 3pm–7pm; Aug 21–April Mon–Fri 9am–4pm; ☎84/310-900); and IBUSZ at Fő utca 174 (May–Sept Mon–Fri 8am–6pm, Sat 8am–4pm; Oct–April Mon–Sat 8am–4pm; ☎84/311-481). All three offices handle money exchange and **accommodation** bookings, but can get completely swamped in summer, when it's wise to book ahead. The alternative is to hope for a vacancy at a pension, pay through the nose at a lakeside hotel, or resign yourself to a private room, possibly in a distant suburb, or a campsite far from the centre.

*HOTELS AND PENSIONS*

**Hotel Balaton**, Petőfi sétány 9 (☎84/310-655). The cheapest of the four Pannonia high-rise hotels next to each other on the waterfront, sharing the same private beach. ④.

**Hotel Europa**, Petőfi sétány 19 (☎84/313-411). The most expensive of the high-rise hotels on the waterfront, this has recently been refurbished and all rooms have television.

**Hotel Napfény**, Mártirok utca 8 (☎84/311-408). Nondescript seventies low-rise, right in the thick of things by the pier. Rooms have balconies overlooking the lake and promenade. Rates include half-board. March 15 to October. ⑤.

**Csengei Panzió**, Erkel utca 31 (☎84/316-991). Small pension in a villa just west of the centre. All rooms have bath. ②.

**Moló Panzió**, Petőfi sétány 1 (☎84/312-244). Old union holiday home close to the pier offering cheap but basic rooms with shared bathrooms. Due to be renovated. June to Sept 15. ②.

**Hotel N.G.K.M.**, Petőfi sétány 4 (☎84/311-506). Ministerial holiday home, the name of which changes as ministries are shuffled round, but this is still written outside. Moderate comfort close to the lakeside in the centre of town. ④.

**Oázis Panzió**, Szigliget utca 5 (☎84/313-650). Relatively quiet, cheap place, 500m west of the Sió Canal and one block in from the lake, with single, double and triple rooms. May–Sept. ②.

**Rádió Inn**, Beszédes József sétány 77 (☎84/311-634). By the shore, twenty minutes' walk east from the centre. This holiday home for journalists has a beach and tennis courts. Rooms have balconies and bath. ⑤.

**Tengerszem Panzió**, Karinthy Frigyes utca 4 (☎84/310-146). Friendly set-up spread over twelve buildings forming a sort of compound in the older part of town, two minutes' walk from lakefront. ③.

*HOSTELS AND CAMPSITES*

**Aranypart Camping**, Szent László utca 183–185 (☎84/352-801). Beachfront campsite 5km east of the centre, where Siófok merges into Balatonszabadi. No shade, but a great waterchute. April–Sept. ②.

**Ezüstpart Camping**, Október 23 tér. Fairly large, shadeless site, 4km west of the centre (bus #1 from the Baross Bridge). April–Oct. ②.

**Trade School Holiday Home**, Erkel Ferenc utca 46 (☎84/310-131). Hostel west of the centre with double rooms and shared bathrooms. June–Aug. ②.

## Eating, nightlife and entertainment

Siófok's **restaurants** include the *Csárdás*, at Fő utca 105, a traditional Hungarian joint with the ubiquitous gypsy music; and the *Fogas*, opposite the bus station, one of many places that specialize in fish dishes. Siófok has more than its fair share of sleazy **nightlife**, but you should have a good time (and not be ripped off) at the *Casablanca* disco at Fő utca 184, by the *Fogas* restaurant, offering sixties and eighties hits, or at two techno clubs, *Flört*, just off Fő utca, on the east bank of the canal, and *Paradiso*, down on the harbour side.

As the birthplace of Imre Kálmán, **operetta** dominates summer entertainment, with performances of his works (usually in German) in the Cultural Centre (*Kulturális Központ*) behind the water tower. There are also regular pop and **rock concerts** on one of the *strand* by the hotels in the centre of town. In mid-July Siófok hosts an **international folklore festival**, with parades and dancing by troupes from around the world. Tourinform can give details of the latest in events.

## The town and beaches

The bustling **centre** of town lies east of the Sió Canal that flows into Balaton, ten minutes' walk from the shoreline, where you'll find the bus and train stations, tourist offices, shops and discos. There are two waterfront resort areas: **Aranypart** (Gold Shore) to the east of the canal, and **Ezüstpart** (Silver Shore) to the west. Though the central stretch of shoreline consists of paying **beaches** (daily 8am–7pm; 150–200Ft), there are free *strand* 1km further along at both resort areas. Having larger hotels and more nightlife in the vicinity, Aranypart is the livelier and noisier of the two. You can rent **windsurfing** boards and small **sailing** boats at most beaches, while **horse-riding** and **pleasure cruises** can be arranged through Siótour (see p.171).

With its high-rise hotels and packed beaches, there's little trace of Siófok's pre-war reputation as a quietly elegant resort, nor much evidence of the town's long history. The canal that the Romans began in 292 AD was later made use of by the Turks, who stationed a fleet of 10,000 men here to confront the Austro-Hungarian fleet across the water at Balatonfüred. A small **gallery** at the top of the water tower on Szabadság tér displays photos of Siófok a century ago and offers a view of the town today, though you have to climb over 120 steps to get there (same hours as Tourinform, see p.171; free). The streets between the train station and the shore are an enjoyable place to wander around, with avenues of plane trees screening some magnificent turn-of-the-century **villas**, many of them turned into garishly decorated restaurants or pensions.

It seems somehow appropriate that the most famous son of Siófok was the composer of operettas **Imre Kálmán** (1882–1953), who was born in a house near the train station at what is now Kálmán Imre sétány 5, where there's a **museum** featuring his piano, desk and dressing gown, as well as photos and programmes from operettas such as the *Countess Maritza* and the *Csárdás Princess*, unfortunately without any explanations in English.

From the station, you can walk east along Fő utca for ten minutes to reach the striking modern **Lutheran Church** (May–Sept Mon–Sat 9am–noon & 2–6pm, Sun 2–6pm; Oct–April Sun only 11am–noon), designed by the visionary architect Imre Makovecz (see p.143). It not only embodies his ideas about organic architecture and nationhood, but constitutes a rebuke to the immorality and materialism of Siófok – or at least that's assumed to be the significance of the hollow-eyed face of an old man carved into the wooden facade. The points of the roof are meant to be the shoulders of his sheepskin coat.

# West to Fonyód

Blink as you pass through **ZAMÁRDI**, the next settlement, 8km from Siófok, and you'll miss it – which isn't a great shame. The two sights in the place are across the main road from the station and up the hill, twenty to thirty minutes' walk away. Up Honvéd utca and left along Fő utca you come to a **Tájház**, an old thatched peasant cottage displaying pottery, tiled ovens and old agricultural equipment (June–Aug Tues–Sun 9am–1pm & 2–6pm; 100Ft). Ten minutes further along Fő utca is the **Szamárkő** (Donkey Rock), just off the road to the right, in the first clump of trees. Though it's thought by archeologists to have been a sacrificial site of the ancient Magyars, and claimed by some Christians to bear a child's footprint and the hoof-print of Christ's donkey, you will be hard pressed to spot anything significant at all about it. If you wish to stay, the Viva Balaton **information** office at Petőfi utca 1, near the station (May–Oct daily 8am–8pm; ☎84/348-772), can organize rooms, villas, pensions and camping, but your best bet is to push on.

From Zamárdi, signposts point to **SZÁNTÓDRÉV**, 3km away, which is the point of departure for car ferries to Tihany (see p.182) on the northern shore (March–May & early Sept–Nov every hour; June to early Sept every 40min). It's a cheaper place to stay than Tihany, what with the *Rév Hotel* at Szent István út 162, five minutes' walk from the ferry (☎84/348-245; ④; May–Sept), and *Rév Camping*, by the ferry (☎84/348-859; April–Aug). If you stick to Route 7, a bright yellow car on stilts, 3km west of Szántódrév, alerts you to a cluster of eighteenth- and nineteenth-century farm buildings converted into a "tourist and cultural centre" at **Szántódpuszta** (April 4–Oct 10; 300Ft; check times with Siótour). "Puszta" in

Hungarian has two meanings: one is the flat plains of eastern Hungary, and the other, of which Szántódpuszta is a good example, is a large farmstead common in western Hungary. The restored thatched buildings house a local history exhibition with beautiful old photos, a poor craft display, a blacksmith's workshop that's sometimes in operation, and a Balaton aquarium, plus two restaurants, and a stables offering horse and carriage rides. You can stay here at *Patkó Fogadó* (☎84/348-923; ④), run by the Siótour office at the entrance to the complex.

Shortly after Szántódpuszta, 3km inland, the village of **KŐRÖSHEGY** has a church with some fifteenth-century remnants, where chamber-music concerts are held on Friday evenings in the summer; check with Siótour in Balatonföldvár at Szécheny utca 9–11 (☎84/340-099). Coming by train, the nearest stop is Szántód-Kőröshegy. If you're in the mood for **walking**, aim for the pretty villages further to the south, and the hills beyond, where herds of deer roam.

## Balatonszárszó and Balatonszemes

The boundary of the small town of **BALATONSZÁRSZÓ**, 5km further on, is marked by a cemetery containing the **grave of Attila József**, the tragic proletarian poet. Dismissed by his literary peers and rejected by both his lover and the Communist Party, he threw himself under a local freight train on December 3, 1937. Attila spent his last days in a pension that's now a **memorial museum** at József Attila utca 7 (Tues–Sun: April–Oct 10am–6pm; Nov–March 10am–2pm; 100Ft). It has some interesting photographs, though there are no English captions. There's a campsite, *Tura Camping*, 100m from here by the rail tracks (mid-June to Aug; ①), or try the *Vasmacska Panzió* at József Attila utca 17 (☎84/362-589; ③). Siótour, by the train station (May–Sept Mon–Fri 9am–6pm; ☎84/362-956), can help with accommodation.

**BALATONSZEMES**, 5km further west, has a special feel, with pleasant plane-tree-lined avenues curling down to the lakeside, and an old coaching inn converted into a **Postal Museum** (June–Sept Tues–Sun 10am–6pm), where antique stage coaches stand in the courtyard. Besides **rooms** in the *Lídó Fogadó* at Ady utca 8 (☎84/360-112; ③; May–Sept), there are several **campsites**: *Lídó Camping* at Ady utca 8 (☎84/345-112; ①; April–Sept); *Vadvirág Camping* just off the main road (☎84/360-114; ②; May–Sept); and the *Bagódomb* site, uphill towards the ruined **Bagolyvár Castle** (☎84/345-117; ①; July & Aug ). For information, there's a Siótour near the station (mid-April to Sept Mon–Fri 9am–6pm, Sat 9am–1pm; ☎84/360-057).

## Balatonlelle, Kishegy and Balatonboglár

During the Kádár era, the settlements of Balatonlelle and Balatonboglár were merged into a single entity called Boglárlelle, but since 1991 they have re-established their own identities and also made the most of the revival of the wine industry since then, becoming the main centre of **wine tourism** on the southern shore of the lake.

**BALATONLELLE** does its bit to attract tourists by staging the **Juniális Festival** of music and crafts in June, and **folk dancing** in an old mansion at Kossuth utca 2 during July and August. You can rent private rooms from the Siótour **information** office at Szent István utca 16 (June–Aug daily 8am–7pm; May & Sept Mon–Fri 8am–4.30pm; ☎85/351-086), and there are several **hotels** and pensions on Köztársaság út, including the *Guiseppe* at no. 36 (☎85/350-433; ④; June–Sept). The *Aranyhíd* campsite, at Köztársaság út 53 (☎85/350-449; ②; May to mid-Sept), is expensive by Balaton standards.

Wine lovers should venture 3km inland to **KISHEGY** (you'll have to walk or take a taxi), where you can taste and buy wine in the **Szent Donatus winery** at Kishegyi utca 42 (Mon–Fri 7.30am–4pm; ☎85/354-701). It's another 2km to the *csárda* at the top of the hill (the staff at the winery can direct you), where, in July and August, you can sample wines while gazing over the lake. Draught Holsten can be quaffed at the *Zöld Lugas* on Honvéd utca in Lelle, and, though it looks uninspiring, the *Albatross Étterem* on the main road between Lelle and Boglár is a good place to **eat**.

**BALATONBOGLÁR** hosts a massive annual **wine harvest festival** (*Boglári Szüret*) from August 18 to 20, two stages down by the *Platán strand*, with a big fair and a procession, a competition for the title of Wine Queen, nightly firework displays, and, of course, lots of wine. On neighbouring Várhegy, a spherical **lookout tower** commands a sweeping view from Keszthely to Tihany, while atop Temetődomb (Cemetery Hill), behind the two chapels, there are regular exhibitions by artists from June to August.

Balatonboglár's Tourinform office is at Erzsébet utca 12–14, a couple of minutes' walk up off the main road (mid-June to Aug Mon–Fri 9am–noon & 1–6pm, Sat & Sun 9am–noon; Sept to mid-June 9am–noon & 1–4.30pm; ☎85/353-230). You can book private rooms at Fredo Tourist, Dózsa utca 1 (July & Aug daily 8am–8pm; Sept–June Mon–Fri 8am–4.30pm; ☎85/350-665), while the *Vasutas Üdülő* at Kodály utca 9–15, by the tracks to the east of the station (☎85/350-634; ②), has cheap beds. The *Sellő Campsite* (☎85/350-800; ①; mid-May to Sept) is on the west of the landing stage at Kikötő utca 3.

# Fonyód

**FONYÓD** grew up between the Sipos and Sándor hills and subsequently spread itself along the lakeside. Its built-up shoreline, with bleak modern architecture, is not appealing, and most people come here only for the **ferries to Badacsony** on the northern shore, from where the symmetry of Fonyód's setting is best appreciated. However, there are a couple of places of interest away from the water. Heading uphill along Szent István utca from the station and turning right along winding József utca, you come to some fantastic **villas** high above the lakefront. About five minutes' walk along, the salmon-coloured "**Crypt Villa**" was built above a red marble crypt with room for two by a grieving widower who lived here in seclusion for many years, waiting to join his wife below. A further ten minutes' walk brings you to some more fine villas on the tree-lined Bartók Béla utca promenade, which offer marvellous views across the lake to the Badacsony hills, and can be reached by local buses running from the bus station to the suburb of Bélatelep.

Sticking to Szent István utca and heading up past the IBUSZ office for twenty minutes, you'll find the **Fácán park** on your right, where the earthworks of a medieval castle are still visible. Its Hungarian defenders escaped their Turkish besiegers by using wooden columns sunk below the surface of the water to cross the surrounding marshes, while the Turks were left stranded on the other side.

## Practicalities

Fonyód's bus and train stations and ferry are all conveniently close to the centre of town and the **tourist offices**, with Siótour in the train station (mid-May to mid-Sept daily 8am–noon & 3–7pm; mid-Sept to mid-May Mon–Fri 8am–4.30pm;

☎85/361-850), and IBUSZ a couple of minutes' walk away at Szent István utca 4 (June–Aug Mon–Sat 8am–10pm, Sun 8am–3pm; Sept–May Mon–Fri 8am–4pm; ☎85/360-499).

It's essential to reserve **accommodation** in August, but it should be easier to find at other times of the year. IBUSZ can book you into the former *Szocialista Üdülő*(②), only 700m from the water, and both tourist agencies can arrange private rooms (③). Otherwise, it's a choice between the *Korona Panzió* at Szent István utca 3 (☎85/361-608; ⑤); the *Kilató Panzió* at Bartók Béla utca 48, 3km from the centre (☎85/356-16; ③); and camping or a bungalow (②–③) at the *Napsugár* complex, Komjáth utca 5, in Fonyód-Bélatelep, 2km east of the centre.

From May to August, you can enjoy tasty homestyle Hungarian **food** at the *Présház* restaurant behind Fácán park, which is named after the wine-press that operated here in the eighteenth and nineteenth centuries.

## From Fonyód to the Kis-Balaton

From Fonyód the lakeside sprawl continues another 15km westwards to **BALA-TONKERESZTÚR**, where it's worth a brief stopover to see the **Baroque Church** at the main crossroads, which is entirely decorated with gorgeous frescoes in the style of Maulbertsch. These include portraits of the Festetics family, who owned most of the land around Keszthely (see p.189). Count Kristóf is portrayed at the rear of the church and to the left of the altar, accompanied by his wife Judit Szegedi.

At **BALATONBERÉNY**, 4km further west, you'll find the only **nudist beach** on the southern shore, the agreeable lakeside *Kócsag* **campsite** (☎85/377-154; ①; June–Aug), and a Siótour office on the *strand* (mid-May to mid-Sept Mon–Fri 9am–6pm, Sat 9am–1pm; ☎85/377-701). **BALATONSZENTGYÖRGY**, 3km inland, has nothing to recommend it apart from the fact that you can catch trains from here to Keszthely and Nagykanizsa in southern Transdanubia (see p.189).

At the far end of the lake, reeds obscure the mouth of the River Zala and stretch for miles upstream to the **Kis-Balaton** (Little Balaton). This lake once covered forty square kilometres, but was half-drained in the 1950s to provide irrigation for new crop land, and was nearly destroyed by the dumping of pollutants into the Zala during the 1980s. Its rehabilitation was begun in the 1980s, as attempts were made to improve the quality of water in Lake Balaton. The first stage of the process, diverting water back through the reed beds that act as a filter for the lake, has been completed, but there is much debate about how successful this has been, and whether further steps should be taken. It has certainly restored the area as a paradise for birds and bird lovers, with over eighty breeds of birds found here. The Research Centre in Fenékpuszta, 4km up Route 76 towards Keszthely, arranges **bird-watching tours** for groups; individuals can phone the reserve (☎83/315-341) on the off-chance of being able to tag along.

## The northern shore to Balatonfüred

The **resorts** of Balatonalmádi and Balatonfüred on the **northern shore** of the lake are more genteel than their southern counterparts, with a certain faded elegance, but the crowds of tourists are just as big, outnumbering the locals in **villages** like Alsóörs and Csopak. Though there's little to get excited about on this stretch of the shoreline, it makes a pleasant run-up to the main attractions further west: Tihany, the Badacsony and Keszthely.

Coming from Budapest, the first stop for buses and trains is **BALATON-AKARATTYA** (motorists should turn off the M7 following the signs for Route 71 and Balatonfüred), an agreeable resort whose only "sight" is the trunk of an elm tree in a park near the top of the hill beside Route 71, which the eighteenth-century free-dom fighter Ferenc Rákóczi is said to have tied his horse to. However, some may be attracted by the **nudist campsite** *FKK Piroska* at Aligai út 15 (☎88/381-084; ②; mid-May to late Sept), which is signposted from the main road near the station, a twen-ty-minute walk down Bercsényi lejáró to the shore. The *Hotel Szilfa* at Bercsényi lejáró 3 (☎88/381-994 or 381-558) runs another, non-nudist campsite down by the water, which also has smarter rooms for rent at its premises up the hill (②).

# Balatonalmádi

The first major settlement along the northern shore is **BALATONALMÁDI**, a resort since 1877, which now has a pleasantly faded air, and even in the summer the main crowds pass it by. Its bus and train stations are situated at the top and bottom of the main square, Városház tér, while in July and August boats from Balatonfüred and Tihany arrive at the pier, ten minutes' walk eastwards through the lakeside park.

The best time to visit is during the **Almádi Days** at the end of July, a ten-day cultural festival featuring folk dancing, operetta and a big craft fair around the lakeside area. The **grape harvest** celebration in mid-September is a smaller event – a day of wine and music, with a big procession through the town.

All the sights in the town are church-related. A few minutes' walk west of the centre, the small **Chapel of the Holy Right Hand** (*Szent Jobb Kápolna*), tacked on to the left side of the Church of Szent Imre, at Táncsics utca 47, was originally located in the Royal Palace in Buda and housed the holy right hand of St Stephen, which is now in the Basilica in Budapest (see p.95). During the reconstruction of Buda palace after World War II, the chapel was spared from destruction by Stalinists, and rebuilt at Balatonalmádi in 1957. Peering through the bars of the gate you can see the impressive gold mosaic by Károly Lotz, although the turquoise walls give the whole thing a tacky feel.

Two other unusual churches lie in **Vörösberény**, the older part of town, twenty minutes' walk up Petőfi utca, and along Veszprémi út (ask at the bus station which bus to catch). The Baroque parish church, built in 1779 for the Jesuits, contains interesting frescoes depicting the order's founder, St Ignatius, as well as some con-temporary figures; you can get the key from the *plébánia*, two houses behind the church. Just uphill stands a fortified thirteenth-century Calvinist church, whose shape has undergone many changes over the years; only fragments of frescoes remain and a couple of windows remain from the original. The key is available from the priest's house (*Református Lelkész Hivatal*), directly below the church at Veszprémi út 105. On Fridays in July and August the church hosts **concerts** of Renaissance and Baroque music.

## Practicalities

Tourinform, opposite the train station at Baross Gábor utca 2, behind *McDonald's* (July & Aug Mon–Sat 8.30am–6pm, Sun 8.30am–1pm; rest of the year Mon–Fri 8.30am–4.30pm; ☎88/438-408), can supply **information** on events and accommodation, but doesn't handle bookings. For private rooms, go to IBUSZ, at Petőfi utca 21 (June–Aug daily 8am–6pm; ☎88/338-149), or Balatontourist, further up on the right, at no. 6 (May–Sept Mon–Sat 8.30am–4.30pm; July & Aug Mon–Sat 8.30am–7pm, Sun 9am–noon; Oct–April Mon–Fri 8.30am–3.30pm; ☎88/438-588). The **post office** is at Petőfi utca 19, and there's an OTP bank with an **ATM** at Baross Gábor utca 5/a, just up from Tourinform.

**Accommodation** in Balatonalmádi is tight in July and August, but you should be able to get something even then. If you are not attracted by the view from the kitsch *Hotel Auróra* at Bajcsy-Zsilinszky utca 14, near the ferry (☎88/438-810; ⑤), which has its own pool and sauna, and rooms with balconies and all mod cons, there is the friendly *Hotel Viktória* at Bajcsy-Zsilinszky utca 42 (☎88/338-940; ④), where rooms have TV, telephones and bathrooms. A cheaper option is the *Pedagógus Üdülő* (Teachers' Holiday Home) at Dózsa György utca 13, just behind the Church of St Imre (☎88/338-518; ①; mid-May to Sept), offering basic rooms with basins and shared bathrooms. **Private rooms** (②) are bookable through the tourist offices listed above. The nearest of the three **campsites** in town is the friendly *Kristóf Camping and Motel*, a few minutes' walk from the centre (☎88/338-902; room ④; camping ②; Easter to mid-Oct), which has no direct access to the lake, though you can get to the *strand* next door free of charge. A little further along the shore is *Yacht Camping* (☎88/338-906; ①; mid-May to mid-Sept), where you can swim and rent boats. Both campsites have tourist offices for information and changing money. Cheapest of all is *Bikini Camping*, 300m further along the main road at Óvari utca 70 (☎88/338-302; June to mid-Sept), a smaller, more basic site that's not actually on the lake.

Balatonalmádi has a beach (150Ft) by Városház tér in the centre of town, and a free beach (*szabad strand*) half an hour's walk west at Káptalanfüred. The most charming of the town's **restaurants** is the *Liget Kávéház* at Véghely Dezső út 1, in a Baroque building with period furnishings in the park near the pier, which serves coffee and meals on its terrace (daily 7.30am–midnight).

## Alsóörs and Felsőörs

**ALSÓÖRS**, 5km west of Balatonalmádi by ferry or train, is one of the few places in the country to retain a street called Marx utca. Like many of the villages and towns on the northern shore, the old centre of settlement is away from the lakeside, while the waterfront holiday area has a transient population that far outnumbers the residents of Alsóörs. Formerly a mining village where the rock was used to make millstones, its centre lies fifteen minutes' walk up from the boat station across the main road, while most of the accommodation and the *strand* lie off to the east. The **Turkish House** at Petőfi köz 7 (*Török Ház*; mid-June to Aug daily 3–9pm) is one of the few remnants of the Ottoman occupation here. Located in one of the narrow alleys that wind around the hillside, this Gothic manor house was once inhabited by the local Turkish tax collector and is distinguished by a turban-topped chimney – a sign of wealth in the days when smoke left most houses through a simple hole in the roof. It is now used as an exhibition hall and also hosts the odd wedding.

The *Fogadó az Aranysashoz* at Szegfű utca 13, just across the main road from the *strand* (☎87/447-124; ②–⑤; June to mid-Sept), has **accommodation** in wooden bungalows with shared bathrooms, and is currently building a luxurious villa too. The miners' holiday home (signposted *Hotel Bergarbeiter* by the road) at Füredi utca 24 (☎87/447-131; ②; mid-April to mid-Oct) offers cheap rooms with bathrooms, some with balconies overlooking the lake (as well as the road and train line), while the friendly *Riviera Camping* on the eastern edge of the village (☎87/447-085; ①) has its own beach, as well as access to the town *strand*, where there is a waterslide and canoes for rent. For **eating**, you could try the *Kolompos Restaurant*, in a 150-year-old barn at Fő utca 23, just below the Turkish House (mid-May to Sept), which is signposted from the main road. Prices are at Budapest levels, but it offers a pleasant garden and colourfully presented dishes, such as the "Knife Plate" – beef served on a wooden dish with a knife sticking out.

A few kilometres inland, the small village of **FELSŐÖRS** is notable for its impressive **Romanesque Church**, built from the purple-red sandstone that is characteristic of the surrounding villages. Its tower is carved with ancient ornamental reliefs known as the "Knots of Hercules", designed to ward off demons, while the eighteenth-century Baroque interior includes a fine pulpit. Felsőörs also boasts a good **restaurant**, the *Udvarház*, at Fő utca 22. Six buses a day go to Felsőörs from Alsóörs and Balatonalmádi.

# Csopak

The village of **CSOPAK**, 4km down Route 71 towards Balatonfüred, has made a name for itself in recent years for its **wine**, and this is the main reason for visiting. Arriving by train, walk up the main street, Kossuth utca, to the old village, or, to get to the *strand* and the resort area, walk across Route 71 and then along Fürdő utca; the ferry is a couple of minutes' walk beyond. The only tourist office is Csopaktourist at Veszprémi út 33, in the old village near the top of Kossuth utca (mid-May to mid-Sept; ☎30/957-6115).

There are numerous **wine cellars** around the old village, and many houses advertise dens where you can pop in to taste – and buy – the local hock. Csopak wines are mainly white, of which the best-known is *Olaszrizling*; most locals sell it straight from the barrel. The co-operative Csopak Kistermelői Pinceszövetkezet bottles the wines of a thousand small vineyards in the area and sells them at the large factory-like building behind Csopaktourist (Mon–Thurs 7.30am–3pm, Fri 7.30am–2pm, Sat 8am–noon). Smaller cellars, where you can also eat as you taste the wines, include the Linci Pince at Berekháti utca 34, a few minutes' walk up from the train station (May–Oct daily 5–11pm), and the Söptei Pince at Istenfia utca 5, fifteen minutes' walk west along Füredi utca (June to mid-Oct 11am–11pm). Csopak's Wine Week (*Borhét*) takes place in the third week of August, with wine, singing and dancing down by the waterfront at the entrance to the *strand*.

**Accommodation** is available down near the waterfront at the *Rozmaring Panzió*, a series of low buildings spread over large pleasant grounds by the *strand* at Rozmaring utca 10 (☎87/446-583; ②; May–Aug); the *Youth Resort*, a large complex a few minutes' walk east of the *strand* at Sport utca 9 (*Ifjúsági Üdülő*, ☎87/446-505; ②–③; May–Sept; no IH discounts in July & Aug), which has rooms with showers, and sports facilities to cater for the big groups that stay here; and the *Hotel Piroska* next door at Sport utca 5–7 (☎87/446-576; ④; June–Aug), which is outwardly unappealing but has nice rooms with balconies overlooking the gardens. Two pleasant places to **eat**, both with outside seating and serving traditional Hungarian cuisine, are the *Dobó Restaurant* at the top of Kossuth utca near Csopaktourist, and the *Malom Csárda* in an old watermill ten minutes' walk up at Veszprémi út 3, on the northern edge of the village.

# Balatonfüred

Seventeenth-century chronicles tell of pilgrims descending on **BALATONFÜRED** to "camp in scattered tents" and benefit from the mineral springs. Some 30,000 people come here every year for treatment at the springs, mingling with hordes of tourists, giving this popular Balaton resort a distinctive, sedate air. Füred, as it is often called, is split into two, with the older centre a couple of kilometres away from the lake: here you'll find shops, churches and a market along its Baroque main street, Kossuth utca. Most visitors head for the resort area beside Balaton, whose centrepiece is the leafy Gyógy tér, with its sanatorium, springs and run-down nineteenth-century facades, leading down to a tree-lined lakeside promenade. On either side are beaches and a mix of modern hotels and antebellum villas.

## Arrival and accommodation

The **bus and train stations** are conveniently located next door to each other on Dobó István utca, just off Ady Endre utca, which links the town and resort. Bus #2 or #3, or a twenty-minute walk up Ady Endre utca, brings you to the old town, while a ten-minute walk in the other direction, down Jókai utca, takes you past the Tourinform office on Petőfi utca to the lakeside. Alternatively, bus #1 takes a round-about route to the embankment before heading west along Széchenyi út. **Ferries** from Siófok and Tihany dock at the pier at the western end of the promenade.

The best sources of **information** are both easy to find: Tourinform at Petőfi utca 8, the road down to the centre from the bus and train stations (mid-July to Aug 20 Mon–Sat 9am–7pm, Sun 9am–1pm; April to mid-July & Aug 21 to mid-Oct Mon–Fri 9am–4pm, Sat 9am–1pm; mid-Oct to March Mon–Fri 9am–4pm; ☎87/342-237), and Balatontourist, by the pier at Tagore sétány 1 (June–Aug Mon–Sat 8.30am–6.30pm, Sun 8.30am–noon; Sept–May Mon–Fri 8.30am–4pm; ☎87/342-822). IBUSZ, at Petőfi utca 4a (July–Aug 20 daily 8.30am–6pm; June & Aug 21 to mid-Oct Mon–Fri 8.30am–4pm, Sat 8.30am–1pm; mid-Oct to May Mon–Fri 8.30am–4pm; ☎87/342-028), handles accommodation only. There are ATMs at the OTP **bank** opposite Tourinform, and by the entrance of the sanatorium on Gyógy tér. The **post office** is at Zsigmond utca 14, just up from *Hotel Blaha Lujza*.

### Accommodation

It's always advisable to book **accommodation** ahead, and essential in the period from the last weekend in July to August 20. In the last couple of years, most of the cheaper hotels and dormitories in town have closed their doors, but it's worth asking at Tourinform if the *Széchenyi Ferenc Kollégium* on Iskola utca, up in the main town (☎87/343-844; ①; July & Aug only), is taking tourists. **Private rooms**, the cheapest of which are in the town, can be booked through Balatontourist and IBUSZ. Twenty minutes' walk west of the promenade (bus #1 or #2), at Széchenyi utca 24, lies the huge *Füred* campsite (☎87/343-823; ②–③; mid-April to mid-Oct), offering tennis, water-sports and bungalows on the lakefront.

There are several **hotels** including the *Hotel Blaha Lujza*, Blaha Lujza utca 4 (☎87/343-094; ③), which has rooms with bathroom in the centre of the resort in the Neoclassical summer home of the nineteenth-century actress and singer Lujza Blaha; the *Hotel Fortuna*, Huray utca 6 (☎87/343-037; ③; May–Sept), a modern pension in large grounds next to the Jókai Museum, with bathroom and TV in all rooms and some with balcony; the *Hotel Tagore*, Deák Ferenc utca 56 (☎87/343-173; ④), a pleasant four-storey hotel close to the lake at the eastern end of Tagore sétány, which has rooms with balcony and shower; and the *Korona Panzió*, Vörösmarty utca 4 (☎87/343-278; ④), a decent pension just up the hill from IBUSZ, ten minutes' walk from the waterfront, with TV and bathroom in all rooms.

## The Lakeside

Walking round Balatonfüred's resort area makes you feel like an extra in Robbe-Grillet's film, *Last Summer in Marienbad*, and you almost expect to come across tubercular countesses and impoverished artists. Despite the crowds and a few high-rise hotels, this once elegant spa has managed to retain most of its old Central European charm. The tone is set by the tree-lined promenade that runs east from the pier, where you can admire the view across to the Tihany promontory and the far side of the lake. The promenade is named Tagore sétány after the Bengali poet Rabindranath Tagore who came here in 1926 and planted a tree near the pier in gratitude for his cure. Indira and Rajiv Gandhi and a host of other Indian figures have followed suit, as have various Nobel prize-winners, and the odd Soviet cosmonaut.

A few minutes up from the middle of the promenade, you come to the aptly named **Gyógy tér** (Health Square). Its columned, pagoda-like **Kossuth Well** gushes carbonated water, while other springs feed the sanatorium and cardiac hospital on the northern and eastern sides of the square. Excavations suggest that the Romans were the first to exploit the springs, using the waters to treat stomach ailments and, when mixed with goats' milk whey, as a cure for lung diseases. The hospital's **mineral baths** are reserved for patients. On the western side of the square stand two former trade union holiday homes, the *Árkád Hotel*, where redevelopment work is currently taking place, and the eighteenth-century **Horváth House**, one of the first inns in a land where innkeeping developed late, patronized by writers and politicians during the Reform era. The inn was a sanatorium for uranium miners in the Communist era, but is now closed, awaiting its next transformation.

---

### THE ANNA BALL AND OTHER EVENTS

The big event in Füred's calendar is the **Anna Ball** on the last Saturday of July. Magnate Zsigmond Horváth held the first ball on Anna's Day, July 26, 1825, in honour of his granddaughter Anna, and since the collapse of Communism this traditional social occasion has gained in stature. Crowds gather around Gyógy tér to watch the ball-goers, though the exact location of the ball has moved around in recent years, with the *Annabel Hotel* just behind the sanatorium being the latest setting.

Besides the **sailing competitions** on the lake, Füred has two other regular events in August. On the second weekend of the month, keen swimmers set off on the 3.6km to Tihany – a challenge that attracted over four thousand participants in 1998. The same weekend sees the start of the two-week **Wine Festival** (*Borhetek*), with stalls set up along the promenade, where you can taste local vintages. There are also **concerts** during summer in the Calvinist church on Kossuth utca in the main town (the whitewashed church rather than the red sandstone one at the top of Ady utca).

Running westwards between the two is Blaha Lujza utca, named after the "Nation's Nightingale", who spent her summers here in a **villa** at no. 4 (now a hotel) and had her tea at the *Kedves Cukrászda* across the road. Just past the hotel at the junction with Jókai utca stands the mid-nineteenth-century **Round Church**, modelled on the Pantheon in Rome. Across the road, the **Jókai Memorial House** (April–Oct Tues–Sun 10am–6pm; 100Ft) was built by the nineteenth-century novelist Mór Jókai, whose novels are often compared to those of Dickens; Queen Victoria is said to have been among his fans. He came to Balatonfüred at the age of 37, half-expecting to die from a lung infection, and built the villa as a refuge; he didn't die, however, until the ripe old age of 84. The museum preserves Jókai's furniture and belongings, and includes an excellent coffee house, the *Jókai kávézó*.

## Eating, drinking and activities

Of the **restaurants** down by the lakeside, the *Borcsa* and *Stefánia Vitorlás Étterem* at either end of Tagore sétány, and the *Halászkert*, on Széchenyi tér, specializing in fish dishes, are the most reliable, but are, inevitably, crowded. The *Jókai kávézo*, behind the Jókai Museum, serves decent food as well as coffee and cakes (May–Oct), and Lujza Blaha's favourite coffee shop, the *Kedves*, is open from 8am to 8pm. A slightly quieter place to eat is the excellent *Arany Korona Vendéglő* at Kossuth utca 11, up in the main town, just before the Calvinist church.

With wooded hills on one side and water on the other, Füred offers a good variety of sports. Balatontourist can help with arranging **horse-riding** at the riding school in the Koloska Valley, a few kilometres outside town (☎06-30/367-908). You can rent **bicycles** from outside the big hotels, and pedaloes and **windsurfing** boards at every *strand*, while **yachts** can be rented from Opticonsor on Köztársaság utca 1, Lisa Hajó at *Füred Camping*, and the Fekete Sailing School at Zákonyi utca 8, which also offers sailing lessons. Tennis courts can be found at various locations, including Ferencsik utca 16 and Fürdő utca 24. All the **beaches** either side of the harbour are paying *strand* (daily 8am–6pm; July & Aug till 7pm; 180Ft); the *Városi strand* on Széchenyi utca west of the centre by the *Hotel Marina* is best for swimming (though not for kids, as it drops away quickly).

# Tihany peninsula

A rocky finger of land that was declared Hungary's first national park in 1952, **Tihany peninsula**, 7km west of Balatonfüred, is historically associated with the Benedictine order and a castle (no longer in existence) that withstood 150 years of Turkish hostility. As one of the most beautiful regions of Balaton, Tihany gets swamped with visitors over summer, though it's easy to escape the crowds by hiking into the interior.

The lakeshore road from Balatonfüred passes along the eastern side of the peninsula, through Diós (where Avar graves have been discovered) and Gödrös, entering **Tihany village** above the inner harbour (*Belső Kikötő*), where ferries from Balatonfüred and Siófok arrive. At the tip of the peninsula, 2km on, lies **Tihanyi-rév**, where car ferries cross every half-hour to Siófok. Next to the ferry is the expensive *Club Tihany* resort complex. Besides the paying **beaches** by *Club Tihany* and the Tihany docks, there are free *strand* along the reedier shores between Gödrös and Diós, and south of Sajkod on the other side of the peninsula.

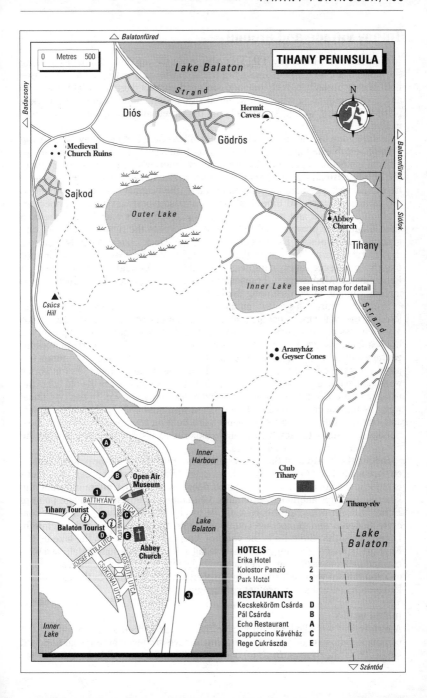

# Tihany village and around

In contrast with Tihany-rév, **TIHANY** village, on the top of the hill halfway along the eastern side of the pensinsula, is a traditional-looking place, full of old houses built of grey basalt tufa, with thatched roofs and porticoed terraces, their windows and doors outlined in white. However, it rivals Szentendre as the most touristy place in Hungary, with folksy stalls lining the streets and parking as expensive as in Budapest.

In days gone by, the village was dominated by a Benedictine abbey overlooking Balaton, established in 1055 at the request of Andrew I and founded, true to the biblical injunction, upon a rocky promontory. Andrew's body lies in the crypt of the **abbey church** – the only one of the Árpád line to remain in the place where he was buried. The building itself is Baroque, the original having succumbed to the ravages of wars and time. Inside are virtuoso **woodcarvings** by Sebestyén Stulhoff, who lived and worked in the abbey for 25 years after his fiancée died (her features are preserved in the face of an angel to the right of the altar), and grandiose **frescoes** by Károly Lotz, Székely and Deák-Ebner. Recently restored, the church (10am–6pm except during mass) provides a magnificent setting for **organ concerts** over summer. The abbey's foundation deed, held at Pannonhalma Monastery in Transdanubia (see p.217), is the earliest document to include Hungarian words among the Latin.

From the church, it's a few minutes' walk down Pisky sétány, a parapet overlooking the waterfront parapet, to a small **Open-Air Museum** (*Szabadtéri Múzeum*; Easter–Sept Tues–Sun 10am–6pm; 100Ft) exhibiting two well-preserved houses. The first, with a beautiful entrance way, was built in the early nineteenth century and inhabited up until 1960; note the cross on the chimney, a common feature in this region. Behind this is an old Fishermen's Guild House, its mud-brick walls clad in thin stone to give an impression of wealth. Inside are the old boats the fishermen used, and a "wooden dog" sledge for fishing on ice. In the traditional way, the mud floor of the veranda is washed with mud daily to deal with the dirt and cracks. Folk dancing performances are held on the open-air stage on most Sunday mornings at 11am. If you want to look round, it's worth getting here on the dot of 10am to avoid the coach tours.

Behind the museum at Batthyány utca 26 is a **pottery workshop**, where earthenware made from the red clay of the area and glazed in bright greens and blues is made and sold; ring at the house next door if it is closed. Continuing along the lakeside walk for another five minutes, you come to the scenic vantage point of **Echo Hill**. An echo can theoretically be produced by standing on a short concrete pedestal and projecting your voice onto the wall of the abbey church. Legend goes that the echo is the voice of a princess, drowned in the lake by the King of the Water following her refusal to fall in love with his son. By taking a well-marked path onwards, you can circumambulate the **Óvár** (Old Castle), a volcanic outcrop riddled with cells carved by Russian Orthodox monks in the eleventh to fourteenth centuries, whence hot springs gush forth.

### Inland walks

A trek inland will allow you to escape the crowds and enjoy the beauty of the peninsula, whose geology and microclimate have produced an unusual flora and fauna. The **Inner Lake** (*Belső-tó*), whose sunlit surface is visible from the abbey church, fills a volcanic crater 25m above the level of Balaton. From its southern bank, you can follow a path for a couple of kilometres through vineyards, orchards and lavender fields to the **Aranyház geyser cones** – rock funnels forced open by hot springs.

The northerly **Outer Lake** (*Külső-tó*) was drained for pasture in 1809, but started to be refilled in 1975. Its reed beds are harvested by hand over winter in the traditional manner, and provide a sanctuary for mallards, gadwalls and other **birds**. On the eastern side of the peninsula, a lookout tower atop **Csúcs Hill** (232m) offers a **panoramic view** of Balaton. The trail, marked in red, takes about one and a half hours to walk.

# Practicalities

Tihany is connected to Balatonfüred by hourly **buses**, which stop in the village on András tér below the abbey church, and at Balatontourist on Kossuth utca. The peninsula is also connected by bus with Balatonudvari, Balatonszepezd and Badacsony to the west. **Ferries** from Balatonfüred and Siófok, and from Badacsony and Keszthely during the summer months, arrive at the inner harbour (*Belső Kikötő*), while from April to November there are boats every half-hour or so between Tihany-rév and Balatonföldvar, and a car ferry to and from Szántód on the southern shore (560Ft per car & 140Ft per person). Regular buses link the ferries with the upper village.

**Information** is available in Tihany village from Balatontourist at Kossuth utca 20 (June 20 to Aug 20 daily 8am–6.30pm; May to June 19, Aug 21 to mid-Oct Mon–Fri 8.30am–4.30pm, Sat 8.30am–1pm; ☎87/448-519) and Tihany Tourist at Kossuth utca 11 (April–Oct daily 9am–7pm; ☎87/448-481). You can change money at both offices.

## Accommodation
**Private rooms** (③) can be booked during the summer months through Balatontourist or Tihany Tourist. Alternatively, if you simply wander the streets you'll see plenty of *Zimmer frei* signs dotted around. Hotels here are none too cheap.

**Adler Panzió**, Felső Kopasz hegy 1 (☎87/448-755). A decent pension at the southern end of the upper village, with a swimming pool and sauna. Rooms have showers and TV. April to Oct 23. ④.

**Erika Hotel**, Batthyány utca 6 (☎87/448-010). New plush pension in the centre of the village with a swimming pool and fifteen rooms decorated in staggeringly bad taste. ⑤.

**Kolostor Panzió**, Kossuth Lajos utca 14 (☎87/448-408). A pleasant new air-conditioned pension in the centre of Tihany, with a couple of cheaper "tourist rooms", plus access to the beach of the *Club Tihany* down by the ferry. Easter–Oct. ③–⑤.

**Park Hotel**, Fürdőtelepi utca 1 (☎87/448-611). On the east side of the peninsula, with lovely lawns sloping down to the water and private swimming. The hotel has two wings: the Castle, a grand mansion confiscated by the Communist Party as their summer house, and the Park, a cheaper, modern building next door. May to mid-Oct. ⑤–⑥.

## Eating and drinking
While **bars** and snack stalls cluster round the dock at Tihany-rév, **restaurants** are concentrated in the village, with some less expensive, less frequented wine cellars and restaurants in the streets around the inner lake (*Belső-tó*). Homestyle

Hungarian cuisine with frills is the rule in Tihany, and you'll be paying Budapest prices at any restaurant. The *Kecskeköröm Csárda*, Kossuth utca 19 (10am–11pm), has a good reputation, but it remains to be seen whether the new management can maintain it. The *Fogas Csárda* at no. 1 (daily 11am–11pm) specializes in fish, and the *Pál Csárda*, up at Visszhang utca 19, has a pretty, vine-shaded courtyard, while the dearer *Echo Restaurant* on Echo Hill (Mon–Sat 10am–10pm) offers a lovely view. For coffee, the *Cappuccino Kávéház*, opposite the far end of the Fisherman's Guild House, is a good bet, as is the *Rege Cukrászda*, which has fab views and delicious cakes.

# West towards Keszthely

Although **the shoreline** between Tihany and Keszthely is dominated by holiday homes and nondescript resorts, there are some sights en route at Örvényes, Balatonudvari and Badacsonyörs, while the local vineyards make a few visits to wine cellars a temptation. The biggest wine centre is on the slopes of the **Badacsony Hills**, whose picturesque village draws big crowds throughout the summer. For walkers, there is plenty to explore in the hinterland, from the volcanic shapes around Badacsony Hill to the beautiful Kál Basin further north. Buses run along the shore from Füred to Keszthely, while trains run to Badacsony, where you can change for Keszthely.

## Örvényes, Balatonudvari and Badacsonyörs

As you enter **ÖRVÉNYES**, 2km west of Tihany by Route 71, notice the still-working eighteenth-century **watermill** (*vizimalom*; May to Oct 14 daily 9am–4pm; 100Ft), one of the few that wasn't demolished in the 1950s to clear the way for state milling collectives. A collection of trade implements and diagrams showing how the mill worked makes it worth a quick stop. Nine kilometres further on, the roadside cemetery by the football pitch in **BALATONUDVARI** features **heart-shaped tombstones** (a popular motif in Austria and Germany during the eighteenth century), although how this cemetery took shape is not known.

Another 12km brings you to **RÉVFÜLÖP**, the jumping-off point for the Kál Basin. It is also the scene of the **swim across Balaton** that takes place on the last Saturday in July; in 1998, seven thousand made it to Balatonboglár. The Tourinform office at Villa Filip tér 8/b, just up from the main road, can give any information needed (June–Sept daily 9am–5pm; Oct–May Mon–Fri 8am–4pm; ☎87/463-092).

Shortly before **BADACSONYÖRS**, 9 km west, signposts point up the hill to the **Folly Aborétum** (April–Nov Tues–Sun 10am–5pm; 120Ft), a ten-minute steep walk uphill that rewards visitors with excellent views and a small park offering a peaceful contrast to Balaton. This private collection of cedars and pines from all over the world was started in 1905, and it takes about an hour to walk round. A few minutes further along Route 71 is *Balaton Camping* (☎87/471-253; ①; mid-May to mid-Sept). The road opposite leads to an excellent wine cellar at Mandulás utca 6, the *Hörpintő Borozó*, where you can taste (and buy) the wines of István Szabó and enjoy excellent homestyle food (mid-May to mid-Sept daily 5–11pm, mid-July to Aug 20 noon–11pm; ☎87/471-720).

# The Badacsony

A hulk of volcanic rock with four villages at its feet, backed by dead volcanoes ranged across the Tapolca basin, **the Badacsony** is one of Balaton's most striking features. When the land that was to become Hungary first surfaced, molten magma erupted from the seabed and cooled into a great semicircle of **basalt columns**, 210m high, which form Badacsony's southeastern face. The rich volcanic soil of the lower slopes has supported **vineyards** since the Age of Migrations, when the Avars buried grape seeds with their dead to ensure that the afterlife wouldn't be lacking in wine. Nowadays, the harvest consists of *Zöldszilváni*, *Szürkebarát* (Pinot Gris), *Olaszrizling*, and *Kéknyelő* (Blue Stem); the last variety is exclusive to the region. The **wine harvest festival** in the village of Badacsony during the second week in September is a time of street processions, folk dancing and music – and of course lots of wine to be drunk.

## Badacsony village and nearby walks

Although trains and buses also call at the other villages – Badacsonytomaj, Badacsonylábdihegy and Balatontördemic – it is **BADACSONY** proper that gets all the tourists, who arrive by ferry from Balatonboglár, Fonyód and Szigliget, and in high summer it's absolutely packed. Whatever your means of transport, you'll arrive in the midst of a mass of stalls selling folksy crafts, wine and fried fish. If you don't fancy embarking on the **wine trail** immediately, you can pay a visit to the **Egry Museum**, just over the level crossing on Egry sétány (May–Sept Tues–Sun 10am–6pm; 100Ft), exhibiting the paintings of József Egry, a local artist who died in 1951. Born into a poor family, Egry worked as a locksmith and roofer before winning a scholarship to the Academy of Fine Arts. His paintings capture the changing light and moods of Balaton.

From May till October you can take one of the **jeep-taxis** leaving from in front of the post office on Park utca, and for 400Ft you'll be transported 3km uphill through the vineyards to the charming **Róza Szegedy House** (*Szegedy Róza Ház*; May–Sept Tues–Sun 10am–6pm; Oct 10am–5pm; 100Ft). Róza Szegedy met her future husband, poet Sándor Kisfaludy, on the slopes of the Badacsony in 1795, and when they married five years later they used her Badacsony house as a summer home; its views proved to be an inspiration to his poetry. The museum contains mainly modern furniture, including an ornate card table, though the bed in Róza's room upstairs was her own. A wine bar now operates in the former winepress room.

From the museum you can follow a path up to the **Rose Rock** (*Rózsakő*), where it's said that if a man and woman sit upon it with their backs to Balaton and think about each other, they'll be married by the end of the year. The trail continues through the beechwoods to the **Kisfaludy lookout tower** (437m), about an hour's walk from the museum, and on another twenty minutes to the **Stone Gate** (*Kőkapu*), two massive basalt towers flanking a precipitous drop.

For **longer hikes** into the hills further north, offering an escape from the crowds, it's a good idea to buy a 1:80,000-scale map of the region from one of the tourist offices. A four-kilometre walk northwest from the Stone Gate will bring you to **Gulács-hegy**, a perfectly conical hill (393m) near the Nemesgulács halt for trains en route to Tapolca. The **Szent György-hegy** (415m), on the far side of the tracks, boasts some impressive basalt **organ pipes** and the region's finest vineyards, where *Szürkebarát* is produced. A few kilometres to the east, the 375-metre-high **Csobánc-hegy** is crowned by a **ruined castle**; this hike will probably take the best part of a day and leave you closer to Tapolca than Balaton. Don't be alarmed if you hear bangs in the fields around you: it's just the local way of scaring birds off the grape crop.

## Practicalities

Badacsony's **train station** is in the centre of the village, just by the **ferry** pier. Beyond Badacsony the line veers northwards up to Tapolca in the Bakony, so it's easier to continue along the shore **by bus**, changing at Balatonederics if necessary.

Maps and **information** are available from Tourinform, Badacsony tomaj Római út 55 (☎87/472-023); Balatontourist, in the Capitano shopping centre between the lakeside and the train line (July & Aug Mon–Sat 8.30am–6.30pm, Sun 8.30am–noon; May, June & Sept Mon–Fri 8.30am–4.30pm, Sat 8.30am–noon; ☎87/431-249); IBUSZ, at the same place (☎87/431-292); Miditourist at Park utca 6 and 53 (☎87/431-028); and Cooptourist at Egry sétány 1 (☎87/431-134), which all work the same hours.

### *ACCOMMODATION*

Given the popularity of the place, **accommodation** here is scarce, and you may find it easier to go to nearby Badacsonytomaj (see below), which has cheaper options. All four tourist offices rent private **rooms** (②) and there are plenty of households advertising *Zimmer frei*. Pensions range from the friendly and central but run-down *Hársfa Panzió* at Szegedy Róza út 1 (☎87/431-293; ①; May–Sept) to the flashier *Volán Panzió*, a neo-Baroque heap with a 1980s annexe, five minutes' walk further on at Római út 168 (☎87/431-013; ④; April–Nov). Rooms have TV and minibar, and there's a pool and fancy garden too. Badacsony's **campsite** is on the shore, fifteen minutes' walk west of the ferry pier (☎87/431-091; ①; mid-June to mid-Sept).

**BADACSONYTOMAJ**, 1km east on the road to Balatonfüred, offers a good alternative for accommodation, with cheaper rooms, a pleasant atmosphere, bus and train connections to Badacsony, and no crowds. Five minutes up from the station, near the church, the friendly *Egry József Fogadó* at Római út 1 offers simple accommodation with shared bathrooms (☎87/471-057; ①; April–Sept). A few minutes' walk further along Római út brings you to the *KSH Üdülője* (☎87/471-245; ②), the holiday home of the Central Statistical Office at nos. 42–44, which has rooms with and without bathrooms and is just five minutes from the lake. A few steps along the same road, opposite the Tourinform office, the classier *Borbarátok* ("Wine Friends") pension at no. 78 (☎87/471-597; ③) makes its own wine; rooms here have bathroom and TV.

### *EATING AND DRINKING*

There are various **restaurants** to choose from in Badacsony. The *Halászkert* at Park utca 5 is centrally located, but can be crowded and pricey. The crowds thin out as you climb the Badacsony and you are rewarded with the *Bormúzeum Pince* ("Wine Museum Cellar"), a restaurant housed in an eighteenth-century winepress house at Hegyalja út 6, near the Róza Szegedy House. Best of the lot is the *Kisfaludy Ház* by the museum, which offers excellent food, Hungarian gypsy music, and fabulous views of the lake. In Badacsonytomaj, the restaurant at the *Borbarátok* is the best option.

# Szigliget

After the crowded Badacsony, the **Szigliget peninsula** is a marked contrast. Both the main road and the train line go inland of the picturesque village of **SZIGLIGET**, giving it a pleasant secluded feel – indeed, locals are proud that there is no disco here. Though the peninsula has been built up with holiday homes, these are mainly privately owned, and accommodation is almost entirely in private houses. Earlier inhabitants of the region included a people known as the Lads, who occupied this area when the Magyars entered the region in the tenth century.

Access is by **bus** running between Tapolca and the train station at Balatontördemic (eight buses daily), serving all points around the peninsula. The centre of the village lies on the west of the peninsula at the top of Kossuth utca, with the castle ruins above. Here you'll find two tourist information offices: Naturtourist at no. 48 (May–Sept daily 10am–6pm; ☎87/461-399), and another one, *Famili Balaton* at no. 51 (Whit Sunday to Sept daily 9am–5pm; ☎87/461-207). Both these can help with **accommodation**, or you can try one of the many places advertising *Zimmer frei*.

The centre of the village is dominated by a former Esterházy mansion (closed to the public), now a holiday resort for the Writers' Union, and the ruins of **Szigliget Castle**, a twenty-minute signposted walk uphill. Originally commissioned in 1260 by Pannonhalma Monastery in the wake of the Mongol invasion, the present remains date from the sixteenth century. During the Turkish occupation, the Hungarian fleet moored at Szigliget under the protection of the castle, but in the seventeenth century lightning struck the castle and burnt it down. Just below the ruins is the *Vár Vendéglő*, a restaurant that caters mainly for big tourist groups but has well-appointed outdoor seating. The **Esterházy Wine Museum** at Kossuth utca 3 (☎87/461-044; June–Sept Mon, Wed Fri noon–10pm) offers tours round its beautifully decorated eighteenth-century cellars. Heading down Kossuth utca for 2km you come to the *strand*, which is slightly quieter than your average Balaton beach (May–Sept daily 9am–6pm; 150Ft); boats from Keszthely and Badacsony arrive at the port 500m further on. Just before the turning for Balatontördemic, another couple of kilometres on, are the remains of a twelfth-century church with a restored octagonal tower.

# Keszthely and around

A tradition of freethinking that dates back to the eighteenth century gives **KESZTHELY** a sense of superiority over other resorts, and its university ensures that life isn't wholly taken over by tourism. Perched at the far western tip of the lake, and the hub of several ferry, bus and train routes, the town gracefully absorbs thousands of visitors during peak season and yet manages not to look bleak and abandoned the rest of the year. With the Belváros and Festetics Palace to admire, and a thermal lake awaiting bathers at nearby Hévíz, Keszthely is one of the most appealing towns on Balaton.

## Arrival, information and accommodation

**Arriving** by ferry near the main *strand*, you can walk up Erzsébet királyné útja to the centre in roughly fifteen minutes. The **train and bus stations**, with services to Budapest, the Bakony and major towns in Transdanubia, are further south, at

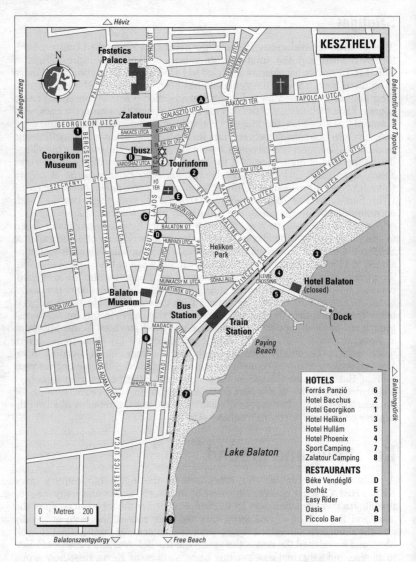

the bottom end of Mártírok útja, but most buses entering town drop passengers on downtown Fő tér, sparing them a 600-metre trudge along Kossuth utca.

Kezthely's main axis, Kossuth utca, runs from the bus and train stations through Fő tér, where the downtown begins and Kossuth utca turns pedestrian, continuing on up to the gates of the Festetics Palace. Of the six **tourist offices** in the pedestrian section of Kossuth utca, by far the best is Tourinform at no. 28 (May & June Mon–Fri 9am–5pm, Sat & Sun 9am–1pm; July & Aug Mon–Fri 9am–6pm, Sat &

Sun 9am–1pm; Sept–April Mon–Fri 8am–4pm; ☎83/314-144). The others include IBUSZ at no. 27 (May–Sept Mon–Sat 8am–6pm, July & Aug daily 8am–8pm; Oct–April Mon–Fri 8am–4pm; ☎83/314-321); and Zalatour at no. 1, near the palace, where staff speak German (May–Sept Mon–Sat 8am–9pm, Sun 8am–noon; Oct–April Mon–Fri 8am–5pm, Sat 8am–noon; ☎83/312-560). There's an **ATM** at the bank at Kossuth utca 38, and the main **post office** is further down at no. 44.

## Accommodation

Cheap accommodation is limited in Keszthely since, unusually for a university town, there is no dormitory accommodation for tourists (though it's worth checking with Tourinform whether this is still the case). **Private rooms** (②–③) are bookable through any of the tourist offices above; alternatively, searching the backstreets south of the station should turn up something, or you could always catch a bus #15 for nearby Hévíz (see p.193).

*HOTELS AND PENSIONS*

**Hotel Bacchus**, Erzsébet királyné utca 18 (☎83/314-096). New hotel close to Fő tér offering rooms with balcony, TV and bathroom. ⑤.

**Forras Panzió**, Római út 1 (☎83/314-617). Pension near the lake and a few blocks west of the station. ③.

**Hotel Georgikon**, Georgikon utca 20 (☎83/315-730). Rooms with bath in a renovated manor house. ④.

**Hotel Helikon**, Balaton-part 5 (☎83/315-944). Luxury high-rise eyesore with 232 rooms, sauna, pool and tennis courts – and a causeway leading to its own island in Balaton. ⑥.

**Hotel Hullám**, Balaton-part 1 (☎83/312-644). Palatial nineteenth-century mansion on the waterfront, with use of the *Helikon*'s facilities. May–Oct. ⑤.

**Hotel Phoenix**, Balaton-part 3 (☎83/312-631). A motel-style place just behind the presently defunct *Hotel Balaton*. April–Oct. ④.

*CAMPSITES AND HOSTELS*

**Castrum Camping**, Móra Ferenc utca 48 (☎83/312-120). 1km north of the station, this site, aimed at motorists, is not on the shore. April–Oct. ①.

**Sport Camping**, Csárda utca (☎83/312-842). A noisy and unappealing campsite with bungalows situated beside the tracks, behind the *Helikon Hotel*. Mid-May to Sept. ①.

**Zalatour Camping**, Balaton-part (☎83/312-782). Ten minutes' walk south of *Sport Camping*; a large and attractively located site with bungalows for four people and tennis courts. May–Sept. ①.

# The Town

Walking uphill along Mártírok útja from the train and bus stations, you'll pass the **Balaton Museum** at the junction with Kossuth utca (April–Sept Tues–Sun 10am–6pm; Oct–March Tues–Sat 9am–5pm; 150Ft), which covers the region's history and wildlife, with artefacts dating back to the first century AD, when road-building Romans disrupted the lifestyle of local Celtic tribes. Mock-up displays of fishing and thatching scenes are used to illustrate the life of the lakeside population. Ten minutes' walk up Kossuth utca and a right turn down Helikon utca brings you to the new **Wine Museum** (*Borház*; daily 10am–6pm; 100Ft entry, 300Ft for a wine-tasting session), featuring exhibits on the making of wine and a display on barrel-making in the courtyard. Heading on up Kossuth utca brings you to **Fő tér**, a strangely shaped square in the middle of which stands the **Trinity Statue**, erected in 1770. The much remodelled **Church of Our Lady of the Hungarians** was originally built in the fourteenth century, and still retains a Gothic rose window above its portal. From here on, Kossuth utca is pedestrianized and given over to cafés, buskers and strollers, with a **flea market** on Wednesday mornings.

Heading towards the Festetics Palace, you'll pass a plaque on the right at Kossuth utca 22 marking the **birthplace of Karl Goldmark**. Born in 1830, the son of a poor Jewish cantor who enrolled him in Sopron's school of music, Goldmark went on to study at the Vienna Conservatory. Almost shot as a rebel for giving concerts in Győr during the 1848 Revolution, he survived to compose *Merlin*, *Zrínyi* and *The Queen of Sheba*. In the courtyard behind is the newly restored **synagogue**, dating from 1852. If it's closed you can arrange to get keys from István Goldschmidt (☎83/312-458). The **Marzipan Museum and Pastry Shop** at Katona József utca 19 (daily 9am–6pm), just below the palace gates, is well worth a stop for anyone with a sweet tooth.

Keszthely has three **beaches**: a free *strand* at the end of Lóczy Lajos utca east of the centre and two more paying beaches: *Városi strand*, near the ferry dock, with its own quay, and the *Helikon strand* between the two campsites further south (both daily 8.30am–7pm; 150Ft and free after 5.30pm). You can rent **windsurfing** gear at both of the paying beaches.

### The Festetics Palace and Georgikon

The imposing neo-Baroque **Festetics Palace** assumed its present form in 1887, and with three hundred halls and rooms it is one of the largest, and most expensive to get into in Hungary (April–Sept Tues–Sun 10am–6pm, midsummer till 7pm; Oct–March Tues–Sun 9am–4.30pm; 700Ft). The Festetics family are chiefly remembered for Count György, founder of Keszthely's agricultural university, the Georgikon in 1797. During the early nineteenth century, the palace's salons attracted the leading lights of Magyar literature and became Hungary's first public forum for criticism. More recently, there was a national scandal in 1989 when it was discovered that a porn version of the life of spy Mata Hari had been filmed here while school parties were touring other parts of the palace.

The highlights of the palace are a gilt, mirrored **ballroom** and the **Helikon Library**, a masterpiece of joinery by János Kerbl, containing 52,000 books in diverse languages. Chinese vases and tiled stoves jostle for space with portraits of the family racehorses and dachshunds (whose pedigrees are proudly noted), and the pelts and heads of tigers, bears and other animals shot by Count Windishgrätz. Regular **concerts** are held here over summer; ask Tourinform for details.

The **Georgikon**, founded by Count György, was the first of its kind in Europe. Students attending the three-year course lived and worked together in a cluster of whitewashed buildings at Bercsényi utca 67, where dairy and viticulture equipment, cartwright's tools and old Ford tractors are now displayed (daily 9am–6pm; 60Ft). The Georgikon was the forerunner of today's **Agricultural University**, a green and daffodil-yellow pile halfway along Széchenyi utca.

# Eating, drinking and entertainment

The friendly *Oasis* restaurant, down Szalasztó utca from the palace at Rákóczi tér 3 (Mon–Fri 11am–6pm, Sat & Sun 11am–4pm), has an excellent salad and vegetarian self-service bar, while the *Béke Vendéglő* at Kossuth utca 50 has a pleasant atmosphere and good homestyle Hungarian food. From June until August, the *Borház* at Helikon utca 4 offers Hungarian food cooked in the traditional way on an open fire. The *Easy Rider* at Kossuth Lajos utca 79 across from the post office, and the *Kolibri* nearby are both popular bars with students, as is the cheap and friendly *Piccolo Bar* at Városház utca 9.

Keszthely hosts a wide variety of festivals and cultural events every summer, the highlight being the **Balaton Festival** at the end of May every year, which brings concerts and theatre to venues across town, including the lakeside, the Balaton Museum, and the pedestrian stretch of Kossuth utca; ask at Tourinform for details. In May of even-numbered years, the **Helikon Festival of Chamber and Orchestral Music**, a celebration featuring young musicians, takes place in the palace. In July and August there are frequent philharmonic concerts at the palace, organ recitals at the Lutheran church on Wednesdays or Fridays, and pop music and cinema showings at the open-air stage (*Szabadtéri színpad*) on Sörház utca. Another regular event is the five-day **Wine Festival**, starting on the first weekend of August, with folk music and dance performances. Stalls selling wine and offering tastings are set up on the avenue between the *Helikon* and *Hullám* hotels near the lake. The summer months are further enlivened by rock, folk and jazz concerts on Fő tér, and buskers and jugglers along Kossuth utca.

# Hévíz

**HÉVÍZ**, 8km east of Keszthely, boasts the second-largest **thermal lake** (*Gyógy-tó*) in the world after Lake Tarawera in New Zealand. The temperature rarely drops below 30°C even during winter, when steam billows from the lake and its thermal stream, and Indian waterlilies flourish on its surface. The lake is replenished by up to eighty million litres of warm water a day gushing up from springs 1km underground, and is completely flushed out every couple of days.

Exploited since medieval times for curative purposes as well as for tanning leather, the lake was salubriously channelled into a bathhouse by Count György Festetics in 1795. By the end of the nineteenth century, Hévíz had become a grand **resort**, briefly favoured by crown princes and magnates like those other great spas of the Habsburg empire, Karlsbad and the Baths of Hercules. They'd be hard-pressed to recognize it today, with high-rise hotels and tacky bars setting the tone.

Although the wooden terraces and catwalks surrounding the **baths** (*Tófürdő*; daily 8.30am–6pm; 400Ft) have a vaguely *fin-de-siècle* appearance, the general ambience is modern, with people sipping beer or reading newspapers while bobbing on the lake in rented inner tubes. Prolonged immersion isn't recommended on account of the slightly radioactive water, though mud from the lake is used to treat locomotive disorders. The busiest months are May and September, when the water is at its optimum temperature for bathing.

## Practicalities

With half-hourly buses from Fő tér in Keszthely, there's no need to linger in Hévíz, but, should you decide to stay, there's plenty of **accommodation**, except in May and September, when the town is at its fullest. Private rooms (②) can be booked through Hévíz Tourist at Rákóczi utca 2 (Mon–Fri 9am–5.30pm, Sat 9am–1.30pm; ☎83/341-348) and Zalatour at no. 8 (May–Sept Mon–Fri 8am–7pm, Sat 8am–6pm, Sun 9am–1pm; Oct–April Mon–Fri 8am–7pm, Sat 8am–1pm; ☎83/341-048). Otherwise, Kossuth and Zrínyi utcas are both teeming with

*Zimmer frei* signs. At the southern end of the lake, the four-star *Castrum Gyógycamping* rents plots for tents and trailers at high rates (☎83/343-198; ②).

Cheaper **hotels** include the *Amazon*, Széchenyi utca 23 (☎83/340-482; ③), a basic hotel near the centre of town, with rooms with showers; and the *Piroska Panzió*, Kossuth utca 10 (☎83/342-698; ③), a small pension close to the lake, with six rooms with shower and fridge. The *Park Hotel*, Petőfi utca 26 (☎83/341-193; ⑤) is the classiest place in town – an elegant thirty-room hotel near the lake with use of the *Thermál Hotel's* indoor and outdoor pools and sauna; while the *Hotel Thermál*, Kossuth utca 9–11 (☎83/341-180; ⑦) is one of the most expensive hotels in town, with the full range of facilities including indoor and outdoor pools, tennis courts, sauna and solarium.

Hévíz's nightlife is pretty sleazy, while its **restaurants** are very tourist-oriented. Some claim that the *Tavirózsa* and the *Magyar Csárda* on Tavirózsa utca, fifteen minutes' walk southwest of the centre, are the best of the pack, but it is a close thing. Another establishment with a good name is the *Rózsakert* on Rákóczi utca in the centre of town.

# The Bakony

**The Bakony** range cuts a swathe across central Transdanubia, as if scooped from the ground to provide space for the lake and piled as a natural embankment behind the lowlier Balaton highlands. Abundant vineyards testify to the richness of the volcanic soil, and mineheads to the mineral wealth beneath it. With dense woods and narrow ravines, the Bakony was the Hungarian equivalent of Sherwood Forest during the centuries of warfare and turmoil, and the setting for a dozen castles, the finest of which stand at **Sümeg** and **Nagyvázsony**. The regional capital, **Veszprém**, boasts a wealth of historic architecture and serves as a base for trips, while **Tapolca** is currently enjoying a revival, belying its old reputation as a dour mining centre. During autumn, pink crocuses spangle the meadows between Sümeg and Balaton, and huge sunflower fields abound nearer Sárvár, and, if you want to do some walking, the hills around **Zirc** and **Bakonybél** are ideal.

Access to the western end of the Bakony is from Tapolca, where **buses** and **trains** go to Sümeg. Buses also run from here via Nagyvázsony and Nemesvámos towards Veszprém, the main transport hub, from where buses serve all the Bakony villages and towns, as well as the major Route 8 to Herend.

## Tapolca

**TAPOLCA** is a charming small town that's also something of a transport hub, with regular **buses** and **trains** from Keszthely, including *nosztálgia* **steam trains** in July and August (Tues–Sun at around 4pm), and services to and from Balatonfüred and Veszprém. While the train station is 1.5km west of the town centre, served by regular buses, the bus station is on Deák Ferenc utca, a minute's walk from the main square, **Fő tér**. Here you are within a short walk of the main sights: the Cave Lake to the west and the Mill Lake and city museum to the south.

Tapolca was turned from a small village into the capital of Hungary's mining industry in the 1960s, swamping the Baroque centre with modern blocks on all sides. One of the biggest draws in town, the **Cave Lake** (*Tavasbarlang*; April, May, Sept & Oct Tues–Sun 10am–5pm; June–Aug 10am–6pm; 160Ft entry, 300Ft to rent a boat), where you can explore about 100m of the cave on foot, and paddle a boat round a further 300m. The cave was robbed of its water by mining until 1990, when the mine was closed and the water returned. The entrance to the lake is at Kisfaludy utca 3, a minute's walk from Fő tér along Kossuth Lajos utca and up to the left.

Just behind Fő tér to the south is the picturesque **Mill Lake** (*Malomtó*), fed by thermal springs. The old watermill is now the *Hotel Gabriella*, and the mill wheel still hangs precariously outside. In the group of buildings behind the hotel, signs point you to an old school housing the **School Museum** (*Iskola* or *Városi Múzeum*; June–Aug Tues–Sun 9am–4pm; Sept–May Tues–Fri 9am–4pm, 60Ft), where you can see old desks and school uniforms among other accessories from a hundred years ago; there's also a teacher's bedroom next door.

### Practicalities

Tourinform at Deák Ferenc utca 20, opposite the bus station, can help with **information** of all kinds (June–Aug Mon–Fri 9am–5pm, Sat 9am–noon; Sept–May Mon–Fri 9am–5pm; ☎87/323-415), while Balatontourist at Deák utca 7 (June–Aug Mon–Fri 8am–4pm, Sat 9am–11.30am; mid-July to Aug 20 Mon–Fri 8am–5pm; Sept–May Mon–Fri 8am–3.30pm; ☎87/323-179) also books accommodation. The main **post office** is at Deák utca 19, and there is an **ATM** at the OTP bank at Fő tér 2.

You can book **private rooms** through Balatontourist, and there is **accommodation** at two elegant establishments next to the main tourist sites: the *Szent György Panzió* at Kisfaludy utca 1 (☎87/413-809; ③), which has rooms with bathrooms, and the *Gabriella Hotel* at Batsányi tér 7 overlooking the Mill Lake (☎87/412-642; ③–④), which has rooms with showers and some with minibars. Both have **restaurants** too.

# Sümeg

**SÜMEG**, 14km north of Tapolca, has always been a big tourist attraction, with its dramatic-looking castle overshadowing the Belváros: it dates from the eighteenth century, when Sümeg was the seat of the bishops of Veszprém. Arriving by train, it's a ten-minute walk into town along Darnay Kálmán utca, whereas the bus station is on Flórián tér, at one end of the main street, Kossuth Lajos utca.

Baroque mansions line Deák utca, leading down from Kossuth Lajos utca to the **Church of the Ascension** (April–Oct daily 8am–noon & 1–4pm); if shut, ask for the key at the *plébánia*, across the road at Biró Marton utca 3. Outwardly unprepossessing, the church contains magnificent **frescoes** by Maulbertsch, who, with a team of assistants, managed to cover the whole interior within eighteen months, mostly in biblical scenes. Exceptions are the rear wall, which depicts his patron, Bishop Biró (1696–1762), and the wall facing the choir, which shows the churches Biró sponsored in Sümeg and Zalaegerszeg. In the former, the man kneeling before the bishop has Maulbertsch's features, as does the shepherd in the Adoration scene.

Retracing your steps to cross Kossuth utca you come to Kisfaludy tér. To the left is the city museum, the **Kisfaludy Museum** (April–Oct 10am–6pm; Nov–March Mon–Fri 8am–4pm; 145Ft), which houses archeological finds from the area and furniture and other objects belonging to Sándor Kisfaludy, the romantic poet of Balaton. Up from the square behind the trees, the crumbling, overgrown **Bishop's Palace**, commissioned by Bishop Biró in the mid-eighteenth century, is currently being renovated. On the right side of the square is the second-oldest building in town after the castle, the **Franciscan Church and monastery**, originally dating from the seventeenth century, though the present church owes more to alterations the following century. The church hosts special celebrations on September 13, when the miraculous statue of the Virgin draws crowds of believers. Heading up Vak Bottyán utca to the right of the church, a five-minute walk brings you round past the former **Bishop's Stables** (*Váristálló*), where horses are still kept today, and there is a funny old Hussar exhibition tucked away in what seems to be the stable office (no opening times or entrance fee; just ask). By now you are at the souvenir stalls that lead up from Route 84 to the entrance of the castle.

## Sümeg Castle

The most impressive sight in town is **Sümeg Castle** (May–Aug daily 9am–6pm; Sept–April daily 10am–4pm weather permitting; ☎87/352-737; 500Ft), one of the best-preserved fortifications in Hungary and worth visiting just for its tremendous views alone. It dominates Sümeg from a conical limestone massif, a unique Cretaceous outcropping among the basalt of the Bakony. Built during the thirteenth century as a defence against marauding Mongols, the castle was reinforced several times over the next few hundred years. It proved impregnable to the Turks, but eventually fell to the Habsburgs in 1713.

From June to August each year the so-called "Castle Captain", who is currently renting the castle, organizes evenings of folk dancing, gypsy music, jousting and the like, which cost 3000Ft including supper. In the daytime, medieval knights wander round inviting tourists to join in spear- and axe-throwing.

## Practicalities

Tourinform, at Kossuth utca 13 (May to mid-Oct Mon–Fri 9am–5pm, Sat 9am–1pm; July & Aug same hours, plus Sun 9am–1pm; mid-Oct to April Mon–Fri 7.30am–3.30pm; ☎87/352-481), is the place for **information**. Besides *Zimmer frei* signs all around town, **accommodation** possibilities include the new and comfortable *Hotel Kapitány* at Tóth Tivadar utca 19, round the far side of the Várhegy (☎87/352-598; ②), which has minibars and en-suite facilities in all the rooms and can supply information on balloon rides and other activities in the area. Closer to the centre, the *Király Fogadó* at Udvarbíró tér 5 (☎87/352-605; ②–③) is beautifully set behind the Bishop's Palace, but hard to find – walk down the side of the Kisfaludy Museum and head up to the right; or there is the more basic *Hotel Vár*, also signposted under its old name, *Hotel Tourist*, in a 1960s block behind the Franciscan Church at Vak Bottyán utca 2 (☎87/352-414; ②–③; closed Jan). The *Nelli Panzió* is a converted 1980s villa at Tapolcai utca 4 by Route 84, on the eastern edge of town (☎87/352-511; ②–③). Horse lovers might want to take the basic student accommodation at Vároldal utca 5, above the stables (*Váristálló*) by the entrance to the castle (☎87/352-367; ③). The *Kisfaludy Étterem* at Kossuth utca 13, and the **restaurants** in the *Hotel Kapitány* and the *Király Fogadó* are the best places to eat.

# Nagyvázsony, Nemesvámos and Balácapuszta

En route between Tapolca and Veszprém, there are two places redolent of the Bakony's history which are worth stopping off for – Nagyvázsony, which is also accessible by bus from Balatonfüred, and an old highwaymen's inn near Nemesvámos, only 6km outside Veszprém.

NAGYVÁZSONY, a sleepy market town 20km from Tapolca, harbours **Kinizsi Castle** (April–Oct daily 9am–dusk; 100Ft), given by King Mátyás to Pál Kinizsi, a local miller who made good as a commander. Formidably strong, he is said to have wielded a dead Turk as a bludgeon and danced a triumphal jig while holding three Turks, one of them between his teeth. During the sixteenth century, this was one of the border fortresses between Turkish and Habsburg-ruled Hungary. It is now a ruin, except for the pale stone keep housing an exhibition of weapons and fetters, and the chapel across the way containing Kinizsi's red marble sarcophagus.

The town livens up in the first weekend of August, when there are three or four days of **show-jumping and jousting** in the former Zichy mansion at Kossuth utca 12, north of the castle. The mansion is now the *Kastély Hotel* (☎80/364-109; ④), and during this period it is essential to reserve a place here, or above the mansion's stables in the cheaper *Lótel* – a play on the Hungarian word for horse, *ló* (same phone; ②). Closer to the castle, there is the *Vázsonykő Pension* at Sörház utca 2 (☎80/364-344; ②), where you can also get good Hungarian home cooking.

Approaching Veszprém, you can't miss the roadside *Vámosi Csárda* (or *Betyár Csárda*), an eighteenth-century **inn**, 600m before the village of **NEMESVÁMOS**. If you ignore the odd modern fixture and today's clientele, it's possible to imagine it as it once must have been: servants hurrying from the tap-room with its huge casks to the cellar, where swineherds, wayfarers and outlaws caroused, seated upon sections of tree trunk. Poor though most were, Bakony folk were proud of their masterless lives among the oak forests, esteeming the *kondás*, with his herd of pigs, and the highwaymen who robbed rich merchants. These highwaymen called themselves *szegénylegények* ("poor lads"), and the most audacious, Jóska Savanyú, claimed the tavern as his home.

Another 300m past the inn, a turning to the right leads to the **ruins of a Roman villa** in the middle of the countryside, 3km away at **BALÁCAPUSZTA** (May–Sept Tues–Sun 10am–6pm; 100Ft). Its reconstructed frescoes and mosaics convey an impression of the lifestyle of wealthy Roman colonists in the early centuries of the Christian era.

# Veszprém

VESZPRÉM spreads over five hills cobbled together by a maze of streets that twist up towards its old quarter on a precipitous crag overlooking the Bakony forest. Like Székesfehérvár, it became an episcopal see in the reign of Prince Géza, who was converted to Christianity in 975. It was here in 997 that King Stephen crushed a pagan rebellion with the help of knights sent by Henry of Bavaria, father of his queen, Gizella. During medieval times, Veszprém was the seat of the queen's household and the site of her coronation – hence its title the "Queen's Town". Utterly devastated during the sixteenth century and rebuilt after 1711, its Várhegy and downtown parks are now juxtaposed with apartment buildings, a technical university and chemical factories. Being only 15km from Lake Balaton, Veszprém is a good base for visiting the resorts without having to stay there, and for excursions to Nagyvázsony, Nemesvámos and Herend.

## Arrival and information

**Arriving** at the train station 2km out to the north, catch bus #1, #11, #14V or #20 to the tall tower block near downtown Szabadság tér (built by the Communists so that the view of the town would not be dominated by the castle and cathedral); the

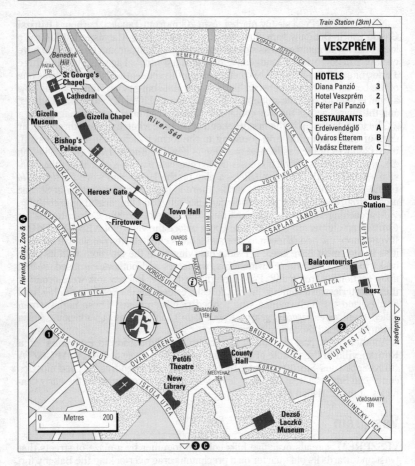

intercity **bus depot** (which has a left-luggage office) is more conveniently situated five minutes' walk northeast of the town centre. From Szabadság tér, you can head north towards Várhegy or strike out into the lower town. **Drivers** coming in from the west cross the 150-metre-long Valley Bridge over the River Séd, glimpsing the Várhegy en route to the centre.

**Information** is available from Tourinform at Rákóczi utca 3 (June–Aug Mon–Fri 9am–6pm, Sat 9am–1pm; Sept–May Mon–Fri 9am–5pm; ☎88/404-548), Balatontourist at Kossuth utca 21 (Mon–Fri 8am–4.30pm, Sat 9am–noon; ☎88/429-630), or from IBUSZ, opposite, at Kossuth utca 10 (Mon–Fri 9am–5.30pm; ☎88/427-604).

## Accommodation

Both Balatontourist and IBUSZ can book private **rooms** (②), and Balatontourist can find **beds** (①) in the *Tetőfedő Szakkollégium* at Tüzér utca 42 (July, Aug & all weekends; ☎88/423-022), accessible by bus #5 from the centre of town, or alternatively in the student hostel (same prices) at Egyetem utca 12, beyond Veszprém University, 1km south of the centre (bus #2Y, #4, #8 or #14Y). The Theological Academy (*Hittudomány Akadémia*) at Jutási út 11 is easier to reach, being twenty minutes' walk up the main road from the station (buses into town pass it) and has double rooms in July and August (☎88/426-116; ②).

**Diana Panzió**, József Attila utca 22 (☎88/421-061). Ten-room pension with a good restaurant in an attractive villa on the road towards Tapolca (bus #4 from the train station or the town centre). ③.

**Éllő György Apartment**, József Attila utca 25 (☎88/420-097). Smart villa 1km out from the centre on the Tapolca road. ④.

**Péter Pál Panzió**, Dózsa György utca 3 (☎88/324-097). Friendly pension with small rooms close to the centre and car-parking facilities. ③.

**Hotel Veszprém**, Budapest út 6 (☎88/424-677). Centrally located seventies low-rise with 76 rooms – those at the back overlooking Kossuth Lajos utca are considerably quieter. ④.

**Hotel Villa Medici**, Kittenberger Kálmán út 11 (☎88/321-273). A flashy new four-star hotel down by the entrance to the zoo. Price includes use of the sauna and pool. ⑤.

## Várhegy

The Castle district is presaged by **Óváros tér**, a triangular plaza overlooked by Art Nouveau buildings on one side and Baroque and Rococo edifices on the other, including the Baroque **Town Hall**, originally built as the home of the Kaposvári family. Most are painted in pinks, blues and the shade known as "Maria Theresa yellow" – the colour scheme the empress ordained for public buildings throughout the Habsburg empire. Behind nos. 7–8 rises the Baroque **Firetower** (*Tűztorony*; April 15 to Oct 15 daily 10am–6pm; 100Ft), which you can climb for a fine view of Veszprém's rooftops. Access is via the **Heroes' Gate**, a neo-Romanesque portal commemorating the dead of World War I, and into the courtyard at Vár utca 17. The tower's medieval base once formed part of the castle. A traditional recruiting tune is played every hour on the hour by a carillon in the dome.

Continue for five minutes along Vár utca, past well-preserved eighteenth-century buildings, and you'll come to a **Piarist Church and Monastery** (May–Oct daily 9am–5pm; 20Ft), now used for temporary exhibitions, whose facade bears three Greek letters encapsulating the Piarist credo "Mary, Mother, God". Soon after, the street broadens out into the main square, **Szentháromság tér** (Trinity Square), where classical music concerts are held during the summer. The square is dominated by the **Bishop's Palace**, a typically massive Baroque pile by Jakab Fellner, with the distinction of having had the first flush toilets in Hungary, installed in the late eighteenth century. During its construction, workmen unearthed a vaulted chamber believed to be part of Queen Gizella's palace, which stood on the site until the fourteenth century. Dubbed the **Gizella Chapel** (May–Oct daily 9am–5pm; 20Ft), it contains Byzantine-style frescoes of the apostles from the thirteenth century. Across the square, at no. 35, you can view the **Gizella Museum** (May–Oct daily 9am–5pm; 100Ft), an ecclesiastical collection of votive statues, chasubles and suchlike.

Behind the Trinity Statue in the centre of the square looms Veszprém **Cathedral**. Having been razed and resurrected half a dozen times since the eleventh century, its current neo-Romanesque incarnation, dating from 1907–10, has only a Gothic crypt to show for its origins. However, a glass dome behind the cathedral shelters the excavated remains of **St George's Chapel** (mid-April to mid-Oct Mon–Tues & Sun 10am–6pm; 30Ft; access from Vár utca), where Stephen's son Imre is said to have taken an oath of celibacy. His canonization, like that of Stephen and the latter-day King László, cemented the Árpáds' adherence to Catholicism and gave the Hungarians their own saints with whom to identify. Statues of Stephen and Gizella duly watch over the parapet at the far end of Vár utca, while a flight of steps round the far side of the cathedral leads down to **Benedek Hill**, the spur which commands a panoramic view of the Séd Valley and the Bakony forest.

## The lower town

Returning to Óváros tér, head on down past the Tourinform office on Rákóczi utca, and at the lights in Szabadság tér turn right onto Óvári Ferenc út to find the Art Nouveau **Petőfi Theatre**, built in 1908. The first large building in Hungary to be constructed from reinforced concrete, it boasts a circular stained-glass window entitled *The Magic of Folk Art*, whose symbolic figures represent the attachment of Hungarians to their land. Its designer, Sándor Nagy, was one of the Gödöllő Pre-Raphaelites; another of his designs, *The Hunting of the Magic Deer*, a depiction of a Magyar myth, decorates the rear of the building. Theatre tickets can be purchased at the Petőfi ticket office at Szabadság tér 7 (Mon–Fri 9am–5pm).

A five-minute walk past the Eclectic-style **County Hall** brings you to the **Dezső Laczkó Museum**, behind the trees at Erzsébet sétány 7 (Tues–Sun: April–Sept 10am–6pm; Oct–March 10am–2pm; 100Ft), which features an array of local history exhibits from all periods, including Roman mosaics unearthed in the villa at Balácapuszta, regional folk costumes, and material on the Bakony's highwaymen. Next door stands the **Bakony House** (same hours, and entry on the same ticket), a 1930s clone of a traditional homestead, filled with peasant artefacts.

Two more sights lurk on Kittenberger utca. About ten minutes' walk along Jókai utca, below the castle, is an antique **watermill** – one of many that once lined the banks of the Séd – followed by the **Kittenberger Zoo** (daily: May–Sept 9am–6pm; Oct–April 9am–3pm; 260Ft), named after the nineteenth-century zoologist Kálmán, where the lions and tigers have hardly enough room to pace their cages.

## Eating, drinking and entertainment

One of the best **restaurants** in town is the *Vadásztanya Étterem* in the *Diana Panzió*, serving game and meat. In the centre of town on Óváros tér is the elegant *Óváros Étterem*, which spills out onto the pavement in summer, while ten minutes south is a good pizzeria on Egyetem utca opposite the college dormitory. If you find yourself at the zoo, you can cheer yourself up with good food at least: by the main entrance is the expensive new restaurant in the *Villa Medici*. Next to the entrance on the far side of the zoo is the friendly and cheap *Erdei Vendéglő*, serving game and the usual Hungarian fare. In the evening the peacocks jump over the fence from the zoo to join you on the terrace for their supper. A good bar where the younger crowd go to eat and dance is *Unplugged* on the corner of Budapest út and Bajcsy-Zsilinszky utca.

One of the largest events in the Veszprém calendar is the **Gizella Days** (*Gizella Napok*), held every year in the second week of May in honour of István's wife. Concerts, exhibitions and dance events mark the occasion.

# On from Veszprém

Heading northwest **towards Szombathely** (see p.233), the famous porcelain factory at Herend is an easy stop-off, with the possibility of scenic detours for those with their own transport. The route more directly north **towards Győr** (see p.212) plunges through the heart of the Bakony, emerging onto the Little Plain to pass by Pannonhalma, with its famous monastery.

## West towards Szombathely

Twelve kilometres west of Veszprém, **HEREND**'s famous **porcelain factory** makes for an enjoyable day-trip or an interesting stopover en route to Szombathely. A pottery was founded in the village by Vince Stingl in 1826, and in 1851 Herend porcelain gained international renown when Queen Victoria ordered a chinoiserie dinner service at the Great Exhibition. Other famous buyers have included Tsar Alexander II, Kaiser Wilhelm I, the Shah of Iran and the British royal family. The factory's **museum** (April Mon–Sat 8.30am–4.30pm; May–Oct daily 8.30am–4.30pm; Nov–Dec 20 & March Mon–Fri 10am–3pm; 200Ft) displays hand-painted dinner services, vases and statuettes – many of which are rather over the top.

After Herend the scenery deteriorates around Ajka, but 6km beyond Devecser (where the rail line turns northwards towards Celldömölk), there's a great view of the Bakony from a lookout tower near **Sómlóvásárhely**. In clear weather Mount Kőris (see p.202) and even the Austrian Alps may be visible.

## North towards Pápa and Győr

Heading north towards Győr, the train tracks and Route 82 follow the River Cuha through the Bakony Hills up to Pannonhalma (see p.217) and Győr. The first stop en route is the small town of **ZIRC**, dominated by the yellow towers of the large **Cistercian Abbey** at its centre. From the train station it's a ten-minute walk into town, while the bus station is right beside the abbey and the Balatontourist office at Deák Ferenc utca 2 (Mon–Thurs 8.30am–4pm, Fri 8.30am–3.30pm, Sat 9am–noon; ☎84/414-163). The church, which has altar paintings by Maulbertsch, is currently undergoing restoration but still open, while the adjacent abbey houses a **natural history museum** on the first floor (daily 9am–5pm; 130Ft), and a **library** with Empire-style furnishings (Tues–Sun 10am–noon & 2–4pm; 100Ft), named after Antal Reguly (1819–58), the pioneer of Finno-Urgic linguistic research, who was born in Zirc. A short walk along Széchenyi utca and down to the left brings you to the **Arborétum** (May–Sept Tues–Sun 9am–5pm; March 15 to April & Oct same days 9am–4pm), which used to belong to the abbey. Its tall trees provide an oasis of coolness on a hot day.

Should you wish to stay, Balatontourist can help with private **accommodation**, and there are several pensions. The cheapest is the *Erdőalja Panzió* on Pintérhegyi Erdősor, a twenty-minute walk out along Deák Ferenc utca and up to the right on the edge of the town (☎30/378-889; ①–③). This former hunting lodge has small dark rooms with shared bathrooms on the corridor, and a bungalow that sleeps five. Alternatives near the centre are the *Jeskó Panzió* at Kossuth Lajos utca 28 (☎88/414-390; ②), which has quieter rooms at the back away from the road, and the *Király Fogadó* at no. 68, behind the petrol station (☎88/416-189; ③).

From Zirc you can head into the Bakony Hills in two directions. Route 82 continues northwards past the village of **CSESZNEK**, 11km away, where a **ruined castle** (daily until sunset; 100Ft) on a steep hill affords a fine view of the region. Founded in the thirteenth century, steady decay, followed by an earthquake in 1810, have reduced the castle to its present, paltry state, and with only a shell of the original castle remaining there is little to see once you climb up there except the view, though it looks very striking from a distance. Buses offer the best access, with ten a day from Zirc going right to the village. Trains stop some distance away at Porva-Csesznek, but the journey is a scenic one, winding between cliffs, over bridges and through tunnels, along a line built in 1896.

**BAKONYBÉL**, 17km to the west and served by six daily buses from Zirc, is situated at the foot of **Mount Kőris**, the highest peak in the Bakony at 713m. Several **hiking trails** emanate from the village. There is a variety of **accommodation**, including the *Tamás Panzió* at Jókai út 62 (☎88/461-121; ②), which is not very friendly but has excellent views; the *Aliz Panzió* at Pápai út 108, at the far end of the village (☎88/461-046; ②), overlooking the forest; and the *Gerence Fogadó* at Fürdő út 42, a few minutes' from the village (☎88/461-042; ①), an old hiking hostel with basic facilities.

# Pápa

Thirty kilometres beyond Bakonybél, between the Bakony Hills and the Little Plain, the small town of **PÁPA** grew up in the Middle Ages as a milling village, with 26 mills along the Tapolca stream. It missed out on the nineteenth-century industrialization drive, thus preserving its elegant Baroque centre, though during the Communist era the Tapolca suffered the same fate as many other streams and springs in the region, being destroyed by pollution and mining. Today, the town is best known for its Calvinist school, one of the few religious schools to remain in church hands during Communist times, whose illustrious alumni include the national poet Sándor Petőfi and the novelist Mór Jókai.

**Arriving** by bus, you'll be dropped five minutes' walk east of the centre, while the train station is half an hour's walk from the centre, to the north. All the sights in town are concentrated on Fő utca and Kossuth utca, leading off Fő tér, where Tourinform and Balatontourist share an office at no. 12 (Mon–Fri 8.30am–4pm, Sat 8.30–11am; ☎89/324-282).

Dominating the main square is the Catholic **Church of St Stephen**, built by Jakab Fellner and József Grossman in 1774–86, with frescoes by the Austrian painter Maulbertsch from the life of the saint (not the Hungarian king but the original martyr). The church was commissioned by Bishop Károly Esterházy, who had the same team build the U-shaped mansion behind the church on the ruins of the old castle. The finest Baroque parts of the **Esterházy Mansion** are closed "for an unforeseen period", as the notice says. Now the building, which desperately needs renovation, hosts a small gallery and occasionally rocks to the sound of the local pop bands rehearsing.

Walking down Fő utca, the street leading south from the main square, there are delightful Baroque buildings on either side – few butchers can boast such a nice ceiling and chandelier as the one at no. 2. At no. 6, the **Calvinist History and Art Museum** (*Református Egyházművészeti Múzeum*; May–Oct Tues–Sun 9am–5pm; 80Ft), housed in the former chapel, has temporary exhibitions downstairs and a few pieces of peasant-style painted church furniture from the eighteenth and nineteenth centuries upstairs. When the chapel was built in 1783, Catholic restrictions required that it should not face onto the street, and should have no tower. Later the congregation was allowed to build a larger church just down the road on Március 15 tér.

Across the road from the church, at no. 12, is the delightful **Blue Dyers' Museum** (*Kékfestő Múzeum*; Tues–Sun: May–Sept 9am–5pm; Oct–April 9am–4pm; 150Ft). Blue dyeing was a method of dyeing cotton that was popular among the German communities of western Hungary, went into a decline after the postwar deportation of Germans and was an endangered craft by the 1960s (when the museum opened), but is now back in fashion with Hungarians. The museum fronts a workshop that was run by the Kluge family from 1783 until 1957, where the original vats and drying attic can still be inspected and demonstrations are held, and you can also buy blue-dyed items.

Alternatively, you can walk through the archway on Fő tér and down the pedestrianized **Kossuth utca**, full of turn-of-the-century shops and buildings. By turning left down Petőfi Sándor utca, you can find the house, no. 11, where Petőfi lived while attending school in Pápa, which is right next to the school itself. Further down on the left is an empty **synagogue**, a beautiful relic of a community that barely survived the Holocaust. The family living at Eötvös utca 24 holds the key.

Though Pápa has a limited range of **accommodation**, you shouldn't have trouble finding a room even in high summer. Balatontourist can book private rooms in town, while the *Griff Hotel*, in the Baroque row on Fő tér (☎89/312-000; ④–⑤), is the most central, and has one apartment with a box window overlooking the square. The *Főnix* on Jókai utca 4, just past the Blue Dyers' Museum (☎89/324-361; ②), has an incredibly tasteless bar ceiling, but is conveniently located. The *Griff* has a café spilling onto the pavement at the front, and a restaurant at the back which serves Hungarian specialities, as does the *Vadásztanya*, at Rákóczi út 21, leading off Kossuth utca.

## travel details

**Trains**

**Budapest (Déli Station)** to: Balatonfüred (every 1–2hr; 2hr–2hr 30min); Siófok (8 daily; 1hr 30min); Székesfehérvár (every 1hr–1hr 30min; 1hr); Veszprém (5 daily; 2hr 15min–3hr).

**Balatonfenyves** to: Csisztapuszta (Tues–Sun every 1hr–1hr 30min; 45min–1hr 30min).

**Balatonfüred** to: Budapest (every 1–2hr; 2hr–2hr 30min).

**Balatonszentgyörgy** to: Nagykanizsa (every 1–2hr; 45min).

**Székesfehérvár** to: Balatonfüred (hourly; 30min–1hr); Budapest (every 1hr–1hr 30min; 1hr); Komárom (every 1hr–1hr 30min; 1hr 15min–1hr 45min); Siófok (hourly; 30min); Szombathely (7 daily; 2hr 30min–3hr 45min); Veszprém (hourly; 45min–1hr).

**Tapolca** to: Celldömölk (every 1hr–1hr 30min; 1hr 15min); Sümeg (every 1hr–1hr 30min; 1hr 30min); Szombathely (4 daily; 1hr 30min).

**Veszprém** to: Budapest (4 daily; 1hr 45min–2hr 15min); Győr (4 daily; 2hr 30min); Szombathely (4 daily; 1hr 15min).

**Buses**

**Budapest (Erzsébet tér)** to: Balatonfüred (2 daily; 2hr 15min); Herend (2 daily; 2hr 45min);

Hévíz (2 daily; 4hr); Keszthely (2 daily; 3hr 45min); Nagyvázsony (2 daily except Sun; 3hr); Siófok (3 daily; 1hr 45min–2hr 15min); Sümeg (2 daily; 4hr 30min); Székesfehérvár (every 40–60min; 1hr 15min); Veszprém (every 1hr–1hr 30min; 2hr 15min); Zirc (4 daily; 2hr 30min).

**Badacsony** to: Keszthely (hourly; 1hr); Székesfehérvár (2 daily; 2hr 15min).

**Bakonybél** to: Budapest (3 daily; 3hr 15min).

**Balatonfüred** to: Győr (every 30–1hr 30min; 2hr); Nagyvázsony (every 1hr 30min; 45min); Sopron (1 daily; 4hr); Tapolca (1 daily except Sun; 1hr 30min); Tihany (hourly; 30min); Veszprém (every 30min–1hr 30min; 30min).

**Hévíz** to: Keszthely (every 30min; 15min); Pécs (2 daily; 4hr 15min); Zalaegerszeg (1 daily; 2hr).

**Keszthely** to: Hévíz (every 30min; 15min); Pécs (2 daily; 3hr 45min); Sümeg (1 daily; 1hr); Szombathely (hourly; 2hr 30min); Zalaegerszeg (1 daily; 1hr).

**Siófok** to: Győr (1 daily; 3hr); Mohács (1 daily; 3hr); Pécs (1 daily; 3hr); Szekszárd (1 daily; 1hr 45min); Veszprém (1 daily; 1hr).

**Sümeg** to: Győr (3 daily; 2hr 15min); Keszthely (1 daily; 45min); Sárvár (2 daily; 1hr 15min); Sopron (2 daily; 2hr 15min).

**Székesfehérvár** to: Badacsony (1 daily; 2hr 30min); Budapest (every 40–60min; 1hr); Kalocsa

(1 weekly; 3hr); Pécs (1 daily; 4hr); Szekszárd (2 daily; 2hr); Veszprém (every 40–90min; 1hr); Zalaegerszeg (2 daily; 4hr 15min).

**Tapolca** to: Balatonfüred (1 daily except Sun; 1hr 30min); Nagyvázsony (8 daily; 45min); Sümeg (hourly; 30min); Veszprém (every 2hr; 1hr).

**Veszprém** to: Budapest (every 1hr–1hr 30min; 2hr 15min); Győr (4 daily; 2hr); Harkány (1 daily; 4hr); Herend (hourly; 30min); Nagyvázsony (7 daily; 25min); Nemesvámos (hourly; 25min) Siófok (1 daily; 1hr 30min); Székesfehérvár (every 60–90min; 1hr); Szekszárd (2 daily; 3hr 45min); Tapolca (7 daily; 1hr).

**Zirc** to: Budapest (3 daily; 2hr 30min).

## International trains

**Balatonszentgyörgy** to: Zagreb (1 daily; 4hr).

**Fonyód** to: Zagreb (June–Sept 2 daily; 2hr).

**Siófok** to: Vienna (1 daily; 5hr); Zagreb (1–3 daily; 2hr 30min).

**Székesfehérvár** to: Vienna (1 daily; 5hr 45min); Zagreb (1–3 daily; 6hr).

## International buses

**Balatonboglár** to: Vienna (July–Aug 1 weekly; 5hr 15min).

**Balatonföldvár** to: Banská Bystrica (July–Oct 1 weekly; 5hr 30min).

**Balatonszeped** to: Vienna (July–Aug 1 weekly; 5hr 15min).

**Hévíz** to: Vienna (July–Aug 1 daily; 6hr 30min).

**Keszthely** to: Graz (June–Sept 1–2 daily; Oct–May 2 weekly; 4hr 30min).

**Siófok** to: Bratislava (July–Aug 1 daily; 5hr 15min); Brno (July–Aug 1 daily; 7hr); Galanta (July–Aug 1 daily; 4hr 15min); Semmering (July–Aug 1 daily; 6hr); Trnava (July–Aug 1 weekly; 5hr 30min); Vienna (July–Aug 1 weekly; 5hr).

**Veszprém** to: Nitra (1 daily; 4hr 30min); Vienna (3 weekly; 4hr 30min).

**Zalakros** to: Vienna (1 daily; 4hr 45min).

## Ferries

**Badacsony** to: Balatonboglár (July–Aug 5 daily; 1hr); Balatonföldvár (July–Aug 1 daily; 2hr 45min); Fonyód (mid-April to mid-Oct 11 daily; 45min); Siófok (June–Aug 1 daily; 4hr 30min); Tihany (June–Aug 1 daily; 3hr).

**Balatonboglár** to: Badacsony (July–Aug 11 daily; 30min); Révfülöp (July–Aug 7 daily; 30min).

**Balatonföldvár** to: Balatonfüred (4 daily; 1hr); Keszthely (July–Aug 1 daily; 5hr); Siófok (4 daily; 2hr); Tihany (4 daily; 30min).

**Balatonfüred** to: Balatonföldvár (4 daily; 1hr); Siófok (8 daily; 1hr); Tihany (6 daily; 30min).

**Fonyód** to: Badacsony (mid-April to mid-Oct 10 daily; 30min).

**Keszthely** to: Badacsony (July–Aug 5 daily; 45min); Balatonföldvár (1 daily; 5hr).

**Révfülöp** to: Balatonboglár (July–Aug 7 daily; 30min).

**Siófok** to: Badacsony (July–Aug 1 daily; 4hr 30min); Balatonföldvár (4 daily; 2hr); Balatonfüred (7 daily; 1hr); Tihany (6 daily; 1hr 15min).

**Szántódrév** to: Tihany-rév (early March–Nov every 40–60min; 10min).

**Tihany** to: Badacsony (July–Aug 1 daily; 2hr 30min); Balatonföldvár (4 daily; 30min); Balatonfüred (4 daily; 30min); Siófok (4 daily; 1hr 15min).

**Tihany-rév** to: Szántódrév (early March–Nov every 40–60min; 10min).

# CHAPTER FOUR

# TRANSDANUBIA

**T**ransdanubia – the *Dunántúl* – is a region of considerable charm and variety, boasting, in the north, lakeside Tata, Győr's antique waterfront, and Sopron's cobbled streets, while in the south of the region are the rolling **Mecsek Hills** and the vineyards of **Villány** and **Szekszárd**. More than any other region in Hungary, Transdanubia is a patchwork land, an ethnic and social hybrid. Enclosed to the north and the east by the River Danube, its valleys, hills, forests and mud flats have been a melting pot since Roman times, when the region was known as Pannonia. Settled since then by Magyars, Serbs, Croats, Germans and Slovaks, it has been torn asunder and occupied by the Turks and the Habsburgs, and only within the last 150 years has it emerged from a state of near-feudalism.

Though **Szombathely** has the most to show for its Roman origins, with its Temple of Isis and other ruins, every main town has at its core a fortified castle – stark testimony to centuries of warfare. Constant upheavals decimated medieval culture, leaving only the **Pannonhalma Monastery** and a few superb churches such as those at **Ják** and **Velemér**. Around each weathered *vár* (castle) stands a Belváros, with rambling streets and squares overlooked by florid Baroque and the odd Gothic or Renaissance building. **Tata**, **Kőszeg** and **Győr** provide fine examples of the genre; so too does **Sopron**, the most archaic, and **Pécs**, which boasts a Turkish mosque and minaret.

While several towns host spring or summer **festivals** of classical music, drama, folk music and dancing, the most interesting event is the masked Busójárás Carnival at **Mohács**, seven weeks before Easter. During summer, concerts are also held in two unique settings – the **Esterházy Palace** at **Fertőd** and the rock chambers of **Fertőrákos** – both close to Sopron and **Nagycenk**, where you can ride antique steam trains on the **Széchenyi Railway**. At the monthly **market** in Pécs, you'll sense the peasant roots underlying many Transdanubian towns, whose sprawling *lakótelep* (apartment buildings) house recent immigrants from the countryside.

### ACCOMMODATION PRICE CODES

All accommodation in this guide is graded according to the price bands given below. Note that prices refer to the **cheapest available double room in high season** or the price of **two people sharing a tent** in a campsite. 100Ft is roughly equivalent to $0.45 or DM1. For more details, see p.24.

| | | |
|---|---|---|
| ① Under 2000Ft | ④ 6000–8500Ft | ⑦ 20,000–27,000Ft |
| ② 2000–4000Ft | ⑤ 8500–13,000Ft | ⑧ 27,000–40,000Ft |
| ③ 4000–6000Ft | ⑥ 13,000–20,000Ft | ⑨ over 40,000Ft |

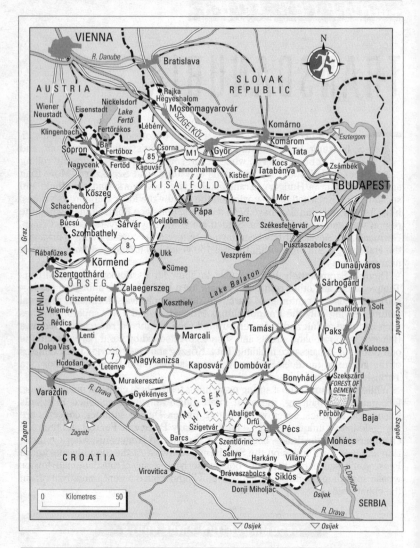

# NORTHERN TRANSDANUBIA

Most of **Northern Transdanubia** consists of the **Kisalföld** (Little Plain), a fertile but dreary landscape that focuses your attention on the region's towns. **Tata** is delightful, with a medieval castle cocooned amid Baroque and Neoclassical buildings. There's another castle, on a grander scale, in the Belváros of **Győr**. This city is equally proud of its ballet company and football team, and is also a base for excursions to **Pannonhalma**, Hungary's most impressive monastery, and the wetlands of the **Szigetköz** with abundant birdlife.

The main transport routes interconnect at **Komárom**, the chief border crossing between Hungary and Slovakia, and **Mosonmagyaróvár**, the last town before Vienna and Bratislava. All the towns en route are served by frequent trains from Budapest's Déli or Keleti stations, and can also be reached by bus from the Erzsébet tér depot. The toll-paying stretch of motorway between Győr and Austria is reputedly the most expensive in Europe, and blissfully empty.

# Zsámbék and Tatabánya

West of Budapest, the wooded **Vértes Hills** form a prelude to the Kisalföld and harbour two places worth a mention. **ZSÁMBÉK** is the site of a **ruined Romanesque church** from the thirteenth century, whose arches and walls are as romantic as a Piranesi drawing. Built for the Premonstratensians by the Ainard family, who were of French descent and came over during the Angevin monarchy, the church later passed to the Pauline order, and was destroyed by an earthquake in 1763. Zsámbék can be reached by bus from Széna tér (near Moszkva tér) in Budapest – bring a picnic and make an afternoon of it. To get an idea of what the church once looked like, check out the replica on Lehel tér in Budapest constructed during the 1930s.

You can't miss **TATABÁNYA**, an ugly mining town on the Budapest–Vienna route, surrounded by ravaged countryside. Its only sight, the giant bronze **Turul Statue**, perched on a mountain top overlooking the grimy sprawl, can be glimpsed from a train carriage window. Erected in 1896 to commemorate the thousandth anniversary of the Magyar conquest, it shows the legendary bird of prey clutching the sword of Árpád in its talons. The Turul's wingspan measures 14m and the sword is 12.5m long.

The only reasons for a closer encounter with Tatabánya are its summer **Jazz Festival** and the chance to go **walking** in the Vértes Hills, where the **ruined Vitány Castle** broods on a crag 5km south of town; catch a bus to Vértessomló and walk up. Legend has it that the cowslips that grow around here during April are able to guide you towards hidden treasure.

Tatabánya's bus and train stations are ten minutes from Fő tér, the main square, where the *Árpád Hotel* (☎34/310-299; ④), IBUSZ (Mon–Fri 8am–4pm; ☎34/310-897), and Komturist (Mon–Fri 9am–4pm; ☎34/311-936) are located. Private rooms (②) or *Nomád Camping* at Tolnai út 14 (☎34/311-507; ①; May–Sept) provide a cheaper alternative to the hotel.

# Tata

In total contrast to Tatabánya, modern **TATA**, 13km away, is a small lakeside town interlaced with canals and streams, at its most charming on misty mornings, when its castle, mills and riding school appear as wraiths from olden days on the shores of the central lake. There's enough to see in a leisurely day, plus horse-riding, fishing and swimming for the more actively inclined.

Historically, Tata had the misfortune to be right on the war-torn border between Turkish and Habsburg Hungary for 150 years. It was almost wholly

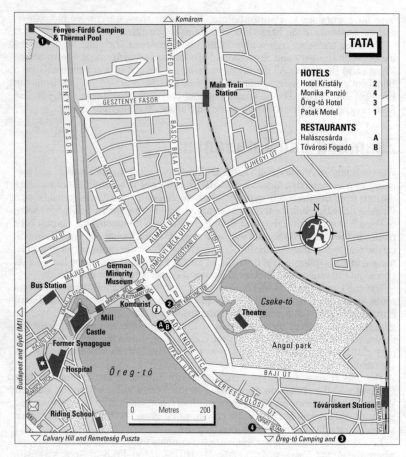

rebuilt in the eighteenth century under the direction of the Moravian-born architect Jakab Fellner, resulting in an extremely harmonious Baroque town centre up on the hill, which has been left untouched by later developments in the Tóváros (Lake Town) to the east, where most of the tourist facilities are located.

## The Town

While Tópart utca, running beside the **Old Lake** (*Öreg-tó*), offers a more scenic approach to the castle, the most direct route is along Alkotmány utca, past the **German Minority Museum** at no. 1 (April–Oct Tues–Sun 10am–6pm; Nov–March Wed–Fri 10am–2pm, Sat & Sun 10am–4pm; 100Ft). Swabians, Bavarians and other German settlers have long inhabited Transdanubia, and Tata (like Székesfehérvár and Pécs) was almost entirely German-speaking for many centuries. In keeping with their ethic, the folk costumes are less flamboyant than Magyar attire. The museum is housed in the former Nepomucenus Mill, built in

1758, straddling a weir. The **Cifra Mill**, dating back to the sixteenth century, stands 50m further east, at Bartók Béla utca 3.

Just beyond lies Tata's moated **castle** (April–Oct Tues–Sun 10am–6pm; Nov–March Wed–Fri 10am–2pm, Sat & Sun 10am–4pm; 150Ft). Once the hunting lodge of King Sigismund, it was badly damaged by both the Turks and the Habsburgs, and only one of the original corner towers remains. Its residential "keep" was reconstructed in 1897 for a visit by Franz Josef II, and now contains a museum of Roman miniatures and faïence by the eighteenth-century local craftsman Domokos Kuny. In the grounds by the road is an old chapel used for art exhibitions (same hours; 30Ft).

From here you can wander up Rákóczi utca towards the Baroque old town laid out by Fellner, which begins at Hősök tere. On the right, Tata's former synagogue is now the **Roman-Greek Statue Museum** (April–Oct Tues–Sun 10am–6pm; 80Ft), containing life-sized plaster casts of the Elgin Marbles, Hercules and Laocoön. Across the square stands an impressive, decrepit pile that was formerly an **Esterházy mansion**, where the Habsburg King Francis took refuge from Napoleon in 1809 and later signed the Schönbrunn peace treaty. It has been a mental **hospital** since World War II.

The climax to Fellner's endeavours occurs further along on Kossuth tér, where his statue stands in front of the twin-spired **Great Church** designed by himself and József Grossman, which wasn't completed until seven years after Fellner's death in 1780. A crag behind the church is named **Calvary Hill** and has a crucifixion monument, to which a more secular age has added an outdoor **Geological Museum** (April–Oct Tues–Fri 10am–4pm, Sat & Sun 10am–6pm; 80Ft), a **nature reserve** and a **lookout tower** offering fine views of the town (May–Oct daily 9am–5pm; 50Ft).

East of busy Ady Endre utca, which is also the main road up to Komárom, peace returns as you turn off by the *Hotel Kristály* into Erzsébet királyné tér, leading to the 200-hectare **Angol Park** (English Park) surrounding the **Small Lake** (*Cseke-tó*). Laid out in 1780 in the naturalistic English style, the park contains an outdoor **theatre** and **swimming pool**, and a fake ruined church cobbled together from Roman and Benedictine stonework. Hungary's Olympic team has its main training facility along the southern edge of the park.

On the western shore of the Old Lake is a grandiose **Riding School** (*Lovasiskola*), modelled on the Spanish Riding School in Vienna, which has been going for over a century. It offers lessons, point-to-point races through the woods, extended riding tours and, in the autumn, hunting. Komturist or the *Hotel Kristály* (see overleaf) can supply details, and also tell you about **angling** in the lakes out towards the **thermal pool** on the edge of town, reached by bus #3. Rowing **boats** (*csónak*) and pedal boats (*vízibicikli*) can be rented beside the Old Lake.

## Remeteségpuszta and Kocs

**Remeteségpuszta**, south of town, is a former **game park** with a hotel catering to wealthy hunters, and is a nice place to visit; take bus #4 to the end of the line. You can stay at the *Diana Vadász ház* (☎34/381-335; ①), which also arranges riding. Lastly, it would be churlish not to mention **Kocs**, 11km southwest of Tata, where the **coach** (far lighter and more comfortable than the wagons used up to then) was invented in the seventeenth century – not that the village has anything much to show for it.

## Practicalities

**Arriving** by train, you'll be deposited at the main (Vasútállomás) station, 1km north of the Tóváros (bus #1), or at the Tóvároskert Station, 600m east (bus #5). The intercity bus station is only a few blocks north of the castle. Motorists coming off the M7 drive through the old town round to the top of Ady utca.

**Information** is available from Tourinform at Ady utca 9 (June–Aug Mon–Fri 8am–5pm, Sat 8am–noon; Sept–May Mon–Fri 8am–4pm; ☎34/384-806) and Komturist at no. 3, in the Fenyves store (May–Sept Mon–Fri 9am–5pm, June & Aug also Sat 9am–noon; Oct–April Mon–Fri 8am–4pm; ☎34/480-380). The **post office** is on Kossuth tér in the old town, and there's an **ATM** opposite Tourinform.

### Accommodation

You can book **private rooms** (①) through Komturist or aim for one of Tata's agreeable **campsites**: *Fényes-Fürdő*, by the thermal baths, where bus #3 terminates (☎34/381-591; ①; May to Sept); or *Öreg-tó* on Fáklya utca, between the Old Lake and the highway (☎34/383-496; ①; May to Sept), which has bungalows (②–③) and tennis courts. To get there from Tóvároskert Station, follow Székely Bertalan utca to the end, then Öveges József utca.

**Hotel Kristály**, Ady utca 22 (☎34/383-577). Noisy location on the main road, but its 200-year-old dining room is appealing. Doubles and singles with showers or baths. ④.

**Hotel Gottwald**, Fekete út 1 (☎34/381-760). Grand new hotel on the southwest shore of the lake. ④.

**Monika Panzió**, Öregtó-part (☎34/383-208). Large rooms by the lake near *Öreg-tó* campsite, fifteen minutes' walk south of Tourinform. ③.

**Patak Motel**, Fényes fasor, near the thermal baths to the north of the centre (☎34/382-853). The latest name for a clutch of bungalows with tennis courts and a sauna; bus #3 goes there. ②.

**Öreg-Tó Hotel/Youth Hostel**, Fáklya utca 4 (☎34/487-960). A complex offering single and double rooms (②), dormitory rooms (①) and two-person bungalows (①), beyond the *Monika Panzió*.

### Eating, drinking and festivities

Besides the classy **restaurants** in the *Kristály* and *Gottwald* hotels (the latter's is especially recommended), there are two agreeable places by the lake – the *Halászcsárda*, serving freshly caught fish, and the *Tóvárosi Fogadó* next door. There's also the *Öreg-tó Étterem* at Ady utca 33. For ice cream, check out the *Gelato* stand at the *Hotel Kristály*.

On the last weekend in June, Tata holds a **Water-Music-Flower Festival**, featuring concerts and dancing, a flower show, and a craft fair in the castle grounds.

# Komárom

**KOMÁROM**, 18km northwest of Tata, is the main crossing between Hungary and Slovakia, linked by a 500-metre-long road and rail bridge to Komárno, across the Danube. The two towns formed a single municipality until 1920 and ethnic Magyars still predominate on the Slovak side, where streets and shops are signposted in both languages. Though neither town has much to offer in the way of sights, the easy crossing and good **connections** between Komárno and Bratislava make this a useful stepping stone en route to the Slovak capital.

The confluence of the Danube and the Váh has been a fortified crossing-point since Roman times, reaching its apotheosis in the nineteenth century with three Habsburg fortresses that are quite irrelevant today. The largest and most accessible is the **Monostori Fortress** near the train station, which covers over a hundred square kilometres and contains 4km of underground passages. Guided **tours** in Hungarian are in theory for groups only (☎34/344-152; 150Ft), but you may be able to join a party or even persuade the guide to show you around (dress warmly and bring a torch). If not, there is a **museum** (Tues–Sun 9am–4pm; 50Ft) relating the history of the fort, which was occupied by Soviet troops from World War II until the early 1990s.

The **Igmándi Fortress**, 2km down Igmándi utca from the centre, contains nothing more than a display of stonework from a Roman site outside town (May–Sept Tues–Sat 1–5pm, Sun 10am–3pm; 80Ft), while the star-shaped **Csillag Fortress**, east of the centre, serves as a storage depot and isn't open at all. You'll get more joy out of the **thermal bathing complex** on Táncsics utca, ten minutes' walk from the station, which is open all year (May–Sept daily 9am–7pm; Oct–April Tues & Thurs 9am–8pm, Wed & Fri–Sun 9am–6pm; 200Ft).

Komturist at Mártírok útja 19 (Mon–Fri 8am–noon & 12.30–3.30pm; ☎34/341-767), on the main road running parallel to the river, can book **accommodation** in private rooms (①), hotels and pensions, and owns the comfy modern *Thermal Hotel* at Táncsics utca 38, near the baths (☎34/342-447; ③), and the *Hotel Juno* at Bem utca 21 (☎34/340-568; ④). There are campsites attached to both hotels, and a third site, *Solaris*, at Táncsics utca 34–36 (☎34/342-551; ①), which is open all year and has apartments with shared showers (②). Rates at all these places include admission to the baths, unlike at the seedy *Béke Hotel*, Bajcsy-Zsilinszky utca 8 (☎34/340-333; ③). The best **restaurants** are in the *Juno* and the *Bogáncs Étterem*, beside the *Thermal* hotel.

# Into Slovakia: Komárno

It takes five minutes to walk from Komárom train station to the bridge, which is usually thronged with people **crossing the border**. Both countries' passport controls are at the Slovak end of the bridge, where formalities are straightforward; only Australians and New Zealanders need visas. If you don't fancy walking, the information desks in Komárom and Komárno train stations can tell you the time of the next bus running from one to the other (every couple of hours). There are regular local trains from Komárno to **Bratislava**, 110km away, eliminating the need to use international services (which cross the border here at night). If you're **entering Hungary**, there are fairly frequent trains and buses from Komárom to Budapest, Győr or Esztergom (for the Danube Bend).

At ulica Palatinova 32, the small **Podunajské Museum** (Tues–Sun 10am–noon & 2–4pm) pays tribute to two local sons, **Franz Lehár** and **Mór Jókai**. The former, the composer of the *Merry Widow*, was born here in 1870 and initially followed in his father's footsteps as bandmaster with the local garrison, while Jókai was a prolific writer of sentimental novels. You'll need Slovak or Hungarian to appreciate the displays. The museum stands next to a small **Orthodox Church** (*Pravoslávny kostol*) built in the early eighteenth century by Serbian refugees who had fled from the Turks. Komárno's **bus and train stations** are 2km northwest of the main street, Záhradnícka Slovanská, where the tourist office at Zupná 5 (Mon–Fri 9am–5pm) can arrange **accommodation** in one of the town's hotels or pensions.

# Győr

The industrial city of **GYŐR**, 120km from Budapest (pronounced "Dyur"), harbours a waterfront Belváros stuffed with Baroque mansions and churches, where streets bustle and restaurants vie for custom. With so much to enjoy around the centre, you can easily forget the high-rise apartments and factories that form the rest of Győr, whose Rába Engineering Works, producing trucks and rolling stock, is one of the country's most successful industries. The city also makes an excellent base for excursions to Pannonhalma Monastery (see p.217).

Győr's **history** owes much to its location at the confluence of three rivers – the Rába, Rábca and Mosoni-Duna – in the centre of the Kisalföld. The place was named Arrabona by the Romans, after a local Celtic tribe whom they subjugated, while its current name derives from *gyürü*, the Avar word for a circular fortress. During the Turkish occupation of Hungary, Győr's castle was a Habsburg stronghold and the town was known as Raab (after the Rába River). After its military role diminished, Győr gained industrial muscle and a different kind of clout. In the 1956 Uprising, its town hall was occupied by a radical Provisional National Council that pressed the Nagy government to get Soviet troops out and to quit the Warsaw Pact immediately.

## Arrival and accommodation

Győr's **bus and train stations** are on the southern edge of the centre, behind the very grand wedding-cake-like town hall, only ten minutes' walk from the Belváros along Baross Gábor utca and across Szent István út – a veritable windtunnel of an avenue that separates the new and old towns.

The best source of **information** is Tourinform, in a pavilion on the corner of Baross utca and Arany János utca (June–Aug Mon–Fri 8am–8pm, Sat 9am–4pm, Sun 9am–1pm; April, May & Sept Mon–Fri 8am–6pm, Sat 9am–4pm; Oct–March Mon–Fri 9am–4pm, Sat 9am–3pm; ☎96/311-771), conveniently located near a bank and **ATM**. They can also provide information on the **museum opening hours**, which are limited from October till April, and may only open on request. Ciklámen Tourist at Aradi vértanúk utca 22 (April–Oct Mon–Fri 8am–4.30pm, Sat 8am–noon; Nov–March Mon–Fri 8am–4.30pm; ☎96/316-557) and IBUSZ at Kazinczy utca 3 (June–Aug Mon–Fri 8am–5pm, Sat 8am–noon; Sept–May Mon–Wed 8am–4pm, Thurs 8am–5pm, Fri 8am–3pm; ☎96/311-700) also provide information, **change money** and book rooms.

### Accommodation

Ciklámen Tourist and IBUSZ (see above) can book private **accommodation** (②–③), but this is in short supply over summer, while in the autumn, hotels tend to be filled with conference delegates. The cheapest option is a room (①) at the *Széchenyi Főiskola kollégium* at Hédervári út 3, across the bridge in Révfalu, which usually has a few rooms all year round, though they go fast. All the campsites are some distance from the town centre.

*HOTELS AND PENSIONS*
**Corvin Panzió**, Csaba utca 22 (☎96/312-171). A small modern pension three blocks east of the bus station. ③.

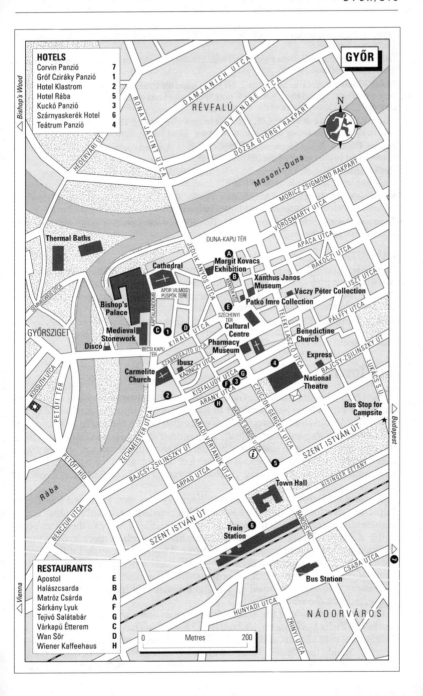

**GYŐR**

**HOTELS**
| | |
|---|---|
| Corvin Panzió | 7 |
| Gróf Cziráky Panzió | 1 |
| Hotel Klastrom | 2 |
| Hotel Rába | 5 |
| Kuckó Panzió | 3 |
| Szárnyaskerék Hotel | 6 |
| Teátrum Panzió | 4 |

**RESTAURANTS**
| | |
|---|---|
| Apostol | E |
| Halászcsarda | B |
| Matróz Csárda | A |
| Sárkány Lyuk | F |
| Tejivó Salátabár | G |
| Várkapu Étterem | C |
| Wan Sör | D |
| Wiener Kaffeehaus | H |

Bishop's Wood

RÉVFALÚ

Thermal Baths

DUNA-KAPU TÉR

Cathedral

Margit Kovacs Exhibition

Xanthus Janos Museum

Váczy Péter Collection

Patkó Imre Collection

APOR VILMOST PÜSPÖK TÉRE

Bishop's Palace

SZÉCHENYI TÉR

Cultural Centre

Benedictine Church

GYŐRSZIGET

Medieval Stonework

Disco

BECSI KAPU TÉR

Pharmacy Museum

Express

Carmelite Church

Ibusz

National Theatre

Bus Stop for Campsite

Town Hall

Train Station

Bus Station

NÁDORVÁROS

Vienna

Budapest

Rába

0    Metres    200

Mosoni-Duna

**Duna Panzió**, Vörösmarty utca 5 (☎96/329-084). A nice hotel with antique furniture, near Dunakapu tér. ③–④.

**Gróf Cziráky Panzió**, Bécsi kapu tér 8 (☎96/310-688). An elegant and pricey pension smack in the centre of town. ④.

**Hotel Klastrom**, Zechmeister utca 1, off Bécsi kapu tér (☎96/315-611). Occupying the 200-year-old priory behind the Carmelite Church, this hotel has a beautiful restaurant and inner courtyard, and lovely views of the river. ④.

**Hotel Rába**, Árpád út 34 (☎96/315-533). A large well-equipped 1970s block by Tourinform; best to avoid rooms facing directly onto the busy Szent István út. ⑤.

**Kuckó Panzió**, Arany János utca 33 (☎96/316-260). A seven-room pension in an old townhouse, right in the centre of the old town. ③–④.

**Pető Panzió**, Kossuth Lajos utca 20 (☎96/313-412). Across the bridge on Győrsziget, near the synagogue, accessible by bus #1 or #1Y from Aradi vértanúk útja. ③–④.

**Szárnyaskerék Hotel**, Révai Miklós utca 5 (☎96/314-629). The "Winged Wheel Hotel", as its name translates, occupies the old hostel building across from the train station. ②–③.

**Teátrum Panzió**, Schweidel utca 7 (☎96/310-640). Ten-room pension in the southeast part of the Belváros facing the National Theatre. ②–③.

*CAMPSITES*

**Napsugár**, Külső Veszprémi út 19 (☎96/411-042). 5km south of the centre; take the Kismegyer bus from the bus station. Can be noisy, as it's near the railway line.

**Pikenő**, 10-es Fő út (☎96/316-461). By the old main road to Budapest, 5km east of the centre. Take a bus towards Szentiván from the bus station.

**Kiskuti Camping**, Kiskút-liget (☎96/318-986). A big site 3km east of the centre, beyond the stadium, with bungalows (②–③). To get there catch bus #8 from Szent István út, opposite Lukács Sándor utca. Open mid-April to mid-Oct.

# The Town

Almost everything of interest in Győr lies within the **Belváros**, a web of streets and alleys stretching from Széchenyi tér to Káptalandomb, near the confluence of the Rába and Mosoni-Duna. Protected by preservation orders and traffic restrictions, it is a pleasure to wander around. Heading up pedestrianized Baross Gábor utca from the train station, antique sidestreets beckon on your left, narrow and shadowy with overhanging timbered houses – the perfect setting for a conspiracy. Indeed, Communists met secretly during the Horthy years at no. 15 on Sarló köz, a cobbled alley forking off Kazinczy utca.

Turning off Baross Gábor utca down Kazinczy utca, you come out into **Bécsi kapu tér**, overlooking the River Rába, which reputedly escaped flooding in the eighteenth century thanks to a miracle-working statue of Mary of the Foam occupying a chapel beside the former **Carmelite Church**. Entering the church through a portal whose inscription proclaims "I worked zealously for the Lord of Hosts", you'll find a richly decorated high altar and other furnishings carved by Franz Richter, a lay brother in the order. Behind the church stands the erstwhile monastery, subsequently used as a refugee centre and military prison and now converted into the *Hotel Klastrom*.

On the eastern side of the square are two **mansions** with finely wrought ironwork. The Zichy Palace at no. 13, built in 1778–82, has a balconied Zopf-style facade bearing the coat of arms of the Ott family, who owned it at a later date. Next door, at no.12, stands the Altabek House, with two corner oriel windows dating back to the sixteenth century, and a Baroque portico. Just around the corner, at Király utca

4, is the so-called Napoleon House, where the emperor stayed during a visit in 1809, and which now contains a **picture gallery** of mostly nineteenth-century works (May–Sept Tues–Sun 10am–6pm; limited winter opening; 80Ft).

From Bécsi kapu tér you can carry on uphill to the surviving bastions of Győr's sixteenth-century **castle**, where visitors can see a courtyard full of Roman and medieval stonework and underground casements (May–Sept Tues–Sun 10am–6pm; 80Ft). The castle successfully resisted the Turks for decades – unlike the town, which was frequently devastated.

## Káptalandomb and the waterfront

**Káptalandomb** (Chapter Hill) has been crowned by a **cathedral** (daily 9.15am–noon & 2–6pm; free) ever since King Stephen made Győr an episcopal see in the eleventh century, so the existing building incorporates Romanesque, Gothic and Baroque features. Just inside the entrance, the Gothic Hederváry Chapel contains a **reliquary bust of St László**, the canonized monarch who ruled from 1077 to 1095. Sensitively moulded and richly enamelled, it is a superb example of the goldsmith's art from the workshop of the Kolozsvári brothers. The frescoes inside the cathedral were painted by Maulbertsch, who decorated numerous Hungarian churches in the eighteenth century, while the Bishop's throne was a gift from Empress Maria Theresa.

The building behind the cathedral, to the southeast, at Apor Vilmos püspök tere 2, houses the **Miklós Borsos Collection** of paintings and sculptures by the self-taught artist who designed the Kilometre Zero monument in Budapest (May–Sept Tues–Sun 10am–6pm; see Tourinform for winter opening; 80Ft). On the other side of the cathedral lies the **Bishop's Palace** (*Püspökvár*), a much remodelled edifice whose oldest section dates from the thirteenth century, but which is not open to the public at present.

From here you can walk down Káptalandomb, past the Zopf-style Provost House at no. 15, to reach **Duna-kapu tér**, a waterfront square alongside which Danube grain ships once moored, and where food **markets** are still held on Wednesdays and Saturdays. Notice the iron weathercock on top of the well – an allusion to the one that the Turks fixed above the town's gate, boasting that they would not leave Győr until it crowed.

## Around Széchenyi tér

Heading up Jedlik Anyos utca from Duna-kapu tér, you'll find the **Ark of the Covenant**, a splendid Baroque monument erected by Emperor Karl III by way of an apology for the Habsburg soldiers who knocked the monstrance from a priest's hands during a Corpus Christi procession in 1727. At the same junction, on the corner of Káposztás köz (Cabbage alley), is the **Margit Kovács Collection** (May–Sept Tues–Sun 10am–6pm; limited winter opening; 50Ft). Kovács was born in Győr in 1902, and this is just as delightful as the museum of her work in Szentendre (see p.133).

On the other side of the road, Kenyér köz (Bread Alley) and Szappanos köz (Soap Alley) lead to **Széchenyi tér**, traditionally the main square, overlooked by eye-like attic windows from the steep roofs of surrounding buildings. Notice the **Iron Stump House** at no. 4, so-called after a wooden beam into which travelling journeymen hammered nails to mark their sojourn. It now contains the stimulating **Imre Patkó Collection** of African art . (May–Sept Tues–Sun 10am–6pm; limited winter opening; 50Ft). Next door is the **Xantus János**

**Museum** (May–Sept Tues–Sun 10am–6pm; limited winter opening; 80Ft), named after a locally educated nineteenth-century archeologist who emigrated to America and subsequently travelled in China. You can buy a leaflet in English describing the varied and fascinating artefacts relating to local history, while the collection of tiled stoves needs no explanation.

On the south side of the square, beyond an ornate **Marian Column** commemorating the recapture of Buda from the Turks, stands the Benedictine **Church of St Ignatius**, designed by the Italian Baccio del Bianco in the 1630s. A painting in the sanctuary by the Viennese artist Troger depicts the saint's apotheosis. Beside the adjacent monastery is the **Pharmacy Museum** (Mon, Tues, Thurs & Fri 8am–4.30pm, Wed 10am–4.30pm; 80Ft), a beautifully furnished seventeenth-century apothecary's that still functions as a pharmacy. North of the square, at Nefelejcs utca 3, an ex-hospice with two minuscule Renaissance-style yards contains the fabulous **Péter Váczy Collection** of seventeenth- and eighteenth-century Hungarian and European furniture. It's also worth seeing the **City Gallery** at Király utca 17, a venue for contemporary art exhibitions in a fine old building.

### Across the river

Should you want a change of scenery, walk across the bridge over the Mosoni-Duna to the **Révfalu** district, where a fifteen-minute walk will bring you to the **Bishop's Wood** (*Püspök-erdő*), a large park with deer and other fauna. Alternatively, you can cross the Rába via a small island linked by bridge to Bécsi kapu tér and the **Győrsziget** district. On the far side there's a **swimming pool** that's open during the summer and an outdoor **thermal bath** open year-round (Mon–Fri 6am–8pm, Sat & Sun 7am–6pm; 250Ft). Down Kossuth utca stands a domed former **synagogue** at no. 5, built in 1869, which is sometimes used for concerts, particularly during the Mediawave festival (see opposite). Ask at the music academy next door whether you can get inside.

# Eating, drinking and entertainment

Győr has recently taken off in terms of places to eat and drink, with Western European and American-style bars and pubs rubbing shoulders with more traditional Hungarian places. Note that most eating places **close early**, around 10pm.

**Apostol**, Széchenyi tér 3. Pleasant, quiet place with reasonable prices.

**Halászcsárda**, Apáca utca 4. Friendly atmosphere, good fish dishes, and music in the evenings.

**Matróz Csárda**, Duna-kapu tér 3. A reasonably priced option on the northern edge of the old town.

**Pátió**, Sarló köz 7. Smart place to eat, and not too expensive. Also has a beautiful coffee shop.

**Sárkány Lyuk**, Arany János utca 29. The "Dragon Hole" is a local hangout with good, inexpensive Hungarian food.

**Tejivó Salatbár**, Kisfaludy utca 30. Specializes in salads and real fruit milkshakes. Closes at 5pm Mon–Fri, and 1pm on Saturday.

**Várkapu Étterem**, Bécsi kapu tér 7. The place to go if you want to indulge yourself. Wide choice of dishes.

**Wan Sör**, Király utca 9. A beer and pizza place up a small alley that draws a young crowd.

## Drinking

Győr's **watering holes** include the *Szürkebarát Borozó* at Arany János utca 20 and the *Vár-borozó*, midway along Király utca. The *Yankee Pub* on the island in the middle of the Rába across from Bécsi kapu tér is an American-style saloon, which serves tasty food and has a disco upstairs. **Patisseries** such as the *Wiener Kaffeehaus* in the court-yard at Arany János utca 18–20 do cocktails and liqueurs as well as coffee and cakes. Alternatively, catch a #4 bus out to the Nádorváros district to enjoy the old-fashioned ambience of the *Bergmann Cukrászda* at Attila utca 31 (Wed–Sun 10am–6pm).

## Entertainment

Culture vultures should look out for performances by the **Győr Ballet Company**, which achieved international renown under its founder Iván Márko, formerly the lead dancer of Maurice Béjart's Twentieth Century Ballet Company. Although Márko has moved on and foreign critics now disparage the company, locals still cherish it, and performances always sell out at the brashly tiled **National Theatre**, on the corner of Bajcsy-Zsilinszky út and Czuczor Gergely utca (tickets from Kisfaludy utca 25).

The **Cultural Centre** at Czuczor Gergely utca 17 is a regular venue for foreign **films**, exhibitions and concerts, especially during the **Mediawave festival** in late April/early May – one to two weeks of avant-garde film, theatre and music. The **Summer Events** from mid-June to mid-July is a larger festival of music, theatre and dance at venues throughout the town. Tourinform can give details of all the **entertainment** on offer. The city's **football** team, Győr ETO, is a great source of pride, and has in the past humbled such foreign clubs as Manchester United at their stadium in the eastern suburbs (bus #8).

# Pannonhalma Monastery

Twenty kilometres southeast of Győr, the low-lying Kisalföld meets a spur of the Bakony, a glorious setting for the fortress-like **Pannonhalma Monastery** atop St Martin's Hill (282m). According to Anonymous, the medieval chronicler, it was here that Árpád was "uplifted by the beauty of Pannonia" after the Magyar con-quest, and Prince Géza invited the **Benedictine Order** to found an abbey in 969. The Order helped Géza's son Stephen weld the pagan Magyar tribes into a Christian state, and remained influential until its suppression in 1787 by Emperor Josef II. Re-established by his successor, the Benedictines thereafter confined themselves to prayer and pedagogy.

The monastery manifests a variety of styles, its chiefly Romanesque wings con-trasting with the Baroque exterior of the **basilica** and a Neoclassical **tower**. Purists lament the church's neo-Romanesque interior, remodelled by Ferenc Storno in 1867. Notice the marble sepulchres containing the bones of two abbots and a princess. An exquisitely carved portal leads into Gothic **cloisters** dating from the first quarter of the thirteenth century, when Pannonhalma was remod-elled under Abbot Oros, who later gave King Béla IV 220 kilos of silver to help him rebuild the country after the Mongol invasion. On the wall by the doorway are some fifteenth-century graffiti – "Hic fuit".

Although Pannonhalma's most sacred **treasures** are displayed on only a couple of days around August 20, its medieval codices and ancient books are permanently on show in the Empire-style **library**. The 300,000-volume collection includes the foundation deed of Tihany Abbey. Dating from 1055, this is the earliest known document to include Hungarian words (55 of them) amongst the customary Latin. The **art gallery** displays a portrait of King Stephen and paintings by Italian, Dutch and German artists of the sixteenth and seventeenth centuries, plus new works marking the monastery's millennium, which was celebrated in 1996.

Visitors are only admitted on **guided tours** (in English March 21 to Oct 11 Tues–Sun at 11am & 1pm; 650Ft; in Hungarian year-round, hourly except midday Tues–Sun 9am–4pm, June–Sept 9am–5pm; 450Ft). Churchgoers have a choice of two **masses** on Sunday: a Hungarian one at 9am or a Latin one at 10am, the latter complete with Gregorian singing. Fully fledged **organ recitals** usually occur on Easter Monday, Whit Monday, August 20, October 23 and December 26, drawing crowds of music lovers; book at least a week in advance through Pax Tourist (see below). Another profitable sideline is the selling of **lavender** (*levendula*) from the fields surrounding the monastery. Shops advertise lavender oil's efficacy as a remedy for depression, insect bites, and moths in clothes.

## Practicalities

The monastery can be reached from Győr by any bus or train heading for Veszprém (or vice versa). The train station is 2km away, but buses run right up to the monastery, following Petőfi utca through Pannonhalma village, and Hunyadi utca as it winds uphill. **Information** is available from Tourinform in the cultural centre at Petőfi utca 25 (☎96/471-733), or Pax Tourist at Vár 1, near the entrance to the monastery (Tues–Sat 9am–4pm, Sun noon–4pm; ☎96/570-191).

While neither can arrange private **accommodation**, Pax Tourist can give a few addresses. Three agreeable Alpine-style places with wooden balconies are the elegant *Pax Hotel* at Dózsa György utca 2, just off Petőfi utca (☎96/470-006; ⑤), the *Pannon Panzió* at Hunyadi utca 7B (☎96/470-041; ④), and the *Familia Panzió* at Béke utca 61, 600m off Petőfi utca (☎96/470-192; ③). The *Panorama* campsite (☎96/471-240; ①) is beautifully sited on the hillside at Fenyvesalja utca 4a, 300m south of the village centre.

Of the several **restaurants** in the village, the *Szent Márton* near the monastery (which runs it) is more expensive than the *Pannon Panzió* down the hill, whose food is just as good.

# Northwest to the border

Driving to (or from) Vienna or Bratislava, you have the option of stopping over at Mosonmagyaróvár, or detouring off the M1 motorway to visit Lébény or the Szigetköz region.

Detouring off the highway to **LÉBÉNY**, 20km beyond Győr, is only recommended if you're a fan of ecclesiastical architecture, since the village's sole attraction is a thirteenth-century **Benedictine Church** that once came under the jurisdiction of Pannonhalma. Though touted as one of the oldest and finest examples of Romanesque architecture in Hungary, it was actually restored to its original style after receiving a Baroque face-lift from the Jesuits in the mid-seventeenth century.

On the other side of the highway lies the **Szigetköz** or "island region", bounded by the meandering Mosoni-Duna and the "old" or main branch of the Danube. This picturesque wetland abounds in rare flora, **birdlife** and fish, making it something of a paradise for hikers and naturalists alike. Unfortunately, the **Gabčíkovo**

**hydroelectric barrage** has reduced water levels sharply, thus badly affecting the ecology and wildlife of the region. If you want to explore the region on horseback, there are lots of local **riding** stables; Tourinform in Mosonmagyarovár (see below) has details on this, as well as on boat hire on the river and bike hire. The minor road that traverses Szigetköz, running between Győr and Mosonmagyaróvár, is ideal for **cyclists**. The village of **Lipót**, 2km off the road, offers **accommodation** in the form of the *Hort-Duna Panzió* (☎96/216-196; ②) and a basic campsite (May–Sept). Other accommodation possibilities include the 300-year-old *Kastély Hotel* in Hédervár at Fő út 47 (☎96/213-576; ⑤), and the *Dunaponti Panzió* in Mecsér at Ady Endre út 45 (☎96/213-386; ③); both places rent out bikes.

# Mosonmagyaróvár

**MOSONMAGYARÓVÁR** is a fusion of two settlements near the confluence of the Mosoni-Duna and Lajtha rivers. While **Moson** is utterly prosaic, dominated by the main road that runs through the middle of it, **Magyaróvár** is a pleasant old town with a picturesque castle and bridges. Both are visibly prosperous, thanks to all the Austrians who come here to shop or to receive inexpensive medical attention, and townsfolk travel to work in Austria. If you have the choice, the best time to visit is late autumn, when the crowds have thinned and the first pressing of grapes takes place at **vineyards** in the locality.

The chief attraction is **Magyaróvár Castle**, at the north end of the town (follow the signposts for Bratislava). Founded in the thirteenth century to guard the western gateway to Hungary, it gave the town its medieval name, Porta Hungarica. Much remodelled since then, it now houses a section of Keszthely's Agricultural University and a small exhibition on the fauna of the Hanság region (Mon–Fri 10am–6pm; free).

The cobbled streets running down through the town are worth exploring, even if they have been strongly kitschified for the big tourist crowds that come across the border from Austria. On Fő utca, the main road running round the west side of the old centre, the **Cselley Ház** at no. 19 (March 15 to Oct Tues–Sun 10am–6pm; Nov to March 14 Tues–Sun 10am–2pm; 120Ft) is one of the oldest buildings in the town, with some features dating back to the fourteenth century. It's notable for its stone-framed windows, wrought-iron window-grilles, and its panelled ceilings on the first floor. It houses an **Exhibition of Fine and Applied Arts** from the seventeenth century onwards, as well as the collection of an art-loving doctor, including paintings by some of the big names in Hungarian art such as Munkácsy Mihály. In the basement are Roman stoneworks. Following Fő útca on down for ten minutes to the junction with Kossuth utca, you come to the **Hanság Museum** at Szent István Király út 1 (Tues–Sun: May–Sept 10am–5.30pm; Oct–April 10am–2pm; 120Ft), with its classical front, which has one of the oldest provincial collections in Hungary, covering local history from prehistoric times up to the event which made the town notorious in 1956, when secret police opened fire on a crowd of demonstrators.

## Practicalities

From the bus and train **stations** in Moson, buses #1, #2, #5 and #6 run along Szent István Király út, past Tourinform at Kápolna tér 16 (May–Sept Mon–Fri 8am–5pm, Sat 8am–1pm; Oct–April Mon–Fri 8am–4pm, Sat 8am–1pm; ☎96/206-304), into Magyaróvár, where Ciklámen Tourist at Fő utca 8 (Mon–Thurs

8am–4.15pm, Fri 8am–noon & 12.30pm–3.15pm, Sat 8am–noon; ☎96/211-078) can supply **information** and **change money**.

**Private rooms** (②) are available from both tourist offices and are advertised around town. For those with transport, *Vizpart Camping* in Dunakiliti (☎96/224-579), 12km north of the town, near the Danube, is a better option than the crowded *Magyar Autóklub* site by the river at Gabona rakpart 6 (May to mid-Oct; ☎96/215-883), which has bungalows (③). Of the **hotels**, the *Szent Flórián Hotel*, Fő utca 127 (☎96/213-177; ⑤), is an attractive, comfy establishment, with wheelchair access, on the southern edge of Magyaróvár's old town; the pleasant *Solaris* on Lucsony utca 19, five minutes' walk east of the castle along a leafy quiet road (☎96/215-300; ④), has rooms with minibar and TV; the *Lajtha Hotel*, Palánk utca 3 (☎96/211-824; ③), is a one-star place a few minutes east of the castle, behind a new shopping centre.

Of the several **restaurants** spilling out onto Magyar utca, the *Magyaros Vendéglő* at no. 3 is the best option in downtown Magyaróvár. For tasty Hungarian cooking beyond the tourist zone, track down the *Csülökház Étterem* at Frankel Leo utca 2, near the junction with Marx Károly utca, en route to Moson, or the *Vadásztanya Vendéglő* at Kossuth utca 75.

## Border crossings

Mosonmagyaróvár is the last stop before two major border crossings. **Rajka**, 19km north, handles traffic bound for the Slovak capital of Bratislava, 15km away, while **Hegyeshalom** is the main road and rail crossing into Austria, from where it's 45km to Vienna. While the latter used to be famous for its queues of Ladas and Trabants carrying families of Hungarians to the hypermarkets on the Austrian side, traffic now moves quickly in both directions.

# WESTERN TRANSDANUBIA

**Western Transdanubia**, part of the region bordering Austria and Slovenia, has a sub-Alpine topography and climate, ideal for wine-growing and outdoor pursuits. Its Baroque towns and historic castles evince centuries of Habsburg influence and doughty resistance against the Turks. From the beautiful town of **Sopron**, you can visit the Esterházy Palace at **Fertőd** before heading south to **Kőszeg** and **Szombathely**, and thence to **Sárvár** or the picturesque **Őrség region**. This itinerary is possible by public transport, since Sopron is easily accessible by express trains and buses from Budapest or Győr, whereas other places are easier to reach using local services. Starting from Balaton, however, it's easier to work your way north via Szombathely or **Zalaegerszeg** (in which case, you should backtrack through the following sections).

# Sopron

With its 115 monuments and 240 listed buildings, **SOPRON** can justly claim to be "the most historic town in Hungary". Never having been ravaged by Mongols or Turks, the inner town retains its medieval layout, with a mélange of Gothic and Baroque that rivals the Várhegy in Budapest – and here there are even fewer cars on the streets. Sopron is also a major wine-producing centre and the base for excur-

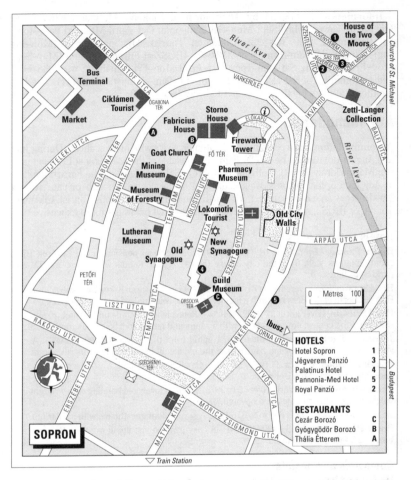

sions to the Esterházy Palace and the vintage steam train at Nagycenk amongst others. Its proximity to Vienna means that Austrians have long come here to shop, eat
out and get their teeth fixed (there are dentists everywhere in Sopron). While the
local economy benefits, visitors will find that prices are almost at Budapest levels and
accommodation can be in short supply in the high season. Should you be visiting in
the winter, be warned that most of the museums are closed from October until April.

## Arrival and information

From Sopron's **train station**, it's just 500m up Mátyás király utca to Széchenyi
tér, on the southern edge of the Belváros. Arriving by Intercity **bus**, it's five minutes' walk along Lackner Kristóf utca to Ógabona tér, on the northwest side of the
Várkerület that surrounds the Belváros.

**Information** is offered by Tourinform at Előkapu 11, just north of the Firewatch Tower (May–Sept Mon–Sat 9am–6pm; Oct–April Mon–Fri 9am–4pm, Sat 9am–noon; ☎99/338-892); Ciklámen Tourist, Ógabona tér 8 (Mon–Fri 8am–4.30pm, Sat 8am–1pm; ☎99/312-040); IBUSZ at Füredi sétány 9 (May–Sept Mon–Fri 8am–5pm, Sat 8am–1pm; Oct–April Mon–Fri 9am–5pm; ☎99/338-695); and Lokomotiv Tourist at Új utca 1 (Mon–Fri 9am–5pm; ☎99/311-111). The last handles bookings for the Széchenyi Railway (see p.228).

# Accommodation

**Accommodation** is at a premium over summer, so it's wise to book ahead. During July and August **dormitory beds** (①) might be available at the *kollégium* at Erzsébet utca 9 or Mátyás király utca 21 (both just down from Széchenyi tér), or the *Faipari Egyetem* at Ady utca 5, ten minutes' walk southwest of the centre. Though **private rooms** (②–③) are scarce over summer, it's worth enquiring at Lokomotiv Tourist, Ciklámen Tourist or IBUSZ, since most of the alternatives listed below are more expensive.

## Hotels and pensions

**Diana Panzió**, Lővér körút 64 (☎99/329-013). Nine-room pension in the Lővérek Hills, twenty minutes' walk from the city centre (bus #1 or #2). Rooms with fridge and TV, and parking facilities. ③.

**Hotel Sopron**, Fövényverem utca 7 (☎99/314-254). A plush place on Koronázó-domb (Coronation Hill) just north of the Belváros, with a nightclub, sauna, solarium and tennis courts. ⑥.

**Hotel Szieszta**, Lővér körút 37 (☎99/314-260). Refurbished ex-trade union hotel, 20 minutes' walk from the centre, now renovated with a sauna and tennis courts, on bus route #1. ④.

**Jégverem Panzió**, Jégverem utca 1, just uphill from the Belváros (☎99/312-004). A converted eighteenth-century inn named after the old ice pit in the middle of its restaurant. ④.

**Palatinus Hotel**, Új utca 23 (☎99/311-395). Small modern hotel, with an agreeable ambience, in the heart of the Belváros. ⑤.

**Pannonia-Med Hotel**, Várkerület 75 (☎99/312-180). A lovely old building with wrought-iron balconies, recently completely renovated. ⑤–⑥.

**Sas Fogadó**, Lővér körút 69 (☎99/316-183). A seven-room guesthouse with a solarium. ③.

**Royal Panzió**, Sas tér 13 (☎99/314-481). A cosy pension just uphill from the Belváros and boasting a four-star restaurant. ⑤.

## Campsites and hostels

**Brennbergi Panzió/Youth Hostel**, Brennbergi utca (☎99/313-116). To the west of the city centre (bus #3 or #10 from the bus station). Open mid-April to mid-Oct. Charges by the bed. ①.

**Lővér Camping** (☎99/311-715). Located 4km south of the centre and accessible by hourly bus #12 from Deák tér and the intercity bus station. Open all year, with chalets (②–③) over summer. Bookings through Ciklámen Tourist. ①.

**Ózon Camping**, Erdei Malom köz 3 (☎99/331-144). A four-star site with a few rooms (②), in the garden district 5km outside town, off the #10 bus route. Mid-April to mid-Oct. ①.

# Around the Belváros

Compact and easily explored on foot, the Belváros is where most of the sights are located. While Templom utca provides a direct route from Széchenyi tér to the heart of the Belváros, you'd be foolish not to detour along the first turning to the right, to admire **Orsolya tér**. At the centre is the Maria Fountain (*Mária Kút*), dating from 1780, which is worth a look, though it no longer operates as a fountain. This romantic-looking cobbled square gets its name from an Ursuline convent that once occupied the site of the **Church of the Virgin**, sandwiched between two neo-Gothic edifices dripping with loggias, one of which contains the **Catholic Collection of Ecclesiastical Art** (May–Sept Mon & Thurs 10am–4pm, Sun 11am–4pm; 100Ft). The square was the site of the Salt Market in olden days, and animals were butchered under the arcades of the building at no. 5. Today, this houses a museum, with temporary displays only.

From Oroslya tér you can head north up **Új utca** (New Street), which is actually one of Sopron's oldest thoroughfares. Its chunky cobblestoned pavements follow a gentle curve of arched dwellings painted in red, yellow and pink, with a view of the Firewatch Tower above them. During the Middle Ages it was called Zsidó (Jewish) utca and housed a flourishing mercantile community, until they were accused of conspiring with the Turks and expelled in 1526, only returning to Sopron in the nineteenth century. At no. 22, a tiny medieval **synagogue** (April–Oct daily except Tues 9am–5pm; 100Ft) stands diagonally opposite another one that now contains a tax office. At the end of the street you emerge onto Fő tér.

## Fő tér

The focal point of **Fő tér** is the cherubim-covered **Holy Trinity Statue**, which local Protestants took as an affront when it was erected in 1700 by Cardinal Kollonich, who threatened: "First I will make the Hungarians slaves, then I will make them beggars, and then I will make them Catholics." Behind it stands the triple-aisled **Goat Church** built for the Franciscans in 1300, where three kings were later crowned and Parliament convened on seven occasions. Its curious name stems from the legend that the church's construction was financed by a goatherd whose flock unearthed a cache of loot – in gratitude for which an angel embraces a goat on one of the pillars of its interesting Gothic and Baroque interior.

Before crossing the square to visit the mansions on its northern side, check out the **Pharmacy Museum** at no. 2 (May–Sept Tues–Sun 9am–5pm; 60Ft), which preserves the Angel apothecary's founded by Tóbiás Marb in 1601. Though remodelled since then, its Biedermeier-style walnut furnishings and artefacts from the Dark Ages of pharmacology certainly deserve a look.

Directly opposite the church stands the **Fabricius House** at no. 6 (May–Sept Tues–Sun 10am–6pm; 40Ft), which unites a Baroque mansion built upon Roman foundations with a patrician's house from the fifteenth century. A Renaissance stairway leads up to a small museum of archeological finds, also noted for its "whispering gallery", while the Gothic cellar contains three large Roman statues unearthed during the construction of the town hall. Next door at no. 7 is the **Lackner House**, named after the seventeenth-century mayor who bequeathed it to Sopron; his motto "Fiat Voluntas Tua" ("Thy will be done") appears on the facade.

The Renaissance **Storno House** at no. 8 has the finest pedigree, however. King Mátyás stayed here in 1482–83, as did Franz Liszt in 1840 and 1881. It is still owned by descendants of Ferenc Storno, painter, architect and master chimney-sweep, who restored Pannonhalma and other medieval churches during the nineteenth century. The family's private collection of Liszt memorabilia and Roman, Celtic and Avar relics are displayed in an enjoyably eccentric **museum** on the second floor (May–Sept Tues–Sun 10am–6pm; 150Ft).

## The Firewatch Tower

North of Fő tér rises Sopron's symbol, the **Firewatch Tower** (*Tűztorony*; April–Oct Tues–Sun 10am–6pm; 120Ft), founded upon the stones of a fortress built by the Romans, who established the town of Scarbantia here during the first century AD. As its name suggests, the tower was intended to give warning of a fire anywhere in town. Its sentries, while standing watch, blew trumpets to signal the hours. Ascending from its square tenth-century base, up through a cylindrical seventeenth-century mid-section, you emerge onto a Baroque balcony offering a stunning **view** of Fő tér and the Belváros.

At the base of the tower stands the **Gate of Loyalty**, erected in honour of the townfolks' decision to reject the offer of Austrian citizenship in 1921. The motif shows Hungaria surrounded by kneeling citizens and Sopron's coat of arms, which henceforth included the title "Civitas Fidelissima" (the most loyal citizenry). Walking through the gate, you'll emerge onto **Előkapu** (Outer Gate) utca, where the houses are staggered for defensive purposes, and "errant burghers" and "gossiping, nagging" wives were once pinioned in stocks for the righteous to pelt with rotten food.

At the junction with the Várkerület, you can cross the road to examine the colourfully tiled facade of the **Golden Lion Pharmacy** at no. 29, or head to the right along the boulevard to espy a section of the **medieval town walls** on the right.

### Templom utca

**Templom utca**, a picturesque street of Baroque facades, heads south from Fő tér. Standing just around the corner from the Goat Church on Fő tér is the square's finest sight, a fourteenth-century **chapterhouse** behind the Baroque facade of no. 1, whose Gothic pillars and vaults are decorated with images of the seven deadly sins and the symbols of the Evangelists (mid-March to mid-Oct daily 10am–noon & 2–5pm; free).

While you won't miss much by skipping the Museum of Forestry at no. 4 (April–Sept 1–5pm; Oct–March 10am–1pm; closed Wed; 150Ft), the **Mining Museum** at no. 2 (10am–2pm; closed Tues; 30Ft) occupies a former Esterházy mansion where Haydn often stayed, and has some curious artefacts from the Brennberg pits near Sopron, the oldest coal mines in Hungary. A medieval building given an extra floor in the 1770s contains the **Lutheran History Museum** (April–Sept Tues, Wed & Fri–Sun 10am–4pm), which explains how all the Evangelical churches were confiscated in 1674, obliging Lutherans to worship at home until the authorities relented. The adjacent **Lutheran Church** dates from 1782, but only acquired its Romanesque bell-tower eighty years later, due to restrictions on the faith decreed by Emperor Josef II. On the other side, the profusely ornamented Töpler House at no. 22 is named after a physician who devoted his life to fighting epidemics, while the courtyard of no. 15 contains a neo-Renaissance loggia.

# Beyond the Belváros

While the Belváros is spectacular, there is more to see as you move out of the centre, with art and architecture to the north, a folly to the west, and beautiful countryside to the south.

**Ikva híd**, crossing a narrow stream which used to flood noxiously in the nineteenth century, points towards some more sights. Off to the right at Balfi utca 11

is the private **Zettl-Langer Collection** (daily 10am–noon; 150Ft) of porcelain,
earthenware and weaponry, assembled by a nineteenth-century businessman.

A five-minute walk up Dorfmeister and Szent Mihály utca from Ikva híd takes
you past the **House of the Two Moors** (so-called after the turbaned statues
flanking its gate) on your left, to the partially Gothic **Church of St Michael** further uphill, whose gargoyles leer over a decaying thirteenth-century Chapel of St
Jacob. Nearby stand the tombstones of Soviet soldiers killed liberating Sopron
from the Arrow Cross puppet government, which massacred hundreds of
hostages before fleeing with the Coronation Regalia in April 1945.

### The Fool's Castle

In the western garden suburbs, 3km from the centre, at Csalogány köz 8, lurks a
bizarre **"Fool's Castle"** (*Taródi-vár*), similar to Bory's Castle in Székesfehérvár
(see p.166), which was built by a local eccentric early this century. It is still inhabited by his descendants, who allow visitors to enter several rooms crammed with
paintings and curios, and sometimes take paying guests. There are no set hours,
but you can usually gain admission whenever someone's at home; the curator
charges whatever she can get away with. To get there, take bus #1 from
Széchenyi tér, which drops you near the covered pool (*Fedett Uzsoda*) outside
town, walk 50m back, turn left onto Tölgyfa sor, and then left again at the end.

### The Lővérek Hills and the Burgenland

South of town, the sub-Alpine **Lővérek Hills** are a standing invitation to hikers.
Bus #1 or #2 will drop you at the *Hotel Lővér* near the start of the path up to the
**Károly lookout tower** (daily: April–Oct 9am–6pm; Nov–March 9am–4pm), which
offers marvellous views of the surrounding countryside. Although several **hiking
trails** continue into Austria, only locals are allowed to pass through the low-key
checkpoints. Both sides of the border are inhabited by bilingual folk engaged in
viticulture, following the division of the **Burgenland** region between Hungary and
Austria (which got the lion's share) after the collapse of the Habsburg empire – an
amicable partition, it seems, since nobody complains about it today.

# Eating, drinking and entertainment

Sopron is stuffed with **places to eat**. For traditional Hungarian fare, try the
*Várkerület Söröző* at Várkerület 83, or the cheap and cheerful *Expresszó Ételbár*
by the Storno House on Fő tér, where the nearby *Corvinus Söröző* serves tasty
pizzas. There are many options behind the Várkerület, such as the terrace of the
*Barokk Restaurant* at Várkerület 25, overlooking the Ikva, or the delightful *Sopron
Halászcsárda* with a garden (closes 9pm; ☎99/338-403; booking advisable) on
Fővényverem utca, where you'll also find the agreeable *Fekete Bárány*. More
centrally, there's the authentically Magyar *Thália Étterem* on Színház utca, with
cheesy keyboard music, which stays open until 6am.

Hearty red *Kékfrankos* and white, apple-flavoured *Tramini* are best sampled in
**wine cellars** such as the *Gyógygödör Borozó* at Fő tér 4 (Tues–Sun 9am–9pm).
The *Cezár Borozó* on the corner of Oroslya tér and Hátsókapu utca (9am–9.30pm)
boasts vintage oak butts and leather-aproned waiters. For beer, try the *Rókalyuk*
pub opposite the *Várkerület Söröző*. The *Stefánia Cukrászda*, in a building with a
charming arcaded courtyard at Szent György utca 12, was once a safe house for
a Lutheran priest, and today offers good **cakes and coffee**.

Sopron is at its liveliest during the **Spring Days** (late March) and **Festival Weeks** (mid-June to mid-July), when all manner of concerts and plays are staged at the Petőfi Theatre on Petőfi tér and the Liszt Cultural Centre on Széchenyi tér. You can get details from Tourinform and tickets from the festival office at Széchenyi tér 17. In mid-October the town hosts a festival to celebrate the Grape Harvest, when there is wine-tasting, folk dancing and music.

# Around Sopron

To the east of Sopron lies the **Hanság region**, a once extensive swampland that has gradually been drained and brought under cultivation since the eighteenth century. Prone to thick fogs, the area is traditionally associated with tales of elves and water sprites, and with the dynastic seats of the Esterházy and Széchenyi families at Fertőd and Nagycenk. The most obvious feature on the map is the shallow, reedy expanse known to Hungarians as **Lake Fertő** and to Austrians as the Neusiedler See, which was out of bounds under Communism to prevent escapes, but is now being developed as a nature reserve and resort, noted for its wild beauty and varied **birdlife**. It can be reached by bus from Sopron (every 1hr 30min–2hr), and is especially good **cycling** country, having a cycle track all the way around it, with campsites en route and *Zimmer frei* signs in most of the villages. This track forms part of a longer track from Sopron to Fertőd via Fertőrákos, which is highly recommended. There are hourly buses to all of the following places from the depot on Lackner Kristóf utca in Sopron.

## Fertőrákos Quarry

**FERTŐRÁKOS**, 8km north of town, presumably gets its name "cancerous slough" from the local **quarry** (daily: March–April 8am–5pm; May–Sept 8am–7pm; Oct 8am–5pm; Nov, Dec & Feb 8am–4pm; 60Ft), where limestone has been hewn since Roman times. Vienna's St Stephen's Cathedral and Ringstrasse were built with stone from Fertőrákos, where quarrying only ceased in 1945. The result is a cyclopean labyrinth of gigantic chambers and oddly skewed pillars, resembling the mythical cities imagined by H.P. Lovecraft; animal and plant fossils attest that the land was once submerged beneath a prehistoric sea. **Concerts** are staged in the quarry during the Sopron Festival Weeks (tickets available from the Sopron festival office).

Everything in the village is situated on Fő utca, the main street running downhill from the quarry, where a five-minute walk downhill brings you to the **Crystal Museum** at no. 97 (Tues–Sun 10am–5pm; 100Ft), followed by the former Bishop's Palace at no. 153, which dates back in parts to the Middle Ages and should reopen as a **local history museum** (daily 10am–5pm for groups of ten or more) once renovation is finished in 1999.

Should you feel like **staying**, an old peasant dwelling at Fő utca 194 has been converted into the cosy *Horváth Ház* (☎99/311-383; ③), or there's the basic *Vízmalom Hostel* at no. 141 (☎99/355-034; ②), where beds can be reserved through Lokomotiv Tourist in Sopron. Many households also offer rooms and it's worth enquiring at the Bishop's Palace, where the *Kastély Hotel* (☎99/355-040; ②) is due to reopen.

# East to the Esterházy Palace

The Esterházy Palace at Fertőd lies 27km east of Sopron along a minor road that connects with the route to Fertőrákos at **BALF**, which has been a **spa** since Roman times. Alas, its *fin-de-siècle* facilities were wrecked during World War II and the modern *Kurhotel-Schloss Balf* (☎99/314-266; ⑤) lacks the aesthetic appeal of the prewar hotel, though its stately grounds give an idea of how the resort once looked, and the water of the spa is as good as ever (Tues–Sun 10am–5pm; 1200Ft). Balf also boasts a fish restaurant, a year-round campsite (☎99/357-024), and majestic views out over the lake when weather conditions are right.

The village of **FERTŐD**, 20km further, began life as an appendage to the palace and was known as "Esterháza" until the family decamped in 1945. As you enter the village, postwar housing gives way to stately public buildings endowed by the Esterházys, presaging the palace at the eastern end – which is impossible to miss so long as you stay on the main street. En route you'll pass the post office, an ATM and the train station (turn right outside if you arrive there); buses stop close to the palace and the Tourinform office, which is at Madách sétány 1 (mid-April to mid-Oct Mon–Fri 8am–6pm, Sat 8am–noon; mid-Oct to mid-April Mon–Fri 8am–4pm; ☎99/370-544).

## The Esterházy Palace

Built on malarial swampland drained by hundreds of serfs, the **Esterházy Palace** was intended to rival Versailles and remove any arriviste stigma from the dynasty (see box overleaf). Gala balls and concerts, hunting parties and masquerades were held here even before it was completed in 1776, continuing without a let-up until the death of Prince Miklós "the Ostentatious" in 1790. Neglected by his successor, who dissolved the orchestra and moved his court back to Eisenstadt, the palace rapidly decayed. Its picture gallery, puppet theatre and Chinese pavilions disappeared, while its salons became storerooms and stables. Though basic repairs were made after World War II, restoration only began in earnest in the 1950s, and is still unfinished due to the prodigious cost.

Ornate Rococo wrought-iron gates lead into a vast horseshoe courtyard where hussars once pranced to the music of Haydn, Esterházy's resident maestro. The U-shaped wings and ceremonial stairway sweep up to a three-storey Baroque facade, painted a rich ochre. **Guided tours** (Tues–Sun: May–Sept 9am–noon & 1–5pm; Oct–April 9am–noon & 1–4pm; 600Ft) cover 25 of the 126 rooms in the palace, whose decaying splendour speaks of its one-time magnificence. The highlights of the ground floor are the panelled and gilded **Sala Terrena** and several blue-and-white **chinoiserie salons**, their walls painted by fairly mediocre artists – unlike the superb fresco on the ceiling of the **Banqueting Hall** upstairs, by J.B. Grundemann, which is so contrived that Apollo's chariot seems to be careering towards you across the sky whatever angle you view it from.

An adjacent room displays **Haydn memorabilia** from the period following his appointment as the Esterházy *Kapellmeister* in 1761, though the exhibition mainly consists of photocopied texts and old Hungaroton record sleeves. Haydn subsequently took over the direction of palace orchestra, opera house and marionette theatre, and wrote six great masses for performance here between 1796 and 1802. The palace also witnessed the premiere of Beethoven's Mass in C, personally conducted by the maestro in 1807. **Concerts** are held here in the summer

### THE ESTERHÁZY FAMILY

Originally of the minor nobility, the **Esterházy family** began its rise thanks to **Miklós I** (1583–1645), who married two rich widows and sided with the Habsburgs against Transylvania during the Counter-Reformation, for which he was rewarded with the title of Count. His son Paul was content to make his mark by publishing a songbook, *Harmonia Celestis*; but **Miklós II** "the Ostentatious" (1714–90) celebrated his inheritance of 600,000 acres and a dukedom by commissioning the palace in 1762. Boasting "anything the Kaiser can do, I can do better!", he spent 40,000 gulden a year on pomp and entertainment. Thereafter the family gradually declined, until under the Communists they were expropriated and "unpersoned". Today, one descendant drives trams in Vienna, while two others (from a separate branch of the family) are respected figures back home: the writer **Péter Esterházy** and his cousin, **Marton Esterházy**, formerly centre forward on the national football team. Internationally, however, the best-known bearer of the family name is **Joe Esterhasz**, the Hollywood scriptwriter of *Basic Instinct* and *Showgirls*.

months on Saturday and Sunday evenings; ask for a brochure from the ticket office. The tour over, you can wander around the neglected **French Gardens** at the back.

### Practicalities

The prospect of **staying at the palace** is almost irresistible. Rooms (②) with shared showers are available on the second floor of the east wing all year round, though it's essential to book over summer (☎99/370-971). Its furnishings are pretty basic, but the wing is enchanting, with lovely views. Alternatively, there are two pensions **in the village** – the dubious *Eszterházy Panzió* at Fő utca 20 (☎99/370-012; ②–③), and the preferable *Újvári Vendégház* at Kossuth utca 57/a (☎99/371-828; ③), which is signposted near the palace – while for campers there's *Dori Motel Camping Fertőd*, signposted up the road opposite (mid-April to mid-Oct; ☎99/370-193), which has tent pitches (①) and bungalows (③).

While the *Arkád* and *Gránátos* restaurants are sited just outside the palace, for really good food it's worth travelling a few kilometres down the road towards Sopron, to the village of Fertőszéplak, where you'll find the *Polgármester Vendéglő* behind the church at Széchenyi utca 39.

## The Széchenyi Mansion and Railway

Another feudal seat worth investigating lies 13km southeast of Sopron, near **NAGYCENK**. Buses from Sopron can drop you at the **Széchenyi Mansion** (*kastély*) on Route 84 (the Budapest road), 800m outside the village, which is on the Balaton road. As the family home of Count Széchenyi, "the greatest Hungarian" (see box opposite), it has never been allowed to fall into ruin, and was declared a museum in 1973. The museum (Tues–Sun: April–Oct 10am–6pm; Nov–March 10am–2pm; 150Ft) includes portraits and furniture from his household – the first in Hungary to be lit by gas lamps and to have flush toilets – and details his achievements, leading naturally into an exhibition on Hungarian industry since Széchenyi's day. Sadly the whole thing has a rather sterile feel to it, and the Hungarian labels on the exhibits leave you little the wiser.

Adjoining the mansion is a 200-year-old **Stud Farm** (Mon, Tues & Thurs–Sun 9am–5pm, Wed 1–5pm; ☎99/360-026), where **horse-riding** can be arranged. If you'd rather go for a walk, cross the road running past the mansion's front garden to find a lovely **avenue of limes** that's now a nature conservation area. At the far end of the three-kilometre-long avenue, there used to be a cell inhabited by the "Nagycenk Hermit", whom the Széchenys employed to pump the church organ on Sundays.

Just up the road to the left of the avenue is a shining example of Hungary's heritage industry – the **Széchenyi Railway**. This outdoor museum of **vintage steam trains** comes alive every weekend from April to October, when hundred-year-old engines run along a special line, past fields full of stooks of drying reeds, to terminate at Fertőboz, 4km away (though some turn back earlier). Advance details and tickets can be obtained from Lokomotiv Tourist in Sopron, or you can just turn up and hope for the best. Bicycles may be taken on the trains.

Down in the **village** stands the neo-Romanesque **Church of St Stephen**, designed by Ybl in 1864. Its portal bears the Széchenyi motto "If God is with us, who can be against us?" Across the road is a cemetery containing the **Széchenyi Mausoleum**, with a chapel decorated by István Dorfmeister, and a crypt including the graves of István and his wife Crescentia Seilern.

---

### COUNT SZÉCHENYI

**Count István Széchenyi** (1791–1860) was the outstanding figure of Hungary's Reform Era. As a young aide-de-camp he cut a dash at the Congress of Vienna and did the rounds of stately homes across Europe. The "odious Zoltán Karpathy" of Bernard Shaw's *Pygmalion* (and the musical *My Fair Lady*) was based on his exploits in England, where he steeplechased hell-for-leather, but still found time to examine factories and steam trains. Back in Hungary, he pondered solutions to his homeland's backwardness and offered a year's income from his estates towards the establishment of a Hungarian Academy. In 1830 he published *Hitel* (Credit), a hard-headed critique of the nation's feudal society.

Though politically conservative, Széchenyi was obsessed with **modernization**. A passionate convert to steam power after riding on the Manchester–Liverpool railway, he invited Britons to Hungary to build rail lines and the Lánchíd. He also imported steamships and dredgers, promoted horsebreeding and silk-making, and initiated the taming of the River Tisza and the blasting of a road through the Iron Gates of the Danube. Alas, his achievements were rewarded by a melancholy end. The 1848 Revolution and the triumph of Kossuth triggered a nervous breakdown, and, although Széchenyi resumed writing after his health improved, he committed suicide during a relapse.

---

## Practicalities

While private rooms advertised around the village are a less expensive option, it's tempting **to stay** at the comfortable *Kastély Hotel* in the west wing of the mansion (☎99/360-061; ⑤), whose guests can make free use of the spa facilities at Balf, and rent bicycles to visit nearby Lake Fertő. As an alternative to **eating** in the hotel's rather pricey dining room, there's the *Gyura Vendéglő* in the old train station building, which also does half portions at half price if you're not up to a full Austro-Hungarian-sized dish.

# Kőszeg and around

Nestled amidst the sub-Alpine hills along the Austrian border, the small town of **KŐSZEG** cherishes its status as the "Hungarian Thermopylae", and a town centre which can justifiably claim to be the prettiest in Hungary. While its castle recalls the medieval Magyar heroism that saved Vienna from the Turks, its Baroque houses and *bürgerlich* ambience reflect centuries of Austrian and German influence, when Kőszeg was known as Güns. Despite a summer blitzkrieg of tourists that briefly arouses excitement and avarice, this is basically a sleepy, old-fashioned town where people still leave fruit outside their houses and trust you to leave money for it.

## Arrival and accommodation

On **arrival** at Kőszeg's bus station, walk 150m up Kossuth utca to the Várkör, a horseshoe-shaped road that follows the course of the long-demolished medieval town walls; most things of interest lie within this area. Arriving at the train station in the south of town, catch a #1, #1A or #1Y bus as far as the junction of Fő tér and the Várkör.

Maps and **information** are available from Savaria Tourist at Várkör 69 (Mon–Fri 8am–4pm, Sat 8am–noon; ☎94/360-238) and IBUSZ, at Várkör 35–37 (Mon–Fri 8am–4pm, Sat 8am–noon; ☎94/360-376). You can **change money** at both these offices, or else use the ATM at Kossuth utca 18. If you're planning to visit all four of Kőszeg's museums, it makes sense to buy a **day ticket** (*napibérlet*; 250Ft), from either of the tourist offices, which covers them all.

### Accommodation

For private **rooms** enquire at either tourist office, or try Express at Városház utca 5 (Mon–Fri 8am–4pm, Sat 8am–noon; ☎94/360-247), which handles reservations in student hostels. There is a **campsite** by the swimming pool on Strand sétány (mid-April to mid-Oct; ①; ☎94/360-981).

**Írottkő Hotel**, Fő tér 4 (☎94/360-373). Central, modern and comfy – the best option for those who can afford it. ⑤.

**Jurisics (Tourist) Hostel**, in the yard through the first gate of the castle (☎94/360-227). Dormitory beds (①) and a few double and triple rooms. ②.

**Gyermeküdülő**, Űrhajósok utca 2 (☎94/360-169). A handsome old building in the green belt, ten minutes' walk southeast of the centre. Tennis facilities. ②.

**Arany Strucc Hotel**, Várkör 124 (☎94/360-323). "The Golden Ostrich" is the oldest hotel in Hungary, with bags of charm but fairly simple double rooms with showers. ③.

**Várkör Panzió**, Hunyádi János utca 19 (☎94/360-972). Flashy new ten-room pension west of the centre on the road leading up towards the Arborétum. Breakfast not included. ③.

## The Town

From **Fő tér**, where the **Church of the Sacred Heart** stands aloof from two hotels, Városház utca leads off to the **Heroes' Tower** (Tues–Sun 10am–5pm;

100Ft). Erected to mark the four-hundredth anniversary of the siege of Kőszeg, this fake medieval portal was one of several commemorative gates raised in the 1920s and 1930s, when Hungary was gripped by nostalgia for bygone glories and resentment towards the Successor States. You can climb the 27-metre-high tower for a view of the square below and the storks' nests perched on top of each chimney. The entrance to the tower also leads to the former Baroque General's House, the **Tábornok Ház**, containing examples of bookbinding and other historic crafts.

Beyond the archway lies **Jurisics tér**, a cobbled square whose antique buildings are watched over by two churches and a statue of the Virgin. The most eye-catching facades are those of the **Town Hall** (embellished with oval portraits of the Hungarian coat of arms and the Virgin and Child) and the beautifully sgraffitoed no. 7, now a pizzeria, on the eastern side of the square, where the pillory stood in medieval times. There's more to see inside the **Golden Unicorn Pharmacy Museum** at no. 11 (Tues–Sun 10am–5pm; 80Ft), which preserves an eighteenth-century apothecary's; there's another such establishment at Rákóczi utca 3, just south of Fő tér (March–Oct Tues–Sun 10am–5pm; 80Ft).

Past Jurisics tér's fountain (where a brass band often plays on Sundays and holidays), the Baroque **Church of St Emerich** precedes the older **Church of St James**, a handsome Gothic edifice containing the tomb of Miklós Jurisics (see below) and frescoes dating back to 1403. From here you can head north to Várkör, where you'll find a former **synagogue** at no. 38, which can only be viewed from the street. Built in 1859, the redbrick complex resembles an outlying bastion, having two crenellated towers with slit windows, and originally included a *yeshiva* and a ritual bath. Its dereliction is a sad reminder of the provincial Jewish communities that never recovered from the Holocaust, for – unlike the Budapest ghetto – their extermination was scheduled for the summer of 1944, when Eichmann's death-machine still ran at full throttle. Oddly, a **Lutheran bell-tower** stands next to the synagogue. When the Lutheran church behind it was built in 1783, József II had decreed that non-Catholic churches could not have bell-towers or steeples; this bell-tower was only built in 1930.

From Várkör you can head up Hunyadi utca to the west for ten minutes to the **Chernel Arboretum** of sub-Alpine trees (Mon–Thurs 8am–4pm, Fri 8am–2pm; 60Ft), or the same distance in the opposite direction to an outdoor **swimming pool** across the river: follow Kiss János utca eastwards from Várkör – a signpost in Fő tér points towards the *strand*. Otherwise, head back the other way to the castle.

## The Castle

The Turks swore that **Kőszeg Castle** was "built at the foot of a mountain difficult to climb; its walls wider than the whole world, its bastions higher than the fish of the Zodiac in heaven, and so strong that it defies description". Since the castle is actually quite small, with not a mountain in sight, the hyperbole is probably explained by its heroic defence during the month-long **siege of 1532**, when Sultan Süleyman and a hundred thousand Turks were resisted by four hundred soldiers under Captain Miklós Jurisics. After nineteen assaults the Sultan abandoned campaigning until the following year, by which time Vienna was properly defended. Today's visitors to the castle won't find anything dramatic when they cross the moat into an ugly yard that postwar additions have done nothing to enhance, or among the weapons and other relics in its **museum** (Tues–Sun 10am–5pm; 120Ft), but in summer the castle comes to life with the staging of **medieval games** in the moat and concerts in the yard (see overleaf).

# Eating, drinking and entertainment

Aside from hotel **restaurants**, the centre can offer the *Kulacs Étterem* at Várkör 12 (daily 6am–10pm) and the *Kék Huszár* on Károly Róbert tér, behind the castle (Tues–Sun; closes 9pm). Two excellent cheaper places are the *Betérő az Aranykoszorúhoz* at Temető utca 59 (closes at 9pm) and the *Szarvas Étterem* on Rákóczi utca.

For **drinking**, try the *Bécsikapu Söröző* on Rajnis utca, opposite St James' Church, or the beer garden at the back of the *Kék Huszár*. If you enjoy quaffing wine in medieval surroundings, the vaulted ceiling and high Gothic windows of the *Old Cellar* at Rajnis utca 10 provide an ideal setting. The best coffee in town is to be had at the *Ibrahim Kávézó* on Fő tér. You can buy cakes and pastries at Soproni Zoltán's lovely old-fashioned shop next to the *Café Senator* on Rákóczi utca. For nightlife, you have the choice of two **discos** in the castle, the *Monte Carlo* and the *Black Cat*.

Wine lovers are well catered for in Kőszeg, with a **Grape Festival** on April 24 (a tradition dating back to 1740), the **Summer Festival** in July and August, with theatre and opera in the castle yard, and a **Wine Festival** in September.

# Around Kőszeg

There are plenty of opportunities for **hiking** in the delightful countryside, with a well-signposted trail through the hills to the **Óház lookout tower**, 5km away. Set out along Temetö utca and then head back into town past the Fountain of the Seven Leaders, a spring with seven waterspouts named after the Magyar tribal chieftains, and a church with shrines of the stages of the cross. At the bottom of the hill you can turn left to reach a boating lake, or bear right for town, passing a chamber in the hillside where **St Stephen's Crown** was hidden for ten days in 1945, as it was being smuggled out of Hungary.

If you want to explore further afield, there are three attractive villages grouped south of Kőszeg. Local buses bound for Velem can drop you off in the pretty village of **CÁK** , 6km south of Kőszeg, with a protected row of old thatched cottages (April–Oct Tues–Sun 10am–6pm; 60Ft), actually little more than wattle-and-daub hovels with straw hats on, used at one time for wine-making and storage. The *csárda* near the bus stop is a good place for lunch, and if you want to continue you can pick up the walking trails, marked with a yellow stripe, to the neighbouring villages of Bozsok and Velem.

**VELEM**, 4km further down the road, is famous for its handicrafts and holds a **craft festival** in August. You can get information from Savaria Tourist at Rákóczi utca 73 (☎94/360-029), and reasonable rooms in the *Gomba Panzió* (☎94/360-036; ②–③). **BOZSOK**, 5km further on to the southwest, is basically a one-street village, with a seventeenth-century manor house in a lovely park at Rákóczi utca 1 serving as the *Castle Hotel* (☎94/360-960; ④); its rooms are comfy but disappointingly dull. A cheaper option is the *Szilvia Panzió* at Rákóczi utca 120 (☎94/361-009; ②), which also has **camping** facilities. The local riding school offers **pony trekking** in the region.

Lastly, there's the resort of **BÜKFÜRDŐ**, 16km east of Kőszeg, which is much touted for its healing waters and 18-hole golf course, but wildly expensive by Hungarian standards, and fairly soulless. The **spa complex** was obviously constructed to lure Western tourists and their money to Hungary, and the golf course is a kind of manicured Country Club, again run primarily for the benefit of foreigners, though native nouveaux riches can also be seen on the links.

# Szombathely and around

Commerce has been the lifeblood of **SZOMBATHELY** ("Saturday market") ever since the town was founded by Emperor Claudius in 43 AD to capitalize on the Amber Road from the Baltic to the Mediterranean. Savaria, as it was then called, soon became the capital of Pannonia, and a significant city in the Roman empire. It was here that Septimus Severus was proclaimed emperor in 193 AD and Saint Martin of Tours was born in 317. Under Frankish rule in the eighth century, the town, known as Steinamanger, prospered through trade with Germany. Nowadays, it is Austrians who boost the economy, flooding across to shop, get their hair done or seek medical treatment in the town which they have nicknamed "the discount store".

From a tourist's standpoint, the chief attractions are the outdoor Village Museum (*Skanzen*) and Roman ruins, and a Belváros stuffed with Baroque and Neoclassical architecture. Szombathely is also the base for a side trip to the beautiful Romanesque church at Ják and, further out, Sárvár Castle, home of the infamous "Blood Countess" Báthori. If you're here at Easter time, there are colourful religious processions in Szombathely and other towns in the region.

## Arrival, information and accommodation

Arriving at the **train station**, walk west along Széll Kálmán utca to get to the centre (just under 1km), or catch a #2, #3, #5, #7, #7Y or #11 bus to Mártírok tere, close to Fő tér. The intercity **bus station** is next to the Romkert, near the cathedral, so arriving there makes things even easier. As is often the case, the Belváros is compact enough to cover on foot with no risk of getting lost.

**Information** can be obtained from the helpful Savaria Tourist at Mártírok tere 1, on the corner of Király utca (Mon–Fri 8am–5pm, Sat 8am–noon; ☎94/312-348), a second branch on Savaria tér at the bottom of Király utca, or the Szombathelyi Turisztikai Iroda at Király utca 11 (Mon–Fri 10am–noon & 1–5pm, Sat 10am–1pm; ☎94/341-810). Train information and tickets are available from MÁV Tours, Thököly utca 39. You can **change money** at any of the tourist offices, or use the ATMs outside Savaria Tourist on Savaria tér and the Budapest Bank, Kőszegi utca 1–3, just off Fő tér. The **post office** is at Kossuth utca 18.

### Accommodation

The cheapest form of accommodation are dormitory **beds** (①) in the *kollégium* facing the cathedral or one of the colleges 50m west of the bus station – available over summer and at weekends all year round through IBUSZ, Fő tér 44 (Mon–Fri 8am–4pm, Sat 9am–noon; ☎94/314-141), or Savaria Tourist. *Tópart* **campsite** at Kondics utca 4, by the Anglers' Lake, a ten-minute walk from the Village Museum (☎94/314-766; May–Sept), has huts sleeping two (②) or four (④).

Of the **hotels**, *Hotel Claudius*, at Bartók körút 39, where the ring road passes near Lake Gondola (☎94/313-760; ⑤) is a modernistic pile, with sauna, gym and restaurant; the centrally located *Hotel Savaria*, Mártírok tere 4 (☎94/311-440; ⑤), is a turn-of-the-century establishment with a ritzy restaurant; and *Alvég Panzió*, Izsó utca 18 (☎94/312-015; ③), is in the suburb of Szentkirály (bus #17 from the central

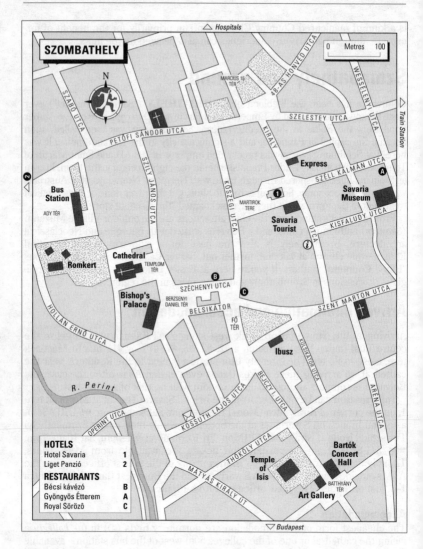

**SZOMBATHELY**

HOTELS
Hotel Savaria — 1
Liget Panzió — 2

RESTAURANTS
Bécsi kávézó — B
Gyöngyös Étterem — A
Royal Söröző — C

bus station). *Liget Panzió*, Szent István park (☎94/314-168; ③) is a motel-style place in a park, fifteen minutes' walk west of the centre, or take bus #7 or #7Y).

## The Belváros

**Exploring the Belváros** doesn't take long unless you spend time in its museums and galleries, and if your appetite for both is limited it's best to make a beeline for the cathedral and the Romkert, and conserve some enthusiasm for the Village Museum. Otherwise, it may be worth buying a day ticket (300Ft) that covers the

Savaria, Smidt and Village museums and the Romkert (sold at all of these places). Note that winter opening times are uncertain; enquire at Savaria Tourist for details.

To get an idea of Szombathely's history, start with the **Savaria Museum** at Kisfaludy utca 9 (Tues–Sun 10am–5pm; 100Ft), which is also accessible through the park from Széll Kálmán utca. This local archeology display starts with mammoth tusks and works through to Roman times, the latter represented by reliefs of mythical figures and other stonework.

Further west, the Belváros turns monumental around Berszenyi Dániel tér, dominated by the **County Hall** and an eighteenth-century **Bishop's Palace** whose facade is crowned by statues of Prudence, Justice, Fortitude and Temperance. In one of its wings, the intriguing **Smidt Museum** (Tues–Fri 10am–6pm; 100Ft) represents the fruits of a life-long obsession. As a boy, Lajos Smidt scoured battlefields for souvenirs and collected advertisements and newspapers, diversifying into furniture and pictures as an adult. The destruction of many items during World War II only spurred him to redouble his efforts during retirement and, finally, he founded this museum to house his extraordinary collection. Highlights include huge Celtic swords, Austro-Hungarian uniforms, the dancing slippers of Széchenyi's wife, and clocks galore.

### The Cathedral, the Romkert and Bartók Concert Hall

Szombathely's **Cathedral**, a few paces north of Berzsenyi Dániel tér, postdates the great fire that ravaged the town in the late eighteenth century, which explains why it is Neoclassical rather than Baroque or Gothic. Unfortunately, its exuberant frescoes by Maulbertsch were destroyed when US bombers attacked the town in the last months of World War II, and painstaking structural restoration has stopped short of recreating his work. A glass-fronted coffin in the south aisle contains the grisly remains of a mitred saint.

Around the corner lies the **Romkert** or Garden of Ruins (April–Nov Tues–Sat 9am–5pm; 80Ft), comprising a crossroads and some fine segments of mosaic floor from Roman Savaria. Recent archeological research would suggest this was either the site of the Basilica of St Quirinus, the largest church in Pannonia, or, more likely, the Roman Governor's Palace.

Another relic of ancient Savaria only came to light in 1955, when construction work along Rákóczi utca uncovered the **Temple of Isis**, dating from the second century AD, one of only three such temples extant in Europe. Unfortunately, however, the ruins are closed for the present. Just south of the temple, the **Szombathely Gallery** hosts temporary exhibitions.

Across the road from the gallery stands Szombathely's former **synagogue**, a lovely piece of neo-Byzantine architecture, built in 1881 and now home to the **Bartók Concert Hall** and music college. Sadly, all that now remains of the town's Jewish presence is a plaque recording that "4228 of our Jewish brothers and sisters were deported from this place to Auschwitz on 4 June, 1944".

# Beyond the Belváros

Szombathely's northern suburbs harbour two more attractions which can be reached by bus #2 from Petőfi utca. The **Kámoni Arboretum** (Tues–Sun: March–Oct 8am–6pm; Nov–Feb 8am–4pm; 80Ft) contains 2500 different kinds of trees, shrubs and flowers, with an especially varied assortment of roses, while just up the road is the grandly named **Gotthárd Astrophysics Observatory**

(*Csillag Vizsgáló*; Mon–Fri 9am–4pm; 100Ft), with an interesting exhibition on cosmology.

Northwest of the centre lie the **Rowing Lake** (*Csónakázótó*) and the **Anglers' Lake** (*Horgásztó*), two smallish ponds where locals fish and go boating near an outdoor **thermal bath**. Bus #7 takes you to both lakes and to the **Village Museum** (*Skanzen*) at Árpád utca 30, beyond the Anglers' Lake (April–Oct Tues–Sun 10am–6pm; 100Ft). Eighteenth- and nineteenth-century farmsteads are reconstructed here, culled from 27 villages in the Őrség region, and furnished with all the necessities and knick-knacks, making an architectural progression from log cabins to timber-framed wattle-and-daub dwellings. Every other month there are demonstrations of traditional folk crafts and dances of the region.

The green-belt district south of the lakes includes a small **game park** (*Vadaszkert*) with deer, pheasants and other wildlife – nothing to get too excited about, but a nice place for a picnic. The park is situated on Víztorony utca, southwest of the *Liget Panzió*; alight from bus #7 on Jókai utca and walk past the water tower for ten minutes.

## Eating, drinking and entertainment

Despite its size and relative prosperity, there isn't a great choice of **restaurants** in Szombathely. The *Gyöngyös Étterem* at Széll Kálmán utca 8 (closed Mon) offers good value for money, as does the chandeliered restaurant in the *Hotel Savaria*, though it doesn't deign to list prices on its menu, and it's worth checking whether the *Pannónia Étterem* on Savaria tér has reopened yet. Another option is the *Royal Söröző* on Fő tér, which serves tasty meals and draught beer and has tables outside, while the *Saláta bár*, at the end of Belsikátor utca, offers a few vegetarian salads (open till 8pm). On the same street is a patisserie with amusingly low stools, and there's a nice café at Széll Kálmán utca 5.

There is a strong musical tradition in Szombathely, and the town even has its own orchestra, the **Savaria Symphony**, and an early music ensemble, the Capella Savaria. There are also several cultural festivals, the most important of which are the **Spring Days** in late March and the **Autumn Festival** in September to mid-October. The international **Bartók Festival** in late July is another highlight, with seminars and concerts. At other times of the year, ask what's happening at the Bartók Concert Hall, the hideous 1960s **Cultural Centre** on Március 15 tér, or the cultural hall on Ady tér, west of the bus station.

## Around Szombathely: Ják

With hourly buses from Szombathely to **JÁK**, 10km southwest, you can easily pay a visit to Hungary's most outstanding **Romanesque abbey church** (daily: April–Oct 8am–6pm; Nov–March 10am–2pm; free), which is far more impressive than the scaled-down replica in Budapest's Városliget. The church is sited on a hilltop overlooking the feudal domain of its founder Márton Nagy (1220–56), who personally checked that his serfs attended Sunday services – and whipped any who failed to do so.

The church is similar in plan to its ruined contemporaries at Zsámbék (see p.207) and Lébény (see p.218), and likewise influenced by the Scottish Benedictine church in Regensburg, the point from which Norman architecture spread into Central Europe. Its most striking feature is the magnificent **portal** on the western facade, where Christ and his apostles surmount a six-ordered Norman zigzag arch. The church was restored in the 1890s by Frigyes Schulek, the architect of the Fishermen's Bastion in Budapest, who added the stumpy spires atop Ják's towers. For a 50Ft coin, you get four minutes of light to view the **frescoes**, which the English-speaking priest may take the time to explain. In the north aisle is an exquisite medieval **altarpiece**, recently discovered in the nearby church of St James; a kiosk outside sells books on the surrounding area. There are several *Zimmer frei* signs around the village, but there's nothing much else to see, so you might as well return to Szombathely or push on elsewhere.

# Sárvár

**SÁRVÁR**, 25km east of Szombathely on the River Rába, is the most recently developed **spa centre** in Hungary, following the discovery of hot springs 25 years ago. The spas were developed to attract hard currency from German and Austrian tourists and still do a roaring trade, but aside from wallowing and quaffing, the town's only real attraction is the fortress that gives Sárvár its name – "Mud Castle".

While this description might have been appropriate in the Dark Ages, it hardly applies to **Sárvár Castle** today (Tues–Sun 10am–6pm; 120Ft). Modified by many owners over the centuries, its pentagonal layout and palatial interior is owed to the **Nádasdy family**, particularly Tamás Nádasdy, who hired Italian architects and made this a centre of Renaissance humanism. It was here that the first Hungarian translation of the New Testament was printed in 1541. The **Festival Hall** is decorated with Dorfmeister frescoes of biblical episodes, allegories of art and science, and murals depicting the "Black Knight" Ferenc Nádasdy routing the Turks. In the castle **museum** are weapons, uniforms and memorabilia associated with Tamás and his son Ferenc, but barely a reference to the latter's wife, the infamous Countess Báthori (see box overleaf).

From the castle you can follow the signs to the **thermal baths** by the bridge over the River Rába, 1km along Rákóczi utca. The complex includes both indoor and outdoor hot pools and special treatment facilities; ask at the *Sport Hotel*. There are **tennis courts** and a **riding school** in the vicinity.

## Practicalities

Sárvár is accessible by hourly trains and irregular buses from Szombathely. The castle stands at the centre of town, with the train station to the north (bus #1 or #1Y), the bus station 500m west along Batthyány utca, and the thermal baths to the southeast. Savaria Tourist, by the entrance to the castle (Mon–Fri 8am–noon & 1–5pm, Sat 8am–noon; ☎95/320-578), can supply **information**, change money and book rooms. The main **post office** is at Várkerület 32 near the castle, and there is an **ATM** at Kossuth tér 1.

### Accommodation

Even during the busiest period in August you should be able to get private accommodation (②) through Savaria Tourist or tent-space at the *Thermal* campsite near the baths (☎95/320-228; mid-March to Oct), which can be reached by taking bus #1Y to the end of the line.

**Hotel Thermal**, Rákóczi út 1 (☎95/323-999). The town's most expensive hotel, with its own indoor and outdoor thermal pools, sauna, gym and curative facilities. ⑦.

**Lisztes Vendégház**, Rákóczi út 57/A (☎95/320-456). Simple modern house in the centre of town. ③.

**Platán Fogadó**, Hunyadi utca 23 (☎95/326-906). A small pension en route to the castle, with shared showers and toilets and its own restaurant. ③.

**Sport Hotel**, Rákóczi utca 46A (☎95/324-444). Comfy hotel offering a gym, sauna, free entrance to the thermal baths and discounts at the local riding school. ⑤.

**Thermal Panzió**, Temető utca 1A (☎95/320-377). A modern pension, whose price includes free entry to the baths. ③.

**Vadkert Fogadó**, Vadkert utca (☎95/320-045). Rustic-style pension in an old hunting lodge between the castle and the baths. ④.

## Eating and entertainment

The *Platán*, *Sport* and *Vadkert* hotels all have good **restaurants**, the latter specializing in game dishes, while the *Matróz Vendéglő* on Árpád utca is the place for fish. More elegant are the *Várkapu*, opposite the entrance to the castle, and the *HBH* by the *Thermal Hotel*.

Sárvár's annual **International Folklore Festival** is celebrated in mid-August in the castle's courtyard. At intervals over summer there are also so-called **History Days**, with concerts, traditional dancing and singing.

---

### COUNTESS ERZSÉBET BÁTHORI

**Countess Erzsébet Báthori** has gone down in history as *Die Blutgräfin* (The Blood Countess), who tortured to death over six hundred women and girls, sometimes biting chunks of flesh from their necks and breasts – the origin of legends that she bathed in the blood of virgins to keep her own skin white and translucent. Yet there's a strong case that the accusations arose from a conspiracy against her by the Palatine of Hungary, **Count Thurzó**, and her own son-in-law, Miklós Zrínyi, grandson of the hero of Szigetvár.

Born in 1560, the offspring of two branches of the Báthori family (whose intermarriage might explain several cases of lunacy in the dynasty), Erzsébet was married at the age of fifteen to Ferenc Nádasdy and assumed responsibility for their vast estates, which she inherited upon his death in 1604. To the chagrin of her sons-in-law and the Palatine, she refused to surrender any of them. Worse still from a Habsburg standpoint, the election of her nephew, "Crazy" Gábor Báthori, as Prince of Transylvania, raised the prospect of a Báthori alliance that would upset the balance of power and border defences on which Habsburg rule depended.

In December 1610 Thurzó raided her residence at Aachtice, and claimed to have caught her literally red-handed. Under torture, her associates testified to scores of **secret burials** at Sárvár, Aachtice, and elsewhere, and the Countess was immediately walled up in a room at Aachtice, where she died in 1614. Although Thurzó amassed nearly three hundred depositions, no trial was ever held, as the death of Gábor Báthori reduced her political significance to the point that it served nobody's interests to besmirch the Nádasdy and Báthori names.

While there's little doubt that there was a **conspiracy** against the Countess, it's hard to believe that she was totally innocent. There were accusations of her cruelty at Sárvár even before her widowhood, and the theory that the tortures were actually medical treatments doesn't explain the most atrocious cases. Probably the best one can say is that she was a victim of double standards in an era when brutality was rife and the power of nobles unbridled.

# Körmend, Szentgotthárd and the Őrség

The hilly region to the **south of Szombathely** is defined by the River Rába, which flows from the Styrian Alps across the Little Plain to join the Danube at Győr. Its valley forms a natural route into Austria, straddled by two small towns with a sub-Alpine ambience and historic links with the now independent state of **Slovenia**. Though neither merits a special trip, Körmend and Szentgotthárd make pleasant stopovers en route to the border, and good jumping-off points for the Őrség region, further south. Both towns are accessible by train from Szombathely.

## Körmend

**KÖRMEND**, 25km from Szombathely, boasts a massive Baroque **Batthyány-Strattman Mansion**, a grand building with four corner towers built upon the foundations of the town's medieval castle, just off Szabadság tér, whose present-day use hardly does justice to it. The small **local history museum** (April–Oct Tues–Sun 9am–noon & 1–5pm; 100Ft) has some intriguing objects and pictures of the old town, but no English information, while in another building overlooking the entrance courtyard is a small **Shoe Museum** (Mon–Fri 9am–5pm, Sat 8am–noon; free), whose exhibits include the footwear of various ethnic groups and a few distinguished Hungarian personalities. The **arboretum** beside the mansion is a conservation area, with many old trees and allegedly the finest magnolias in Hungary; access is from the river-facing side of Rákóczi út.

Körmend's **train and bus stations** are five minutes' walk north from the centre of town. Savaria Tourist at Rákóczi út 11 (Mon–Fri 9am–5pm, Sat 8am–noon; ☎94/410-161) can supply **information** and book private rooms, if available. Otherwise you can **stay** at the *Rába Hotel* at Bercsényi utca 24, near the station (☎94/410-089; ②), or the *Halászcsárda Panzió* by the river at Bajcsy-Zsilinszky utca 20 (☎94/410-069; ②), which has a decent fish restaurant.

## Szentgotthárd

Twenty-nine kilometres west of Körmend and 5km off the road to the Rábafüzes/Heiligenkreuz border crossing, **SZENTGOTTHÁRD** is a pleasant Baroque town that grew up around a twelfth-century Cistercian abbey. The influence of nearby Austria is manifest in its tidy streets and ubiquitous recycling bins. The former presence of Slovenes here is evinced by a collection of their costumes in the **Pável Ágoston Museum** (Tues–Sun 10am–6pm; 80Ft), which, like the Dorfmeister fresco in Szentgotthárd's **Baroque Church**, also commemorates the Battle of Mögersdorf in nearby Austria in 1664, when European mercenaries under General Montecuccoli repulsed a Turkish army. Tradition has it that one hundred Turks drowned in the River Lapincs, which joins the Rába at Szentgotthárd. A mere stream in summer, it becomes an icy torrent as the snow thaws in the Styrian Alps. Otherwise, bicycle rental is available in some of the neighbouring villages in the Őrség (see overleaf).

### Practicalities

Szentgotthárd's **bus and train stations** are both east of the River Rába, which you cross as you walk towards the church steeple; from here continue up to the right to the town centre. Savaria Tourist at Kossuth út 2 (Mon–Fri 8am–5pm, Sat 8am–noon; ☎94/380-029) can help with money-changing, **information** and **accommodation**. The *Motel Alpokalja*, an uninspiring modern block on Füzesi út, the main road running from the north (☎94/380-169; ②), is worth trying, as is the *Rézi Panzió* on Mártírok útja (☎94/380-797; ③). The best restaurant in town is probably the *Café Picasso* in the centre of town at Széll Kálmán tér 18, next door to the *Tiffany Bar* – a hangout for local youth (daily 9am–10pm). For a taste of authentic working man's Hungary, try the nearby *Sikátor Vendéglő* off Deák Ferenc utca (closed Sun evening), where they serve Szalon Sör, brewed in Pécs.

# The Őrség

The forested **Őrség region** has guarded Hungary's southwestern marches since the time of the Árpáds. Dotted with hilltop watchtowers and isolated hamlets, every man here was sworn to arms in lieu of paying tax. The people became used to their freedom and refused to be bound into serfdom by the Batthyány family, whose seat was at nearby Körmend. Moist winds from the Jura Mountains make this the rainiest, greenest part of Hungary, while the heavy clay soil allows no form of agriculture except raising cattle, but provides ample raw material for the local pottery industry. Until well into this century, when the region declined as villagers migrated to Zalaegerszeg, houses were constructed of wooden beams plastered with clay. Whether tourism and the encouragement of crafts will revive the Őrség remains to be seen; meanwhile, its soft landscapes and folksy architecture are a powerful attraction.

There are several **approaches**, depending on your starting point. Trains from Szombathely to Szentgotthárd are met by buses to Őriszentpéter via Szalafő – two of the nicest villages. Alternatively, you could head for Zalalövő by train from Körmend or Zalaegerszeg (four daily) and travel on to Őriszentpéter (14km) via Pankasz, hitching or hiking if a bus doesn't materialize. Given the limited services and quiet roads, cycling is the best way of **getting around**. Bikes can be rented at several villages, but it's wise to bring waterproof clothing for the inevitable drizzles.

## Őriszentpéter
**ŐRISZENTPÉTER** is the obvious base for exploring the region, a straggling village made up of groups of houses (*szer*), built on nine separate ridges to escape flooding, each with one road bearing the same name – Városszer, Szikaszer, etc – and numbered round in a circle. In June the village hosts the **Őrség Fair**, with folk music, dancing and handicrafts. The village has bus connections to Szentgotthárd, Körmend and Zalalövő, and boasts the best tourist facilities in the region, including a tourist **information** office at Városszer 55 (Mon–Fri 9am–5pm; ☎94/429-019). The *Őrségi Fogadó*, next door (☎94/428-046), has rooms (④) and camping facilities (mid-April to mid-Oct), while there are cheaper **rooms** advertised along Templomszer, and at Városszer 58 (☎94/428-037; ②). You can get decent **meals** at the *Bognár Étterem*, Kovácsszer 98, and the *Lukács Vendéglő*, Városszer 27, but the best place to try the local speciality *dödölle* (fried potato and onion dumplings served with soured cream) is the *Centrum Étterem* at the main crossroads (daily 6am–10pm). **Pony trekking** can be arranged from the house at Szikaszer 18.

On the edge of the village, beside the road to Szalafő, stands a beautiful thirteenth-century **Romanesque church** with a finely carved portal and traces of frescoes inside, which can only be properly seen by attending Sunday mass (9.30am; not the first Sun of the month), as the stairs up to the choir loft that provide access at other times offer a poor view of the interior.

## Szalafő Village Museum

The village of **SZALAFŐ**, 6km up the road from Őriszentpéter, likewise consists of small separate settlements on adjacent ridges. From the church and bar that constitute the centre, it's 3km to Pityerszer, a mini **Village Museum** (April–Oct Tues–Sun 10am–6pm; 100Ft) of heavy-timbered houses, typical of the region, that gives a good idea of life as it was five or six decades ago. Notice the little hen ladders that run up the sides of the houses. There are two buses every day from Őriszentpéter to Szalafő-felső, the end stop, and you'll find the museum a further kilometre's walk in the same direction. Tickets are sold at the *büfé* across the road from the museum, where you can also get refreshments.

If you happen to be here on **May 1**, look out for **dancing** around the tall, slender may tree. The origins of this ritual have long been lost, but many pine trees in the Órség region are stripped of their lower branches as teenaged boys shin up to retrieve bottles of champagne suspended from the higher branches. Some even plant may trees in their girlfriends' gardens in the middle of the night.

Lots of houses advertise **rooms** for rent; try the one at Csörgőszer 20 (☎94/428-623; ③), run by the same people who run the bar in the centre of the village. They can also direct you to several houses selling delicious goat and cow cheese (*sajt*) and milk (*tej*). The *Hubertus Vendégház* at the entrance to the village serves hot **meals**.

## Other villages in the region

Seven kilometres east of Őriszentpéter at **PANKASZ**, you can stop to admire the rustic **wooden bell-tower**; follow signs off the main road to the *Posta* for 200m. **Bikes** and **rooms** can be rented at **HEGYHÁTSZENTJAKAB**, 3km further north, off the road between Zalalövő and Pankasz, where you will find the comfortable *Trófea Panzió* (☎94/426-230; ⑤) and a popular swimming **lake**, the *Vadása tó*.

More appealing, though, are two villages along a minor road **south of Őriszentpéter**. In the hills along the Slovenian border, 12km away, the tiny village of **MAGYARSZOMBATFA**, with a population of three hundred, preserves the old tradition of **Habán pottery**, sold through the local *Fazekasház* (*fazekas* is the Hungarian for "potter"). The road continues 6km southeast to **VELEMÉR**, whose single-aisled Romanesque church contains beautiful frescoes from 1377. To view them, ask for the key at the house signposted *Templomkulcs*. The church lies across the fields, hidden in the trees, about 500m from the main road. There are two or three buses a day to Velemér from Őriszentpéter via Magyarszombatfa.

### CROSSING INTO SLOVENIA

Hungary has two **border crossings into Slovenia**. Most traffic heads to the Rédics/Dolga Vas crossing, 30km south on Route 75, running down from Keszthely.The Hodos/Salovci crossing is quieter; the turn-off is midway between Őriszentpéter and Magyarszombatfa.

# Zalaegerszeg

The county capital **ZALAEGERSZEG**, familiarly known as Zala, began to meta-
morphose after the discovery of oil in 1937, and is now the most industrialized
town in southwestern Hungary, with a population of 70,000. Despite the futuristic
television tower featured on tourist brochures and the bleak downtown area of

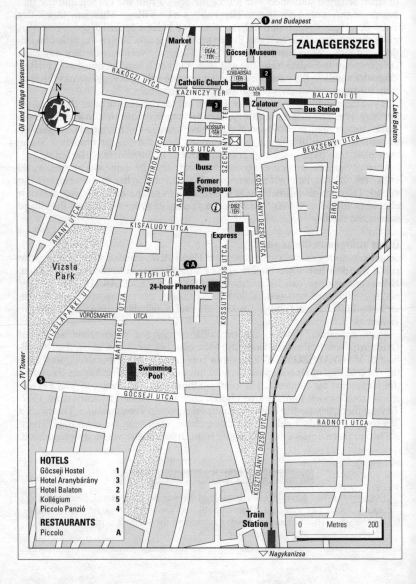

ZALAEGERSZEG

HOTELS
Göcseji Hostel     1
Hotel Aranybárány   3
Hotel Balaton     2
Kollégium       5
Piccolo Panzió    4

RESTAURANTS
Piccolo        A

housing estates and landscaped plazas, Zala hasn't totally forgotten its past: vestiges of folk culture from the surrounding region are preserved in two museums and an annual festival.

Zala's north–south axis, Kossuth utca, is pretty drab until it reaches several squares at the northern end, more like wide streets than plazas, where Baroque and Art Nouveau buildings offer a touch of colour and an idea of how Zala looked before postwar planning changed its appearance. It's somehow appropriate that the town's most famous sons exemplify the Hungarian genius for making the best of an adverse situation.

The sculptor **Zsigmond Kisfaludi Strobl** enjoyed early success with busts of British royals and Hungarian aristocrats, and then switched to producing glorified Workers (and the Liberation Monument in Budapest) under Communism, earning himself medals and the nickname "Step from Side to Side". You can chuckle over his oeuvre at the **Göcsej Museum** at Batthyány utca 2 (Tues–Sun: April–Sept 10am–6pm; March 15–30 & Oct 10am–5pm; Nov to March 14 10am–3pm; 150Ft). In the immediate vicinity, Deák tér bears a statue of the local politician **Ferenc Deák**, who negotiated the historic Compromise between Hungary and the Habsburg empire in 1867 that created the Dual Monarchy. Off to the northwest is a lively **market** selling Göcsej cheese and other local produce.

Heading south, it's five minutes' walk to Zala's former **synagogue**, an unmistakeable, lilac-painted edifice at Ady Endre utca 14. As it's now a concert hall and gallery, one is usually able to peek in to see the Eclectic-style interior, designed by József Stern in 1903, though it has been marred by lurid stained-glass windows and a massive organ, installed in the 1960s.

## The Oil and Village museums

Zala's main attractions are two outdoor museums near a dead tributary of the River Zala on the northwestern outskirts of town (bus #1, #1Y or #8Y). Giant pumps, drills and other hardware dominate the **Oil Museum** (April–Oct Tues–Sun 10am–6pm; 100Ft), which examines the history of the petroleum industry in Hungary. Unfortunately for the economy, exploratory drilling in the 1950s and 1960s discovered far more hot springs than oil, and the most promising field was found to straddle the Romanian border, so domestic production amounts to a fraction of Hungary's requirements.

The **Village Museum** next door (Tues–Sun: April–Sept 10am–6pm; March 15–30 & Oct 10am–5pm; Nov to March 14 10am–3pm; 150Ft) assembles traditional dwellings, barns and artefacts from the surrounding **Göcsej region**. Traditionally, this was so poor and squalid that no one would admit to being a part of it, and enquirers were always hastily assured that its boundaries began a few miles on, in the next village.

# Practicalities

**Arriving** at the intercity bus station, it's a few minutes' walk to Zalatour, Kovács tér 1 (Mon–Fri 8am–5pm, Sat 8am–noon; ☎92/311-443), while if you're riding a bus (#1, #7, #10 or #11) into the centre from the train station, you can stop by at Tourinform, Kossuth utca 17–19 (Mon–Fri 10am–1pm & 3–6pm, May–Sept also Sat 10am–1pm;☎92/316-160), which is the best source of **information**. You can change **money** at Zalatour or use the ATM at Kisfaludy utca 15–17, near Tourinform. Zala's main **post office** is at Kossuth tér 6A.

## Accommodation

Aside from the chance of dormitory beds (①), the cheapest **accommodation** is a private room (②) from Zalatour or IBUSZ at Eötvös utca 6–10 (Mon–Fri 8am–5pm; ☎92/311-458).

**Aranybárány Hotel**, Széchenyi tér 1 (☎92/314-100). The very comfortable "Golden Lamb" is in a fine old building in the centre, with a 1970s extension. ⑤.

**Claudia Vendégház**, Körmendi út 16 (☎92/321-255). A six-room pension with bowling alley. Discounts for stays of more than one night. ②–③.

**Balaton Hotel**, Balatoni út 2A (☎92/314-400). Hideous modern block, but very central, just across from the bus station. ④.

**Számviteli Főiskola Kollégium**, Vizslaparki út 48 (☎92/312-560). Fairly basic double (②) and triple (③) rooms near the Youth Park, ten minutes' walk from the centre, usually available all year round.

**Gőcseji Hostel**, Kaszaházi utca 2 (☎92/311-580). A cheap hostel sharing a building with a Chinese restaurant, which may explain the odours. ②.

**Piccolo Panzió**, Petőfi Sándor utca 16 (☎92/314-932). Family pension with garden restaurant and minibars in the rooms. Booking essential. ③.

## Eating and entertainment

Of the hotel **restaurants** offering decent food, the best one is at the *Piccolo Panzió* (see above), which is closed on Sunday. Local **entertainment** consists of whatever's on at the cultural centre off Ady utca, or at the Sportscsarnok, a few blocks east along Balatoni út, while for nightlife, try the wonderfully seventies nightclub in the *Aranybárány Hotel* (Tues–Sat), or the *Hangulat* music bar on Kossuth utca. Though its future is uncertain, it's also worth asking about the **Göcsej Days**, a folklore festival previously held in August, which may resume in the future if Zala can afford it.

# SOUTHERN TRANSDANUBIA

Heading for **southern Transdanubia** from Zala, Budapest or Balaton, it's best to aim directly for **Pécs**, the region's attractive capital. Although the **Völgység**, the valley region between Lake Balaton and the **Mecsek Hills**, is pretty to drive through, none of the towns is really worth stopping for. Travelling from Balaton by train, however, you might have to change at **Nagykanizsa** or **Kaposvár**, and can take in their sights between connections. Express trains from Budapest to Pécs usually run via Dombóvár, while intercity buses are routed through **Szekszárd**, the nicest small town in the region, within reach of the lovely **Forest of Gemenc**. On the way back to Budapest, trainspotters can visit the museum of locos at **Paks**, while devotees of 1950s' Socialist-Realist aesthetics will relish the steel town of **Dunaújváros**.

# Nagykanizsa

**NAGYKANIZSA** (pronounced "Nodge-konizha") is a quiet backwater that makes a pleasant stopover, but isn't worth a special trip. In its day it was a proud fortress town straddling the River Principális, which together with Szigetvár and Siklós bore the brunt of Turkish assaults during the first decades of the occupation and finally succumbed. Unlike the others, the fortress at Nagykanizsa no longer exists, and the town is best known for its brewery, producing a brand named Kanizsai Kinizsi after the folk hero Pál Kinizsi, a miller's son of legendary strength who reputedly once used a millstone as a tray to serve a drink to a woman he admired.

The compact centre of Nagykanizsa consists of two leafy squares connected by Fő út. Coming in from the train station you'll pass a large well-tended **Jewish cemetery** (Mon–Fri 8am–4pm, Sun 8am–1pm), attesting to the big community that once existed here; if it's closed, ask for the key from Sasvári Lajos at Őrház utca 6. The **synagogue**, in the courtyard of Fő út 6 (Tues–Sat 2–6pm; free), was built in 1821 with the support of Count Fülöp Batthyány, whose ancestors settled Jewish families on their estate. In April 1944, all three thousand Jews were deported to Auschwitz; only three hundred survived, of whom about 120 are still alive to meet in the prayer rooms in the courtyard opposite the synagogue, which was sold off to the municipality in 1982. Though sometimes used for concerts, it remains in a sorry state, and even had its chandelier stolen in 1997.

Across the road at Fő út 5, the **Thury György Museum** (Mon–Fri 9am–3pm; 80Ft) mounts temporary exhibitions and displays a few Roman sarcophagi in its entrance way. You'd do better to go looking for the **parish church** on Zárda utca, built with masonry from the town's fortress, and originally a mosque where Nagykanizsa's last Turkish overlord, Mustafa Pasha, is buried in a tomb into which baptismal fonts have been cut. To get there, retrace your steps to Ady utca and turn left just beyond the post office at no. 10.

Alternatively, head up Fő út to reach Deák tér, a pleasant square with several café terraces overlooking a bizarre **statue** of the poet Petőfi urging a twentieth-century soldier to throw a grenade at the nearest row of shops. The monument honours the 48th Infantry Regiment in which he served in 1848–49, though it chiefly refers to their World War I campaigns, and was created in the Horthy era by Kisfaludi Strobl.

### Practicalities

**Arriving** by bus you'll be dropped on the western side of Erzsébet tér, in the centre; coming from the train station you can walk there in fifteen minutes or catch a bus (#21 or #23) along Ady utca, which runs down from Fő út. Zalatour at Fő út 13 (Mon–Fri 8am–5pm, Sat 8am–noon; ☎93/311-185) can supply **information**, change money (there are also ATMs at Deák tér 15 and Ady utca 6), and book dormitory beds (in summer) and private rooms. Other **accommodation** includes the pricey *Hotel Central* at Erzsébet tér 23 (☎93/314-000; ⑤), the grungy *Tourist Hostel* at Fő út 24 (☎93/312-340; ②), but there is a good pension, the *Hugi Panzió* at Kiraly utca 20 (☎93/319-400; ③). The best **places to eat** are the *Kremzner Étterem*, Deák tér 11, and the *Ady*, Ady utca 5 (closed Sun). In summer you can go **rowing** on the Lower Town Wood Lake (*Alsóvárosierdő-tó*), a few kilometres east of town on the Kaposvár road (bus #17 from the bus station). The nearest road crossing into Croatia is at Letenye, 26km west of town, where the *Arany Bárány*, Szabadság tér 1 (☎93/343-047; ②), has basic accommodation if needed.

# Kaposvár

Capital of Somogy county, the industrial town of **KAPOSVÁR** has an elegant centre with numerous Art Nouveau and classical buildings, making it a pleasant place to stroll around. Apart from being famous for its theatre and as the birth-place of József Rippl-Rónai, the father of Hungarian Art Nouveau, Kaposvár is a stepping stone for walks in the **Zselic nature conservation area**.

Most things are located along or just off the main street, Fő utca. The **Somogy County Museum** at no. 10 (Tues–Sun: April–Oct 10am–4pm; Nov–March 10am–3pm; 80Ft) contains the usual mix of local ethnographic and historical material, as well as a gallery of contemporary art. Confusingly, it is sometimes known as the Rippl-Rónai Museum; he was born on this street, at no. 19, above the Golden Lion Pharmacy, though the museum doesn't contain any of his paintings.

You'll find these at the **Rippl-Rónai Villa** on Fodor József utca, in the suburb of Rómahegy, 3km southeast of the centre (*Emlekház*; Tues–Sun: April–Oct 10am–6pm; Nov–March 10am–4pm; 100Ft); take bus #15 from the bus station. Born in 1861, he first studied in Munich and then under the academic painter Munkácsy before refining his own style in Paris, influenced by Postimpressionism and Art Nouveau. His return home in 1902 marked the end of his "black period", when some of his best-known works such as *Lady with a Black Veil* were produced, and the start of a "sunlit" one reflecting "the colours that surround me in my new house and garden". In his later years he abandoned oils and turned to crayon. The villa contains pictures from each phase, plus furniture, glassware and ceramics.

Nature lovers will enjoy **walking in the Zselic region** south of Kaposvár, with its watermeadows, woods and rolling hills. Maps are available from bookshops in Kaposvár, showing marked trails; you can follow the one from the village of **SZENNA**, 9km away (hourly buses from stand 11 of Kaposvár's bus terminal). This harbours one of Hungary's smallest *Skanzen* (April–Oct 10am–6pm; Nov–March 10am–4pm; 100Ft), consisting of six farmhouses and an eighteenth-century Calvinist church, transplanted from elsewhere in the region to a site opposite the main bus stop at Rákóczi utca 2. If you want to stay, **rooms** are available at Kossuth utca 21 (☎82/484-027; ③).

# Practicalities

Kaposvár's **stations** are close to each other, with local buses next to the train station on Budai Nagy Antal utca and long-distance services across the road on Áchim András utca. If you're carrying on to Pécs by train, note that reservations are required on the expresses (make reservations with MÁV Tours, through the passageway at Fő utca 21). To reach the centre of town, head up Teleki or Dózsa György utca, both of which lead to Fő utca. Here, you can get **information** from Tourinform at no. 8 (Mon–Fri 9am–5pm, Sat 9am–noon; July 20 to Aug 20 Mon–Fri 9.30am–5.30pm, Sat 9.30am–1.30pm; ☎82/320-349), or Siotour at no. 1 (Mon–Fri 8am–4.30pm; ☎82/320-537). IBUSZ at Dózsa György utca 5 is only useful for accommodation. You can **change money** at any of these, or use the ATMs in the bank or business centre on Széchenyi tér, off which is the post office at Bajcsy-Zsilinszky utca 15.

## Accommodation

A **private room** (②) from any of the agencies will prove more convenient than *Deseda* **campsite** 6km northeast of town (☎82/312-030; ①), which can be reached by bus #8 or #18 from the station, or by alighting at the Toponár stop on the Siófok–Kaposvár branch line.

**Borostyán Hotel**, Rákóczi tér 3 (☎82/320-735 or 321-746). Sadly over-restored Art Nouveau building near the train station. ⑤.

**Csokonai Fogadó**, Fő utca 1 (☎82/312-011). Kaposvár's nicest hotel, in a renovated eighteenth-century building above Siotour. Breakfast not included. Reservations advised. ③.

**Flamingó Panzió**, Füredi utca 53 (☎82/416-738). A guesthouse in a former workers' hostel, 2km out on the road towards Balatonlelle (bus #10 or #11A). Rooms with TV, fridge and bathroom (②), and cheaper ones with shared facilities next door. ①.

**Pálma Panzió**, Széchenyi tér 6 (☎82/420-227). Small, centrally located pension just up from the business centre. ③.

### Eating, drinking and entertainment

After Pécs, Kaposvár has more good **restaurants** than any town in southern Transdanubia. The *Csokonai Fogadó* (see above) serves tasty home cooking, the *Arany Szarvas* ("Golden Stag") at Fő utca 46 specializes in game dishes, and *Borostyán Hotel* on Rákóczi tér has a dining room pandering to the nouveau riche, plus a coffee shop. For a change, you could try Greek food at the *Görög Taverna*, in a cellar on the corner of Fő utca and Irányi Dániel utca. Over summer, cafés and bars spill out onto the pedestrianized stretch of Fő utca.

Kaposvár's **Csiky Gergely Theatre**, opposite the Golden Eagle Pharmacy, is one of the best in Hungary and has gained kudos abroad with its performances of *The Master and Margarita*; tickets are available from the ticket office, *Színház Jegypénztár*, at Fő utca 8. During the town's **Spring Festival** in late March, there are concerts in the **Liszt Concert Hall** at Kossuth utca 21. **Nightlife** centres on the *Top Cat* club by the Greek taverna, which is open till 4am.

# Pécs and the Mecsek Hills

After Budapest, **PÉCS** (pronounced "Paych") is probably the finest town in Hungary. Its tiled rooftops nestle against the slopes of the Mecsek Hills, and the sprawling modern housing estates can easily be forgotten once you are inside the old town. Pécs has a reputation for art and culture, boasting many excellent art galleries and museums, some fine examples of Islamic architecture, and the biggest market in western Hungary. As Transdanubia's leading centre of education, its population of 150,000 includes a high proportion of students, giving Pécs a youthful profile. The city is overlooked by the **Mecsek Hills**, where the Turks planted fig trees that still flourish, and where uranium has been mined since the 1950s.

Though prehistoric settlements existed here, the first town was Sopianae, settled first by the Celts and later by the Romans, who raised it to be the capital of the new province of Pannonia Valeria. Made an epicospal see by King Stephen, the town, known as Quinque Ecclesiae or Fünfkirchen (Five Churches), became a university centre in the Middle Ages. Under Turkish occupation (1543–1686) its character changed radically, its Magyar/German population being replaced by Turks and their Balkan subjects. Devastated during its "liberation", the city slowly recovered, thanks to local viticulture and the discovery of coal in the mid-eighteenth century. While the pits now face closure due to bankruptcy, Pécs's uranium mines are still going strong.

## Arrival, information and accommodation

**Arriving** at the train station, you can stash your luggage near platform 1 before catching a bus north into the centre. Any bus up Szabadság utca can drop you at the Zsolnay Monument on Rákóczi út, while bus #30 runs to Széchenyi tér via

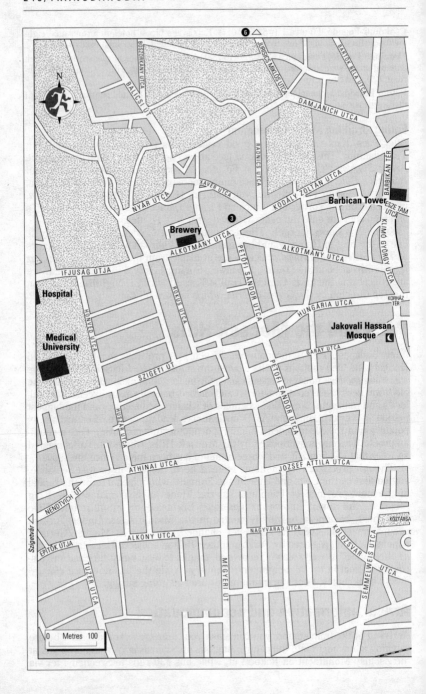

N

Szigetvár

**6**

BOSZORKÁNY UTCA

BALICSI U

JURISICS MIKLÓS UTCA

BARTÓK BÉLA UTCA

DAMJANICH UTCA

BARBIKÁN TÉR

RADNICS UTCA

XAVÉR UTCA

NYÁR UTCA

KODÁLY ZOLTÁN UTCA

ESZE TAM

GYÖRGY UTCA

KLIMÓ GYÖRGY UTCA

**Barbican Tower**

**3**

**Brewery**

ALKOTMÁNY UTCA

ALKOTMÁNY UTCA

PETŐFI SÁNDOR UTCA

IFJÚSÁG ÚTJA

RÓKUS UTCA

HONVÉD UTCA

HUNGÁRIA UTCA

KÓRHÁZ TÉR

**Hospital**

**Jakovali Hassan Mosque**

**Medical University**

GARAY UTCA

SZIGETI ÚT

PETŐFI SÁNDOR UTCA

HUSZÁR UTCA

JÓZSEF ATTILA UTCA

ATHINAI UTCA

KÖZTÁRSA

NENDTVICH ÚT

NAGYVÁRAD UTCA

KOLOZSVÁR UTCA

SEMMELWEIS UTCA

ALKONY UTCA

ÉPÍTŐK ÚTJA

MEGYERI ÚT

TÜZÉR UTCA

0  Metres  100

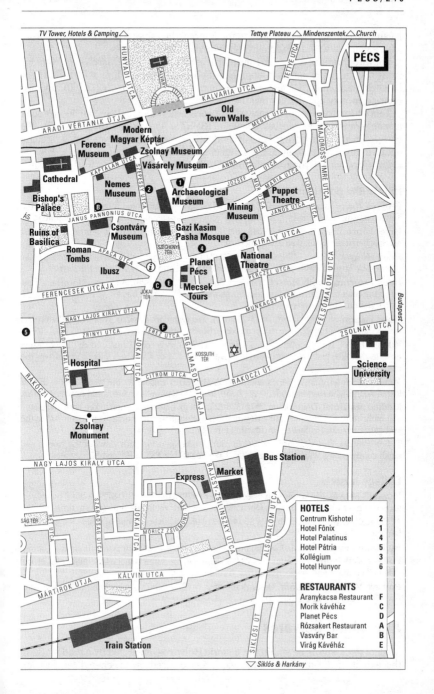

PÉCS

CALVARY

HUNYADI UTCA
TETTYE UTCA
KALVARIA UTCA
ARADI VÉRTANÚK ÚTJA
MEGYE UTCA
DR. MAJOROSSY IMRE UTCA

Old
Town Walls

Modern
Magyar Képtár

Ferenc
Museum

Zsolnay Museum

Vásárely Museum

KÁPTALAN UTCA
SZEPESSY UTCA
ANNA UTCA
SZENT MÓR UTCA
MÁRIA UTCA
JÓZSEF UTCA
FLÓRIÁN UTCA

Cathedral

Nemes
Museum

❷

Archaeological
Museum

❶

Puppet
Theatre

Bishop's
Palace

❻

JANUS PANNONIUS UTCA

Mining
Museum

JÁNOS UTCA

ÁS

Ruins of
Basilica

Csontváry
Museum

Gazi Kasim
Pasha Mosque

❻

KIRÁLY UTCA

Roman
Tombs

APÁCA UTCA

SZÉCHENYI
TÉR

❹

National
Theatre

FELSŐMALOM UTCA

Ibusz

ⓘ

Planet
Pécs

PERCZEL UTCA

FERENCESEK UTCÁJA

JÓKAI
TÉR

Ⓒ Ⓔ

Mecsek
Tours

MUNKÁCSY UTCA

ZSOLNAY UTCA

NAGY LAJOS KIRÁLY ÚTJA

TÉREZ UTCA

ZRÍNYI UTCA

JÓKAI UTCA

Ⓕ

IRGALMASOK UTCÁJA

KOSSUTH
TÉR

✡

Science
University

❺

VÁRADI ANTAL UTCA

Hospital

✉

CITROM UTCA

RÁKÓCZI ÚT

RÁKÓCZI ÚT

Zsolnay
Monument

NAGY LAJOS KIRÁLY UTCA

BAJCSY-ZSILINSZKY UTCA

Bus Station

Express

Market

SÁG TÉR

RÉT UTCA

SZABADSÁG UTCA

JÓKAI UTCA

MÓRICZ ZSIGMOND

ALSÓMALOM UTCA

MÁRTIROK ÚTJA

KÁLVIN UTCA

SIKLÓSI ÚT

Train Station

Budapest ▷

| HOTELS | |
|---|---|
| Centrum Kishotel | 2 |
| Hotel Fônix | 1 |
| Hotel Palatinus | 4 |
| Hotel Pátria | 5 |
| Kollégium | 3 |
| Hotel Hunyor | 6 |

| RESTAURANTS | |
|---|---|
| Aranykacsa Restaurant | F |
| Morik kávéház | C |
| Planet Pécs | D |
| Rózsakert Restaurant | A |
| Vasváry Bar | B |
| Virág Kávéház | E |

▽ *Siklós & Harkány*

Irgalmasok utcája, passing close to the intercity bus station on Zólyom utca, from where you can walk to Széchenyi tér in under fifteen minutes.

For **information**, drop into Tourinform at Széchenyi tér 9 (March–Oct Mon–Fri 9am–5.30pm, Sat & Sun 9am–2pm; Nov–Feb Mon–Fri 9am–4pm; ☎72/213-315) or Mecsek Tours at no. 1 (Mon–Fri 9am–5pm, Sat 9am–1pm; ☎72/213-300). You can **change money** at either, or use the **ATM** at Széchenyi tér 8.

Tourinform has a comprehensive list of **accommodation** in Pécs, but doesn't book private rooms – unlike Mecsek Tours and IBUSZ at Apáca utca 1 (☎72/212-157). The cheapest beds are in college halls of residence; some are open at weekends throughout term time, others only in the summer vacation (June to late Aug). The *Familia Privát Camping* at Gyöngyösi utca 6 (☎72/329-938) is the nearest official campsite.

## Hotels and pensions

**Fenyves Panorama Hotel**, Szőlő utca 64 (☎72/315-996). Balconied rooms to the west of the Tettye plateau; accessible by bus #34 or #35 from the bus station or the Zsolnay Monument. ④.

**Hotel Főnix**, Hunyadi út 2 (☎72/311-680). Popular modern place with a central location just off Széchenyi tér. Book well in advance. ⑤.

**Hotel Hunyor**, Jurisics Miklós utca 16 (☎72/315-677). A fifty-room hotel in the Mecsek Hills, reached by bus #32, with a nice garden and restaurant and lovely views of the city. ⑤.

**Hotel Laterum/Youth Hostel**, Hajnóczy utca 37 (☎72/315-829). A revamped workers' hostel on the road to Szigetvár, a few kilometres west of centre; take bus #2, #4 or #27 to the MOL petrol station. Open year-round. ②.

**Hotel Palatinus**, Király utca 5 (☎72/233-022). Renovated *fin-de-siècle* pile right in the centre, with a magnificent lobby and modern rooms. Shame about the breakfasts. ⑥.

**Kikelet Hotel**, Károlyi Mihály utca 1 (☎72/310-777). A recently restored Art Deco resort hotel in the hills, just over 1km from the centre (bus #34 or #35), with superb views over the city. ⑤.

**Mandulás Hotel**, Ángyán János utca 2 (☎72/315-981). Campsite in the woods below the TV tower. Rooms with showers and toilets (②–③). Bus #34 stops outside. Open mid-April to mid-Oct.

**Mediterrán Hotel**, Dömörkapu (☎72/336-222). An ex-hostel gone upmarket, with TV, phone and bathrooms throughout, and a view of the hills dominated by a quarry; take bus #35 to the end of the line, and follow signs downhill for 300m. ⑤.

**Toboz Panzió**, Fenyves sor 5 (☎72/325-232). A quiet pension with views of the woods and small comfy rooms with minibar and TV. Take bus #34 or #35 to Károlyi Mihály utca. ④.

## College hostels

**Hunyadi Mátyás Fiúkollégium**, Széchenyi tér (☎72/310-875 or 310-872). A boys' hall of residence run by Cistercian monks. Open all summer and weekends during term time. ①.

**JPTE Kollégium**, Damjanich utca 30 (☎72/310-055). University hall of residence with four-bed rooms. Open June–Aug. ①.

**Kollégium**, Kodály utca 20. College hostel located 500m west of the cathedral. ①.

**Pollack Kollégium**, Jókai utca 8 (☎72/315-846). On the same street as the main post office. Open all summer and weekends during term time. ①.

**Pollack Mihály Kollégium**, Boszorkány út 2 (☎72/310-387). An outlying fallback option. Bus #30 to the end of the line. ①.

# Around the Belváros

Most of Pécs' sights lie within the historic **Belváros**, encircled by a road marking the extent of the medieval town walls, and centred on Széchenyi tér. Passing

Kossuth tér en route to the centre, don't miss one of the city's finest monuments, an elegant **synagogue** built in 1865 (May–Oct Mon–Fri & Sun 10am–noon & 12.30–4pm; 40Ft). Its carved and stuccoed interior is beautiful but haunting, emptied by the murder of over four thousand Jews now listed in a *Book of Remembrance* – ten times the number that live in Pécs today. Thanks to local efforts, state support and contributions from abroad, this was one of the first synagogues in Hungary to be restored, in the 1980s.

Further uphill, as Irgalmasok utcája nears Széchenyi tér, you'll spot the **Zsolnay Fountain** in front of a church to your right. Local Zsolnay ceramics are typified by polychromatic, metallic-looking glazes; the bulls' heads on the fountain are modelled on a gold drinking vessel from the "Treasure of Attila".

Before entering Széchenyi tér, take a look at **Király utca**, traditionally the *korzó* where townsfolk promenade. Among the buildings worth noting here are the Art Nouveau **Hotel Palatinus**; the **Nendtvich House** at no. 8, with its ceramic ornamentation; the **National Theatre**, surmounted by a statue of Genius; and the **Vasváry House** at no. 19, with its allegorical figurines. Unfortunately the elegant aspect of the street has been marred by a chemist and other eyesores.

## Széchenyi tér

With its art galleries and tourist offices, modern-day **Széchenyi tér** is centuries removed from its Turkish predecessor, a dusty square crowded with "caravans of camels laden with merchandise from India and the Yemen". At its top end stands the Catholic church (*Belvárosi templom*), whose ornate window grilles and scalloped niches denote its origins as the **Mosque of Gazi Kasim Pasha** (April 15 to Oct 15 Mon–Sat 10am–4pm, Sun 11.30am–4pm; Oct 16 to April 14 Mon–Sat 10am–noon, Sun 11.30am–2pm; donations acccepted), which the Turks built from the stones of a medieval Gothic church. The vaulted interior and Islamic prayer niche (*mihrab*) are decorated with Arabic calligraphy.

Contemporary artwork is exhibited in the **Pécsi Gallery** on the western side of the square (Mon–Fri noon–6pm, Sat 10am–6pm; 65Ft). It's worth a quick look in case there's anything remarkable, but with so many art collections in Pécs it pays to be selective. On the northern side of the square, the **Archeological Museum** (Tues–Sun: April–Oct 10am–4pm; Nov–March 10am–2pm; 120Ft) covers the history of the region from prehistoric times to the Magyar conquest, but pales in comparison to the real Roman tombs a few streets over on Apáca utca (see overleaf). Dominating one side of the square is the vast yellow ochre hulk of the *Nádor Hotel*, now disused and awaiting its fate. At this point, you have the option of three routes to the cathedral – along Káptalan, Janus Pannonius or Apáca utca – via a clutch of museums.

## Káptalan utca

Káptalan utca has no fewer than five museums virtually next to each other. The **Zsolnay Museum** at no. 2 is a must for its vases, plaques and figurines from the Zsolnay Ceramics Factory, founded in 1868 by Vilmos Zsolnay and the chemist Vince Wartrha, the inventor of eosin glaze. Some pieces are exquisite, others totally kitsch, but they deserve a look either way. In the basement are sculptures by Amerigo Tot, whose *Erdély Family* with its clamped grave-posts symbolizes the plight of the ethnic Hungarians of Romania.

Across the road at no. 3, the **Vasarely Museum** (Tues–Sun: April–Oct 10am–6pm; Nov–March 10am–4pm; 200Ft) exhibits lurid Op Art canvases by Viktor Vasarely, who was born in this house in 1908, but made his name in Paris

and New York. The **Modern Magyar Képtár**, next door to the Zsolnay Museum
(Tues–Sun: April–Oct 10am–6pm; Nov–March 10am–4pm; 120Ft), presents a *tour
d'horizon* of Hungarian art since the School of Szentendre, with a large section
devoted to constructivist evocations of the proletarian struggle by Béla Uitz
(1887–1972), who lived for fifty years in the Soviet Union. The **Nemes Museum**
at no. 5 honours the surrealist Endre Nemes, who was born in nearby Pécsvárad
in 1909, but spent most of his life in Sweden. Diagonally across the street at no. 6,
right by Dóm tér, the **Martyn Museum** (Tues–Sun: April–Oct 10am–6pm;
Nov–March 10am–4pm; 120Ft) showcases work by Ferenc Martyn, an early
exponent of non-figurative painting, who died in 1986.

## The Csontváry Museum

If you only visit one place in Pécs, make it the **Csontváry Museum** at Janus
Pannonius utca 11–13 (Tues–Sun: April–Oct 10am–6pm; Nov–March 10am–4pm;
200Ft). Kosztka Tivadar Csontváry (1853–1919) was born in the same year as Van
Gogh, and his artistic career was similarly affected by madness and the pursuit of
"the path of the sun". His fascination with Hebrew lore and the Holy Land was
expressed in huge canvases – *Baalbek*, *Mary's Well at Nazareth* and *Pilgrimage* –
while his hallucinatory vision of nature produced *Tatra*, *Storm on the Great
Hortobágy* and *Solitary Cedar*.

After his death, these works came close to being sold as tarpaulin, but at the
last moment were purchased by an architect. When Picasso later saw an exhibition of Csontváry's work in Paris, he asked to be left alone in the room for an hour
and then remarked, "I did not know there was another great painter in our century besides me", and later told Chagall, "There you are, old master, I bet even
you could not paint something like this."

## Roman remains on Apáca utca

The necropolis of Sopianae lay more or less beneath Apáca utca (Nun Street),
where several **Roman tombs** decorated with scenes of the Gates of Paradise
have been excavated in the courtyard of no. 9. After the Romans went home and
waves of migrating tribes swept across Hungary, the tombs were used as refuges
and modified accordingly. Across the road are the less impressive **remains of a
chapel**, likewise dating from the third or fourth century AD. Opening hours for
both sites are irregular, but the tombs are worth seeing if they're open. If not,
another excavated ruin can be found nearby on Szent István tér.

## Around Dóm tér

Szent István tér, the lower, park-like extension of the square before the cathedral,
harbours **ruins** of what was either a subterranean basilica or early Christian mausoleum from the fourth century (Tues–Sun 10am–6pm; 200Ft). Decorated with
frescoes of the Fall and Daniel in the Lions' Den, it contains a white marble sarcophagus and some skeletal remains.

Just uphill, **Dóm tér** is overshadowed by a huge, four-towered **cathedral** that
has been endlessly rebuilt since a basilica was founded here in the eleventh century. Though a crypt and side chapels from eleventh- to fourteenth-century
churches have been incorporated in the cathedral, its outward form is neo-
Romanesque, the style chosen to replace Mihály Pollack's previous Baroque
design. Its lavish blue and gold murals are by Lotz, Székely and other historicist
painters of the 1890s. The whole interior has recently been given an overhaul.

The neo-Renaissance **Bishop's Palace** to the west of the square is embellished with a modern statue of Liszt waving from the balcony, which might have amused its former bishops, Janus Pannonius, who was also a humanist poet, and György Klimó, founder of its library, who told borrowers: "You don't have to pay for anything. Depart enriched. Return more frequently." Around the corner to the south, a circular **barbican tower** punctuates the old town walls, giving access to Klimó György utca.

### Around the periphery

From the tower, you can head uphill and on to Aradi Vértanuk útja to see a section of the **old town walls** – once a massive crenellated rampart 5500 paces long, buttressed by 87 bastions – erected after the Mongol invasion of the thirteenth century. Above the tunnel, 300m along, is a small garden with a decaying **Calvary Chapel**, offering a fine view of the Belváros.

Alternatively, head downhill around the peripheral boulevard – henceforth Rákóczi út – to find the inconspicuous **Jakovali Hassan Mosque** (April–Sept daily except Wed 10am–1pm & 1.30–6pm; 120Ft). Unlike its counterparts at Szigetvár (see p.255) and Eger (see p.280), this sixteenth-century mosque is still intact (though its minaret is closed), bearing traces of friezes and arabesque carving. The attractive *minbar* pulpit and kilims adorning its cool white interior are gifts from the Turkish Ministry of Culture. Around the corner on Ferencesek utca, you can see the ruins of a Turkish bath outside the *Minaret* restaurant.

A small **Ethnographic Museum** (Tues–Sun: April–Oct 10am–6pm; Nov–March 10am–4pm; 120Ft) containing folk costumes from the Baranya region can be found at Rákóczi út 15. On the way back to the centre you can see the **Zsolnay Monument**, with an image of the factory's founder gazing benevolently over the junction with Szabadság utca; and the Romantic-style **post office** on Jókai utca, roofed with Zsolnay tiles.

# Around Pécs

For a fresh perspective on Pécs, catch bus #33 from Kossuth tér up to the **Tettye plateau**, where a ruined sixteenth-century palace, later used as a Dervish monastery, stands in a park. Higher up and further out from the centre, **Misina Hill** (534m) is crowned by a **Television Tower** with an observation platform (Feb–Oct Sun–Thurs 9am–9pm, Fri & Sat 9am–11pm; Nov–Jan daily 9am–4pm; 170Ft) and a café with a retro 1970s ambience, accessible by bus #35 from Kossuth tér or the train station. Should you care to walk back from the plateau, Havihegyi út offers a succession of views as it winds around the hillside, with several picturesque backstreets slinking down past the **All Saints' Church**, whose pastor supplements his income by selling poultry.

All kinds of livestock and farming paraphernalia appear at the monthly **Pécs Market**, a huge country fair held on the first Sunday of every month at a site 3km southwest of the Belváros; take bus #3 or #50 from outside the Konzum store on Rákóczi út and ask to be dropped off at the *Vásártér* market on Megyeri út. On other Sundays, there's a lively flea market on the same site.

# Eating, drinking and entertainment

For tasty, cheap **meals**, you can't beat the *Aranykacsa* at Teréz utca 4. To dine in style, try the magnificently decorated *Dóm Étterem* at Király utca 3; the *Cellárium* beside the *Hotel Főnix* at Hunyadi út 2; or *Tettye* 1km out from the centre, in the hills at Tettye tér 4 (bus #33 from Kossuth tér), which has live music and a glowing reputation. In summer, the beer garden of the *Rózsakert* on Janus Pannonius utca is very pleasant. For **coffee and cakes**, try the stylish *Morik Kávéház* on Jókai tér or the *Virág Cukrászda* opposite Mecsek Tours on Széchenyi tér.

The *Pécsi Sörfőzde* or Pécs **brewery**, just off Rókusalja utca, produces some of Hungary's best beers – Szalonsör, Gilde, Goldfassl and the brown version of Szalon. As the brewery doesn't run tours, the *Rókus* beer cellar or the homely *Kiskorsó* restaurant are the nearest you can get to the source. Sticking to the centre of town, the liveliest **pubs** are on Király utca. *Vasváry* at no. 19 is the coolest hangout; *Planet Pécs* at no. 2 is open till 2am for music and dancing; while if you're gasping for a Double Diamond, there's the *John Bull*.

Pécs's **opera** and **ballet** companies are highly regarded, and tickets for performances at the National Theatre on Király utca can be hard to obtain – ask about cancellations at the box office an hour before the show starts. Tourinform can give details of **concerts** and other events at local cultural centres, including the annual **Pécs Days** festival in September. For children, there's a **puppet theatre** on the corner of Mária and Szent Mor utca.

## The Mecsek Hills

The karstic **Mecsek Hills** north of Pécs offer panoramic views and trails fanning out from the television tower through groves of sweet chestnuts and almond trees. If you fancy some **hiking**, buy a 1:40,000 map of the hills, available from most bookshops or tourist offices in town. Alternatively, you can catch a bus (every 1hr–1hr 30min) from the intercity depot out to Orfű or Abaliget, two popular resorts forty minutes' ride from town, where **accommodation** can be pre-booked through Mecsek Tours in Pécs.

ORFŰ features four artificial **lakes** surrounded by sports facilities, restaurants and accommodation, with an antique **mill** to the east of the smallest lake. Besides private rooms there are several **campsites** on the terraced slopes. *Orfű Camping* at Dollár utca 1 (☎72/378-501; ①; mid-April to mid-Oct) has plenty of space, bungalows with baths (③), and bikes and windsurfing boards for rent. Other options include the *Laterum Motel*, Dollár utca 10 (☎72/378-454; ②); *Cedrus Vendégház*, Hermann Otto utca 77 (☎72/336-134; ②); and *Molnár Panzió*, Széchenyi tér 18A (☎72/378-563; ②). *Muskátli*, near the last, is the best **restaurant** in Orfű.

A few kilometres further west, the larger settlement of **ABALIGET** has an outdoor **thermal pool** and a 640-metre-long **stalactite cave** inhabited by blind crabs beside one of its lakes. Should you wish to stay, there are lots of rooms for rent on Kossuth utca, and two campsites: *Abaliget* (☎72/378-530; ①), by the lake, with bungalows and a restaurant; and *Forrás* (☎72/390-777; ①), near the thermal baths.

# Szigetvár

**SZIGETVÁR**, 33km west of Pécs, rivals Kőszeg for its heroic resistance to the Turkish invasion. Every Hungarian child is taught the story (see opposite), which is enshrined in poetry and music, and the subject of a colossal painting in the Hungarian National Gallery in Budapest. Although a striking new community centre designed by Imre Makovecz has aroused some attention, and the local **thermal baths** are as agreeable as any, it is the **castle** and **relics of the Turkish occupation** that are still the main attractions of this dusty town.

Szigetvár's sights can all be easily explored on foot. On the way to the castle from the bus station, it's worth stopping off at the sixteenth-century **Turkish House** at Bástya utca 3, a simple brick building across the road from the market near the bus station. Originally a caravanserai, it now displays a modest collection of Turkish artefacts (mid-May to Sept Tues–Sun 9.30am–2.30pm; 30Ft).

Turn left along Szecsődi Máté utca and up Rákóczi utca, where you'll come to a shoe factory at no. 7, festooned with awards won in the 1950s, their red stars now crudely effaced. This presages a grander act of revisionism on **Zrínyi tér**, where what was built as the **Mosque of Ali Pasha** in 1596 was converted into a Baroque church in the late eighteenth century; only the Turkish-style windows around the back betray its origins. The frescoes inside date from 1788 (daily 8am–noon, once restoration is finished). At this point your eyes will be drawn by the twin towers of Makovecz's **Cultural Centre**, a bizarre structure resembling an alien spacecraft come to earth. During its construction the town council ran out of money and refused to trim other budgets to fulfil Makovecz's conception of the project, to his outrage, resulting in the fact that the inside of the theatre wasn't finished. You can inspect it at close quarters on József Attila utca, not far away.

Returning to Zrinyi tér and turning right past a snarling lion statue on to Vár utca, you'll pass the *Török Kávéház* at no. 1, a café decorated with Turkish motifs that maintains a **local history museum** in a vaulted room out back (daily 9am–9pm; 30Ft), exhibiting Habsburg-era shop signs, folk carvings, embroidery, weaponry and old photos of Szigetvár.

## The Castle

As the town's name, Island Castle, suggests, this quadrilateral fortress was once surrounded by lakes and marshes. Under local strong man Bálint Török, it resisted sieges by the Turks in 1541 and 1554, but its finest hour came in 1566, when 2400 soldiers under **Miklós Zrínyi**, governor of Croatia, resisted the onslaught of 100,000 Turks for 33 days. Enraged by the loss of 20,000 troops and the failure of his seventh attempt to march on Vienna, **Sultan Süleyman** died of apoplexy before the siege finally wore down the defenders. Spurning offers of surrender, Zrínyi donned his court dress before leading a final, suicidal sally when they could no longer hold out.

A **mosque** was erected after the castle's capture, which you'll find past a typically dour Soviet war memorial at the foot of the massive brick ramparts and through a gateway. Its minaret has long since disappeared, but the interior survives, complete with ornamental grilles, Koranic inscriptions, and frescoes depicting the deaths of Zrínyi and Süleyman (added later by the Hungarians). At no time, however, was the sultan buried here – though his viscera once reposed in another mosque in town (see overleaf).

In an adjacent **museum**, built as the summer house of Count Andrássy, coloured miniatures of Turkish life are counterpointed by praise for Magyar heroism (Tues–Sun: May–Sept 9am–6pm; April & Oct 9am–4pm; 120Ft). Copies of the epic *Szózat* (Appeal) are on display, penned by Zrínyi's grandson, himself a general. A cry for liberty and a call for endurance, this seventeenth-century poem was adapted as a chorale by Kodály in 1956. Its single performance at the Budapest Academy turned into an emotional symbolic protest against the Rákosi regime. Chanting crowds took up the refrain, "*Ne Bántsd a Magyart!*" ("Let the Magyars alone!"), causing government members who were there to walk out.

## The Hungarian-Turkish Friendship Park

One of those ideas that appeal to politicians but leave the public cold, the **Hungarian-Turkish Friendship Park** (*Magyar-Török Barátság Emlékpark*) was opened in 1994 by Turkey's prime minister, as a token apology and symbol of reconciliation. While a stone commemorating the death of Süleyman on the spot where his tent once stood (and he presumably expired) was acceptable, local people objected to a larger-than-life statue of the sultan until the Turks commissioned one of Zrínyi, whereupon it was agreed to place them side by side rather than confronting one another.

For the record, Süleyman's heart and innards were buried by his son, Selim II, in a **mosque** built nearby shortly after his death, and taken back to Constantinople when campaigning ceased. After the Turks were finally driven out, the mosque was turned into a church, though its past was acknowledged by a plaque. The strength of the gates suggests that vandalism has been a problem.

The park is 3km north of Szigetvár on the left-hand side of the road to Kaposvár, so it's accessible by bus – unlike the mosque, which is 3km down the road towards Zsibót. The *Domolos Kastély Hotel* in Zsibót is best avoided, however tempting it may look.

## Practicalities

Szigetvár's **bus and train stations** are about 500m down Rákóczi utca from the main square, Zrínyi tér, from where it's a short walk north along Vár utca to the castle.

As most visitors **stay** just a few hours in Szigetvár, Mecsek Tours in the *Hotel Oroszlán* on Zrínyi tér (Mon–Fri 8.30am–4pm; ☎73/310-116) doesn't try hard to please, and has few private rooms for rent. The *Oroszlán* (☎73/310-116; ④) itself is soulless compared to the cosy *Kumilla Hotel* at Olay Lajos utca 6, behind the Makovecz building (☎73/310-150; ③). It's worth asking at the castle whether the cheap *Kazamata Tourist Hostel* that used to exist in the grounds has reopened.

The best **places to eat** are the *Florián* and the *Kisváros*, both a little way out of town on József Attila utca. Mecsek Tours can **change money** and there are banks with ATMs at Vár utca 4 and Széchenyi utca 4. The post office is at József Attila utca 27–31.

# South of Pécs

The area south of Pécs offers many attractions. Those in search of a therapeutic wallow in yet another thermal bath should visit **Harkány**, while nearby **Siklós**, Hungary's southernmost town, has a fifteenth-century castle. **Villány** is a must for the wine aficionado, with its extensive vineyards and cellars producing some of Hungary's finest red wines.

## Harkány

Thirty-four kilometres south of Pécs, **HARKÁNY**'s main draws are its open-air **thermal pool** and indoor **baths** (daily 9am–6pm & 8–11pm; 350Ft for the pool,

1000Ft for the baths and pool), with a section for wallowing in **hot mud**, thera-peutically rich in sulphur and fluoride. The open-air *strand* can be entered from Kossuth utca to the west or Bajcsy-Zsilinszky utca to the east, while the entrance to the spa is on Zsigmond sétány on the south side of the compound, in the middle of town. Aside from this, there's not much else to visit except a small **market** near the bus station and an early nineteenth-century **Calvinist Church** on Kossuth utca.

**Arriving** by train, a fifteen-minute walk up Táncsics Mihály and then Arany János utca will bring you close to the Kossuth utca entrance to the *strand*; the bus station is at the southern end of Bajcsy-Zsilinszky utca, on the far side of the baths. **Information** is available from Tourinform on Kossuth utca 2 (May–Sept Mon–Sat 9am–7pm, Oct–April Mon–Fri 9am–4pm; ☎72/479-624) or Mecsek Tours by the Bajcsy-Zsilinszky ucta entrance (May–Sept Mon–Fri 8am–5pm, Sat 8am–noon; Oct–April Mon–Fri 8am–4pm; ☎72/480-322). Mecsek can also arrange cheap private **rooms** and **car rental**, and runs the nondescript *Hotel Drava*, Bartók Béla utca 3 (☎72/480-434; ②–④), and *Thermal* **campsite**, Bajcsy-Zsilinszky utca 6 (mid-April to mid-Oct), which has a basic hotel (②), motel (①), and four-bed bungalows. Or there's the *Baranya Hotel* opposite the baths on Bajcsy-Zsilinszky utca (☎72/480-160; ④).

## Siklós

Most buses plough on a further 5km across the dusty plain to **SIKLÓS**, another one-horse town huddled around a castle, although its fortunes have been trans-formed by an influx of **Croatian shoppers**: goods here cost far less than in Croatia due to high tariffs and VAT there. The local market is a cornucopia of goods and every shop advertises its wares in Croatian, but unless you're looking for a fake pair of Reeboks the only real attraction is the castle.

To get to the castle from the **bus station**, follow the main street, Felszabadulás utca, up to Kossuth tér, past the post office on Florián tér, and the OTP and K&H banks. Arriving by **train**, it's a ten-minute walk up Táncsics Mihály utca to the bot-tom of Kossuth tér, just below the castle.

Opposite the faded Baroque town hall on **Kossuth tér**, no. 12 was the **birth-place of George Mikes**, the émigré writer known for his parodies of British life in the 1960s. A couple of steps down the road to the right stands the sixteenth-century **Malkocs Bej Mosque** (Tues–Sun: mid-April to mid-Oct 9am–noon & 12.30–4pm; mid-Oct to mid-April 9am–4pm; 40Ft), stuffed with Turkish knick-knacks and recently over-restored.

**Siklós Castle** (Tues–Sun: mid-April to mid-Oct 10am–5.30pm; mid-Oct to mid-April 10am–4pm; 90Ft) remained in private hands from its foundation in the fif-teenth century up until 1943, when it was confiscated by the state. Bastions and rondellas form an impressive girdle around a mansion once occupied by the enlightened Casimir Batthyány, who freed his serfs in 1847. His tomb is in the Gothic chapel, located (with no sense of incongruity according to medieval values) within whipping distance of a dungeon filled with instruments of torture. Sadly, the museum here is less interesting than the view from the ramparts.

Should you need one, local **rooms** are bookable through Mecsek Tourist in Harkány or Pécs. There is no tourist office in Siklós, and the only hotel in town, the *Központi*, is being renovated, though its gloomy **restaurant** still functions. You can get an excellent strudel at the oddly named *Hamburger Cukrászda* by the entrance to the market on Felszabadulás utca (daily 6am–6pm).

## Villány

Fifteen kilometres east of Siklós, acres of vineyards lap the slopes of Mount Szársomlyó, producing red wine under the appellation Villányi. The village of **VILLÁNY** is of Swabian (German) origin, as you might guess from its neatness and uniformity, with pots of geraniums outside all the houses and everything signposted for the benefit of visitors; from the train station, out beyond the co-op winery, buses run along the main road, Baross utca, into the centre.

The local viticultural tradition goes back two thousand years, though you won't find anything that ancient in the **Wine Museum**, in a 200-year-old cellar at Bem József utca 3, down the main road to the left (Tues–Sun 9am–5pm; free). You can sample local **wine** at many places on Baross utca and Diófas tér – the names to look out for are Gere and Bock, whose wines have an international reputation. Bock's are labelled Jammertal (German for Valley of Lamentation), after a battle in 1687 where the Turks were hacked to death amid the Drava bogs. Wine lovers should also investigate the Polgár, Blum and Tiffán cellars in Villánykövesd, 2.5km down the road towards Pécs. Another local attraction is the **Villány artists' summer camp**, whose presence is evidenced by bronze totems and concrete erections on the hillside.

In Villány, one can **stay** at the comfy *Gere Panzió*, Diófas tér 4 (☎72/492-195; ③), the *Bock Panzió* at Batthyány utca 15 (☎72/492-388; ③), where József Bock has his cellar, or houses in the village advertising beds (*falusi szálláshely*). The *Júlia Vendéglő* at Baross utca 43, and the *Fülemüle Csárda*, ten minutes' walk past the station on the road to Villánykövesd, serve the best **meals**. There's an ATM at the OTP bank at Baross utca 27.

# Mohács

The small town of **MOHÁCS**, beside the Danube, is a synonym for defeat. As a consequence of a single **battle** here in 1526, Hungary was divided and war-torn for 150 years and lost its independence for centuries thereafter. The state was tottering before Mohács, however: its treasury depleted, and with an indecisive teenager on the throne. Only after Süleyman "the Magnificent" had taken Belgrade and was nearing the Drava did the Hungarians muster an army, which headed south without waiting for reinforcements from Transylvania, engaging the Turks on August 29.

Legend has it that an olive tree planted two hundred years earlier by Louis the Great suddenly became barren on that day, while the king's scribe records how the young Louis II gave orders for the care of his hounds before riding out to meet his fate. Attacking first, the Magyars broke ranks to loot the fallen and suffered a crushing counter-attack by Turkish janissaries and cavalry, which caused a rout. Louis was crushed to death by his horse when trying to ford a stream, and the twenty thousand Hungarian dead included five hundred nobles and scores of prelates, leaving the country unable to organize resistance as the Turks advanced on Buda.

## The battlefield and town

The battle occurred 7km south of Mohács, at a site thenceforth known as Sátorhely (Place of the Tent), which in 1976 was declared a **memorial park**

(*Emlékpark;* April–Oct daily 9am–5pm; 150Ft) to mark the 450th anniversary of the battle. By coincidence, it was also the site of a later battle in 1687 between Habsburg and Turkish forces, where the latter were defeated. Though easily reached by Route 56 (buses heading from Mohács towards Nagynyárád, Majs, Lippó, Bezedek or Magyarbóly run past), there's little to see but a bunker-like edifice containing maps of each side's deployments and endless texts in Hungarian – bar a wreath-laying ceremony on Mohács Memorial Day (August 29).

In Mohács itself, there is a small commemorative **museum** next to the Orthodox church at Szerb utca 2 (Tues–Sat: April–Sept 10am–5pm; Oct–March 10am–4pm; 40Ft). The **Kanizsai Dorottya Museum** at Városház utca 1 (same hours; 40Ft) focuses on the diverse ethnic groups that repopulated Mohács in the late seventeenth century. On Széchenyi tér stands an impressively ugly **Votive Church**, built to commemorate the 400th anniversary of the battle; and the **Town Hall**, where the Sultan's calligraphic signature is engraved on one of the windows.

Aside from those above, the River Danube rolling through town disconcertingly near street level is the only "sight" for 364 days of the year. Each spring, however, exactly seven weeks before Easter, the streets come alive with the annual **Busójárás Carnival**. With its procession of grotesquely masked figures waving flaming torches, who cross the Danube in wooden boats to chase away the winter, the carnival assumes a macabre appearance at night. Originally, it was probably a spring ritual intended to appease the gods, but over time participants also began to practise ritualistic abomination of the Turks to magically draw the sting of reality. Similar carnivals are held in Serbia and Croatia, where many of the revellers at Mohács travel from.

# Practicalities

While the **train station** is half an hour's walk north of the centre, the **bus station** is close to Szabadság utca, the main street running eastwards across Széchenyi tér and on to the Danube embankment near the ferry landing-stage. Here Mecsek Tours, in the foyer of the *Hotel Csele* (Mon–Fri 8am–4.30pm; ☎69/311-825), can supply **information** and private rooms (②), which are also available from IBUSZ, Szabadság utca 4–6 (Mon–Fri 8am–noon & 1–4pm, Sat 8am–noon; ☎69/311-531).

Though it's essential to reserve **accommodation** at carnival time, you needn't otherwise bother at the *Hotel Csele* (☎69/311-825; ④), where the best rooms are on the river-facing side of the second floor. Alternatively, there's the year-round *Arena Camping* at Dunaszekcső, 12km north along Route 56 (☎69/335-161; ①), which has a menagerie of animals, lovely views of the river, a restaurant, rooms (②) and bungalows (②).

For **eating**, you can choose between the posh *Halászcsárda* beside the hotel, which has a terrace overlooking the river and plays Hungarian gypsy music, or the *Veli Aga Vendéglő* at Szentháromság utca 7, just along from the Holy Trinity statue, whose cuisine has a Turkish flavour.

Moving on, there are **buses** to Szekszárd and Budapest (leaving around 7am & 2.40pm), and to Baja and Kecskemét or Szeged on the Great Plain (5–6 daily), which are more convenient than trains, since travellers aiming for Szekszárd or Baja are obliged to take a branch line 28km north to Bátaszék to get a connection. There is a **border crossing** into Croatia at Udvar, 11km south of town, and there are daily international buses to Osijek and Slavonski Brod.

# Szekszárd and the Forest of Gemenc

The chance to sample red wine produced in vineyards dating from Roman times and to buy inexpensive black pottery makes **SZEKSZÁRD** the prime stopover between Pécs and Budapest. Baroque squares, leafy streets and ancient wine cellars make this an ideal base to explore the wild, marshy Forest of Gemenc – while in June, early August and mid-September several festivals are held.

**Arriving** at the bus or train station on Pollack Mihály utca, it's a ten-minute walk up pedestrianized Bajcsy-Zsilinszky utca to the central intersection of two main axes: the park-like Mártírok tere that eventually leads uphill to Béla tér, and the busy Széchenyi utca, crossing it at right angles.

In a neo-Renaissance pile at the eastern end of Mártírok tere, the **Wosinsky Museum** (April–Oct Tues–Sun 10am–6pm; Nov–March Tues–Sat 10am–4pm; 50Ft, free on Tues) has a rich collection of Roman artefacts and peasants' costumes, as well as workshops and replicas of the shops that existed about a century ago. Behind the museum is an old **synagogue**, now used as a concert hall, whose interior is as tawdry as the facade is magnificent (Tues–Sun 10am–6pm; free).

The final uphill stretch beyond Széchenyi utca leads to Béla tér, where porticoed buildings tilt perceptibly around a statue marking the plague of 1730. The Neoclassical palace on the south side was built in 1828 by Mihály Pollack, on the site of an abbey church from the time of the Árpáds – the foundations are visible in the courtyard. Inside, a small **Liszt Memorial Exhibition** (*Liszt Emlék kiallitás*; April–Oct Tues–Sun 10am–6pm; Nov–March Tues–Sat 9am–3pm; 50Ft) commemorates Liszt's four visits to Szekszárd, and displays the piano that he played and a few of his scrawls.

At the top end of the square, Babits utca runs off towards the **House of Mihály Babits** (April–Oct Tues–Sun 10am–6pm; Nov–March Tues–Sat 9am–3pm; 50Ft), a homely residence exhibiting photos and manuscripts related to the journal *Nyugat* (West). This avant-garde publication was edited by Babits and included the Village Explorers' exposés of rural life in interwar Hungary, launching the literary careers of Endre Ady and Gyula Illyés. Alas for Attila József, the finest poet of that era, Babits refused to publish his work in *Nyugat*, earning József's eternal hostility. Babits went to his graveside to ask his forgiveness.

## Wine and festivities

Szekszárd's dark, rich "ox-blood" **wine** (*Szekszárdi Vörös*) was exported as far afield as Britain and Turkey in the 1700s, and Franz Liszt, Pope Pius IX and Emperor Haile Selassie are all said to have been admirers. Today, wine lovers can join tours of the vineyards arranged by Provincia Tourist (see opposite), or visit several excellent private vintners such as the Vesztergombi family, which has a shop at the top of Béla tér (Mon–Fri 10am–noon & 1–6pm, Sat 10am–noon) selling *Vida* and *Sárosdi*, as well as their own wines, and a cellar on Kadarka utca, uphill behind the square. Aliscavin, the former state winery, also has a cellar and a shop below the palace, on your right as you enter Béla tér (Mon–Fri 10am–6pm, Sat 10am–4pm, Sun 10am–2pm).

Many other private cellars open their doors during the **Wine Days** (*Bornapok*) in June, when there are tastings and craft fairs. During the **grape harvest** (mid-Sept to mid-Oct), the whole town is in a festive mood, and visitors are welcome to participate in picking and pressing the grapes, and enjoy the music, wine and song.

Another event worth attending is the **folklore festival at Decs** at the beginning of August. Though only 8km from Szekszárd, this village was traditionally isolated by marshes yet *au courant*, as its menfolk worked as bargees, bringing home the latest news and fabrics from Budapest. Their wives wore be-ribboned silk skirts and cambric blouses with lace inserts, and later acquired a taste for lime green and yellow metallic thread, making their **costumes** as lurid as rave attire.

### Visiting the Forest of Gemenc

The **Forest of Gemenc** is a remnant of the wilderness of woods, reeds and mud-land that once covered the Danube's shifting, flood-prone banks. Only at the beginning of this century was the river tamed and shortened by 60km, ending the annual flooding of its backwaters and the *Sárköz* (Mud Region). However, marshes and ponds remained to provide habitats for boar, wildcats, otters, deer, ospreys, falcons, bald eagles, black storks and other **wildlife**. Nowadays, the forest is a nature reserve of sorts (although the deer are fair game for Western hunters), with **boat trips** on its backwaters and a **miniature train line** through the forest. Unfortunately, its terminals at **Bárányfok** (bus #7 from town) and **Pörböly** (on the main line between Bátaszék and Baja) are awkward to reach, and there are only three trains a day (leaving Bárányfok at 10am & 2pm; Pörböly at 7.30am). All in all, it's easier to sign up for a Provincia Tourist **excursion** in Szekszárd, which includes a ride on the train and a visit to the Gemenc excursion centre.

### Practicalities

Tolna Tourist, in a striking pink mock castle at Széchenyi utca 38 (May–Oct Mon–Fri 8am–4.30pm, Sat 8am–noon; Nov–April Mon–Fri 8am–4.30pm; ☎74/312-144), can arrange wine tours and excursions to the Forest of Gemenc, as well as supply **information** and book private rooms – also available from IBUSZ at Széchenyi utca 20 (June–Sept Mon–Fri 8am–4.30pm, Sat 9am–noon; Oct–May Mon–Fri 8am–4.30pm; ☎74/319-822). The main post office is at Széchenyi utca 11–13, and there's an ATM at Mártírok tere 5–7.

Private rooms aside, **accommodation** boils down to the 1970s *Hotel Gemenc*, Mészáros Lázár utca 4 (☎74/311-722; ④), behind the Wosinsky Museum; the *Alisca Hotel* (☎74/312-228; ④), Kálvária utca 1, above Béla tér, which has fine views over town; or the *Illyés Gyula Pedagógiai Főiskola kollégium*, ten minutes' walk north of the centre at Mátyás király utca 3 (☎74/412-133; ①), which has guest rooms throughout the year. There's a campsite 5km north of the centre, at the junction of Route 6 (☎74/312-458; mid-March to mid-Nov).

Though Szekszárd's gastronomic efforts are less remarkable than its wine, you can enjoy tasty **meals** in the *Séd Söröző* by the Babits House, or the gloomy *Gastrolux* on Garay tér (daily 9am–midnight). For **entertainments**, check out the alternative arts centre Zug at Béla tér 6, which hosts concerts, films and other events and has a bar open until 10pm; or drop into the *Szász Söröző* off Béla tér for a game of pool or darts.

# Szekszárd to Budapest

The road and train line between Szekszárd and Budapest pass through dreary countryside punctuated by three towns that might tempt you to make a stopover – **Paks**, **Dunaföldvár** and **Dunaújváros**. If not, and you're driving, consider a scenic detour along minor roads through the pretty villages of Högyész, Gyonk and Cece, before rejoining the trunk route at Dunaföldvár, which – aside from Baja – has the only bridge across the Danube. Irregular **car ferries** from Fadd-Dombori, Gerjen, Paks and Dunaújváros also enable motorists to cross over to the Great Plain (covered in Chapter Six).

# Paks

**PAKS**, 52km north of Szekszárd, is the site of Hungary's only **nuclear power station**, four Soviet-designed pressurized water reactors which supply up to forty percent of the country's electricity. Bar some anxiety in the aftermath of Chernobyl, the issue of nuclear power has never aroused much public concern in Hungary except among communities living near the site of proposed nuclear waste dumps, and in Paks itself people are quick to point out that the plant gets good marks from international safety inspectors.

At the **Railway Museum**, beside the river, two kilometres north of town (daily 8am–6pm; 100Ft), vintage steam trains – some dating back to the great rail expansion of the 1880s – are displayed in an old station. You can get there by bus #1 from the main train station south of downtown Paks, which follows Dózsa György út through the centre of town.

The same bus takes you past the remarkable **Catholic Church** on Hősök tere, built by Imre Makovecz. A strikingly organic structure made of wood, its separate bell-tower has three spires topped by a cross, a crescent and a sun sign – which provoked letters to the press condemning the "Satanic forces" behind it, despite Makovecz's claim that they were early Christian symbols. You can get the key to the church at Hősök tere 19.

The remaining sights are on Szent István tér, the main square in the north of town, where a small **City Museum** (Mon & Tues 10am–4pm, Wed–Sun 10am–6pm; 50Ft) displays the usual Bronze Age, Roman, Celtic and Magyar artefacts, plus a table used by the statesman Deák. More excitingly, there's the **Paks Gallery** at Szent István tér 4 (Tues–Sun 9am–5pm; free), set up by local artist Károly Halász, whose stimulating exhibition of contemporary Hungarian works is hung within a cool white conversion of a grand classical building that was only the third casino the country when it was built in 1844. Later it became a hotel.

## Practicalities

If you're **arriving** by train it's better to get off at the Paks Duna-part station near Szent István tér rather than the main station over a kilometre south of the centre, where the bus station is located near the bottom of Dózsa György út. Both are connected to the centre by regular buses. While Tourinform at Szent István tér 2 (June–Aug Mon–Fri 9am–5pm, Sat 9–11am; Sept–May Mon–Fri 9am–5pm; ☎75/421-575) can supply information, Viking Tours at Kossuth utca 1–3 (May–Oct 9am–noon & 1–5pm; Nov–April Mon–Fri 9am–noon & 1–5pm, Sat 9am-noon; ☎75/310-475) are responsible for booking private rooms – which are the only alternative **accommodation** to the modern *Duna Hotel* at the bottom of Dózsa György út 75 (☎75/421-913; ②), opposite an ATM.

The *Halászcsárda* fish **restaurant** at Dunaföldvár utca 5A, fifteen minutes' walk upriver from the main square, has a terrace with fine views of the river, and a good reputation, despite the reactor being a mile downstream.

## Dunaföldvár

DUNAFÖLDVÁR is by far the prettiest and smallest of the three towns en route to Budapest. Its name derives from the sixteenth-century fortress that was hastily erected to guard the Danube after Belgrade fell to Süleyman's army, of which only the keep – known as the **Turkish Tower** – has survived. After the Turks were finally driven out, the town was repopulated by outsiders, as its Baroque **Serbian Orthodox Church** attests. Besides some elegant **Art Nouveau buildings** in the centre, it's possible to inspect **craft workshops** such as that of the blue-dyer (*kékfestő*) Vadász Istvánné, at Duna utca 6. Visits can be arranged through Tourinform, Rákóczi utca 2 (☎75/341-176), which can book private rooms if required.

## Dunaújváros

In total contrast, DUNAÚJVÁROS (Danube New Town), 20km upriver, is a monument to Stalinist economics, created around a vast ironworks which the Party saw as the lynchpin of its industrialization strategy for the 1950s. The construction of Sztálinváros (as the town was originally called) was trumpeted as a feat by Stakhanovites, though much of the heavy work was performed by peasants and "reformed" prostitutes living under appalling conditions. Yet, at the same time, it embodied a striving for a brighter future for the working classes – a paradox that has assumed a new form today, as this incarnation of the planned economy has weathered the transition to capitalism better than "traditional" industrial towns like Ózd.

*THE TOWN*

The town's appeal lies in its **Bauhaus and Socialist-Realist aesthetic**, making it an ideal location for a pop video, though its uniform rows of blocks make orientation difficult. A tall redbrick block on Városháza tér serves as the main landmark in the centre, whence Vasmű út runs to the Iron Works. On Városháza tér, in the centre of town, the former Party headquarters now houses the **Intercisa Museum** (Sat & Sun 2–6pm, and on alternate weeks Tues–Fri 10am–2pm or 2–6pm; 100Ft), which relates the history of this site from Roman times, represented by beautiful glass shells, to the Stalinist era. This latter is epitomized by a book of 14,800 signatures presented to Party Secretary Rákosi "demanding" that Sztálinváros be built – although it doesn't go into much detail about the suffering involved. A few minutes' walk brings you to a **sculpture park** of rusting iron supplied by the works, with lush views over the river.

A few minutes' walk brings you to the glass-fronted **Dózsa Cinema** on Ságvári tér, facing a group of stone frogs that in the summer spout water across the pond. Further on to the right, Babits utca leads onto **Bartók tér**, featuring a store with mosaics depicting workers and peasants building the town.

Next door, the **Bartók Cultural Centre** combines classical, Egyptian and Bauhaus motifs, while through the archway a school of the same era has separate doors for boys and girls, topped by reliefs of idealized children at study. Leading away from the square is Majus 1 út, one of the first streets to be built in 1950, and a must for lovers of the Bauhaus style.

Continuing along Vasmű út you'll pass a **statue of a foundry worker** relaxing, which Party officials complained should show the worker working, not resting, and was consequently not put up until 1961. Another fifteen minutes' walk brings you to the entrance of the **Iron Works**, like something out of a Cecil B. De Mille set, with enormous frescoes of joyous workers above a Neoclassical portico. The works cover a huge area, almost as big as the town itself, and have managed to survive by being fragmented into private firms, some foreign-owned, that pay no local taxes, though they continue to employ thousands of people.

To check out where Dunaújváros is going nowadays, visit the new **Institute of Contemporary Art** at Vasmű út 12, which mounts temporary exhibitions of Hungarian and foreign works, and has a coffee bar and an **Internet café** (Tues–Sun 10am–6pm; 100Ft).

*PRACTICALITIES*

There are regular bus services into the centre from the train station, 2km south, while the bus terminal is within easy walking distance; buses into town often stop at Városháza tér.

As you'd expect, Dunaújváros is hardly geared up for tourists, with a single **tourist office** at Vasmű út 41 (Mon–Fri 7.30am–4.30pm; ☎25/413-922), which can book private rooms (②) or beds in the *kollégium* at Dózsa György út 33 (☎25/410-811; ①; Jul & Aug), if you don't fancy **staying** at the *Dunaferr Hotel*, É pítők útja 2 (☎25/481-073; ②). There is also a campsite (☎25/310-285; ①; May–Sept), with an open-air bathing area, on a small island 3km north of the centre, accessible by bus #24 or #26.

Dunaújváros is surprisingly good for **eating**, with authentic Greek food at the *Napsugár Taverna*, Vasmű 11; Tex-Mex at *Geronimo* on Ságvári tér; tasty pizzas at *Da Tibor* and good Hungarian food at the *Corsó* – both just off Aranyvölgy út, northwest of the centre. *Dali*, alongside the Bartók Cultural Centre, is the best coffee house (2pm–midnight), while the 24-hour *Kis Csillag* on Devecseri utca near the cinema has good food and **live music**. Hungarian and foreign bands play at *Muvi* down by the Fun Fair (*Vidámpark*), near the entrance to the Iron Works, while *Remix* down by the campsite is a disco-cum-pizzeria.

## travel details

**Trains**

**Budapest (Déli or Keleti Station)** to: Győr (10 daily; 1hr 20min–1hr 50min); Komárom (10 daily; 1hr 30min–2hr); Pécs (4 daily; 3hr); Sopron (5 daily; 3hr 30min); Székesfehérvár (every 1hr–1hr 30min; 1hr); Szekszárd (3 daily; 3hr); Tata (4 daily; 1hr 15min).

**Dombóvár** to: Pécs (4 daily; 1hr–1hr 30min).

**Fertőboz** to: Nagycenk (April–Oct 4 departures Sat & Sun; 30min).

**Győr** to: Sopron (6 daily; 1hr); Veszprém (4 daily; 2hr 30min).

**Körmend** to: Szentgotthárd (every 1–2hr; 30min); Szombathely (every 1–2hr; 30min); Zalalövő (6 daily; 30min).

**Kőszeg** to: Szombathely (every 1hr–1hr 30min; 30min).

**Mohács** to: Pécs (4 daily; 2hr 30min); Villány (every 1–2hr; 30min).

**Nagycenk** to: Fertőboz (April–Oct 4 departures Sat & Sun; 30min).

**Nagykanizsa** to: Balatonszentgyörgy (every 1–2hr; 45min); Budapest (every 1–2hr; 3–4hr); Pécs (5 daily; 1hr 30min–3hr).

**Pécs** to: Dombóvár (every 1hr–1hr 30min; 1hr–1hr 30min); Mohács (3 daily; 1hr 30min); Nagykanizsa (5 daily; 1hr 30min–3hr); Szombathely (2 daily; 4hr 30min); Villány (5 daily; 1hr).

**Sopron** to: Budapest (5 daily; 3hr); Győr (5 daily; 1hr); Szombathely (7 daily; 1hr 30min).

**Szekszárd** to: Budapest (3 daily; 3hr).

**Szentgotthárd** to: Körmend (every 1–2hr; 30min); Szombathely (every 1–2hr; 1hr).

**Szombathely** to: Körmend (every 1–2hr; 30min); Kőszeg (every 1hr–1hr 30min; 30min); Nagykanizsa (4 daily; 1hr 30min–2hr 30min); Pécs (2 daily; 4hr 30min); Sopron (8 daily; 1hr 30min);

Székesfehérvár (6 daily; 2hr 15min–2hr 45min); Szentgotthárd (every 1–2hr; 1hr); Tapolca (4 daily; 1hr 45min).
**Zalaegerszeg** to: Budapest (3 daily; 3hr 30min); Zalalövő (7 daily; 30min).
**Zalalövő** to: Körmend (4 daily; 30min); Zalaegerszeg (7 daily; 30min).

## Buses
**Budapest (Erzsébet tér)** to: Dunaújváros (4 daily; 1hr 30min); Győr (every 40min–1hr; 1hr 15min–2hr); Harkány (1 daily; 4hr 30min); Mohács (2–3 daily; 4hr); Pécs (5 daily; 4hr); Siklós (1 daily; 5hr); Sopron (2 daily; 3hr 45min); Szekszárd (8 daily; 3hr 15min); Szombathely (2 daily; 4hr 15min); Zalaegerszeg (1 daily; 4hr 45min).
**Győr** to: Balatonfüred (every 30–90min; 2hr); Budapest (every 40min–1hr; 1hr 15min–2hr); Kalocsa (1 weekly; 5hr); Pannonhalma Monastery (every 30min–1hr 30min; 30min); Siófok (1 daily; 3hr); Sümeg (5 daily; 2hr 15min); Székesfehérvár (1 daily; 2hr); Szombathely (3 daily; 2hr 30min); Tapolca (1 daily except Sun; 4hr); Veszprém (1 daily; 2hr); Zalaegerszeg (2 daily; 4hr 30min).
**Harkány** to: Budapest (1 daily; 4hr 15min); Pécs (3 daily; 35min); Siklós (hourly; 1hr); Szekszárd (3 daily; 2hr 15min).
**Kaposvár** to: Hévíz (2 daily; 2hr 30min); Pécs (every 1hr–1hr 30min; 2hr); Siófok (1 daily; 2hr); Szekszárd (2 daily; 2hr 15min); Zalaegerszeg (1 daily; 3hr).
**Komárom** to: Esztergom (3 daily; 1hr 30min); Sopron (2 daily; 1hr 45min).
**Kőszeg** to: Budapest (2 daily; 4hr); Sopron (5 daily; 2hr); Szombathely (5 daily; 30min).
**Mohács** to: Siófok (1 daily; 3hr); Szekszárd (1 daily; 1hr).
**Paks** to: Baja (2 daily; 1hr 30min); Budapest (hourly; 2hr); Pécs (6 daily; 2hr); Szekszárd (hourly; 25min).
**Pécs** to: Abaliget (hourly; 1hr); Békéscsaba (1 daily; 5hr 30min); Harkány (3 daily; 45min); Hévíz (1 daily; 4hr 30min); Kaposvár (every 60–90min; 2hr); Keszthely (4 daily; 4hr); Orfű (hourly; 1hr); Siklós (hourly; 1hr); Siófok (1 daily; 3hr); Székesfehérvár (1 daily; 4hr 30min); Szekszárd (every 1–2hr; 1hr 15min); Szigetvár (every 60–90min; 1hr); Zalaegerszeg (2 daily; 4hr 15min).
**Sárvár** to: Sopron (2 daily; 1hr 15min); Sümeg (2 daily; 1hr); Szombathely (2 daily; 1hr).

**Siklós** to: Budapest (1 daily; 5hr); Harkány (hourly; 1hr); Pécs (hourly; 1hr).
**Sopron** to: Baja (1 daily; 9hr 30min); Balatonfüred (1 daily; 4hr); Budapest (3 daily; 3hr 45min); Esztergom (2 daily; 4hr); Fertőd (hourly; 1hr); Fertőrákos (hourly; 1hr); Győr (3 daily; 2hr); Hévíz (3 daily; 3hr); Komárom (2 daily; 2hr 45min); Kőszeg (5 daily; 2hr); Sárvár (2 daily; 1hr 15min); Sümeg (3 daily; 2hr 15min); Szekszárd (1 daily; 8hr); Szombathely (1 daily; 1hr 45min); Zalaegerszeg (1 daily; 3hr).
**Szekszárd** to: Baja (2 daily; 1hr); Budapest (hourly; 2hr 30min); Kecskemét (1 daily; 2hr); Mohács (4 daily; 1hr); Paks (every 30min; 25min); Pécs (every 1–2hr; 1hr 15min); Siófok (1 daily; 2hr); Szeged (2 daily; 3hr); Székesfehérvár (2 daily; 2hr); Veszprém (2 daily; 3hr 45min).
**Szigetvár** to: Nagykanizsa (5 weekly; 2hr 30min); Pécs (every 1hr–1hr 30min; 1hr).
**Szombathely** to: Budapest (2 daily; 3hr 45min); Ják (hourly; 30min); Keszthely (3 daily; 2hr 30min); Nagykanizsa (3 daily; 2hr 45min); Körmend (hourly; 1hr); Kőszeg (3 daily; 25min); Sárvár (2 daily; 1hr); Sopron (4 daily; 3hr 15min); Zalaegerszeg (6 daily; 1hr 30min).
**Tata** to: Esztergom (every 1hr–1hr 30min ; 1hr 30min); Komárom (hourly; 1hr); Tatabánya (every 20min; 15min).
**Zalaegerszeg** to: Győr (2 daily; 4hr 30min); Kaposvár (1 daily; 3hr); Keszthely (hourly; 1hr); Körmend (1 daily; 1hr); Nagykanizsa (1 daily; 1hr); Pécs (2 daily; 4hr 30min); Sopron (1 daily; 3hr 15min); Székesfehérvár (2 daily; 4hr 15min); Szigetvár (2 daily; 3hr 45min); Szombathely (1 daily; 1hr 20min).

## International trains
**Győr** to: Bratislava (3 daily; 5hr); Vienna (8 daily; 1hr 45min).
**Nagykanizsa** to: Zagreb (June–Sept 2 daily; 3hr 30min).
**Pécs** to: Osijek (2 daily; 4hr).
**Sopron** to: Vienna (1 daily; 1hr); Wiener Neustadt (4 daily; 1hr).
**Szombathely** to: Graz (3 daily; 3hr).
**Tatabánya** to: Bratislava (1 daily; 6hr).

## International buses
**Dunaújváros** to: Komárno (1 daily; 4hr 30min); Vienna (2 weekly; 7hr).
**Győr** to: Galanta (1 daily; 2hr 30min).

**Kaposvár** to: Bratislava (June–Oct 2 weekly; 5hr).

**Lenti** to: Ljubljana (1 daily; 5hr 30min).

**Mohács** to: Osijek (1 daily; 3hr).

**Mosonmagyaróvár** to: Bratislava (2 weekly; 1hr 30min); Vienna (4 weekly; 2hr).

**Sárvár** to: Neunkirchen (July–Aug 1 daily; 4hr); Vienna (June–Sept 1 weekly; 3hr); Wiener Neustadt (1 daily; 5hr).

**Sopron** to: Baden (1 daily; 3hr 30min); Bratislava (1 daily; 3hr); Forchenstein (2 weekly; 1hr 30min); Oberpullendorf (1 daily; 1hr 30min); Semmering (1 daily; 5hr); Vienna (1–2 daily except Sun; 1hr 45min).

**Szombathely** to: Bratislava (1 daily; 3hr 30min); Oberpullendorf (1 daily; 2hr 45min); Oberwart (1–2 daily; 1hr 45min); Stergersbach (July–Aug 1 daily; 2hr 30min); Vienna (2 daily; 3hr).

# CHAPTER FIVE

# THE NORTHERN UPLANDS

H ungary's **Northern Uplands** boast beautiful wooded hills, karstic rock
formations, ruined castles and tranquil villages, as well as three major
wine-producing regions, offering some of the best wines in the world. Top
of the list is **Eger**, which combines a fabulous castle and Baroque town
centre with a viticultural pedigree that's only surpassed by **Tokaj**, in the foothills
of the **Zemplén Hills**, where some of Hungary's finest wine and prettiest villages
are to be found. The scenery gets more impressive the further north you go, as
do the **ruined castles**, which can be seen at villages like **Füzér** and
**Boldogkőváralja**. In the more westerly Cserhát region, the museum village of
**Hollókő** and the castles at **Somoskő** and **Salgóbánya** are as romantic as any in
Hungary, though the best preserved is at **Sárospatak**, on the eastern lowlands
bordering the Great Plain. The other great attraction is likewise remote from
Budapest but worth the journey – the amazing **Aggtelek stalactite caves**.

Historically, the Uplands were more important than they are today, both strategically and economically. Most of the fortresses here saw active service against
the Turks and the Habsburgs, particularly during the War of Independence
(1703–11), led by Ferenc Rákóczi II. In between times, commerce and culture
thrived in tandem with highland Slovakia, until the Treaty of Trianon in 1920
severed the links that sustained old market towns like **Balassagyarmat**, while
industrialization gave rise to utilitarian towns that did well under Communism but
have since become Hungary's "Rust Belt". **Miskolc**, however, is redeemed by its
proximity to the scenic **Bükk Hills** and the *fin-de-siècle* spa of **Lillafüred**.
Another aspect of the region is its Jewish heritage, which draws many Jewish-
Americans to places like **Sátoraljaújhely**, **Gyöngyös** and **Verpelét** in search of
their ancestors. The old synagogues and cemeteries here are even more neglected

---

### ACCOMMODATION PRICE CODES

All accommodation in this guide is graded according to the price bands given below.
Note that prices refer to the **cheapest available double room in high season** or
the price of **two people sharing a tent** in a campsite. 100Ft is roughly equivalent
to $0.45 or DM1. For more details, see p.24.

| | | |
|---|---|---|
| ① Under 2000Ft | ④ 6000–8500Ft | ⑦ 20,000–27,000Ft |
| ② 2000–4000Ft | ⑤ 8500–13,000Ft | ⑧ 27,000–40,000Ft |
| ③ 4000–6000Ft | ⑥ 13,000–20,000Ft | ⑨ over 40,000Ft |

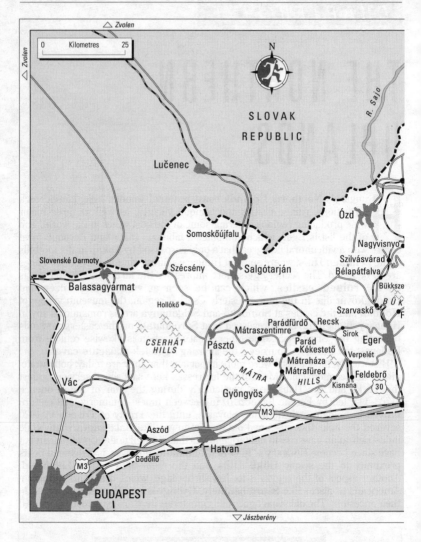

than the former aristocratic mansions that also languished under Communism, though these are now slowly being restored – most impressively at **Gödöllő**, outside Budapest.

## Approaches to the Uplands

Although the westerly Cserhát Hills are accessible by train from Vác on the Danube Bend, the commonest **approaches** are **from Budapest** or the Great Plain. Several trains leave the capital's Keleti Station daily, passing through Hatvan and Füzesabony en route to Miskolc and Szerencs, from where branch

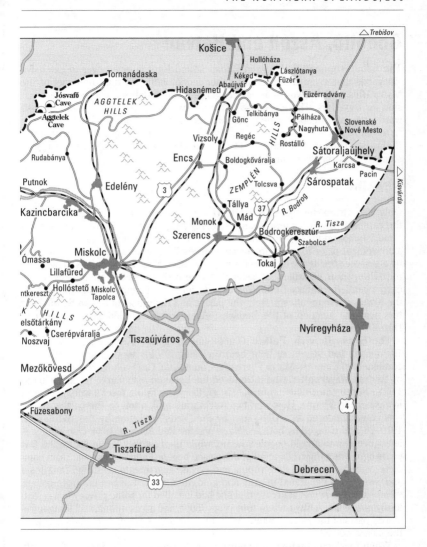

lines head further north. Buses from the Népstadion terminal run directly to Hollókő and Eger, and the HÉV line makes Gödöllő an easy day excursion from the capital. Driving to Eger or Miskolc, the fastest route is the M3 motorway that currently runs as far as Füzesabony, where drivers transfer onto the one-lane Route 3 (E71).

Coming **from the Great Plain**, frequent trains from Nyíregyháza call at Tokaj and Szerencs, before branching off towards Miskolc and Sátoraljaújhely, and there are regular services from Karcag, Tiszafüred and Szolnok to Hatvan and Füzesabony.

# Gödöllő, Aszód and Hatvan

The rolling countryside between Budapest and Eger is given over to extensive vineyards that eventually become rather monotonous, so that the onset of the Mátra Hills at Gyöngyös and the scenic route via Feldebrő are a welcome diversion for travellers. There are also a few places worth visiting as you head eastwards out of Budapest along the M3 motorway – notably **Gödöllő**, whose Grassalkovich Palace and artistic legacy are impressive enough to rate a trip from Budapest. Though the same can't be said about **Aszód** and **Hatvan**, a brief stopover is probably justified.

## Gödöllő

Only 30km from Budapest, **GÖDÖLLŐ** is readily accessible by HÉV train from the capital's Örs Vezér tere Station (50min) and makes a pleasant stopover for motorists bound for Eger or Miskolc, but as few express trains stop here it's not a convenient place to interrupt a train journey. This small Baroque town used to be a summer residence of the Habsburgs, whose palace rivalled the splendour of the "Hungarian Versailles" at Esterháza (see p.227), while the influence of the early twentieth-century Gödöllő Artists' Colony is still apparent in Hungary, as the town's museum attests. Both the palace and the museum are on **Szabadság tér**, near the junction of the Budapest–Aszód road and Gödöllő's main street, Dózsa György utca.

The **Grassalkovich Palace** (Tues–Sun: April–Oct 10am–6pm; Nov–March 10am–5pm; last tickets an hour before closing; 250Ft) was commissioned by a confidante of Empress Maria Theresa's, Count Antal Grassalkovich, and designed by András Mayerhoffer, who introduced the Baroque mansion to Hungary in the 1740s. In the nineteenth century, "Sissy", Emperor Franz Josef's wife, preferred living here to Vienna. However, two world wars took a toll on the palace, which was commandeered as a GHQ first by the "Reds" and then by the "Whites" in 1919–20, and pillaged by both the Nazis and the Red Army in 1944. One wing was later turned into an old people's home, while the rest was left to rot until a few years ago, when the restoration of the palace began. Though this is far from complete, you can visit the state rooms and private apartments used by Franz Josef and Sissy – his decorated in grey and gold, hers draped in her favourite colour, violet – and the secret staircase that she had installed for some privacy in a relentlessly public life. A fifty-minute **tour** costs 350Ft, and a longer one, including unrestored parts of the palace, 400Ft. An English-language *Guide to Gödöllő* is sold at the palace bookshop.

When the **local history museum** at no. 5 Szabadság tér reopens (probably Tues–Sun 10am–6pm; 100Ft), it's sure to focus on the **Gödöllő Artists' Colony**. Founded in 1901, the colony was inspired by the English Pre-Raphaelites and the Arts and Crafts movement of William Morris and John Ruskin, whose communal, rural ethos it took a stage further. Members included Aladár Körösfői Kriesch, who wrote a book about Ruskin and Morris, Sándor Nagy, whose home and workshop may become a separate museum, and the architect Károly Kós. Though the colony dispersed in 1920, its stamp on the decorative arts persisted until the 1950s, while Kós's work has been a major influence on Imre Makovecz and his protegés, who dominate today's architectural scene.

If you have the time and inclination for a stroll, there's a huge **arboretum** on the road to Isaszeg, 3.5km south of the junction (Sat & Sun 9am–dusk). Along this road you'll find several stately old trees and buildings, since this whole area on the edge of town used to be part of the palace grounds. If you head 3km down the road towards Aszód, you'll see a Transylvanian-style wooden gateway fronting a **Capuchin Church** that has been a place of pilgrimage ever since workmen dug up an ivory statue of the Virgin in 1759. The Grassalkovich family vault is situated here, and one can also see the grave of Pál Teleki, the wartime prime minister who committed suicide in protest at Hungary's participation in the Nazi invasion of Yugoslavia.

### Practicalities

**Arriving** by HÉV train, get off well before the terminal at the Szabadság tér stop, which is bang in the centre of town; the bus station is only a minute's walk from Gödöllő Tourist in the Petőfi Cultural Centre at Szabadság út 6 (Mon–Thurs 9am–5pm, Fri 9am–4pm; ☎28/420-685). You can also get **information** from Tourinform in the palace ticket office (Tues–Sun: April–Oct 10am–6pm; Nov–March 10am–5pm; ☎28/415-402). With Budapest so close there's little point in **staying** in one of Gödöllő's pricey pensions, though in July and August you can get cheap rooms at the Agricultural University on Páter Károly utca, just east of the main train station (☎28/430-183; ①). The *Carnevale* pizzeria at Dózsa utca 12 is very handy, but the best **restaurant** is the *Napsugár* on Rét utca, 3km north of the centre (bus #5, #15 or #44 from the depot on Szabadság út), which is hideously kitsch but serves tasty, reasonably priced meals (11am–11pm; closed Tues & Wed).

# Aszód

In **ASZÓD**, 10km further east, the main Szabadság tér is likewise dominated by a gorgeous, decrepit Baroque pile in faded Maria Theresa yellow. The former **Podmaniczky Mansion** also dates from the eighteenth century and was damaged during the war; unlike the Grassalkovich Palace, it was promptly restored, but then stood totally empty for forty years, typifying the Communists' ambivalent attitude to the national heritage. It functions as an archive now, as well as a student dormitory, and the staff of the *kollégium* section along the left-hand side can guide visitors to the former ballroom, whose ceiling fresco by J. L. Kracker is in bizzare contrast to the dreary corridors leading to the *díszterem* (ceremonial hall). The **war memorial** outside the mansion is unusual for bearing a menorah as well as a cross, in remembrance of those who died in the Holocaust – about a quarter of Aszód's prewar population was Jewish.

A few minutes' walk to the right of the mansion, a small **Petőfi Museum**, in an erstwhile Lutheran grammar school at Petőfi utca 6 (March 15 to Oct Tues–Sun 10am–4pm; Nov to March 14 Fri–Sun 10am–4pm; 60Ft), contains material about the poet-revolutionary Sándor Petőfi, who studied here for three years, as well as the usual mix of local archeological, ethnographic and historical exhibits. Some of Hungary's earliest biplanes were produced at the local airplane factory, whose militant workers earned the town the name "Red Aszód" for their role in the 1919 revolution.

Regular **buses** between Aszód and Hatvan run right past Szabadság tér. From the train station, east of the centre, you can board mainline services to Budapest and Miskolc, or local ones to Balassagyarmat (see overleaf).

# Hatvan

**HATVAN**, whose name (meaning "sixty") refers to its distance from Budapest in kilometres, straddles a crossroads between the the the Northern Uplands, the Great Plain and the capital, and was a market town until its wholesale industrialization this century, since when any incentive to linger has been hard to find. Given its pivotal role in the **transport** system, however, you might have an hour to kill between changing buses or trains. While the train station is 2km away down Grassalkovich út, the bus terminal is on Kossuth tér in the old town centre, east of the River Zagyva, alongside a **museum** (Tues–Sun 10–4pm; 60Ft) featuring temporary exhibitions of local art and history, and another, folornly empty, **Grassalkovich mansion**.

Should you be obliged to **stay**, the *Kristály Kastély*, resembling a fancy hunting lodge, is incongruously sited outside a sugarbeet factory on the corner of Boldogi út and Grassalkovich út, near the station (☎37/341-188; ②). It's preferable to the *Park Hotel* at Kossuth tér 14 (☎37/345-409; ①), as a place to **eat**, too. **Buses** fan out from Hatvan to Szolnok, Gyöngyös, the Mátra settlements, and as far afield as Eger.

# The Cserhát Hills

The **Cserhát Hills**, like their loftier neighbours, the Mátra and the Börzsöny, were once continuously forested, with a chain of fortresses guarding the valleys and passes into Slovakia, which formed part of Hungary until 1920. The Treaty of Trianon not only sundered economic ties, but stranded ethnic minorities on both sides of the redrawn border – Magyars in Slovakia, and **the Palóc** in Hungary. The Palóc, though probably of Slovak origin, are noted for their antiquated Hungarian dialect and fantastic costumes that are still worn (with an eye for the tourist trade) at the museum village of **Hollókő**, though you'll learn more about their traditions from the Palóc museum in **Balassagyarmat**.

Elsewhere, the region's feudal past is represented by picturesquely **ruined castles** at **Salgóbánya** and **Somoskő**, and the Forgách mansion at **Szécsény**, which conjure up images of the warlords and counts who held sway before industrialization – a process embodied by the town of **Salgótarján**, with its nineteenth-century mineshafts and Socialist-Realist monuments.

## Balassagyarmat

After losing its medieval fortress and most of its inhabitants to the Turks, **BAL-ASSAGYARMAT** (pronounced "Bolosho-dyarmot") was repopulated by Germans, Slovaks and Czechs in the eighteenth century, when its prosperity was reflected in the Baroque edifices along its main street. This archetypal provincial town produced two of Hungary's leading nineteenth-century writers: Imre Madach, whose play *The Tragedy of Man* is widely held to be Hungary's greatest classical drama, and Kálmán Mikszáth, whose short stories satirized the landed gentry.

Today, the town has little to show for its status as the "Palóc capital" except for an imposing nineteenth-century **county hall** on Köztársaság tér, the main square, and the **Palóc Ethnographical Museum** in a grand, eclectic-style building in Palóc Park, a few minutes' walk down Bajcsy-Zsilinszky út (Tues–Sat 10am–4pm; 100Ft). The exhibition covers every aspect of Palóc life from the cradle to the grave, with all kinds of homemade artefacts and a fantastic collection of folk costumes. Another exhibition housed in two thatched cottages behind the museum presents the traditional Palóc way of life *in situ* (May–Sept Tues–Sun 10am–4pm; 100Ft). En route to Palóc Park from Köztársaság tér, you'll pass the small **City Gallery** on the corner of Bajcsy-Zsilinszky út (Tues–Sun 10am–noon & 1–5pm; 100Ft), exhibiting work by local artists.

### Practicalities

Balassagyarmat's **bus station** lies a block or so north of the central Köztársaság tér, while the **train station** is fifteen minutes' walk south along Kossuth utca. Almost everything else is located on the main Rákóczi fejedelem utca, which runs across Köztársaság tér: namely IBUSZ at no. 61 (Mon–Fri 9am–4pm; ☎35/300-415), the post office at no. 24, an ATM at no. 44, the cheap *Balassa* restaurant at no. 34, and the agreeable *Orchidea* coffee house, further down, at the end of the block.

Aside from private rooms (②), bookable through Tourinform in Szécsény (see below), and IBUSZ in Balassagyarmat, there is the *Club Panzió* at Teleki út 14, a few minutes' walk from the post office (☎35/312-824; ②), and a small campsite on the edge of town on the Budapest road, should you wish **to stay**. If not, there are hourly **buses** to Salgótarján and three a day to Szécsény (see below), plus a weekday service to Lučenec in Slovakia.

# Szécsény

Less than an hour's bus ride from Balassagyarmat, the small town of **SZÉCSÉNY** is ennobled by the **Forgách Mansion**, a vivid yellow Baroque pile occupying the site of a medieval fortress that was blown up by the Habsburgs during the War of Independence. As the Forgáchs were previously noted for their Habsburg sympathies, it's ironic that their mansion was the site of the Hungarian Diet's election of Ferenc Rákóczi II as ruling prince and commander-in-chief of the Magyar forces, and the declaration of the union of Hungary and Transylvania in 1705. Today it houses the **Kubinyi Ferenc Museum** (May–Sept Tues–Sun 10am–6pm; Oct–April Tues–Sat 10am–4pm; 100Ft), with hunting and local archeology exhibits, while the gatekeeper's lodge contains a collection of religious artefacts collected by Sándor Csoma Körösi, who travelled widely in Asia and compiled the first Tibetan–English dictionary. Down the road, to the right of the mansion, stands a **bastion** from the old fortress, exhibiting instruments of torture and engravings showing their use, which staff at the museum will open on request; other remnants of the old **town walls** can be seen in the vicinity.

The mansion is situated on Ady Endre utca, a few minutes' walk from Fő tér, where you'll find an eighteenth-century **Firewatch Tower** that has listed three degrees since the town was bombed in 1944. The Leaning Tower of Pisa it's not, but from mid-May to mid-September you can ascend it to enjoy a bird's-eye view of town; an exhibition on local ornithology and history is due to open here in 1999.

More intriguingly, you can visit a **Franciscan church and monastery** (*Ferences templom & kolostor*) on Erzsébet tér, to the west of the Tourinform office on Rákóczi út, which dates back to the Middle Ages. There are guided tours from Tuesday to Saturday (at 10am, 11am, 2pm, 3pm & 4pm; 60Ft); though, unless you understand Hungarian, they raise more questions than they answer. You can also enter from the far end of Ady Endre utca, beyond the Forgách mansion.

## Practicalities

Tourinform at Rákóczi út 90/B, just west of Fő tér (May–Oct Mon–Fri 8am–4pm, Sat & Sun 10am–6pm; Nov–April Mon–Fri 8am–4pm; ☎32/370-777), can supply **information** and private **rooms** (①), while the *Agro Hotel* next door (☎32/370-382; ②) is a cheaper alternative to the *Panzió Paradisó*, in the servants' quarters of the mansion at Ady utca 14 (☎32/370-427; ③). The *Paradiso*'s **restaurant** serves regional specialities like *tócsni* (potato pancake), and its Saturday night **disco** is occasionally pepped up by erotic shows. There's an ATM at the OTP bank beside the town hall on Fő tér.

# Hollókő

From Szécsény there are hourly buses to **HOLLÓKŐ** (Raven Rock), 16km further south, where a ruined fortress overlooks a **museum village** on UNESCO's world cultural heritage list. Following a fire in 1907, Hollókő's whitewashed Palóc houses were rebuilt in traditional style with broad eaves and carved gables. The old dwellings may now be largely owned by Budapest intellectuals who can better afford the upkeep – their original owners having long since installed themselves in flats on the outskirts – but the village has lost none of its striking appearance. Hollókő's apotheosis comes on August 20, when local dance groups and international folk troupes in gorgeous costumes perform at the **Palóc Festival** (*Palóc szötés*).

At other times, traditional Palóc dress is chiefly worn by old ladies attending vespers at Hollókő's wooden-towered **church** – outwardly austere, but decorated inside in vibrant colours and with flowers. Once, each village had its own style of homespun attire: in Őrhalom, for example, the Hollókő-style cap was transformed into a bonnet by the insertion of a stiff cardboard lining. Fine examples from various localities are displayed in the **Folk Museum** at Kossuth utca 82 (April–Sept Tues–Sun 10am–6pm; Oct–March Thurs 10am–2pm, Fri noon–2pm, Sat & Sun 10am–4pm; 50Ft). This Palóc house follows the Magyar peasant custom of having one room where the family lived and slept, and a parlour solely used for storing bedding and entertaining guests; its curator jokes that the jug and basin by the door was the bathroom. Three wells served the whole village until 1959, when piped water and electricity arrived on the same day.

To delve further into Palóc crafts, visit the *Szövőház* or **Weaving House** at no. 94 (Easter–Oct Tues 10am–2.30pm, Wed–Sat 10am–5.30pm, Sun 10am–4.30pm; 60Ft), which contains a workshop and sells local textiles; and the **Táj és a nép** exhibition at no. 99 (Tues & Thurs–Sun: April–Oct 9am–5pm; Nov–March 10am–3pm; 120Ft), featuring handpainted furniture. Weaving, woodcarving and folk-dancing **courses** can arranged through ID-Ker kft (see opposite). Look out, too, for the superb **exhibition** of photographs of Palóc villages by Irén Ács, at Kossuth utca 75 (daily 10am–5pm; 50Ft).

Lastly, walk up to the **ruined castle** on the hilltop, which is signposted near the church (10min), and also accessible by a steeper path through the woods, seldom used by visitors, which you can reach by carrying on down to the edge of the village and turning left uphill. Although the tumbled ramparts and single surviving tower are a far cry from their former glory as the original seat of the Illés family, the **view** over the village is wonderful.

## Practicalities

Hollókő is directly **accessible by bus** from Budapest's Népstadion terminal (2 daily; 2hr), and connected by hourly services to Szécsény and Salgótarján, plus four a day to Pásztó, the jumping-off point for the Mátra Hills. Buses run through the modern part of Hollókő before dropping visitors at the top of Kossuth utca, the main street running down to the church.

**Information** is available from ID-Ker kft, at Kossuth utca 46, near the bus stop (☎32/379-273), and at no. 68 (Easter–Sept daily 9am–3pm; Oct–Easter Mon–Thurs 9am–3pm; ☎32/379-266), both of which can reserve **rooms** (②), some furnished with Palóc wardrobes and embroidered bolsters. Alternatively there's the year-round *Panoráma* complex, half an hour's walk from the centre at Orgona utca 31 (☎32/379-048), comprising a campsite, bungalows (①) and a small pension (②). Your best bet for **eating and drinking** is *Muskátli* at Kossuth utca 61.

# Salgótarján and around

After folksy Hollókő, **SALGÓTARJÁN** whacks you with Brutalist modernity. Scarred since the nineteenth century by industrial squalor and poverty, this mining town was extensively rebuilt during the 1960s – a tardy response to workers' demonstrations in 1956, when the ÁVO secret police shot dead 131 strikers in the aftermath of the Uprising. Court proceedings against the alleged murderers began in 1994, but locals are sceptical of the outcome and doubtful that senior officials who gave the orders will ever be brought to justice. Even the numbers of those killed is disputed. Fewer than forty names appear on the memorial on December 8 tér, south of the centre, along Rákóczi út.

From a visitor's standpoint, the town's interest lies in its **industrial heritage**, and the chance to visit two romantic **ruined castles** near the Slovak border – though if you happen to be around in early May there's a **jazz festival** to enliven things.

## The Town

**Arriving** at the train station, 300m west of the centre, or the bus depot on the far side of the tracks, aim for the outdoor market, a block behind which, on Ady út, lies the entrance to the defunct "József" pit, now a **Mining Museum** (*Bányamúzeum*; Tues–Sun: April–Sept 9am–3pm; Oct–March 10am–2pm; 100Ft). Cramped and muddy, filled with props, tools and cables, the tunnels only lack the dust, danger and noise of a working mine, but the explanatory leaflet still bids visitors "good luck", the traditional miners' greeting.

If the museum induces nostalgia for the days when Communist countries regarded factories and Five Year Plans as something to celebrate, you can arrange to visit a **Glass Factory** at Huta út 1, ten minutes' walk south of the centre, down Rákóczi út (Mon–Fri 9am–1pm; ☎32/410-433, or contact Nógrád Tourist (see overleaf)), where you can see glass being blown and engraved; there are finished products for sale, too.

The only other "sights" are on the main square at the top end of Rákóczi út, where a huge statue of a gun-toting 1919 revolutionary, and a matching couple of people releasing doves of peace, are all that distinguishes **Fő tér** from its surroundings, other than the outsized *Karancs Hotel*.

## The ruins at Salgóbánya and Somoskő

In contrast with the grimness of the town, the surrounding countryside is well endowed with volcanic rock formations and picturesque ruins. Regular buses from Salgótarján's terminal run 8km north to the village of **SALGÓBÁNYA**, overlooked by a **ruined castle** (Tues–Sun 9am–5pm; 60Ft), which broods atop a 625-metre-high basalt cone. Constructed after the Mongol invasion of the thirteenth century, it later belonged to Count István Werbőczy, author of the Tripartium law which bound the peasants to "perpetual serfdom" following the peasants' revolt of 1514. The castle was blown up during the Turkish occupation, but it's still worth visiting the ruins, which command superb views of the highlands further north. You can stay in the *Hotel Medves* just below (☎32/435-066; ②).

Most buses carry on to **SOMOSKŐ**, a hamlet near the Slovak border. Just across the border, another **ruined castle** squats upon vast blocks of eroded stone. Founded during the fifteenth century, its five towers survey impressive **basalt formations** (*bazaltömlés*) resembling giant organ pipes. It used to be possible to visit both sites on organized tours, but this arrangement has now lapsed and they can only be reached from Slovakia, so you'll need a pair of binoculars to get the best from the view. The *Somosi Fogadó*, in Somoskő village (☎32/435-229; ①), is the only place to stay.

## Practicalities

In Salgótarján you can get **information** from Nógrád Tourist at Erzsébet tér 5, a few minutes' walk south of Fő tér (April–Sept Mon–Fri 8am–5pm, Sat 8am–noon; Oct–March Mon–Fri 8am–4pm; ☎32/316-940), or IBUSZ at Rákóczi út 10 (Mon–Thurs 8am–4pm, Fri 8am–3pm; ☎32/421-200), both of which can arrange private **rooms** (②). The best pension in town is the *Galcsik Fogadó* at Alkotmány utca 2, near the bus station (☎32/316-524; ②), a bright new building with good facilities. Otherwise, there's the *Karancs Hotel* (☎32/410-088; ③), or a chalet at *Tó-Strand Camping*, 5km from the centre, at the end of the #6 bus route (☎32/311-168; ①–②; April to mid-Oct), though if you're going to travel that far out it's better to go the whole hog and stay at Salgóbánya or Somoskő (see above).

The best place to eat is the restaurant in the *Galcsik Fogadó*, while the *Godó Cukrászda* at Rákóczi út 12 does delicious **cakes**. In early May each year Salgótarján comes to life with an international **Dixieland Jazz Festival**, held in the József Attila cultural centre on Fő tér; ask Nógrád Tourist for details.

If you're dependent on public transport, **moving on** amounts to heading northeast towards Ózd or south towards the Mátra region, assuming that you don't take a bus to Lučenec in Slovakia. Since the remote Aggtelek caves are the only reason for passing through Ózd, and bus connections are unreliable, **south** seems the obvious direction to take. Along the way to Hatvan (by bus or train), ore-buckets and slag hills disappear, giving way to vineyards and fields, and you can change buses at **Pásztó** and head **into the Mátra** by a scenic route – though services from Hatvan to Gyöngyös run more frequently.

# Gyöngyös and the Mátra Hills

Hungarians make the most of their highlands, and the **Mátra Hills**, where Mount Kékestető just tops 1000m, are heavily geared to domestic tourism. Mount Kékestető itself is a popular place for winter sports, despite the relatively lacklustre resort facilities at Mátraháza and Mátraszentimre. In the summer, families ramble the paths between picnic sites and beer gardens, unaware of the wild boar and deer that live deeper in the thickets of oak and beech. Few of the Mátra settlements have much of interest beyond their amenities, but the hills and forests are, in any case, the main attraction.

The Library, Pannonhalma Monastery

Pannonhalma Monastery

Fertőd Palace

Eger's Cathedral

Topiary, Fertőd Palace

The Zsolnay fountain, Pécs

The Bishop's Palace, Székesfehérvar

A Komondor, the largest Hungarian dog

Paprika drying near Villany

The nine-arched bridge at Hortobágy

Northern Uplands farmhouse

Vineyards in the Tokaj-Hegyalja region

Roadside conversation, Szatmár region

Bugac Puszta

# Gyöngyös

Most visitors approach the Mátra via **GYÖNGYÖS** (pronounced "Dyurn-dyursh"), the centre of the Gyöngyös-Visonta **wine** region, where white wine grapes predominate. Gyöngyös itself is a mellow town with enough museums and Baroque monuments to rate an hour or two of sightseeing before pushing on into the hills.

The town's central **Fő tér** is a long, thin square surrounded by Baroque and Art Nouveau buildings, reconstructed after a fire in 1917. On the northeast corner stands **St Bartholomew's Church** (9am–noon), originally Gothic but heavily remodelled in the eighteenth century, when the small building behind it was a music school. Across the road at Szent Bertalan utca 3, the Baroque **House of the Holy Crown** is so named because the Crown of St Stephen was brought here three times for safekeeping between 1806 and 1809. By ringing the bell you can gain admission to a splendid **Ecclesiatical Treasury** of vestments, books and medieval chalices (Tues–Sun 10am–noon & 2–5pm; 50Ft), and view a ceiling fresco that includes a picture of Hungary's last monarch painted in the 1920s, whose last legislative action was to approve the rebuilding of the town after the 1917 fire. The anti-monarchist regime of the time condemned the fresco as illegal, as it depicted a king.

Five minutes' walk east along Kossuth utca brings you to the former Orczy mansion at no. 40, housing the **Mátra Museum** (Tues–Sun: April–Oct 9am–4pm; Nov–March 10am–2pm; 180Ft), whose local archeology and history section, including photos of the great fire, has some English explanations. The wildlife section upstairs includes tableaux on hunting, and a dazzling collection of minerals, butterflies and other Mátra wildlife, while downstairs, live lizards and birds from around the world appear in a **Mikroárium** (same hours; 80Ft).

By heading south from the museum, past the bus station, and turning right, you come to a **Franciscan Church** endowed by the Báthori family (see p.223), whose coat of arms – three dragon's teeth surrounded by a dragon biting its own tail – appears in the chancel. The Franciscan library on the first floor has exhibitions of illuminated manuscripts (Tues–Fri 2–4pm, Sat 10am–noon; 20Ft).

Before the Holocaust Gyöngyös had a considerable Jewish population, as evinced by the **Great Synagogue** on Vármegye tér, west of Fő tér, a Moorish-Gothic hybrid designed in 1929 by Lipót Baumhorn that once belonged to the Reform community, but now sadly serves as a carpet warehouse. Their Orthodox co-religionists used the older **Memorial Synagogue**, a Neoclassical edifice next door, built in 1816, that nowadays houses a local TV station.

## Practicalities

Arriving at the train station, simply follow Kossuth utca past the terminal for the narrow-gauge line, the Mátra Museum and the main crossroads until you come to central Fő tér. The bus station is 100m south of the crossroads, on Koháry út. Tourinform at Fő tér 13 (July–Sept Mon–Fri 8.30am–5pm, Sat 8.30am–noon; Oct–June Mon–Fri 8.30am–4pm; ☎37/311-155) is the best source of **information**, though you can also try IBUSZ at Kossuth utca 6 (May–Sept Mon–Fri 8am–6pm, Sat 8am–noon; Oct–April Mon–Fri 8 am–4pm; ☎37/311-861), or Mátra Tourist in an ugly modern building at Hanisz tér 2, off to the north of the main square (June–Aug Mon–Fri 8.30am–5pm, Sat 8am–1pm; Sept–May Mon–Fri 8.30am–5pm; ☎37/311-565).

The plushest **accommodation** in Gyöngyös is the three-star *Hotel Mátra* on Fő tér (☎37/312-057; ④), although the *Vincellér Panzió* at Erzsébet királyné utca 22 (☎37/311-691; ③) has a good restaurant and offers better value for money; cheaper private rooms (②) are available from all the tourist offices, where you can also make bookings at the Mátra resorts (see below). Other **eating** possibilities include the *Kékes Étterem* on Fő tér, opposite Tourinform, and the humble but popular *Kulács Vendéglő* on Pater Kis Szalész út 10, near the post office behind Tourinform (Mon–Fri 9am–8.30pm, Sat till 3pm). Next door there's a wine cellar that's open longer hours.

To quit town in style, head for the terminus of the **Mátravasút**, a narrow-gauge train line on Kossuth utca, just beyond the Matra Museum, which runs to Mátrafüred in the hills (see below), with departures roughly every hour until nightfall.

# The Mátra villages

Though most tourists head straight for Mátrafüred, there are several picturesque **villages** at the foot of the Mátras that are relatively undiscovered, and right in the heart of the **wine country**. With your own transport it's feasible to explore the region thoroughly, but travellers dependent on local buses may have to settle for the village of **GYÖNGYÖSPATA**, 12km west of Gyöngyös. This has a fifteenth-century **Gothic church** with a fine doorway and an imposingly high Baroque altar; keys are held in the house just uphill or at the addresses listed on the door. If you feel like staying, try the *Patavár Panzió* at Fő út 47 (☎37/364-486; ②). Alternatively, you can follow a minor road for 20km in the direction of Eger to reach **KISNÁNA** and view a **ruined castle** destroyed by Ottomans in the sixteenth century, before carrying on to Verpelét (see p.280). There's a small museum inside the ruins, with a lapidarium (May–Sept Tues–Sun 9am–1pm; 50Ft).

From Gyöngyös, **buses** run every hour or so to Mátrafüred and Mátraháza, and four or five buses a day pass through Parád, Recsk and Sirok on their way to Eger. Recsk and Sirok are also accessible via the branch train line down from **Kál-Kápolna** (the station before Füzesabony on the Budapest–Miskolc line). Anyone intending to visit Sirok or Feldebrő, or go walking in the hills, should buy a large-scale **hiking map** (*A Mátra turistatérképe*) beforehand. Egertourist in Eger and Tourinform in Gyöngyös can help find accommodation in the villages.

## Mátrafüred and Sás-tó

The Mátravasút is the fun way to get from Gyöngyös to **MÁTRAFÜRED**, and takes no longer than the bus, dropping passengers off at the centre of this sloping, popular spa settlement. Private **rooms** (②) can be arranged through Tourinform in Gyöngyös, or there's the three-star *Hotel Avar* at Páradi út 5 (☎37/320-131; ④), which organizes tennis and horse-riding, or the less expensive *Hegyalja Panzió*, a former trade union resort at Béke út 7 (☎37/320-027; ②). For eating, there are endless buffets in the centre of the village.

Four kilometres uphill from Mátrafüred, on the bus route between Gyöngyös and Mátraháza, lies **Sás-tó** (Sedge Lake). More of a large pond than a lake, it's a friendly place full of Hungarians boating and fishing amid the usual snack stands. If you feel like **staying**, *Sas-tó Camping* (☎37/374-025; ①; April to mid-Oct) is an attractive complex with a 28-room motel and bungalows. At 8pm the restaurant closes and action shifts down to the **disco** and bars in Mátrafüred. Heading on, you can easily walk from Sás-tó to Mátraháza along the footpath through the forest, where **wild boars** reputedly lurk.

## Mátraháza and Mount Kékestető

MÁTRAHÁZA, 9km north of Mátrafüred, is a small village consisting mainly of ex-trade union hostels converted into hotels, plus a few bars, though there are plenty of enjoyable walks in the vicinity. The chalet-style *Bérc Hotel* (☎37/374-095; ③) is a clean and pleasant place to stay, as is the friendly *Hotel Pagoda*, in the centre of the village (☎37/374-013; ②). The latter consists of three Communist-style buildings, one of which houses the village's most reliable restaurant.

From Mátraháza, you can easily make a quick bus trip to **Mount Kékestető**, the highest point (1015m) in the Mátra range. Two **ski runs** (*sípálya*) descend from the summit (you can rent skiing equipment at the slope and the car park), which is crowned by a nine-storey telecommunications **tower** offering an impressive view of the highlands (Tues–Sun: April–Oct 9.30am–4pm; Nov–March 9.30am–3pm; 160Ft). The *Hotel Hegycsúcs* at the top of the hill has a sauna and gym (☎37/367-086; ④).

## Parád and Parádfürdő

About 10km to the northeast, a group of similarly named villages gathers around **PARÁD**, where Count Károlyi tried to set an example to other nobles in 1919 by distributing land to his serfs. The settlement has an old **Palóc House** full of costumes and artefacts (Tues–Sun 9am–5pm; 60Ft), and an exhibition of **wood-carving**, signposted *Fafaragó Kiállítás* (daily 9am–7pm; 50Ft). Inexpensive **accommodation** is available at the *Palócz Fogadó* on Kossuth utca (☎36/364-053; ②).

A popular **thermal spa** where the sulphurous, fizzy water is said to benefit digestive complaints, **PARÁDFÜRDŐ** really deserves a visit for its **Coach Museum** (*Kocsimúzeum*; April–Oct daily 9am–5pm; Nov–March Tues–Sun 10am–4pm; 65Ft). The splendid collection includes vehicles for state occasions, hunting and gallivanting around in. For the record, the coach, which superseded the cumbersome wagon throughout Europe, was actually invented in a Hungarian village called – one might have guessed it – Kocs, west of Budapest (see p.209). Some beautiful horses can be seen in adjacent stables, which were designed for the Károlyi family by Miklós Ybl, the architect of Budapest's Opera House.

Follow the signposts from the main road to the eastern end of the village to find cheap **rooms** in the *Muflon Fogadó* at Peres utca 8 (②), which has a **restaurant** (daily except Tues 4–10pm); the *Valentin Panzió* at no. 16 (☎36/364-295; ②); and the *Boroka Mini Hotel* at no. 18 (☎36/364-527; ③).

## Recsk

Mention **RECSK**, a village 2km east of Parádfürdő, and many older Hungarians will share recollections of terror. During the late 1940s and early 1950s, thousands of the tens of thousands of citizens arrested by the ÁVO were sentenced to labour in the quarries southwest of here. Half-starved and frequently beaten by their jailers, prisoners died of exhaustion or in rockfalls, or more usually while sleeping in muddy pits open to the sky.

Closed by Imre Nagy in 1953, **Recsk concentration camp** was effaced by a tree plantation during the Kádár years, and not until 1991 were its victims commemorated. A stone **monument** symbolizing repression and a bronze model of the camp stand near the still-working quarry, 4.5km up from the village (look for the *Kőbánya* signs).

## Sirok, Verpelét and Feldebrő

The bus from Parádfürdő to Eger stops at **SIROK**, 8km further east, en route to Eger – the place to visit if you're wild about romantic views. On a mountain top above the village, 1.5km northeast of the train station, there's a ruined thirteenth-century **castle** from which you can admire the mingled peaks of the Mátra, the Bükk and Slovakia. The village itself is also lovely, its old houses nestling among cliffs and crags, and there's a **campsite** at the end of the road towards the castle (☎36/361-558; ①; May–Sept).

Antiquity buffs can head 11km south to **VERPELÉT**, with their own transport, where the **Jewish cemetery** on the far side of the village has gravestones from as long ago as 1628, many richly carved or tilting at crazy angles. The cemetery is tended by a Roma gypsy family living nearby, who can help you climb into the grounds.

Four kilometres further down the road, **FELDEBRŐ** boasts one of the oldest church crypts in Hungary, containing twelfth-century **frescoes** influenced by Byzantine art, and the **grave of King Aba** (1041–44), one of the ephemeral monarchs between the Árpád and Angevin dynasties. Keys for the crypt (Tues–Sat 9am–noon & 1–6pm, Sun & holidays 1–6pm) are held by a grumpy guy at Szabadság tér 19, nearby. The local **linden leaf wine** (*Debrői hárslevelű*) is good for refreshing weary travellers, as you can discover in **wine cellars** such as the one at Árpád út 2.

### Füzesabony

Though it's not in the Mátra, **FÜZESABONY** rates a mention as a **road and rail junction** between Route 3 and the main line to Miskolc, and the branch routes north to Eger. Other than that, it gained some notoriety in 1997 when its mayor returned the wrong video to a local store and a home movie of him having sex with prostitutes fell into the hands of his opponents, who made six hundred copies and posted them to everyone in his town, forcing his resignation.

# Eger and around

Situated in its own sunny valley between the Mátra and the Bükk, **EGER** is famed for its wine, its minaret, and the heroic legend attached to its castle, which overlooks a florid Baroque town centre. With by far the liveliest atmosphere of anywhere in the Northern Uplands, this is a must on anyone's itinerary.

From Eger, buses and local trains head to various villages bordering the Bükk national park, notably Szilvásvárad, near the Szalajka Valley to the north, and Cserépváralja to the northeast, just below the "rocking" stones in the Felső-szoros ravine. Thus you can enter the Bükk Hills from the west, or cut straight through on a bus to Miskolc, and re-enter them by train from Lillafüred (see p.288) after you've finished with Eger. There are also regular buses and trains to Budapest.

## Arrival and information

The best source of **information** is Tourinform at Dobó István tér 2 (May–Oct daily 9am–6pm; Nov–April Mon–Fri 9am–5pm, Sat 9am–2pm; ☎36/321-807), who can also help out with information about **horse-riding** and other activities on offer in the region. There is also Egertourist at Bajcsy-Zsilinszky utca 9 (May–Sept Mon–Fri 10am–6pm, Sat 9am–noon; Oct–April Mon–Fri 9am–5pm; ☎36/411-724) and IBUSZ at Széchenyi utca 9 (June–Sept Mon–Fri 8am–6pm, Sat 8am–1pm; Oct–May Mon–Fri 8am–4pm, closed 12.25–1.25pm for lunch; ☎36/311-451). The post office is at Széchenyi utca 20–22.

# Accommodation

Eger is a popular destination, so it's advisable to **book ahead** to get the place of your choice, though there are usually **private rooms** (②) available beyond the centre. Tourinform has a list, but won't do bookings, which are handled by Egertourist and IBUSZ (see above), Express at Széchenyi utca 28 (Mon–Fri 9am–5pm, Sat 9am–1pm; ☎36/427-757) and Villa Tours at Deák út 55 (April–Sept Mon–Fri 10am–8pm, Sat 10am–6pm, Sun 2–6pm; Oct–March Mon–Fri 10am–6pm; ☎36/417-803).

The cheapest option is **student hostels** (*kollégium*), bookable through Express or Villa Tours. Multi-bed rooms can be found at Klapka György utca 10 (☎36/313-943; ①; summer daily; winter Sat & Sun only), and Pozsonyi utca 4–6 (☎36/324-122; ①; mid-June to Aug).

*HOTELS, MOTELS AND PENSIONS*

**Bacchus Panzió**, Szépasszonyvölgy (☎36/428-950). A classy place with a restaurant and secure parking, close to the wine cellars outside town. ⑤.

**Flóra Hotel**, Fürdo utca 5 (☎36/320-211). A block near Eger's thermal baths, with free admission for guests. All rooms have TV and minibar, and many have balconies. ⑤.

**Fortuna Panzió**, Kapás utca 35A (☎36/316-480). West of the first junction on Deák út as you come up from the train station, en route to Szépasszonyvölgy. All rooms have TV and fridge. ③.

**Hotel Park-Eger**, Szálloda utca 1–3 (☎36/413-233). A three-star establishment made up of the older *Park* and the modern *Eger*. Both are identically priced and have a few rooms overlooking the Archbishop's garden, which are the nicest. Facilities include a swimming pool, sauna and bowling alley. ⑤.

**MÁV Turista Szálló**, Állomás tér 2 (☎36/410-132). Plain but clean four-bed rooms in the train station building – great for sleepless nights. ①.

**Minaret Hotel**, Knezich utca 4 (☎36/410-020). A comfy three-star establishment, with a swimming pool, which faces the minaret, making it almost irresistible. ④.

**Senátor-ház Hotel**, Dobó István tér 11 (☎36/320-466). A lovely eighteenth-century inn near the castle. It only has eleven rooms (with bathroom, TV, minibar and hair dryer), so book ahead. ⑤.

**Szépasszony Fogadó**, Szépasszonyvölgy (☎36/310-777). A simple guesthouse out near the valley, offering rooms without breakfast. ③.

**Tourist Motel**, Mekcsey utca 2 (☎36/429-014). Just off Szarvas tér. Rooms sleeping two to four people, with or without bathroom. The more of you there are, the lower the price is. ①–②.

*CAMPSITES*

**Autós Caravan Camping**, 3km north of the centre by bus #10 or #11 (☎36/410-558). Two-person bungalows (②) and huts (①), tent space, a restaurant and snack bar. Open mid-April to mid-Oct.

**Tulipán Camping**, across the road from the riding centre, at the entrance to the Szépasszony Valley (☎36/410-580). Small site, open July & Aug.

# The Town

One of the oldest Magyar settlements in Hungary, Eger was a flourishing Renaissance centre at the time of the Turkish invasion, when it found itself on the front line after the occupation of Buda. To general amazement, its castle withstood the **siege of 1552**, when two thousand soldiers and Eger's **women** (who hurled rocks, hot soup and fat), under the command of **István Dobó**, repulsed a Turkish force six times their number – a victory immortalized in Géza Gárdonyi's novel *Egri Csillagok* (*Eclipse of the Crescent Moon*). During the siege of 1596, however, the castle was held by foreign mercenaries who surrendered after a week, whereupon the Turks sacked Eger, leaving only "blackened walls and buildings razed to the ground" and "the naked bodies of Christians baking in the sun, in some places four yards high".

By the time the Turks were driven out in 1687, Eger had only 3500 inhabitants, including 600 Muslims who subsequently converted to Christianity. Its **revival** in the eighteenth century was directed by the episcopal see, which commissioned much of the Baroque architecture that gives Eger its characteristic appearance. This was largely financed by the local vineyards, whose robust red *Egri Bikavér* – known abroad as **Bull's Blood** – is still a major money-earner, both from direct sales and the tourism that it generates. Under Communism, local co-ops had little incentive to aim for quality and a lot of fairly rough stuff was produced (which is still on sale), but in recent years, independent producers such as Thummerer have done much to raise standards.

While the town's cultural traditions are celebrated by a **Baroque Festival** in July and early August, it's fitting that the major event is the **Harvest Festival** (*Szüret*) in September, with two weeks of wine-related events, including folk dancing and a parade of floats. Though finding somewhere to stay could be a bit problematic, this is the best time to visit – particularly if you enjoy drinking wine.

Travellers **arriving** at the bus station, near the cathedral, can stroll into the centre. Coming from the train station, walk up the road to Deák Ferenc út, catch bus #10 or #12 and get off just before the cathedral. Within the centre of the town, orientation is simple and everything is within walking distance.

## The Cathedral and Lyceum

**Eger Cathedral**, occupying a site hallowed since the eleventh century, looms above a flight of steps flanked by statues of saints Stephen, László, Peter and Paul, by the Italian sculptor Casagrande. Constructed between 1831 and 1836, this ponderous Neoclassical edifice was architect József Hild's rehearsal for the still larger basilica at Esztergom. Its interior was largely decorated by J. L. Kracker, who spent his last years working in Eger. Particularly impressive is the frescoed cupola, where the City of God arises in triumph as evildoers flee the sword. Close by, facing Széchenyi utca, stands the **Archbishop's Palace**, a U-shaped Baroque pile with fancy wrought-iron gates. In the right wing of the palace you'll find the treasury and a history of the bishopric of Eger (Mon–Sat: April–Oct 9am–5pm; Nov–March 10am–2pm; 80Ft).

The florid, Zopf-style **Lyceum**, opposite the cathedral, was founded by two enlightened bishops whose proposal for a university was rejected by Maria Theresa. Now a teacher training college (named after Ho Chi Minh during the Communist era), the building is worth visiting for its **library** (Mon–Fri 9.30am–1pm, Sat & Sun 9.30am–noon; 150Ft), whose beautiful floor and fittings

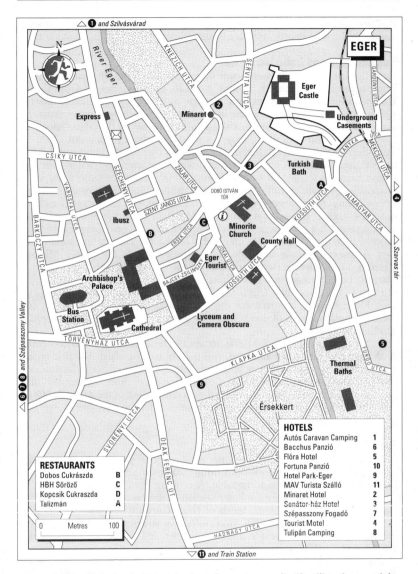

**EGER**

△ **1** and Szilvásvárad

River Eger

N

Express

Minaret ●

**Eger Castle**

**Underground Casements**

CSIKY UTCA

KNEZICH UTCA

SERVITA UTCA

GÁRDONYI UTCA

**Turkish Bath**

DOBÓ ISTVÁN TÉR

**Ibusz**

SZÉCHENYI UTCA

SZENT JÁNOS UTCA

ZALÁR UTCA

ÉRSEK UTCA

**A**

KOSSUTH UTCA

LEÁNYKA UTCA

MÉCSEY UTCA

ALMAGYAR UTCA

**B**

**C**

(i)

**Minorite Church**

**County Hall**

**Eger Tourist**

BAJCSY-ZSILINSZKY

TÁRKÁNYI UTCA

KOSSUTH UTCA

▷ Szarvas tér

▷ **4**

**Archbishop's Palace**

BARKÓCZY UTCA

**Bus Station**

**Cathedral**

TÖRVÉNYHÁZ UTCA

**Lyceum and Camera Obscura**

KLAPKA UTCA

FÜRDŐ UTCA

**Thermal Baths**

**5**

△ **6 7 8** and Szépasszony Valley

**9**

Érsekkert

SVORÉNYI UTCA

DEÁK FERENC ÚT

**HOTELS**

| | |
|---|---|
| Autós Caravan Camping | 1 |
| Bacchus Panzió | 6 |
| Flóra Hotel | 5 |
| Fortuna Panzió | 10 |
| Hotel Park-Eger | 9 |
| MAV Turista Szálló | 11 |
| Minaret Hotel | 2 |
| Senátor-ház Hotel | 3 |
| Szépasszony Fogadó | 7 |
| Tourist Motel | 4 |
| Tulipán Camping | 8 |

**RESTAURANTS**

| | |
|---|---|
| Dobos Cukrászda | B |
| HBH Söröző | C |
| Kopcsik Cukraszda | D |
| Talizmán | A |

0 Metres 100

HADNAGY UTCA

▽ **11** and Train Station

are made of polished oak. There is also a huge trompe l'oeil ceiling fresco of the Council of Trent by Kracker and his son-in-law. The lightning bolt and book in one corner symbolize the Council's decision to establish an Index of forbidden books and suppress all heretical ideas.

While in the building, it's definitely worth checking out the **observatory**, at the top of the tower in the east wing (same hours and ticket as the library), where a nineteenth-century **camera obscura** projects a view of the entire town from a bird's-eye perspective. The camera's monocled curator gleefully points out lovers kissing in the backstreets, unaware of surveillance.

## Kossuth utca and Dobó István tér

From the Lyceum and Provost House across the way, **Kossuth utca** leads past a Franciscan church, where a mosque stood in Turkish times, and the **County Hall**, whose magnificent gates were wrought by Henrik Fazola – notice the stork with a snake in its beak and a vine in its claws, on the county coat of arms. The same man who designed the gates was also responsible for the prison bars in the old Eger jail at Kossuth utca 9, now a small **local history museum** (April–Oct Tues–Sun 9am–4pm; 80Ft). If your Hungarian is up to it, the curator will deliver an enthusiastic lecture on Eger's local swimming team and water polo club, whose members formed the basis of Hungary's Olympic team. Otherwise, printed information is available in English detailing the exhibits of each room.

Continuing along Kossuth utca across the bridge, you pass on your right the deserted "Buttler House" that featured in Mikszáth's novel, *A Strange Marriage*, and on your left a synagogue now transformed into a shop. Alternatively, follow Bajcsy-Zsilinszky or Érsek utca into **Dobó István tér**, the starting point for further sightseeing. Along one side of the square stands the former **Minorite Church**, a twin-towered Baroque edifice completed in 1771. The Latin inscription above its entrance asserts that "Nothing is Enough for God". The small exhibition of Palóc folk art next door (April–Oct Tues–Sun 9am–5pm; 60Ft) is also worth a visit. More striking, however, are the action-packed **statues of warriors** commemorating the siege of 1552, including several women wreaking havoc on Turkish assailants.

A short distance from Dobó István tér are two relics of the Turkish occupation. A slender, fourteen-sided **minaret**, rising forty metres above Knezich utca, is Eger's most photographed structure, and, despite looking rather forlorn since its mosque was demolished in 1841, it offers fine views from its balcony (daily 9am–5pm; 40Ft). If the door is locked, the reception desk of the adjacent *Minaret Hotel* will loan you a key. A passing glance suffices for the unimpressive remains of a **Turkish bath**, en route to Eger Castle.

## Eger Castle

With every approach covered by batteries of cannons, you can easily appreciate why **Eger Castle** (daily 9am–5pm, Mon *Kazamata* and Hall of Heroes only; 250Ft, 120Ft Mon) was so formidable. Ascending from its lower gate past the Gergely Bastion, you enter the inner section of the castle through the Várkoch Bastion. On top of this lies the **tomb of Géza Gárdonyi**, on which is inscribed "Only his body lies here". The ticket office is straight ahead. If you feel so inclined, you can also invest in a historical video and English-language cassette for a do-it-yourself tour.

One of the few Gothic structures left in northeastern Hungary, the **Bishop's Palace** harbours a **museum** containing tapestries, Turkish handicrafts and weaponry. On the ground floor are temporary exhibits and a "**Hall of Heroes**" (*Hősök terme*), where István Dobó is buried amid a bodyguard of siege heroes carved in best Stakhanovite style. The adjacent **art gallery** boasts several fine Munkácsys and three romantic Transylvanian landscapes by Antal Ligeti.

To the east of this complex lies a jumble of medieval foundations signposted as a "Romkert" – **Garden of Ruins**. Here stood Eger's Gothic cathedral, which was damaged by fire in 1506 and used by the Turks as a gunpowder magazine during the first siege "to spite the Christians". To the south, tour groups gather outside the concrete tunnel entrance to the *Kazamata* or **underground galleries**, a labyrinth of sloping passages, gun emplacements, deep-cut observation shafts and mysterious chambers.

### Out from the centre: the Szépasszony Valley

Although the **Wine Museum** at Városfal utca 1 (Tues–Sat noon–10pm; free) offers a display of viticultural implements to whet your palate, it's more fun to go drinking in the **Szépasszony Valley**, just west of town (accessible by taxi). The "Valley of the Beautiful Women" is surrounded by dozens of vineyards producing four types of **wine** – *Muskotály* (Muscatel), *Bikavér* (the famous Bull's Blood), *Leányka* (medium dry white with a hint of herbs) and *Médoc Noir* (rich, dark red and sweet – coats your tongue black). Though the valley has suffered at the hands of mass tourism, it is still fun to visit, particularly outside peak season.

Finding the right **wine cellar** is a matter of luck and taste – some are dank and gloomy, some serve wines of ambrosial quality and others will pour you a trickle of vinegar. Certain cellars also have their own **musicians**, who appear only when tourist numbers have reached critical volume. Most cellars are open daily until 8pm or later, depending on custom. Particularly recommended are those at no. 31, whose proprietor Mr Szilágyi speaks English (try his excellent *Médoc Noir*), and no. 32 where János Birincsik stocks some fine old wines, including a vintage *Bikavér*.

Getting back into town can be a challenge unless you're prepared to hoof it (it's a twenty-minute walk). Getting hold of a taxi is hard, as they tend not to pick up the phone. Your best bet, if you really don't want to walk, is to arrange before you go for a taxi to come and pick you up.

En route between the valley and the town you'll pass a large **Jewish cemetery**, which was desecrated by local **skinheads** in 1994. For some reason, Eger seems to have more than its fair share of them, and their occasional presence at drinking venues merits a word of warning.

## Eating, drinking and activities

With a dozen restaurants and takeaways around the centre, **eating out** in Eger is never a problem. For a full meal, your best options are the *Talizmán* at Kossuth utca 19 and the *HBH Söröző*, just off Dobó István tér. Other restaurants in the centre are inclined to be tourist traps, so if you're aiming to economize it's better to check out the backstreets on the periphery. For toasted sandwiches and other snacks, try the *Szenátor Ház* in the hotel of the same name, which also does coffee and cakes. Eger's most elegant patisseries are the *Dobos Cukrászda* at Széchenyi utca 6 and the *Kopcsik Cukrászda* at Kossuth utca 28; the latter is famous for its parfaits and cakes iced with marzipan in the style of Palóc and Matyó embroidery.

For **drinking**, head out to the cellars of the **Szépasszony Valley** to sample the local wines. If you get hungry, there are plenty of snack bars and one or two restaurants to choose from, so there's no need to take a picnic.

### Activities

Contact Tourinform if you're interested in **horse-riding** in the Szépasszony or Szalajka valleys, or **aeroplane tours** over town (May–Aug, weather permitting). Riding is also good at Nagyegyed, 2km northeast of town on the road to Noszvaj, where you can get simple accommodation at the stud itself, the *Mátyás Udvarház* (☎36/312-804), and where the saddle-shy can enjoy carriage rides. Alternatively, head for the **thermal baths** and **swimming pool** (May–Sept daily 8.30am–7.30pm), where half the town comes to wallow and splash at weekends during summertime – look out for the pool's pebbly bottom. Folk or rock **concerts** are sometimes held in the open-air theatre at the end of the Szépasszony Valley.

## Up to Szilvásvárad and the Szalajka Valley

The road and rail line skirt the western foothills of the Bükk as they wiggle northwards towards Putnok. Twelve kilometres out from Eger the scenery is promisingly lush around **SZARVASKŐ** (Stag Rock), a pretty village with a **ruined castle** and two basic **hotels**: the *Turistaszálló* (☎36/352-085; ①) and the *Debmut* (☎36/352-057 or 52/412-233 for reservations; ①), both on Rózsa utca. Further on, quarries and an ugly cement factory spoil the view at **BÉLAPÁTFALVA**, where the sole reason to stop is a well-preserved Romanesque **abbey church** (Tues–Sun 9am–4pm; 40Ft), founded by French Cistercian monks in 1232. To get to the church, follow the signpost off the main road for 2km. On chilly days, the caretaker can be found at Rózsa utca 42 – look for the *apátság gondnok* (abbey wardens) sign on the right shortly after leaving the main road.

### Szilvásvárad

Eight kilometres further north, **SZILVÁSVÁRAD** occupies a dell beside wooded hills rising to the east. Once the private estate of the pro-Fascist Pallavicini family, and then a workers' resort after 1945, nowadays it is chiefly known as a breeding centre for **Lippizaner horses** (see box below) and the site of Hungary's annual coach-driving championship, the **Bükk Trophy**, usually held the last weekend in August. Those who feel inspired to go **horse-riding** themselves should head for the Péter Kovács stables, just out of town on the main highway to Eger (☎36/355-155; 2000Ft per hour in German, 1200Ft per hour in Hungarian).

You don't have to be mad on horses to enjoy the **Horsebreeding Exhibition** at Park utca 8 (Tues–Sun 9am–5pm; 60Ft), which is reached via the Transylvanian-style wooden gate just beyond the *Hotel Lipicai*. The exhibition includes a collection of coaches and a stable of beautiful white Lippizaners. The totemic columns in the park around the stud farm are dedicated to the memory of the farm director's beloved mount, Zánka, who died in harness of a heart attack

---

### LIPPIZANER HORSES

Descended from Spanish, Arabian and Berber stock, **Lippizaner horses** are bred at six European stud farms. The original stud was founded at Lipica in Slovenia in 1580 by the Habsburg archduke Karl, but when Napoleon's troops invaded Italy its horses were brought to Mezőhegyes in southern Hungary for safekeeping. During the recent wars in former Yugoslavia, a similar rescue mission was carried out by the Austrians. Lippizaner horses are comparatively small in stature – 14.3 to 15.2 hands – with a long back, a short, thick neck and a powerful build. They are usually white or grey. Like their counterparts at the famous Spanish Riding School in Vienna, Szilvásvárad's horses are trained to perform bows, provettes and other manoeuvres that delight dressage cognoscenti.

– evoking the time of the Magyar conquest, when favourite horses were buried in graves.

Except during the coach-driving championships, there shouldn't be any problem with **accommodation**. On the road in from Eger you'll find the *Hotel Lipicai* (☎36/355-100; ②) and the more basic *Szalajka Fogadó* (☎36/355-257; ②), while at Park utca 6 is the reasonably priced *Szilvás Kastély Hotel* and *Panzió* (☎36/355-211; ③), with tennis courts and other facilities. There's a campsite (open year-round) attached to the latter, and another one, *Hegyi Camping*, at Egri út 36 (☎36/355-207; May to mid-Oct). You can also rent private rooms (①) – look for signs advertising *Zimmer frei*.

## The Szalajka Valley

If you don't fancy walking a couple of kilometres, it's possible to travel by narrow-gauge train from Szilvásvárad into the **Szalajka Valley**, which really begins at *szikla-forrás*, a gushing rock cleft beyond the food stalls and captive **stags** that guard its approaches. Signposted just off the main path is an outdoor **Forestry Museum** (*Erdei Múzeum*; April–Nov Tues–Sun 9am–4pm; 100Ft) exhibiting weathered huts and tools, including an ingenious water-powered forge, once used by the charcoal-burners and foresters of the Bükk. Trout is on every restaurant's menu round here, freshly caught from the streams of the Szalajka Valley.

Higher up, the valley is boxed in by hills, with paths snaking through the woods to the triangular **Istállóskői cave** (*barlang*) and the barefaced **Mount Istállóskő**, which at 959m is the highest in the Bükk range. The second-highest, Bálvány, can be reached by footpath from Istállóskő (8km) or from Nagyvisnyó (9km), the next settlement after Szilvásvárad and on the same branch train line.

# The Bükk Hills

Beech trees – *bükk* – cover the hills between Eger and Miskolc, giving the region its name. Unlike most of the northern hills, the **Bükk** were formed from sedimentary limestone, clay slate and dolomite, and are riddled with sink-holes and caves that were home to the earliest tribes of *homo sapiens*, hunters of mammoths and reindeer. As civilization developed elsewhere, the Bükk declined in importance, except as a source of timber, until the start of the nine-teenth century, when Henrik Fazola built a blast furnace in the Garadna Valley, exploiting the iron ore which spurred the industrialization of Miskolc and Ózd. Despite this, almost four hundred square kilometres have been declared a **national park and wildlife refuge**, which can be explored superficially by train and bus, or more thoroughly if you're prepared to do some hiking.

If you are planning to **walk**, a hiking map (*Bükk hegység*) is essential. Since paths are well marked and settlements are rarely more than 15km apart, it's hard to go far astray on foot, but a few **preparations** are advisable. Food and supplies should be purchased beforehand, together with insect repellent/bite cream and a canteen. Drinking water (*ivóvíz*) isn't always available, though many of the springs are pure and delicious. To be sure of **accommodation**, make reservations through Egertourist in Eger, or ask for help from Tourinform there. If need be, you can also sleep in shelters (*esőház*) dotted around the hills.

The Bükk is particularly lovely in autumn, when its foliage turns bright orange and yellow, contrasting with the silvery tree trunks. Among the mountain flora are violet-blue monkshood which blooms at the end of summer, yellow lady's-slipper, an endangered species in Europe, and the Turk's-cap lily. The undergrowth is home to badgers, beech martens, ermines and other animals, and you might encounter rock thrushes and other birds in abandoned quarries, or see an imperial eagle cruising overhead. The seldom glimpsed "smooth" snake isn't poisonous. In spring, look out for limekilns and charcoal-burners in the forests.

### Approaches from Eger

Starting **from Eger**, the most direct approach to the hills is to take a bus, getting off somewhere along the route to Miskolc, or the branch train line up to **Felsőtárkány** – an ideal starting point for walks and a lovely village in its own right, with parks, ponds and vine-laden gardens. Paths also lead into the Bükk from Bélapátfalva, Szilvásvárad and Nagyvisnyó, north of the range (see pp.286 and 287), and from villages to the south, accessible by bus from Eger. On the south side, arrowheads and other remains were found in the **Subalyuk Cave**, a Paleolithic dwelling 2km from **Bükkzsérc** and **Cserépfalu**, at the start of one of the footpaths. Further east "rocking stones" and hollowed-out pillars, used by medieval beekeepers and known as "hive rocks", line the rocky **Felső-szoros ravine** north of **Cserépváralja**.

**Accommodation** is offered by two villages on this side of the hills. In Felsőtárkány are the *Park-Hotel Táltos*, Ifjuság út 1 (☎36/434-760; ②; March to late Nov), and the cheaper *Szikla Fogadó*, Fő utca 313 (☎36/434-604; ②). Alternatively, **Noszvaj**, 13km from Eger, has a clutch of guesthouses, plus a Baroque mansion converted into the *De La Motte Kastély Hotel* at Dobó utca 10 (☎36/463-090; rooms in annexe ③, apartments in main house ⑤). Inside, the house is bizarrely decorated with rather kitsch frescoes; tours are 200Ft for non-guests. Allegedly there were once some voluptuous nudes in the master bedroom, until a new mistress of the house had them painted over.

### Approaches from Miskolc

The Bükk can also be visited **from Miskolc** (see p.290), which offers a number of approaches. From Újgyőri főtér in the western part of the city (bus #101 from Tiszai Station), a #68 bus will take you to **Bükkszentlászló**. From here you can either walk or hitch via **Bükkszentkereszt**, a small village with a quaint glass-blowing museum, to **Hollóstető**, 6km on, which is on the Miskolc–Eger bus route, though services are infrequent. Bükkszentkereszt offers **private rooms** as well as the *Bükk Fogadó* (☎46/390-165; ③), while Hollóstető has a **campsite** with **bungalows** (May to mid-Sept).

The easiest approach, however, is to aim for **Lillafüred** (see below), a small resort that's accessible by bus #5 or #105 from Majális Park in the western part of the city (bus #1 from Tiszai Station), or by narrow-gauge train from Miskolc's Killian Észak terminal (served by bus #101).

The train and buses #5 and #115 continue via Újmassa to Ómassa, further up the valley. All these places are marked on the "Environs of Miskolc" map on p.294.

## Lillafüred and its caves

**LILLAFÜRED** ("Lilla Bath") was named after Lilla, the wife of Count András Bethlen, who established the place as a resort in 1892. Despite its weekend popularity, Lillafüred can still be peaceful and romantic, with its lake and grand hotel set amidst wooded hills. Out of season, the whole place seems rather forgotten.

The village's principal attractions are three **stalactite caves** (*barlang*) that can be visited on guided tours, starting every hour or so from each cave entrance (daily: mid-April to mid-Oct 9am–5pm; mid-Oct to mid-April 9am–4pm; 150Ft). Tucked away above the Miskolc road, the **Szeleta Cave** was found to contain Ice Age spearheads and tools. The **Anna Cave**, beside the road up to the hotel, has a long entrance passage and six chambers linked by stairs formed from lime-stone. If your appetite for stalactites is still unsatiated, walk 1km down the road towards Eger to find the **István Cave**, which is longer and less convoluted, with a "cupola hall" of stalactites, various pools and chambers. Bats can usually be seen roosting above your head.

Two hundred metres beyond this stands the wooden **house of Ottó Herman**, where the naturalist and ethnographer spent many years trapping and mounting local wildlife until his death in 1914. Stuffed boars, birds and rodents, plus an extraordinary collection of giant beetles are the main attraction, but you can also see Ottó's top hat and butterfly nets, and a letter from Kossuth. **Lake Hámori**, just north of Lillafüred, is used for **boating** during the summer and **ice-skating** in winter.

## Accommodation

Dominating the resort is the grand *Palota Hotel* (☎46/331-411; ⑤), a nostalgic creation built in 1927 in the style of a medieval hunting lodge – note the windows in its restaurant, the *Mátyás Terem*, which represent towns from the former Hungarian territories lost in the Treaty of Trianon. Just around the bend from the *Palota*, the friendly *Szikla Turistaház* (☎46/401-469; ①) offers alternative lodg-ings in the form of an old army bunker built into the cliffs overlooking the lake. Though plain, the rooms are spotless, with views of the lake to boot; there's also a restaurant serving tasty home-cooked meals. Another possibility, albeit less memorable, is the *Ózon Szálló* at Erzsébet sétány 19 (☎46/379-200; ②), where the slightly more expensive rooms have a balcony.

# Újmassa and beyond

Open trains filled with shrieking children continue from Lillafüred up the Garadna Valley, which cleaves the Bükk plateau. At **ÚJMASSA**, the next stop, a **nineteenth-century foundry** (Tues–Sun 9am–5pm) attests to the work of **Henrik Fazola**, a Bavarian-born Eger locksmith, and his son Frigyes, who first exploited the iron ore deposits of the Bükk. Nearby are the sooty camps of **charcoal-burners**, who still live for part of the year in the forest.

**ÓMASSA**, further up the valley, is the last stop on the train and bus routes. From here it's a few hours' walk up a well-marked path to **Mount Bálvány**, south of which lies the "Great Meadow" (*Nagymező*), where wild horses graze. A ski chalet and the summits of **Nagy-Csipkés** (822m) and **Zsérci-Nagy-Dél** (875m) can be reached to the east, but more impressive crags lie to the south – **Tárkő** (950m) and **Istállóskő** (959m). The land drops rapidly south of Tárkő, and water from the plateau descends through sinkholes, bursting forth in a spring at **Vörös-kő** (Red Rock). During winter, when the plateau is covered with snow, the entrances to these **sink-holes** are marked by rising steam.

# Miskolc and the Aggtelek Range

To the north and east of Bükk National Park are the three cities that comprise Hungary's "Rust Belt", a region afflicted by the collapse of its heavy industry in the 1990s. **Miskolc**, straddling the transport network, is hard to avoid and holds more promise than you'd imagine, with a surreal downtown and an impressive castle and "thrashing" cave baths in the suburbs – plus a first-division football team, and a summer festival of performing arts. Alas, **Ózd** and **Kazincbarcika** have no such redeeming features, except their transport links to more appealing destinations like the wonderful **stalactite caves at Aggtelek** near the Slovak border.

## Miskolc

Due to the closure of its steel factory and other industries, **MISKOLC** (pronounced "*Mish*-koltz") has suffered from high unemployment and a sharp rise in

DOWNTOWN MISKOLC

**HOTELS**

| Feketebarány | 5 |
| Gösser Udvar | 1 |
| Hotel Pannónia | 2 |
| Korona Panzió | 4 |
| Székelykert Panzió | 3 |

**RESTAURANTS**

| Biggaton | D |
| Gösser Udvar | A |
| Pálos | B |
| Rori Cukrászda | C |

▽ *Miskolc-Tapolca and Budapest*

racist attacks on its Roma minority, to which the city council responded at one point by prosposing that they all be moved to an outlying housing estate, until dissuaded by a national outcry. However, the city puts a brave face on its woes, at least around the centre, whose main street retains much of its prewar charm, surrounded by relics of the city's Greek and Jewish communities, and nineteenth-century artisans' dwellings with gardens dwarfed by concrete high-rises. Aside from the Queen's Castle and the spa resort of Miskolc-Tapolca, everything of interest is in the city centre.

## Arrival and information

The main **points of arrival** are the Tiszai Station, 1km east of the centre (tram #1 or #2; bus #1 or #101 for the castle or Majális Park, aiming for Lillafüred or the Bükk Hills), and the intercity bus station on Búza tér, from where you can either walk into the centre, or head straight for Miskolc-Tapolca by bus #2 from the adjacent local bus station. Should you arrive at the Gömöri train station instead, walk down to Zsolcai kapu, catch any bus heading west and alight near Ady utca.

The best source of **information** is Tourinform on the ground floor of the International Trade Centre, Mindszent tér 1 (May–Sept Mon, Tues & Thurs 7am–3.30pm, Wed 7am–4.30pm, Fri 7am–noon, Sat 8am–1pm; rest of year Mon–Fri only same hours; ☎46/348-921), followed by IBUSZ in the courtyard at Széchenyi út 18 (May–Sept Mon–Fri 8am–6pm, Sat 8am–1pm; Oct–April Mon–Fri 8am–4pm; ☎46/324-090 or 324-411). Borsod Tourist at Széchenyi út 35 (June–Aug Mon–Fri 8am–4.30pm, Sat 9am–noon; Sept–May Mon–Fri 8am–4.30pm; ☎46/350-666) and Express at no. 56 (May–Sept Mon–Fri 8am–4.30pm, Sat 8am–noon; Oct–April Mon–Fri 8am–4pm; ☎46/349-530) are less helpful.

## Accommodation

Though **private rooms** are bookable through all of the tourist offices except Tourinform, they tend to be in outlying housing estates, so you're better off paying extra to stay in a **hotel** or **pension** in the centre. The cosy *Gösser Udvar* at Déryné utca 7 (☎46/357-111; ③) has a restaurant, as does the plush *Hotel Pannónia* at Kossuth utca 2 (☎46/329-811; ④). At the foot of the Avas Hill, the *Székelykert Panzió* occupies an old town house at Földes utca 4 (☎46/411-222; ③), and the *Korona Panzió* a modern block at Kis Avas 18, across the road (☎46/358-400; ②).

As usual, student **hostels** (bookable through Express) are the cheapest option for solo travellers. The best is the *Karács Teréz Kollégium* (☎46/370-495; ①) at Győri kapu 156 (bus #1 or tram #1 or #2), open daily from late June to late August, and at weekends throughout the year. Another good one is the *Bólyai kollégium* at Egyetem út 17, in the hilly Egyetemváros district south of town (☎46/365-111; ①), which is open the same times as the *Karács*; take bus #12 from Hösök tere to the last stop.

Private **rooms in Miskolc-Tapolca** (②) can be arranged through Borsod Tourist at Károlyi Mihály utca 1 (May–Oct 9am–6pm daily; ☎46/368-917). Among the options on and off the main road, the *Bástya Panzió* at Miskolc-Tapolcai utca 2 is right by the baths (☎46/369-154; ③); the *Pallaz Panzió* at Bencések utca 3 is in a quiet location (☎46/368–770; ③); and the *Hotel Junó* at Csabai utca 2–4 (☎46/364-133; ③) is a high-rise three-star hotel overshadowing the resort. **Bungalows** and tent space can be rented at two **campsites**: *Éden Camping* at Károly Mihály utca 1 (☎46/368-917; ①–③; mid-April to Oct), a kind of manicured parking lot near the *Hotel Junó*; and *Autós Camping*, 2km along Iglói utca (☎46/367-171: ①–②; May to mid-Sept), a leafier site, popular with motorists.

# The City

On the main downtown **Széchenyi út**, an eclectic mix of boutiques and restaurants interspersed with Baroque facades painted pea green and sky blue or in the last stages of decrepitude, gives the impression of a boom and slump happening simultaneously. Here you'll find the recently restored **National Theatre** (*Nemzeti Színház*), which apart from musicals like *Fiddler on the Roof* also stages some good straight drama, and has an alternative theatre run by the ex-rock star Péter Müller. Opened in 1823, it was the first Hungarian-language theatre in the country, fourteen years before Budapest acquired one. Miskolc's thespian tradition is celebrated in the **Theatre Museum**, just around the corner at Déryné utca 3 (Tues–Sat 9am–5pm; 100Ft). At the far, western end of Széchenyi út, a new statue of its namesake, Count Széchenyi, appears to be doing a painful form of yoga on **Városház tér**, which looks especially atmospheric with its town hall spotlit at night.

## North of Széchenyi út

A century ago, Miskolc was distinguished by its Greek and Jewish communities – the former descended from refugees from the Turks, who fled here during the seventeenth century, and the latter migrating from Sub-Carpathian Ruthenia after it was incorporated within the Austro-Hungarian Empire. Though both are now a shadow of their former size and significance, their places of worship are among the finest monuments in Miskolc.

On the south side of **Hősök tere** is an **Orthodox Synagogue** designed by Ludwig Förster, the architect of the great synagogue in Budapest, whose magnificent but crumbling interior seems painfully empty on major feast days – only 175 Jews now live in Miskolc, whereas the prewar Jewish population numbered 16,000, of whom 14,000 were sent to the death camps; ask at the office behind the synagogue for the keys. On the far side of the square stands a former **Minorite Church** and monastery, dating from 1729–40.

Heading left onto **Deák tér** you'll encounter a splendid, newly restored neo-Renaissance pile designed by György Lehóczky in 1927 for the **Forestry Commission** (*Erdőigazgatóság*), an important institution in this region of wooded hills. Next door stands the **Feledy Museum** (Tues–Sat 9am–5pm; 100Ft), devoted to the work of local artist Gyula Feledy, which reflects his preoccupation with the world of Orthodox Christianity. Greek Orthodox and Uniate religious art from all over Hungary is exhibited in the **Orthodox Ecclesiastical Museum** further along at no. 7 (Tues–Sat: May–Sept 10am–6pm; Oct–April 10am–4pm; 100Ft).

The finest sight in the town is the eighteenth-century **Greek Orthodox Church**, screened by trees, which contains a sixteen-metre-high **iconostasis** in the naturalistic Greek style, to the left of which is the *Black Mary of Kazan*, an icon presented by Catherine the Great of Russia, hung with tokens representing prayers for children, health and marriage. There is also a jewelled cross from Mount Athos, brought by the first Greek settlers. You can visit during Sunday Mass at 10.30am, or by applying to the Orthodox Ecclesiastical Museum at other times. Originally there were about 250 Greek families in Miskolc, who traded in wine and lived around Búza tér, but the quarter was pulled down in the 1960s, and only about four families remain from the community.

Further north on the slope above Petőfi tér, the Gothic-style **Plank Church** is undergoing a painstaking reconstruction after suffering at the hands of a local arsonist. This kind of wooden church is rare in Hungary but common in northern

Romania, where architecture of this type reached its zenith in the eighteenth century. The interior is nothing special, however.

### Avas Hill
South of Széchenyi út, a beautiful domed *fin-de-siècle* **bathhouse** (currently closed) presages the **Ottó Herman Museum** at the foot of Avas Hill (Tues–Sun 10am–6pm; 200Ft), exhibiting a collection of folk costumes, minerals and pottery. The pile of broken mugs is a result of the tradition at wakes of drinking and then smashing your mug. Just uphill stands a Gothic **Calvinist Church** dating from 1560, which features a detached **wooden belfry** (as required by Counter-Reformation ordinances) and Baroque pews decorated with flower motifs, added later.

From here, a maze of paths snakes upwards to the **TV Tower** and observation platform on the summit. The right-hand paths climb through an extraordinary shantytown of miniature villas and rock-hewn **wine cellars**, some up to 50m deep, guarded by savage dogs. In the summer and early autumn you can roam all over the hill sampling local wine, and even food at some of the bigger cellars. Ten minutes' walk down Mendikás dülő past the TV tower is a **Jewish Cemetery** with beautifully carved gravestones dating back to the eighteenth century, and memorials to those killed during the war. On weekdays until late afternoon a caretaker will let you in if you ring the bell.

## Around Miskolc

The oldest building in Miskolc is the **Queen's Castle**, located 7km west of the centre in the suburb of Diósgyőr, beyond the steelworks (*Diósgyőr vár*; April–Nov Tues–Sun 10am–6pm; 250Ft). Built for King Louis between 1350 and 1375, the castle marked the introduction of the southern Italian type of fortress to Hungary. Though eminently defendable, it served chiefly as a royal holiday home and a residence for dowager queens. Today it is the main site for summer concerts, festivals and events in the city. Blown up in the Rákóczi wars, it has been crudely restored with breeze blocks and poured concrete, but the views from its towers of Miskolc and the Bükk Hills are as splendid as ever. To get there, catch a #1 bus to the *Ady Endre Művelődési Ház* and walk towards the four stone towers poking above the rooftops.

If you feel like a relaxing bath, head out to **MISKOLC-TAPOLCA**, a resort suburb twenty minutes' ride from Búza tér (bus #2). Crammed with holiday homes and school parties, its main attractions are an outdoor **pool** (late May to mid-Sept daily 8am–6pm), complete with rowing boats, water slides, electronic cars and rides; and the *barlang fürdő* or **cave baths** (daily 9am–1pm & 2–6pm and until 5pm on Wed; 400Ft), a series of dimly lit warm-water grottoes discovered in the 1920s culminating in a twelve-metre-high waterfall known as the "pounding shower", which should get your circulation going if nothing else. Visitors who go **mushroom hunting** in the Bükk can have their fungi checked at the *Gomba Vizsgálat* hut near the #2 bus stop (mid-May to mid-Nov Sat, Sun & holidays 1–6pm). There are snack stands aplenty and a **disco** in the *Hotel Junó*, as well as a wide range of hotels and private rooms (see p.291).

## Eating, drinking and entertainment

The *Hotel Pannónia* on Széchenyi út boasts the smartest **restaurant** in Miskolc, and a snazzy patisserie, the *Rori Cukrászda*. Cheaper downtown options include the

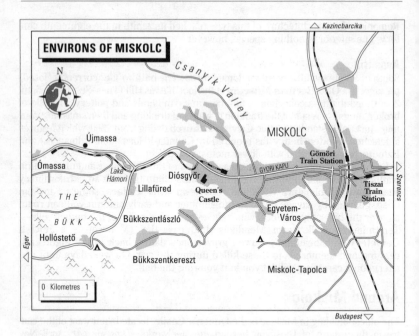

*Gösser Udvar* at Déryné utca 7, *Pálos* at Árpád utca 1, and the *Biggaton* pizza joint on Kossuth utca, while the outdoor market beside the local bus terminal on Búza tér abounds in **snacks**. Going **drinking**, you can choose between the *Mona Lisa* next to the Theatre Museum for cocktails, the *Big Ben Caffe* at Kossuth utca 8, the *Speed Bar* on Hunyadi utca, or the Euro-clone *John Bull Pub*, beside the *Speed Bar*.

The city is at its liveliest during the **Miskolc Summer Festival** (June–Aug) when jazz, classical music and operas are performed at the Queen's Castle and in Miskolc-Tapolca. Among its highlights is the **Kaláka Folklore Festival** in July, one of the largest folk gatherings in the region, attended by musicians and dancers from all over Hungary and abroad. The national holiday on **August 20** is marked by equestrian displays and a folk fair in the Queen's Castle. Tickets for all these events are available at the National Theatre ticket office at Széchenyi út 23 (☎46/344-862), while Tourinform and IBUSZ can give details. The Borsodi beer festival in the first week of September is celebrated in the centre of Miskolc with live music and cheap beer.

**Nightlife** in Miskolc revolves around the *Piramis Disco* on Középszer utca (which has billiards), the *Bahnhof Music Club* at Csaba vezér út 91/93, and two live music venues at Győri kapu 27: the *Vian Klub* and *Ifúsági és Szabadidő Ház*. Look out for flyers for Saturday night raves in the TV Tower, too. The *Villa Bar* on Megyesalja utca has good home-brewed beer and pool, while across the road is a trendier place frequented by Miskolc's biking fraternity who prefer commercial lager out of chipped glasses served by rude staff. In Miskolc-Tapolca over summer, there are regular raves and parties in the *Hotel Junó*, and visiting DJs and groups appear at other venues, as advertised.

# Kazincbarcika and Ózd

A planner's dream and a resident's nightmare, **KAZINCBARCIKA** was created in the fifties for the purpose of manufacturing chemicals and energy from
the coal deposits of the north. Laid out in a grid, its endless rows of numbing-
ly identical housing estates (*lakótelep*) are ineffectually separated from the
town's industrial zone by five hundred metres of withered grass. Unlike Ózd,
its industrial mono-culture has weathered the transition to capitalism, and its
**chemical plant** not only continues to employ half the town but even hosts a
popular **disco**, *Akropolisz*, on Saturday nights. Of the three villages that originally stood here, only the **churches** of Barcika and Sajókazinc and the eighteenth-century **wooden belfry** of Berente remain. Though they're hardly
worth staying the night for, the *Hotel Polimer* on Szent Flórián tér lives in hope
(☎48/311-911; ②).

## Ózd

**ÓZD** has been harder hit by industrial decline than anywhere else in Hungary, as
is evident from the burnt-out blocks of flats, squatted by destitute Roma who hunt
for scrap metal in the grounds of the **derelict foundry** in the centre of town. In
Communist times it spewed smoke into the air – as vividly depicted in Márta
Mészáros's film *Nine Months*, about a factory girl at the Ózd works – and employed
three-quarters of the population. Nowadays, though the smokestacks still dominate the skyline, the only things working are the ex-workers' swimming pool, and
the *Rio* **disco**. However, there are signs of an upturn in Ózd's fortunes, with
American and Swedish business tentatively moving in, and a new hotel under way.

# Stalactite caves in the Aggtelek Hills

Like the Bükk, the **Aggtelek range** bordering Slovakia displays typical **karstic**
features such as gullies, sinkholes and caves, caused by a mixture of water and car-
bon dioxide dissolving the limestone. The **Baradla caves**, between the villages of
Aggtelek and Jósvafő, and the **Béke caves** to the southeast constitute an amazing
subterranean world with Stygian lakes and rivers, waterfalls, countless stalactites
and 262 species of wildlife. Set in remote countryside that's ideal for walking,
cycling, and bird-watching, the caves are deservedly popular with tourists.

Getting to the Aggtelek entails catching an early bus from Budapest, Miskolc
or Eger; or travelling later in the day, starting from Ózd, which has daily services
around 8am, noon & 3pm, less frequently at weekends, or Putnok, where there
are **buses** to Aggtelek and Jósvafő every hour and a half. Putnok, linked to Ózd,
Eger, Miskolc and Kazincbarcika by rail, is the last outpost of IBUSZ and the last
place you'll find any banks. Alternatively, slow **trains** from Miskolc to
Tornanádaska can drop you at the Jósvafő-Aggtelek station, 10km east of Jósvafő,
whence regular buses run to both villages (less frequently on Sundays).

### Jósvafő and Aggtelek

Aside from the fortified church with its picturesque cemetery in **JÓSVAFŐ**, and
the algae-green lake outside **AGGTELEK**, both villages are fairly unremarkable.

Shops are few and social life centres around the church and "drink shop" (active from 4pm). **Information** is available from Naturinform at the entrance to the caves (☎48/343-029). Jósvafő has a tourist house at Rákóczi utca 1 where you can **stay** the night, or there's the *Tengerszem Hotel* at Tengerszem oldal 2, by the entrance to the caves, a couple of kilometres outside the village (☎48/343-159 or 350-006; ②), which is surrounded by forest and hiking trails. Accommodation in Aggtelek consists of the seventy-room *Hotel Cseppkő* at Gyömrői út 2, pic-turesquely situated on a hill by the entrance to the caves (☎48/343-075; ②), and the *Karszt Üdülő* at Deák utca 11 in the village (☎46/382-181; ②). There is also the *Baradla Camping* complex right by the cave entrance (☎48/343-073; ①–②), which has four-bed chalets, apartments and a hostel. Both the *Tengerszem* and the *Cseppkő* have **restaurants** and display local bus schedules in their lobbies. The tourist office or hotels can tell you about the classical music **concerts** that are held in the caves between June and September and at New Year.

## Visiting the caves

Both sets of caves are open daily from 8am to 6pm (Oct–April until 4pm), but hourly guided tours begin only once at least five people have assembled at one of the entrances (*bejárat*), the last one leaving an hour before closing.

The main **Baradla cave passage** twists underground for 22km, and there is a range of **tours** you can take. There are one-hour tours from both ends (400Ft from Aggtelek, 300Ft from Jósvafő), or you can do a combined tour (700Ft). The **Aggtelek end** of the passage is more convoluted and thus more rewarding for shorter tours. No description can do justice to the variety and profusion of **stalactites and stalag-mites**, whose nicknames can only hint at the fantastic formations, glittering with cal-cite crystals or stained ochre by iron oxides. Among them is the world's tallest sta-lagmite, a full 25m high. In the "Concert Hall", boats sway on the "River Styx", and the guide activates a tape of Bach's *Toccata in D minor* to create a *Phantom of the Opera* type ambience. **Longer tours** (500Ft) of five to seven hours begin at the Red Lake (*Vörös-tó*) entrance, situated in the Cool Valley (*Hideg völgy*) between the two villages, and require some stamina: it's a long time to clamber around dank, muddy caves, however beautiful they are. You need to book in advance on ☎48/343-073.

Guided tours around the **Béke caves** are also fairly demanding. Although they contain a sanatorium, the underground air being judged beneficial to asthmatics, most of the caves are, in fact, untamed, even unexplored, and as recently as 1973 a new passage was found when cavers penetrated a thirty-metre waterfall. You'll need boots and warm, waterproof clothing, and visitors are issued with helmets. **Underground wildlife** – bats, rodents and bugs, mostly – keeps out of sight, and is easiest to view in the **Cave Museum** by the Aggtelek entrance (Tues–Sun 10am–6pm; 100Ft), which also has photos and mementoes.

## Excursions in the vicinity

The surrounding countryside is riddled with smaller caves and rock formations, clearly marked on the hiking **map** (*Aggtelek és Jósvafő környéke*) sold at the Aggtelek cave entrance. This also shows the **border zone**, where armed guards still patrol with dogs, notwithstanding the demise of Communism – it's always a good idea to carry your passport when hiking. For those with a car or bike, lots of attractive **villages** are within reach in this part of the highlands, for example **RUDABÁNYA**, where the ten-million-year-old jawbone of *Rudapithecus hungari-cus*, an ancient primate, can be seen at the mine where it was excavated – though the mine now faces closure, spelling doom for the community. There is also a delightful old church with a painted panelled ceiling.

# Tokaj and the Zemplén Hills

**TOKAJ** is to Hungary what Champagne is to France, and this small town has become a minor Mecca for wine lovers. Squeezed onto a narrow strip of land between Tokaj Hill and the confluence of the rivers Bodrog and Tisza, its sloping streets and pastel-painted dwellings are rife with wine cellars and nesting storks, overlooked by lush vineyards climbing the hillside towards the "Bald Peak" and the inevitable television tower. Though it looks prosperous and laid-back, Tokaj is far from rich, and most people have to work hard to get any kind of living from the vineyards. The price of grapes and wages for agricultural labourers are so low that in 1998, protesting growers and field-hands blocked the roads with tractors. For those with money to invest, however, there are exciting prospects for exports.

In Tokaj, you can sample local wines in the famous Rákóczi cellar, or countless other, humbler places. To see a working winery, take a trip to Tarcal, Mád or Tolcsva – pretty villages that well deserve a visit if you've got the time.

**The Zemplén range** is largely unspoiled by industry and tourism, and richly textured by nature and history. Its volcanic soil and microclimates provide a favourable environment for diverse wildlife, particularly snakes and birds of prey, while the architecture reflects a tradition of trade and cultural exchange between the Great Plain and the Slovakian highlands. Tokaj absorbs most of the region's tourists, surprisingly few of whom make it up to **Sárospatak**, site of the superb Rákóczi castle, or to little **Zemplén villages** such as Füzér and Boldogkőváralja, and the castles that loom over them. For **accommodation** in the villages contact Tourinform in Miskolc, Sárospatak or Tokaj, or Express in Sátoraljaújhely.

## Approaches via Szerencs

Approaching Tokaj and the northern Zemplén from Miskolc you're bound to pass through **SZERENCS**, a drab little town with a reeking factory that's responsible for most of the chocolate produced in Hungary. If you've got time to kill between connections, check out the **Zemplén Museum** in a **fortified manor** that dominates the centre of town, at the far end of Rákóczi út (May–Oct Tues–Sun 10am–4pm; Nov–April Tues–Thurs 10am–4pm, Fri 10am–1pm; 100Ft). It was here that István Bocskai was elected Prince of Hungary, an event recalled by a number of exhibits. The museum also boasts the world's third-largest **collection of postcards** – 700,000 of them, donated by a local doctor.

For those with more spare time – or a sweet tooth – there's the **chocolate factory's museum** by the main gates on Route 37 (Sat & Sun 9am–1pm; free). Its curator will deliver a ninety-minute spiel in Hungarian given half a chance, though it only takes ten minutes to inspect its collection of sugar packaging from around the world, old photos and dull documentation. Sadly, visitors aren't able to visit the factory itself, which is now owned by a French company.

Should you need to **stay**, there's the agreeable *Hotel Huszárvár* built onto the fortified manor (☎47/362-518; ③). Besides **trains** to Tokaj, Szerencs is the starting point for the branch line up to Hidasnémeti, via villages on the western side of the Zemplén; and for **buses** to Monok, Mád and Tállya in the Tokaj-Hegyalja (see pp.300–301).

# The Town

**Arriving** at the train station or the main bus stop directly outside, take your bearings from the map posted there before heading north along Bajcsy-Zsilinszky utca into the **old centre** of Tokaj – a ten-minute walk. The main street that runs northwards through the centre has recently been spruced up and pedestrianized, so you can

## TOKAJI WINES

**Tokaji wines** derive their character from the special soil, the prolonged sunlight and the wine-making techniques developed here. Heat is trapped by the volcanic loess soil, allowing a delayed **harvest** in October, by which time many of the grapes are overripe and botrytized (attacked by a rot that shrivels them and makes them incredibly sweet). It is these **Aszú grapes** that make the difference between regular *Hárslevelű* (linden leaf) and *Furmint* wine, and the special wines sold in short, stubby bottles under the names *Szamorodni* and *Aszú*, whose qualities depend on the number of hods (*puttony*) of *Aszú* added to 136-litre barrels of ordinary grapes. *Szamorodni* is a word of Polish origin meaning "as it comes". It is typically golden in colour and can be dry or sweet, but never as sweet as *Aszú*. Another crucial factor is the ageing of the wine in cellars encrusted with a black odourless **mould** called *penész*, which interacts with the fermentation process.

Tokaj wine has collected some notable **accolades** since the late Middle Ages. Beethoven and Schubert dedicated songs to it; Louis XVI declared it "the wine of kings, the king of wines"; Goethe, Voltaire, Heine and Browning all praised it; and Sherlock Holmes used it to toast the downfall of von Bork, after troubling Watson to "open the window, for chloroform vapour does not help the palate".

In the Communist era, collective wineries tended to level standards down to the lowest common denominator, but also produced such gems as a 1972 6-*puttonyos* that was recently voted the best dessert wine in the world. Since 1990 foreign investors have fallen over themselves to get involved, resulting in what is known as the **Tokaji Renaissance**. Tokajis from the old days tend to be a richer brown-red in colour due to oxidization, which doesn't occur in the state-of-the-art stainless steel tanks used by foreign wineries. Some like the new style, others prefer the old. You can decide for yourself on **tours and tastings** at wineries in the region, of which the following are recommended:

**Degenfeld** in Tarcal. Bought by a German sewing-machine magnate for his Hungarian wife, it has brand-new cellars fronted by a pretty house set among chestnut trees, and is in the process of being turned into a hotel.

**Disznókő** outside Tarcal. Its new French owners began by scrubbing all the mildew off the cellar walls, to the horror of the locals. The new winery was designed by Makovecz (note the circular tractor shed) and has a restaurant and pension attached (☎47/369-139).

**Hétszőlő** in Tokaj. A Franco-Japanese venture that owns the Rákóczi cellars on the main street and most of the vineyards around town. See opposite for details.

**Megyer-Pajzos** in Sárospatak. Now owned by a French company, this famous seventeenth-century cellar is associated with Prince Rákóczi. See p.306 for details.

**Oremus** in Tolcsva. A wise investment by the Spanish, as it was this winery that produced the 1972 6-*puttonyos* mentioned above.

**Royal Tokaji** in Mád. Miles of old cellars lined with oak barrels and smothered in mould. Owned by a British firm.

admire its Baroque facades without any fear of being run over by a Lada. Three land-marks en route are the rainbow-striped *Hotel Tokaj* by the bridge over the Tisza; the former Rákóczi-Dessewffy mansion at Bajcsy-Zsilinszky utca 15–17 (owned by the Franco-Japanese investors Hétszőlő, and not open to the public); and the Zopf-style **town hall** at Rákóczi utca 44, just short of the main square, **Kossuth tér**.

**Wine** is omnipresent, with cellars at every step, all kinds of wine-making equipment displayed in shop windows, and barrel staves piled in people's backyards. The venerable **Rákóczi cellar** at Kossuth tér 15, where 20,000 hectolitres of wine repose in 24 cobwebbed, chandelier-lit passages, is the most famous in Tokaj and a place of pilgrimage (May–Oct daily 10am–7pm). On the outside wall is a plaque commemorating Máté Szepsi Lackó (1567–1633), a Calvinist minister who invented *Aszú* wine. The cellar now belongs to a foreign firm, but functions much as it previously did. However, you'll get more personal service in smaller **private cellars** in the backstreets above the main street, such as Hímesudvar at Bem utca 2, five minutes up from Kossuth tér. Once a hunting lodge owned by the eighteenth-century nobleman János Szapolyai, it now houses the cellars of the Várhelyi family, where you can taste wines and nibble *pogácsa*.

On Bethlen Gábor utca, just past Kossuth tér, the **Tokaj Museum** (Tues–Sun 9am–5pm; 200Ft), in a lovely building with an old wooden staircase, has an excellent local history exhibition, including a recreation of a drawing room from a Greek wine-trader's house, and Judaica from the former **synagogue** behind the museum. Prewar Tokaj had a large Jewish population, which handled most of the wine trade in conjunction with a smaller number of Greek families – hence the **Jewish cemetery** a few kilometres north along the main road, the keys for which are available from the house just beyond it.

If you fancy a longer walk, follow the road behind Kossuth tér uphill to the summit of Tokaj's 516-metre-high "**Bald Peak**". The route takes you past dozens of vineyards, each labelled with its owner's name. The tower is accessible by road too, but you have to drive round the hill via the village of Tarcal. From the summit you can scan the distant Great Plain and the lush green Tokaj-Hegyalja – the hilly wine-producing region.

Other **activities** in Tokaj include rowing, cycling, water-skiing, and swimming in the Tisza. Between mid-June and the end of August there are **riverboat cruises** from Tokaj to Sárospatak, further down the Bodrog (2hr 30min).

## Practicalities

For **information** on wine tours and the Tokaj-Hegyalja villages, drop into Tourinform at Serház utca 1, just past the hotel on the way into town (April–Oct Mon–Fri 9am–5pm, Sat 9am–1pm; Nov–March Mon–Fri 9am–4pm; ☎47/353-390).

Private **accommodation** (②) is available from Tokaj Tours, right next door (Mon–Fri 9am–5pm; ☎47/353-323), or by following *Zimmer frei* signs around town, many of which lead to Óvár utca 6, which has its own (overpriced) wine cellar, or Bajcsy-Zsilinszky utca 19. Rooms at Bethlen Gábor utca 49, on the north side of town, come slightly cheaper because guests share a toilet – literally, as it has two doors, one from each room. Doubles with bathrooms and quadruples without can be found at the *Széchenyi Kollégium*, Bajcsy-Zsilinszky utca 15–17 (☎47/352-355 ), from June till late August, and at weekends the rest of the year.

Moving upmarket, there's the pleasant *Makk Marci Panzió* at Liget köz 1, on the corner of Rákóczi út (☎47/352-336; ③); the *Lux Panzió* at Serház utca 14, down towards the river from Kossuth tér (☎47/352-145; ③); and the waterfront *Hotel Tokaj* (☎47/352-344; ④), with balconied rooms facing the river. At the far end of Bethlen Gábor utca, the *Torkolat Panzió* (☎47/314-517; ③) loans bikes and canoes to guests free of charge; bikes cost 1000Ft a day for non-residents.

Additionally, there are three **campsites**: *Unió Vízitelep* on Bodrogkereszturi út (☎47/352-927; mid-April to mid-Sept), which has bungalows and hot and cold showers; and the *Pelsőczy* (☎47/352-626) and *Tisza Camping* (☎47/352-927) sites, across the bridge to the left and right, the last of which also has bungalows.

The choice of **places to eat** is limited, with the touristy *Halászcsárda* at Bajcsy-Zsilinszky utca 23 and the restaurant in the *Hotel Tokaj* attracting most trade, though the pizzeria attached to the *Makk Marci Panzió*, and the *Róna Étterem* near the *Torkolat Panzió* on Bethlen Gábor utca offer better value for money.

# The Tokaj-Hegyalja

The southern slopes of the Zemplén form the distinctive region known as the **Tokaj-Hegyalja**, which is largely devoted to producing wine. Most of its beautifully sited villages are accessible by bus from Tokaj or Szerencs (many are also served by the train line from Szerencs to Hidasnémeti), but the paucity of tourist accommodation (ask Tourinform in Miskolc – see p.291 – for a list of private rooms) may oblige you to stick to day-trips – you can stop off at one or two villages a day, depending on schedules.

In **MÁD**, 11km east of Szerencs, it's worth enquiring about **tasting tours** at the British-owned **Royal Tokaji cellars** at Rákóczi utca 35, in the centre of the village, which is also home to the renowned vintner István Szepsy (allegedly descended from the inventor of *Aszú*), who can be found at Táncsics utca 57.

---

## LAJOS KOSSUTH

**Lajos Kossuth** was the incarnation of post-Napoleonic bourgeois nationalism. Born into landless gentry in 1802, he began his political career as a lawyer, representing absentee magnates in Parliament. His parliamentary reports, advocating greater liberalism than the Habsburgs would tolerate, were widely influential during the Reform Era. While in jail for sedition, Kossuth taught himself English by reading Shakespeare. Released in 1840, he became editor of the radical *Pesti Hírlap*, was elected to Parliament and took the helm during the 1848 Revolution, whereupon his eloquent idealism tragically fulfilled its latent demagogic chauvinism.

After Serbs, Croats and Romanians rebelled against Magyar rule and the Habsburgs invaded Hungary, the Debrecen Parliament proclaimed a republic with Kossuth as de facto dictator. Having escaped to Turkey after the Hungarians surrendered in August 1849, he toured Britain and America, espousing liberty. So eloquent were his denunciations of Habsburg tyranny that London brewery workers attacked General Haynau, the "Butcher of Vienna", when he visited the city. Karl Marx loathed Kossuth as a bourgeois radical, and tried to undermine his reputation with articles published in the New York *Herald Tribune* and the London *Times*. As a friend of the Italian patriot Mazzini, Kossuth spent his last years in Turin, where he died in 1894.

While the train station lies ten minutes' walk down Bányász utca, visitors arriving by bus will pass a folk Baroque-style **synagogue**, built in 1765, whose ornate ceilings are rotting with damp while pigeons desecrate its pews. The talisman-sized key is held at Kossuth út 73, below the former **Rabbi's house** and arcaded **Yeshiva** (religious school), long divided into flats and sunk into disrepair. On the northern edge of Mád lies an old **Jewish Cemetery**, which is also locked; ask around for the key.

**TÁLLYA**, 9km further towards Gönc (see overleaf), is another wine-producing village with hundreds of barrels maturing in seventeenth-century **cellars** near a former Rákóczi mansion. In the village **church** you can view the font where Lajos Kossuth was baptized, while on the road up to the TV tower, the former synagaogue has been been turned into an art gallery where exhibitions and **concerts** are held during the Zemplén Days in late August; Tourinform has details.

**MONOK**, 10km northwest of Szerencs, was the **birthplace of Kossuth**, whose childhood home is now a **museum** (Tues–Sun 10am–1pm & 3–6pm; 100Ft) that casts his career (see box opposite) in the most favourable light. Monok's other famous son is Miklós Németh, Hungary's Prime Minister during the transition from Communism to democracy in 1989.

Some 30km north of Tokaj and 2km off the road to Sárospatak, **TOLCSVA** can be reached by the hourly bus from Tokaj to Komlóska. Its erstwhile Rákóczi manor at Kossuth Lajos utca 55 beyond the two churches in the centre is now a **Wine Museum** (Tues, Fri, Sat & Sun 4–6pm; 60Ft), while the hillside is honeycombed with 2.5km of cellars full of local **linden leaf wine** (*Tolcsvai Hárslevelű*). Tolcsva's Spanish-owned **winery** produces some of the finest modern Tokajis.

The village of **SZABOLCS**, 10km east, on the far side of the River Tisza, was once important enough to lend its name to a county in northeastern Hungary. Here you'll find the only surviving earthworks fortress (*földvár*) in Central Europe, dating from the ninth century, the eighteenth-century **Mudrány Mansion** at Petőfi utca 38 (May–Sept Tues–Sun 10am–6pm), and a **Calvinist Church** with fifteenth-century frescoes that was built as a Catholic church in the eleventh century.

## The western Zemplén

The western flank of the Zemplén is dotted with **villages** whose remote and sleepy existence today belies their historic significance. Unlike the other parts of Hungary with medieval churches and ruined castles, there's rarely another tourist in sight, even though the scenery everywhere is great. In contrast to the rounded sedimentary hills on the western side of the valley, the volcanically formed Zemplén often resemble truncated cones called *sátor* (tent). If all of this appeals, and you don't mind the lack of bright lights and facilities, the region is well worth exploring.

Though private **transport** is definitely advantageous, most places are accessible by local buses or trains up the Szerencs–Hidasnémeti branch line. The scarcity of **accommodation** could be more of a problem unless you bring a tent, or encounter sympathetic locals. Try to buy a hiking **map** (*Zempléni hegység*) even if you don't intend to go **hiking**. There are two maps: *északi,* covering the northern part, and *déli* the south, showing all the villages mentioned below.

The route described below approximately follows the **Hernád Valley** up towards the river's source in the Slovakian highlands, and the **border crossing** into Slovakia at Tornyosnémeti (by road) and Hidasnémeti (by rail).

## Boldogkőváralja and Vizsoly

Best reached by road, since the village lies 2.5km from its train stop, **BOLDOGKŐVÁRALJA** is dominated by a massive **castle** (April–Oct Tues–Sun 8am–4pm; 100Ft) upon a volcanic mound. Erected in the thirteenth century to discourage a return visit by the Mongols, it commands a spectacular view of the Zemplén Hills, and the surrounding woods are rife with red squirrels. In summer, you can **stay** at the *Tekerjes Fogadó*, beside the village church on Kossuth utca (☎46/387-701; ①), but it's closed over winter as it doesn't have any heating.

At **VIZSOLY**, 2km from its train station, Korlát-Vizsoly, a thirteenth-century **Calvinist Church** harbours fantastic frescoes of Jesus's Ascension (leaving his footprints behind) and St George and the dragon, which were only discovered in 1940 after being lost for many centuries, and have recently been restored. A Latin inscription on the chancel wall reads "If you did not come to pray in this place then leave as you have come." The church also contains an original edition of the **Vizsoly Bible**, the first Hungarian translation of the Bible, by Gáspár Károlyi, dean of Gönc, in 1590, which was printed in the house across the road and played a formative role in the development of Hungarian as a written language. Keys to the church are held at the priest's house (*református lelkesz*) at Szent János út 123, where it's possible to **stay** at the *Károlyi Gáspár Ifjúsági Tábor* (☎46/387-187; ①) in summertime. There are regular **buses** to Abaújszantó and a daily service to Miskolc and Szikszó.

## Gönc and Regéc

Thirteen kilometres further up the valley, amid ravishing countryside, the village of **GÖNC**, accessible by buses from Hidasnémeti as well as by train, was a thriving trade centre in the Middle Ages. It was here that Dean Károlyi was born and translated the Vizsoly Bible, and Sárospatak's Calvinist College took refuge during the Counter-Reformation. Subsequently, the village became famous for making the 136-litre oak **barrels** (*Gönci hordok*) used to store Tokaj wine – sadly no longer made here.

The most tangible relic of this history is the white **Hussite House** on Kossuth utca (April 15 to Oct 15 Tues–Sun 10am–6pm; 100Ft), whose Calvinist inhabitants could escape into the maze of cellars beneath the village via a door in the cellar of the house. Notice the Gönc barrel, and the weird bed that pulls out from a table upstairs. If it's shut, the old woman at Rákóczi utca 80, across the stream, and off to the right, can let you in; she was born in the Hussite House.

Gönc is very picturesque but facilities are minimal, with nowhere to eat, and a single bar, where locals get stuck into *pálinka* at 10am – you can even buy alcohol at the flower shop. However, there is year-round **accommodation** at Arany János utca 1/B (☎46/388-477; ①), plus the *Diákotthon* at Károlyi utca 21 (☎46/388-052; ①) over the summer.

Some might enjoy a hard day's **hiking to REGÉC**, along an ill-marked path skirting the 787-metre-high Gergely-hegy (bring a compass, food and water). Regéc is the site of another **ruined castle**, which is also accessible by two buses a day from Encs, on the Miskolc–Hidasnémeti line, leaving around noon and 2pm.

## Telkibánya, Abaújvár and Kéked

Buses from Hidasnémeti to Gönc carry on to **TELKIBÁNYA**, 9km to the east (also served by two buses from Sátoraljaújhely, on the other side of the hills), whose **museum** on Múzeum utca (Tues–Sat 10am–4pm) has a fine collection of

Zemplén crystals, pottery and carved heads. The Children's Camp (*Gyermektábor*) at Fürdő utca 17 offers self-catering **accommodation** during summer, and also out of season if you phone ahead (☎46/388-507; ①), and there are private rooms at Múzeum utca 10 (☎46/388-463; ①).

Buses from Gönc and a limited service (two daily on weekdays) from Hidasnémeti, 4km away, to Hollóháza (see p.309) can get you to **ABAÚJVÁR**, 9km to the north of Gönc. This pretty village has a picturesque **Calvinist Church** with battered frescoes from 1332; ask for the key on Rákóczi utca, below the church. Another 4km along the way to Hollóháza, buses call at **KÉKED**, which boasts a **fortified manor** (Tues–Sun 10am–4pm; 100Ft) containing rustic knick-knacks and antiques that belonged to the present mayor's grandmother prior to its expropriation in 1947. There are hopes to turn it into a hotel, which will bring employment opportunities. Meanwhile, you can **stay** at the *Kéked Fogadó* at Fürdő utca 13, near an **outdoor bath** in the forest (☎46/388-077; ②; May–Aug), fed by a cold-water spring.

# Sárospatak

Half an hour's train journey from Szerencs, **SÁROSPATAK** (Muddy Stream) basks on the banks of the River Bodrog – a graceful, serene spot with almost unlimited expanses of green. The town once enjoyed a significant role in Hungarian intellectual life, thanks to its **Calvinist College**: Magyars given to hyperbole used to describe Sárospatak as the "Athens on the Bodrog". In the last twenty years, some fine examples of **Makovecz architecture** have drawn attention to the town, but Sárospatak's main claim to fame is still its historic association with the **Rákóczi family**, whose **castle** is one of the main sights in town.

The Rákóczi family played a major role in Transylvania and Hungary during a turbulent era. Shortly after **György I Rákóczi** acquired Sárospatak Castle in 1616, his Transylvanian estates – and political influence – were augmented by marriage to the immensely wealthy **Zsuzsanna Lorántffy**. In 1630 the nobility elected him Prince of Transylvania, hoping that György would restore the stability enjoyed under Gábor Bethlen – which he did.

Alas, **György II** was as rash as his father was cautious, managing to antagonize both Poland and Vizier Mehmet, whose invasion of Transylvania forced the clan to flee to Habsburg-controlled Hungary in 1658. Here the Counter-Reformation was in full swing, and Magyar landlords and peasants reacted against Habsburg confiscations by sporadically staging ferocious revolts of "dissenters" (*kuruc*). Though the original revolt, led by Imre Thököly, was bloodily crushed, conspirators gathered around György's son **Ferenc I**.

By 1703, the insurgency had become a full-scale **War of Independence**, led by **Ferenc II**, whose irregular cavalry and peasant foot soldiers initially triumphed. By 1711, however, the Magyars were exhausted and divided, abandoned by their half-hearted ally Louis XIV of France, and Ferenc fled abroad as his armies collapsed under the weight of Habsburg power, to die in exile (in Tekirdag, Turkey) in 1735.

## The Town

From the bus or train station it's about ten minutes' walk into the town centre, via Táncsics Mihály utca and Rákóczi út. If you're not laden with baggage, take a

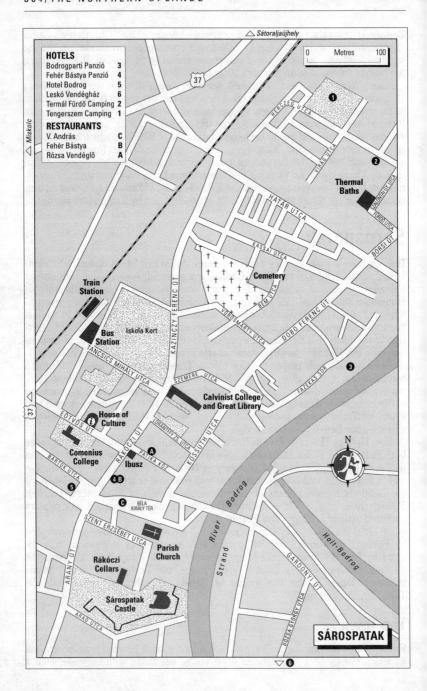

△ *Sátoraljaújhely*

**HOTELS**

| | |
|---|---|
| Bodrogparti Panzió | 3 |
| Fehér Bástya Panzió | 4 |
| Hotel Bodrog | 5 |
| Leskó Vendégház | 6 |
| Termál Fürdő Camping | 2 |
| Tengerszem Camping | 1 |

**RESTAURANTS**

| | |
|---|---|
| V. András | C |
| Fehér Bástya | B |
| Rózsa Vendéglő | A |

0   Metres   100

◁ *Miskolc*

37

HERCEG UTCA

VIRÁG UTCA

**❶**

**❷**

SZAUNCÁLY UTCA

FÜRDŐ UTCA

**Thermal Baths**

HATÁR UTCA

KASSAI UTCA

BORSI ÚT

† † † † †
† † **Cemetery**
† † † †
† † † †

KAZINCZY FERENC ÚT

VÖRÖSMARTY UTCA

BEM UTCA

DOBÓ FERENC ÚT

**Train Station**

**Bus Station**

Iskola Kert

TÁNCSICS MIHÁLY UTCA

SZEMERE UTCA

FAZEKAS SOR

**❸**

**Calvinist College and Great Library**

EÖTVÖS ÚT

ⓘ **House of Culture**

RÁKÓCZI ÚT

PATAKA KÖZ

TORÁNTEY S. UTCA

KOSSUTH UTCA

Ⓐ

BARTÓK UTCA

**Comenius College**

**Ibusz**

❹Ⓑ

**❺**

Ⓒ

BÉLA KIRÁLY TÉR

N

SZENT ERZSÉBET UTCA

River Bodrog

Strand

GÁRDONYI ÚT

Holt-Bodrog

**Parish Church**

ARANY ÚT

**Rákóczi Cellars**

**Sárospatak Castle**

ARAD UTCA

DÓZSA GYÖRGY UTCA

**SÁROSPATAK**

▽ **❻**

detour through the **Iskola Kert** (School Garden), full of statues of alumni from the **Calvinist College** across the park (Mon–Sat 9am–5pm, Sun & holidays 9am–1pm; closed Easter, Whitsun & Oct 31). Founded in 1531, the college achieved renown under the rectorship (1650–54) of the great Czech humanist **Jan Comenius**, who published several textbooks with the support of György Rákóczi. During the Counter-Reformation, it was forced to move to Gönc, and then to Slovakia, before returning home in 1703. Illustrious graduates include Kossuth, Gárdonyi, the writer Zsigmond Móricz and the language reformer Ferenc Kazinczy. Like the Calvinist College in Debrecen, it has long-standing ties with England and runs an international **summer language school**. Since regaining control in 1990, the church has striven to make the college an educational powerhouse once again. Hour-long **tours** take in the Neoclassical **Great Library** (*Nagykönyvtár*), to the right of the main entrance, and a **museum** of college history. The modern building in the courtyard was designed by Makovecz (see below).

## The Makovecz buildings
Passing through the centre of town you can see a succession of buildings by the visionary architect Imre Makovecz, whose association with Sárospatak dates back to 1972, when Makovecz was on the Party's blacklist. His first project for the council was the **department store** on the corner of Rákóczi út and Bartók utca, quite anodyne by Western standards, but far removed from the then prevailing brutalist style. Next came the **House of Culture** on Eötvös utca, whose silvery, insectile facade conceals an amazing wooden auditorium; followed by an **apartment building** on the corner with Rákóczi út, manifesting his passion for asymmetry and organic forms, rooted in a fascination with ancient Celtic and Magyar culture. In the 1990s Makovecz returned to Sárospatak to embellish the Calvinist College and build a delightful **school** on Arany út, just past the castle.

## Sárospatak Castle
In a park outside the centre, **Sárospatak Castle** (Tues–Sun: March–Oct 10am–6pm; Nov–Feb 10am–5pm; 300Ft) is a handsome mélange of Gothic, Renaissance and Baroque architecture, both doughty and palatial. Grouped around a courtyard in the Renaissance wings, the **Rákóczi Museum** dotes upon the dynasty, even down to a series of watercolours depicting the stages of Ferenc II's exile. Heavy inlaid furniture, jewellery, monstrous stoves, and a banqueting hall complete with piped court music recreate domestic life, while other rooms contain life-size paintings of fearsome cavalry and the moustachioed portrait of Ferenc II that is much reproduced.

A romantic loggia, like a prop from *Romeo and Juliet*, links the residential wings to the fifteenth-century keep, known as the **Red Tower**. Guided tours (in Hungarian only) take you around the dungeons and underground wells, the labyrinth of galleries used by gunners and a series of impressive halls. The **Knights' Hall**, remaining somehow austere despite its throne and stained-glass windows, hosted sessions of Parliament during the Independence War. Plots were hatched by Ferenc I in the adjoining circular balcony room, beneath a ceiling decorated with a stucco rose – the rose being a cryptic warning to guests to be discreet (hence the expression "sub rosa", meaning conspiratorial). Beyond the courtyard is a sloping grass bank, now a nature conservation area, running down to the river. The castle **café** is a good place for coffee.

### The Rákóczi Cellars and Parish Church

The **Rákóczi Cellars** in the vicinity of the castle are the most impressive in the Zemplén. Hewn out by prisoners from the castle dungeons in the seventeenth century, they are thickly coated in a black *penész*, the "noble mould", whose presence is considered vital to the flavour of local **wine**. There is a famous niche with a bench in it where Ferenc Rákóczi himself used to come and smoke a pipe and plot the overthrow of the Habsburgs. The cellar is now owned by **Megyer-Pajzos**, a French company with a Hungarian name. Although **tours and wine-tasting** (Mon–Fri 7am–7.30pm) are only for groups of five or more, individuals can phone to find out if one is scheduled (☎47/311-902).

A minute's walk away, further up Szent Erzsébet utca, stands Sárospatak's **Parish Church** (Tues–Sun 10am–2pm). Though much remodelled since the fourteenth century, with painted-on rather than genuine vaulting, it remains one of the largest Gothic hall churches in eastern Hungary. Its huge Baroque altar was brought here from the Carmelite church in Buda Castle after their order was banned in 1784. Look out for posters advertising **organ recitals**.

## Practicalities

Pending the opening of a Tourinform in the House of Culture on Eötvös út (☎47/311-811), you can get **information** from IBUSZ at Rákóczi út 15 (Mon–Fri 8am–4pm; ☎47/311-244), which is also the place to book **private rooms** (②), or **beds** in a local *kollégium* (①–②) over summer.

The next step up in **accommodation** is the *Fehér Bástya Panzió* at Rákóczi út 39 (☎47/312-400; ②–③), where the cheaper rooms share a bathroom, but they all have TV. If you fancy a place with a riverside garden and canoes to rent, go for the *Bodrogparti Panzió* at Fazekas sor 46, twenty minutes' walk from the centre (☎47/312-623; ③). Further out across the river, the *Leskó Vendégház* at Dózsa György út 30/b (☎47/312-375; ③) is quieter still. With the *Hotel Borostyán* beside the Rákóczi cellars closed at present, the only **hotel** is the soulless mid-rise *Bodrog* on Rákóczi út (☎47/311-744; ③–⑤).

Of the two **campsites**, thirty minutes' walk away, *Termál Fürdő Camping* on Határ út (☎47/312-180; ①; April–Sept) is next to the town's thermal baths, while *Tengerszem Camping* (☎47/312-744; ②; April to mid-Oct) has bungalows and good facilities, but charges higher rates all round.

The best places to **eat** are the modern *Fehér Bástya* on Rákóczi út, and the more stylish *V András* restaurant and café on Béla Király tér, where you can sit outside in summer (closes 3pm on Sun). On Patika köz, off Rákóczi út, the old-fashioned working-class *Rózsa Vendéglő* (daily 6am–7pm) is just a few doors along from the *Black Cats* Irish pub, Sárospatak's youth hangout.

Ask at the House of Culture about **concerts**, plays and other events, especially during the **Music Days** (*Zenei Napok*) in July and August. Less highbrow activities include wallowing in the **thermal baths**, sunbathing beside the Bodrog, or **fishing** in the Holt-Bodrog tributary; ask at IBUSZ.

## East to Karcsa and Pácin

Karcsa and Pácin are both readily accessible by bus from Sárospatak or Sátoraljaújhely. On the edge of **KARCSA**, 20km east of Sárospatak, stands a tenth-century **Romanesque Church** with a Gothic nave and a freestanding belfry. The keys are next door, at the house with the *Belyegzés* sign. In **PÁCIN**, 4km further on, there's a fifteenth- to sixteenth-century **Renaissance manor** exhibiting peasant furniture (Tues–Sun: May–Sept 10am–6pm; Oct–April 9am–4pm; 100Ft). The kitchen cupboard carries a picture of a woman slaving over the stove, shouting "Hurry up, it's eleven o'clock!" to her husband who sits by the fire.

# Sátoraljaújhely and around

Easier to reach than it is to pronounce ("*Shah*-tor-oll-yah-oowee-hay"), **SÁTORAL-JAÚJHELY** is the last Zemplén town before the border crossing to Slovenské Nové Mesto in Slovakia. Formerly a thriving county town, it was relegated to a backwater by the Treaty of Trianon and the provincial mergers which made Sárospatak the Zemplén "capital", while its once prosperous Jewish wine-trading community was wiped out in the war. Unless you happen to be searching for an ancestor, the reason for coming is to catch buses to the villages (see overleaf) rather than to see the town itself – unless your visit happens to coincide with its **international folk dancing festival** in August or September, which alternates every year between being for children or adults; 1999 is an adults' year.

From the bus and train stations 1km south of the centre, follow Fasor utca until it joins Kossuth utca, beside the striking new red and yellow Reynolds tobacco factory. Across the main road lies a direly neglected **Jewish cemetery**, one of two in Sátoraljaújhely, where Jews amounted to forty percent of the population at the turn of the century. Further uphill, past a Gothic parish church, one reaches a cluster of Baroque edifices around Kossuth tér. It was from the balcony of the **Town Hall** at no. 5 that Kossuth first demonstrated his talent for oratory, during the Zemplén cholera epidemic and riots of 1830. In the middle of the square stands an almost unrecognizable Soviet war memorial covered with ivy. Rounding off the air of desolation, there's a dull local history exhibition in the **Kazinczy Museum** on Dózsa utca, down to the right past Kossuth tér (Tues–Sat 9am–3pm; 100Ft).

If you fancy some walking, the wild ravines and forested slopes of **Mount Magas** (509m) loom just outside town to the west. These heights saw bitter fighting between Magyars and Slovaks in 1919, and between partisans and Nazis in 1944.

## Practicalities

On Kossuth tér you can book local private rooms (which are pretty limited) through IBUSZ at no. 26 (Mon–Fri 8am–4pm), and **accommodation** throughout the Zemplén at Express at no. 22 (Mon–Fri 8am–4.30pm; ☎47/322-563), which is also just about the only place in town that'll change money. Otherwise there's the drab but clean *Hotel Zemplén* at Széchenyi tér 5–7 (☎47/322-522; ③–④), or the slightly cheaper *Hotel Henriette* at Vasvári Pál utca 16, a few doors down from the museum on the corner of Dózsa György utca (☎47/323-118; ③), both of which are very central.

Your options for **eating** are more or less limited to the *Hotel Zemplén*'s dining room, a *Halászcsárda* on Kossuth tér that serves "Hungover" fish soup, and the unpretentious *Zemplén Bisztró* at Dózsa György utca 2. Local youths go **drinking** at the *Pipa* bar near the station, or at *Caffe Henriette* on Vásvari Pál utca.

# Around Sátoraljaújhely

In the highlands beyond Sátoraljaújhely there are more villages that are just as lovely as those on the western side of the Zemplén. With a car, you can visit half a dozen of them in a day and not feel cheated if a couple are less appealing than expected. Relying on local buses, you'll have to go for a simpler itinerary and be more selective. Local buses enable one to reach Füzér (three daily), Pálháza (eight daily), Hollóháza (six daily), Karcsa and Pácin (hourly), and Telkibánya (twice daily on weekdays).Tourinform in Miskolc has information on lodgings in local houses, and Express in Sátoraljaújhely can also help. The following itineraries are basically structured around bus routes.

## Towards Pálháza and Rostállo

This route can be a long excursion, or even a prelude to hiking over the Zemplén, depending on your inclinations. There are three buses daily from both Sátoraljaújhely and Sárospatak via Szépmalom and Füzérradvány to Pálháza, from where you can reach Rostállo in the hills.

At **SZÉPMALOM** ("Beautiful Mill"), 5km from Sátoraljaújhely, a park beside the road contains the elaborate **mausoleum of Ferenc Kazinczy** (Tues–Sun 10am–6pm; 100Ft), which also has a nice restaurant in the park. It was largely thanks to Kazinczy and his associates that Hungarian was restored as a literary language in the nineteenth century rather than succumbing entirely to German, as the Habsburgs would have preferred.

Six kilometres later, buses stop by an avenue of pines leading to the **Castle Garden** (*Kastély Kert*) surrounding a derelict manor house on the edge of **FÜZÉRRADVÁNY**, whose arboretum of variegated oaks and pines provides a haven for vipers and other wildlife (daily 9am–5pm; 100Ft). If the main gates are closed, follow the road round to the left and ask at the lodge. Work is under way to convert the manor house into a hotel and museum. In the village there's a youth camp, the *Ifjúsági Tábor*, that sometimes lets **rooms** (①) from April to October, bookable through Express in Sátoraljaújhely, or you can stay at the *Nagy-Tanya Fogadó* across the road (☎47/370-550; ①).

Another kilometre or so on up the main road lies **PÁLHÁZA**, the place to board the **narrow-gauge train** that runs 9km up to Rostalló (45min). This *erdei vasút* (forest railway) runs three times daily between mid-April and mid-October, to coincide with buses for Sátoraljaújhely and Sárospatak. Its terminal is near the *Pálháza Ipartelep* bus stop, ten minutes' walk from the main road down towards Kőkapu. Mrs. Ulicskané offers rooms at Vörösmarty utca 10, at the eastern end of the village (☎47/370-278; ①), or there is the *Megálló Turistaház* at Dózsa György utca 160 (☎47/370-121; ①). To really get away from it all, you can stay at the *Kőkapu Kastely*, an old hunting lodge in woods overlooking a rowing lake (☎47/370-032; ③). The best rooms are in the lodge itself, rather than in the annexe. You can rent bikes and boats, and there is a small restaurant, too. Though connected to Pálháza by road (8km), there aren't any buses.

**ROSTALLÓ**, the bus terminus 1km further on, is the starting point for **hikes** in various directions – mostly ambitious ones for which you need proper equipment and a map. A good objective is **István kut** (Stephen's Well), a silver birch wood between Rostalló, Háromhuta and Regéc, noted for its special flora and diverse butterflies.

# Füzér, Hollóháza and Lászlótanya

If one excursion is your limit, the village to aim for is **FÜZÉR**, a stopover for buses between Sátoraljaújhely and Hollóháza, only 9km from Pálháza. An idyllic place of vine-swathed cottages, dignified elders and wandering animals, Füzér enjoys an exceptionally temperate climate and maintains its traditional ways less self-consciously than museum villages like Hollókő – though a single old dwelling has been preserved as a *tájház* for visitors to poke around. Depending on the time of day, Füzér's social centre shifts from the tiny folk Baroque **church** to the *italbolt* ("drink shop") and then the bus stop, for the last buses to Hollóháza (Mon–Fri 2.20pm; Sat, Sun & holidays 8.50pm) or Sátoraljaújhely (Mon–Fri 2.30pm; Sat, Sun & holidays 6.50pm).

The ruined **Perényi Castle** is almost directly overhead, although screened by trees and the precipitous angle of the hill. Erected in case the Mongols should return, it served as a repository for the Hungarian crown from 1301 to 1310, while foreign rivals squabbled over the throne. At a later date it was owned by Countess Báthori, who is said to have murdered several victims here. From the huge Gothic arches of its ruined chapel there's a magnificent view of the sleepy village below, the blue-green hills along the border and the distant Plain beyond – the whole scene enlivened by flocks of swifts swooping and soaring on the powerful thermals. Due to the microclimate, the hillsides abound in **wildlife**, with special flora, vipers, birds of prey and – sometimes – wolves and wildcats. **Accommodation** can be found at the school (②) on Kossuth utca, downhill from the bus stop – cross the bridge and turn right – where you should contact Bodnár Józsefné, or ask about rooms in houses on Petőfi utca.

The **porcelain factory** in the village of **HOLLÓHÁZA** was founded in 1831, and has a **museum** relating its history (April–Oct Tues–Sun 10am–5pm; Nov–March Tues–Fri 10am–4pm, 2nd & 4th Sat in the month 10am–4pm; 160Ft), with a shop (Tues–Sat 10am–4pm) selling unbelievably lurid, flowery examples. When the factory shop is closed, an outlet selling seconds is open round the corner. At the top end of the village is a small modern **church**, one wall bearing the stations of the cross by the ceramicist Margit Kovács. Having seen both, there might be time for a hearty meal at the *Nagymilic Étterem* at Károlyi utca 46, before pushing on to Lászlótanya, or catching one of the **buses** across the hills to Kéked and Abaújvár (see p.303).

About 6km by road from Hollóháza or a four-kilometre hike from Füzér, the tiny hamlet of **LÁSZLÓTANYA** gets its name from the former **hunting lodge** of Count László Károlyi, which stands only 400m from the Slovak border. During the early 1950s, the lodge served as a holiday resort for top Communist officials, notably the then Party leader Mátyás Rákosi, the route being lined by ÁVO guards during his visits. This mock Tudor folly is currently closed for refurbishment, but it's worth checking whether work has finished (☎47/305-008), as it may well reopen as a hotel. Rákosi slept in the suite at the top of the stairs, if you're curious to know.

## travel details

### Trains

Aszód to: Balassagyarmat (7 daily; 1hr 30min).

Balassagyarmat to: Aszód (7 daily; 1hr 30min); Diósjenő and Vác (5–6 daily; 1–2hr).

**Budapest (Keleti Station)** to: Eger (3 daily; 2hr); Miskolc (11 daily; 1hr 45min–2hr 15min).

**Eger** to: Budapest (4 daily; 2hr); Putnok (5 daily; 3hr).

**Füzesabony** to: Debrecen (5 daily; 2hr); Eger (every 1hr–1hr 30min; 30min); Hortobágy (5 daily; 1hr); Tiszafüred (5 daily; 30min).

**Gyöngyös** to: Mátrafüred (hourly; 1hr).

**Hatvan** to: Salgótarján (every 1hr–1hr 30min; 1hr–1hr 30min).

**Miskolc** to: Kazincbarcika (every 2hr; 30min); Nyíregyháza (every 1hr–1hr 30min; 2hr); Ózd (every 2hr; 2hr); Putnok (every 2hr; 1hr); Sárospatak (3 daily; 1hr 20min); Sátoraljaújhely (5 daily; 1hr–1hr 30min); Szerencs (hourly; 30min). Tornanádaska (8 daily; 2hr);

**Sárospatak** to: Karcsa and Pácin (3 daily; 30min); Pálháza (2 daily; 1hr); Miskolc (3 daily; 1hr 30min).

**Szerencs** to: Boldogkőváralja (4 daily; 1hr); Gönc (4 daily; 1hr 15min); Mád (8 daily; 15min); Sárospatak (hourly; 1hr); Tállya (8 daily; 30min); Tokaj (7 daily; 35min).

### Buses

**Budapest (Népstadion)** to: Aggtelek (1 daily; 5hr); Balassagyarmat (every 1–2hr; 2hr 30min); Eger (every 1hr 30min; 3hr); Lillafüred (1 daily; 3hr 30min); Mátraháza (4 daily; 2hr).

**Aggtelek** to: Budapest (1 daily; 5hr); Eger (1 daily; 4hr).

**Balassagyarmat** to: Budapest (every 1–2hr; 2hr 30min); Salgótarján (hourly; 1hr); Szécsény (hourly; 1hr).

**Eger** to: Abádszálok (2 daily; 1hr 15min); Aggtelek (1 daily; 4hr); Békéscsaba (2 daily; 5hr); Budapest (every 1hr 30min; 3hr); Debrecen (1 daily; 2hr 45min); Gyöngyös (1 daily; 1hr 30min); Gyula (1 daily; 5hr 30min); Hajdúszoboszló (1 daily; 3hr 15min); Hortobágy (1 daily; 2hr 30min); Jászberény (1 daily; 2hr); Kecskemét (2 daily; 4hr); Mátraháza (1 daily; 2hr); Miskolc via the Bükk (2 weekly; 2hr 30min); Recsk (1 daily except Sun; 1hr 45min); Salgótarján (3 daily except Sun; 2hr); Sirok (1 daily except Sun; 1hr 30min); Szeged (1 daily; 5hr); Szilvásvárad (hourly; 1hr); Szolnok (1–3 daily; 2hr 30min); Tiszafüred (2 daily; 1hr 15min).

**Füzesabony** to: Tiszafüred (hourly; 45min).

**Gyöngyös** to: Abádszálok (1 daily; 2hr); Debrecen (1 daily; 4hr 30min); Eger (1 daily; 1hr 30min); Mátrafüred (every 20min; 30min); Mátraháza (hourly; 45min); Miskolc (1 daily; 3hr 15min) .

**Hatvan** to: Gyöngyös (hourly; 30min); Hollókő (3 daily; 1hr 30min).

**Hollókő** to: Hatvan (3 daily; 1hr 30min); Szécsény (3 daily; 45min).

**Mátraháza** to: Eger (1 daily; 2hr); Gyöngyös (1 daily; 45min); Miskolc (1 daily; 4hr).

**Miskolc** to: Aggtelek (1 daily; 3hr); Békéscsaba (1 daily; 5hr); Bükkszentkereszt (1 weekly; 1hr); Bükkszentlászló (every 20min; 45min); Debrecen (1 daily; 2hr); Eger via the Bükk (2 weekly; 2hr 30min); Eger via Noszvaj (1 daily; 2hr 15min); Hajdúböszörmény (1 daily; 1hr 30min); Jászberény (1 daily; 5hr); Lillafüred (every 20min; 30min); Mátraháza (1 daily; 4hr); Miskolc-Tapolca (every 10min; 15min); Nyíregyháza (1 daily except Sun; 2hr); Ómassa (every 20min; 45min); Recsk (1 daily except Sun; 1hr); Sirok (1 daily except Sun; 1hr 15min).

**Ózd** to: Aggtelek (1 daily; 1hr 30min); Debrecen (2 daily; 3hr 45min); Miskolc (2 daily; 3hr 30min).

**Paradfürdő** to: Debrecen (1 daily; 4hr); Eger (1 daily; 1hr); Hajdúszoboszló (1 daily; 4hr 30min); Tiszafüred (1 daily; 2hr 45min).

**Putnok** to: Aggtelek (5–6 daily; 30min).

**Salgótarján** to: Balassagyarmat (3 daily; 1hr); Budapest (hourly; 2hr 30min); Gyöngyös (3 daily; 1hr 30min); Hatvan (2 daily; 1hr 30min); Ipolytarnoc (hourly; 30min); Kecskemét (1 daily; 3hr); Miskolc (2 daily; 3hr); Pásztó (hourly; 1hr).

**Sárospatak** to: Sátoraljaújhely (hourly; 20min).

**Sártoraljaújhely** to: Füzér (hourly; 45min).

**Szécsény** to: Hollókő (1 daily; 45min).

### International trains

**Miskolc (Tiszai Station)** to: Košice (5 daily; 2hr); Poprad Tatry (1 daily; 3hr 45min).

**Salgótarján** to: Częstochowa (1 daily; 10hr 15min); Katowice (1 daily; 9hr).

### International buses

**Balassagyarmat** to: Banská Bystrica (June–Sept 1 daily; 3hr); Lučenec (June–Sept 1 daily; 3hr 15min); Žilina (June–Sept 1 daily; 4hr 45min).

**Eger** to: Banská Bystrica (June–Aug 1 daily; 4hr); Lučenec (daily except Sun; 3hr 30min).

**Miskolc** to: Košice (2–4 weekly; 2hr 30min); Rožňava (1–2 daily except Sun; 3hr); Uzhgorod (1 daily; 7hr); Velké Kapušany (July–Sept 2 weekly; 3hr); Zemplinska Yirava (June–Sept 3 weekly; 3hr 30min).

**Ózd** to: Rimavská Sobota (5 weekly; 1hr 30min); Uzhgorod (1 daily; 8hr 30min).

**Salgótarján** to: Lučenec (1–3 daily; 1hr 30min).

**Sárospatak** to: Trebiyov (1 daily; 1hr 45min); Velké Kapušany (July–Sept 2 weekly; 2hr).

**Sátoraljaújhely** to: Trebiyov (June–Sept 1 daily; 1hr 15min); Velké Kapušany (June–Sept 2 weekly; 1hr 30min).

# CHAPTER SIX

# THE GREAT PLAIN

Covering half of Hungary, the **Great Plain** (*Nagyalföld*) is awesome in its flatness. It can be as drab as a farmworker's boots or it can shimmer like the mirages of **Hortobágy National Park**, which, along with **Kiskunság**, preserves the traditional landscape and wildlife of the region. In the villages, often with names prefixed by *Nagy-* or *Kis-* (Big or Little), the most characteristic sight is an isolated whitewashed farmstead (*tanya*) with a rustic artesian well, surrounded by flocks of geese and strings of paprika hanging out to dry. Marcell Iványi's short film *The Wind*, which won an award at Cannes in 1996, wonderfully captures the visual and emotional impact of this landscape.

By contrast, there's a keen rivalry between **Debrecen** and **Szeged** as to which is the more sophisticated city. Szeged deserves the accolade if restaurants, architecture and festivals are the main criteria, but both have plenty of students and a high cultural profile. On a lesser scale this also goes for **Kecskemét** and **Hódmezővásárhely**, the most attractive of the many small towns on the Plain. During the summer, visitors can go to **festivals** in Debrecen and Szeged, the equestrian Bridge Fair at Hortobágy on August 19 to 20, and the *Téka Tábor* folk festival at **Nagykálló** in late July, while the pilgrimages to **Máriapócs** and the tomb of the "miracle rabbi" in Nagykálló cast a fascinating light on religious life.

## The Puszta: a brief history

The word *puszta* is nowadays practically synonymous with the Great Plain, but it's actually a name that describes the transformation of this huge lowland. During medieval times **the Plain** was thickly forested, with hundreds of villages living off agriculture and livestock-rearing; the mighty **River Tisza**, fed by its tributaries in Transylvania and Maramures, determined all. Each year it flooded, its hundreds of loops merging into a "sea of water in which the trees were sunk to their crowns", enriching the soil with volcanic silt from the uplands and isolating the villages for months on end. However, the Turkish invasion of 1526 unleashed a scourge upon the land: 150 years of nearly unceasing warfare. The peasants who survived fled to the safer *khasse* (tribute-paying) towns like Szeged and Debrecen, leaving their villages to fall into ruin, while vast tracts of forest were felled to build military stockades, or burned simply to deny cover to the partisans (*Hajdúk*). Denuded of vegetation, the land became swampy and pestilent with mosquitoes, and later the abode of solitary swineherds, runaway serfs, outlaws (*betyár*) and wolves. People began calling it **the puszta**, meaning "abandoned, deserted, bleak", and something of its character is conveyed by other words and phrases with the same root; for example *pusztít* (to devastate), *pusztul* (to perish, be ruined), and *pusztulj innen* (Clear out of here!). Not surprisingly, most people shunned it, or ventured in solely out of dire necessity.

Yet another transformation began in the nineteenth century, as an unexpected consequence of Count Széchenyi's flood-control work along the Tisza, when soil alkalinity increased the spread of **grassland**. Suitable only for pasturage, in time this became the "Hungarian Wild West", complete with rough-riding *csikósok* (cowboys), and wayside *csárdák* (inns), where lawmen, gypsies and outlaws shared the same tables, bound not to fight by the custom of the *puszta*. It was a man's world – women and children remained in the farmsteads close to town – and nineteenth-century romantics like Sándor Petőfi rhapsodized over it as the incarnation of Magyardom: "My world and home... the Alföld, the open sea".

By the 1920s reality had crushed romance. Irrigation enabled landowners to enclose common pasture for crops, while mechanization denied the evicted share-croppers and herders even the chance of work on the big estates. Most of Hungary's landless peasants, or **"three million beggars"**, lived on the Plain. Their efforts to form agrarian leagues were violently opposed by the gentry and gendarmerie, particularly in the Viharsarok region, meaning the "Stormy Corner".

True to their promises, the Communists distributed big estates amongst the peasantry and **nationalized land** "for those who till it" in 1947. Two years later, however, following the dictates of Stalinism, the peasants were forced to join state-run co-operative farms. Treated as socialist serfs, they unanimously dissolved "their" co-operatives in 1956 and reverted to subsistence production, vowing to prevent the landlords from returning. In response to this, the Party pursued a subtler **agricultural policy** from the sixties onwards, investing in ever larger co-operative and state farms, while allowing peasants to sell the produce of their "household plots" (limited to 1.5 acres), which accounted for half the meat and seventy percent of the fruit and vegetables produced in Hungary. By Eastern European standards the co-operatives were successful, producing a grain surplus that earned one third of Hungary's hard currency income, though the urge to be master of their own land remained strong amongst the peasantry.

In the 1990 election, the **Smallholder's Party** won a majority of votes cast on the Plain by pledging to dissolve the co-operatives and return the land to its pre-1947 owners. The ensuing compromise worked out by the coalition government gave co-operative members the option of leasing or owning land. Though many became **independent farmers**, they lacked the capital for modern equipment and storage facilities, to the detriment of quality, while the emphasis on export crops meant that in 1994–95, Hungary even had to import potatoes, traditionally the poor man's food. The birth pangs of the new agricultural system are proving longer and harder than anyone expected, and it will be years before Hungary regains its standing as the breadbasket of Eastern Europe.

## Getting there

With its often monotonous vistas and widely spaced towns, the Plain is something most people cross as much as visit and, if you're pressed for time, large areas can be skipped with a clear conscience. The region between the Danube and the Tisza is chiefly notable for Szeged, Kecskemét and Kiskunság National Park, while Debrecen, Hortobágy and the Nyírség are the highlights beyond the River Tisza. Few other places merit more than an excursion or a stopover, though visitors keen on rural life or cycling might want to consider more off-the-beaten-track destinations.

**Intercity trains** are the fastest way of reaching the larger towns of Debrecen and Nyíregyháza to the east and Kecskemét and Szeged to the south from Budapest. **Buses** from Budapest's Népstadion terminal are the best way of reaching towns such as Kalocsa and Baja, which are awkward or impossible to reach

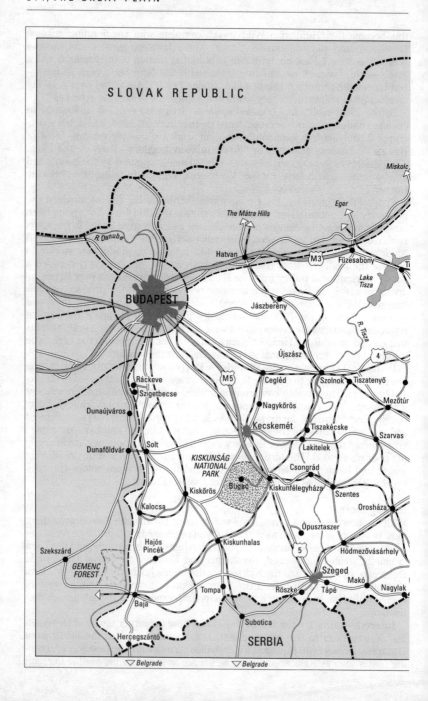

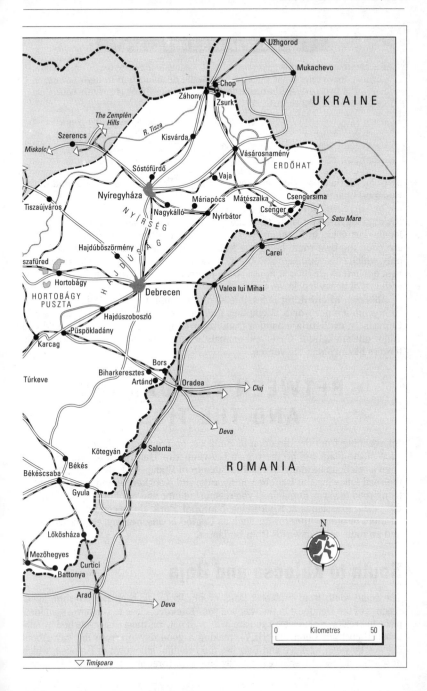

---

**ACCOMMODATION PRICE CODES**

All accommodation in this guide is graded according to the price bands given below. Note that prices refer to the **cheapest available double room in high season** or the price of **two people sharing a tent** in a campsite. 100Ft is roughly equivalent to $0.45 or DM1. For more details, see p.24.

① Under 2000Ft      ④ 6000–8500Ft      ⑦ 20,000–27,000Ft
② 2000–4000Ft      ⑤ 8500–13,000Ft      ⑧ 27,000–40,000Ft
③ 4000–6000Ft      ⑥ 13,000–20,000Ft      ⑨ over 40,000Ft

---

by train. All these services are covered under "Travel Details" at the end of the Budapest chapter.

For **drivers**, the best route south is the M5, which runs as far as Kiskunfélegyháza en route to Szeged, and has two toll-paying stretches (1200Ft for the last 40km to Kecskemét, 500Ft thereafter). Road connections to the east are poor, the best route being the M3, also tolled, and presently to Füzesabony only, which cuts south along Route 33 towards the Hortobágy and Debrecen. The best non-toll alternative is Route 30 via Hatvan; Route 4 via Szolnok is very slow with lots of heavy trucks on the road.

Although **hitchhiking** is feasible along the trunk routes to Baja, Szeged and Debrecen, it's not worth attempting it elsewhere unless there's no alternative. Conversely, **cyclists** are banned from major (single-digit) roads, but should find minor ones delightful. Carts and animals are more common than cars, and wild flowers bloom along the verges.

---

# BETWEEN THE DANUBE
# AND THE TISZA

---

Approaching from the direction of Budapest or Transdanubia, your first experience of the Plain will be the region **between the Danube and the Tisza**. Its chief attractions lie along two main routes from Budapest: **Kalocsa** and **Baja**, on the road following the Danube southwards; and **Kecskemét** and **Szeged**, on the trunk road towards Romania. If you're short of time and want to see something of the *puszta* grasslands at **Kiskunság National Park**, the second itinerary has a lot more to offer. Other towns, such as **Cegléd** or **Jászberény**, can easily be visited en route or as day-trips from Budapest.

## South to Kalocsa and Baja

The route south from Budapest leads eventually to laid-back **Baja**, on the lower reaches of the Danube. On the way you pass **Ráckeve**, close to Budapest – an ideal place to break your journey if you are in a car. If not, it is most easily reached by suburban train from Budapest (HÉV), making a good day-trip from the city. About halfway between Ráckeve and Baja lies the beautiful little town of **Kalocsa**, which despite its sleepy atmosphere is actually one of the three archbishoprics in Hungary.

# Ráckeve and Szigetbecse

The town of **RÁCKEVE**, 46km south of Budapest, is a diminutive counterpart to Szentendre on the Danube Bend, likewise founded by Serbian (*Rác*) refugees and rich in Baroque architecture, but far less touristy, despite being easily accessible from Budapest. Hourly HÉV trains from Budapest's Vágóhíd terminal on Soroksári út take an hour and a quarter and are met by buses into the centre of town. Motorists should turn off the main road just beyond Kiskunlacháza, and cross the bridge onto Csepel Island, where the town is situated. Its main street, Kossuth utca, runs parallel to the Danube, where townsfolk go sunbathing and swimming.

Ráckeve's finest sight is the magnificent **Serbian Orthodox Church** at Viola utca 1 (Tues–Sat 10–noon & 2–5pm, Sun 2–5pm; 100Ft), whose blue and white tower, topped by a gilded cross, rises above the rooftops to the west of the town centre. The oldest Orthodox church in Hungary, dating from 1487, it has a Baroque iconostasis and frescoes painted by Tódor Gruntovich between 1765 and 1771, using traces of the original fifteenth-century ones as a guide. The oldest part of the church is the nave, whose colours are dimmed by age; the narthex and freestanding bell-tower are sixteenth-century additions. Mass is still celebrated on important Orthodox holidays, though the congregation mainly comes from neighbouring villages like Lórév, which have preserved their Serb character. The custodians will open the door if you ring the bell of their house in the grounds.

Also look out for the **Savoy Mansion** on Kossuth utca, a grandiose fusion of Italian and French Baroque with a Neoclassical dome and other nineteenth-century additions. The original building was commissioned by Prince Eugene of Savoy, shortly after his armies drove the Turks from Hungary, and was constructed between 1702 and 1722 according to the designs of J L Hildebrandt. Restored in the 1970s after decades of neglect, it is now a hotel, the *Savoyai-Kastély* (☎24/485-253; ②–③). Other **accommodation** is offered by *Hidláb Camping*, across the bridge and to the right at Dömsödi utca 2 (☎24/385-501; ②), which also has bungalows (③). The *Fekete Holló* on Kossuth utca does tasty **meals**, but the service is appallingly slow.

From Ráckeve you can catch a local bus or taxi 4km to the village of **SZIGET-BECSE**, where the renowned Hungarian-born photographer **André Kertész** spent much of his childhood. A small **museum** at Makádi út 40 (April–Sept Mon–Thurs 8am–4pm, Fri 8am–noon, Sat & Sun 10am–5pm; donations accepted) exhibits over sixty of his early works, ranging from pictures of Szigetbecse to scenes from World War I, including one of troops sitting on a collective latrine. On weekdays you have to get the key from the mayor's office (*polgármesteri hivatal*) at Petőfi utca 34, ten minutes' walk away.

# Kalocsa

Around 120km south of the capital, **KALOCSA** makes a pleasant and convenient stopover, with regular buses passing through en route to Baja further south. The town is promoted for its flowery **embroidery** and "**painting women**", who made it their business to decorate everything in sight, and also as Hungary's "**paprika capital**". If you happen to be here around September 8, when the harvest season officially begins, head out to the surrounding countryside to see the paprika fields transformed into a sea of red.

From the bus station at the far end of Kalocsa's main street, it's a twenty-minute walk to the cathedral and archbishop's palace at the other end of Szent István király út. By the bus station, you can't miss the 22-metre-high **Chronos 8 light tower**, a bequest from the locally born Parisian conceptual sculptor Nicolas Schöffer, some of whose smaller kinetic works are exhibited in the **Nicolas Schöffer Museum** at Szent István király út 76 (Tues–Sun 10am–noon & 2–5pm; 60Ft). Fifteen minutes' further on, the **Viski Károly Museum** at no. 25 (Tues–Sun 9am–5pm; 100Ft) has a dazzling collection of nineteenth-century Magyar, Swabian (*Sváb*) and Slovak (*Tót*) folk costumes. The overstuffed bolsters and quilts on display were mandatory for a bride's dowry. Further along, at no. 6, the **Paprika Museum** (May–Oct Tues–Sun 10am–noon & 1–5pm; 100Ft) lacks intelligible captions or the allure of paprika alfresco, but you'll get the gist of the exhibits easily enough (see box below).

Carrying on to the old main square, Szentharomság tér, you'll find Kalocsa's Baroque **Cathedral**, designed by the prolific András Mayerhoffer in the early eighteenth century. Don't miss the richly attired embalmed bishop that adds a bizarre touch to its pink and white interior, nor the ornate gold pulpit. The nearby **Archbishop's Palace** (May–Sept Tues–Sun 10am–5pm; 120Ft) dates from the same period, but its grandeur recalls the medieval heyday of Kalocsa's bishopric, when local prelates led armies and advised monarchs. Its 120,000-volume **library** contains medieval illuminated manuscripts, a Bible signed by Luther, and impressive frescoes by Maulbertsch. The library was founded by Archbishop Patachich, who was transferred to Kalocsa from his previous post as a punishment for founding a theatre there, and henceforth stuck to books. His apartments were lodged between his chapel and his library, with a door connecting the two, as can still be seen.

Following Kossuth utca off to the right as far as the hospital, you'll see a signpost for the thatched **Folk Art House** on Tompa utca (*Népművészetek Háza* or *Tájház*; March 15 to Oct 15 Tues–Sun 10am–5pm; 100Ft). Several of its rooms are

---

## PAPRIKA

More **paprika** is grown around Kalocsa and Szeged than anywhere else in Hungary. Revered as "red gold" (*piros arany*), no one really knows when this member of the *Capsicum* genus was first introduced. Some theories ascribe its introduction to the Age of Migration via the Balkans, while others even credit Christopher Columbus. Its consumption received an important boost during the Napoleonic Wars thanks to continental blockades, which compelled Europeans to find a substitute for pepper.

The nineteenth-century preference for milder paprika spurred cross-fertilization experiments, which led to the discovery of capsaicin, produced by the plant in response to drought and sunlight and responsible for its piquancy. Inventions such as the Pálffy roller frame eased the laborious task of chopping and grinding, while the plant's nutritional qualities were investigated by **Dr Albert Szent-Györgyi** of Szeged University, who won the 1933 Nobel Prize for synthesizing vitamin C (paprika is also rich in vitamin A).

More recently, there was national outrage over the **paprika scandal** of 1994, when it was discovered that powdered paprika was being laced with red lead to look extra ruddy. To protect the public and the reputation of the national condiment, all supplies were withdrawn from shops until the source of the contamination had been identified and fresh, certifiably pure, paprika became available.

decorated with exuberant floral murals, traditionally found in the *tiszta szoba* or "clean room" of peasant households, where guests were entertained. In Kalocsa, almost uniquely, these were painted by groups of women who were respected artisans. Also displayed is a host of Kalocsa embroidery. This has changed considerably over the decades, with embroiderers working entirely in white in the nineteenth century, till blue and red slowly crept into the designs; then, in the 1920s, when the Kalocsa folk dance troupe became more widely known, it was decided to brighten up the costumes so that they would be more startling on stage. Hence the present multicoloured, rather twee, designs.

### Practicalities

**Arriving** by bus, you might be allowed to jump off on Kossuth utca near Szentháromság tér, rather than alighting at the bus station at the junction of Szent István király út and Route 51. Kalocsa's train station is on Mártírok tere, a fifteen-minute walk along Kossuth utca from the archbishop's palace.

You can get **information** from IBUSZ at Szent István király utca 23 (May–Sept Mon–Fri 8am–6pm, Sat 8am–noon; Oct–April Mon–Fri 8am–4pm; ☎78/462-674), or Korona Tours in Room 13 of the *Hotel Kalocsa* (Mon–Fri 7.30am–4.30pm; ☎78/461-819). Private **rooms** from IBUSZ or the *Hotel Piros Arany* at Szent István király út 37 (☎78/462-220; ③) are affordable alternatives to the beautifully restored and quite luxurious *Hotel Kalocsa* on Szentháromság tér (☎78/461-244; ⑤), whose **restaurant** is the best in town. A cheaper option for eating is the *Barokk Kávéház* by the cathedral, which serves pizzas and has pool tables. You'll find ATMs at Szent István király út 28 and 45, and the post office at no. 44. There are **buses to Baja**, 76km south, every thirty to ninety minutes.

# Hajós Pincék

**Hajós Pincék**, 35km from Baja on the Kecskemét road, is an extraordinary village: no one lives here at all, the entire settlement being devoted to wine cellars – 1260 of them in all. The mainly Swabian population of the surrounding area has been storing and fermenting wine here for centuries, and you can sample it to your heart's content in the cellars along every street. St Orbán's day on May 25 is the day all the vintners come out in force to celebrate the coming harvests with folk dancing and the like. Though there are visitors here all year round, summer is the best time to visit, as you are more likely to find someone in the labyrinth of cellars who will invite you to sample and buy their wine. The *Judit Panzió* at Borbiró sor 1 (☎78/404-832; ②) offers accommodation and also has a restaurant. Buses run from Baja and Kalocsa, and there is a daily bus direct from Budapest.

# Baja

**BAJA**, on the shady banks of the Sugovica-Danube, is a restful town with an almost Mediterranean climate, whose culinary pride is manifest in a **Fish Soup Festival** in mid-July. Baja fish soup (*halászlé*) is a rich mix of carp, catfish, pike-perch and paprika that's more like a freshwater bouillabaisse than a soup. Indeed, Baja currently holds the world record for the greatest amount of fish soup cooked in one place at one time. During the last week in May, there's another festival called the **Summer Days**, with the emphasis on folk dancing and crafts. At other times Baja is a nice place to rest up, but short on sights and excitement.

In the heart of town, imposing civic edifices and the massive, cobbled **Szentháromság tér** overlooking the Sugovica River and Petőfi Island, recall Baja's importance before the Treaty of Trianon relegated it to a minor border town. On Roosevelt tér, off the main square's southeast corner, the **Turr István Museum** (April–Oct Tues–Sun 10am–4pm; 80Ft) is named after a Hungarian general who fought alongside Garibaldi in Italy, just as many Poles and Italians aided Hungary against the Habsburgs. At present there's only a small exhibition on 300 years of local history, including the farcical attempt by Karl VI to regain the Habsburg throne (see box opposite), but the ethnographic and natural history sections upstairs should reopen at some point.

Icon buffs should try to visit the **Serbian Orthodox Church** on Táncsics utca, one of two ministering to locals of Serbian descent; its irregular opening hours are posted outside. There is also a German high school catering to a smaller community of Swabians, whom the Habsburgs encouraged to settle here after the Turks were evicted. From the church, a short walk down Telcs Ede utca brings you to Munkácsy Mihály utca and a fabulous Neoclassical **Synagogue** (now serving as a library), with a monument to the town's 5705 victims of Fascism. The building has been sensitively restored, leaving the ceiling paintings and ornaments as they were, and visitors are welcome to admire what was once the spiritual base of a proud and thriving community. Heading back towards Szentháromság tér, you pass the **Nagy István Gallery** on Arany János utca (April–Oct Tues, Thurs & Sun 10am–4pm; 80Ft), where a collection of paintings by the Alföld School is displayed, Nagy himself being the group's best-known proponent.

Across the river from the main square lies **Petőfi Island**, where Baja's festivals are held – a nice place to go boating, swimming or fishing. It was from here that the last Habsburg emperor was ignominiously deported by a British gunboat, after the failure of his putsch in 1921.

## Practicalities

On **arrival** at the bus station on Csermák Mihály tér, it's a twenty-minute walk along Eötvös utca through the modern downtown to Szentháromság tér, or an extra five minutes if you start from the train station on Szegedi út. Downtown, you can get **information** from IBUSZ, Táncsics Mihály utca 5, behind the Bacsker department store (May–Sept Mon–Thurs 8am–6pm, Fri 8am–2pm, Sat 8am–noon; Oct–April Mon–Thurs 8am–4.30pm, Fri 8am–2pm; ☎79/321-644). There's an ATM on the corner of Szentháromság tér and Deák utca.

If you can't afford the comfortable seclusion of the *Hotel Sugovica* on Petőfi Island (☎79/321-755; ④), try the *Kolibri Panzió* at Batthyány utca 18 (☎79/321-628; ②), or the old-fashioned *Hotel Duna*, Szentháromság tér 5 (☎79/323-224; ②). The cheapest **accommodation** is at the *IYHF Youth Hostel* on Petőfi Island near the bridge (☎79/324-022; ①–②; ten percent discount for IYHF card holders; mid-June to late Aug), or the *József Eötvös College* at Szegedi út 2 (☎79/324-451; ①; mid-June to Aug). *Sugovica Camping* on Petőfi Island (☎79/321-755; May–Sept) is an agreeable site with huts and chalets (②), and pheasants strutting around at dawn.

The spacious café on the corner of Szentháromság tér and Eötvös utca is a popular meeting place, and other cafés spill onto the square over summer. Besides hotel **restaurants**, there is the excellent *Véndió Étterem* just across the bridge on Petőfi Island, and two places offering a change from Hungarian cusine: the lively *Laguna Pizzeria* on Babits Mihály utca, south of the *Korona Panzió*; and the *Fondő kert* (Fondue Garden) at Kossuth utca 19, which serves good salads but no fondue.

## THE LAST OF THE HABSBURGS

Although the Habsburg Empire ended with the abdication of **Karl IV** and the establishment of republics in Austria and Hungary in 1918, the dynasty refused to die. In October 1921, Karl attempted to regain the Hungarian throne by flying into Baja, where a royalist force awaited him with trucks supplied by Major Lehár (cousin of Franz, composer of *The Merry Widow*). However, their advance on Budapest was swiftly halted by regular troops, and a British gunboat transported Karl into exile in Madeira. His widow **Zita** was barred from Austria until 1982 for refusing to renounce her claim, and only returned thereafter to be buried in Vienna.

Meanwhile, their son **Otto** had become a Euro MP and roving ambassador to the former Habsburg territories. An apocryphal story has it that when asked if he would be watching the Austria–Hungary football match, Otto replied, "Who are we playing?" More recently, his son **György** has been given the role of travelling ambassador for Hungary (notwithstanding his Austrian citizenship), and in 1997 married Eilika von Oldenburg in Budapest's St Stephen's Basilica – an event covered live on Hungarian television.

For **nightlife**, check out the *Rock Café* serving herb teas and booze to students in a cellar beside an Indian clothes shop on Széchenyi utca, or the *Amnesia* disco in a factory on Szegedi út, on the edge of town. Other discos and parties organized by different colleges are flyposted around town.

# Jászberény

**JÁSZBERÉNY**, 50km east of Budapest, merits a mention for its historic links to the **Jász** (Jazygians), an Iranian-speaking people who migrated here from around the Caspian Sea at the beginning of the thirteenth century. Granted feudal privileges by Béla III, they prospered as cattle-breeders, tanners and furriers, each extended family owning several farms and a town house. A dozen settlements with names prefixed by "Jász-" denotes the extent of the Jászság region, which remained semi-autonomous until the 1890s, by which time the people had become totally assimilated. As Patrick Leigh Fermor wrote, "this entire nation seems to have vanished like a will o' the wisp, and only these place-names mark the points of their evaporation". Today, Jászberény celebrates the folk traditions of another ethnic group – the Csángó of eastern Transylvania – with an annual festival.

## The Town

Leafy **Lehel vezér tér** is more like a street than a square, but indisputably the heart of town, flush with Baroque piles and festooned with plaques and other memorials to local worthies and 1956 martyrs. The Déryné Cultural Centre at no. 33 (☎57/411-294) is the venue for the **Csángó Festival** in the first week in August, a chance to hear haunting music from the eastern Carpathians, where the ancestors of the Csángó (literally, "wanderer") fled to during the fifteenth, eighteenth and nineteenth centuries. The festival also provides an opportunity to buy embroidered quilts, tablecloths, jackets and other Csángó handicrafts.

To delve into the town's Jazygian heritage, cross the square and visit the **Jász Museum** at Táncsics Mihály utca 5 (Tues–Sun 9am–5pm; 50Ft). Its star exhibit is the ivory **Lehel Horn**, intricately carved with hunting scenes. According to Jász tradition this belonged to a Magyar general, Lehel, whom the German emperor Otto I defeated near Augsburg in 955. Legend has it that Lehel begged to be allowed to blow his horn before being executed and, when the last notes had faded, suddenly stabbed Otto to death with it. Alas for legend, the horn is reckoned to be of eleventh- or twelfth-century Byzantine origin, and it was Lehel, not Otto, who perished at Augsburg.

## Practicalities

There are regular buses from Budapest, Cegléd and Szolnok on the Plain, and from Hatvan in the Northern Uplands. The bus station on Petőfi tér is five minutes' walk from Szentháromság tér, which opens off Lehel vezér tér; the train station lies 1km further out past the bus station, on Rákóczi út. The best source of **information** on local events is Tourinform in the Cultural Centre (mid-June to mid-Sept Mon–Fri 8am–5pm, Sat 8am–noon; mid-Sept to mid-June Mon–Fri 8am–4.30pm; ☎57/411-976), though there's also an IBUSZ at Szövetkezet utca 7/a (June–Aug Mon–Fri 8am–4pm, Sat 8am–noon; Sept–May Mon–Fri 8am–4pm; ☎57/412-143).

Private **accommodation** from IBUSZ (②) may be preferable to the motel-like *Hotel Touring* at Serház út 3 near the bus station (☎57/412-051; ②), or the slightly cheaper *Kakukkfészek Panzió* at Táncsics utca 8, near the museum (☎57/412-345; ②), which only has shared bathrooms. During July and August, the cheapest beds (①) are in local *kollégium* such as the ones at Rákóczi út 15 and 53. For **food**, try the pub-like *Stella Étterem* at Réz utca 1, off past the museum, or you can get a toasted sandwich and a coffee in the Cultural Centre's buffet (Mon–Fri 8am–5pm). The town's **thermal baths**, at Hatvani út 5, just west of the centre, have an outdoor *strand*, sauna and indoor pool (May–Sept Tues–Sun 9am–6pm; 150Ft).

# Cegléd and Nagykőrös

**CEGLÉD** straddles two major rail lines across the Great Plain, linking Budapest with Debrecen to the east, and Kecskemét and Szeged to the south. With an hour or so to kill between connections, you can check out the **Kossuth Museum** in a large turn-of-the-century building on the corner of Rákóczi út and Múzeum utca, between the train station and the centre (Tues–Sun 10am–5pm; 80Ft). It was in Cegléd that Lajos Kossuth launched his drive for volunteers to defend the gains of the 1848 Revolution, principally the abolition of serfdom. The museum preserves the oak table on which he stood to speak, while a statue marks the site on Szabadság tér, down Rákóczi út, near the bus terminal. Kossuth's son, Ferenc, was a parliamentary representative here, and his collection of family relics is exhibited in the museum, along with displays on local archeology and folk culture.

Another clue to the region's history is provided by **NAGYKŐRÖS**, further down the line towards Kecskemét. Like other settlements with names ending in "-kőrös", it recalls the **Kőrös people** who raised sheep and tumuli on the Plain during the Neolithic era (5500–3400 BC). Aeons later, it was briefly dubbed the "Weimar of Hungary" due to the seven academicians teaching here in the 1850s. They are commemorated by a statue outside the museum on Ceglédi út, ten minutes' walk from the central Szabadság tér. Housed in a former hussars' barracks, the **Arany János Museum** (May–Sept Tues–Sun 10am–6pm; 100Ft) commemorates the life and works of the nineteenth-century poet, librettist and balladeer, János Arany, and has a history section featuring Kőrös figurines, and nineteenth-century wooden grave markers from the region. If you walk along the side of the **ornamental garden** (*Cifrakert*) for another ten minutes you'll reach the *Cifra Csárda*, a restaurant with a good reputation.

While the bus station is right on the main square, the train station lies 1km out along Kossuth utca. Country Tours on Széchenyi tér, just west of Szabadság tér (Mon–Thurs 9am–5pm, Fri 9am–3pm; ☎53/355-794), can supply information and book rooms in the *Központi Hotel* (②) above the *Salon Pizzeria* across the square, or private houses (③). There are frequent buses to Cegléd, Jászberény and Kecskemét.

# Kecskemét and around

Hungarians associate **KECSKEMÉT** with *barackpálinka* (the local apricot brandy) and the composer Kodály (who was born in what is now the train station), but its cultural significance doesn't end there. Ranking just behind Szeged and Debrecen as a centre of higher education and the arts, Kecskemét rivals both cities in terms of festivals and museums, and surpasses them architecturally. Given this sophistication, you would never imagine that its name derives from the Hungarian word for "goat" (*kecske*).

Besides being one of the most attractive towns on the Plain, Kecskemét is readily **accessible** from Budapest (by train from Nyugati Station or bus from Népstadion), and there are equally regular services from Szeged (plus less frequent buses from Baja and Cegléd), making it an ideal day excursion from either city, and the prime stopover between them. The town is also a good base for **excursions** to the Kiskunság National Park, with the option of relaxing along the River Tisza, or getting right back to nature by horse-riding or renting a farmhouse in the surrounding countryside.

## The Town

Although nothing remains of medieval Kecskemét, its size can be judged from the ring boulevard (*körút*), which follows the old moat. Unlike most towns in the region, it was spared devastation by the Turks, as the Sultan took a liking to it. Waves of refugees settled here, and Kecskemét became the third-largest town in Hungary, its various religious groups co-existing in harmony. This fortunate history, underpinned by agricultural wealth, explains its air of confidence and the flamboyant, eclectic **architecture**, skilfully integrated with modern buildings by town-planner József Kerényi. To enhance its charms, the centre of town consists of two open squares that merge into a single verdant expanse, with traffic diverted several blocks away. To get there from the bus or train station, follow Nagykőrösi utca or Rákóczi út for ten minutes until you reach Szabadság tér, where the monumental architecture begins.

### Szabadság tér

The northern end of Szabadság tér is characterized by three strikingly different buildings. On one corner of Rákóczi út stands a white, onion-domed former **Synagogue**, built between 1862 and 1871 in the Moorish style, which was sacked by the Nazis when they deported Kecskemét's Jews in 1944, and transformed by

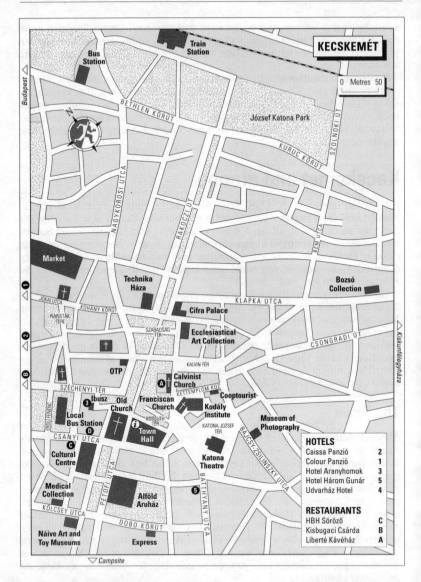

the Communists into a **Technika-háza** or science club, with a hideous Socialist-Realist interior. Across the road, the **Cifra Palace** resembles a scene from *Hansel and Gretel* on acid, with ceramic mushrooms sprouting from psychedelic tiles above a gingerbread-like facade. Designed by Géza Markus in 1902, this wonderful example of Art Nouveau (termed the "Secessionist style" in Hungary) now houses the **Kecskemét Art Gallery** (Tues–Sun 11am–6pm; 100Ft), whose collection includes work by the Jewish painter István Farkas, who died in Auschwitz. Upstairs is a splendid peacock ballroom with enamel tiles and Art Nouveau motifs that was once a casino. Carry on up the stairs and you'll emerge onto a terrace affording a close-up view of the palace's chimneys and gables. Originally built to house small shops and flats, the building is one of the architectural gems of Kecskemét, though it has been sadly neglected over the last fifty years.

The Transylvanian-Gothic hulk diagonally opposite the Cifra Palace is one of two buildings in Kecskemét in the style known as **National Romanticism**. Built between 1911 and 1913 as a Calvinist college, this one is a "mature" example of the genre that coincided with Hungary's millennial anniversary and campaigns to "Magyarize" ethnic minorities, reflecting the triumphalist yet paranoid *Zeitgeist* of the 1890s and 1900s. Its steeply pitched roofs and intimidating tower hark back to the vernacular architecture of rural Hungary and Transylvania, regarded as pure wellsprings of Magyar culture. It now houses a library, a Calvinist high school and the **Collection of Ecclesiastical Art** (Tues–Sun 10am–6pm; 70Ft; entrance on Villám utca). Its highlights are a rustic painted wooden ceiling saved from a church near Lake Balaton just before the whole edifice collapsed, peasant grave markers and a small wooden bell-tower.

### Kossuth tér and around

To the south, across Kossuth tér, is the building that started the whole National Romanticism movement: the **town hall**, designed by Ödön Lechner and Gyula Pártos in 1893. Like Lechner's later works in Budapest, it is richly ornamented with Zsolnay tiles inspired by the decorative traditions of Magyar folk art and nomadic Turkic cultures. However, the building itself is a Renaissance-Baroque pastiche, whose lack of "authentic form" was criticized by later National Romanticists such as Károly Kós. Its Grand Hall contains gilded murals by Bertalan Székely, who decorated the interior of the Mátyás Church in Budapest. Unfortunately there are no regular hours for visits – ask at Tourinform round the corner about access to the hall. The bells outside play snatches of Kódaly, Handel, Beethoven, Mozart and Erkel at regular intervals.

With five churches in the vicinity you can afford to be selective; the three most interesting are on Kossuth tér. Next to the town hall stands the so-called **Old Church**, which is Catholic and Baroque. Designed by Oswald Gáspár, an eighteenth-century Piarist father, its facade is decorated with reliefs commemorating the Seventh Wilhem Hussars and local heroes of the War of Independence. In the summer months you may be able to climb the church tower, which gives you an excellent view of the city. The **Calvinist Church** was founded in 1683 and enlarged in the 1790s, when its "Red Tower" was added. Its meeting hall contains frescoes similar to those in the town hall. The **Franciscan Church** to the east is really the oldest one, but Baroque restoration has obscured its medieval features. Around the corner on Kéttemplom köz (Two Churches Lane) stands the former Franciscan monastery, which now houses the **Kodály Institute** (see box overleaf).

### Kecskemét museums

The diversity of Kecskemét's architecture is matched by that of its museums. One of the most rewarding is the **Museum of Photography** on Bajcsy-Zsilinszky utca (Wed–Sun 10am–5pm; ☎76/483-221; 100Ft), which features temporary exhibitions of photos and a permanent display of vintage cameras and other apparatus. The building was originally a dance hall, but was converted into a synagogue in

1918 and sold off by the decimated Jewish community after the last war. The museum retains such original features as the female gallery and the painted ceiling on which Rabbi Lowe's sacred animals appear.

A few blocks south of the centre on the corner of Gáspár András and Hosszú utca, the **Toy Museum** (Tues–Sun 10am–12.30pm & 1–5pm; 100Ft) occupies an airy wooden building, specially designed by Kerényi. It contains a delightful collection of nineteenth- and twentieth-century toys, and its helpful English-speaking staff also organize children's workshops. The adjacent **Naive Art Museum** (Tues–Sun 10am–5pm; 100Ft) exhibits naïve paintings from pre-World War I to the present day. Should you need an antidote to all this cuteness, wander round the corner to the **Medical Collection** at Kölcsey utca 3 (May–Sept daily 10am–2pm; 50Ft), which includes several gory exhibits.

Fans of Magyar folk art should head 500m south towards the junction of Petőfi utca and the ring boulevard (bus #1, #11 or #22). One block back, at Serfőző utca 19A, the **Museum of Hungarian Folk Craft** (Tues–Sun 10am–5pm; 200Ft) exhibits a wealth of textiles, pottery and embroidery from the 1950s onwards; call ☎76/327-203 to arrange a guided tour. Last but not least there's the extensive **Bozsó Collection** (Fri–Sun 10am–6pm; 100Ft) of antique furniture and other artefacts, assembled by a local artist. The collection is housed at Klapka utca 34,

---

## ZOLTÁN KODÁLY AND JÓZSEF KATONA

For a small town, Kecskemét has made a not inconsiderable contribution to national culture, and its Spring Days festival features the work of its two famous sons.

Through his researches into the folk roots of Hungarian music, **Zoltán Kodály** (1882–1967) was inspired to compositions that eschewed the Baroque and Western strains his colleague Bartók termed "New Style". He also revolutionized the teaching of music, inventing the "Kodály method" that is now applied throughout Hungary and around the world. Kodály's belief that music can only be understood by actively participating in it remains the guiding principle of Kecskemét's **Institute of Music Teaching** (*Zenepedagógiai Intézet*). Students on the **one-year course** are exhorted to approach music through the human voice, "the most easily accessible instrument for all", and build upon their national folk traditions when teaching children – a task Kodály considered supremely important, claiming "No one is too great to write for the little ones. In fact one has to strive to be great enough." For those who want to know more, there's an exhibition in the institute itself, at Kéttemplom köz 1–3.

The town can also boast of **József Katona** (1791–1830), the "father" of Hungarian romantic drama, who was born and died in Kecskemét. His masterpiece, *Bánk Bán* (later made into an opera by Erkel), revolves around the murder of Gertrude, the German-born queen of King Andrew II, by his vassal Bánk. Katona himself expired of a heart attack outside the town hall, the spot now marked by a cloven block. The fallible organ was preserved in a jewelled casket, and his name was bestowed upon Kecskemét's playhouse. Designed by the Viennese architects who built the Vígszínház in Budapest, it is a smaller version of the same and was erected in 1896. During the 1980s, the **Katona Theatre** was directed by film-maker Miklós Jancsó, whose avant-garde productions scandalized many townsfolk. There is now a **museum** dedicated to the playwright at Katona József utca 5, near the Photography Museum (Tues–Sun 10am–2pm; 50Ft), though its literary exhibits lack any explanation in English, and the period furniture isn't actually Katona's own.

500m east of the Cifra Palace, in a Baroque residence that once belonged to György Klapka, a general in the 1848 Hungarian War of Independence.

## The Pannónia Filmstudió

Kecskemét is also the home of the **Pannónia Filmstudió**, whose entire output consists of animated cartoons – short films, television series, advertisements and training films. Famous Hungarian children's cartoons like *János Vitéz, Leo and Fred* and *King Mátyás* were all made by these skilled animators. Phone ☎76/481-788 to enquire if the studio is running **guided tours**. It is located at Liszt Ferenc utca 21, beyond the train station, off Ceglédi út, and can be reached by bus #18 from Rákóczi út.

# Practicalities

Most things of practical use to tourists are concentrated in the centre. The best source of **information** is Tourinform on the corner of the town hall (April–Oct Mon–Fri 8am–5pm, Sat & Sun 9am–1pm; Nov–March Mon–Fri 8am–5pm, Sat 9am–1pm; ☎76/481-065). IBUSZ is on the ground floor of the *Hotel Aranyhomok* across the square (Mon–Fri 7.30am–4pm, Sat 7.30–11am; ☎76/322-955); Cooptourist is at Kéttemplom köz 9–11 (Mon–Fri 8.30–noon & 1–5pm; ☎76/481-472); and Express is slightly further out, on the first floor of Dobó körút 11 (Mon 10am–4.30pm, Tues–Fri 8am–4.30pm; ☎76/329-236). The main post office is at Kálvin tér 10–12, just off Szabadság tér, and there is an ATM at the OTP bank, Szabadság tér 5.

## Accommodation

During the summer holidays you may be able to get cheap **beds** in the colleges at Jókai tér 4 (☎76/486-977) or Izsáki utca 10 (☎76/321-916), bookable through Express, Cooptourist or IBUSZ. **Private rooms** (①) from Cooptourist and other agencies are also good value, or there's the *Autós* **campsite** with chalets at Sport utca 5, past the *Szauna Hotel* (☎76/329-398; ①; mid-April to mid-Oct), which is accessible by bus #22. Alternatively, ask Tourinform about lodgings on one of the old isolated farms (*tanya*) in the countryside around Kecskemét.

**Caissa Panzió**, Gyenes tér 18 (☎76/481-685). A fifth-floor pension on a quiet square, ten minutes northwest of Kossuth tér. Caissa is the patron saint of chess, and the owner is an avid fan of the game, who organizes tournaments in the pension. ②–③.

**Colour Panzió**, Jókai utca 26 (☎76/483-246). On a busy road in from Budapest, north of the centre, this pension is named after the paint shop below, run by the same owner. ②.

**Hotel Aranyhomok**, Széchenyi tér 2 (☎76/486-286). Named after the "golden sands" of the *puszta*, the chief asset of this place is its prime location, overlooking Kossuth tér. Rooms with bathrooms, minibar, TV, and phone. ⑤.

**Hotel Három Gunár**, Batthyány utca 1–7 (☎76/483-611). Smart, comfortable place near the theatre. Rooms have bathrooms en suite, as well as minibar, TV, and phones. ④.

**Hotel Udvarház**, Csányi utca 1–3 (☎76/413-912). Just off Kossuth tér, on the first floor of a shopping complex, this new hotel has agreeable rooms (some with air-conditioning) and secure parking. ④.

**Szauna Hotel**, Csabay Géza körút 2 (☎76/481-859). Well-equipped hotel with a sauna and gym, beside the thermal baths, 2.5km south of the centre; buses #1 and #11 stop nearby. ④.

## Eating and drinking

Apart from the **restaurants** in the *Udvarház* and *Aranyhomok* hotels, there are several decent places to eat in the centre. The plush *Liberté Kávéház* on Szabadság tér has a great terrace overlooking the square and serves full meals as well as coffee and cakes. For Bavarian beer and meaty dishes, there's the *HBH* on Csányi utca, near the Old Church. For a Magyar nosh-up try the *Kisbugaci Csárda* at Munkácsy utca 10, beyond Széchenyi tér, in a quarter that is full of tree-lined older streets (daily noon–midnight). Across the road from the bus station on Széchenyi tér there's a restaurant serving falafel, and the *Italia Pizzeria,* which does a quick pizza and pasta.

Though most of the above are feasible **drinking** spots, Kecskemét's students prefer places like the *Bahia Teázó* on Wesselényi utca, a gloomy cavern housing an Oriental boutique of the same name, where it's acceptable to sit and talk for ages over a fruit tea or a shot of spirits. Two agreeable **patisseries** are the *Fodor Cukrászda* near the *Liberté Kávéház,* and the *Delicatesse Cukrászda* (7am–10pm) in an arcade on the corner of Kossuth and Széchenyi tér. The outdoor **market** is good for cheap snacks and fresh produce.

### Entertainment and excursions

Kecskemét is at its liveliest during the **Spring Days** in late March, a feast of music and drama, coinciding with Spring Days in Budapest, and the **Week Festival** in late August, featuring street theatre, pageants, wine-tasting and craft fairs on Szabadság tér and Petőfi utca. At other times there are concerts and fairs at the Erdei Ferenc Cultural House on Deák Ferenc tér, and shows at the **Ciróka Puppet Theatre**, Budai utca 15. You can get details of all these events from Tourinform.

At weekends there are likely to be **discos** in the cultural centre, the *Hotel Aranyhomok*, or the *Júlia Presszó* above the Univer grocery store on Petőfi utca. Also look out for **raves and events** organized by the three colleges, advertised by flyers at the *Bahia Teázó* (see above).

The countryside around Kecskemét is ideal for **horse-riding**, with numerous riding schools and stables known to Tourinform. There are also scores of **farmsteads** that welcome tourists who enjoy riding, walking, fishing or simply relaxing in rural surroundings. For details and bookings, contact Mrs Ferenc Palásti of the *Kiskunsági Vendégvárók Egyesület* at Csongrádi utca 25 (☎76/486-230).

The town also makes a good base for **excursions** to the Tisza resorts and the Kiskunság region (see opposite). Bus #2 from Széchenyi tér can drop you at the Átrakó terminal for narrow-gauge trains to Kiskunság National Park, while Bugac Tours at Szabadság tér 5/a (☎76/481-643) handles bookings to the Bugacpuszta (see p.330).

### International connections

Besides numerous destinations on the Plain and Eger in the Northern Uplands, the intercity bus station is also the point of departure for **buses to Romania and Yugoslavia**. These are used by ethnic Hungarians returning to Miercurea Ciuc, Oradea, Cluj and Tîrgu Mureş in Romania (designated by their Hungarian names as Csíkszereda, Nagyvárad, Kolozsvár and Marosvásárhely), or Subotica in the Voivodina region of Former Yugoslavia. Foreigners are obliged to have visas for both countries. Yugoslav ones can only be obtained from a consulate, in advance; the Romanians issue them at the border, but it's safer to get one beforehand.

## Around Kecskemét: Lakitelek and Tiszakécske

Thirty kilometres east of Kecskemét are several low-key **resorts** where you can swim in the Tisza or wander beside it as it meanders through woodlands and meadows. Lakitelek and Tőserdő make for a relaxed excursion from Kecskemét or Kiskunfélegyháza, while Tiszakécske is more of a family holiday centre. **From Kecskemét**, five trains daily stop at Lakitelek en route to Kunszentmárton; to reach Tőserdő you can take the same trains from Kecskemét, alighting at the Szikra station, or catch the bus. **From Kiskunfélegyháza**, the four daily Szolnok trains call at Lakitelek, Tiszakécske and Tőserdő.

The village of **LAKITELEK** is famous for hosting the conference that gave birth to the Hungarian Democratic Forum (*MDF*), the centre-right party with nationalist leanings which went on to win the 1990 elections. The conference was held in the backyard of Sándor Lezsák, who led the party into a coalition with Fidesz in 1998, but seems likely to find his party swallowed up by its increasingly powerful partner. The "spirit of Lakitelek" is invoked by the party's politicians, who return to press the flesh at the local **festival** of folk music and dancing (*Lakitelek Falunapok*) on the first weekend in July.

Another local attraction is the lovely **Lakitelek-Tőserdő**, a sylvan nature reserve 4km away. Turning off the main road beside the *Tősfürdő* or **thermal baths** (May–Aug daily 9am–5pm; 200Ft), a path runs 1km down to the *Holtág*, a dead branch of the river that's nice for swimming and boating, with cheap **restaurants** and a campsite (mid-May to mid-Sept; ☎76/449-011). Up the road there is **accommodation** at the *Tölgyfa Fogadó* at Napsugár utca 6 (☎76/449-037; ②) and another campsite, *Autóscamping*, up by the baths (May–Sept; ☎76/449-012). The Tőserdő train station is a couple of kilometres south, on the main road.

**TISZAKÉCSKE**, further north, has more of a tourist industry outside town. Hourly buses run from the train station to the centre, passing by several rooms for rent, before heading to the riverside resort area (*Üdülő telep*), which has horse-drawn carts and a **children's railway** (May–Sept; 100Ft), **thermal baths** (daily 9am–5pm; 250Ft), and both free and paying **campsites**.

# The Kiskunság

The **Kiskunság** region, to the south of Kecskemét, is called "Little Cumania" after the Cumanian (*Kun*) tribes that settled here in the Middle Ages. This sandy tableland was unfit for anything but raising sheep until, in the nineteenth century, it was laboriously transformed by afforestation and soil husbandry to yield grapes and other fruit. While Magyars esteem this as "Petőfi country", where their national poet was born, its prime attractions for visitors are Kiskunság National Park and the exhibition complex at Ópusztaszer.

## Kiskunfélegyháza

To Hungarian ears, **KISKUNFÉLEGYHÁZA** suggests people and paths converging on the "House of Cumania". The present town was actually created by Jazygian settlers in the 1740s, but the name is nevertheless appropriate as the Cumanian original was wiped out by the Turks. As regional capital, it is a rural foil to urbane Kecskemét, a town that lives by geese-breeding and market gardening, with storks' nests on the chimneys and draw-wells in the courtyards. Like many small towns on the Plain, its main street follows the primary trade route of old and its main square is sited at the crossroads with the secondary route.

If that wasn't clear enough, Petőfi tér is embellished with a majolica-encrusted **town hall** in the National Romantic style. Built by József Vass and Nándor

Morbitzer in 1912, its facade is adorned with embroidery motifs typical of the region, as are the staircase and main hall. Diagonally opposite is the **Swan House** (*Hattyuház*), where Petőfi's father had a butcher's shop and the poet spent his childhood. His statue outside is decked with flowers and flags on March 15, the anniversary of the 1848 Revolution. His life is documented with newspaper articles, maps and suchlike at the **Petőfi Ház**, just past the bus station at Petőfi utca 7 (April–Sept Wed–Fri 9am–noon; 30Ft). Five minutes' walk south, at Móra utca 19, is a museum with exhibits on **Ferenc Móra**, writer, journalist and antiquarian, who was born at this house in 1879 (April–Sept Wed–Fri 9am–noon; 30Ft).

However, it's better to walk 300m up the main road in the direction of Kecskemét to visit the **Kiskun Museum** (mid-March to late Nov Wed–Sun 9am–5pm; 100Ft) in an eighteenth-century manor house. Exhibits on the Cumanians and Jazygians and modern paintings of rural life by László Holló pale before a section devoted to the **history of prisons**, in the very cell where the famous *betyár* Sándor Rózsa languished in 1860. The old **windmill** in the courtyard comes from the village of Mindszent by the River Tisza, where Cardinal Mindszenty was born. For a break from museums, you could go for a soak in the **thermal baths** at Blaha tér 1, down towards the train station (6am–7pm; 150Ft).

### Practicalities

The bus station is on the eastern side of Petőfi tér, and the train station fifteen minutes' walk in the opposite direction along Kossuth utca. You can get **information** from Kiskun Tours in the town hall (Mon–Fri 9am–5pm; ☎76/463-229) and **accommodation** at the cheerful *Oázis Panzió*, Szegedi út 13, 500m south of the centre (☎76/461-913; ④), with TV and minibar in every room; or the fairly basic *Mónika* (☎76/466-022; ②) and *Borostyán* (☎76/466-785; ②) pensions at Szőlő utca 1. Although coach parties get taken to the *Aranyhegyi Csárda*, you'll do better **eating** at the *Csillag Vendéglő*, Szegedi út 41, or the Chinese *Kinai Étterem* on Móra tér, which is right beside an Irish pub. Another place to drink is the wonderfully named *Aszpirin Bar* on Kossuth utca. More likely, though, you'll simply catch the first **bus** out to Bugac (every 60–90min) or Ópusztaszer (2–3 daily), the highlights of this region.

# Kiskunság National Park

The 30,000 hectares of **Kiskunság National Park** consist of several tracts of land, the largest of which starts 3km beyond the village of **BUGAC**. Buses from Kiskunfélegyháza can drop you near the entrance to the park (April–Oct daily 10am–5pm). From here a sandy track runs 3.5km past flower-speckled meadows and lounging shepherds, to a **farm** where *csikósok* (cowboys) in white pantaloons stage equestrian displays, riding bareback and standing up with much cracking of whips.

Among the **animals** bred here are grey long-horned cattle, Merino sheep and Mangalica pigs (said to make the finest bacon). The surrounding reedy marshes support diverse birdlife and flora – including rare blue globe-thistles in August – and serve as baths for water buffalo, which plod back to their barns at sunset. In the wooden **Shepherds' Museum** (same hours as park) you can see felted cloaks and hand-carved pipes, and a grotesque tobacco pouch made from a ram's scrotum.

Apart from Bugac Tours' excursions from Kecskemét (see p.328), there are two ways of **getting there**. The narrow-gauge train from Kecskemét is the fastest and most enjoyable method, but drops visitors at the Bugac felső terminal, ninety minutes from the farm, whereas buses from Kiskunfélegyháza drop you nearer to the entrance of the park. To catch the horse show you must get the first train (leaving 7.50am) or an early bus, since events are scheduled for groups, who then travel by buggy to a "typical" *csárda*. You can **stay** near Bugac at the *Bugaci Lovas Hotel* (☎76/372-522; ③; mid-March to mid-Nov), which also offers bungalows.

# Kiskőrös

Although **KISKŐRÖS** deserves a mention as the **birthplace of Sándor Petőfi**, who made Byron look tame (see box overleaf), the thatched **Petőfi House** preserved as a museum at Luther tér 2 (Tues–Sun 9am–5pm; 100Ft) offers little enlightenment to non-Hungarian speakers. Nearby stands the first Petőfi statue in a country where every town has at least one feature named after him. Such is the cult of Petőfi (which the Communists tried to appropriate, but which Hungarian youth reclaimed as a symbol of rebellion) that Kiskőrös was elevated to the rank of a city on the 150th anniversary of his birth, in 1972. On the edge of town is a small nature reserve, the **Szücs Moorland Wood**.

    **Rooms** are available from the helpful Marco Polo Travel Agency, Martini utca 1 (Mon–Fri 10am–noon & 1–5pm; ☎78/312-273), or the *Hotel Kiskőrös* at Petőfi utca 112, on the edge of town (☎78/311-983; ④). **Meals** are served in the *Kurta kocsma* on József Attila utca, and the *Fürdő Vendéglő* by the **thermal baths**, whose temperature is a constant 58°C (daily 9am–5pm; 200Ft).

# Kiskunhalas

**KISKUNHALAS** has more going for it than Kiskőrös, especially if you happen to be around for the **Grape Harvest Festival** in September, when folk dancing and other celebrations enliven the squares around its Art Nouveau town hall. Another more specialized attraction of Kiskunhalas is its tradition of **lace making**, a medieval industry whose revival in the 1890s was owed to local schoolteacher Maria Markovits, who studied patterns and samples from before the Turkish occupation. Other crafts, such as saddlemaking, are also pursued here.

    A whistle-stop tour could begin at the **Thorma János Museum** opposite the town hall (Tues–Fri 10am–6pm, Sun 9am–1pm & 2–5pm; 100Ft), which features local history and the oeuvre of painter Tibor Csorba (1906–85), who taught here before moving to Poland. The **House of Collections** (same hours and price) displays temporary exhibits at Bokányi Dezső utca 4, while **saddlemaker** Balázs Tóth welcomes visitors to his workshop at Vas utca 1. Don't miss the **Lace House** at Kossuth utca 37A (Tues–Sun 9am–5pm; 80Ft), a treasury of tablecloths, ruffs and petticoats, some composed of 56 different types of stitches. The statue outside is of Maria Markovits. Other sights include an old **windmill** on Kölcsey utca, to the right of the main road, 1km north of the centre (Sat & Sun 10am–6pm; 100Ft), and a lovely classical **synagogue** at Petőfi utca 1 (by arrangement with Sándor Reihold, Révész utca 6; ☎77/422-058).

    At weekends, people make for the **thermal baths** on Dr. Monszpart László utca, ten minutes west of the centre (daily 10am–6pm; 270Ft), or go **fishing** at Sóstó pond, 3km north of town.

## Practicalities

Kiskunhalas is accessible by train or bus from Baja or Kiskunfélegyháza. Its train station lies 1km east of the centre on Kossuth utca, while the bus station is located just west of Hősök tere, where Proko Travel at no. 1 (Mon–Fri 9am–5pm; ☎77/421-984) can supply **information** and arrange private **rooms**, which are cheaper than the Art Nouveau *Klub Hotel* on Bethlen Gábor tér in the centre (☎77/423-069; ③), or the less agreeable *Hotel Csipke* on Semmelweiss tér, near the baths (☎77/421-455; ④). Kiskunhalas has two campsites: one by the baths and the other at Sóstó; the last has wooden bungalows, open all year round (☎77/422-222; ②). The post office is at Bethlen tér 6, and there's an ATM at Bokányi Dezső utca 5–7.

# Ópusztaszer Historical Park

**Ópusztaszer National Historical Memorial Park**, just outside the village of the same name (April–Oct Tues–Sun 9am–5pm), commemorates the conquest of the seven Magyar tribes who crossed the Carpathians and spread out across the plains, each claiming a territory – an event known in Hungarian history as the *honfoglalás*, or "land-taking". The park supposedly marks the site of their first tribal "parliament" after the land-taking, in about 896 AD, although the only evidence for this comes from Anonymous, writing 300 years later. A huge memorial was erected here for the millennial anniversary celebrations of 1896, and in 1945 the Communists symbolically chose Ópusztaszer for the first distribution of land amongst the peasants.

Both themes are implicit in the diverse exhibits of the historical park. The **Village Museum** of households from southern Hungary is juxtaposed against combine harvesters, steam trains and aeroplanes. A ruined thirteenth-century monastery attests to Christian traditions, while the early freebooting, pagan Magyars are celebrated in the **Cyclorama** by Árpád Feszty. This monumental canvas depicting Prince Árpád leading the tribes into the valley of Munkács was originally exhibited in Budapest's City Park. Damaged in the siege, it has only recently been restored

---

## SÁNDOR PETŐFI

Born on New Year's Eve 1822, of a Slovak mother and a Southern Slav butcher-innkeeper father, **Sándor Petőfi** was to become obsessed with acting and poetry, which he started to write at the age of fifteen. As a strolling player, soldier and labourer, he absorbed the language of working people, writing lyrical poetry in the vernacular, to the outrage of critics. Moving to Budapest in 1844, Petőfi fell in with the young radical intellectuals who met at the *Pilvax Café*; from this time on, poetry and action were inseparable. His *Nemzeti Dal* (National Song) was declaimed from the steps of the National Museum on the first day of the 1848 Revolution ("Some noisy mob had their hurly-burly outside so I left for home," complained the director). Mindful of the thousands of landless peasants encamped outside the city, Parliament bowed to the demands of the radicals and voted for the abolition of serfdom.

During the War of Independence, Petőfi fought alongside General Bem in Transylvania, and disappeared at the battle of Segesvár in July 1849. Though he was most likely trampled beyond recognition by the Cossacks' horses (as foreseen in one of his poems), Petőfi was rumoured to have survived. In 1990, entrepreneur Ferenc Morvai announced that Petőfi had been carted off to Siberia by the Russians, married a peasant woman and later died there. The Hungarian Academy refused to support Morvai's expedition to uncover the putative grave, and it was subsequently reported that forensic analysis had proved the corpse to be that of a Jewish woman.

---

**THE LEGEND OF ATTILA**

The lower reaches of the Tisza are associated with the **legend of Attila the Hun**, who died in 453 AD of a nasal haemorrhage following a night of passion with his new bride, Kriemhild. The body of the Scourge of God was reputedly buried in a triple-layered coffin of gold, silver and lead, and then submerged in the Tisza at an unknown spot – unknown because the pallbearers were slain before the Huns departed. Archeologists have yet to find it, but the legend gains credence from the "treasure of Attila". Thought to have belonged to a Hun general, the treasure was discovered at Nagyszentmiklós (in what is now Romania) and is currently held by Vienna's Kunsthistorisches Museum.

---

and put back on show. The whole park reeks of nationalism, with at least ten maps of Greater Hungary showing how the empire looked before World War I, and hundreds of displays dedicated to the number of Magyars around the world. Don't bother paying extra to see the dreary waxworks.

**ÓPUSZTASZER** itself lies 10km east of Kistelek on the Kecskemét–Szeged road. Direct **buses** to the village are scarce except on national holidays, but it's worth checking out the timetables in Kiskunfélegyháza or Szeged. Alternatively, you could try hitching from Kistelek, a stop for buses along the highway. On the way to the park on Árpád liget you'll find the *Szeri Csárda* restaurant and next door the basic *Szeri Camping* (☎62/375-123; ①; May–Oct), with **horse-riding** facilities across the way.

# Szeged

**SZEGED** straddles the River Tisza like a provincial Budapest, as cosmopolitan a city as you'll find on the Great Plain, whose friendly atmosphere is mainly thanks to the students from the university. The old city's eclectic good looks have been saved by placing the ugly modern housing and industry over the river, in Újszeged. Though Kőrös folk settled here four to five thousand years ago, and the town flourished after 1225 because of its royal monopoly over the salt mines of Transylvania, Szeged's present layout dates from after the **great flood** of March 1879, which washed away all but 300 homes and compelled the population to start again from scratch. With aid from foreign capitals (after whom sections of the outer boulevard are named), the city bounced back, trumpeting its revival with huge buildings and squares where every type of architectural style made an appearance.

During Communist times **Szeged University** (*JATE*) was at the forefront of student protests in 1956, and one of the seedbeds of the peace movement and punk rock scene in the eighties. More recently, the wars in Yugoslavia led to a boom cross-border **smuggling** and Mafia activity, which made Szeged notorious in Hungary and enriched the local economy at a time when other cities were feeling the pinch.

## Arrival, orientation and information

To get to the old city or Belváros from the **train station**, take tram #1, while from the intercity **bus terminal** on Mars tér it's a five-minute walk. The Belváros, on the west bank of the Tisza, is encircled by Tisza Lajos körút and an outer ring

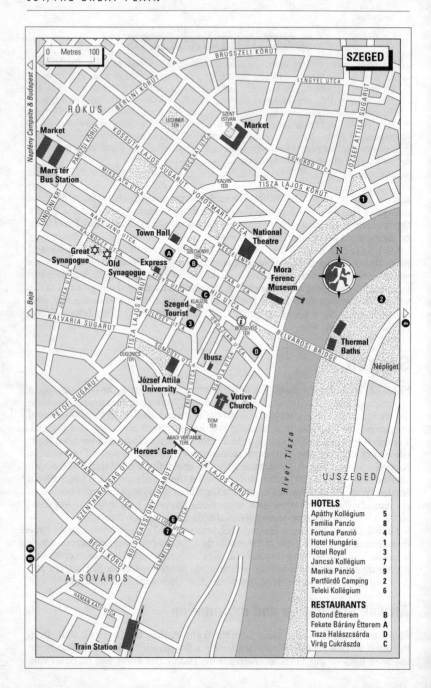

# SZEGED

0  Metres  100

Napfény Campsite & Budapest

RÓKUS

Market

Mars tér
Bus Station

Town Hall

Great
Synagogue
Old
Synagogue
Express

Szeged
Tourist

József Attila
University

Heroes' Gate

ALSÓVÁROS

Train Station

BRUSSZELI KÖRÚT
LENGYEL UTCA
BERLINI KÖRÚT
PÁRIZSI KÖRÚT
KOSSUTH LAJOS SUGÁRÚT
BOCSKAI UTCA
LECHNER TÉR
SZENT ISTVÁN TÉR
Market
SÖHORDÓ UTCA
JÓZSEF ATTILA SUGÁRÚT
MIKSZÁTH UTCA
VÖRÖSMARTY UTCA
KÁLVIN TÉR
TISZA LAJOS KÖRÚT
LONDONI KRT
NAGY JENŐ UTCA
HAJNÓCZY UTCA
WESSELÉNYI UTCA
National
Theatre
SZÉCHENYI TÉR
VÁR UTCA
Mora
Ferenc
Museum
KÍGYÓ UTCA
HÍD UTCA
KLAUZÁL TÉR
TISZA LAJOS KÖRÚT
JÓSIKA UTCA
KÖLCSEY UTCA
OROSZLÁN UTCA
ROOSEVELT TÉR
KÁLVÁRIA SUGÁRÚT
SOMOGYI UTCA
DUGONICS TÉR
BELVÁROSI BRIDGE
Thermal
Baths
Népliget
Ibusz
PETŐFI SUGÁRÚT
ZRÍNYI UTCA
OSKOLA UTCA
Votive
Church
DÓM TÉR
ARADI VÉRTANÚK TERE
BATTHYÁNY UTCA
VITÉZ UTCA
SZENTHÁROMSÁG UTCA
BOLDOGASSZONY SUGÁRÚT
TISZA LAJOS KÖRÚT
UJSZEGED
River Tisza
BÉCSI KÖRÚT
SEMMELWEIS UTCA
HÁMÁN KATÓ UTCA

Baja
Beja

N

## HOTELS
| | |
|---|---|
| Apáthy Kollégium | 5 |
| Familia Panzío | 8 |
| Fortuna Panzío | 4 |
| Hotel Hungária | 1 |
| Hotel Royal | 3 |
| Jancsó Kollégium | 7 |
| Marika Panzió | 9 |
| Partfürdő Camping | 2 |
| Teleki Kollégium | 6 |

## RESTAURANTS
| | |
|---|---|
| Botond Étterem | B |
| Fekete Bárány Étterem | A |
| Tisza Halászcsárda | D |
| Virág Cukrászda | C |

boulevard, with radial avenues emanating from the park-like Széchenyi tér and other downtown squares – the most important of which are Klauzál tér, with its tourist offices and cafés, and Dóm tér, overshadowed by the colossal Votive Church. For a map and **information**, drop into Szeged Tourist, Klauzál tér 7 (May–Aug Mon–Fri 9am–5pm, Sat 9am–1pm; Sept–April Mon–Fri 9am–5pm; ☎62/425-731); Tourinform, Viktor Hugo utca 1 (Mon–Fri 8am–4pm; ☎62/425-711 or 425-966); or IBUSZ at Somogyi utca 11 (May–Sept Mon–Fri 8am–6pm & Sat 9am–1pm; Oct–April Mon–Fri 8am–4pm; ☎62/471-177).

## Accommodation

You should be able to get some form of **accommodation** in Szeged at any time, though the city's resources can be strained during the Festival Weeks in July and August. **Private rooms** (①) from Szeged Tourist, IBUSZ or Alföld Tours at Somogy utca 21 (Mon–Thurs 8pm–4.30pm, Fri 8am–3.30pm; ☎62/421-070) are the best value for money if you can get somewhere in the centre. **Dormitory beds** in colleges in the vicinity of Dóm tér are more expensive, such as the *Apáthy Kollégium* at Apáthy István utca 4 (☎62/455-729; ②), or the *Teleki* at no. 5 (☎62/454-000; ②) and *Jancsó* at Semmelweis utca 7 (☎62/455-041; ②). The first two function during July and August and the last has vacancies at weekends throughout the year. All are bookable through Express at Kígyó utca 3 (Mon–Thurs 8am–4pm, Fri 8am–3pm; ☎62/481-411). In addition to the campsites, there is a **nudist camp** in Kiskundorozsma, 10km outside the city (☎62/426-021), and one could also feasibly **stay in Hódmezővásárhely**, a thirty-minute bus ride from Szeged (see p.339).

### Hotels and pensions

**Hotel Hungária**, Maros utca 2 (☎62/480-580). One of the oldest hotels in Szeged, located by the river to the north of the Belváros, and rated with three stars. ④.

**Hotel Royal**, Kölcsey utca 1 (☎62/475-275). As comfortable as the *Hungária*, and dead central, though higher prices for foreigners still exist here. The Romanian gymnast Nadia Comaneci briefly took refuge here after defecting in 1989. ⑤.

**Familia Panzió**, Szentháromság utca 71–73 (☎62/441-802). A hospitable pension south of the town centre, which gets good marks from travellers. ②–③.

**Fortuna Panzió**, Pécskai utca 8 (☎62/431-585). In Újszeged, on the other side of the River Tisza from the city centre. ③.

**Marika Panzió**, Nyíl utca 45 (☎62/443-861). A small place in the Alsóváros, south of the train station, complete with protected parking and a swimming pool. ③.

### Campsites

**Napfény Camping**, Dorozsmai út 2 (☎62/421-800). In the western suburbs of the city near the start of the Budapest highway (bus #78). Open May–Sept. ①.

**Partfürdő Camping**, Középkikötő sor (☎62/430-843). A dearer site, near the *strand* and thermal baths in Újszeged. Open May–Sept. ②.

## The Town

**Dóm tér** is the most impressive feature of the inner city. Flanked by arcades with twisted columns and busts of illustrious Hungarians, this 12,000-square-metre expanse was created in 1920 by demolishing a network of backstreets, to accommodate a gigantic **Votive Church** (Mon–Sat 9am–6pm, Sun 9.30–10am, 11–11.30am & 1–6pm), which the townsfolk had pledged to erect after the flood. Built of brown brick in the neo-Romanesque style, its portal is surmounted by a statue of the Virgin whose image recurs inside the church in peasant costume, wearing embroidered "Szeged slippers". Visitors are dwarfed by the white, blue and gold interior, where the organ, with its 10,180 pipes and five manuals, benefits from superb acoustics.

The eight-sided **Demetrius Tower** out in front dates from the eleventh century, but was largely rebuilt by Béla Rerrich, who designed the square. A chiming clock plays the folk song "Szeged, a famous town" at midday. On the northeastern corner of Dóm tér stands an eighteenth-century **Serbian Orthodox Church** with a magnificent iconostasis framed in pear-wood, while on the south side of the square crowds gather every day at 11am and 1pm to watch the **Music Clock**, whose figures move round to the rich sound of the bells. During the summer festival the bells also play at 8.15pm.

In the summer rows of seats are banked opposite the Votive Church for Szeged's festival, where local operas are performed. When performances (which start with everyone standing for the national anthem) finish, the crowds flood out towards the **Heroes' Gate** (*Hősök Kapuja*), which links Aradi vértanúk tere with Boldogasszony sugárút. Though its origins are no longer publicized, the gate was raised to honour Horthy's henchmen, the "Whites", who gathered here in 1919, waiting for the Romanian army to defeat the Republic of Councils before they fanned out across Hungary to persecute Jews and "Reds" in the "White Terror". Stone guardsmen still flank the archway, but Horthy's murals have been erased by dirt and time.

## Szeged University

Many of the buildings to the west of Dóm tér are related to **Szeged Universty**, whose main building overlooks Dugonics tér and a **Water Music Fountain** where students congregate during breaks. Locally known by its Hungarian initials, JATE, the university is named after the poet **Attila József**, whom it expelled in 1924 for a poem which began "I have no father, I have no mother, I have no god and I have no country" and continued "with a pure heart, I'll burn and loot, and if I have to, even shoot". Attila's bitterness was rooted in his childhood, when his mother, a poor washerwoman, died of starvation. Later he was expelled from the Communist Party for trying to reconcile Marx and Freudian pyschology and, despairing of abject poverty, finally jumped under a train at Lake Balaton. Though unappreciated during his lifetime, Attila's poetry is now recognized as some of the best in the language. Elderly Hungarians weep upon hearing his sentimental "Mama", while anarcho-punks relish lines such as "Culture drops off me, like clothes off a happy lover".

Head on past the university, take a left turn, and you'll come to the so-called **Black House** on the corner of Somogyi and Kelemen utca. This Romantic-style edifice is actually painted brown and white, but the ironmonger who lived here in the nineteenth century always told peasants "You can find me in the Black House". It now houses a local history exhibition (Tues 10am–3pm, Wed–Sun 10am–5pm; 40Ft). If you carry on up Somogyi utca and bear right onto Fekete sas utca you'll find the fabulous **Reök Palace** on the corner of Kölcsey utca. Built for Iván Reök, a nephew of the painter Munkácsy, this Art Nouveau masterpiece by Ede Oszadszki Magyar is now owned by a bank, which has restored its facade and retained some of its interior features too. Look out for the siren over the entrance with her Medusa-like coils of hair.

## Around the waterfront and Széchenyi tér

Alternatively, head northwards from Dóm tér towards Roosevelt tér and the **Móra Ferenc Museum** (Tues 10am–3pm, Wed–Sun 10am–5pm; 100Ft). Its Neoclassical facade cloaks a typical mix of *objets d'art* and artefacts of local significance, notably a huge painting of the flood. More interesting is the display on the Avars, the people displaced by the arriving Magyars. The fountain in front of the museum is a favourite meeting place in the summer. At the back is another smaller **museum** featuring a geological display of the city (Tues–Sun 10am–2pm), which is sited on the **remains of a castle** that later served as a prison for the outlaw Sándor Rózsa and for convicts who laboured on the river towpaths during the eighteenth century. As in Debrecen, this was a time of mass witch trials organized by the church elders, when victims were tortured to make them confess.

From here you can walk up west past the **National Theatre** to spacious, verdant **Széchenyi tér**, Szeged's inner-city park. On the far side stands a neo-Baroque **town hall**, likened by the poet Mihály Babits to "a lace-covered young woman dancing in the moonlight". The two allegorical **fountains** outside, known as "The Blessed and the Angry", symbolize the benevolent and destructive aspects of the River Tisza. The town hall is linked to a neighbouring building by a charming "Bridge of Sighs", modelled on the one in Venice.

## The Jewish quarter and beyond

Beyond Tisza Lajos körút, Szeged is shabbier and more utilitarian, but not devoid of sights, especially in the former **Jewish quarter** around Hajnóczy utca. The classical **Old Synagogue**, dating from 1843, bears a plaque showing the height of the water during the flood, but is only open during the summer festival, when it serves as a theatre. Far grander and more alluring is the Secession-style **Great Synagogue** with its entrance on Jósika utca (April–Sept 9am–6pm; Oct–March 9am–2pm; closed Sat). One of the largest synagogues in Europe, it was built between 1900 and 1903 by Lipót Baumhorn, who designed 22 synagogues throughout Hungary, this one being regarded as the finest example of his work. Its magnificent dome, executed in blue stained glass, represents the world, with 24 columns for the hours of day and night, white flowers for faith, and blue stars for the infinity of the cosmos. The stained-glass windows illustrate texts from *The Flora of the Jews*, by Rabbi Immanuel Löw, who was the Chief Rabbi here in the early part of the century.

Around the outer boulevard (bus #11 or #21), to the south, parts of the **Alsóváros** or "lower town" resemble a village, with ochre-painted cottages and rutted streets. This quarter was traditionally inhabited by paprika-growers, and centres around the **Alsóvárosi Church** on Mátyás király tér, begun in the late fifteenth century. Its reworked Baroque interior contains the *Black Madonna*, a copy of the famous Madonna of Częstochowa, and the focus of attention during the reconsecration ceremonies at the annual melon harvest festival.

Two busy outdoor **markets**, on Mars tér in the Rókus quarter, and Szent István tér between the inner and outer boulevards, are well worth a visit. To the north of the centre (tram #3 from Dugonics tér), there's a **zoo** with a large collection of small monkeys and South American animals.

# Eating, drinking and entertainment

Szeged has lots of eating places and watering holes, and is famous for its sausages and for dishes such as *halászlé* (fish soup) and *halpaprikás* (fish in paprika sauce). The smartest of its **restaurants** is the *Alabárdos* at Oskola utca 13 (closed Sun), which specializes in fish and game dishes; reservations are advisable (☎62/420-914). Less expensive but also good are the fish-oriented *Tisza Halászcsárda* at Roosevelt tér 12; the *Botond Étterem*, housed in an old printing workings at Széchenyi tér 9 (daily 9am–midnight); and the cheap and cheerful *Fekete Bárány* at Kossuth sugárút 5. Fish lovers should make a pilgrimage to the *Kiskörösi-Halászcsárda*, the smaller of two thatched restaurants out towards the fishing village of Tápé (bus #73 or #73Y), where the Prince of Wales (later Edward VIII) often came in the 1890s. The *Jazz Kocsma* on Kálmány Lajos utca 14 has good Mexican-stye food, or try the *Mojo Bar* on Alföld utca behind the university (open till 10pm only) for pizzas, while for **cakes and ices** you can't beat the *Virág Cukrászda* on Klauzál tér – though its languid service and high prices might drive you to the cheaper, stand-up *Kisvirág* outlet across the square.

## Nightlife and entertainment

As you'd expect of a university town, there are regular **raves and parties** at the *JATE Klub* at Toldi utca 2, behind the university, which seethes with activity on Friday and Saturday nights (8pm–4am; ☎62/421-245) and the *Szote Klub* at Dóm tér 13 (☎62/455-773). Two other popular student **hangouts** are the *Mojo Bar* near the university (see above), and the *Bounty Bar* at Wesselényi utca 2, across from the National Theatre. For dancing, there's also the *Sing-Sing Disco* near Mars tér, and the Juhász Gyula Cultural Centre at Vörösmarty utca 5–7, which has discos on Thursday and Friday and **live music** on Saturdays, while the *Tisza Gyöngye*, by the baths across the river, is an occasional disco venue. The student paper *Szegedi Egyetem*, sold at newspaper stalls, carries up-to-date information about what's on.

Other forms of **entertainment** are likeliest during the concert season (Sept–May) and the **Szeged Weeks** (roughly July 20 to Aug 20), a huge festival of drama and music. Events are advertised around town, and **tickets** are available from the *Szabadtéri jegyiroda* ticket agency at Deák utca 28–30 (Mon–Fri 10am–5pm, Sat 10am–1pm; ☎62/471-411). In July there is also the Szeged beer festival, when pubs and restaurants put up tents in town, and the beer flows.

## Outdoor activities

On hot summer weekends people flock to the **swimming pool** or the grassy *Partfürdő strand* in Újszeged across the river, undeterred by its less than clean reputation, while in winter wallowing in the outdoor **thermal baths** becomes the favoured pastime. A less crowded place to get some fresh air is the **botanical garden** (*Fűvészkert*) at the end of the #70 bus line.

There are opportunities for **excursions** from the city, using buses leaving from Mars tér, or a hired car from ISA Rent a Car at Kállay utca 13 (☎62/431-577), and IKESZ kft at Kossuth Lajos Sugárút 112 (☎62/471-200). With a few days' notice, Tourinform can arrange **bird-watching** expeditions to the **Fehér-tó Nature Reserve**, a haven for 250 kinds of migratory **birds**, as well as **horse-riding** trips, **angling**, **boating**, **hiking** and **cycling** tours, and even an **archery course** at Ópusztaszer (see p.332).

# THE SOUTHERN PLAIN
# BEYOND THE TISZA

The **Southern Plain** beyond the Tisza is sunbaked and dusty, with small towns that bore the brunt of the Turkish occupation and often suffered from droughts, giving rise to such paranoia that "witches" were burned for "blowing the clouds away" or "selling the rain to the Turks". Resettled by diverse ethnic groups under Habsburg auspices, they later attracted dispossessed Magyars from Transylvania, who displaced the existing communities of Swabians, Serbs, Slovaks and Romanians. In the fifties, geologists scoured the region for oil, but almost every borehole struck thermal springs instead, hence the numerous **spas** in this region. The most attractive towns are **Hódmezővásárhely**, **Gyula** and **Szarvas**, while the famous stud farm at **Mezőhegyes** is another attraction.

**Approaches** are largely determined by where you cross the river. Crossing over at Szeged, the main trunk route heads towards Békéscsaba. Csongrád, further upriver, marks the start of a less clear-cut itinerary which might include Szarvas and Mezőtúr. The more northerly route from Szolnok to Debrecen is covered under the Northern Plain (see p.346).

# East from Szeged

Heading on from Szeged there are two basic routes: northeast towards Békéscsaba via **Hódmezővásárhely**, or southeast through **Makó** to the Romanian border. Counting the lovely park at nearby **Mártely**, Hódmezővásárhely is better endowed with sights than Makó, but the latter is closer to the stud farm at **Mezőhegyes**, with its horse-riding.

## Hódmezővásárhely

**HÓDMEZŐVÁSÁRHELY**'s tongue-twisting name can be translated as "marketplace of the beaver's field", though it's disputed whether the *hód-* prefix really derives from the Magyar word for "beaver". That aside, this long-established market town has the distinction of being the second-largest municipality in Hungary, incorporating several distant settlements. Most of its sights are around the main square, Kossuth tér, and the street leading north, Szántó Kovács János utca. The grandeur of the square hints at the town's former importance, which its current mayor, the businessman András Rapcsák, is striving to restore. The best time to visit is during the **Hungarian Riding Festival** on the last weekend in September, which includes coach driving, stunt riding and falconry. The **Autumn Art Festival** in October is a more academic event, with conferences on the Alföld School of painters (see overleaf).

The southern edge of the town centre is defined by a **levy** built after the great flood that ravaged Szeged. Safely ensconced within its walls, the Bethlen Gábor grammar school houses an old library of 25,000 volumes, while downtown, Kossuth tér is dignified by an eighteenth-century **Calvinist Church** and an imposing **town hall** (Mon–Fri 8am–3pm), whose magnificent banqueting hall is hung with pictures of local heroes and historical figures; ask the porter who will let you visit if the hall is free. On the other side of the square is a huge bank topped with a four-metre statue of Mercury, and the *Fekete Sas Hotel*, currently being restored to its former glory, where merchants once gathered to trade agricultural products from all over the Balkans, storing their money in the bank and gambling the profits in the casino opposite the hotel (now a youth centre).

On Szőnyi utca around the side of the town hall, the **Alföldi Gallery** (Tues–Sun 10am–6pm; 50Ft) exhibits scenes of *puszta* life by local artist János Tornyai. He died in 1936, but his oeuvre was recently enhanced by the discovery of 700 canvases in a Budapest attic. Work by other local artists hangs in the **Tornyai János Museum** at Szántó Kovács utca 16, north of Kossuth tér (Tues–Sun 11am–5pm; 50Ft), whose archeological collection includes a 5000-year-old statue of a fertility goddess known as "the Venus of Kökénydomb". Across the street stands a fine Baroque **Greek Orthodox Church**, whose "Nahum iconostasis" from Mount Athos is named after an obscure seventh-century prophet; mass is held here on the last Sunday of each month. Still more impressive is the florid Art Nouveau **Synagogue** on Szent István tér, east of Kossuth tér, the outside of which has recently been restored to the 1906 design of Gyula Müller. To see how the interior is progressing, ask for the key at the town hall.

Hódmezővásárhely is renowned for its **pottery**, and each district of the town has a different style. The most distinctive is the black pottery based on Turkish designs, fired in a manner dating back to Neolithic times. Examples are displayed in the **Csúcs Potter's House** (Tues–Sun 1–5pm; 50Ft), twenty minutes' walk north of the centre at Rákóczi utca 101, and in the **Folk Culture House**, two thatched cottages at Árpád utca 21, near the levy (*Tájház*; Tues–Sat 10am–5pm; 50Ft), which also displays peasant costumes and furniture. To buy pottery or watch it being made, visit the workshop of János Szénási at Eke utca 41, past the Csúcs House, or János Mónus at Táncsics Mihály utca 26/a, near the synagogue.

From town there are regular buses 10km out to **Mártely**, a gorgeous **park** beside a tributary of the Tisza, with boats for rent and hand-woven **baskets** for sale. Ideal for picnics and **horse-riding**, it's a nice spot in which to relax and unwind, featuring a **campsite** with chalets and apartments (☎62/242-753; ②–③).

## Practicalities

All trains to Hódmezővásárhely stop at two stations, Népkert, south of the centre, and the main station to the east, both of which are connected to the centre by local buses. Buses from Szeged run right through the centre before terminating at the main train station rather than the intercity bus terminal, in Bocskai út, where buses from elsewhere wind up. In the centre, Szeged Tourist at Szőnyi utca 1 (mid-June to mid-Sept Mon–Fri 8am–5pm, Sat 9am–noon; mid-Sept to mid-June Mon–Fri 8am–5pm; ☎62/241-325) can supply **information** and organize private **rooms**. Behind the synagogue, the *Fáma Hotel* at Szeremlei utca 7 (☎62/222-231; ③) has rooms with en-suite facilities, TV and minibar – far comfier than beds in the *Kereskedelmi Szakközépiskola Kollégium* at Hóvirág utca 1 (☎62/242-011; ①). Another option for those with transport is the *Vándorsólyom Fogadó* (☎62/241-900; ②), a country inn 2km out along the road to Orosháza, where guests can go cross-country riding or carriage driving. *Termál Camping* at Ady utca 1 (☎62/245-072; ①; June–Aug) is right beside the outdoor **thermal baths** (daily 7am–7.30pm; 180Ft).

The best place for Hungarian **food** is the *Bagólyvár* at Nagy Imre utca 31, east of the centre. On Hősök tére, you can sample Serbian specialities at the costlier *Phoenix*, or drop in for a beer and a game of pool or bowls at the *Casino Söröző*. Another good, inexpensive Hungarian restaurant is the *Bandula* at Pálffy utca 2, north of the centre.

## Makó and Mezőhegyes

Aside from being the "onion capital" of Hungary, the faded town of **MAKÓ** is notable for its therapeutic **baths in radioactive Maros mud**, and for being the birthplace of Joseph Pulitzer, who won fame as a journalist and publisher in America in the nineteenth century and founded the Pulitzer Prize. It was here, too, that the poet Attila József was sent to school after his mother died, had his first verses published, and made several attempts to commit suicide between 1912 and 1913. His former domicile is now the **Attila Memorial House** at Kazinczy utca 8 (*Epersit Ház*; Tues 11am–4pm Wed–Sun 10am–5pm; 20Ft), while his name graces the **Attila József Museum** on the corner of Kazinczy and Megyeház utca (Tues 11am–4pm Wed–Sun 10am–5pm; 40Ft). A typical collection of local paintings and artefacts, it also documents the history of Máko's onion trade and features a wagon-builder's workshop in the yard. You can also track down a desolate crenellated **Orthodox Synagogue** at Eötvös utca 15, near the bus station to the northeast of the main square, Széchenyi tér. The train station lies in the opposite direction, on Lonovics sugár út.

Though there's no **accommodation** in town, motorists are served by two campsites from May to September: one beside the River Maros, 500m out towards Szeged (✆62/211-914; ①), the other 2km along the road to the Romanian border (✆62/212-232; ①), past the *Fenyő Panzió* at Batthyány utca 38/b (✆62/212-951; ②). There are also a few chalets and a grassy area for tents at Magyarcsanád, a fuel stop 8km from the **Nagylak border crossing**.

At **MEZŐHEGYES**, 30km northeast of Szeged, a stud for breeding Lippizaner horses was founded in 1785. Today the **stud farm** breeds **Gidrán and Nonius horses**, the latter having been introduced from Normandy in 1810 to produce resilient cavalry chargers. There is a covered **riding school** offering horse or carriage rides (1800Ft/3000Ft an hour), and you can stay at the *Hotel Nónius* at Kozma utca 32 (✆68/467-321; ③), which also organizes visits to the stables. A tour of the buildings and coach museum costs 2000Ft, and has to be booked in advance.

# Békéscsaba and around

Travelling by road from Szeged to Debrecen, you're almost bound to pass through **BÉKÉSCSABA**, the "sausage capital" of Hungary. While carnivores might be attracted by its Kolbász Festival, a more compelling reason for a stopover is to visit the old border fortress town of **Gyula**, a far livelier place, with one of the hottest baths in Hungary. As Gyula is only 20km from Békéscsaba, you can easily get there and back by bus in a day.

Settled by the Magyars at the time of the land-taking, the region around Békéscsaba was left virtually devoid of life by the Turkish wars and the War of Independence, until it was revived by settlers from all over the Habsburg empire, making it the most ethnically diverse town in eighteenth-century Hungary. The town itself was rebuilt by Slovaks, whose characteristic folk costumes and handicrafts are exhibited in an ornate **Slovak House** at Garay utca 21 (*Slovák Tájház*; Tues–Sun: April–Nov 10am–noon & 2–6pm; Dec–March 10am–noon; 80Ft), which you can find by bearing off the main Szent István tér along Baross utca, and turning right.

Other oddments relating to the Slovaks can be found in the **Munkácsy Museum** at Széchenyi utca 9, a short way off the square along the Gyula road (Tues–Sun: April–Nov 10am–6pm; Dec–Mar 10am–4pm; 100Ft). The museum is named after the nineteenth-century romantic painter Mihály Munkácsy, several of whose dark landscapes and historical pictures are displayed here, while a neighbouring building contains a historical exhibition on the different groups of settlers (covered by the same ticket). Munkácsy himself lived nearby as a teenager at Gyulai út 5, in what is now the **Munkácsy Memorial House**, a fine porticoed domicile containing period furniture and paintings (Tues–Sun: April–Oct 10am–6pm; Nov–March 9am–5pm; 50Ft).

If you're here in late October, you can go to the **Kolbász Festival**, celebrating Békéscsaba's role in the meat-processing industry, with folk music and dancing events accompanying demonstrations of pig-slaughtering and sausage-making. *Kolbász* is crude but tasty salami-style sausage.

## Practicalities

From the train and bus stations on the edge of town, bus #1, #1G, #2 or #7 can get you to the start of the pedestrian stretch of Andrássy út, from where it's fifteen minutes' walk to the main square, passing two **tourist offices** en route: Express at Andrássy út 29–33 (Mon–Fri 8am–4pm; ☎66/324-201) and Békéstourist at no. 10 (Mon–Fri 8am–4pm; ☎66/323-448). On Szent István tér you'll find IBUSZ at no. 9 (May–Sept Mon–Fri 8am–7pm, Sat 9am–noon; Oct–April Mon–Fri 8am–4pm; ☎66/325-554), an ATM at no. 3, and the post office across the road at Szabadság tér 1–3. If you feel like a wallow, the **Árpád thermal baths** are on the east bank of the canal (May–Sept daily 6am–7pm; Oct–April Tues–Sun 7am–7pm; 200Ft); bus #8 runs fairly close by.

Private rooms, or dormitory beds at weekends and in the summer, are the cheapest form of **accommodation**, followed by two rather unappealing hotels along the Gyula road (bus #4 or #9): the *Sport* (☎66/449-449; ②) and the *Trófea* (☎66/441-066; ③). If you can afford it, a better choice is the *Fiume*, a beautifully restored prewar hotel on the corner of Szent István tér (☎66/443-243; ⑤), which contains the only real restaurant in town, the *HBH Bajor*. Across the square, *Club Narancs* is a hangout for young people, with occasional live music, while coffee and cakes are available at the *Cukrászda* on Andrássy út.

# Gyula

**GYULA**, en route to the Romanian border, is the prettiest town in the Körös region, with the most to show for its history. Named after a tribal chieftain from the time of the land-taking, the town was heavily fortified by the Angevins but quickly succumbed to the Turks, who held its castle for nearly 130 years. After the Turks were evicted, Gyula was rebuilt as a twin town, with Hungarian Magyargyula on one side of the Élővíz Canal, and German–Romanian Németgyula on the other. Though this distinction ceased long ago, you'll still hear

German and Romanian spoken in town: Germans come here for the thermal baths and Romanians to trade. Gyula's lively character, however, is largely due to its sizeable student population, rather than its tourists.

## The Town

All the town's sights are within ten minutes' walk of the small squares that comprise downtown Gyula, north of the canal. West of Erkel tér, the **Ladics House** at Jókai utca 4 (Tues–Sun 9am–5pm; 100Ft) is a fascinating nineteenth-century bourgeois home preserved down to the last antimacassar, though, unfortunately, lacking much information in English. In the same direction, the **Erkel Museum** at Ápor tér 7 (Tues–Sun 9am–5pm; 100Ft) pays homage to Ferenc Erkel, the nineteenth-century composer of Hungary's national anthem, who was born in Gyula; while the **György Kohán Museum** at Béke sugárút 35, just north of the centre (Wed–Sun 9am–5pm; 100Ft), exhibits some of the 3000 works that its namesake bequeathed to his home town – mostly bold depictions of horses, women and houses.

The main attractions, however, lie out along Kossuth utca, to the east. Shortly before reaching the castle you'll pass an exhibition hall called the **Dürer Terem**, named after the German artist Albrecht Dürer, whose jeweller father migrated from Gyula to Germany. (Their original surname was Ajtóssy, from the Hungarian for "door"; Dürer has an identical root in the German word *Tür*.) Though its temporary exhibits can be rewarding, there is nothing related to its namesake.

Gyula's fourteenth-century **Castle** (*vár*) is the only brick fortress to have survived in Hungary (Tues–Sun: May–Sept 9am–5pm; Oct–April 10am–6pm; 100Ft). Its walls are three metres thick and originally incorporated every defensive feature known in Europe at that time. Its Powder Tower is now a wine bar, while in July and August the courtyard provides a stage for the **Castle Plays** on historical themes. Erkel used to compose in the park beside the castle under the shade of an oak known as "**Erkel's Tree**", which still stands. In the grounds nearby are the popular **Thermal Baths** (*Várfürdő*; May–Sept daily 8am–7pm; Oct–April Mon–Fri 8am–7pm, Sat & Sun 2–7pm; 290Ft), a complex of 22 pools ranging in temperature from 46°C to 92°C – the latter can only be endured after you've acclimatized yourself, and then only for a very short time. There is also a large outdoor pool, likewise full of peaty-coloured water, where people lark about. Not far away, on Gróza tér, you can visit the **Greek Orthodox Church**.

## Practicalities

The only drawback to Gyula is the fifteen-minute walk into the centre from the train station at the northern end of Béke sugárút, or the bus station to the south of the canal on Vásárhelyi Pál utca. All the **tourist offices** are central: Tourinform at Kossuth utca 7 (May–Sept Mon–Fri 9am–7pm, Sat 9am–1pm; Oct–April Mon–Fri 9am–5pm; ☎66/463-421); IBUSZ at Harruckern tér 10 (same times; ☎66/463-084); Békéstourist at Vásárhelyi utca 2 (Mon–Thurs 8am–4.30pm, Fri 8am–3.30pm; ☎66/463-028); and Gyulatourist just across the bridge at Eszperantó tér 1 (June–Aug Mon–Fri 8am–5pm, Sat 8am–noon; Sept–May Mon–Fri 8am–5pm; ☎66/463-026). There's a **24-hour currency exchange** at Hétvezér utca 5.

**Accommodation** abounds, with all the above offices booking private rooms, while Tourinform and Gyulatourist handle beds in vacant colleges. The *Hotel Aranykereszt*, beside Gyulatourist (☎66/463-194; ④), has rooms with phone and TV, and its own bowling alley, while similar rooms and secure parking are available at the *Vali Panzió* on Kossuth utca, near the castle. *Termál Camping* at Szélső utca 16 (☎66/463-551; ①) and the smaller *Mark Camping* at Vár utca 5 (☎66/361-473; ①) can both be found in the vicinty.

The most popular place **to eat** is the *Asia Indonesian Restaurant* on Városház utca, which makes a welcome change from Hungarian cuisine – though if that's what you'd prefer, the *Aranykereszt*'s restaurant is fine, while for plainer food and beer there's the *Sörpince* on Vértanúk útja, nearby. Don't miss the tiny *Százéves Cukrászda* at Jókai utca 2, which is the **oldest patisserie** in Hungary after *Ruszwurm*'s in Budapest. Furnished in the Biedermeier style and painted in shades of crème de menthe and chocolate, it includes a small museum of pastry-chef's utensils. The *Kézműves* at Városház utca 21 is another fine coffee house, though not as old.

# Csongrád, Szarvas and Mezőtúr

An alternative route across the Tisza is via Csongrád, east of Kiskunfélegyháza, a good base for visiting Szarvas and Mezőtúr before joining the main route to Debrecen at Kisújszállás. In many ways this region has even less to offer than places further south, but frequent **buses** mean that you needn't stay long in a town if it doesn't appeal. Trains, on the other hand, are not much use here unless you strike lucky or juggle timetables. The country roads around here are excellent for **cycling**, especially in the late summer when the verges are awash with purple sea lavender.

## Csongrád

The town of **CSONGRÁD** derives its name from the "Black Castle" (*Czernigrad*) erected at the confluence of the Tisza and Körös by the Bulgar princes who conquered this region in the early ninth century, before the coming of the Magyars. Though long since vanished, it lends its name to the Öregvár (Old Castle) district, whose narrow streets are full of 200-year-old thatched **fishermen's houses** restored to a state that their original owners would scarcely recognize, with a **Tájház** at Gyökér utca 1, displaying vintage domestic artefacts *in situ* (May to Oct Tues–Sun 1–5pm; free).

In the 1840s Count Széchenyi organized an association of riparian landowners with the aim of making the Tisza navigable, curtailing its floods, and reclaiming nearly 4000 square kilometres of swampland. The embankments were thrown up by thousands of day-labourers who wandered from site to site with their barrows. Their lives are commemorated in the **Tari László Museum** at Iskola utca 2, just off Kossuth tér in the centre of town (Tues–Fri 1–5pm, Sat & Sun 9am–noon; 80Ft). Like most towns on the Plain, Csongrád has a **thermal bath** located on Dob utca, around the corner from the *Hotel Tisza* on the tree-lined main street, Fő utca (May–Sept Tues–Sun 7am–10pm; Oct–April Mon 7–10am, Tues–Fri 7am–7pm, Sat & Sun 8am–7pm; 190Ft).

### Practicalities
Whereas it's a twenty-minute walk along Zrínyi utca from the train station to the centre (which has shifted from the Öregvár since Széchenyi's day), the bus terminal lies only a few blocks from Fő utca, where Szeged Tourist at no. 14 (Mon–Fri 9am–5pm; ☎63/483-069) can supply **information** and **accommoda-**

---

### SUICIDES

Csongrád county has the unenviable distinction of the highest **suicide** rate in Hungary: over twice the national average of fifty cases per 100,000 people every year, which is the highest of any nation in the world. Nobody is sure why this is, but theories are legion. Many Hungarians believe it's in their genes, citing the old saying that "the Magyar takes his pleasures sadly" and the fact that the next most suicidal people are their ethnic cousins, the Finns. Both countries have many isolated dwellings and a high incidence of alcoholism, and winter on the Great Plain can be as harsh as in Finland, with the *puszta* as monotonous as the Karelian forests. Yet while both countries share a prevalance of suicide in rural areas, other factors are specific to Hungary. Besides the local custom of parading the deceased through the streets in an open coffin – thought to encourage attention-seekers – Hungarian history and culture is full of suicides, from military heroes like Zrínyi to the poet Attila József (whose death under a train at Lake Balaton is emulated by several people every year), and 17-year-old Csilla Molnár, who killed herself shortly after becoming Miss Hungary in 1986. Some cases are simply known for their oddity: for one woman in Kaposvár, the final straw was the death of Bobby in the TV series *Dallas*.

---

**tion**. Between May and September you can rent fishermen's cottages (③–⑤) sleeping two or four people; a couple have heating and are available in winter too. Other options are the modern *Hotel Tisza* at Fő utca 23 (☎63/483-594; ④); the older *Erzsébet Hotel* at no. 3 (☎63/383-960; ③), whose spacious rooms and free entry to the thermal baths make amends for its dingy exterior; and the pleasant *Köröstoroki* campsite near the *strand* on the river 3km away (☎63/483-631; ①), which is accessible by bus. For **meals**, try the *Csuka Csárda* at Szentesi út 1, the *Garden* at Vasút utca 60, towards the train station, or the more touristy *Kemence Csárda* at Öregvár 54, past the Tájház. The *Bohém Kávéház*, a few doors down from the tourist office, is a popular hangout for the younger generation.

## Szarvas

**SZARVAS** ("Stag") feels peculiarly spacious, with a broad main street intersected by wide roads. The town was laid out like a chessboard in the eighteenth century by the enlightened thinker Samuel Tessedik, who served as a Lutheran priest in the town until his death in 1820. Aside from the bronze statue of a stag, the main sights in the centre are the **Tessedik Samuel Museum** on Vajda Péter utca (Tues–Sun: May–Oct 10am–6pm; Nov–April 10am–4pm; 100Ft), with local history displays, and the **Slovak House** at Hoffmann utca 1 (Jan–Oct Tues–Fri 1–4pm, Sat 10am–noon; 40Ft). Like Békéscsaba, Szarvas was populated by Slovak settlers after the withdrawal of the Turks in 1722, athough the domestic items and folk costumes on show in the house date from the late nineteenth century.

The town's principal attraction, however, is the **Arboretum**, a few kilometres out along the road to Mezőtúr, beside a backwater of the River Körös (daily: mid-March to mid-Nov 8am–6pm; mid-Nov to mid-March 8am–4pm; closed Dec 15 to Jan 5; 150Ft). This 82-hectare park contains 1600 different plants in its five arboreal collections. The oldest of the five is the *Pepikert* (Pepi's Garden), laid out by Count Pál "Pepi" Bolza in emulation of the grounds of Schönbrunn Palace in

Vienna. You can also get there by rented **boat**, which makes a nice little excursion; contact Tourinform or call ☎66/311-400 for details.

### Practicalities

Private **accommodation** is bookable through Tourinform in the Cultural House at Kossuth tér 3 (Mon–Fri 8am–5pm; ☎66/661-140), their branch in the Arboretum (June–Sept daily 10am–3pm), Szarvas Tours at Kossuth út 60 (May–Sept Mon–Fri 10am–4pm, Sat 9am–noon; Oct–April Mon–Fri 10am–4pm), or Pegasus Tours at Szabadság út 6–10 (May–Sept Mon–Thurs 8am–5.30pm, Fri 8am–4.30pm, Sat 9am–1pm; Oct–April Mon–Thurs 8am–4.30pm, Fri 8am–3.30pm; ☎66/312-860 ext 4). Tourinform also provides **information**. Friday and Saturday night techno discos in the *Hotel Árpád* at Szabadság út 32 (☎66/312-120; ②) make the newer *Lux Panzió* at no. 35 (☎66/313-417; ③–④) a better option, while just across the river on the edge of town are the *Mohosz Üdülő* (☎66/312-702; ②) and *Liget Camping*, which has rooms too (☎66/311-954; ③). For **meals**, the *Lux Panzió* has a good restaurant, or try the *Halászcsárda*, by Route 44, across the bridge west of town, or *Ciprus Csárda*, oposite it.

## Mezőtúr and Túrkeve

A quaint old ferry takes you over the river, as you head north from Szarvas to Mezőtúr, before you come to a region known as the *Sárrét* (Swampland), nowadays largely drained, but still rich in flora, frogs and insects. The quiet town of **MEZŐTÚR**, 19km from Szarvas, has an exhibition of local **pottery** in the former synagogue at Damjanach utca 1 (a sight in its own right), but mainly serves as a base for trips to **TÚRKEVE**, 16km further north. Here you can see a big exhibition of sculptures by the Finta brothers at the **Finta Museum** on Attila út (Tues–Thurs & Sun 9am–5pm, Sat 9am–noon). The brothers left Hungary in the 1920s in search of fame and fortune, Sándor Finta moving to Paris and Gergely making it as far as New York. The most striking work displayed is Gergely's *Human Destiny*, a giant hand poised to absorb a helpless figure.

**Accommodation** is available in both towns. In Mezőtúr there is the *Berettyó Fogadó* at Kossuth tér 8 (②), while Túrkeve offers a choice between the *Kevi Fogadó* at Kenyérmezei út 27 (②), or private rooms at Petőfi tér 3–5 (①–②), Árpád utca 3A or Kenyérmezei út 8B. **Buses** link both towns to Kisújszállás, along the main road and train line between Szolnok and Debrecen.

# THE NORTHERN PLAIN BEYOND THE TISZA

The **Northern Plain** has more to offer than the south, with **Hortobágy National Park**, the friendly city of **Debrecen** and picturesque villages around the headwaters of the River Tisza. In July and August, you can catch colourful **festivals** at Nagykálló, Hortobágy and Debrecen, while in September there's a carnival at Nyíregyháza. The region is also noted for its **pilgrimages**, and long history of religious fervour. Debrecen is the centre of Hungarian Protestantism, dubbed "the Calvinist Rome", the village of Máriapócs is a focus for Greek Catholics and

Roma believers, while the tomb of the "miracle rabbi" at Nagykálló is a vestige of the rich Hasidic culture that existed here before the Holocaust.

Most travellers head directly for Debrecen along the M3 via Gyöngyös and cut down past Tiszafüred along Route 33, or take the slower trunk route from Budapest, which crosses the Tisza at Szolnok. Since the intervening towns have little to offer, and most places are best reached from Debrecen, the following sections have been structured accordingly.

# Szolnok and around

Sited at the confluence of the Zagyva and Tisza rivers, **SZOLNOK** has never been allowed to forget its importance as a bridgehead. Once the Mongols had stormed its castle in the thirteenth century, there was nothing to stop them riding on to Buda. In this century, the town's seizure by the Red Army foretold its inexorable advance in 1944 and again in 1956, when it crushed the Uprising. Given this history, it's not surprising that most of Szolnok consists of postwar blocks, or that the population turned out to jeer the Soviets goodbye in 1990.

Along the main axis through the centre, the **János Damjanich Museum** at Kossuth tér 4 (Tues–Sun: April–Oct 10am–6pm; Nov–March 10am–4pm; each section 50–100Ft, free on Tues) bears the name of the general who trounced the Habsburg army just up the road in 1849. It has separate sections devoted to Bronze Age, Roman and medieval artefacts; folk crafts and implements; nineteenth-century interiors; and work by the Szolnok Artists' Colony, whose leading members were László Mednyánszky (1852–1919) and Adolf Fényes (1867–1945).

Heading south from the centre towards the banks of the Tisza, several Art Nouveau buildings on Szapáry utca presage Szolnok's former **synagogue**, a magnificent creation by Lipót Baumhorn in the last years of the nineteenth century. Gutted during the war like so many others, it was turned into an art gallery in the 1960s, which retains some original features (Tues–Sun 9am–5pm). On Templom út nearby stands a handsome Baroque Franciscan church, where **organ concerts** are held in summer.

With more time to kill, it's worth investigating the Tabán district beside the Zagyva, a twenty-minute walk east along the main street and off to the left. One of the oldest parts of Szolnok, it used to be a poor quarter of fishermen and bargees, but has now become a Brookside-like estate. As a reminder of the past, one thatched house on the river side has been preserved as a **Tájház** (May–Sept Thurs–Sun 1–5pm; 40Ft), with its interior as it would have looked in the 1930s, when fisherman Sándor Kovács and his family lived here; the adults slept on the bed and their six children on the dirt floor.

## Practicalities

Szolnok's **bus station** is on Ady Endre utca, a couple of minutes' walk north of the main Baross utca, and its **train station** is west of the city centre on Jubileumi tér (bus #24, #8, #7, #6 or #15). The city is sited along the main road and rail line from Budapest to Debrecen, and serves as a terminus for trains to Kiskunfélegyháza via Lakitelek, and a nexus for buses to Jászberény, Cegléd, Tiszafüred and other towns on the Plain.

You can get **information** from Tourinform at Ságvári körút 4, opposite the bus station (July & Aug Mon–Fri 8am–4pm, Sat 9am–noon; rest of year Mon–Thurs

8am–4pm, Fri 8am–3pm; ☎56/424-803); IBUSZ at Szapáry utca 24 (May–Oct Mon–Fri 8am–5pm, Sat 9am–noon; Nov–April Mon–Fri 8am–4pm; ☎56/423-602); or the sluggish Express at Kossuth út 18 (Mon–Thurs 8am–3.45pm, Fri 8am–1pm; ☎56/424-010).

Apart from private **accommodation**, the *Tisza Hotel* at Verseghy park 2 (☎56/371-155; ⑤) is a wonderfully old-fashioned place with its own thermal bath (closed mid-July to mid-Aug) and a fine patio overlooking the river. It's preferable to the gloomy *Pelikán Hotel* at Jászkürt út 1, in the centre (☎56/423-855; ④), or the *Touring Hotel* (☎56/379-805; ③) or *Sport Motel* (☎56/376-206; ①) on Tiszaligeti sétány, in the neglected resort area across the river (accessible by bus #15), where one also finds Szolnok's campsite (☎56/424-403) and **thermal baths**.

For Hungarian **food**, the restaurant in the *Tisza Hotel* has a grand ambience and a riverside summer garden, but you can get similar dishes for less at *Bajnok*, Baross utca 3, west of the *Pelikán Hotel*, or the nearby *Róza Vendéglő*, Konstantin utca 36; for a change of cuisine, try the *Alexander Pizzeria* at Táncsics utca 16. The *Irish Pub* at Szapáry utca 24 is a lively drinking place, and you an get coffee and cakes at the *Tünde Cukrászda*, a few doors along.

# Karcag

**KARCAG**, 85km east of Szolnok, was once a major settlement of the Cumanians, whose costumes and pottery are displayed in the **Győrffy István Museum** at Kálvin utca 4 (Tues–Sun 10am–noon & 2–6pm; 80Ft). Although much of the town's Cumanian identity has been lost, a couple of aspects still survive, including a thriving local tradition of **pottery**, as a visit to the **Kántor Sándor Fazekas Tájház** at Erkel utca 1 (April–Oct Tues–Sun 10am–noon & 2–6pm; 80Ft) will confirm. **Food** based on traditional recipes, such as *kunsági pandurleves*, a soup made of chicken or pigeon and seasoned with ginger, garlic, nutmeg and paprika, is also still made; you can try it at the *Kunsági Étterem* at Dózsa út 1, and the *Mészáros Vendéglő* at Madarasi út 63. Karcag is also the location of the largest rice-hulling mill in Europe, which processes the rice grown around Hortobágy. On the

---

### ADMIRAL HORTHY

In September 1994 Hungarian journalists descended on the town of Kenderes, near Karcag, to cover the reburial of Admiral Miklós Horthy, who died in exile in 1957. Of noble birth, he served as an aide to Emperor Franz Josef and was appointed naval commander-in-chief just before the collapse of the Dual Monarchy. Following the rout of the Republic of Councils in Hungary, Horthy organized the "White Terror" against Jews and leftists, and became Regent in 1920. Described by Count Károlyi as the "Hungarian Quisling", it was Horthy who led Hungary into its fateful alliance with Hitler and Mussolini, in return for territory lost under the Treaty of Trianon. By 1944, however, he was secretly pursuing an armistice with the Allies, which the Germans forestalled by occupying Hungary and deposing him. Sent to Berlin under "protective custody", he was granted refuge in Portugal and died on the Algarve. Reburying Horthy at his ancestral seat in Hungary was inconceiveable until the post-Communist era, when it rekindled the old debate between conservatives nostalgic for his nationalistic leadership, and liberals who revile him as a dictator.

**accommodation** front, there's the *Fehér Holló* at Püspökladányi út 3 (☎50/313-555; ④), and half a dozen tourist motels and a campsite in nearby **BEREKFÜRDŐ**, whose main attraction is its small and very popular **spa park** with three outdoor baths (daily 8am–7pm).

# Debrecen

Once upon a time, **DEBRECEN** was the site of Hungary's greatest livestock fair, and foreigners tended to be snooty about "this vast town of unsightly buildings", with its thatched cottages and a main street that became "one liquid mass of mud" when it rained, "so that officers quartered on one side were obliged to mount their horses and ride across to have dinner on the other". Even so, none denied the significance of Debrecen (pronounced "*Deb*-retzen"), both economically and as the fount of **Hungarian Calvinism**. From the sixteenth century onwards there wasn't a generation of lawyers, doctors or theologians that didn't include graduates from its Calvinist College. The city is still renowned for its university and teacher-training colleges, but equally for its hard-headed commercialism, which has made Debrecen the second most populous city in Hungary, and the richest on the Plain. More pertinently for visitors, it hosts three major **festivals** plus a mega Flower Carnival on August 20; its restaurants, pubs and nightlife are as good as any on the Plain; and the city makes an ideal base for **excursions** to Hortobágy National Park and the Hajdúság and Nyírség regions.

## The City

Tram #1 follows the old, much maligned **Piac utca** (Market Street) through the centre of town and out to the university. On the way in from the train station you'll pass the former **County Hall** at no. 54, its facade crawling with Zsolnay pyrogranite statues of Hajdúks (see p.355); an ornate corner house (no. 51) and the Romantic-style **Small Church**, whose bastion-like top replaced an onion dome that blew off during a storm in 1909. The Secessionist pile opposite, with a gilded portal, was originally a savings bank rivalling the Gresham Building in Budapest for opulence. Debrecen's coat of arms, a phoenix arising from the ashes, appears on the **town hall** at no. 20, shortly before the road widens into **Kossuth tér** and **Kálvin tér**, dominated by two monumental edifices.

### The Great Church and Calvinist College

The **Great Church** (*Nagytemplom*) is an appropriately huge monument to the *Református* faith that swept through Hungary during the sixteenth century and still commands the allegiance of roughly one third of the population. Calvinism took root more strongly in Debrecen than elsewhere, as local Calvinists struck a deal with the Turks to ensure their security and forbade Catholics to settle here after 1552. In 1673, the Catholic Habsburgs deported 41 Calvinist priests (who ended up as galley slaves), but failed to shake the faith's hold on Debrecen. A reconciliation of sorts was achieved during the pope's visit in 1991, when he laid a wreath at their memorial.

The church itself (Mon–Sat 9am–4pm, Sun noon–4pm; 40Ft) is a dignified Neoclassical building designed by Mihály Pollack. Its typically austere interior accommodated the Diet of 1849 that declared Hungary's secession from the

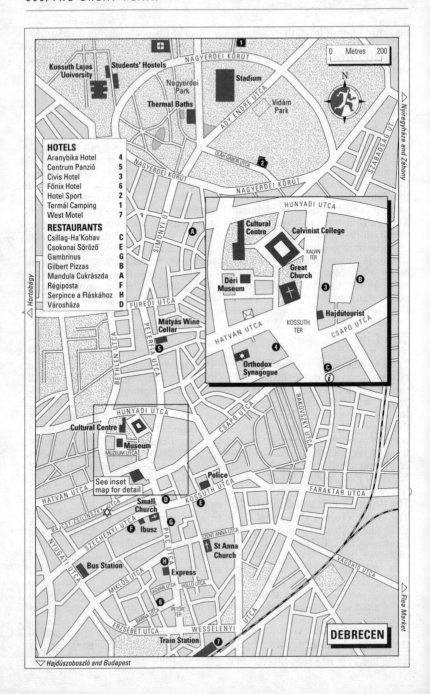

## WITCHCRAFT

The early Calvinists' hatred of popery was only exceeded by their animus towards pagan beliefs among the peasantry of the Plain, who regarded *táltos* (village wise men) with benevolence, while fearing *boszorkány*, their female counterparts. Until the eighteenth century, women accused of **witchcraft** were able to plead that they were beneficent *táltos* (for example Frau Bártha, who claimed to have learned *táltos* skills from her brother), but as the Calvinists' grip tightened this defence became untenable. Midwives were particularly vulnerable as it was popularly believed that the murder of a relative or newborn child was a prerequisite for acquiring their "magical" skills, but women in general suffered from the Calvinists' witch-hunting zeal, which also found scapegoats in herbalists, beggars and vagabonds.

**Witch trials** were finally banned by Maria Theresa in 1768 after some scandalous trials in Szeged when "witches" had confessions tortured out of them. By the nineteenth century the bloody deeds of Debrecen's forefathers were buried beneath platitudes eulogizing the "Calvinist Rome".

Habsburg empire. The *Rákóczi-harang* – forged from cannons used in the Rákóczi War of Independence – is the largest **bell** in Hungary. From the tower you can get an excellent view of the city (same times; 70Ft).

Around the back on Kálvin tér stands the **Calvinist College** (*Református Kollégium*), where students were compelled to rise at 3am and be in bed by 9pm until the end of the eighteenth century. The college motto, inscribed over the entrance, is *orando et laborando* ("praying and working"). Though venerable in appearance, this is not the original college founded in 1538, but an enlarged nineteenth-century version. It was here that the Provisional National Assembly of left-wing and centre parties met under Soviet auspices late in 1944, unwittingly conferring legitimacy on the Soviet occupation. Visitors can inspect a **Museum of College History** (Tues–Sat 9am–5pm, Sun 9am–1pm; 60Ft), whose exhibits include a meteorite which landed near the town in 1857, as well as the **Oratory** and **Library** upstairs.

### The Déri Museum

The beguiling **Déri Museum** (Tues–Sun: April–Oct 10am–6pm; Nov–March 10am–4pm; 80Ft) is fronted by statues by Ferenc Medgyessy that won a prize at the 1937 Paris Expo. Its ethnographic collection includes the richly embroidered shepherds' cloaks (*szűr*) which played a significant role in local courtship rituals. A herdsman would "forget" to remove his finest *szűr* from the porch when he left the house of the woman he was courting, and if it was taken inside within an hour a formal proposal could be made. Otherwise, the cloak was hung prominently on the veranda, giving rise to the expression *kitették a szűrét* ("his cloak was put out"), meaning to get rid of an unwanted suitor.

A separate gallery (same times; 100Ft) contains **paintings** depicting romantic and patriotic themes by Viktor Madarász, Bertalan Székely and **Mihály Munkácsy**. Pride of place is given to the last's vast canvas *Ecce Homo*, an allegorical representation of good and evil, truth and falsehood, which toured the world in the 1890s. Having viewed it in Dublin, James Joyce commented: "It is a mistake to limit drama to the stage; a drama can be painted as well as sung or acted, and *Ecce Homo* is a drama."

## Other sights in the centre

Given the focus on Calvinism, it's easy to overlook the existence of other faiths in Debrecen. Before the war there were over 9000 Jews and eight synagogues, of which only two remain in the backstreets west of Kálvin tér. The eclectic-style **Orthodox Synagogue** on Pásti utca is so derelict that the Jewish community is negotiating with the council to turn it into a cultural centre, but the building next door is used as a prayer house in the winter, when the nearby **Status Quo Synagogue** on Kápolnási utca is too big to heat. Built to serve the Status Quo Jews in 1909, it has recently been restored and may be visited (call ☎52/415-861 if the door is locked). Its pale pastel decor and *bemah* are as austere as a Calvinist church, unlike the rich interiors of the synagogues of Szeged and Budapest.

If ecclesiastical architecture is your thing, consider tracking down **St Anna's Church**, a couple of blocks east of Piac utca, which is Catholic and Baroque and originally belonged to the Piarist order. Above the portal you can discern the coat of arms of its founder, Cardinal Csáky. Next door is the former Piarist grammar school, with an exhibition on their educational methods (mid-Sept to late May Mon–Fri 8am–2pm). The street on which it stands was previously called Béke útja (Avenue of Peace), which raised a mordant chuckle amongst the townsfolk, as it leads to a slaughterhouse beyond the **Greek Orthodox Church** on Attila tér.

## Nagyerdei Park and Kossuth Lajos University

North of Kálvin tér the city turns greener and quieter, with stylish residences lining the roads to **Nagyerdei Park**. In the western section you'll find the **thermal baths** (daily: April–Oct 8am–8pm; Nov–March 8am–6pm; 300Ft), an indoor complex fed by springs of sulphurous "brown water" (*bárna-víz*) rising up from beneath the park. Elsewhere you may notice hemp, growing wild; the plants are so low in THC that they're not worth smoking, but local *táltos* have been known to boil bushels in cauldrons, to some effect.

Beyond the reedy lake and wooden footbridge rises the columned bulk of **Kossuth Lajos University**, fronted by fountains where newlyweds pose for photos. The university's **Hungarian language courses** in mid-January, late May and mid-July draw students from nations as diverse as Sweden and Australia (☎52/329-117; *nyariegy@tigris/klte.hu*). Beyond the campus lies a **Botanical Garden** (daily 9am–4pm; free).

## Markets

Though the great bi-monthly fairs "held here since time immemorial" no longer take place, Debrecen's **fruit and vegetable market** is a pungent, compulsive affair. The indoor market (*vásárcsarnok*), next to the supermarket on Csapó utca (Mon–Sat 4am–3pm, Sun 4–11am), is awash with kerchiefed grannies hawking pickles, meat, soft cheese and strange herbs, the air filled with smells and Magyar interrogatives ("*Hogy a… ?*" is slang for "how much is the… ?").

Debrecen's **flea market**, known as the **Noisy Market** (*Zsibogó Piac*), is held in an industrial quarter of the city (8am–noon or 1pm; closed Wed). Take a #30 bus from the train station and get off where everybody else does, just past the cigarette factory (*Dohánygyár*). The market is across the road and through a portal, its 800-odd stalls selling clothes, tools, loads of junk and a few antiques. It is also a place to exchange forints or hard currency for Romanian lei, Czech crowns and other currencies – and to get ripped off, if you're not careful.

# Practicalities

Tram #1, running from the **train station** to the baths and university, makes sight-seeing a cinch, though if you arrive at the **bus station** off Széchenyi utca you'll have to walk into the centre, at least as far as Piac utca. The best places for **information** are Tourinform at Piac utca 20 (June–Aug 8am–8pm; Sept–May Mon–Thurs 9am–5pm, Fri till 4pm; ☎52/412-250), and Hajdútourist at Kálvin tér 2/A (June–Aug Mon–Fri 8am–5pm, Sat 8am–12.30pm; Sept–May Mon–Fri 8am–4.30pm; ☎52/415-588), though IBUSZ (mid-May to mid-Sept Mon–Fri 8am–4pm, Sat 8am–noon; rest of year Mon–Thurs 8am–4pm, Fri 8am–2pm; ☎52/415-555) can also help. Express at Piac utca 77 (May–Sept Mon–Fri 8.30am–4.30pm, Sat 9am–1pm; Oct–April Mon–Fri 8.30am–4.30pm; ☎52/418-332) is really only useful for booking accommodation. The **post office** is on Hatvan utca 5–9, and there's a 24-hour **pharmacy** at Széchenyi utca 1.

## Accommodation

It's wise to make **reservations** during the annual festivals (many hotels are booked a year ahead of the Flower Carnival), though you should be able to find something at short notice the rest of the time. The cheapest accommodation is in **colleges**, charging by the bed. Express can arrange places on Friday and Saturday throughout the year, and daily throughout July and August, though vacancies are scarce at this time. A likely venue is the *kollégium* annexe behind the university. The next step up are **private rooms** (②) from Hajdútourist or IBUSZ. Other options are listed below, with the exception of the seedy *Hotel Debrecen* opposite the station, which is best avoided.

### HOTELS AND PENSIONS

**Aranybika Hotel**, Piac utca 11–15, off Kossuth tér (☎52/416-777). Established in 1690, the 250-room *Aranybika* is reputedly the oldest hotel in Hungary, though most of today's building dates from the early twentieth century, and the furnishings are standard socialist Hungarian. It has a huge restaurant with stained glass windows, a casino and a gym. ④–⑤.

**Centrum Panzió**, Péterfia utca 37A (☎52/416-193). Plain but comfortable pension, a few blocks north of the Great Church. ③.

**Cívis Hotel**, Kálvin tér 4 (☎52/418-522). A flash establishment opposite the Great Church, with its own sauna (free for guests) and massage parlour; TV and minibar in every room. ⑤.

**Főnix Hotel**, Barna utca 17 (☎52/413-355). On a quiet street off Petőfi tér, a few blocks from the station. Rooms with basins and shared bathrooms, or private showers and TV. ②–③.

**Hotel Sport**, Oláh utca 5 (☎52/417-655). Variable rooms in Nagyerdei Park, with a solarium, sauna and bowling alley next door. ②.

**West Motel**, Petőfi utca 12 (☎52/347-915). A noisy place by the station with double and triple rooms. No breakfast. ①–②.

### CAMPSITES

**Dorcas Camping**, Vekeri tó (☎52/441-119), 6km south of town near Lake Vekeri (bus #26 from the bus station). Bungalows and facilities for horse-riding and angling. Open mid-April to Sept.

**Termál Camping**, Nagyerdei körút 102 (☎52/412-456). Tent-space and chalets (①–③) northeast of Nagyerdei Park. Open May–Sept. ①.

## Eating

Although the *Aranybika's* dining room is wonderful, its food is nothing special, and for that kind of money you'd do better at **restaurants** like the *Gambrinus* at Piac utca 28B (11am–11pm), the *Régiposta* (Old Post Office) at Széchenyi utca 6, in an arcaded building where Charles XII of Sweden stayed the night in 1714, which sometimes has gypsy music, or the *Csokonai Söröző* on Kossuth utca, where customers roll three dice at the end of the meal and don't have to pay if the right symbols come up (Mon–Fri noon–11pm, Sat & Sun 4–11pm; ☎52/412-958; booking is advisable). The *Városháza* at Piac utca 20 offers Baroque surroundings and well-cooked traditional dishes, while *Csillag-Ha'Kohav* at Piac utca 10 prides itself on being eastern Hungary's only Israeli restaurant, offering a special Friday menu.

For **cheaper meals**, try the excellent *Serpince a Fláskához* at Miklós utca 4, which serves regional specialities. Out towards the university the *Aranykakas* on the corner of Mikszáth and Martonfalvi utcas offers hearty food at prices that appeal to the locals, while the trendier *Retro* on Bajcsy-Zsilinszky utca does pizza, pasta and Magyar dishes till late. Otherwise there's the inevitable *McDonald's* on Piac utca, or *Gilbert Pizzas* in the mall off Kálvin tér (noon–10pm). Excellent ice cream can be found at the *Mandula Cukrászda* at Ember Pál utca 6, just off Simonyi út, before Nagyerdei Park.

## Drinking and nightlife

Pubs are all the rage in Hungary at the moment, and the *John Bull* at Piac utca 28 (☎52/424-026) is one of Debrecen's liveliest **drinking** spots, with regular live music nights. Another popular place is the *Flamingó Bar* on Jerikó utca out beyond the Cultural Centre. The *Mátyás Pince* on Péterfia utca (daily 11.30am–midnight) has a nice ambience and an enjoyable rigmarole of serving wine from glass spigots, while the *Fácán Kakas* at Marothy György utca 38, nearby, features a great courtyard and dreadful music.

For up-to-date info on **nightlife** and events, get hold of *Debreceni, Nyíregyházi Est*, a free bi-weekly listings guide available in cinemas, tourist offices and bars. The *Klinika Mozi* at Nagyerdei körút 98 (☎52/411-600) hosts concerts and raves with visiting DJs, while the *Utópia Disco* on Vágóhíd utca varies its diet of parties with body-building shows (a big thing in Hungary).

## Festivals

Debrecen endeavours to dispel its austere image with three major festivals. In late March, the **Spring Festival** (*Tavaszi Fesztivál*) of music and drama coincides with events in Budapest, though Debrecen claims to have originated the custom. There's often something worth watching at the **Csokonai Theatre** on Kossuth utca, an exotic-looking Moorish structure named after the locally born poet, Mihály Csokonai Vitez. In early July, the week-long **Bartók International Choir Competition**, held in odd-numbered years, alternates with the biennial **International Military Bands** festival. Best of all is the **Jazz Festival** (*Dzsessz Napok* or *Jazzfeszt*) in early September, featuring top Hungarian musicians and a few foreign acts; see Hajdútourist or posters around town for details.

A more predictable event occurs on August 20, when the **Flower Carnival** trundles north along Egyetem sugárút – thirty floats laden with flowers, bands and operatically dressed soldiers. People hang from windows en route, cheer wildly when the band plays tunes from *István a király* (*Stephen the King*, a patriotic rock opera) and surge behind the last float towards the stadium, where the show continues into the late afternoon. In the evening there's a **fireworks** display outside the Great Church.

# The Hajdúság

The **Hajdúság** region around Debrecen takes its name from the **Hajdúk** communities who occupied eight derelict villages here during the early seventeenth century. Originally Balkan cattle drovers-cum-bandits who fought as mercenaries against the Turks, they were unfettered by feudal servitude and infamous for their ferocity and bisexuality. Their ranks were swollen by runaway serfs and homeless peasants, and they formed a guerilla army, led by István Bocskai, which turned against the Habsburgs in the winter of 1604–5. After Bocskai achieved his ambition to be Prince of Transylvania, the Hajdúk were pensioned off with land to avert further disturbance. The result was a string of settlements with names prefixed *Hajdú-*, where the Hajdúk farmed, enjoyed the status of "nobles" (*natio*) and, if necessary, were mustered to fight.

## Hajdúböszörmény

This military heritage is apparent in the layout of **HAJDÚBÖSZÖRMÉNY**, 20km northwest of Debrecen, where old houses stand in concentric rings around a walled core that was once a Hajdúk fortress. Its pristine Bocskai tér is overlooked by a Calvinist church, Baroque town hall and **Hajdúság Museum** (daily: April–Sept 10am–6pm; Oct–March 10am–4pm; 100Ft), whose local history exhibits include a 1659 engraving of "Giorgio Ragozzi" (better known as György Rákóczi), and relics of the Communist era such as the red star that once adorned the town hall. For a romantic view of olden days, check out the *puszta* scenes in the home of the nineteenth-century artist Miklós Káplár, on Hortobágy utca.

Though private **rooms** are available from Hajdútourist on Fő utca (Mon–Fri 8am–5pm; ☎52/371-416), the *Káplár* **campsite** at Polgári út 92–100, 1km from the centre, off Route 35 (☎52/371-388; April–Oct), is more enticing. It is actually a converted *Skanzen* of wattle-and-daub thatched houses (③), with antique furnishings, indoor and outdoor cooking facilities and a restaurant playing gypsy music, with lots of tent space and bikes for hire. At the junction of Polgári út and Route 35 are two picturesque **cemeteries**, one full of the boat-shaped wooden grave posts typical of the region, the other overgrown with cornstalks.

## Hajdúszoboszló

A spa since 1927, **HAJDÚSZOBOSZLÓ** gets about one and a half million visitors each year, far more than anywhere else in the Hajdúság. Surveying the wallowing, guzzling crowds in the steaming brown waters of its **thermal baths** (daily 7am–6pm; 300Ft), you might try the old Hajdúk war cry, *Huj, huj, hajrá!*, to clear some space before jumping in yourself. Away from the baths, things are more relaxed, with tennis courts for rent in the park, and cafés and quaint old buildings around Hősök tere, guarded by a comically fierce statue of Bocskai.

Twenty metres of **fortress wall**, part of the fifteenth-century defences, lurk behind the inevitable Calvinist church on Hősök tere. Around the corner at Bocskai

utca 12, the **Bocskai Museum** (Tues–Sun: May–Sept 9am–1pm & 3–7pm;
Oct–April 9am–1pm & 2–6pm; 60Ft) exhibits photos of nineteenth-century Hajdúk
villagers, and assorted military relics – among them Bocskai's embroidered silk
banner, given pride of place alongside the town's charter. Although Bocskai comes
across as a benevolent leader, he didn't balk at betraying another group who fought
for him: the Székely of Transylvania, who were butchered when they had outlived
their usefulness during the so-called "Bloody Carnival". Another building at no. 21
houses a folklore and ethnographic display, and there are temporary exhibitions at
no. 11; the same ticket is valid for all three.

On the edge of town, around the train station, the atmosphere is more rural.
Chunky whitewashed cottages, their vegetable gardens fringed with sunflowers,
shimmer in the heat, while errant cows, old women and wagon-loads of pigs move
slowly in the dazzling sunlight.

## Practicalities

Buses #1, #4 and #6 run from the **train station** into the centre, terminating at the
**bus station** near the baths. Most things are on or just off the main Szilfákalja út,
which is also Route 4 between Budapest and Debrecen. Both Tourinform at
Szilfákalja út 2 (July & Aug Mon–Fri 8.30am–5.30pm, Sat 9am–noon; Sept–June Mon
& Fri 8.30am–noon, Tues–Thurs 8.30am–4.30pm, Sat 9am–noon; ☎52/361-612), and
Hajdútourist at József Attila utca 2 (Mon–Fri 8am–4.30pm, Sat & Sun 8am–1pm;
☎52/362-214), can supply **information** and private rooms (②) if needed. The fanci-
est **hotels** are the *Mátyás Király* (☎52/360-200; ④) and *Barátság Gyógyszálló*
(☎52/361-744; ③) on Mátyás király sétány, near the baths, and the *Béke Gyógyhotel*
(☎52/361-411; ③), attached to the baths. Two cheaper options on József Attila utca
are the *Start Panzió* at no. 18 (☎52/365-981; ②), and the run-down but friendly
*Délibáb* at no. 4 (☎52/360-366; ②). The campsite beside Debreceni út (☎52/362-427;
①; May–Sept) has a hotel (③), multi-bed bungalows (④) and apartments (⑤).

# Hortobágy National Park

Petőfi compared the **Hortobágy puszta** of the central Plain to "the sea, bound-
less and green". In his day, this "glorious steppe" resounded to the pounding
hooves of countless horses and cattle being driven from well to waterhole by
mounted *csikósok* (horse-herds) and *gulyások* (cowboys), while Racka sheep
grazed under the surveillance of Puli dogs. Medieval tales of cities in the clouds
and nineteenth-century accounts of phantom woods, or the "extensive lake half
enveloped in grey mist" which fooled John Paget, testify to the occurrence of
**mirages** during the hot, dry Hortobágy summers. Caused by the diffusion of
light when layers of humid air at differing temperatures meet, these *délibáb*
sporadically appear at certain locations – for example north of Máta, south of
Kónya, and along the road between Cserepes and the *Kis-Hortobágyi Csárda*.

Over the ages tribes have raised burial mounds (*kurgán*), some dating back
4000–5000 years. One of them served as the site of a duel between Frau Bártha
of Debrecen and two rival *táltos*. Nowadays, the grasslands have receded and
mirages are the closest that Hortobágy gets to witchcraft, but the *puszta* can still
pass for Big Sky country, its low horizons casting every copse and hillock into
high relief. You should, however, be prepared for a relatively costly touristic
experience – the *puszta* comes packaged at Hortobágy.

# Around the Hortobágy

The 730-square-kilometre **Hortobágy National Park** is a living heritage museum, with cowboys demonstrating their skills, and beasts strategically placed along the way to the **nine-arched stone bridge** (depicted in a famous painting by Tivadar Csontváry) that lies just west of **HORTOBÁGY** village. In the village itself stands the much restored **Great Inn** (*Nagycsárda*), a rambling thatched edifice dating from 1871 that's now a touristy restaurant. Across the road you'll find the *Pastormúzeum* or **Shepherds' Museum** (April–Oct daily 9am–5pm; 200Ft), whose embroidered *szűr* (cloaks), carved powder horns and other objects were fashioned by plainsmen to while away solitary hours. Status had great significance within their world: horse-herds outranked shepherds and cowherds, who, in turn, felt superior to the *kondás* or swineherd. Beneath the stars, however, all slept equally, only building crude huts (*kunyhó*) or sharing the protection of a reed screen (*szárnyék*) with their animals in bad weather.

Across the bridge and 2km north, the stud farm at **Máta** is the place to witness equestrian displays and go riding in horse-drawn carriages; tickets are sold from the Epona stall by the Shepherds' Museum, and events take place in the *Epona Lovasfalu* (horse village), a massive new tourist development tacked onto Máta that is also the venue for an international **Horse Show** (*Nemzetközi Lovas Napok*) on the first weekend of July. The biggest event of the year is the annual **Bridge Fair** on August 19–20, a Magyar rodeo occasioning the sale of leatherwork, knives and roast beef, which is staged by the bridge near Hortobágy.

## Wildlife

Wildlife is dispersed all over the park, but for the convenience of visitors there is a **Hortobágy Animal Park** (*Pusztai Állatpark*), devoted to the distinctive breeds of the Great Plain: hairy Mangalica pigs, corkscrew-horned Racka sheep, silvery-grey horned cattle, water buffalo and Puli sheepdogs, with information on each in English. Its observation tower affords a fine view of the nine-arched bridge and the surrounding *puszta*. The park lies across the bridge from the village and 800m down to the left (daily 9am–6pm; 300Ft).

Exploring further afield is getting easier as the park becomes more visitor-friendly. **Visitor passes** (500Ft a day) for four protected areas are available from Pusztainform, and a Visitor Centre is due to open by the Shepherds' Museum in 2000. **Bicycles** are the best way to get around this flat terrain; you can get the addresses of locals renting bikes from Pusztainform.

The Hortobágyi-halastó lakes, 6km west of Hortobágy village and turn right, are great for **bird-watching** – especially storks, buzzards, mallards, cranes, terns and curlews – with lodgings at the lakeside *Öregtói Vendégház* (④), bookable through Pusztainform. Most trains stop at the Halastó halt, the next station west of Hortbágy. Elsewhere in the park, little ringed plovers, stone curlews and pratincoles favour dry sheep-runs, while red-footed falcons behave unusually for their species, forming loose groups in abandoned rooks' nests. Millions of migratory birds pass through in spring and autumn – the thousands of cranes that fill the skies in late September make an incredible sight and sound. There's less to see at the bird reservation southwest of Nagyiván, although large colonies of storks nest in the villages of Nagyiván and Tiszacsege till the end of August.

Wild **mammals** can be found all over the *puszta* – boars near Kecskéses in marshy thickets, otters at Árkus and by the canals and fishponds, ground squirrels near Kónya in the northern grasslands, and roe deer can be found in the reeds, meadows and copses between Óhat and Tiszaszőlős.

## Practicalities

A succession of small tourist inns gives advance notice of the park to drivers approaching via the Debrecen–Füzesabony road, but **getting there** by train offers a subtler transition from farmland to *puszta*. Services from Debrecen (towards Tiszafüred and Füzesabony) are better than trains from Nyíregyháza, which leave you stranded at Óhat-Pusztakócs, several kilometres west of Hortobágy village. During summer there might even be a "nostalgia" steam train from Debrecen. Buses, calling at Hortobágy en route between Eger and Hajdúszoboszló (or direct from the latter during high season), are another option. Although cycling is the best way of getting around, some of the sites are within walking distance of train halts along the Debrecen–Tiszafüred, Tiszafüred–Karcag and Nyíregyháza–Óhat–Pusztakócs lines.

Most amenities are concentrated at the western end of Hortobágy village, where Hajdútourist in the Galéria behind the *Great Inn* (April–Oct Mon–Fri 9am–7pm, June–Aug also Sat & Sun 9am–4pm; ☎52/369-039) can provide a **map** of the park and explain the various **programmes** on offer, while Pusztainform migrates from the Shepherds' Museum (April–Oct daily 9am–5pm; ☎52/369-119) to Czinege utca 1 down the road towards Debrecen (Nov–March Mon–Fri 9am–4pm; ☎52/369-105).

Both tourist offices can supply private rooms (②) and point you in the direction of *Puszta Camping*, just down the river bank from the museum (☎52/369-300; ①; May–Oct). Other **accommodation** in the vicinity includes the friendly but rundown *Hortobágy Fogadó* at Kossuth utca 3, in the centre of the village (☎52/369-137; ②); the more salubrious *Hortobágy Hotel* on the eastern outskirts (☎52/369-071; ③; April–Oct); and the *Pásztortanya Vendégfogadó* 5km west of the village by the main road (☎52/369-127; ②), which has a good restaurant.

The last offers pricey **flying trips** over the park (9000Ft for three passengers for 10min), while the *Epona Lovasfalu* (☎52/369-092; ⑥) in Máta is a lavish resort hotel with its own swimming pool, fitness centre and **riding school**.

# Lake Tisza

Created by damming the upper reaches of the river, **Lake Tisza** has become a new centre for tourism. It's not as developed as Lake Balaton, but then much of it is marshy and less attractive, and the authorities permit motorboats to buzz around the southern end of the lake near Abádszalok and Kisköre, the most Balaton-like area. Tiszafüred is slightly quieter, with fishing and bird-watching, swimming and canoeing.

**TISZAFÜRED** is the most developed of the resorts, and a transport junction between the Plain and the Northern Uplands. Its bus and train stations are ten minutes' walk from the centre; head up Vasút út to Kossuth tér and follow the main street, Fő út. The only "sights" are the **Kis Pál Museum** on Tariczky sétány near Kossuth tér (Tues–Sun 10am–noon & 2–6pm; 60Ft), where fishing features prominently in the local history display; and the **Pottery House** (*Fazekasház*) at Malom utca 12 up the far end of the main street, turning right opposite the

Calvinist church (same hours; free). The real lure is swimming and sunbathing, either in a dead branch of the Tisza twenty minutes' walk down Ady utca towards the lake, where you can hire canoes, or on the river itself at Tiszaörvény, accessible by regular buses from Tiszafüred, with **horse-riding** on offer at Füredi út 1 (☎59/353-936) and Esze Tamás utca 2/b (☎59/351-814). There are also **thermal baths** (May–Oct daily; 150Ft) in Tiszafüred, near Tourinform.

The **tourist offices** are sited to catch visitors, with Tourinform at Húszöles utca 21A, south of Kossuth tér along the Debrecen road (June–Aug Mon–Fri 8am–7pm, Sat & Sun 8am–4pm; Sept–May Mon–Fri 8am–4pm; ☎59/353-000), and IBUSZ at Fő út 30, in the centre (May–Sept Mon–Fri 9am–4pm, Sat 9am–noon; Oct–April Mon–Fri 9am–4pm; ☎59/353-488). Both can supply private rooms, though it's advisable to book ahead in high season. This also applies to the ritzy *Aurum Panzió* at Ady Endre út 29, towards the lake (☎59/351-338), or the *Hableány Hotel* at Hunyadi utca 2, in Tiszaörvény (☎59/353-000), which offers fishing and boat hire. Tiszafüred has three campsites: *Tóparti Kemping* (☎59/351-132; ①; April–Oct) and *Flotta Camping* (☎59/352-424; ①; mid-April to mid-Oct) by the lake, and *Termál Camping* opposite Tourinform (☎59/352-911; ①; April–Oct).

At **ABÁDSZALÓK** to the south, the noisy and crowded *Füzes Hotel* (☎59/355-408; ③) and campsite at Feltáro utca 1 is near a beach that rents boats, but a better alternative is the small campsite signposted on the road in from Tiszafüred, or even camping rough further along the shore – though you'll never escape other holidaymakers entirely.

# Szabolcs-Szatmár county

North of Debrecen, the Plain ripples with low ridges of wind-blown sand, anchored by birches, apple groves and tobacco fields. The soft landscape of the *Nyírség* (Birch Region) makes a pleasant introduction to **Szabolcs-Szatmár**, an area scorned by many Magyars as the "black country", mainly a disparaging reference to the region's large Roma population. More densely settled than other parts of the Plain, Szabolcs would be wholly agricultural if not for industrialized Nyíregyháza, straddling the main routes to the Northern Uplands, the Erdőhát villages and Ukraine. Historically isolated by swamps, and then severed from Transylvania and Ruthenia in 1920, the region has remained poor and backward in comparison with the rest of Hungary and was badly hit by recession in the 1990s.

If your interest in **rural life** is limited, stick to **Nyíregyháza**, with its Village Museum, or **Nyírbátor**, with its striking churches – both conveying something of the character of the region. For anyone seeking the challenge of remote areas, encounters with rural Roma, or the folk customs and architecture of old Hungary, though, the county has much to offer. Though sufficient accommodation and transport exists to make independent travel feasible, the only **tourist offices** are in Nyíregyháza. They can, however, supply information on the whole region, and book private accommodation in many towns and villages.

## Nyíregyháza

**NYÍREGYHÁZA** has grown into the Big Apple of Szabolcs county thanks to the food-processing industry developed to feed the Soviet market during the 1960s and 1970s. The collapse of this market has hit the region badly, though other

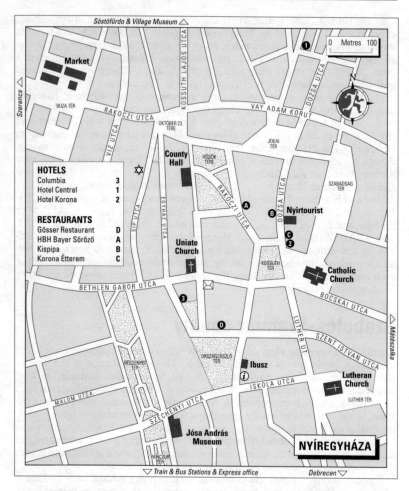

Within the map:

Sóstófürdo & Village Museum △

Market

BUZA TÉR

Szerencs △

RÁKÓCZI UTCA

KOSSUTH LAJOS UTCA

VIZ UTCA

OKTÓBER 23. TÉRE

VAY ADAM KORUT

DÓZSA UTCA

DÓZSA UTCA

JÓKAI TÉR

**County Hall**

HŐSÖK TÉRE

SZABADSAG TÉR

**HOTELS**
Columbia          3
Hotel Central     1
Hotel Korona      2

**RESTAURANTS**
Gösser Restaurant    D
HBH Bayer Söröző     A
Kispipa              B
Korona Étterem       C

SÍP UTCA

EGYHÁZ UTCA

RÁKÓCZI UTCA

Ⓐ
Ⓑ  **Nyírtourist**
Ⓒ
❷

**Uniate Church**

KOSSUTH TÉR

**Catholic Church**

BETHLEN GÁBOR UTCA

BOCSKAI UTCA

❸

Ⓓ

Mátészalka △

LUTHER UT

SZENT ISTVÁN UTCA

BESSENYEI TÉR

ORSZÁGZÁSZLÓ TÉR

**Ibusz**
ⓘ

ISKOLA UTCA

**Lutheran Church**

LUTHER TÉR

MALOM UTCA

SZÉCHENYI UTCA

**Jósa András Museum**

RENCZÚR TÉR

**NYÍREGYHÁZA**

▽ Train & Bus Stations & Express office          Debrecen ▽

businesses have sprung up in response to the flood of shoppers and traders from the CIS. The town itself (pop. 121,000) has a core of old buildings girdled by factories and housing estates, with a garden suburb, **Sóstófürdő**, to the north. The best time to come is the first Saturday in September, when a **carnival** inaugurates the month-long **Nyírség Autumn** arts festival.

A trawl of the downtown area yields several monuments that cast a bit more light on Nyíregyháza's history. Its confessional diversity is symbolized by three **churches** – Catholic on Kossuth tér, Lutheran on Luther tér, and Uniate on Bethlen utca – plus a **synagogue** at the top of Síp utca. The latter has recently been restored and contains some lovely murals; if closed, ask for the key at the *Izraelita Hitközösség* (☎42/310-565). Ethnographic and archeological material appears in the **Jósa András Museum**, beyond pastel-hued Országzászló tér (Tues–Sat 9am–4pm, Sun 9am–2pm; 100Ft), along with rooms devoted to the painter Gyula Benczúr and the epicurean writer Gyula Krúdy, both of whom were born in Nyíregyháza in the mid-nineteenth century.

However, the most cosmopolitan place in town is the **"Comecon Market"** on Rákóczi út (not to be confused with the regular daily market on Búza tér nearer the centre), where Ukrainians, Magyars, Poles and Romanians barter and sell everything from fur hats to cars. The best times to go are weekend mornings and weekday afternoons (bus #1A from the centre), but check with the tourist office before setting out, as the location and timing can change.

### Sóstófürdő and the Village Museum

Nyíregyháza's chief attraction is the leafy resort of **Sóstófürdő** ("Salty Lake Bath"), 7km north of the city. Buses and trains bring you to the striking but defunct *Krudy Hotel*, from where the Village Museum is a short walk to the left, and the baths straight ahead. There is also a branch of Tourinform in the old water tower (May–Sept daily 9am–5pm). Should you fancy a wallow, the **thermal baths** are on Blaha Lujza sétány (mid-May to mid-Sept daily 9am–7pm; 230Ft; 120Ft after 4pm), near the Igrice tourist complex and lake, where boats can be rented.

The main reason for coming, though, is the outdoor **Village Museum** (Tues–Sun: April to mid-June 9am–5pm; mid–June to Aug 9am–6pm; Sept–Oct 9am–5pm; ☎42/479-704; 100Ft). This *Skanzen* represents architecture from five different ethnographic regions within the county, complete with Roma dwellings set firmly at the end of the village, a form of segregation that still exists today. With clothes hanging on the washing-line, tables laid and boots by the hearth, the farmsteads appear to have been abandoned by their occupants only yesterday, leaving mute testimony to their lives in a nineteenth-century Szabolcs village. In this world, the size of the barns and stables denoted a family's wealth, as did the presence of a Beam Gate opening onto the street: "A gate on a hinge, the dog is big, the farmer is great", runs an old proverb. Other clues to social standing are the knick-knacks beloved of the "sandled nobility" or petty gentry, and the placing of a bench between two windows in Orthodox households. A single communal bowl speaks volumes about life in the poorest dwellings, but it's worth renting an audioguide in English to learn more. There is a café in the village tavern, and a restaurant, too.

### Practicalities

Arriving at the **bus or train station** on Petőfi tér, 1km south of the centre, you can obtain a street map from Express at Arany utca 2, before catching bus #8 or #8A downtown, riding on to Sóstófürdő at the end of the line if you prefer. It is also accessible by a narrow-gauge line from Nyíregyháza's main station, the Balsa-Dombrád line. Most other buses leave from Jókai tér, in the centre. Tourinform (Mon–Fri 9am–5pm; ☎42/312-606) and IBUSZ (Mon–Thurs 8am–4pm, Fri 8am–3pm, Sat 8am–noon; ☎42/312-695) on Országzászló tér are better for **information** than Nyírtourist on Dózsa György utca (Mon–Fri 8am–4pm; ☎42/490-344).

**Accommodation** is broadly divided between Sóstófürdő and the centre. In **Sóstófürdő**, just past the Village Museum turn-off, you'll find *Fenyves Camping* and its hostel (☎42/402-036; ①; June–Aug); and *Igrice Camping* and the *Summer Village* near the baths (☎42/479-705; mid-May to Sept), the latter offering fancy bungalows (⑤) and humbler chalets (①). The *Svájci Lak* ("Swiss Chalet") by the water tower boasts of having once accommodated Gyula Krúdy and the singer, Lujza Blaha, and now has minibars, TVs and phones in its rooms (☎42/405-793;

④). Further up the road is the *Paradise Hotel* at Sóstói út 76 (☎42/402-011; ③). In July and August and at weekends throughout the year you may also be able to get beds (①) in the *Tanárképző Főiskola*, 3km from the centre of town at Sóstó út 31/b (☎42/402-488 or ask at Express or IBUSZ).

**Downtown** offers a choice between three fancy establishments, the *Hotel Central* on Nyár utca (☎42/411-330; ④), the *Hotel Korona* at Dózsa György utca 1–3 (☎42/409-300), and the *Columbia Pension* at Egyház út 1 (☎42/313-108; ③) – plus a seedier truck-drivers' stopover, the *Palmero Panzió* at Széchenyi utca 16 (☎42/315-777; ②).

The *Kispipa* across the street from Nyírtourist is your best bet for **eating**, though the cheap self-service *Korona Étterem* (11am–3pm) is also recommended. More expensive places that are equally good for **drinking** are the *John Bull Pub* within the *Hotel Korona* complex, the *Gösser Restaurant* on Országzászló tér and the *HBH Bayer Söröző* on Hősök tere. There's a *Cyber Café* at Szarvas utca 1–3 on the eighth floor of the former Communist Party headquarters (Mon, Wed, Fri 2–5pm). Nyíregyháza's liveliest **nightspots** are the *Bahnhof Music Club* at Bethlen Gábor utca 24, which has regular concerts and visiting DJs (Thurs–Sat at 8pm), and the *Shamrock Irish Pub* on Korányi Frigyes utca, featuring every beer you can imagine, and seventies sounds (open daily).

## Nagykálló and Máriapócs

"Go to **NAGYKÁLLÓ!**" used to be a popular insult east of the Tisza, referring to the large mental asylum in this small town of converging houses painted a flaky ochre. The asylum still stands at one end of the long and eerily empty main square, but such visitors as the town receives come for quite different reasons. The big attraction is the annual *Téka Tábor*, a workshop-cum-**festival of Hungarian folk arts** held in a weird "barn" shaped like a Viking's helmet, amid a cluster of other buildings designed by Imre Makovecz, 2km north of the centre. The event occurs in late June and lasts about ten days; you can obtain the exact dates from the Nagykálló Cultural Centre at Báthori utca 1 (☎42/263-141), the Téka Együttes in Budapest (☎06/309-401-242; *teka@mail.datanet.hu*), or tourist offices in Debrecen or Nyíregyháza.

For Hasidic Jews, however, Nagykálló is a cradle of the Satmar sect, one of the largest in the diaspora (see box opposite). Two reminders of Nagykálló's once sizeable Jewish population can be found on Nagybalkáni út, running off the other end of the main square from the asylum. A plaque at the top of the street on the right indicates the former Jewish school, while the Jewish cemetery further down harbours the **tomb of Rabbi Isaac Taub**, one of the most revered of the Hungarian Hasidic rabbis, who was called "the miracle rabbi" and credited with writing the plaintive folk tune *Szól a kakás már* (The cock has crowed). Hundreds of pilgrims come in early spring (7th of Adar by the Jewish calendar) to ask for his help. The key to his shrine (in the red and yellow building behind the wall) is available from András Barna at Széchenyi utca 6, near the main square.

**MÁRIAPÓCS**, off the road between Nagykálló and Nyírbátor, is a place of pilgrimage for the Orthodox and Catholic faithful, and especially for the Roma. Its **Orthodox Church** contains an icon of the Virgin that has been seen to shed tears since 1696, and there are crutches and other tokens of infirmity attesting to miraculous cures. Now that old identities are reasserting themselves across the

## THE SATMAR HASIDS

The pilgrims who come and pray at Rabbi Taub's tomb are members of the **Satmar sect**, which originated in the town of Satu Mare (Szatmár in Hungarian) in what is now Romania. Like the better-known Lubavitchers, the Satmars follow **Hasidism**, a form of Judaism founded by Jewish mystics in southern Poland in the mid-eighteenth century as a movement of spiritual renewal. The rabbinical authorities of the day denounced the Hasidim, or "pious ones", on the grounds that "they conduct themselves like madmen... and turn over like wheels with the head below and the legs above". Their ecstatic worship and emphasis on song and dance as an expression of joy, their strict laws on dress, diet and everyday life, and their use of Yiddish appealed to the poor village communities of Jews, and the movement won millions of adherents in Poland, Romania, Hungary and the Ukraine.

It was only because so many Hasids emigrated to the US, Canada, Britain and Australia between the 1890s and 1930s that Hasidism survives today. In Central and Eastern Europe, the distinctively dressed Yiddish-speaking Hasid communities were easy targets for the Fascists, and there was little opposition to the Holocaust from local Gentiles. With frightening ease a whole way of life was cleaned out of the region, leaving only vandalized synagogues and cemeteries. In Hungary ninety percent of provincial Jews perished, whereas about half of the Jews of Budapest survived (few of whom were Hasids). The traditions of the old country are now preserved by the descendants of emigrants, who now return to visit the tombs of the great rabbis in Nagykálló, Bodrogkeresztúr and Sátoraljaújhely.

Carpathians, Máriapócs has become a spiritual focus for ethnic Magyars and Uniate Christians in Romania, Slovakia, Ukraine and the Voivodina – in 1991, 200,000 worshippers from all round the region attended an open-air papal mass here. **Pilgrimages** occur on August 15 (the Feast of the Assumption), and the Saturday closest to September 8, which is particularly holy to Roma. The train station is at least 3km from the village, making buses a better bet. For **accommodation** there is the colourful *Fekete Bárány Fogadó* by the station (☎42/385-722; ②–③), which has a restaurant.

# Nyírbátor and around

The tangled history of Trans-Carpathia has also left its mark on **NYÍRBÁTOR**, an attractive small town whose name recalls the **Báthori family**, a Transylvanian dynasty which veered between psychopathic sadism and enlightened tolerance. Both attributes are subtly manifest in Nyírbátor's two exquisite churches, which were equally funded by the Báthoris in an age when religious strife was the norm. Both lie a short distance from the main square, Szabadság tér, which is ten minutes' walk from the bus and trains stations on Ady Endre utca. The churches are a superb venue for **concerts** of choral and chamber music from mid-July to early September, the high point being the **Music Days** in August; details from Tourinform in Nyíregyháza.

## The Calvinist Church

Sited on a grassy hillock above Báthori utca, the **Calvinist Church** was originally founded as a Catholic church in the 1480s, complete with a fourteen-seat pew that's now in the National Museum in Budapest. At the back of its web-vaulted

Gothic nave lies the **tomb of István Báthori**, whose sleeping figure indicates that he died in bed, but reveals nothing of the character of this Transylvanian Prince. Hungarian history judges him a shrewd ruler, forgiving his machinations against the Transylvanian Saxons, and the bouts of orgiastic cruelty for which István atoned by endowing churches. Scholars are less willing, however, to dismiss the tales about his cousin, the "Blood Countess" Báthori. It's possible that she, too, is buried here, as her body was reputedly removed from Aachtice after relatives of her victims protested, and it might well have been reburied in the Báthori crypt at Nyírbátor.

When the church turned *Református* in the late sixteenth century, it was obliged to erect a freestanding **wooden bell-tower**, since only Catholic churches were permitted stone belfries during the Counter-Reformation. From its wide-skirted base, the tower rises to a defiant height of thirty metres, with a spire like a wizard's hat sprouting four mini-towers known as *fiatorony* ("sons of the tower"), symbolizing a civic authority's right to execute criminals. Its hand-cut shingling and oak-pegged joists and beams can be inspected from the crooked stairway up to the balcony and bell chamber.

## The Minorite Church and Báthori Museum

István Báthori's other legacy to Nyírbátor is located on Károlyi Mihály utca, and signposted from the main square. Paid for by the spoils of war against the Turks (who, perhaps appropriately, gutted it in 1587), the **Minorite Church** contains fantastic Baroque wood carvings from Eperjes in Slovakia. The altars swarm with figures wearing disquieting expressions, suggestive of István's soul but actually commissioned by János Krucsay around 1730. To gain admission, ring at the side door marked *plébánia csengője*, which leads to an exhibition of photos of ancient Szabolcs churches.

Next door you'll find the **Báthori Museum** (Mon–Fri 8am–4pm; 100Ft), where various relics with unintelligible captions trace the history of the dynasty, whose estates included most of **Szatmár**. Though predominantly inhabited by Hungarians, this region was bisected as a result of the Treaty of Trianon, which allotted the provincial capital (nowadays called Satu Mare) and its surroundings to Romania. Relations have been awkward, if not hostile, ever since, which partly explains the small number of border crossings in these parts.

## Practicalities

**Accommodation** in Nyírbátor is better than average, with the pleasant *Mátyás Panzió* at Hunyadi utca 8 (☎42/281-657; ②) and the flashier *Bástya Hotel* next door, west of the main square (☎42/281-657; ③), and the *Hotel Hódi* in a beautiful old town house at Báthori utca 11 (☎42/281-012; ④), plus the small *Holdfény Camping* on Széna tér (☎42/281-494; ①; mid-June to late Aug). Private rooms are bookable through the tourist office in Nyíregyháza.

Tasty **meals** can be had at the restaurant in the *Hotel Hódi* or the cheaper *Kakukk* at Szabadság tér 21 (open till 9pm), while for dessert you can head for the *Csekő Cukrászda* at Bajcsy-Zsilinszky út 62. There's an outdoor **market** on the corner of Váci and Fürst utcas.

On weekdays there are two **buses** a day between Nyírbátor and Mátészalka, 21km away, which, like the buses for the nearby villages, depart from the station forecourt.

# Mátészalka, Nagyecsed and Vaja

A shabby fusion of flaking estates and low yellow houses, **MÁTÉSZALKA**'s sole claim to fame is that it's the birthplace of the parents of the actor **Tony Curtis**. When he paid a visit recently he was fêted and driven around in a carriage, but though he promised funds nothing has come of it. To make its present poverty more galling, Mátészalka was once at the forefront of progress as the first town in provincial Hungary to be lit by electricity – though as the carts, wood carvings and ceramics in the **Szatmár Museum** at Kossuth út 5 (Tues–Fri 10am–4pm, Sat & Sun 10am–3pm; 100Ft) attest, its urbanity was merely a veneer on what was, and still is, an extended village. On the same street stands Mátészalka's former **synagogue**, locked and disintegrating like the rabbi's house behind it at no. 37.

The museum and synagogue can be found by turning right off Bajcsy-Zsilinszky utca, leading off the main square, Hősök tere, which is ten minutes' walk from the bus and train stations. If you need **to stay**, the Swiss-chalet-style *Kristály Panzió* at Eötvös utca 17 (☎44/312-036; ②) is preferable to the *Szatmár Hotel* on Hősök tere (☎44/310-428; ③), or booking a private room through IBUSZ in Nyíregyháza (there is no tourist office in Mátészalka). More likely, though, you'll want **transport** to somewhere else. There are regular buses to Nagyecsed and Vaja (see below), and both buses (ten daily, two at weekends) and trains (three–four daily) to Csenger and Fehérgyarmat in the Erdőhát region. Other slow trains (five daily) run up to Vásárosnamény and Záhony, and across the border to Carei in Romania.

The small town of **NAGYECSED**, 15km south, deserves a mention as the birthplace of the **"Blood Countess" Báthori**, the most notorious of the Báthori clan (see p.238). In the 1560s Ecsed was a palatial Renaissance court surrounded by mires and quicksands, where the family's ancestor Vid Báthori reputedly slew a dragon (hence the Báthori coat of arms, a dragon coiled around three dragon's teeth). It was here that Erzsébet Báthori spent her childhood till she was sent to marry Ferenc Nádasdy at Sárvár. Alas for sensation-seekers, nothing remains of the palace but a few stones.

A tangible relic of the past is the **fortified manor** (Tues–Sun: April–Oct 9.30am–5.30pm; Nov–March 8am–4pm; 80Ft) 14km northwest of Mátészalka in **VAJA**, the feudal seat of Ádám Vaj, an early supporter of Rákóczi's campaign against the Habsburgs. Within its thick stone walls, visitors in felt slippers shuffle across the parquet from room to room, gaping at painted furniture and the grand meeting hall, the *Rákóczi-terem*. The school next door can sometimes provide **accommodation** (☎44/385-317).

# The Erdőhát

The **Erdőhát** is Hungary's most isolated region, a state imposed by nature and confirmed by history. Meandering and flooding over centuries, the headwaters of the Tisza and its tributaries carved out scores of enclaves beneath the flanks of the Subcarpathians, where dense oak forests provided acorns for pig-rearing and ample timber for building. Though invaders were generally deterred by Escedi Swamp and similar obstacles, scattered communities maintained contact with one another through their intricate knowledge of local tracks and waterways. When

the borders came down like shutters in the twentieth century, people were suddenly restricted to three tightly controlled frontier crossings, which have been only partially relaxed since the demise of Communism.

Roads are poor and motor vehicles are rare in these parts, but if you're interested in rural customs and architecture that's almost extinct elsewhere in Hungary, the Erdőhát **villages** are worth the effort. Two small towns, Fehérgyarmat and Vásárosnamény, serve as jumping-off points for the region.

## Fehérgyarmat and Vásárosnamény

Much of the southern Erdőhát is accessible from **FEHÉRGYARMAT**, a small town whose main street is one long park. The train station is ten minutes' walk south of the centre, while the bus station is at the foot of the main street along Móricz Zsigmond út. Its only sights are a Calvinist church with a **medieval tower** topped by a Transylvanian wooden spire, and the **Szatmár-Bereg National Conservation Museum** at Vörösmarty utca 1 (Tues–Sun 9am–5pm; 50Ft), with a collection of paintings and photos of the local flora and fauna. As the only **accommodation** is the grotty *Hotel Szamos* by the bus station (☎44/362-211; ②) you'd do better staying in one of the villages. **Buses** fan out to Tivadar (hourly), Gyügye (less frequently), Csaroda (Mon–Sat two daily), Vásárosnamény and Csengersima (both Mon–Sat five daily; one on Sun), while **trains** to Zajta (two–three daily) can drop you at Nagyszekeres or Gacsály.

Villages in the northern Erdőhát are generally easier to reach by bus from **VÁSÁROSNAMÉNY**, an erstwhile trading post on the "salt road" from Transylvania, whose **Beregi Museum** at Rákóczi utca 13 (Tues–Fri 8.30am–4.30pm, Sat & Sun 8am–4pm; 50Ft) displays local embroidery and cast-iron stoves from Munkachevo, with a room devoted to Erdőhát funerary customs. Local **accommodation** is surprisingly good, with a fancy new hotel in the *Marianna Centre* on Szabadság tér (☎45/470-401; ③) and the likewise decent *Fehér Hotel* at Bereg köz 1–4 (☎45/471-073; ③), opposite the police station. The *Turista szálló* at Szabadság tér 26 (☎45/480-060; ①) is a humbler option. There's also a **campsite** across the Tisza in Gergelyiugornya (☎45/371-076; ①; May to mid-Sept), a small resort whose holiday homes are raised on stilts as protection against flooding; hourly buses run here from June to August 25. **Buses** run from Vásárosnamény to Tákos, Csaroda and Vámosatya every couple of hours. An interesting feature of the **train** ride north to Záhony is the abundance of tank-loading ramps from the Warsaw Pact days, now overgrown and rusting away.

## Around Szatmárcseke and Túristvándi

If you don't fancy staying in Fehérgyarmat, there's a small **campsite** in **TIVADAR**, 10km north of town and within walking distance of Tarpa (see over-leaf). The riverbank here has a *strand* whose water is cleaner than at Vásárosnamény downstream, where the Tisza is joined by the polluted Szamos. As far as sights go, however, there's more to recommend the villages on the other side of the river, further east.

The cemetery at **SZATMÁRCSEKE**, 20km northeast of Fehérgyarmat, contains a number of boat-shaped oaken **grave markers** (*kopjafa*), probably representing the ships that were supposed to transport the souls of the dead to the other world in ancient Finno-Ugric mythology. Beside the entrance is a map indicating Hungarian populations around the world, while nearby is the mausoleum of **Ferenc Kölcsey**, born locally in 1790, who penned the words to Hungary's national anthem. Between April and October, visitors can **stay** at the *Kölcsey Fogadó*, Honvéd utca 6 (44/377-868; ①), which has a **restaurant** attached.

A few kilometres to the south, **TÚRISTVÁNDI** has a picturesque **wooden watermill** whose workings are demonstrated should a group of tourists materi-alize. The key to the mill is kept at the house on the corner, across the main road.

Other fine examples of wooden architecture used to grace Nemesborzova, Vámosoroszi and Botpálad, until they were removed to Szentendre's Village Museum in the 1970s. However, **TISZACSÉCSE** retains the thatched cottage where the novelist and critic **Zsigmond Móricz** was born in 1879, and also affords fine views across the plain towards the Carpathian mountains.

## Further south

The southern Erdőhát is notable for its beautiful churches, folksy adaptations of Gothic or Baroque architecture. Slow trains bound for Zajta can drop you off at **NAGYSZEKERES** or **GACSÁLY**, whose churches feature striking wooden **bell-towers**. Even more appealing is the tiny **church** in **GYÜGYE**, its coffered ceiling decorated with astrological symbols (illuminated in turn by a sunbeam during the course of the year, so the priest says). Gyügye is easily reached by bus from Fehérgyarmat, or you can walk there in an hour from Nagyszekeres.

Committed church buffs might also visit **CSENGER**, where the **Catholic Church** dates from the Middle Ages. Built of red and black brick, it similarly features a superb coffered ceiling with folk Baroque paintings. Csenger is the terminal of the branch line down from Mátészalka; the last train back leaves at 8pm. Should you need **accommodation**, there's the *Csenger Panzió* at Hősök tere 11 (☎44/341-335; ②).

Although **CSENGERSIMA**, a few kilometres north, has been designated a 24-hour **crossing into Romania** – it also happens to be one of the least crowded – the Romanian officials at Petea may refuse to admit travellers after dark. There are five **buses** daily (one on Sun) between Csengersima and Fehérgyarmat, but none across the border.

## North of the Tisza

Another clutch of villages lies north of the Tisza, in the region known as *Bereg*. While some are only accessible from Vásárosnamény, others, such as Csaroda and Tákos, can also be reached from Fehérgyarmat.

**TÁKOS** harbours a wattle-and-daub Protestant **church** dubbed the "Peasants' Notre Dame", with bold floral designs on its gallery and a coffered ceiling painted by Ferenc Asztalos in 1766. As in most village churches, the men sit up front and the women at the back. If the church is shut, track down the lady who has the key around the corner at Bajcsy-Zsilinszky utca 40; she might also be able to help with **accommodation**.

In **CSARODA**, 2km east, is a thirteenth-century **Gothic Church** with a shingled spire – the oldest church in eastern Hungary. Originally built as a Catholic church in the eleventh century, it was decorated a couple of centuries later with frescoes of various saints including Helen, the "smiling saint" (who isn't smiling here). In 1552 the building was turned into a Calvinist church, and red and blue floral designs similar to those found on shepherds' cloaks were added. These were later painted over, remaining hidden from view until the 1960s when restorers brought them back to life by covering them overnight with raw minced meat. The church is normally open from 1 to 6pm daily, but the woman who lives opposite, at Kossuth utca 15, will open it for you if it's closed. Across the road, an old peasants' house has been turned into an exhibition of rural artefacts with a pub/restaurant attached. For **rooms**, ask at József utca 20 (②), en route to the church.

The restorers have also been at work in **TARPA**, to the southeast, where a large horizontal "dry" **mill** (*száraz-malom*) with an intricate conical roof stands amongst the cottages. Another formidable-looking **wooden bell-tower** can be found in **VÁMOSATYA**, 18km northwest of Csaroda.

# Around Kisvárda and Záhony

The fruit-growing area northeast of Nyíregyháza is called the *Rétköz* (Meadow Land) or *Tiszakanyár* (Tisza Bend). Though pretty to drive through, there is little to attract visitors beyond Kisvárda, midway along the road and train line to Záhony, the only border crossing into Ukraine.

## Kisvárda

KISVÁRDA is a backwater **spa** with a **ruined castle** used for staging plays in the summer. Despite being undamaged in the war, a random selection of buildings along the main street have been replaced by ugly modern structures, spoiling the look of Fő utca, which leads to the main square. Just off Fő tér at Csillag utca 5 stands an old **synagogue** with an ornamental ceiling and stained-glass windows, housing the **Rétköz Museum** of local history (April–Oct Tues–Sun 9am–5pm; 80Ft). For **accommodation** there is the *Stil Panzió* at Városmajor utca 60, out beyond the castle (☎45/410-791; ②), a wooden structure with shared showers, which offers secure parking, and the *Bástya Hotel* at Krucsay Marton út 2, in the centre of town (☎45/421-100; ②), with en-suite bathrooms, while motorists could also stay at the *Kastély Vendégház* in the village of Dombrád, 14 km to the west at Erzsébet utca 24 (☎42/444-029; ②).

---

### INTO THE UKRAINE

Obtaining **Ukrainian visas** is an uncertain business, best done at the Ukrainian Embassy in Budapest or elsewhere, and *not* at the border. The **road crossing** is a narrow bridge, easily found by following the traffic, but notorious for robberies and car thefts. Even **customs** at Chop on the Ukrainian side may be out to extort cash or confiscate desirable items. The reason for this becomes apparent once you enter Trans-Carpathia, the mountainous region traditionally known as **Ruthenia**, control of which has passed from Hungary to Czechoslovakia to the USSR to the Ukraine within the last eighty years. This forgotten corner of Central Europe is as poor and backward as Albania, with a tradition of emigration that took Andy Warhol and Robert Maxwell to their adoptive countries. Its ethnic mix includes Hungarians, Slovaks, Roma and Romanians, not to mention a large number of Ruthenians (*Rusyns*), who cling to their Uniate faith.

The main road and rail line run through **UZHGOROD** (also a border crossing into Slovakia), known as *Ungvár* to its Hungarian-speaking inhabitants. Another road heads east to **MUKACHEVO** (*Munkács*), the site of a last-ditch battle against the Habsburgs during the Kuruc War. From here, the road continues across the mountains towards the Ukrainian city of Lvov, via the **Verecke Pass** through which Árpád led the Magyar tribes into the Carpathian Basin.

---

## Záhony and Zsurk

ZÁHONY is the "front line" between relatively prosperous, westernized Hungary and the impoverished masses of the former Soviet Union. When travel restrictions were eased in 1990, people flooded in from Ukraine and Russia to trade goods for foodstuffs at the "**free**" **market** on the edge of town, until controls were reimposed the following year. Since then, spivs and dealers from Hungary and Poland drive across the border to do business in Uzhgorod, using Záhony as a base. Unless you relish hobnobbing with such characters, however, the only reason to come here is another picturesque **church** with a wooden belfry, in the nearby village of **ZSURK**.

Should either prospect appeal, it's possible to stay at the *Európa Panzió* at Ady Endre út 4, near the station in Záhony (☎45/425-835; ②). There are **trains** from here down to Nyíregyháza and Debrecen, but you are not allowed to board international expresses running in either direction.

## travel details

### Trains

**Budapest (Keleti or Nyugati Station)** to: Békéscsaba (5 daily; 2hr 30min); Debrecen (11 daily; 2hr 30min–3hr 30min); Kecskemét (12 daily; 1hr 30min); Nyíregyháza (11 daily; 3hr–3hr 30 min); Szeged (8 daily; 2hr 30min).

**Baja** to: Bátaszék (7 daily; 20min); Budapest (4 daily; 4hr); Kiskunhalas (7 daily; 1hr 15min);.

**Békéscsaba** to: Budapest (5 daily; 2hr 30min); Szeged (7 daily; 2hr).

**Debrecen** to: Budapest (11 daily; 2hr 30min–3hr 30min); Hortobágy (5 daily; 1hr); Mátészalka (6 daily; 1hr 30min); Nyírbátor (6 daily; 1hr); Nyíregyháza (every 30min; 30–45 min).

**Kalocsa** to: Kiskőrös (5 daily; 1hr).

**Kecskemét** to: Bugac (3 daily; 1hr); Szeged (7 daily; 1–2hr).

**Kiskőrös** to: Kalocsa (4 daily; 1hr).

**Kiskunhalas** to: Baja (7 daily; 1–2hr).

**Mátészalka** to: Csenger (3 daily; 1hr); Vásárosnamény (4 daily; 30min); Záhony (4 daily; 1hr).

**Nyíregyháza** to: Mátészalka (4 daily; 1hr 30min); Nagykálló (4 daily; 15min); Nyírbátor (4 daily; 1hr 15min).

**Szeged** to: Békéscsaba (6 daily; 2hr); Budapest (8 daily; 2hr 30min); Kecskemét (6 daily; 1hr 15min); Tokaj (hourly; 30min).

### Buses

**Budapest (Népstadion)** to: Baja (every 1–2hr; 3hr 15min); Békéscsaba (3 daily; 4hr); Kalocsa (every 1–2hr; 2hr); Szeged (1 daily; 3hr 45min).

**Baja** to: Budapest (every 1–2hr; 3hr 15min); Kalocsa (hourly; 1hr); Kecskemét (8 daily; 2hr 40min); Mohács (7 daily; 40min); Pécs (9 daily; 2hr); Szeged (8 daily; 2hr 15min); Szekszárd (11 daily; 40min).

**Békéscsaba** to: Abádszálok (2 daily; 3hr 15min); Békés (hourly; 30min); Budapest (3 daily; 4hr); Debrecen (8 daily; 3hr); Eger (2 daily; 5hr); Gyula

(hourly; 1hr); Hajdúböszörmény (1 daily; 3hr 30min); Miskolc (1 daily; 5hr); Pécs (1 daily; 6hr 30min).

**Csongrád** to: Baja (2 daily; 3hr); Budapest (6 daily; 3hr); Gyula (2 daily; 2hr); Szeged (9 daily; 1hr 15min); Szentes (hourly; 30min).

**Debrecen** to: Abádszálok (1 daily; 3hr 15min); Békéscsaba (6 daily; 3hr 30min); Eger (2 daily; 3hr); Gyöngyös (1 daily; 4hr 45min); Gyula (1 daily; 3hr); Hajdúböszörmény (every 30–90min; 30min); Hajdúszoboszló (hourly; 45min); Hortobágy (1 daily; 1hr); Jászberény (1 daily; 2hr 30min); Miskolc (every 30–90min; 2hr); Nyíregyháza (1 daily; 2hr); Szeged (2 daily; 5hr); Tiszafüred (2 daily; 1hr 45min).

**Gyula** to: Abádszálok (1 daily; 3hr 45min); Csongrád (2 daily; 2hr); Debrecen (1 daily; 2hr); Eger (1 daily; 5hr 30min); Miskolc (1 daily; 5hr 15min).

**Hajdúböszörmény** to: Debrecen (every 30–90min; 30min); Miskolc (every 30–90min; 1hr 45min).

**Hajdúszoboszló** to: Debrecen (hourly; 45min); Eger (1 daily; 3hr 15min); Hajdúböszörmény (2 daily; 1hr); Hortobágy (1 daily; 1hr 15min); Miskolc (2 daily; 2hr 45min); Nádudvar (hourly; 30min).

**Hortobágy** to: Debrecen (1 daily; 45min); Eger (1 daily; 2hr 15min); Hajdúszoboszló (1 daily; 1hr 15min); Tiszafüred (1 daily; 1hr).

**Jászberény** to: Cegléd (3 daily; 1hr 15min); Debrecen (1 daily; 4hr 30min); Kecskemét (3 daily; 2hr); Miskolc (1 daily; 4hr 45min); Parádfürdő (1 daily; 2hr 15min).

**Kalocsa** to: Baja (hourly; 1hr); Győr (1 weekly; 5hr); Székesfehérvár (1 weekly; 3hr).

**Kecskemét** to: Cegléd (hourly; 30min); Eger (2 daily; 4hr); Gyöngyös (2 daily; 3hr); Jászberény (2 daily; 2hr); Kiskunfélegyháza (hourly; 45min).

**Kiskunfélegyháza** to: Bugac (every 60–90min; 1hr); Kecskemét (hourly; 45min).

**Nyíregyháza** to: Debrecen (1 daily; 2hr); Miskolc (daily except Sun; 2hr).

**Szeged** to: Békéscsaba (4 daily; 2hr); Csongrád (1 daily; 1hr 15min); Debrecen (2 daily; 5hr); Hodmezővásárhely (1 daily; 1hr 30min); Miskolc (1 daily; 6hr 30min); Tiszafüred (1 daily; 5hr).

**Szolnok** to: Eger (2–3 daily; 2hr 30min); Jászberény (1 daily; 1hr 15min).

**Tiszafüred** to: Hodmezővásárhely (1 daily; 4hr 30min); Miskolc (2 daily except Sat & Sun; 1hr 30min); Szeged (1 daily; 5hr); Szentes (1 daily; 3hr 45min).

### International trains

**Békéscsaba** to: Arad (1 daily; 3hr); Bucharest (1 daily; 13hr).

**Debrecen** to: Baia Mare (1 daily; 5hr 30min); Belgrade (1 daily; 7hr 45min); Braşov (July–Sept 1 daily; 12hr); Chop (1 daily; 4hr); Cluj (July–Sept 1 daily; 7hr 30min); Satu Mare (1 daily; 6hr); Valea lui Mihai (2 daily; 3hr).

**Kecskemét** to: Belgrade (1 daily; 5hr 30min); Chop (1 daily; 6hr 45min).

**Szeged** to: Chop (1 daily; 8hr).

**Szolnok** to: Arad (4–5 daily; 4hr); Baia Mare (1 daily; 4hr 30min); Belgrade (1 daily; 6hr); Braşov (4 daily; 11hr); Bucharest (5 daily; 13hr 45min); Cluj (1 daily; 8hr); Košice (1 daily; 4hr 45min); Satu Mare (2 daily; 7hr 45min); Sibiu (1 daily; 11hr 30min).

### International buses

**Baja** to: Subotica (1 daily; 2hr).

**Békéscsaba** to: Arad (4 weekly; 4hr); Timişoara (1 daily; 5hr).

**Csongrád** to: Arad (2 daily; 3hr).

**Debrecen** to: Košice (4 weekly; 4hr); Mukachevo (3 weekly; 7hr); Oradea (March–Sept 1 daily; 3hr 30min); Satu Mare (March–Sept 1 daily; 5hr); Uzhgorod (1 daily; 6hr).

**Gyula** to: Subotica (1 daily; 5hr).

**Hajdúszoboszló** to: Oradea (March–Sept 3 weekly; 4hr); Satu Mare (March–Sept 2 weekly; 5hr); Trebišov (June–Sept 2 weekly; 5hr).

**Kecskemét** to: Subotica (1 daily except Sun; 3hr); Tatranská Lomnica (July–Aug 1 daily; 9hr).

**Nyíregyháza** to: Košice (1 daily; 3hr); Satu Mare (1 daily; 4hr); Uzhgorod (1 daily; 5hr).

**Szarvas** to: Arad (2 weekly; 5hr); Timişoara (2 weekly; 6hr).

**Szeged** to: Arad (1 daily; 4hr); Novi Sad (1 daily except Sun; 4hr); Subotica (4–5 daily except Sun; 2hr); Timişoara (1 daily; 5hr); Zrenjanin (1 daily; 4hr).

**Szolnok** to: Baia Mare (1 daily; 9hr); Oradea (1 daily; 4hr 30min); Satu Mare (1 daily; 7hr 30min).

# PART THREE

# THE

# CONTEXTS

A BUDAPESTI ZENEI HETEKEN

Nádor étterem

Nádor kávéhá

Pannonia étte

Drinkbár

Nádor söröző

Mecsek cukrászda

Minaret étterem

10124
KECSKEMÉT
SZEMÉLYV. 2. OSZT.
TELJESÁRÚ
MENETJEGY
48
0

# HISTORICAL FRAMEWORK

The region of the Carpathian basin known as Hungary (*Magyarország*) changed hands many times before the Magyars arrived here at the end of the ninth century, and its history is marked by migrations, invasions and drastic changes, as Asia and Europe have clashed and blended. Over the centuries borders have shifted considerably, so geographical limits as well as historical epochs are somewhat arbitrary. Transylvania, an integral part of Hungary for hundreds of years, was lost to Romania in 1920, and the plight of its Magyar minority remains a contentious issue, while the situation of ethnic Hungarians in Serbia and Slovakia is also a cause for national concern.

## PREHISTORY

Although recorded history of the area now covered by Hungary begins with the arrival of the Romans, archeological evidence of **Stone Age** (3,000,000–8000 BC) humans has been found in the Istállóskő and Pilisszántó caves in northern Hungary, suggesting that the earliest inhabitants lived by gathering fruit and hunting reindeer and mammoths. The end of the Ice Age created favourable conditions for the development of agriculture and the domestication of animals, which spread up through the Balkans in the Neolithic era, and was characteristic of the **Kőrös culture** (5500–3400 BC): clans living alongside the River Tisza, herding sheep and

goats and worshipping fertility goddesses. As humans became more settled and spread into Transdanubia, evidence survives of mounds (*tell*) full of artefacts, apparently leading towards the rise of the **Lengyel culture** around Lake Balaton.

During the **Bronze Age** (2000–800 BC), war-like tribes arrived from the Balkans and steppes, introducing cattle and horses. Subsequent migrants brought new technology – iron came with the Cimmerians, and the Asiatic Scythians (500–250 BC) brought the potter's wheel and manufactured goods from Greek traders on the Black Sea coast – while the **Celts**, who super-seded them in the early third century BC, intro-duced glassblowing and left mournful sculp-tures and superb jewellery (most notably the gold treasures of Szárazd-Regöly), before being subdued by the Romans.

## THE ROMANS

The **Roman conquest** was initiated by Augustus at the beginning of the Christian era, primarily to create a buffer zone in **Pannonia** between the empire and the barbarians to the east. By the middle of the first century AD Roman rule extended throughout Transdanubia, from the Sava to the Danube; fortified with *castra*, the river formed the *limes* or military frontier. Trade, administration and culture grew up around the garrison towns and spread along the roads constructed to link the imperial heartland with the far-flung colonies in Dacia (Romania) and Dalmatia (Yugoslavia). Pécs, Sopron, Szombathely and Buda were all Roman towns, as archeological finds have revealed. Some of the best-preserved Roman remains are found in these towns, including Buda's amphitheatre and baths, the ruins of Gorsium near Székesfehérvár, and Szombathely's Temple of Isis.

During the fourth century the Romans began to withdraw from Pannonia, handing over its defence to the Vandals and Jazygians who lived beyond the Danube. In 430 these people fell under the invading **Huns**, whose empire reached its zenith and then fragmented with the death of Attila in 453. Other warring tribes – Ostrogoths, Gepidae and Langobards – occu-pied the region for the next 150 years, before being swept aside by the **Avars**, whose empire survived until the beginning of the eighth century, when the region once again came up for grabs for any determined invader.

## THE MAGYARS

The **Magyars'** origins lie in the Finno-Ugric peoples who dwelt in the snowy forests between the Baltic and the middle Urals. Around the first century AD, some of these tribes migrated south across the Bashkiran steppes and fell under the influence of Turkic and Persian culture, gradually becoming tent-dwelling nomadic herders who lived on a diet of mare's milk, horse flesh, fish and berries. Some archeologists believe that they mingled with the ancient Bulgars north of the Caspian Sea (in a land known as "Magna Bulgaria"), before the majority fled from marauding Petchenegs in about 750 and moved westwards to settle on the far bank of the River Don in the so-called Etelköz region, around the year 830. Ties with the Huns and Avars have been postulated, including a common language, but there's more evidence to link the seven original Magyar tribes with three Kavar tribes, known collectively as the Onogur, or "Ten Arrows".

Overpopulation and Petcheneg attacks forced the Onogur to move westwards in 889, and tradition has it that the seven Magyar chieftains elected **Árpád** as their leader, pledging fealty to his heirs with a blood oath. Accompanied by smaller Kun (or Cuman) tribes, the Onogur entered the Carpathian basin in 896, and began the "**land-taking**" (*honfoglalás*) or conquest of the region. Six Magyar tribes settled west of the Danube and in the upper Tisza region, the seventh took the approaches to Transylvania, while the lower Tisza and the northern fringes of the Plain went to the Kuns and Kavars. The Magyars continued to raid for the next seventy years, striking terror as far afield as Constantinople and Orleans (where people thought them to be Huns), until a series of defeats persuaded them to settle for assimilating their gains.

Civilization developed gradually, after Árpád's great-grandson **Prince Géza** established links with Bavaria and invited Catholic missionaries to Hungary. His son **Stephen (István)** took the decisive step of applying to Pope Sylvester for recognition, and on Christmas Day in the year 1000 was crowned as a Christian king and began **converting** his pagan subjects with the help of Bishop Gellért. Royal authority was extended over the non-tribal lands by means of the *megye* (county) system, and defended by fortified *vár* (castle); artisans and priests were imported to spread skills and the new religion; and tribal rebellions were crushed. Stephen was subsequently credited with the foundation of Hungary and canonized after his death in 1038. His mummified hand and the Crown of St Stephen have since been revered as both holy and national relics.

## THE MIDDLE AGES

Succession struggles raged for decades following Stephen's death, and of the sixteen kings who preceded Andrew II (1205–35) only the humane László I (also canonized), Kálmán "the Booklover" and Béla III contributed anything significant to Hungary's development. Fortunately, invasions were few during the eleventh and twelfth centuries, and **German and Slovak immigrants** helped double the population to about two million by 1200. Parts of **Transylvania** were settled by the Magyars and Székely, perhaps before the second half of the eleventh century, when the "lands of St Stephen" were extended to include **Slavonia** (between the Sava and Drava rivers) and the unwillingly "associated" state of **Croatia**. The growth in royal power caused tribal leaders to rebel in 1222, when Andrew II was forced to recognize the "noble" status and rights of **the Natio** – landed freemen exempt from taxation – in the "Golden Bull", a kind of Hungarian Magna Carta.

Andrew's son **Béla IV** was trying to restore royal authority when disaster struck from the east – the **Mongol invasion** of 1241, which devastated Hungary. Hundreds of towns and villages were sacked; refugees fled to the swamps and forests; crops were burned or left unharvested; and famine and plague followed. Population losses ranged from sixty to one hundred percent on the Plain and twenty percent in Transdanubia, and after the Mongol withdrawal a year later (prompted by the timely death of the Khan) Hungary faced a mammoth task of **reconstruction** – the chief achievement of Béla's reign, to which foreign settlers made a large contribution. Renewed domestic feuding (complicated by foreign intervention and the arrival of more Cuman tribes) dogged the reign of Andrew III, and worsened when he died heirless in 1301, marking the **end of the Árpád dynasty**.

### FOREIGN RULE

Foreign powers advanced their own claimants, and for a while there were three competing kings, all duly crowned. **Charles Robert** of the French Angevin (or Anjou) dynasty eventually triumphed in 1310, when his rivals went home in disgust; and despite colonial skirmishes with Venice, Serbia and Wallachia, Hungary itself enjoyed a period of peace, while the Mongols and other great powers were occupied elsewhere. Gold mines in Transylvania and northern Hungary – the richest in Europe – stabilized state finances and the currency. Charles's son **Louis the Great** reigned (1342–82) during a period of expansion, when the population rose to three million; and by war and dynastic aggrandizement crown territory grew to include Dalmatia, the Banat, Galicia and (in theory) Poland. Louis, however, sired only daughters, so that after his demise, another foreigner ascended the throne in 1395 – **Sigismund of Luxembourg**, Prince of Bohemia, whom the nobles despised as the "Czech swine". His extravagant follies and campaigns abroad were notorious, and while Sigismund recognized the growing threat of the Turks he failed to prevent their advance up through the Balkans.

During the fourteenth century, the realm contained 49 boroughs, about 500 market towns and 26,000 villages. Everyone benefited from peace and expanded trade, but the rewards weren't shared evenly, for the Angevins favoured towns and guilds, and, most of all, the top stratum of the Natio, on whom they depended for troops (*banderia*) when war posed a threat. The burden fell upon the **peasantry**, who lacked "free" status and were compelled to pay *porta* (gate tax) to the state, tithes to the church, and one ninth of their produce to the landlords – plus extra taxes and obligations during times of war, or to finance new royal palaces.

Sigismund died in 1447 leaving one daughter, Elizabeth, just as **the Turks** were poised to invade and succession struggles seemed inevitable. The Turks might have taken Hungary then, but for a series of stunning defeats inflicted upon them by **János Hunyadi**, a Transylvanian warlord of Vlach (Romanian) origin. The lifting of the siege of Nándorfehérervár (Belgrade) in 1456 checked the Turkish advance and caused rejoicing throughout Christendom – the ringing of church bells at noon was decreed by the pope to mark this victory – while Hunyadi rose to be *Voivode* or Prince of Transylvania, and later regent for the boy king László. Following Hunyadi's death, László's early demise, and much skulduggery, Mihály Szilágyi staged a coup and put his nephew Mátyás (Matthias), Hunyadi's son, on the throne in 1458.

## RENAISSANCE AND DECLINE

**Mátyás Corvinus** is remembered as the **"Renaissance King"** for his statecraft and multiple talents (including astrology), while his second wife **Beatrice** of Naples lured humanists and artists from Italy to add lustre to their palaces at Buda and Visegrád (of which some remains survive). Mátyás was an enlightened despot renowned for his fairness: "King Mátyás is dead, justice is departed", people mourned. By taxing the nobles (against every precedent) he raised a standing force of 30,000 mercenaries called the Black Army, which secured the realm and made Hungary one of Central Europe's leading powers. However, when he died in 1490 leaving no legitimate heir, the nobles looked for a king "whose plaits they could hold in their fists".

Such a man was Ulászló II (whose habit of assenting to any proposal earned him the nickname "King Okay"). Under his rule the Black Army and its tax base were whittled away by the Diet, which met to approve royal decrees and taxes, while the nobility filched common land and otherwise increased their exploitation of the peasantry. Impelled by poverty, many joined the crusade of 1514, which, under the leadership of **György Dózsa**, turned into an **uprising against the landlords**. Its savage repression (over 70,000 peasants were killed and Dózsa was roasted alive) was followed by the **Werbőczy Code** of 1517, binding the peasants to "perpetual **serfdom**" on their masters' land and 52 days of *robot* (unpaid labour) in the year.

Hungary's decline accelerated as corruption and incompetence bankrupted the treasury, forts along the border crumbled and the revived *banderia* system of mobilization disintegrated. Ulászló's son Louis II was only nine when crowned, and by 1520 the Turks, under Sultan Süleyman "the Magnificent", had resumed their advance northwards, capturing the run-down forts in Serbia. In August 1526 the Turks crossed the Drava and Louis hastened south to confront them at the **battle of Mohács** – a catastrophic defeat for the Magyars, whose army was wiped out together with its monarch and commanders.

## TURKISH CONQUEST: HUNGARY DIVIDED

After sacking Buda and the south, the Turks withdrew in 1526 to muster forces for their real objective, Vienna, the "Red Apple". To forestall this, Ferdinand of Habsburg proclaimed himself king and occupied western Hungary, while in Buda the nobility put **János Zápolyai** on the throne. Following Zápolyai's death in 1541 Ferdinand claimed full sovereignty, but the Sultan occupied Buda and central Hungary, and made Zápolyai's young son ruler of Transylvania. Thereafter Transylvania became a semi-autonomous principality, nominally loyal to the Sultan and jealously coveted by the Habsburgs. The tripartite **division of Hungary** was formally recognized in 1568. Despite various official or localized truces, warfare became a feature of everyday life for the next 150 years, and national independence was not recovered for centuries.

**Royal Hungary** – basically western Transdanubia and the north – served as a "human moat" against the Turkish forces that threatened to storm Austria and Western Europe, who were kept at bay by Hungarian sacrifices at Szigetvár, Kőszeg and other fortresses. Notwithstanding constitutional arrangements to safeguard the Natio's privileges, real power passed to the Habsburg chancellery and war council, where the liberation of Hungary took second place to Austria's defence and aggrandizement, and the subjugation of Transylvania.

**Turkish-occupied Hungary** – *Eyalet-i Budin* – was ruled by a Pasha in Buda, with much of the land either deeded to the Sultan's soldiers and officials, or run directly as a state fief (*khasse*). The peasants were brutally exploited, for many had to pay rent to both their absentee Magyar landlords and the occupying Turks. Their plight is evident from a letter to a Hungarian lord by the villagers of Batthyán: "Verily, it is better to be Your Lordship's slaves, bag and baggage, than those of an alien people." Peasants fled their villages on the Alföld to the safer fields around the expanding "agro-towns" of Debrecen and Szeged, the nexus of the cattle trade which gradually supplanted agriculture, while neglect and wanton tree-felling transformed the Plain into a swampy wasteland – the *puszta*.

The Voivodes of **Transylvania** endeavoured to provoke war between the Habsburgs and Turks, in order to increase their independence from both and satisfy the feudal Nationes. The latter, representing the élite of the region's Magyars, Saxons and Székely, combined to deny the indigenous Vlachs political power, while competing amongst themselves and

extending the borders of Transylvania (then much bigger than today). István Bocskai's Hajdúk forces secured the Szatmár region and Gábor Bethlen promoted economic and social development, but Prince György Rákóczi II aimed too high and brought the wrath of the Sultan down on Transylvania.

**Religion** was an additional complicating factor. The Protestant Reformation gained many adherents in Hungary during the sixteenth century, and, while religious toleration was decreed in Transylvania in 1572, in Royal Hungary the Counter-Reformation gathered force under Habsburg rule. The Turks, ironically, were indifferent to the issue and treated all their Christian subjects (*Rayah*) with equal disdain. After the expulsion of the Turks, Protestant landowners were dispossessed in favour of foreign servants of the crown – a major cause of subsequent anti-Habsburg revolts.

## HABSBURG RULE

After heavy fighting between 1683 and 1699, a multinational army evicted the Ottomans, and the Turks relinquished all claims by signing the **Peace of Karlowitz**. Yet for many years peace remained a mirage, for the Hungarians now bitterly resented Habsburg policy and their plundering armies. The **Kuruc revolt** (1677–85) led by **Imre Thököly** was but a prelude to the full-scale **War of Independence** of 1703–11, when peasants and nobles banded together under **Ferenc Rákóczi II**, György's grandson, and initially routed the enemy. Ultimately, however, they were defeated by superior Habsburg power and the desertion of their ally, Louis XIV of France, and peace born of utter exhaustion came at last to Hungary.

**Habsburg rule** combined force with paternalism, especially during the reign of Empress **Maria Theresa** (1740–80), who believed the Hungarians to be "fundamentally a good people, with whom one can do anything if one takes them the right way". The policy of "impopulatio" settled thousands of Swabians, Slovaks, Serbs and Romanians in the deserted regions of Hungary, so that, in areas such as the "Military Border" along the Sava, Magyars became a minority. By the end of the eighteenth century they formed only 35 percent of the population of the huge kingdom. For the aristocrats it was an age of glory: the Esterházy, Grassalkovich and Batthyány families and their lesser imitators commissioned over 200 palaces, and Baroque town centres flourished. Yet the masses were virtually serfs, using medieval methods that impoverished the soil, and mired in isolated villages. Cattle, grain and wine – Hungary's main exports – went cheap to Austria, which tried to monopolize industry.

The **Germanization** of culture, education, and administration was another feature of Habsburg policy. Yet, though the richest nobles and most of the urban bourgeoisie chose the Habsburg style, the petty gentry and peasantry clung stubbornly to their Magyar identity. The ideals of the **Enlightenment** found growing support among intellectuals, and the revival of the **Magyar language** became inseparable from nationalist politics. **Ferenc Kazinczy**, who refashioned Hungarian as a literary language and translated foreign classics, was associated with the seven **Jacobin conspirators**, executed for plotting treason against the Habsburgs in 1795.

## THE NINETEENTH CENTURY: NATIONALISM AND REFORM

**Magyar nationalism**, espoused by sections of the Natio, became increasingly vocal during the early nineteenth century. Hungary's backwardness was a matter for patriotic shame and self-interested concern, especially after the occurrence of peasant riots in the impoverished, cholera-ridden Zempléni, and the publication of *Hitel* ("Credit"), written by Count István Széchenyi, which scathingly indicted the country's semi-feudal economy. However, most nobles were determined to preserve their privileges. One wrote that "God himself has differentiated between us, assigning to the peasant labour and need, to the lord abundance and a merry life". Moreover, national liberation was seen in exclusively Magyar terms – the idea that non-Magyars within the multinational state might wish to assert their own identity was regarded as subversive.

The **Reform Era** (roughly 1825–48) saw many changes. Business, the arts and technology were in ferment, with Jews playing a major role in creating wealth and ideas (although they remained second-class citizens). The **Diet** became increasingly defiant in its dealings with Vienna over finances and laws, and parliamentarians like Ferenc Deák, Count Batthyány and Baron Eötvös acted in the shadow of the "giants" of the time, Széchenyi and Kossuth, who expounded rival programmes for change.

Count **István Széchenyi**, the landowning, Anglophile author of *Hitel*, was a tireless practical innovator, introducing silkworms, steamboats and the Academy, as well as an unprecedented tax on the Natio to pay for the construction of his life's monument, the Lánchíd (Chain Bridge) linking Buda and Pest. His arch-rival was **Lajos Kossuth**, small-town lawyer turned Member of Parliament and editor of the radical *Pesti Hirlap*, which scandalized and delighted citizens. Kossuth detested the Habsburgs, revered "universal liberty", and demanded an end to serfdom and censorship. Magyar chauvinism was his blind spot, however, and the law of 1840, his greatest pre-revolutionary achievement, inflamed dormant nationalist feelings among Croats, Slovaks and Romanians by making Magyar the sole official language – an act for which his ambitions would later suffer.

### REVOLUTION

The fall of the French monarchy precipitated a crisis within the Habsburg empire, which Kossuth exploited to bring about the **1848 Revolution** in Hungary. The emperor yielded to demands for a constitutional monarchy, universal taxation, wider voting rights and the union of Transylvania with Hungary; while in Budapest the nobles took fright and abolished serfdom when the poet **Sándor Petőfi** threatened them with thousands of peasants camped out in the suburbs. However, the slighted nationalities rallied against the Magyars in Croatia and Transylvania, and the reassertion of Habsburg control over Italy and Czechoslovakia closed the noose. The new emperor Franz Josef declared that Hungary would be partitioned after its defeat, in reaction to which the Debrecen Diet declared **Hungarian independence** – a state crushed by August 1849, when Tsar Nicholas of Russia sent armies to support the Habsburgs, who instituted a reign of terror.

Gradually, brute force was replaced by a **policy of compromise**, by which Hungary was economically integrated with Austria and given a major shareholding in the Habsburg empire, henceforth known as the "Dual Monarchy". The compromise (*Ausgleich*) of 1867, engineered by **Ferenc Deák**, brought Hungary prosperity and status, but tied the country inextricably to the empire's fortunes. Simmering nationalist passions would henceforth be focused against Hungary as much as Austria, and diplomatic treaties between Austria and Germany would bind Hungary to them in the event of war. In 1896, however, such dangers seemed remote, and people celebrated **Hungary's millennial anniversary** with enthusiasm.

## WORLD WAR I AND ITS AFTERMATH

Dragged into **World War I** by its allegiance to the Central Powers, Hungary was facing defeat by the autumn of 1918. The Western or Entente powers decided to dismantle the Habsburg empire in favour of the **"Successor States"** – Romania, Czechoslovakia and Yugoslavia – which would acquire much of their territory at Hungary's expense. In Budapest, the October 30 "Michaelmas Daisy Revolution" put the Social Democratic government of **Mihály Károly** in power, but his government avoided the issue of land reform, attempted unsuccessfully to negotiate peace with the Entente, and finally resigned when France backed further demands by the Successor States.

On March 21, 1919, the Social Democrats agreed on co-operation with the **Communists**, who proclaimed a **Republic of Councils** (*Tanácsköztársaság*) led by **Béla Kun**, which ruled through local Soviets. Hoping for radical change and believing that "Russia will save us", many people initially supported the new regime, but enforced nationalization of land and capital, and attacks on religion, soon alienated the majority. Beset by the Czech Legion in Slovakia and by internal unrest, the regime collapsed in August before the advancing Romanian army, which occupied Budapest.

### THE RISE OF FASCISM

Then came the **White Terror**, as right-wing gangs spread out from Szeged, killing "Reds" and Jews, who were made scapegoats for the earlier Communist "Red Terror". **Admiral Miklós Horthy** appointed himself regent and ordered a return to "traditional values" with a vengeance. Meanwhile, at the Paris Conference, Hungary was obliged to sign the **Treaty of Trianon** (July 4, 1920), surrendering two-thirds of its historic territory and three-fifths of its total population (three million in all) to the Successor States. The bitterest loss was **Transylvania**, whose 103,093 square kilometres and 1.7 million Magyars went to Romania – a devastating blow to national pride.

During the **1920s and 1930s**, campaigning for the overturn of the Trianon *diktat* was the "acceptable" outlet for politics, while workers' unions were tightly controlled and peasants struggled to form associations against the landlords and the gendarmerie, who rigged ballots and gerrymandered as in the old days. Politics were dominated by the *Kormánypárt* (Government Party) led by Count Bethlen, representing the Catholic Church and the landed gentry, which resisted any changes that would threaten their power. Social hardships increased, particularly in the countryside where the **landless peasantry** constituted "three million beggars" whose misery concerned the **Village Explorers** (*Falukutató*), a movement of the literary intelligentsia ranging across the political spectrum. With the Social Democrats co-opted by conservatism and the Communist Party illegal, many workers and disgruntled petits bourgeois turned to the **radical right** to voice their grievances, and were easily turned against Jews and the "Trianon Powers".

Resentment against France, Britain and Romania predisposed many Hungarians to admire **Nazi Germany**'s defiance of the Versailles Treaty – a sentiment nurtured by the Reich's grant of credits for **industrialization**, and Nazi sympathizers within *Volksdeutsche* communities, commerce, the civil service and the officer corps. The rise of **anti-Semitism** gave power to nationalist politicians like **Gyula Gömbös**. At the same time, Hungary's belated industrial growth was partly due to the acquisition of territory from Czechoslovakia, following Germany's dismemberment of the latter. The annexation of Austria made the Reich militarily supreme in Central Europe, and Hungary's submission to German hegemony almost inevitable.

## WORLD WAR II

With the outbreak of **World War II**, the government's pro-Nazi policy initially paid dividends. Romania was compelled to return **northern Transylvania** in July 1940, and Hungary gained additional territory from the invasion of Yugoslavia a year later. Hoping for more, Premier Bárdossy committed Hungary to the Nazi invasion of the USSR in June 1941 – an act condemned by the former Prime Minister, Teleki (who had engineered the recovery of Transylvania), as the "policy of vultures". The Hungarian Second Army perished covering the retreat from Stalingrad, while at home, Germany demanded ever more foodstuffs and forced labour. As Axis fortunes waned Horthy prepared to declare neutrality, but Hitler forestalled him with "Operation Margarethe" – the outright **Nazi occupation of Hungary** in March 1944.

Under Sztójay's puppet government, Hungarian **Jews** were forced into ghettos to await their deportation to Auschwitz and Belsen, a fate hindered only by the heroism of the underground, a handful of people organized by the Swedish diplomat Raoul Wallenberg, and by the manoeuvring of some Horthyite politicians. Mindful of Romania's successful escape from the Axis in August, Horthy declared a surprise armistice on October 15, just as the Red Army crossed Hungary's eastern border. In response, Germany installed a government of the native **Arrow Cross Fascists**, or *Nyilas*, led by Ferenc Szálasi, whose gangs roamed Budapest extorting valuables and murdering people, while the Nazis systematically plundered Hungary. They blew up the Danube bridges and compelled the Russians to take Budapest by storm – a siege that reduced much of Buda to ruins. Meanwhile in Debrecen, an assembly of anti-Fascist parties met under Soviet auspices to nominate a **provisional government**, which took power after the Germans fled Hungary in April 1945.

## THE RÁKOSI ERA

In the November 1945 **elections** the Smallholders' Party won an outright majority, but the Soviet military insisted that the Communists and Social Democrats (with seventeen percent of the vote) remain in government. **Land reform** and limited **nationalization** were enacted, while the Communists tightened their grip over the Ministry of the Interior (which controlled the police) and elections became increasingly fraudulent. **Mátyás Rákosi**, Stalin's man in Hungary, gradually undermined and fragmented the "bourgeois" parties with what he called "salami tactics" (chopping his opponents into small groups and then swallowing them), and by 1948, officially called the **"Year of Change"**, the Communists were strong enough to coerce the Social Democrats to join them in a single **Workers' Party**, and neutralize the Smallholders. Church schools were seized, Cardinal Mindszenty was jailed for "espionage" and the peasants were forced into collective farms. More than 500,000 Hungarians

were imprisoned, tortured or shot in native concentration camps like Recsk, or as deportees in the Soviet Union – victims of the **ÁVO** secret police (renamed the *ÁVH* in 1949), who spread terror throughout society.

Soviet culture and the personality cults of Rákosi (known as "Baldhead" or "Asshole" to his subjects) and Stalin were imposed on the country, and Hungarian classics like the *Tragedy of Man* were banned for failing to meet the standards of Socialist Realism. Under the 1949 **Five Year Plan**, heavy industry took absolute priority over agriculture and consumer production. To fill the new factories, peasants streamed into towns and women were dragooned into the labour force. Living standards plummeted, and the whole of society was subjected to the laws and dictates of the Party. "Class conscious" workers and peasants were raised to high positions and "class enemies" were discriminated against, while Party officials enjoyed luxuries unavailable to the populace, who suffered hunger and squalor.

Although the Smallholders retained nominal positions in government, real power lay with Rákosi's clique, known as the "Jewish Quartet". As elsewhere in Eastern Europe at this time, Hungary saw bitter **feuds within the Communist Party**. In October 1949, the "Muscovites" purged the more independently minded "national" Communists on the pretext of "Titoism". The former Interior Minister **László Rajk** was executed, and his friend and successor (and, later, betrayer), **János Kádár**, was jailed and tortured with others during a second wave of purges. Two years later, following Stalin's death in March 1953, Kremlin power struggles resulted in a more moderate Soviet leadership and the abrupt replacement of Rákosi by **Imre Nagy**. His **"New Course"**, announced in July, promised a more balanced industrial strategy and eased pressure on the peasants to collectivize, besides curbing the *ÁVO* terror. Nagy, however, had few allies within the Kremlin, and in 1955 Rákosi was able to strike back, expelling Nagy from the Party for "deviationism", and declaring a **return to Stalinist policies**. This brief interlude, however, had encouraged murmurings of resistance.

## 1956: THE UPRISING

The first act of opposition came from the official Writers' Union, who, in their November

Memorandum, objected to the rule of force. The Party clamped down, but also began to rehabilitate the Rajk purge victims. During June **1956** the intellectuals' **Petőfi circle** held increasingly outspoken public debates, and **Júlia Rajk** denounced "the men who have ruined this country, corrupted the Party, liquidated thousands and driven millions to despair". Moscow responded to the unrest by replacing Rákosi with **Ernő Gerő**, another hardliner – a move which merely stoked public resentment. The mood came to a head in October, when 200,000 people attended Rajk's reburial, Nagy was readmitted to the Party, and **students** in Szeged and Budapest organized to demand greater national independence and freedom.

In Poland, Gomulka's reform Communists had just won concessions from the Kremlin, and Budapest students decided to march on October 23 to the General Bem statue, a symbol of Polish-Hungarian solidarity. Patriotic feelings rose as about 50,000 people assembled, the procession swelling as it approached Parliament. A hesitant speech there by Nagy failed to satisfy them, and students besieged the Radio Building on Bródy utca, demanding to voice their grievances on the airwaves. In response, the *ÁVH* guards opened fire, killing many. Almost immediately, this triggered a citywide **Uprising** against the *ÁVH*. The regular police did little to control it, and when Soviet tanks intervened units of the Hungarian army began to side with the insurgents.

Over the next five days fighting spread throughout Hungary, despite Nagy's reinstatement as premier and pleas for order. **Revolutionary councils** sprang up in towns and factories and free newspapers appeared, demanding "*Ruszkik haza*" (Russians go home), free elections, civil liberties, industrial democracy and neutrality. Intellectuals who had led the first protests now found themselves left behind by uncontrollable dynamism on the streets. The Party leadership temporized, reshuffled the cabinet and struggled to stay in control, as all the "old" parties reappeared and the newly liberated Cardinal Mindszenty provided a focus for the resurgent Right.

The negotiated **Soviet withdrawal**, beginning on October 29, was merely a delaying tactic, while the Russians regrouped in the countryside before bringing in fresh troops from Romania and the USSR. On November 1, Nagy

announced Hungary's withdrawal from the Warsaw Pact and asked the UN to support **Hungarian neutrality**; that night, Kádár and Ferenc Münnich slipped away from Parliament to join the Russians, who were preparing to crush the "counter-revolution". America downplayed Hungary in the United Nations while the Suez crisis preoccupied world attention, but the CIA-sponsored **Radio Free Europe** encouraged the Magyars to expect Western aid. At dawn on November 4, once Budapest and other centres had been surrounded with tanks under cover of a snowstorm, the **Soviet attack** began.

Armed resistance was crushed within days, but the workers occupied their factories and proclaimed a **general strike**, maintained for months despite **mass arrests**. Deprived of physical power, the people continued to make symbolic protests like the "Mothers' March" in December. Inexorably, however, the Party and *ÁVH* apparatus reasserted its control. Over 200,000 **refugees** fled to the West, while at home thousands were jailed or executed, including Nagy and other leading "revisionists", shot in 1958 after a secret trial.

## KÁDÁR'S HUNGARY

In the aftermath of the Uprising, the new Party leader **János Kádár** ruthlessly suppressed the last vestiges of opposition. After the mid-1960s, however, his name came to be associated with the **gradual reform** of Hungary's social and economic system from a totalitarian regime to one based, at least in part, on **compromise**. Kádár's famous phrase, "Whoever is not against us is with us" (a reversal of the Stalinist slogan), invited a tacit compact between Party and people. Both had been shaken by the events of 1956, and realized that bold changes – as happened in Czechoslovakia in 1967 and 1968 – only invited Soviet intervention, justified by the Brezhnev doctrine of "limited sovereignty".

Having stimulated the economy by cautious reforms in the structure of pricing and management, and overcome opposition within the Politburo, Kádár and Resző Nyers announced the **New Economic Mechanism** (NEM) in 1968. Though its impact on centralized planning was slight, the NEM was accompanied by measures to promote "socialist legality" and make merit, rather than class background and Party standing, the criterion for promotion and higher education.

While generally welcomed by the populace, these reforms angered "New Left" supporters of either Dubček's "Socialism with a human face" in Czechoslovakia or of the Chinese Cultural Revolution, and also, more seriously, conservatives within the Party. With backing from Moscow, they watered down the NEM and ousted Nyers, its leading advocate, from the Politburo in 1973, expelling Hegedüs and other "revisionist sociologists" from the Party later.

Following a power struggle, Kádár was able to reverse the reactionary tide, and reduce constraints on the so-called "second economy". While structural reforms were extremely limited, consumerism, a private sector and even "forint millionaires" emerged during the **1970s**, when Hungary became a byword for **affluence** within the Socialist bloc – the "happiest barracks in the camp", as the joke had it. Mechanics and other artisans with marketable skills were able to moonlight profitably, as demonstrated by the boom in private home-building; and workers and unions acquired some say in the management of their enterprises. This **"market socialism"** attracted the favours of Western politicians and bankers, and before *perestroika* the "Hungarian model" seemed to offer the best hope for reform within Eastern Europe.

In the **1980s**, however, economic and social problems became increasingly obvious, ranging from thirty percent **inflation**, whose effect was felt hardest by the **"new poor"** living on low, fixed incomes, to Hungary's $14.7 billion **foreign debt** (per capita, the largest in Eastern Europe). Despite reformist rhetoric, vested interests successfully resisted the logic of the market, whose rigorous application would entail drastic lay-offs and mass **unemployment** in towns dominated by the unprofitable mining and steel industries. Although frank analyses of Hungary's economic plight started appearing in the media during the mid-1980s, other issues ran up against the limits of state tolerance. These included fears for **the environment** in the wake of Chernobyl and the decision to build a dam at Nagymaros (see Chapter Two); an unofficial **peace movement** that was quickly driven back underground; and any discussion of the Party's "leading role" or Hungary's alliance with the Soviet Union. Discussion of such topics could only be found in **samizdat** (underground) magazines like *Beszélő*, whose publishers were harassed as

dissidents. Although in 1983 the Party announced that "independents" could contest elections, it proved unwilling to let them enter Parliament, as demonstrated by the gerrymandering used against László Rajk in 1986.

Yet the need for change was becoming evident even within the Party, where the caution of the "old guard" – Kádár, Horváth and Gáspár – caused increasing frustration among **reformists**, who believed that Hungarians would only accept income tax and economic austerity if greater liberalization seemed a realistic prospect. Happily, this coincided with the advent of **Gorbachev**, whose interest in the Hungarian model of socialism and desire to bring a new generation into power was an open secret.

## THE END OF COMMUNISM

The **end of Communism in Hungary** was so orderly that it can hardly be termed a revolution, but it did set in motion the collapse of hardline regimes in East Germany and Czechoslovakia. Prefiguring the fate of Gorbachev, the politicians who created an opening for change hoped to preserve Communism by reforming it, but were swept away by the forces which they had unleashed.

At the **May 1988 Party Congress**, Kádár and seven colleagues were ousted from power by a coalition of radical reformers and conservative technocrats. The latter backed **Károly Grósz** as Kádár's successor, but his lacklustre performance as Party leader enabled the reformists to shunt him aside in July 1989, forcing conservatives and hardliners onto the defensive. As the ascendancy of **Imre Pozsgay**, **Rezső Nyers**, **Miklós Németh** and **Gyula Horn** became apparent there was a "traffic jam on the road to Damascus" as lesser figures hastened to pledge support for reforms.

In mid-October 1989, the Communist Party formally reconstituted itself as the **Hungarian Socialist Party** (*MSzP*), dissolved its private militia and announced the **legalization of opposition parties** as a prelude to free elections. To symbolize this watershed, the People's Republic was renamed the **Republic of Hungary** in a ceremony broadcast live on national television, on the thirty-third anniversary of the Uprising.

Meanwhile, the iron curtain was unravelling with astonishing speed. In May, Hungary began dismantling the barbed wire and minefields along its **border** with Austria, and thousands of **East Germans** seized their chance to escape to the West, crossing over via Hungary at a rate of 200 every day. Despite protests from the Honecker regime, Hungary refused to close the border or deport would-be escapees back to the DDR, and allowed 20,000 refugees encamped in the West German embassy in Budapest to leave the country. After the DDR sealed its own borders, frustration spilled over onto the streets of Leipzig and Dresden, where mass demonstrations led to the **fall of the Berlin Wall** (November 9, 1989) and the ousting of Erich Honecker. A week later, the brutal repression of a pro-democracy demonstration in Prague's Wenceslas Square set in motion the "**Velvet Revolution**" in Czechoslovakia, which overturned forty years of Communist rule in ten days. The *annus mirabilis* of 1989 climaxed with the **overthrow of Ceaușescu** in Romania (December 22).

## THE 1990S AND BEYOND

After such events Hungary's first **free elections** since 1945, in 1990, seemed an anticlimax. During the first round of voting on March 6, Pozsgay and the Socialist Party were obliterated, while two parties emerged as front runners. The **Hungarian Democratic Forum** (*MDF*), founded at the Lakitelek Conference of 1987, articulated populist, conservative nationalism, encapsulated in the idea of "Hungarianness", whereas the rival **Alliance of Free Democrats** (*SzDSz*) espoused a neoliberal, internationalist outlook, similar to that of the **Federation of Young Democrats** (*Fidesz*). Two prewar parties revived under octogenarian leaders also participated, namely the **Smallholders' Party** (under the slogan "God, Home, Family, Wine, Wheat and Independence") and the **Christian Democrats**.

Despite being diminished by voter apathy, the **1990 elections** uncermoniously swept the reformist Communists out of power. Their place was taken by a centre-right coalition dominated by the Hungarian Democratic Forum (*MDF*) and its Prime Minister **Jozsef Antall**. A born politician with a schoolmasterly style, Antall relished the opportunity to take a role he had longed for but never expected to get during the Communist years. The model for his Hungary was its prewar state, with the restoration of the **traditions** and the **social hierarchies** that had prevailed at that time. Very much a moderate, his policies rested on the belief that over forty years of Communism had destroyed the true values of Hungarian society. However, not everyone wanted the **Catholic Church** to return to the dominant social position it had enjoyed before the war, and his party's proud belief in restoring the Hungarian nation to its former position sounded to Hungary's neighbours like a revanchist claim on the lost lands of Trianon – an interpretation that was strengthened by Antall's failure to distance himself from the ultra-right-wing nationalism advocated by **István Csurka**.

After Antall's death in 1993, his successor Peter Boross was unable to turn the economy around, and the **1994 elections** saw the **return to power of the Socialists** (reform Communists), assisted by sympathetic media that presented the outgoing government as amateurish and arrogant. To guard against accusations of abusing power as their Communist predecessors had done, the Socialists also brought the Free Democrats into the government. The government's **corruption** became blatant, however, and, though their austerity policies succeeded in bringing an economic up-turn, living standards did not improve for most people.

Despite this, the government still rode high in the opinion polls, helped by the fact that the opposition was in disarray. After its poor showing in the 1994 elections, Fidesz had been repositioned by its leader **Viktor Orbán** to the right of centre, bidding to become the focus of opposition to the Socialist-led government. Orbán adopted phrases about the need to revive national culture that would appeal to the right, and renamed the party Fidesz-Hungarian **Civic Party** (the word for civic – **polgári** – also evokes notions of bourgeois middle-class values). It still seemed, however, that Orbán needed more time to mature as a potential Prime Minister.

Then, in early 1998, the Socialists committed their biggest blunder, announcing that Hungary would go ahead with building the controversial **Nagymaros dam** (see p.154). It was the revenge of Gyula Horn: as a leading figure in the old Communist Party he had given full support to the dam, but it had been condemned as undemocratic; now as Prime Minister of a democratically elected government he could give the go-ahead. At first it looked as if he had got away with it, but as the May **1998 elections** approached, public disillusionment mounted. **Fidesz's win** by a narrow margin came as a surprise to many people – though it was not as unexpected as Csurka's extreme right-wing Hungarian Justice and Life Party (*MIÉP*) breaking the four percent threshold to get into Parliament.

Orbán, given the chance to be the youngest premier in Hungarian history, set about talks with the *MDF* and Smallholders with alacrity in order to form a **coalition** – despite the fact that the prospect of government with the unpredictable Torgyán and his Smallholders worried many Fidesz supporters. Orbán, however, bit the bullet. With a style of leadership that clearly borrows from Britain's Tony Blair, Orbán gives the impression of a man with a mission, dispensing soundbites at every opportunity – everything in Hungary is now *polgári* – though his ruthless style and total control alarms his opponents, who are prone to see the institutions of democracy under threat.

Hungary now seems to be settling down after the transition from Communism, and its political field is narrowing. Fidesz is looking to swallow up the smaller parties of the right, the Christian Democrats, the *MDF*, and perhaps even the Smallholders, while on the left the main party is now the Socialist Party, with the Free Democrats in danger of becoming a fringe party. The major issue for Hungary in the coming years is its relations to Europe. Most Hungarians are fervently behind **membership of the EU**, believing that they will benefit from being under Europe's protective mantle. The new government seems to support it too, though there are several areas of potential conflict to be resolved, such as the desire of most Hungarians to limit **foreign ownership**, which goes against EU directives. With the Fidesz government happy to play the nationalist card, joining Europe looks as if it may become a sticky affair.

# MONUMENTAL CHRONOLOGY

| | | |
|---|---|---|
| 8000 BC | Paleolithic cave-dwellers in the Bükk Mountains. | Remains found at Subalyuk, Szeleta and other caves. |
| 400 BC | Celts enter Transdanubia. | Pottery, glassware; gold treasure of Szárazd-Regöly. |
| 1st–4th c. | **Romans** occupy Pannonia, founding numerous towns. | Ruins at **Aquincum**, **Gorsium**, **Szombathely**, **Pécs**, etc. |
| 896 | Magyar conquest. The Hungarian state and Christianity are established by Stephen I during the eleventh century. | The ruins of the Székesfehérvár Basilica and eleventh-century crypts at Pécs and **Tihany** Abbey are virtually all that remain. |
| 13th c. | Mongol invasion. Castles and new towns are founded during the reign of Béla IV. | **Romanesque churches** at **Ják**, **Zsámbék**, **Őskü**, and **Velemér**, and the **Pannonhalma Monastery**. Ruined *vár* at **Esztergom**, **Füzér** and **Boldogkőváralja**, sited on precipitous crags. |
| 14th–15th c. | Zenith of Hungarian power in Europe under the Angevin monarchs and then Mátyás Corvinus. | Remains of **Buda** and **Visegrád** where **Gothic and Renaissance architecture** attained great heights; **Diósgyőr** castle in Miskolc. |
| 1526–1680s | After defeat at **Mohács**, Hungary is occupied for next 150 years by **Turks** and Habsburgs, and ravaged by warfare. | **Kőszeg**, **Sárospatak**, **Siklós** and other **castles** have remained largely intact; as have a few **Turkish** *türbe*, ex-*djami* and **minarets** at **Pécs** and **Eger**; most medieval towns were destroyed, although on the Plain, Szeged and Debrecen expanded vastly. |
| 1703–11 | Rákóczi War of Independence. | |
| 17th–18th c. | Under **Habsburg rule**, many towns are wholly rebuilt around new centres; while Buda Palace and other monumental buildings are begun. | The **wooden belfrys**, pew-carvings and colourful coffered ceilings found at **Nyírbátor**, **Zsurk**, **Csaroda** and other remote churches in eastern Hungary are partly Gothic, and partly the "folk" equivalent of the **Baroque style**. This combination characterized much of seventeenth- and eighteenth-century architecture, eg in the Belváros of **Győr**, **Veszprém**, **Székesfehérvár**, etc, and at the **Esterházy Palace** in Fertőd. |
| 1830–1880s | After the Reform Era and the struggle for independence (1848–49), Hungary accepts the "Compromise" of 1868. Development of new centres of industry – Miskolc, Salgótarján, Csepel, etc. | The **Chain Bridge** presages a spate of construction in Budapest, where large houses are built alongside the new **boulevards**. **Szeged** rebuilt after 1879 flood. The rise of **Neoclassicism**, with Ybl and Hild's huge basilicas in Eger, Pest and Esztergom, but also **neo-Gothic** – the **Fishermen's Bastion** and **Vajdahunyad Castle** (in 1896, like the Metro) –plus Lechner's attempts to develop a uniquely "**Hungarian Style**" for the **Applied Arts Museum** |
| 1896 | 1000th anniversary of the Magyar conquest. | and the public buildings in **Kecskemét**. |

| | | |
|---|---|---|
| 1918–1919 | Habsburg empire collapses; Hungary briefly becomes a "**Republic of Councils**." | Paintings by the **Group of Eight** (Szombathely Gallery). |
| 1920s & 1930s | Hungary loses two-thirds of its territory to neighbouring states. Regency of **Admiral Horthy**. | Deliberate evocation of past national glories such as the erection of "Heroes' Gates" in **Szeged**, **Kőszeg**, etc. |
| 1944–45 | **Nazis** occupy Hungary; massacre of Hungarian **Jews** and **Gypsies**. Heavy fighting with Soviet army. | Desecration of **synagogues**. Budapest and many towns incur massive damage. This is swiftly repaired. |
| 1948–56 | "**Rákosi era**" characterized by Five Year Plans, police terror and a propaganda blitz. | Crash urbanization and industrialization, with new towns built at **Dunaújváros** and elsewhere. The **Liberation Monument** and other Soviet-style projects are undertaken. |
| 1956 | **Hungarian Uprising**. | Widespread urban damage caused by rioters and police; Budapest is worst affected. |
| 1960s & 1970s | Emergence of "**Kádárism**" and economic reforms to encourage greater public affluence. Hungary becomes a byword for "**consumer socialism**" in Eastern Europe. | The **Metro** is completed. **Modernistic** cultural centres at Győr and Sárospatak are notable examples of 1960s and 1970s **architecture**, while supermarkets, hotels and resorts around Balaton are more typical of the period. |
| 1980s | Economic problems, made worse by energy shortfall after the Chernobyl disaster. | Go-ahead for construction of **Nagymaros dam** and more nuclear reactors at **Paks**. Closure of mines and other loss-making industries is proposed by the state. |
| 1988 | **Grósz** replaces Kadár as Party leader. | |
| 1989 | Grósz replaced by **Németh** and **Pozsgay**. Revolutions in neighbouring Czechoslovakia and Romania. | Nagymaros dam project abandoned. Removal of border fortifications. |
| 1990 | **Free elections** result in **MDF** government. | |
| 1994 | Elections sweep the former Communists to power. | |
| 1998 | Fidesz-Hungarian Civic Party win elections and form centre-right coalition government. | |

# BOOKS

Publishers are detailed below in the form of British publisher/American publisher, where both exist. Where books are published in one country only, UK or US follows the publisher's name. Out of print books are designated o/p. For a gentle introduction to current affairs and literature, look for the Budapest-published *The Hungarian Quarterly*.

## TRAVEL AND GENERAL

**Gerald Gorman**, *Birds of Hungary* (C Helm, UK). The best book available on the ornithological world of the country by a resident expert.

**Gyula Illyés**, *People of the Puszta* (Corvina, UK o/p). An unsentimental, sometimes horrifying immersion in the life of the landless peasantry of prewar Hungary, mainly in Transdanubia. Illyés, one of Hungary's greatest twentieth-century writers, was born into such a background, and the book breathes authenticity. Highly recommended.

**Patrick Leigh Fermor**, *A Time of Gifts* (Penguin); *Between the Woods and the Water* (Penguin). In 1934 the young Leigh Fermor started walking from Holland to Turkey, reaching Hungary in the closing chapter of *A Time of Gifts*. In *Between the Woods and the Water* the gypsies and rusticated aristocrats of the Great Plain and Transylvania are superbly evoked. Lyrical and erudite.

**Ruth Gruber**, *Jewish Heritage Travel: A Guide to Central and Eastern Europe* (Jason Aronson). The most comprehensive guide to Jewish sights in Hungary.

**Imre Móra**, *Budapest Then and Now* (New World Publishing, Budapest). A personal and very informative set of vignettes of the capital, past and present.

**John Paget**, *Hungary and Transylvania* (Ayer, US). Paget's massive book attempted to explain nineteenth-century Hungary to the English middle class, and, within its aristocratic limitations, succeeded. Occasionally found in secondhand bookshops.

**Walter Starkie**, *Raggle-Taggle* (John Murray o/p/Transatlantic Arts o/p). The wanderings of a Dublin professor with a fiddle, who bummed around Budapest and the Plain in search of gypsy music in the 1920s. First published in 1933 and last issued in 1964; a secondhand bookshop perennial.

## HISTORY, POLITICS AND SOCIETY

**Robert Bideleux and Ian Jeffries**, *A History of Eastern Europe: Crisis and Change* (Routledge, UK). Excellent history of the region.

**Judit Frigyesi**, *Béla Bartók and Turn-of-the-century Budapest* (University of California Press). Placing Bartók in his cultural milieu, this is an excellent account of the Hungarian intellectual world at the beginning of the century.

**András Gerő**, *Modern Hungarian Society in the Making: The Unfinished Experience* (Central European University Press, Hungary). A good collection of essays setting Hungary in the context of the Eastern European environment.

**Jörg K Hoensch**, *A History of Modern Hungary 1867–1994* (Longman/Addison-Wesley). A good history of the country on its way from tragedy to tragedy, but with a happy(ish) outcome.

**Bill Lomax**, *Hungary 1956* (Allison & Busby/St Martin's Press o/p). Still probably the best – and shortest – book on the Uprising, by an acknowledged expert on modern Hungary. Lomax also edited *Eyewitness in Hungary* (Spokesman, UK), an anthology of accounts by foreign Communists (most of whom were sympathetic to the Uprising) that vividly depicts the elation, confusion and tragedy of the events of October 1956.

**John Lukács**, *Budapest 1900* (Weidenfeld/Grove Press). Excellent and very readable account of the politics and society of Budapest at the turn of the century, during a golden age that was shortly to come to an end.

**George Mikes**, *A Study in Infamy* (Andre Deusch o/p). Better known in the West for his humorous writings, Mikes here exposes the activities of the secret police during the Rákosi era. Based on captured documents which explain their methods of surveillance and use of terror as a political weapon.

**George Schöpflin**, *Politics in Eastern Europe 1945–92* (Blackwell). An excellent overview of the region in the last fifty years.

**Michael Stewart**, *The Time of the Gypsies* (Westview Press). Based on anthropological research in a gypsy community in Hungary, this superb book presents gypsy culture as a culture, and not as a parasitic body on society, as it is widely perceived in Hungary and elsewhere.

**Peter Sugar** (ed), *A History of Hungary* (L B Tauris). A useful, not too academic, survey of Hungarian history from pre-Conquest times to the close of the Kádár era, with a brief epilogue on the transition to democracy.

**Rudolf L. Tökés**, *Hungary's Negotiated Revolution: Economic Reform, Social Change, and Political Succession, 1957–1990* (Cambridge University Press). Very sound and comprehensive account of the Communist regime's survival, decline and fall.

## ART, FOLK TRADITIONS, ARCHITECTURE AND COOKERY

The Hungarian publisher Corvina publishes a number of books covering Hungary's folk traditions and artistic treasures, mostly translated into English or German. Some editions are available on import, and some of its British titles are available through US publishers of fiction and poetry, but they are cheaper to buy in Budapest – either at Bestsellers at V, Oktober 6 utca, which has a good range and takes orders for books; at bookshops in Váci utca; in museum bookshops; in the Corvina discount shop on the second floor of the big modern building on Vörömarty tér; or in the Book Superstore on the corner of Báthory utca and Honvéd utca near the Parliament.

**Irén Ács**, *Hungary at Home* (Jövendő, Hungary). Excellent collection of photos covering all walks of life in postwar Hungary. A collection of the photographer's work is exhibited in Hollókő in northern Hungary.

**Val Biro**, *Hungarian Folk Tales* (Oxford University Press). Children's tales of dragons and the like in a crisp, colloquial translation.

**Lesley Chamberlain**, *The Food and Cooking of Eastern Europe* (Penguin o/p). A great compendium of recipes, nostrums and gastronomical history, guaranteed to have you experimenting in the kitchen.

**Györgyi Éri et al**, *A Golden Age: Art and Society in Hungary 1896–1914* (Corvina). Hungary's Art Nouveau age captured in a beautifully illustrated coffee-table volume.

**Susan Derecskey**, *The Hungarian Cookbook* (HarperCollins, US). A good, easy-to-follow selection of traditional and modern recipes.

**Tekla Dömötör**, *Hungarian Folk Beliefs* (Corvina/Indiana University Press o/p). A superb collection of social history, folk beliefs and customs.

**János Gerle et al**, *Budapest: An Architectural Guide* (6 BT, Budapest). The best of the new guides to the city's twentieth-century architecture, covering almost 300 buildings with brief descriptions in Hungarian and English.

**Tamás Hofer et al**, *Hungarian Peasant Art* (Constable/International Publications Service o/p). An excellently produced examination of Hungarian folk art, with lots of good photos.

**George Lang**, *The Cuisine of Hungary* (Penguin/Random House). A well-written and beautifully illustrated work, telling you everything you need to know about Hungarian cooking, its history and how to do it yourself.

**Dora Wieberson et al**, *The Architecture of Historic Hungary* (MIT Press, US). Comprehensive and invaluable survey of Hungarian architecture through the ages, placing it in its historical context.

## LITERATURE

Access to Hungarian literature has greatly improved in recent years, and authors like **Péter Nádas** and **Péter Esterházy**, whose dense and very Hungarian style had long been inaccessible to English readers, are now appearing in translation. There are numerous collections of short stories published in Budapest, though the quality of translations varies from the sublime to the ridiculous. Works by nineteenth-century authors such as **Mór Jókai** are most likely found in secondhand bookshops (see p.124).

## ANTHOLOGIES

**Loránt Czigány** (ed), *The Oxford History of Hungarian Literature from the Earliest Times to the Present* (Oxford University Press). Probably the most comprehensive collection in print to date. In chronological order, with good coverage of the political and social background.

**György Gömöri** (ed), *Colonnade of Teeth* (Bloodaxe/Dufour). In spite of its strange title, this is a good introduction to the work of young Hungarian poets.

**Michael March** (ed), *Description of a Struggle* (Picador/Vintage). A collection of contemporary Eastern European prose, featuring four pieces by Hungarian writers including Nádas and Esterházy.

## POETRY

**Endre Ady**, *Poems of Endre Ady* (University Press of America). Regarded by many as the finest Hungarian poet of the twentieth century, Ady's allusive verses are notoriously difficult to translate. *Explosive Country* (Corvina) is a collection of essays about his homeland.

**George Faludy**, *Selected Poems, 1933–80* (McClelland & Stewart/University of Georgia Press o/p). Fiery, lyrical poetry by a victim of both Nazi and Soviet repression. Themes of political defiance, the nobility of the human spirit, and the struggle to preserve human values in the face of oppression predominate. The author's cheerfully resigned biographical account of the 1940s and 1950s and the prison camps of the period, *My Happy Days in Hell*, is also worth reading.

**Ágnes Nemes Nagy**, *Selected Poems* (o/p). Nagy is a major postwar poet, who often speculates on knowledge and the role of poetry in trying to impose order on the world.

**János Pilzinsky**, *Selected Poems* (o/p). Themes of humanity's suffering and sacrifice by a major poet.

**Miklós Radnóti**, *Under Gemini: the Selected Poems of Miklós Radnóti, with a Prose Memoir* (Ohio University Press, US); *Foamy Sky: the Major Poems* (Princeton University Press, US). The two best collections of Radnóti's sparse, anguished poetry. His final poems, found in his coat pocket after he had been shot on a forced march to a labour camp, are especially moving.

**Zsuzsa Rákovsky**, *New Life* (Oxford University Press, UK). Well-received volume translated by the Hungarian-born English poet George Szirtes.

**Albert Tezla** (ed), *Ocean at the Window, Hungarian Prose and Poetry since 1945* (University of Minnesota o/p). A reliable collection of Hungarian literature.

**Sándor Weöres**, *Eternal Moment* (Anvil Press Poetry, UK). The collected poetry of a major Hungarian poet of the postwar period.

## FICTION

**Géza Csáth**, *The Magician's Garden and Other Stories* (Penguin/Columbia University Press o/p); *Opium and Other Stories* (Penguin o/p). Disturbing stories written in the magic realist genre. The author was tormented by insanity and opium addiction, finally killing his wife and then himself in 1918.

**Tibor Dery**, *The Portuguese Princess* (Calder/Northwestern University Press o/p). Short stories by a once-committed Communist, who was jailed for three years after the Uprising and died in 1977.

**Péter Esterházy**, *The Glance of Countess Hahn-Hahn, Down the Danube* (Quartet/Grove). Surreal flow down the river by a playful wordsmith. *Helping Verbs of the Heart*, *A Little Hungarian Pornography* and *She Loves Me* are three more works by this descendant of the famous aristocratic family.

**Tibor Fischer**, *Under the Frog, A Black Comedy* (Penguin/New Press). A fictional account of the 1956 uprising by the son of Hungarian survivor emigrés. Witty and enjoyable.

**Agnes Hankiss**, *A Hungarian Romance* (Readers International). A lyrical first novel by "Hungary's new feminist voice", dealing with a woman's quest for self-identity during the sixteenth century and the timeless conflict between personal and public interests.

**Dezső Kosztolányi**, *Skylark* (Central European University Press, Budapest). A short and tragic story of an old couple and their beloved child by one of Hungary's top writers of the twentieth century, in a masterly translation by Richard Aczél and Anna Édes.

**Gyula Krúdy**, *Adventures of Sinbad* (Central European University Press, Budapest/Random House). Stories about a gourmand and womanizer by a popular Hungarian author with similar interests to his hero. Good translation.

**Zsigmond Móricz**, *Be Faithful Unto Death* (Penguin). This novel by a major figure in late nineteenth-century Hungarian literature is helpful in understanding the way Hungarians see themselves – both then and now.

**Péter Nádas**, *A Book of Memories* (Vintage/Overlook Press). This novel about a novelist writing about a novel caused a sensation when it appeared in 1998. A Proustian account of bisexual relationships, Stalinist repression, and modern-day Hungary in a brilliant translation by Iván Sanders, which captures the flavour of the original without losing any readability.

**Giorgio and Nicola Pressburger**, *Homage to the Eighth District* (Readers International). Evocative tales of Jewish life in Budapest, before, during and after World War II, by twin brothers who fled Hungary in 1956.

**Ernő Szép**, *The Smell of Humans* (Central European University Press, Budapest/Arrow, UK). Another superb and harrowing memoir of the Holocaust in Hungary.

### BIOGRAPHY AND AUTOBIOGRAPHY

**Magda Dénes**, *Castles Burning: A Child's Life in War* (Anchor/Touchstone Books). A moving biographical account of the Budapest ghetto and postwar escape to France, Cuba, and the United States, seen through the eyes of a Jewish girl. The author died in December 1966, shortly before the book she always wanted to write was published.

**Charles Fenyvesi**, *When the World was Whole: Three Centuries of Memories* (Viking, US o/p). A very readable account of Jewish life in Eastern Hungary up until the Holocaust.

**Paul Hoffmann**, *The Man Who Loved Only Numbers: the Story of Paul Erdöss and the Search for Mathematical Truth* (Fourth Estate/Hyperion). The amazing story of a Hungarian-born mathematician who became a legend. Totally dedicated to his goal, he wandered from friend to friend with his possessions in a few carrier bags, concerned with nothing but mathematics. Affectionate, engaging account of this genius and his world.

### FOREIGN WRITERS ON HUNGARY

**Heinrich Böll**, *And Where Were You, Adam* in *Adam and the Train* (Penguin/Northwestern University Press o/p). A superb short novel by one of the major postwar German novelists, consisting of loosely connected and semi-autobiographical short stories describing the panic-stricken retreat of Hitler's forces from the *puszta* before the Red Army in 1944. Told through both Hungarian and German eyes, these stories are a haunting evocation of the chaos, cruelty and horror of the retreat, but also of a rural culture that seems to resist everything thrown at it.

**Hans Habe**, *Black Earth* (NEL o/p). The story of a peasant's commitment to the Communist underground and his disillusionment with the Party in power; a good read, and by no means as crude as the artwork and blurb suggest.

**Cecilia Holland**, *Rakossy* (Hodder/Atheneum o/p), *The Death of Attila* (Hodder/Pocket Books o/p). Two well-crafted historical romances: *Rakossy* is a bodice-ripping tale of a shy Austrian princess wed to an uncouth Magyar baron, braving the Turkish hordes on the Hungarian marches; while *The Death of Attila* evokes the Huns, Romans and Goths of the Dark Ages, pillaging around the Danube.

**Ken Smith**, *Wild Root* (Bloodaxe, UK). A collection of poetry that includes sharp, sympathetic observations on travels in Hungary and elsewhere.

# MUSIC AND RECORDS

Hungarian music enshrines the trinity of Liszt, Bartók, and Kodály: Liszt was the founding father, Bartók one of the greatest composers of the twentieth century, and Kodály (himself no slouch at composition) created a widely imitated system of musical education. When you also take into account talented Hungarian soloists like Perényi, it's clear that this small nation has made an outstanding contribution to the world of music.

## HUNGARIAN COMPOSERS

**Franz Liszt** (1811–86), who described himself as a "mixture of gypsy and Franciscan", cut a flamboyant figure in the salons of Europe as a virtuoso pianist and womanizer. His *Hungarian Rhapsodies* and other similar pieces reflected the "gypsy" side to his character and the rising nationalism of his era, while later work like the *Transcendental Studies* (whose originality has only recently been recognized) invoked a visionary, "Franciscan" mood. Despite his patriotic stance, however, Liszt's first language was German (he never fully mastered Hungarian), and his expressed wish to roam the villages of Hungary with a knapsack on his back was a Romantic fantasy.

That was left to **Béla Bartók** (1881–1945) and **Zoltán Kodály** (1882–1967), who began exploring the remoter districts of Hungary and Transylvania in 1906, collecting peasant music. Despite many hardships and local suspicion of their "monster" (a cutting stylus and phono-graph cylinders), they managed to record and catalogue thousands of melodies, laying down high standards of musical ethnography, still maintained in Hungary today, while discovering a rich source of inspiration for their own compositions. Bartók believed that a genuine peasant melody was "quite as much a masterpiece in miniature as a Bach fugue or a Mozart sonata . . . a classic example of the expression of a musical thought in its most conceivably concise form, with the avoidance of all that is superfluous".

Bartók created a personal but universal musical language by reworking the raw essence of Magyar and Finno-Ugric folk music in a modern context – in particular his six *String Quartets* – although Hungarian public opinion was originally hostile. Feeling misunderstood and out of step with his country's increasingly pro-Nazi policies, Bartók left Hungary in 1940, dying poor and embittered in the United States. Since then, however, his reputation has soared, and the return of his body in 1988 occasioned national celebrations, shrewdly sponsored by the state.

Kodály's music is more consciously national: Bartók called it "a real profession of faith in the Hungarian soul". His *Peacock Variations* are based on a typical Old Style pentatonic tune and the *Dances of Galanta* on the popular music played by gypsy bands. Old Style tunes also form the core of Kodály's work in musical education: the "Kodály method" employs group singing to develop musical skill at an early age. His ideas have made Hungarian music teaching among the best in the world, and Kodály himself a paternal figure to generations of children.

For others Kodály was a voice of conscience during the Rákosi era, writing the *Hymn of Zrínyi* to a seventeenth-century text whose call to arms against the Turkish invasion – "I perceive a ghastly dragon, full of venom and fury, snatching the crown of Hungary. . ." – was tumultuously acclaimed as an anti-Stalinist allegory. Its first performance was closely followed by the Uprising, and the *Hymn* was not performed again for many years; nor were any recordings made available until 1982.

## HUNGARIAN FOLK MUSIC

In Hungary today, folk music has little connection with rural communities, whose taste in music (as in other things) has been transformed by urban influences, television and radio. However, folk music and village life are still closely linked **in Transylvania**, which was seen as a repository of Magyar traditions even in Bartók's day, particularly the Kalotaszeg and Mezőség regions near the city of Cluj, and the Csángó districts of the eastern Carpathians. In Hungary, by contrast, Magyar folk music has enjoyed a revival in towns and cities thanks to the **Táncház**. These dance houses are very popular with young people interested in traditional music and dances, which are mostly from Hungary and Transylvania, but also from the "South Slavs", Slovenia and Bulgaria.

## RECORDINGS

Good quality **records and tapes** produced by Hungaroton retail for half or a third of what you'd pay abroad, which makes it well worth rooting through record shops (*lemezbolt*). After Western and Hungarian **pop**, the bulk of their stock consists of **classical music**. A full discography of the works of Liszt, Bartók and Kodály, directors like Dohnányi and Doráti, and contemporary Hungarian soloists and singers would fill a catalogue, but look out for the following names: pianists András Schiff, Zoltán Kocsis (who has recently turned conductor) and Dezső Ránki; the cellist Miklós Perényi; the Liszt Ferenc Chamber Orchestra, the Budapest Festival Orchestra and the Hungarian Radio and TV Symphony; conductors Iván Fischer and Tamás Vasáry; singers Mária Zádori, Ingrid Kertesi, Andrea Rost, Adrienne Csengery, József Gregor and László Polgar.

For those who like **contemporary music**, the grand old man of the modern Hungarian scene is György Kurtág, while Tibor Szemző produces meditative works, one of which, *Tractatus*, inspired by German philosopher Ludwig Wittgenstein, is quite extraordinary. If you're into ethnomusic, then László Hortobágyi's "Gaia" music is worth listening to. Jazz enthusiasts might like to get a taste of the ethno-jazz sounds of Mihály Dresch, or the compositions of pianist György Szabados.

**Folk and gypsy music** can be bought at all record stores, though you should be warned that a CD with a picture of a gypsy orchestra all dressed up in red waistcoats is not playing "Roma Music", but nineteenth-century wistful melodies known as "*nóta*" – it's worth asking to listen before you buy. For genuine Hungarian

gypsy music, look out for bands such as Kalyi Jag, Ternipe, the Szilvási Band and Ando Drom. For Hungarian folk, watch out for ballad singer Irén Lovász and Budapest Klezmer outfit Da Naye Kapelye, as well as the artists listed below. There are hundreds of great recordings in this enormous field, of which the following offer an introduction.

**VII. Magyarországi Táncház Találkozó.** A great mixture of dances, ballads and instrumental pieces from all over Hungary, recorded at the Seventh Dance House Festival in 1988. One of a series (MK 18152), the Tenth Dance House Festival collection (MK 18190) is also especially good.

**Félix Lajkó**, *Lajkó Félix és zenekara*. The best recording so far of this Hungarian virtuoso violinist from Subotica in northern Serbia. To call this a folk-jazz fusion hardly does justice to this special sound. Lajkó is excellent live, though he can get carried away by his own virtuosity.

**Magyar népzene 3** (Hungarian folk music). A four-disc set of field recordings covering the whole range of folk music, including Old and New Style songs, instrumental and occasional music, that's probably the best overall introduction. In the West, the discs are marketed as "Folk Music of Hungary Vol.1".

**Magyar hangszeres népzene** (Hungarian Instrumental Folk Music). A very good three-disc set of field recordings of village and gypsy bands, including lots of solos (Hungaroton LPX 18045-47).

**Kismet**. Márta Sebestyén, Hungary's leading Táncház singer, who made many recordings with the folk group Muzsikás, has now developed well beyond those horizons to become an international star, thanks first to the Canadian duo Deep Forest, who used her voice in a recording (although they were rather slow to acknowledge their debt) and later to the film *The English Patient*, where she contributed to the soundtrack.

**Muzsikás**. Beautiful arrangements of traditional ballads by the Muzsikás group and Márta Sebestyén, who have been leading the field for over twenty-five years. Highly recommended (Hannibal HNBL 1330).

**Morning Star**. Another good Muzsikás volume. Interestingly, their record company recommended slight changes and a softening of edges for this foreign edition of *Hazafelé*, the original Hungarian recording (Gong HCD 37874).

**The Bartók Album**. Released this year by Muzsikás, featuring Márta Sebestyén and the violinist Alexander Balanescu, this manages to set the music of Bartók in its original context. Three of Bartók's violin duos are presented alongside original field recordings and recordings of his transcriptions by Muzsikás. Bartók's works take on a special dance quality when played by this crowd (HNCD 1439).

**Bonchidától Bonchidáig**. The Kalamajka Ensemble, another leading Táncház group, plays Transylvanian and Csángó ballads and dances (Hungaroton MK 18135).

**Este a Gyimesbe Jártam**. Music from the Csángó region performed by János Zerkula and Regina Fikó; sparser, sadder and more discordant than other Transylvanian music (Hungaroton MK 18130).

**Táncházi muzsika** (Music from the Táncház). A double album of the Sebö Ensemble playing Táncház music from various regions of Hungary. Wild and exciting rhythms (Hungaroton SPLX 18031-32).

**Jánosi Együttes** (Jánosi Ensemble). Another young group, performing "authentic" versions of some of the folk tunes that Bartók borrowed in his compositions. A record that makes a bridge between classical and folk music (Hungaroton SPLX 18103).

**New Wave**. The traditional Hungarian folk band Vízöntő combines its roots with other music (FY 80042).

**Roma Vándor**. Kálmán Balogh is one of the virtuosos of the cimbalom, and can play classical, jazz and traditonal folk. On this live recording he turns this staple of Hungarian gypsy restaurant bands into something much more than entertainment for eating (MWCD 4009) .

**Serbian Music from South Hungary** played by the Vujicsics Ensemble. More complex tunes than most Magyar folk music, with a distinct Balkan influence (Hannibal HNBL 1310).

# *LANGUAGE*

Hungarian is a unique, complex and subtle tongue, classified as belonging to the Finno-Ugric linguistic group, which includes Finnish and Estonian. If you happen to know those languages, however, don't expect it to be a help – there are some structural similarities, but lexically they are totally different. In fact, some scholars think the connection is completely bogus, and have linked Hungarian to the Siberian Chuvash language and a whole host of other pretty obscure tongues. Basically the origins of Hungarian remain a total mystery, and though a few words from Turkish have crept in, together with some German, English and (a few) Russian neologisms, there is not much that the beginner will recognize.

Consequently, foreigners aren't really expected to speak Hungarian, and natives are used to being addressed in **German**, the lingua franca of tourism. It's understood by older people, particularly in Transdanubia, and by many students and business people, besides virtually everyone around Balaton or in tourist offices. For a brief visit it's probably easier to brush up on some German for your means of communication. A few basic Magyar phrases can make all the difference, though. Hungarians are intensely proud of their language, and as a nation are surprisingly bad at learning anyone else's. However, **English** is gaining ground rapidly, and is increasingly widely understood.

In addition to the following list of basic phrases, you'll find a detailed food glossary and a selection of basic words pertaining to transport in Basics. The Rough Guide's *Hungarian for*

*Travellers* is a useful phrasebook also has a wide range of phrases. If you're prepared to study the language seriously, *Colloquial Hungarian* (Routledge) is the best available book. As a supplement, invest in the handy little *Angol–Magyar/Magyar–Angol Kisszótár* dictionaries, available from bookshops in Hungary.

## BASIC GRAMMAR AND PRONUNCIATION

Although its rules are complicated, it's worth describing a few features of **Hungarian grammar**, albeit imperfectly. Hungarian is an agglutinative language – in other words, its vocabulary is built upon **root-words**, which are modified in various ways to express different ideas and nuances. Instead of prepositions – "to", "from", "in", etc – Hungarian uses **suffixes**, or tags added to the ends of genderless **nouns**. The change in suffix is largely determined by the noun's context: for example the noun "book" (*könyv*) will take a final "t" in the accusative (*könyvet*); "in the book" = *könyvben*; "from the book" = *könyvből*. It is also affected by the rules of vowel harmony (which take a while to get used to, but don't alter meaning, so don't worry about getting them wrong!). Most of the nouns in the vocabulary section below are in the nominative or subject form – that is, without suffixes. In Hungarian, "**the**" is *a* (before a word beginning with a consonant) or *az* (preceding a vowel); the word for "**a/an**" is *egy* (which also means "one").

**Plurals** are indicated by adding a final "k", with a link vowel if necessary, giving *-ek, -ok* or *-ak*. Nouns preceded by a number or other indication of quantity (eg: many, several) do *not* appear as plural: eg *könyvek* means "books", but "two books" is *két könyv* (using the singular form of the noun).

**Adjectives** precede the noun (*a piros ház* = the red house), adopting suffixes to form the comparative (*jó* = good; *jobb* = better), plus the prefix *leg* to signify the superlative (*legjobb* = the best).

**Negatives** are usually formed by placing the word *nem* before the verb or adjective. *Ez* (this), *ezek* (these), *az* (that) and *azok* (those) are the **demonstratives**.

### PRONUNCIATION

Achieving passably good **pronunciation**, rather than grammar, is the first priority (see the box on p.398 for general guidelines). **Stress**

## HUNGARIAN WORDS AND PHRASES

### BASICS

| | | | |
|---|---|---|---|
| Do you speak . . . | *beszél . . .* | good evening | *jó estét* |
| English | *angolul* | good night | *jó éjszakát* |
| German | *németül* | how are you? (informal) | *hogy vagy?* |
| French | *franciául* | how are you? (more formal) | *hogy van?* |
| yes – OK | *igen – jó* | could you speak more | *elmondaná lassabban?* |
| no/not | *nem* | slowly? | |
| I (don't) understand | *(nem) értem* | what do you call this? | *mi a neve ennek?* |
| please–excuse me | *kérem–bocsánat* | please write it down | *kérem, írja le* |
| two beers, please | *két sört kérek* | today – tomorrow | *ma – holnap* |
| thank you (very much) | *köszönöm (szépen)* | the day after tomorrow | *holnapután* |
| you're welcome | *szívesen* | yesterday | *tegnap* |
| hello/goodbye (informal) | *szia* | the day before yesterday | *tegnapelőtt* |
| goodbye | *viszontlátásra* | in the morning – in the | *reggel – este* |
| see you later (informal) | *viszlát* | evening | |
| good morning | *jó reggelt* | at noon – at midnight | *délben – éjfélkor* |
| good day | *jó napot* | | |

### QUESTIONS AND REQUESTS

*Legyen szíves* ("Would you be so kind") is the polite formula for attracting someone's attention. Hungarian has numerous interrogative modes whose subtleties elude foreigners, so it's best to use the simple *van?* ("is there?"), to which the reply might be *nincs* or *nincsen* ("there isn't"/"there aren't any"). In shops or restaurants you will immediately be addressed with the one-word *tessék,* meaning "Can I help you?", "What would you like?" or "Next!". To order in restaurants, shops and markets, use *kérek* ("I'd like. . .") plus accusative noun; *Kérem, adjon azt* ("Please give me that"); *Egy ilyet kérek* ("I'll have one of those").

| | | | |
|---|---|---|---|
| I'd like/we'd like | *Szeretnék/szeretnénk* | Do you have anything | *Van valami olcsóbb?* |
| Where is/are . . . ? | *Hol van/vannak . . ?* | cheaper? | |
| Hurry up! | *Siessen!* | a student discount? | *van diák kedvezmény?* |
| How much is it? | *Mennyibe kerül?* | Is everything included? | *Ebben minden* |
| per night | *egy éjszakára* | | *szerepel?* |
| per week | *egy hétre* | I asked for . . . | *Én . . . .-t rendeltem* |
| a single room | *egyágyas szoba* | The bill please | *Fizetni szeretnék* |
| a double room | *kétágyas szoba* | We're paying separately | *Külön-külön* |
| hot (cold) water | *meleg (hideg) víz* | | *fizetünk* |
| a shower | *egy zuhany* | what? – why? | *mi? – miert?* |
| It's very expensive | *Ez nagyon drága* | when? – who? | *mikor? – ki?* |

### SOME SIGNS TO RECOGNIZE

| | | | |
|---|---|---|---|
| entrance – exit | *bejárat – kijárat* | room for rent | *szoba kiadó* |
| arrival | *érkezés* | | (or *Zimmer frei*) |
| departure | *indulás* | hospital | *kórház* |
| open – closed | *nyitva – zárva* | pharmacy | *gyógyszertár* |
| free admission | *szabad belépés* | (local) police | *(kerületi) Rendőrség* |
| women's – men's | *női – férfi mosdó* | caution/beware | *vigyázat!/vigyázz!* |
| toilet | (or *WC* - "Vait-say") | no smoking | *tilos a dohányzás/dohányozni tilos* |
| shop – market | *bolt – piac* | no bathing | *tilos a fürdés/füredni tilos* |

## DIRECTIONS

| | | | |
|---|---|---|---|
| Where's the . . . ? | *Hol van a . . . ?* | a return ticket to . . . | *egy retur jegyet . . .-ra/re* |
| campsite | *kemping* | Do I have to change | *Át kell szállnom ?* |
| hotel | *szálloda/ hotel* | trains . . .? | |
| railway station | *vasútállomás* | towards | *felé* |
| bus station | *buszállomás* | on the right (left) | *jobbra (balra)* |
| (bus or train) stop | *megálló* | straight ahead | *egyenesen előre* |
| inland | *belföldi* | (over) there – here | *ott – itt* |
| international | *külföldi* | Where are you going? | *Hova megy?* |
| Is it near (far)? | *Közel (messze) van?* | Is that on the way to . . . ? | *Az a . . . úton?* |
| Which bus goes to . . . ? | *Melyik busz megy . . .-ra/re* | I want to get out at . . . | *Le akarok szállni . . .-on/en* |
| a one-way ticket to . . . | *egy jegyet kérek . . .* | please stop here | *itt álljon meg* |
| please | *-ra/re csak oda* | I'm lost | *eltévedtem* |

## DESCRIPTIONS AND REACTIONS

| | | | | | | | |
|---|---|---|---|---|---|---|---|
| and | *és* | good | *jó* | quick | *gyors* | ugly | *csúnya* |
| or | *vagy* | bad | *rossz* | slow | *lassú* | Help! | *Segítség!* |
| nothing | *semmi* | better | *jobb* | now | *most* | I'm ill | *beteg vagyok* |
| perhaps | *talán* | big | *nagy* | later | *később* | | |
| very | *nagyon* | small | *kicsi* | beautiful | *szép* | | |

## TIME

Luckily, the 24-hour clock is used for timetables, but on cinema programmes you may see notations like 1/4, 3/4, etc. These derive from the spoken expression of time which, as in German, makes reference to the hour approaching completion. For example 3:30 is expressed as *fél négy* – "half (on the way to) four"; 3:45 – *háromnegyed négy* ("three quarters on the way to four"); 6:15 – "*negyed hét*" ("one quarter towards seven"), etc. However, ". . . o'clock" is . . . *óra*, rather than referring to the hour ahead. Duration is expressed by the suffixes *-től* ("from") and *-ig* ("to"); minutes are *perc*; to ask the time, say "*Hány óra?*"

## NUMBERS AND DAYS

| | | | | | |
|---|---|---|---|---|---|
| 1 | *egy* | 20 | *húsz* | 900 | *kilencszáz* |
| 2 | *kettő* | 21 | *huszonegy* | 1000 | *egyezer* |
| 3 | *három* | 30 | *harminc* | half | *fél* |
| 4 | *négy* | 40 | *negyven* | a quarter | *negyed* |
| 5 | *öt* | 50 | *ötven* | each/piece | *darab* |
| 6 | *hat* | 60 | *hatvan* | | |
| 7 | *hét* | 70 | *hetven* | Sunday | *vasárnap* |
| 8 | *nyolc* | 80 | *nyolcvan* | Monday | *hétfő* |
| 9 | *kilenc* | 90 | *kilencven* | Tuesday | *kedd* |
| 10 | *tíz* | 100 | *száz* | Wednesday | *szerda* |
| 11 | *tizenegy* | 101 | *százegy* | Thursday | *csütörtök* |
| 12 | *tizenkettő* | 150 | *százötven* | Friday | *péntek* |
| 13 | *tizenhárom* | 200 | *kettőszáz* | Saturday | *szombat* |
| 14 | *tizennégy* | 300 | *háromszáz* | on Monday | *hétfőn* |
| 15 | *tizenöt* | 400 | *négyszáz* | on Tuesday | *kedden* etc. |
| 16 | *tizenhat* | 500 | *ötszáz* | day | *nap* |
| 17 | *tizenhét* | 600 | *hatszáz* | week | *hét* |
| 18 | *tizennyolc* | 700 | *hétszáz* | month | *hónap* |
| 19 | *tizenkilenc* | 800 | *nyolcszáz* | year | *év* |

almost invariably falls on the first syllable of a word and all letters are spoken, although in sentences the tendency is to slur words together. Vowel sounds are greatly affected by the bristling **accents** (that actually distinguish separate letters) which, together with the "double letters" *cs, gy, ly, ny, sz, ty,* and *zs,* give the Hungarian **alphabet** its formidable appearance.

## PRONUNCIATION

**A** o as in hot
**Á** a as in father
**B** b as in best
**C** ts as in bats
**CS** ch as in church
**D** d as in dust
**E** e as in yet
**É** ay as in say
**F** f as in fed
**G** g as in go
**GY** a soft dy as in due
**H** h as in hat
**I** i as in bit, but slightly longer
**Í** ee as in see
**J** y as in yes
**K** k as in sick

**L** l as in leap
**LY** y as in yes
**M** m as in mud
**N** n as in not
**NY** ny as in onion
**O** aw as in saw, with the tongue kept high
**Ó** aw as in saw, as above but longer
**Ö** ur as in fur, with the lips tightly rounded but without any "r" sound
**Ő** ur as in fur, as above but longer
**P** p as in sip
**R** r pronounced with the tip of the tongue like a Scottish "r"

**S** sh as in shop
**SZ** s as in so
**T** t as in sit
**TY** ty as in Tuesday or prettier, said quickly
**U** u as in pull
**Ú** oo as in food
**Ü** u as in the German "über" with the lips tightly rounded
**Ű** u as above, but longer
**V** v as in vat
**W** v as in "Valkman," "vhiskey" or "WC" (vait-say)
**Z** z as in zero
**ZS** zh as in measure

# HUNGARIAN TERMS: A GLOSSARY

**ÁFA** Goods tax, equivalent to VAT.

**ALFÖLD** Plain; usually refers to the Great Plain (*Nagyalföld*) rather than the Little Plain (*Kisalföld*) in northwestern Hungary.

**ÁLLATKERT** Zoo.

**ÁRUHÁZ** Department store.

**AUTÓBUSZÁLLOMÁS** Bus station.

**ÁVO** The dreaded secret police of the Rákosi era, renamed the *ÁVH* in 1949.

**BARLANG** Cave; the most impressive stalactite caves are in the Aggtelek karst region.

**BELVÁROS** Inner town or city, typically characterized by Baroque or Neoclassical architecture.

**BORKOSTOLÓ** Wine-tasting.

**BOROZÓ** Wine bar.

**BOTANIKUSKERT** Botanical garden.

**BÜFÉ** Snack bar.

**CASTRUM** (Latin) A Roman fortification.

**CIGÁNY** Gypsy (can be abusive); hence *Cigánytelep*, a gypsy settlement; and *Cigányzene*, gypsy music.

**CSÁRDA** Inn; nowadays, a restaurant with rustic decor.

**CSÁRDÁS** Traditional wild dance to violin music.

**CSIKÓS** (plural *csikósok*) *Puszta* horse herdsman; a much romanticized figure of the nineteenth century.

**CUKRÁSZDA** Cake shop.

**DISZTEREM** Ceremonial hall.

**DJAMI** or **DZAMI** Mosque.

**DOMB** Hill; *Rózsadomb*, "Rose Hill" in Budapest.

**DUNA** River Danube.

**ERDÉLY** Transylvania; for centuries a part of the Hungarian territories, its loss to Romania in 1920 still rankles.

**ERDŐ** Forest, wood.

**ERŐD** Fortification.

**ÉTTEREM** Restaurant.

**FALU** Village.

**FALUSI TURIZMUS** Tourist network for accommodation in villages.

**FOGADÓ** Inn.

**FOLYÓ** River.

**FORRÁS** Natural spring.

**FŐ TÉR** Main square.

**FŐ UTCA** Main street.

**FÜRDŐ** Public baths, often fed by thermal springs.

**GYÓGYFÜRDŐ** Mineral baths with therapeutic properties.

**HAJDÚK** Cattle-drovers turned outlaws, who later settled near Debrecen in the **HAJDÚSÁG** Region.

**HAJÓ** Boat.

**HAJÓÁLLOMÁS** Boat landing stage.

**HALÁSZCSÁRDA / HALÁSZKERT** Fish restaurants.

**HÁZ** House.

**HEGY** Hill or low mountain (**HEGYSÉG** = range of hills).

**HÉV** Commuter train running between Budapest and Szentendre, Gödöllő, Csepel and Ráckeve.

**HÍD** Bridge; *Lánchíd*, the "Chain Bridge" in Budapest.

**HONVÉD** Hungarian army.

**IFJÚSÁGI SZÁLLÓ** Youth hostel.

**ISKOLA** School.

**ITALBOLT** "Drink shop", or a village bar.

**KÁPOLNA** Chapel.

**KAPU** Gate.

**KASTÉLY** Manor house or stately home, country seat of noble families.

**KERT** Garden, park.

**KERÜLET** (ker.) District.

**KIÁLLÍTÁS** Exhibition.

**KINCSTÁR** Treasury.

**KOLLÉGIUM** Student hostel.

**KOMP** Ferry.

**KÖRÚT** *(krt.)* Literally, ring; normally a boulevard around the city centre. Some cities have semi-circular "Great" and "Small" boulevards (**NAGYKÖRÚT** and **KISKÖRÚT**) surrounding their Belváros.

**KŐTÁR** Lapidarium.

**KÖZ** Alley, lane; also used to define geographical regions, eg the "Mud strip" (*Sárköz*) bordering the Danube.

**KULCS** Key.

**KÚT** Well or fountain.

**LAKÓTELEP** High-rise apartment buildings.

**LÉPCSŐ** Flight of steps, often in place of a road.

**LIGET** Park, grove or wood.

**LIMES** (Latin) Fortifications along the Danube, marking the limit of Roman territory.

**LOVARDA** Riding school.

**MAGYAR** Hungarian (pronounced "*Mod*-yor"). Also **MAGYARORSZÁG**, Hungary.

**MALÉV** Hungarian national airline.

**MÁV** Hungarian national railways.

**MEGÁLLÓ** A railway station or bus stop.

**MEGYE** County; originally established by King Stephen to extend his authority over the Magyar tribes.

**MIHRAB** Prayer niche in a mosque, indicating the direction of Mecca.

**MŰEMLÉK** Historic monument, protected building.

**MŰVELŐDÉSI HÁZ/KÖZPONT** Arts centre.

**NYILAS** "Arrow Cross", Hungarian Fascist movement.

**OTTOMANS** Founders of the Turkish empire, which included central Hungary during the sixteenth and seventeenth centuries.

**PALOTA** Palace; *Püspök-palota*, a Bishop's residence.

**PÁLYAUDVAR** *(pu.)* Rail terminus.

**PANZIÓ** Pension.

**PATAK** Stream.

**PÉNZ** Money.

**PIAC** Outdoor market.

**PINCE** Cellar; a **BOR-PINCE** contains and serves wine.

**PLÉBÁNIA** Catholic priest's house.

**POLGÁRMESTERI HIVATAL** Mayor's office.

**PUSZTA** Another name for the Great Plain, coined when the region was a wilderness.

**RAKPART** Embankment or quay.

**REFORMÁTUS** The reformed church, which in Hungary means the Calvinist faith; **REFORMÁTUS LÉLKÉSZ HIVATAL** is the church office.

**RÉV** Ferry.

**ROM** Ruined building; sometimes set in a garden with stonework finds, a **ROMKERT**.

**ROMA** The Romany word for gypsy, preferred by many Roma in Hungary.

**SÉTÁNY** "Walk" or promenade.

**SKANZEN** Outdoor ethnographic museum.

**SÖRÖZŐ** Beer hall.

**STRAND** Beach, or any area for sunbathing or swimming.

**SZABADTÉR** Open-air; as in *színház* (theatre) or *múzeum* (museum).

**SZÁLLÓ** or **SZÁLLODA** Hotel.

**SZENT** Saint.

**SZIGET** Island.

**SZOBA KIADÓ** Room to let.

**SZÜRET** Grape harvest.

**TÁJHÁZ** Old peasant house turned into a museum, often illustrating the folk traditions of a region or ethnic group.

**TANÁCSKÖZTÁRSASÁG** The "Republic of Councils" or Soviets, which ruled Hungary in 1919.

**TÁNCHÁZ** Venue for Hungarian folk music and dance.

**TEMETŐ** Cemetery.

**TEMPLOM** Church.

**TÉR** Square; **TERE** in the possessive case, as in *Hősök tere*, "Heroes' Square".

**TEREM** Hall.

**TÓ** Lake.

**TORONY** Tower; as in **TV-TORONY**, television tower, and **VÍZTORONY**, water tower.

**TÜRBE** Tomb or mausoleum of a Muslim dignitary.

**TURISTA TÉRKÉP** Hiking map.

**UDVAR** Courtyard.

**ÚT** Road; in the possessive case, **ÚTJA** – eg *Mártírok útja*, "Road of the Martyrs".

**UTCA** (*u.*) Street.

**VÁR** Castle; **VÁRROM**, castle ruin.

**VÁROS** Town; may be divided into an inner *Belváros*, a lower-lying *Alsóváros* and a modern *Újváros* section. Also **VÁROSKÖZPONT** The town centre, and **VÁROSHÁZA** Town hall.

**VÁSÁR** Market.

**VÁSÁRCSARNOK** Market hall.

**VASÚTÁLLOMÁS** Train station.

**VENDÉGLŐ** A type of restaurant.

**VÖLGY** Valley; *Hűvösvölgy*, "Cool Valley".

**ZSIDÓ** Jew or Jewish.

**ZSINAGÓGA** Synagogue.

# INDEX

# Small

## *but perfectly informed*

**Every bit as stylish and irreverent as their full-sized counterparts, Mini Guides are everything you'd expect from a Rough Guide, but smaller – perfect for a pocket, briefcase or overnight bag.**

### Available 1998
Antigua, Barbados, Boston, Dublin, Edinburgh, Lisbon, Madrid, Seattle

### Coming soon
Bangkok, Brussels, Florence, Honolulu, Las Vegas, Maui, Melbourne, New Orleans, Oahu, St Lucia, Sydney, Tokyo, Toronto

 *Everything you need to know about everything you want to do*

NOTES

# the perfect getaway vehicle

## low-price holiday car rental.

rent a car from holiday autos and you'll give yourself real freedom to explore your holiday destination. with great-value, fully-inclusive rates in over 4,000 locations worldwide, wherever you're escaping to, we're there to make sure you get excellent prices and superb service.

what's more, you can book now with complete confidence. our £5 undercut* ensures that you are guaranteed the best value for money in holiday destinations right around the globe.

drive away with a great deal, call holiday autos now on **0990 300 400** and quote ref RG.

## holiday autos
miles ahead

*in the unlikely event that you should see a cheaper like for like pre-paid rental rate offered by any other independent uk car rental company before or after booking but prior to departure, holiday autos will undercut that price by a full £5. we truly believe we cannot be beaten on price.